Charleston!
Charleston!

Charleston!
Charleston!

The History of a Southern City

by
Walter J. Fraser, Jr.

University of South Carolina Press

Copyright © University of South Carolina 1989

Published in Columbia, South Carolina, by the
University of South Carolina Press

First paperback edition, 1991

Manufactured in the United States of America

Library of Congress Cataloging-in-Publication Date

Fraser, Walter J.
    Charleston! Charleston! : the history of a southern city / by
Walter J. Fraser.
      p.   cm.
    Includes bibliographical references.
    ISBN 0-87249-643-0
    ISBN 0-87249-797-6 (pbk.)
    1. Charleston (S.C.)—History. I. Title.
F279.C457F69   1989
975.7'915—dc20   89-16760
                                                               CIP

Contents

Contents

Contents

Illustrations

Preface

A book like this has never been written before: a documented synthesis of the life and times of Charleston, 1670 to the present. It has taken more than ten years to complete.

With St. Augustine, New York, and Boston, Charleston ranks among the earliest urban centers in North America. It quickly became a boisterous, brawling sea city trading with distant ports, later a capital of the lowcountry plantations, a Southern cultural oasis and a "summer home for planters"; the most Southern of Southern cities, here the Civil War began and in the twentieth century its metropolitan area evolved into a microcosm of what President Dwight D. Eisenhower called the military-industrial complex.

Soon after I arrived in Charleston in the late 1960s to take a position on the history faculty of one of its most venerable institutions, the Citadel, I was surprised to learn that except for several anecdotal accounts, there was no overview of the city's history. Most major urban centers in the nation have at least one well-documented history; therefore, for Charleston, this book attempts to redress the balance.

Every generation of historians is influenced by the events, the new lines of inquiry, and the interpretations of their age. The recent emphasis on history "from the bottom up," the attempt to bring onto center stage the inarticulate, the masses who leave few records but carry civilizations forward, especially has informed my thinking and writing. Particularly within this context the book provides academic historians with an original synthesis of Charleston and it is hoped that it stimulates other studies of this fascinating city where the record is now silent.

I believe too that the academic historian has an obligation to synthesize history for the inquisitive layperson; otherwise who will keep the educated public aware of the paradoxes and complexities in history and its significance to their daily lives?

This book brings together for the first time under one cover all facets of the life of the city and its inhabitants: the rich and the "movers and shakers," the poor and the obscure, black and

white, heroes and villains, and the institutions—churches and orphanages; prisons, hospitals, and schools; the art and architecture
of the homes and public buildings; the recreational, social, and
intellectual life—the bordellos and bars, societies and clubs, theaters, music, debutante teas, libraries and museums, the literati
and the "Charleston style"; politics and the city government that
has contended with epidemic disease of enormous proportions,
sanitation and military sieges, destructive fires and hurricanes, a
high crime rate, and an economy of booms and devastating busts.
It is all here and more.

Much of this book is a distillation of pioneering studies done
by many professional historians and without which this work
could not have been written. Their numerous books and articles
are cited in the notes. This account is also based on letters, dia-
ries, public documents, and photographs made available to me by
archivists at the William L. Perkins Library of Duke University,
the Southern Historical Collection of the University of North Carolina at Chapel Hill, the National Archives and the Library of
Congress, the Robert Scott Smalls Library of the College of
Charleston, and the Library Society of Charleston; especially
helpful were Allen Stokes, Director, South Caroliniana Library of
the University of South Carolina; David Moltke-Hansen, Director, Harlan Greene, and the staff of the South Carolina Historical
Society, Charleston; Gail McCoy, Archivist, and Ernestine Fel-
lers, Charleston City Archives; Bradford L. Rauschenberg, Director of Research, Museum of Early Southern Decorative Arts,
Winston-Salem, North Carolina; Angela Mack, Gibbes Art Gallery, Charleston; Kathryn Gaillard, Photography Department of
the Charleston Museum; Fred Smith, Reference Librarian, Georgia Southern College Library, Statesboro, Georgia; Lynda Heff-
ley, Secretary, Arts and History Commission, City of Charleston;
and Dr. David Heisser, Head, Reference Services, Tufts University Library, Medford, Massachusetts.

Dr. George Rogers, Jr., Professor Emeritus of History, the
University of South Carolina and dean of the historians of the
state, and his colleague, Bob Weir, read early drafts of the manuscript on the colonial period and offered expert advice and encouragement over the years; likewise, Bertram Wyatt-Brown of
the University of Florida and Emory Thomas of the University of
Georgia read first drafts of the chapter on the era of the Civil War
and provided sound guidance; colleagues at the Citadel and Geor-

gia Southern College—"Bo" Moore, Jamie Moore, and Frank Saunders—offered encouragement; graduate students and graduate assistants at both institutions—Drucilla Berkham, Shirley Gibson, Margaret Canaday Adkins, Ellen Barr, Roger Allen, Michael Morris, Sue Hansen, and Dianne Freeman—shared their research with me.

Solomon Breibart, *the* historian of the Jews in Charleston, Catherine Boykin along with her husband Milton, and Betty Marshall all helped uncover bits of information or provided important nurturing contacts with the city over the years after I left the Citadel for Georgia Southern and a department chairmanship. Bob King, formerly of the University of South Carolina Press, worked closely with me on matters regarding the organization of the manuscript that were crucial, and because of his help the book is much improved. Lee Drago of the College of Charleston offered good advice on the next to final draft.

The Georgia Southern College Foundation and the Citadel Development Foundation provided generous grants that helped defray research expenses; Dr. Warren F. Jones, Dean of the School of Arts and Sciences of Georgia Southern, created an atmosphere conducive to research and writing; masters of the micro-computers, Kelly Carnes, Annaha Featherhill-Pugh, Judy Williams, and Sheri Boyd provided inestimable assistance by typing the many drafts of the manuscript; Warren Slesinger, Acquisitions Manager, and the Director of the University of South Carolina Press, Ken Scott, have been patient.

Finally, but most important, my family encouraged and participated in this long project. I thank my mother, Louise, for reading microfilm on arcane topics and my wife, Lynn, for making editorial suggestions; Jay and Thomas, my sons, who grew to young manhood over the course of this work, I thank for staying out of trouble (most of the time) so I could focus my energies on completing the book.

Walter J. Fraser, Jr.
Georgia Southern College
Statesboro, Georgia
June 1989

Charleston!
Charleston!

I

The Proprietary Colony

1. 1670–1695:
" . . . which you are to call Charles Towne"

Albemarle Point

Great cities are both beautiful and ugly.

In British North America in the eighteenth century the four principal cities were Boston, New York, Philadelphia, and Charleston, and of these perhaps Charleston most abounded in glamour and sordidness. Indeed, from its beginnings to the present day the history of this fascinating city has been rich in paradoxes: slavery and freedom, kindness and cruelty, health and sickliness, enormous wealth and grinding poverty. Fragrant and colorful walled gardens have coexisted with stinking alleys, and magnificent homes with hovels. No other city in North America has experienced such dramatic cycles of boom, bust, and destruction, desperate stagnation and confident vigor.

Charleston and the surrounding countryside are at their most attractive in April. When the first group of British settlers sailed into the harbor in April 1670, what they first saw from the deck of the 200-ton frigate *Carolina* probably took their breath away: vast expanses of marsh grass, giant oaks draped with Spanish moss, towering pines, elegant palmettos, and shrubs no European could name.

The master of the three-masted vessel was Henry Brayne, who knew these waters from previous explorations. Among his passengers were the official governor of the expedition, Colonel William Sayle, whom Brayne considered "ancient and crazie," Captain Joseph West, who was characterized by his fellow passengers as "faithful and stout"-hearted, and Captain Florence O'Sullivan, a brawling Irish soldier of fortune for whom Sullivan's Island was eventually named despite the fact that another officer on the ship described him as an "ill-natured buggerer of children."[1] Also accompanying the expedition was a naval surgeon who had spent enough time among some of the Indians of the area to learn their languages.

The Proprietary Colony

The ninety-three passengers aboard the *Carolina* saw an Indian oyster midden about where the Battery now rises from the waters of the bay. Above and behind the whitening shells was a haze of trees and to the left was the river that Captain Brayne knew as the Ashley. The local Indians called it Kiawah and the Spanish had christened it San Jorge, but Brayne had accompanied an expedition that had named the river in honor of Lord Anthony Ashley Cooper, who was eager that a British colony in which he could profitably invest be established north of Florida and south of Virginia. Into this welcoming river Brayne took his leaking ship for several miles.

He entered the first bold creek on the southwestern bank of the Ashley, today called Old Town Creek, and slowly wound his way between thick, golden marsh grasses until the creek narrowed and a low bluff topped by a dark pine forest rose steeply from the bank at the point now known as Charles Towne Landing. Here the *Carolina* anchored and the passengers and crew went ashore.

They had been at sea for most of seven months, having left England in three ships loaded with 15 tons of beer and 30 gallons of brandy, 59 bushels of flour, 12 suits of armor, 100 beds and pillows, 1,200 grubbing hoes, 100,000 fourpenny nails, 756 fishing hooks, 240 pounds of glass beads, 288 scissors, garden seeds, and a set of surgical instruments.[2]

The expedition had been financed by the True and Absolute Lords Proprietors of Carolina, eight politically powerful Englishmen who held a charter from the Crown granting them the lands stretching from present-day North Carolina into Spanish Florida and westward to the "South Seas." Previous attempts by the Proprietors to plant a colony in Carolina for profit had failed miserably, and only Cooper's driving personality had saved the project from being abandoned. The remarkable instrument of government proposed for the colony, the Fundamental Constitutions of Carolina, prescribed, among many other things, an oligarchic government by a governor and an elected Grand Council, whose power was limited by an Assembly of representatives similar to the British House of Commons.[3]

The crew and passengers were happy to be ashore. Having left England in August 1669, they had touched briefly in Ireland and reached Barbados in October. Two other ships in the expedition were lost and those aboard the *Carolina* were weary of mishaps, gales, and rolling seas. They had stopped briefly at Port Royal, but moved on when they recognized that the Spanish were perilously close.

A few of these first settlers were rich, but most were poor. There were twenty-nine "masters" (or men of property) and "free" persons, and sixty-three indentured white servants bound out to serve their owners for two to seven years in return for the passage to Carolina, and there appears to have been at least one black slave aboard. The status of the immigrants was recognizable by their dress. "Masters" and "free" men wore broad-brimmed felt hats or neckcloths, full-sleeved shirts and full-skirted coats, linen or calico knee breeches, silk stockings, and low-buckled shoes. The male indentures were clad in cheap wool caps, cotton shirts, knee breeches and hose, and low-cut shoes. Female servants wore a neck-to-heels coverall with perhaps a single cotton petticoat underneath and used cloth garters to tie up their knee-length cotton hose.[4]

These first immigrants had come from England or the West Indies to start life anew, to escape debts and spouses, and to acquire land. The Proprietors had promised all free settlers over sixteen years of age 150 acres of land, and an additional 100 acres for every able-bodied man servant they brought with them. "Master" Stephen Bull, of the lesser gentry of Warwickshire, England, one of the richest settlers, brought nine servants and therefore received 1,050 acres. One of the servant girls, Affra Harleston, married First Mate John Coming during the voyage or shortly thereafter.[5]

The colonists christened the settlement Albemarle Point after the Duke of Albemarle, one of the Proprietors. Invisible from the sea, it was an excellent defensive sight. The colonists knew that they had settled in the "very chaps of the Spaniards"—St. Augustine was about 200 miles to the south—and hostile natives lived nearby, but there was a brook on one side of the colonists and a marsh on the other. They began entrenchments, established a militia system to maintain a constant watch, and elected their first Grand Council, sometimes referred to as the Council. In August a combined Indian and Spanish force was so intimidated by the defenses and a sudden squall that they called off an attack on the settlement, leaving behind a fear of Spanish Florida that was to last three generations.

The People and the Place

The colonists cleared the land, extended their defensive perimeter, and built shelters of branches, mud, and eventually clapboards. These tasks interfered with a main objective of the settlement: "to provide for the Belly and to make some Experiment of what the land will best produce." Although no one starved to death as some did at Jamestown in Virginia, many went hungry. The inadequate diet caused among some the "bloody flux," or dysentery, and there were a few cases of "feavers" and the "agues," probably malaria. During the warmer months the surrounding salt marshes swarmed with "pestiferous gnats, called Moschetoes." Captain Joseph West complained that a few of the settlers "were so much addicted to Rum, that they will do little but whilst the bottle is at their nose." Other leaders expressed concern over the low moral standards of the people who "prophanely violate" the Sabbath and commit other "grand abuses." They urged the Proprietors to send to Carolina both a good doctor and a "Godly and orthodox minister."[6]

To assure "a speedy peopling of the place" the Proprietors encouraged immigration, and in September a boat from Bermuda brought white servants and the first black slaves to be recorded by name—"John Sr., Elizabeth and John Jr." The Carolina colony was the only English settlement in North America where slaves were introduced virtually at the outset. In early 1671 boatloads of free men and indentures came from Barbados, England, and New York.

That first winter was a cold one and the colonists were shocked by temperatures that remained below freezing long enough to freeze water to the thickness of an inch, and when this information reached London it gave Lord Ashley pause. If the colony did not make a profit for them, the Proprietors were prepared to cut their losses. Indeed to ensure that the Crown remained interested in the venture, the Proprietors soon were flattering their king, Charles II, by politely insisting that the settlement be named "Charles Town" in his honor rather than Albemarle Point.

In 1672 the population of the colony had grown to 268 men, 69 women, and 59 children, and by this time Anthony Ashley Cooper, who had invested over £3,200 there had become the first Earl of Shaftesbury. The colony never gave him the huge profits he anticipated, nor did the colonists adopt the Fundamental Constitutions, which apparently he and his brilliant friend and physician, John Locke, had so carefully drafted. The Fundamental Constitutions did, however, influence the social and political thought of the colonists by emphasizing religious toleration, vast land grants, and a local aristocracy balanced by a modicum of popular representation through an elected Parliament. It recognized that a reconciliation of the differences between "men that have estates" and "men that are in want" was essential to successful governments. The Carolina Parliament, which over time evolved into the Commons House of Assembly, met for the first time at Charles Town in July 1671.

The tiny settlement embodied the rowdiness of a port from its beginnings, and in 1672 the Grand Council censured those persons selling "strong drink" and thereby contributing to "drunkenness, idleness, and quarreling." Henceforth, any person retailing liquor or beer without a license would be punished according to the laws of England.[7]

Each passing year brought new immigrants from the West Indies—big and middling sugar planters, merchants, artisans, sailors, servants, and slaves. They profoundly affected the life of Carolina for generations. With them they brought their institutions and lifestyles. The Barbadians were members of the Anglican church; their slave code became a model for Carolina's slave law; they came for a society combining old-world elegance and frontier boisterousness. Ostentatious in their dress, dwellings, and furnishings, they liked hunting, guns and dogs, military titles like "Captain" and "Colonel," a big midday meal, and a light supper. They enjoyed long hours at their favorite taverns over bowls of cold rum punch or brandy. In sum, the Barbadian well-to-do worked and played hard, drank and ate too much, spent recklessly, and often died young. Experienced, aggressive, ambitious, sometimes unscrupulous, immigrants from Barbados like the Allstons, Beresfords, Fenwicks, Gibbeses, Logans, Moores, and Middletons were not really interested in the Proprietors' dreams and plans for the colony. Independent and enterprising, they sought the quickest routes to riches, and by 1674 they controlled both the Council and the popularly elected Assembly.[8]

Following a series of clashes and alliances with the local Indians, the Ashley River colonists by the mid-1670s were enjoying an expanding trade in deerskins, furs, and Indian slaves. Contrary to the wishes of the Proprietors, the Carolinians enslaved more Indians for their own use and for export than any other English colony. Successful crops of corn—their main food—peas, and wheat were being raised, as were cattle, poultry, sheep, and hogs, and from the vast pine forests they produced tar, pitch, and lumber products. The furs and naval stores were shipped to England for sale; the meat, lumber, and Indian slaves were traded in the West Indies for rum, sugar, and trinkets. A few within the colony were accumulating some wealth, but it would be some years before Carolinians found a product that could be relied on to make money steadily for them the way tobacco made money for the Virginians.[9]

Oyster Point

From the beginning some immigrants received land grants and located beyond the settlement on Albemarle Point. Directly opposite, across the Ashley, was the tip of a wooded peninsula, the Battery today, but called Oyster Point or White Point by the first colonists because of the mounds of opened and discarded oyster shells left there by the Indians. This piece of land soon attracted settlers. Even the aged and feeble Colonel William Sayle, the colony's first governor, recognized the strategic military importance of Oyster Point at the confluence of the Ashley River and what was soon called the Cooper River, as did a member of the Council, Joseph Dalton, who in January 1671 excitedly described the site to Lord Ashley: "It is as it were a Key to open and shutt this settlement into safety or danger" and the site would be "very healthy being free from any noisome vapors and all the Sumer long refreshed with Coole breathing from the sea."

Other colonists agreed with Dalton. By 1671 John Coming, his new bride, Affra, Henry Hughes, Thomas Norris, William Murrell, Hugh Carteret, and John Norton had been granted land on Oyster Point or lived there. Norton, a carpenter, and his black slave, Emanuel, probably built and lived in the first dwelling. In February 1672 the Council selected Oyster Point as the possible location of a new town. The following April, John Culpeper was directed by the Council to "admeasure and lay out" a site on Oyster Point "in a square as much as Navigable Rivers will permit."[10]

At Oyster Point, by the late 1670s more then twenty houses had been built and about twenty more were at various stages of construction. Entrenchments were being dug and cannon mounted. In December 1679 the Proprietors announced that "Oyster Point is . . . a more convenient place to build a towne on than that . . . pitched on by the first settlers" and that "the people's Inclinations tend thither." Therefore, "Oyster Point is the place wee doe appoint for the port towne . . . which you are to call Charles Towne." All agencies of the government were to be transferred there at once.[11]

In laying out the new town, the Proprietors hoped to avoid the narrow, twisting streets of European cities and may have been influenced by the checkerboard plan proposed for the city of London following the great fire of 1666. Cooper had long dreamed of populous Carolina towns with "regular streets" and "beautiful" buildings, and the Proprietors directed that the streets were to be laid out in "broad and . . . straight lines." People granted town lots were required to construct houses within two years and any owner of a lot who wished to build tenements to let had to construct a substantial, two-story dwelling. "Otherwise," they reasoned, "men may build hovels on them, and soe Keepe others from building good homes capable of the receipt of good Familyes." The Proprietors, who had once considered abandoning the Carolina colony, now told the governor, Joseph West, to "give all possible encouragement" to the building of the new town, believing that a populous port at Oyster Point would "draw a plentiful trade and be a great security to the whole settlement."[12]

Additional guns and munitions were moved from the original settlement and by 1681 the Council had granted at least thirty-three lots on Oyster Point, most of them along the Cooper River. In May 1680 one of the colonists, Maurice Mathews, wrote that the town was being carefully laid out so as to "avoid the . . . irregularities" of other English colonies. Resembling a narrow trapezoid four squares long by three wide, it covered about eighty acres. Present-day Meeting Street marked its western boundary and the present-day streets of Beaufain and Water marked its northern and southern boundaries respectively. Mathews observed that "the town is run out into four . . . great streets of 60 foot wide." Each emptied into a "Square of two ackers" where "we are now building a court house." Land also had been set aside "for a Publick Wharfe, . . . Church Yard, and artillery ground."[13]

One of the first streets cut ran north to south, from a creek that ran where Market Street runs today to another creek that flowed deep into the southeastern end of the peninsula, near where Water Street is today and was referred to only as "a street running parallel with Cooper river." Eventually it was called East Bay Street. Two more streets were laid out paralleling it, one becoming known as Church Street and the other, marking the western boundary of the town, was known as "the great street that runs north and south" until acquiring the name Meeting Street.

Running perpendicular to these streets, from the Cooper River to Meeting Street, was a broad avenue called Cooper Street in honor of Lord Ashley but renamed Broad Street in the 1690s. Two streets were cut parallel to Broad. The one to the north was first referred to as the "little street that leads from Cooper River to Ashley River," later Dock Street, and still later Queen Street; the one to the south eventually took its name from one of its first residents, Robert Tradd, believed to be the first male white child born in the town.

Meandering from south to north, bypassing bold creeks and marshes, ran a wide dirt path. Just beyond the town's northern boundaries it traversed an area the colonists called "the Neck" and passed through great stands of cedar, bay, pine, and oak, which abounded with game. Occasionally bobcats and wolves were seen. The settlers marveled at the fauna and flora found along the path. One was amazed at the "great numbers of Fire Flies, who carry their Lanthorns in their Tails." The path connected the "plantations," or farms, of settlers on the Neck and beyond with the town. Planters around Goose Creek on the Cooper or far up the Ashley used the rivers and the dirt path to transport corn, peas, potatoes, and livestock to town, and Indians brought in skins, venison, and fish along this road, which was first called the Broadway or Broad Path and much later renamed King Street.[14]

The town's population increased rapidly in the early 1680s. In May 1680 Maurice Mathews estimated that there were "in all, men, women, and children, about 1000" inhabitants, and two years later Thomas Newe calculated that the town had "about a hundred houses . . . of wood." "Charles Town" soon became the most common spelling of the port, although "Charles Towne" and "Charles-Towne" were still appearing in documents thirty years later.

To encourage immigration the Proprietors advertised widely, making extraordinary claims for Charles Town. Prospective immigrants were told that the very air there "gives a strong Appetite and quick Digestion," that men find "themselves . . . more light-some . . . and that "the Women are very Fruitful."[15] People came from England, Ireland, and the West Indies expecting Charles Town to make them prosperous and gloriously healthy. However, after long voyages on crowded ships, without fresh fruits and vegetables to eat, many of them arrived desperately ill. Furthermore, the hot, humid climate was different from what most of them were used to, and during their first few weeks ashore, their "seasoning time," they were particularly susceptible to infections—and there were plenty of infections to be contracted in Charles Town and the surrounding lowlands. Most white settlers died before reaching the age of forty, and Charles Town acquired a reputation among the sophisticated of western Europe as being the "great charnel house" of America. Some officials recommended that the settlement be relocated.[16]

Government and Factions

The Proprietors expected new immigrants, especially the Dissenters among them, to reduce the power of the independent-minded Barbadians, and they continued to revise the Fundamental Constitutions in the hope that the colony would adopt them.

Better to organize the local machinery of government, the Proprietors in 1682 directed that three counties be established, Berkeley, Craven, and Colleton, each named to honor a Proprietor. Berkeley County, which included Charles Town, was bounded on the north by Craven and on the south by Colleton. The new county court and other governmental agencies were located in Charles Town, which retarded the growth of the county governments. The governor, and the Council and the Assembly, which usually sat as one body, continued to enact legislation for province and town, and commissioners were appointed to carry out the policies pertaining to Charles Town.

Next the Proprietors dismissed Governor Joseph West and replaced him with Joseph Morton, a well-connected leader of the newly arrived English Dissenters. They knew that West was partially controlled by the Barbadian Anglicans who, against proprietary instructions, were dealing in Indian slaves. Attempts by the Proprietors to prohibit trade with pirates, who often put in at Charles Town for supplies, further annoyed the practical Barbadians, for the freebooters spent lavishly, paying for their provisions in gold and silver coin.

Two factions were developing in Carolina. The antiproprietary men, mostly the older settlers the Barbadian Anglicans, formed one party. Because some of them settled at Goose Creek, they were frequently called "the Goose Creek men." Enterprising and ambitious, they were determined to keep control of the government and continue their lucrative trade with the Indians and pirates. The antiproprietary men resented the distant, meddlesome authorities in England. The Dissenters and the more recent immigrants made up the proprietary party. For years these two factions warred over control of the governorship, the Council, and the Assembly. People's politics in early Charles Town were often determined by where they came from, when they came, and where they worshiped.[17]

Having invested a fortune in the colony, the Proprietors hoped that new immigrants would stimulate its economy. Although Charles Town suffered its first epidemic of malaria in 1684 and 1685, the campaign to attract Dissenters nevertheless succeeded grandly. Pamphlets distributed in Europe depicted Carolina as a haven of religious toleration, and when Louis XIV, in October 1685, revoked the Edict of Nantes, which had guaranteed the rights of Huguenots in France, Charles Town was one of the places they fled to; and from England, Scotland, and Ireland, Quakers, Presbyterians, and Baptists joined them.

To protect the "good air" of the town and make it attractive to immigrants, the Carolina Assembly in the 1680s passed acts ordering homeowners to clean up their lots and to prevent their "Swine going loose . . . about Charles Town." To enforce these laws and to "keep the peace," town constables and their deputies were appointed and armed watches were established from ten o'clock at night until half an hour before sun-up. Perhaps the greatest hazard these men faced was drunken sailors whose favorite sport was beating up the night watch.[18]

Usually the dirt streets were full of mariners because the harbors was full of ships, especially during the peak of the shipping season, December to March. Louis Tibou, a French Huguenot, in 1683 observed: "the port is never without ships and the country is becoming a great traffic center." The swaggering sailors, trappers, and Indians, needed policing and the Council passed an act in the 1680s that called for "the suppression of Idle, Drunken and Swearing Persons." In 1682 the Assembly passed an act "for the observation of the Lord's Day," which later was amended to prohibit anyone entering "punch houses, or tippling houses, during the time of Divine Service." The crackdown on drinking was dramatized in 1684 when one desperate woman, Rebeckah Lee, was arrested for "fetching of drink for an Indian squaw" without a liquor license. She asked the court for mercy, since she was attempting only to "gett a penny" for her small children, "my husband having gone . . . to Sea." Occasionally even leading town officials were removed from office for "frequent drunkenness and scandalous behavior." The colony's first Church of England clergyman, Atkin Williamson, is said to have baptized a bear while drunk.[19]

Anglicans had built Charles Town's first church, St. Philip's, in 1683. Constructed of black cypress on a brick foundation and enclosed by a palisade, it stood where St. Michael's stands today. Dissenters also were establishing churches in Charles Town. By 1686 Huguenot immigrants had begun their "French Church" in upper Church Street, and in lower Church Street a Baptist congregation, led by William Screven, established a church by the 1690s. A "White Meeting House" was built by Presbyterians and Congregationalists in the 1680s on the street marking the town's westernmost boundary, giving this thoroughfare its name, Meeting Street. Quakers worshiped in private homes as early as 1682, and in the following decade they met in a "little house" just to the west of the town's first boundaries.[20]

If there were Roman Catholics in Charles Town in the 1680s, they probably took great pains to disguise their religious preference. To most of the colonists "Catholic" meant "Spanish," and the Spanish attack on the Carolina settlement in 1670, feeble though it was, had left the settlers fearful of another invasion from Florida. In 1682 and 1685 acts of the Assembly subjected the free residents of the town to the common defense in case of attack and provided for the construction of several watch houses, one at Sullivan's Island, another at the mouth of the Ashley River.

The anticipated Spanish attack came in 1686, when 100 Spaniards, blacks, and Indians fell on a small settlement to the south near Beaufort, then moved northward to within twenty miles of Charles Town, looting and burning several plantations. The governor summoned militia across Carolina, but on August 26 "a Hurrican wonderfully horrid and distructive" swept over the Spanish attackers who soon turned back to Florida. It was the first of many hurricanes in the recorded history of the city. A new potential threat to the safety of the Carolinians came in 1689 when war was declared between England and France and those two nations began their long struggle for control of North America.[21]

From the mid-1680s to the early 1690s the Barbadian Anglicans, or Goose Creek men, repeatedly frustrated the Proprietors' plans for governing Carolina, resisting again and again efforts to cajole them into adopting the Fundamental Constitutions. In London the power of Parliament was growing, and the Goose Creek men knew it. In 1690, because the Assembly believed that the proprietary Governor Peter Colleton had acted arbitrarily and without the Assembly's consent on matters, the powerful Goose Creek faction ousted him in favor of Seth Sothell, a Proprietor who had recently arrived in Charles Town. The Proprietors soon replaced Sothell with Philip Ludwell who was empowered to appoint a deputy for North Carolina. Separation of the southern from the northern part of the Carolina grant dates from this time. To placate the Goose Creek men, the Proprietors now permitted the Assembly to sit as a separate body, to initiate legislation, to control its membership, and to elect its speaker. A bicameral legislature had emerged and the Commons House of Assembly rapidly evolved into a major political institution.

In 1692 Anglicans who dominated the Council told the leading French settlers that marriages made by Huguenot ministers were illegal and the children of such unions were illegitimate. Immediately the Huguenots protested to the Proprietors, who admonished the governor to ensure that all Protestants enjoyed "liberty of conscience." Shortly thereafter, the Assembly formally extended religious freedom to all Christian immigrants except Roman Catholics.[22]

Freebooters and Rice

Pirates, some believed, posed as great a threat as the Spanish, but others grew rich by provisioning the freebooters. Only under pressure from the Proprietors had the Carolina government passed an act in 1686 "for the restraining and punishing of Privateers." Thereafter a pirate was occasionally captured and hanged in chains at the entrance to the port "as an example to others," but as one observer explained, only the "poor Pyrats" were hanged; "rich ones appear'd publicly and were not molested in the least."

In the mid-1690s, however, the attitudes of the merchants toward the pirates changed. Profits made in exporting had been gradually but steadily rising, until there was more money to be made in exports than in doing business with buccaneers who preyed on the export trade, and Charles Town was beginning to export rice, a product that promised to become even more lucrative than deerskins.

For 300 years Charlestonians believed, probably correctly, that the first rice seeds planted in Carolina came from Madagascar. It is certain that experimental crops of rice had been grown near a creek bank where Water Street runs today and, after ten years of trials and errors, planters were growing rice in commercial quantities and harvesting it in marketable and exportable condition. Merchants and planters had found *the* crop that was to make some of them the richest men in North America.[23]

The colony was not, however, making money for the Proprietors in England, who were beginning to lose interest in it, and in 1695 they appointed as governor John Archdale, the Proprietor who was most interested in making the colonial venture a success. Prudent and practical, Archdale, a Quaker, took control of the government on August 17. He quickly appointed to key positions settlers who were moderate Dissenters or moderate Anglicans and quietly ignored the extremists on either side. Thrilled by the prospects of getting rich, nervous about the growing number of blacks on the streets of Charles Town, fearful of attacks from Spaniards, Frenchmen, Indians, or pirates, and ravaged by epidemics, some of the Dissenters and Anglicans began to realize that they had much in common.

2. 1695–1708:
" . . . all sorts of people"

Involuntary Immigrants

Imports of West Africans rose faster than exports of rice, for the planting, hoeing, and husking of rice required large gangs of laborers. They knew more about the process than the Carolinians who purchased them and, having been exposed to malaria and yellow fever since infancy, were not as susceptible to those dis-

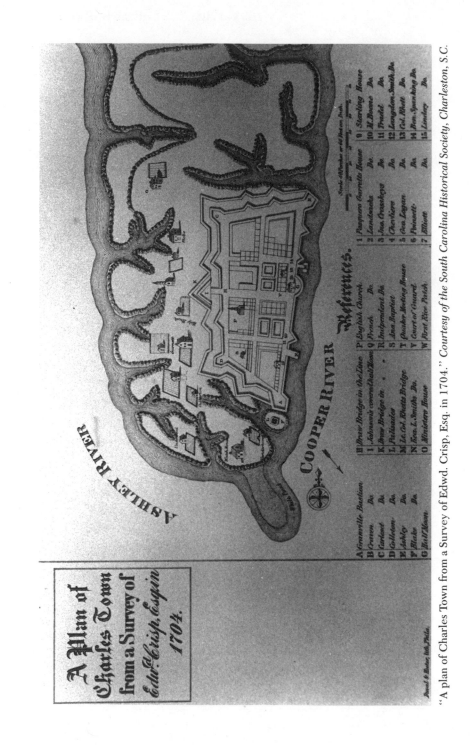

"A plan of Charles Town from a Survey of Edwd. Crisp, Esq. in 1704." Courtesy of the South Carolina Historical Society, Charleston, S.C.

eases as Indian and white laborers, for whom a few weeks in the low-lying, swampy rice fields was often fatal.

In 1696 Carolina's first comprehensive slave law was deemed necessary on the grounds that blacks had "barbarous, wild, savage Natures." The Carolina law was largely copied from Barbadian slave codes, and provided for the policing of slaves and the trial of miscreant slaves.[24]

Hundreds of West Africans passed across Charles Town's new wharfs each year. Some were purchased for labor in the rice fields, others for work in town. Their owners usually gave them a name like Sam, Tom, Doctor, Caesar, Scipio, Moses, Friday, Chloe, Phoebe, or Virtue. If they ran away, the slave law of 1696 provided a severe public whipping of up to forty lashes for the first offense, and persistent runaways were branded, whipped, mutilated, and could be executed, especially if they resisted recapture. In 1697 when three slaves fled Carolina in a bold attempt to reach Spanish Florida, they were captured, returned to Charles Town, and emasculated, one of them dying as a result. His owner, Gabrell Glaze, was paid more than "Sixty five dollars" in compensation.[25]

The dramatic increase in the black slave population of Charles Town and the surrounding countryside alarmed the white inhabitants. In 1701 the Assembly passed a curfew law preventing blacks from "playing the rogue at . . . night" and town constables were to arrest any Afro-American who had no good reason for being abroad and to lock him up until morning, have him whipped "severely," and return him to his owner after a fine was paid.[26]

Wills probated from 1692 to 1700 reflect the new prosperity and hint at the things the people of Charles Town considered important. Heirs inherited Indian and black slaves, real estate, livestock, feather beds, rugs, leather chairs, cedar tables and chests, and brass and iron cooking and eating ware. Men willed silver tobacco boxes, silver tankards and silver-headed canes, swords and pistols; women bequeathed gold rings, watches, lockets, buckles, Bibles, silver bodkins, shoes, and "my best petticoat." Many who made their wills during these years were deeply concerned for their children's education, and a surprising number left funds for the care of "the poor of Charles Town."[27]

With the new prosperity came new taxes. Since the outbreak of war between France and England, the Proprietors had been urging the colonists to fortify the town, but the Assembly, knowing that redoubts could not be constructed without great expense, hesitated. Only when rumors of an impending French attack reached the Assembly in early 1696 did members levy a tax "on Liquors, Etc. imported into, and Skins and Furrs Exported out" of the province so as to pay for fortifications, and a year later the governor of Carolina reported to the Proprietors that the works were underway.[28]

Pestilence, Fire, and Flood

Before long, however, construction of the redoubts and walls came to a sudden halt. During the early summer of 1697 the residents of Charles Town first noticed the signs of a disease terrifying to those who had come from the crowded, unsanitary cities of Europe: high fevers, headaches, vomiting, back pains, followed by festering red eruptions on the skin, were symptoms of smallpox. It swept through the town and raged into the winter months of 1698 killing "200 or 300 persons." Mrs. Affra Coming, who came on the *Carolina* twenty-eight years before, wrote her sister in England that the mortality had been especially high among the Indians who are "unburied, lying upon the ground for the vultures to devouer."

People were still dying in February when an earthquake rumbled through the town, and on the night of February 24 a fire broke out and spread so quickly that in forty-eight hours over fifty families were homeless. "One third" of the town burned and officials reported that the combination of disease and fire "Deadens trade & Discourages Persons . . . to Settle here."[29]

In August 1698 the Proprietors wrote to Carolina's governor expressing sympathy at "your great Disaster" and sent a Mr. Johns, master builder, to direct the rebuilding of the town. A few months later the Assembly authorized the construction of "a House Sixteene foot Long and Tenn foot broad" to be used as a guard house and jail. Nearby a "Pair of Stocks" was to be erected.

In autumn 1698 the Assembly passed the colony's first legislation "for Preventing of Fires." The night watch, which had been "remiss and negligent," was strengthened; the building of stone or brick chimneys was encouraged and they were to be kept clean under penalty of fine; fire commissioners were appointed and authorized to demolish houses to stop fires from spreading, and a tax was levied on homeowners and renters for the purchase of ladders, leather buckets, and fire hooks.[30]

Rebuilding of the town began and work on the fortifications resumed, but by early September 1699 yellow fever, known as "Barbados Fever" or "black vomit," paralyzed the port. Nearly half the Assembly and other government officials were among the victims and business ceased. The town seem deserted except for someone hurrying along with medicines or the death carts rolling by heaping the dead "up one upon another." In the middle of the epidemic a hurricane swept into the town. Survivors remembered a "swelling sea," gale-force winds, and heavy rains, which smashed wharves, undermined the fortifications, and flooded streets. A few people died within the town, while in the harbor a Scottish frigate, the *Rising Sun*, was dashed to pieces and her captain, crew, and ninety-seven passengers perished. A Presbyterian minister, Archibald Stobo, would have been aboard had he not been invited to preach the day before at the Independent Church. A fiery preacher whose contempt for the Church of England was as savage as his hatred of Roman Catholicism, Stobo raised his voice in the colony's religious disputes for years to come.

Like most of Charles Town's yellow fever epidemics, the first one ended only when colder weather killed the mosquitoes that were transmitting the disease that killed approximately 180 inhabitants. It was to be two centuries before the connection between yellow fever and mosquitoes began to be understood.

The colony began the eighteenth century with a confident and efficient campaign to make the seaways safer, which resulted in the public execution of seven pirates in Charles Town in 1700. At about the same time a rumor swept the community that blacks and Indians were plotting to raid the town. An investigation found no substance to the story, but many whites in the colony were affected by a fear of blacks that was to haunt Carolinians for ten generations.[31]

Anglicans and Dissenters

In September James Moore, an ambitious and aggressive Anglican, beguiled the Council into electing him as interim governor and this alarmed the Dissenters. Yet by now if the Presbyterians, Congregationalists, Quakers, and Baptists of the colony were joined by the Huguenots, they could outvote the

Anglicans, and some members of the Assembly enjoyed reminding an Anglican governor that he was no better than his Dissenting neighbor.

Very early in Governor Moore's term of office, while he and the Assembly were still capable of agreeing, legislation was passed to establish a free lending library at Charles Town, one of the first of its kind in North America. Then in 1701 when fears of a Spanish invasion were widespread, he called for the speedy construction of additional defenses and the Assembly authorized the commissioners of the fortifications to build a "brest worke at White Poynt," a "good Substantiall Wall," and gun batteries.[32]

Both religious antagonisms between Anglicans, or "Churchmen," and Dissenters and a struggle for control of the colony's affairs characterized Charles Town politics in the opening years of the eighteenth century. Almost immediately a group of aggressive, sometimes unscrupulous men emerged to lead the Anglican faction while few such bold leaders appeared among the Dissenters. Indeed, in the election of 1701 and subsequent ones, the Dissenters claimed that opposition leaders like Governor Moore, Nicholas Trott, and William Rhett spent election day recruiting unqualified voters—Jews, Quakers, Huguenots, free blacks, white indentured servants—and intimidating opponents in order to elect an Assembly controlled by Anglicans while limiting participation of Congregationalists, Presbyterians, and Baptists.

The Anglicans, who wanted the Church of England to be supported by public taxes, but who were not known for their piety, were at one end of the colony's political spectrum. Indeed, they wished to exclude from public office and polite society everyone who was not a member of the Church of England. The Churchmen felt a profound loyalty to the English monarchy, but had little respect for the colony's English Proprietors. They were eager to profit from the willingness of people in the West Indies and New England to purchase Indian slaves, and given a choice between adding a West African pagan or a Presbyterian member of the British lower classes to the colony's labor pool, the Churchmen were inclined to bring in the black. They also felt it was important to roll back the borders of territories controlled by the Spanish or French.

At the other end of the political spectrum were the Dissenters, "Independents" or Congregationalists, who thought that all churches should be voluntary associations, took their own religious life very seriously, wanted to avoid provoking hostilities from the French, Spanish, and Indians, and found the large numbers of slaves from West Africa disquieting. Though it was diminishing, they also felt some lingering respect for the Proprietors.

Between these two political extremes were several different combinations of religious and political beliefs and practices that made it impossible to divide all the white men in the colony neatly into two parties. None of them would have recognized the term "Anglican," as convenient as it has become for the historian, and although the term "Dissenter" was generally accepted as referring to Presbyterians, Congregationalists, Baptists, and Quakers, the differences between those four denominations, and the differences *within* them, were substantial. Many members of the Church of England in Charles Town, including the rector of St. Philip's, the Reverend Edward Marston, respected the rights of Dissenters and opposed the extremists who were being called Churchmen.

In early February 1702 rumors that war had broken out in Europe again rippled through Charles Town, and Governor Moore stressed the urgency of completing the town's defenses. The Assembly ordered the commissioners of the fortifications to finish the works immediately but refused to vote the additional taxes to do so! Aware that a growing number of the colonists were beginning to enjoy some prosperity, the Assembly was developing a reluctance to tax and spend that was to characterize it for so long and Moore dissolved the body, calling for new elections in March.

One of the colorful characters in the streets of Charles Town at this time was James MacAlpine. Perhaps the town's first music teacher, he also was a champion of the Protestant religion, believing that "the Papists, particularly the Jesuits, were continually plotting his Destruction," and he never went about town without his pistols.[33]

When the new Assembly met in April some legislators demanded an investigation of the recent elections, and an act allowing Roman Catholics to vote was quickly and quietly passed. Strangely inconsistent with the temper of the times, this act was never repealed. It was probably related to the feud between the Churchmen and the Dissenters, but may have been intended to encourage poor Roman Catholics from abroad to come to Carolina. At any rate, the legislators again turned a deaf ear toward Governor Moore's pleas for funds for military preparedness.

Enraged, the governor prorogued the Assembly until May, when he again asked the members " to putt ye Country into a Posture of Defense." A committee was appointed and they agreed that the works were in need of repair, but once more the Assembly refused to vote the necessary funds and the governor sent them home. However, when word arrived that England had officially declared war on France and Spain, and Queen Anne's War was underway, there were enough votes in the Assembly to support the governor's plans to attack the Spanish at St. Augustine. Moore himself led the strike force, which included the itinerant English actor Anthony Aston. Soon after Moore departed, rumors of another slave conspiracy swept Charles Town and the Assembly ordered the constables to take into custody for questioning "Jack Jones & a free Negro and Rebecka Simons a malloto."[34] Again, it may have been a false alarm.

Moore's expedition captured St. Augustine in October, but when Spanish reinforcements arrived he burned the town and retreated toward Carolina. The adventurous young Anthony Aston wrote, "We arrived in Charles Town full of lice, shame, poverty, nakedness, and hunger:—I turned player and poet, and wrote one play on the subject of the country." The performance of this play in Charles Town in 1703 is generally considered the first professional theatrical performance in North America.[35]

The cost of Moore's expedition exceeded the Assembly's authorization by £4,000 sterling and saddled the colony with long-term debt. Moore urged the legislators to emit bills of credit, but his antagonists among them accused him of bungling the invasion and balked at his request. The governor's supporters then stirred up riots and threatened the lives of leading Dissenters. "A drunken crowd with weapons in their hands possessed the streets" for nearly a week in late February 1703.

While a mob held the streets, Governor Moore's interim appointment ended, and Sir Nathaniel Johnson arrived to assume the governorship. One of his first duties was to receive the Reverend Samuel Thomas who had been sent by the Society for the Propagation of the Gospel in Foreign Parts (SPGFP), first organized in England in 1701, as their first missionary to Carolina. His instructions were to take the Yamasee Indians as his flock, but the governor told him that times were not yet propitious for his mission and that there was an area a few miles up the river called

AEtatis: 6
Aprill: 7:
1705

This portrait of Governor Nathaniel Johnson that hangs in the Gibbes Art Gallery was painted in April 1705 by an unknown artist in Charles Town and is one of the earliest known portraits of a public man in America. *Courtesy of the Carolina Art Association, Charleston, S.C.*

Goose Creek that needed more urgently the pastoral care of a priest of the Church of England.[36]

Sailors, Liquor, and Illicit Love

Mixing together in the town's streets were hucksters hawking their wares, indentured white servants, sailors, farmers or "planters," prostitutes, fur traders, African slaves, and sometimes Indian chieftains adorned in ceremonial dress and trailed by a band of retainers. It was a potpourri of nationalities and racial groups and a corresponding Babel of languages and sounds.

The explosive growth of Charles Town made the duties of constables and night watch more difficult. Public inns and taverns sprouted along the waterfront, and prostitution, bastardy, disorder, and public drunkenness increased. The taste of the town's drinking water may have contributed to excessive tippling, for at least one resident found the "Water about Town so Brackish that it is scarcely potable unless mixed with . . . Liquors." Freespending sailors and thirsty Indian traders jammed riverside taverns and punch houses like the Bowling Green House where they could be found "tyed by the Lipps to a pewter engine" of beer, cider, rum punch, brandy, or Madeira wine. These "sparkes," as one who knew them well remarked, thought "little of drinking 15 or 16 pounds [worth] at one Bout."[37]

Sailors were so notorious for causing disorders that in 1703 the night watch was empowered to apprehend and hold until morning any seaman frequenting a public house after dark! The watch also had the authority to question and lock up any "suspicious" persons seen abroad at night "after the tatoo." Female indentured servants sometimes found a quick route to freedom through prostitution, and in May 1703 the Assembly began considering legislation to prevent "Mens Cohabitating with women with whom they are not married, & against Strumpets" and in September passed an "Act against Bastardy."[38]

That same autumn citizens were following intently the town's first major criminal case involving illicit love, intrigue, and murder. It was being tried before chief justice of the Province of South Carolina, Judge Nicholas Trott, Esq., who was descended from an influential English family. Presiding over the Court of General Sessions he heard Pleas of the Crown, mostly criminal cases, and Common Pleas, civil matters. Like the Assembly, the courts met in private dwellings or public taverns.

The trial involved Sarah Dickenson and her lover, Edward Beale, who successfully conspired to murder their spouses. A jury found them and an accomplice, Joshua Brenan, guilty, and Judge Trott sentenced Sarah Dickenson to be "burned to death" and Beale and Brenan to be hanged.[39]

Trott and others, including Governor Nathaniel Johnson, who soon showed himself to be one of the toughest of the Churchmen, evidently managed the elections to the Assembly of November 1703 so as to limit the strength of the most vehement of the Dissenters.

New Defenses

In December the Assembly passed legislation to build a sea wall fronting the Cooper River and to construct entrenchments, parapets, sally ports, gates, and drawbridges around the town. Colonel William Rhett was appointed to oversee the construction and the work began in early 1704. Gangs of bricklayers, carpenters, and slave laborers were pressed into service. Any white man who refused to work could be imprisoned; loitering resulted in reduced wages; if Colonel Rhett did not speedily finish the fortifications, he could be fined.

Granville Bastion, the town's major battery located near the southeastern tip of East Bay Street, was enlarged. Here on a fill of earth and oyster shells a grillage of palmetto logs overlaid by cypress planks was built as the foundation for a fifteen-foot-high brick wall.[40] The new sea wall ran northward from Granville Bastion paralleling the Cooper River and Bay Street. At the foot of Broad Street it connected with the half-moon battery, near the present site of the Exchange building. The wall continued on to Craven's Bastion, at the eastern end of present-day Market Street, and then the line of fortifications turned north paralleling present-day Cumberland Street. At the intersection with Meeting Street the curtain line joined Carteret Bastion and here the entrenchments turned south along Meeting Street. Where the fortifications crossed Broad Street a deep moat was dug, a drawbridge built over it, and another half-moon battery begun. Near the intersection of Meeting and present-day Water streets, at the southwestern angle of the lines, Colleton's Bastion was started. Then the line of entrenchments and redoubts were dug eastward to join Ashley, Blake, and finally Granville bastions, completing the encirclement of the town. Charleston and St. Augustine are the only cities within the present boundaries of the continental United States that were at one time correctly referred to as walled cities. Just beyond the entrenchments, near what is today the corner of Church Street and South Battery, marshland was filled and a brick watch house built.

As more and more persons with their livestock crowded inside the town's fortifications odors increased and became "very offensive." In the early 1700s the Assembly ordered any privy deemed a nuisance to be covered over with dirt. Residents also complained that the air was "infected" by the penning and slaughtering of animals within the town and that "dung and intrails of beasts" were everywhere. Some believed that these conditions "caused many . . . diseases" and eventually the Assembly prohibited the keeping and butchering of livestock within the town. But complaints about the town's "Nasty . . . Streets" continued and finally, in 1710, the Assembly created the post of town scavenger empowered with the authority to levy fines on persons who did not clean the streets before their dwellings and businesses. Nor did the Assembly act speedily to prevent huckstering in the streets despite repeated requests to prohibit it and to establish a central market place, but the Assembly did remain acutely aware of the threat of fire. Since the furnaces kept by townspeople to boil pitch, tar, rosin, and turpentine or for the distillation of whiskey could lead to a general conflagration, the Assembly in 1704 prohibited the production of naval stores and the keeping of large stills.[41]

Within a year of encircling the town with defensive works, town officials were concerned about the damage being done to the fortifications during "this time of danger of invasion" by persons playing about them and the Assembly enacted bills to "prevent such mischiefs." Infractions of the law promised fines and thirty stripes on the bare back. The Assembly also doubled the town watch, and all males "able to bear arms" were required to take their turns in either the militia or the watch.

In 1704 James Moore, the former governor, was in northwestern Florida with an army he financed out of his own pocket with the blessings of Governor Johnson. In a militarily brilliant but brutal campaign, Moore slaughtered and tortured Indians and whites and plundered and laid waste to the Spanish mission system. He withdrew taking 1,000 Indians as slaves and succeeded in extending British control of the trade in Indian slaves, from which he expected to make a handsome profit for himself.

The Assembly, due to meet on May 10, 1704, was suddenly convened by Governor Johnson on April 26. Several days later and before the Dissenters could organize opposition, a bill passed by a slim margin excluding from membership in the Assembly anyone who was not a member of the Church of England.[42] Then in the fall of the year the Assembly passed an act that established the Church of England as the tax-supported church of the colony. All the demoralized Dissenters could do was ask their London lobbyist, Joseph Boone, to attempt to get the two acts disallowed.

Trade with England, Jamaica, Barbados, and the Leeward Islands was growing rapidly, leading one observer to declare that Carolina "was in as thriving circumstances as any colony on the continent of English America." Outward-bound cargoes of naval stores increased sharply when the Crown began offering price supports, or "bounties," in 1704. Over eighty sails a year cleared the harbor during the early years of the eighteenth century. Thousands of Indian slaves captured inland were manacled and marched to Charles Town by traders who were staked financially by some of the canniest merchants the world has known. The men who were on their way to becoming the aristocrats of British North America were beginning to make their fortunes in Charles Town by importing African slaves and exporting Indian slaves.[43]

The town's prosperity had attracted at least one portrait painter by 1705. We do not know his or her name, but in April the artist completed a portrait of Governor Nathaniel Johnson that hangs in the Gibbes Art Gallery today and is one of the earliest know portraits of a public man in America.

While Johnson was sitting for his portrait, Joseph Boone was busy in London. Daniel Defoe, paid a fee and informed of the events that had alarmed the Dissenters of Carolina, wrote a pamphlet entitled *Tyranny of Party*, which helped create a feeling in London that the Exclusion Act and the Church Act passed in Charles Town in 1704 were obnoxious. The Dissenters pointed out to the House of Lords that the Fundamental Constitutions had specifically guaranteed the liberty of the Christian colonists to hold "any speculative opinion in religion," and they protested that in 1703, "when a new Assembly was to be chosen . . . the election was managed with very great . . . injustice, and all sorts of people, . . . Jews, servants, common sailors, and negroes were admitted to vote." On the advice of the attorney general, Queen Anne ordered the Proprietors to void both acts. However, if the

Dissenters believed they had won the struggle for power in Charles Town, they were mistaken. It was the Proprietors who had lost influence, not the Churchmen.

Daily life in the booming boisterous frontier town was grueling and did not yet allow much time for abstract thought or for the arts, except for popular songs and casual dancing in the taverns, but money was changing hands. In warehouses and shops on Bay and Broad streets one could find sugar, rum, molasses, woolens, silks, calico petticoats, scissors, needles, guns, hoes, nails, knives, bullets, flints, ironware, and drinking and looking glasses. By 1706 there were about 3,500 people crowded into the town, which contained about 250 dwellings. Nearly 500 adult white males were earning a living in one aspect or another of the export-import trade, and a few of them were becoming rich and influential. James Moore, however, was not one of those who had a knack for getting rich, and when he died in 1706 he was in debt.[44]

Late in the summer another epidemic of yellow fever hit Charles Town and when Spanish and French commanders at St. Augustine heard of it they planned to attack. On Saturday, August 24, the townspeople saw five puffs of smoke arise from lookout posts on Sullivan's Island signaling an attacking force of five vessels. Alarm guns were fired and messengers were dispatched to alert the county militia who rushed in, camping just outside the town so as not to expose the men to the "fever." The invasion force found the channel through the sandbars at the mouth of the harbor and on August 28 the leaders sent a messenger ashore under a flag of truce and invited Governor Johnson to surrender the town, giving him an hour to respond. The governor replied that he needed less than a minute's time to refuse. Two days later, just before dawn, Spanish soldiers landed on the Neck just to the north of Charles Town. Governor Johnson sent militiamen to engage the Spanish and they killed and wounded about eighteen, talking some sixty prisoners. The next day Colonel William Rhett with several armed brigantines and sloops sailed down the Cooper to attack the French ships, but before Rhett reached them dirty weather blew up and the French ships scattered. To the north and south of Charles Town, French and Spanish raiding parties were beaten back and a French vessel and 230 raiders were captured. Their commanders had underestimated the defensive works at Charles Town and the willingness of the county militia to defend the disease-racked port. While the yellow fever was killing nearly 5 percent of the townspeople, the French and Spanish between them managed to kill only one Carolinian.[45]

"Establishing" the Church of England

Late in 1706 the Assembly again passed an Establishment Act, prescribing the boundaries of ten Church of England parishes in South Carolina and specifying modest public taxation for the maintenance of church buildings and clergy salaries. St. Philip's embraced Charles Town and the surrounding peninsula and received an annual sum of £150 for its rector. The act "established" the Church of England in South Carolina in terms that no English official could disapprove of, and the Dissenters of South Carolina would have to live with it for a long time. They believed, probably correctly, that they saw in the cleverly written act the fine legal hand of Chief Justice Nicholas Trott, against whom they vented much of their anger in the following months. The Dissenters knew they could no longer count on the Proprietors to protect them, for it was the Proprietors who had sent Nathaniel Johnson to govern the colony. Leaders of the Church party and of the Dissenters enlisted the "common sort" of people to continue their bitter disputes in violent confrontations in the streets, one Churchman observing that the "common sort" would "do anything for a glass of liquor." Women became deeply involved in disputes, one citizen noting that "women of the town . . . turned Politicians . . . and have a Club where they meet weekly . . . ."[46]

The protests gradually died away, however. The Churchmen had won by a combination of close cooperation, determination, and political chicanery. Dr. Francis Le Jau, who arrived in 1706 as the representative of the SPGFP, at first thought that the local motive in establishing the Church of England "was grounded upon true zeal for the glory of God," but soon concluded that, rather, it was for "revenge, [and] self interest." Assigned to St. James's parish (Goose Creek), he was invited to celebrate communion at St. Philip's on Easter Sunday, 1707, and was dismayed to find that only twenty-four people received the sacraments.

Annually the Anglican property holders of the parish elected vestrymen, who were responsible for overseeing parish finances, church repairs, the registration of all marriages, births, and deaths, and for establishing a school for the parish children. The vestry of St. Philip's had considerable authority in local government as they appointed church wardens, usually town merchants, who collected funds for the care of the poor and oversaw local elections.

In May 1707 Captain Thomas Walker was commissioned to complete the town's defenses and a work was begun at "Windmill Point," on James Island opposite Charles Town, to guard the southern approach to the harbor. Later this strong defensive point was named Fort Johnson. By the summer of 1708, the Assembly was able to report to the Proprietors that Charles Town was "surrounded with . . . Bastions, . . . Ditched & pallasaded & mounted with Eighty-Three guns."

The port was fortified and prosperous, imports and exports were increasing rapidly, the Spanish had been rebuffed, and the Church of England was established throughout the colony. In a report dated September 17, 1708, Governor Nathaniel Johnson presented the good news to the Board of Trade in London that the colony was flourishing and well populated—there were 9,580 inhabitants of which 3,960 were free white men, women, and children, 120 white male and female servants, 1,400 Indian slaves, and 4,100 Afro-American slaves. Unique among the North American colonies, South Carolina now had a population of more blacks than whites.[47]

❦ 3. 1708–1720: Charles Town's First Revolution

Gideon and Henrietta Johnston

To supervise the church in South Carolina, the bishop of London appointed the Reverend Gideon Johnston as his commissary to the colony and rector of St. Philip's. The ship carrying Reverend Mr. Johnston, his artist-wife Henrietta, and their four children arrived off Charles Town in late summer 1708. It was low tide and the bars at the harbor's mouth were impassable. Anxious to begin his duties, the redoubtable Reverend Mr. Johnston struck out for shore in a small boat with two other men, but a sudden squall drove them ashore far to the south. Johnston later recalled that for days he had nothing "to Eat or Drink . . . but Sea Weeds and his own Urine." Eventually he reached Charles Town prostrate in the bottom of a canoe, suffering from exposure and dehydration.

Johnston received a cool reception at St. Philip's, whose members resented an appointment made 3,000 miles away and made it clear that they preferred to keep their present rector, Richard Marsden. The growing Americanization of the church and the independence of the congregation was reflected in their question: "What has the B[ishop] of London to do with us?" Only after the governor intervened did Marsden resign and the parishioners elect Johnston as their new rector. With his family he moved into the long, narrow, two-story brick parsonage house northwest of the town, just outside the fortifications. Badly in need of repairs, it was surrounded by a small garden and wide, unplanted acres, but the congregation also furnished him "two negro slaves and a stock of cattle." The Johnston household suffered through "fever and ague . . . the seasoning to the country" to which all newcomers were subjected. Johnston found that his £150 a year in Carolina currency was much too meager, for he needed £300 to £400 in Carolina money to live in a style that £100 sterling would buy in London, and he wrote a friend in 1709: "Were it not for the assistance my wife gives me by drawing pictures . . . I shou'd not have been able to live."[48]

Henrietta Johnston began accepting commissions to paint the gentry soon after her arrival. The first American to work in pastels, she depicted her contemporaries with her own combination of skill and naïveté. Her primitive portraits combine enough charm and honesty to make one grateful that more than thirty survive.

Income from Henrietta's paintings, charity, credit extended by Charles Town's shopkeepers, and free medical attention from Dr. John Thomas, a Huguenot physician, saved them from starvation. Johnston believed that Dr. Thomas was the "only person that deserves the name Physician in this place."

Despite hardships, Johnston vigorously pursued his duties as rector of St. Philip's and as commissary, supervising the clergy in the nearby counties and seeking to ensure the establishment of the Church of England. He preached, catechized children, visited the sick, and buried the dead, which he found to be "oftimes very Nauseaus" in hot weather. And he met frequently with the vestry on the care of the poor. Johnston's predecessors at St. Philip's, Edward Marston and Richard Marsden, were jealous of him, and Marston sometimes followed him around town calling him an "Irish rapparee," or bandit, " . . . a covetous, and Schismatical minister." Johnston may have been relieved when Marston got into a fist-fight and was imprisoned and Richard Marsden fled Charles Town charged with indebtedness and fraud.[49]

Commissary Johnston considered his campaign to establish the church in South Carolina "dangerous and difficult Warfare." Two Scotch-Presbyterian preachers gave him trouble. One, a Reverend Mr. Pollock, denounced the Church of England as "a Scandalous Church" and the other, Archibald Stobo, who had been left behind by the 1699 hurricane and now had a church, Johnston found to be "a fierce and violent man." A ship carpenter, William Screven, was the sometime Baptist minister, whom Johnston thought "extremely ignorant." Other Anglican ministers took a similarly haughty and disdainful view of the colony's Baptist clergy. Dr. Francis Le Jau described them as "Cunning and Artful" enough to "ensnare" the "Simple and Ignorant." However, Commissary Johnston did enjoy a cordial relationship with the minister of Charles Town's Huguenot church, the Reverend Mr. L'Escot, whom he came to regard as "a Person of great merit."

By 1713 Johnston was delighted to report to the bishop of London that he believed that the number of Anglicans in the colony exceeded the number of Dissenters. Nevertheless, Presbyterians, Baptists, Independents, and Quakers, in that order, still had sizable congregations and the Johnstons counted many Dissenters among their closest friends. Henrietta painted portraits of them and their families. The commissary's Anglican friends and benefactors included the governor and Colonel William Rhett and his "good Lady" who contributed £30 for the silver of St. Philip's. Yet Commissary Johnston regretted that many of his parishioners remained "a Whimmish and Stubborn people."[50]

Soon after his arrival in Charles Town, appalled by the ignorance, illiteracy, and immorality he encountered, Johnston persuaded influential citizens of the need for a local school, and in April 1710 the Assembly passed an act to establish "a Free School . . . for the instruction of Youth" in grammar, arts and sciences, and the principles of Christianity. Two years later the Assembly voted a house, lands, and £100 a year, for the schoolmaster, requiring that he be a member of the Church of England. John Douglas was appointed the first master of the school and after him John Whitehead, a member of the SPGFP. Yet by Whitehead's death in 1716 no school had been built and there were few books and fewer pupils. A new schoolmaster was not appointed until 1722.[51]

No one felt the need for a new Anglican church in Charles Town more keenly than the rector of St. Philip's. The expanding congregation was outgrowing the small, cypress church, which was badly in need of repairs. Johnston recommended the building of a new church to anyone who would listen, and on March 1, 1711, the Assembly passed an "Act for Erecting a New Brick Church." Johnston and a group of prominent citizens were appointed to raise the money and to oversee the design and construction of the church. The site selected was on "the east side of Church-street, a few poles north of Queen-street" and construction soon began, but was interrupted in the summer by epidemics of yellow fever and smallpox. From August through February 1712 Charles Town endured the worst and the longest "sickly season" in its history.

Commissary Johnston was at the beds or gravesides of his parishioners day and night. Overworked, despondent, often ill himself, Johnston believed the epidemics were God's "Judgement upon the place (for they are a Sinfull People)." Citizens shut themselves up in their houses "for fear of being Infected" and the commercial life of the bustling port came to a halt. On Christmas Day Johnston observed: "Instead of the usual Joy and festivity . . . very few are seen . . . abroad." Before the epidemics ended, 300 to 400 slaves had died and perhaps an equal number of whites, approximately a quarter of the total population of the town.[52]

In June 1712 the Assembly passed an act "for the more effectual Preventing the Spreading of Contagious Distempers" and Gilbert Guttery was appointed the first health commissioner at the modest annual salary of £40. Empowered to board any ship coming into the harbor to determine the state of health of all aboard, Guttery could order that anyone found ill be quarantined in the "pest house" on Sullivan's Island. The pest house was sixteen by thirty feet, and here the quarantined patient would remain under penalty of fine or whipping for leaving until released by the health commissioner.[53]

Life had nearly returned to normal in September 1713 when a hurricane smashed into Charles Town and raged for twelve hours. Vessels were driven ashore, a new lookout post on Sullivan's Island was blown down, huge waves battered the fortifications, and the sea poured into the streets, sweeping away several houses and drowning about seventy persons. The new St. Philip's Church, nearly ready for roofing, suffered extensive damage and for several years after the hurricane no work was done on the building. "The great obstacle," Johnston lamented, was "the Want of Workmen . . . most of them being in the Army."

The Yamasee War

The Yamasee Indian War of 1715 took priority over the building of churches. For years traders financed by Charles Town's merchants had plundered, killed, and enslaved the Indians of the backcountry. Now, at long last, the Yamasees and their confederates—Creeks, Choctaws, and Catawbas—retaliated with devastating suddenness. On Good Friday, April 15, 1715, they fell on frontier settlements eighty miles southwest of Charles Town, butchering about 100 persons, including the wealthy Indian trader and legislator Thomas Nairne, who was roasted to death. The Indians rapidly moved northward, their terrifying war whoops going up along the Combahee and Edisto rivers, and then along the Stono just a few miles south of Charles Town. Raiding parties struck along the upper reaches of the Ashley and Cooper rivers and the Santee, murdering, pillaging, and burning. Refugees streamed into the town and the governor called out the South Carolina militia and led them in a counterattack. Mostly frightened women and children remained in town where they crowded together exposed to an infectious "flux and fever," which "carried away . . . children chiefly."[54]

Terrified by the possibility of an attack on Charles Town itself, leading citizens overcame their fears of arming blacks and, in an unprecedented move, the Assembly ordered that slaves be enlisted and equipped, and by the late summer 400 blacks joined an army of 600 whites in the field. But the sight of armed slaves marching through Charles Town's streets and the nearby countryside unnerved many people, and petitions reached the Assembly asking that the Afro-Americans be disarmed and discharged.

The Carolinians sought help from the Proprietors, but they refused to spend any more money on Carolina and indicated that the colonists should rely on their own resources. The crisis ended only when the Cherokees at the western end of the the colony agreed to aid the Carolinians by attacking the Creeks in early 1716, thus relieving the pressure on Charles Town and helping to end one of the bloodiest and most costly of the Indian wars in colonial America.[55]

Trade had come to a standstill during the war and the colony's indebtedness to London creditors now totaled £100,000. The redemption of £65,000 of paper money printed to finance the war appeared doubtful. Crops to within a few miles of Charles Town had not been planted for several years, buildings and fences had been burned, and livestock slaughtered or carried off. At least 400 Carolinians, mostly farmers, had been murdered and many others had abandoned their fields and fled the colony. Years would pass before crops and the stocks of cattle reached prewar levels. The spring of 1717 brought acute food shortages and soaring prices. "We are ready to eat up one another for want of provisions," one resident asserted.

Governor Robert Johnson, the son of the former governor Sir Nathaniel Johnson, arrived in Charles Town in the summer of 1717. A popular and able leader, Johnson was the last proprietary governor and was subsequently appointed a royal governor of Carolina. The summer after he arrived an epidemic of "small pox and malignant fever" (probably yellow fever again), "carryed off great Numbers of people," in the town, but with colder weather the diseases abated, and by the late autumn one resident observed that "the greatest Plague to us now is by Piracy on our Coast."[56]

The War against the Pirates

In June 1718 the notorious pirate Edward Teach ("Blackbeard"), with four ships and 400 men plundered vessels in the harbor and seized some of their passengers, whom he promised to return for a chest of medicines. If Governor Johnson did not comply, "Blackbeard" threatened to send him the heads of the hostages, including those of Samuel Wragg, a member of the Council, and Wragg's four-year-old son. While Governor Johnson considered the demands, Teach's crew paraded through the town's streets. The governor met his demand and provided nearly 400 pounds of medical supplies. In response "Blackbeard" stripped his hostages of their finery and sent them ashore nearly naked. A few days later the pirates hoisted their sails, leaving Charles Town's inhabitants humiliated and angry.

Johnson asked the Proprietors for several frigates and a large force of soldiers to defend the harbor, but no assistance arrived from England. In late August the black flag again waved off the bar, and ships were seized and their cargoes plundered. Enraged merchants under the command of William Rhett outfitted two sloops, the *Henry* and the *Sea Nymph*, and in September the two vessels carrying a force of 130 men dropped down the Cooper and into the open sea. Rhett's expedition found the notorious Stede Bonnet refitting in the Cape Fear River, and after a furious and bloody exchange of gunfire, Bonnet surrendered. When Rhett entered Charles Town with thirty-five prisoners in early October, he was a hero.[57]

Colonel William Rhett by Henrietta Johnston. *Courtesy of the Carolina Art Association, Charleston, S.C.*

While awaiting trial, most of the pirates were held under heavy guard in the town's Watch House, but Bonnet, known as "a gentleman by birth and education," and his sailing master, David Herriot, were given lodgings at the home of the town marshal. Some people, perhaps fearing that testimony would link them with the freebooters, did not want Bonnet to come to trial. In late October the sentinels posted outside Bonnet's lodgings were bribed with gold and, three days before the trials were scheduled to begin, Bonnet and Herriot escaped. Governor Johnson immediately offered a reward for the fugitives dead or alive.

Bonnet and Herriot fled in a small boat provided by admirers, but bad weather forced them ashore at Sullivan's Island. While Colonel Rhett raised a posse to search for Bonnet, two pirate ships appeared off the coast and rumors flew that they were going to sack the town.

Governor Johnson called an emergency session of the Council and proposed an attack on the pirates. Four vessels lying at the town wharves were pressed into service, fitted out with guns, and disguised as merchant ships. Three hundred men volunteered as crew. Meanwhile, the people of Charles Town were in a punitive mood as the trial of Bonnet's crew began.

The Court of the Vice-Admiralty, Chief Justice Nicholas Trott presiding, convened in a private home on October 28. The attorney general of Carolina, Richard Allen, conducted the prosecution, arguing that impudent and arrogant pirates could no longer be allowed to terrorize citizens, that depredations on the commerce of the colony had to be stopped, and that examples had to be made to ensure the safety of the town. No lawyer came forward to assist the defendants, who pleaded Not Guilty on the grounds that they had been forced into piracy, but Judge Trott interrupted their pleas, denounced them, and sentenced them to death by hanging.[58]

In the early morning hours of November 5 the four ships personally commanded by Governor Johnson rode toward the harbor's mouth. The pirates, believing them to be unarmed merchantmen, attacked, whereupon Johnson ran up the king's colors and gave the pirates a broadside. The freebooters piled on sail and headed for the open sea, but two of Johnson's vessels closed quickly on the pirate ship and for four hours they fought, rolling and pitching, yardarm to yardarm. Around noon Johnson's volunteers leaped aboard the pirate vessel, killed the captain and many of his crew, and clapped the others in irons. Governor Johnson pursued a second ship into the open sea and in midafternoon the pirates surrendered unconditionally. Celebrating citizens crowded the town's wharves to welcome the governor and his prizes. Twenty-six freebooters had been slain and the nineteen taken alive were locked into the Watch House to await trial.

In early November Colonel Rhett and his posse brought in Stede Bonnet, who had been captured on Sullivan's Island. Twenty-nine of Bonnet's men previously condemned to death by Judge Trott were hanged on November 8. Their bodies were left "dancing" for several days as an example and then buried below the high-water mark off White Point. Two days later Stede Bonnet stood trial. Judge Trott declared that Bonnet faced not only physical death but "everlasting burning . . . in fire and brimstone" and Governor Johnson set his date of execution for December 10.

The nineteen pirates captured by Governor Johnson were brought to trial on November 19 and five days later Judge Trott sentenced them to be hanged. They too were buried off White Point.

As the date for Bonnet's execution approached, some townspeople pressured Governor Johnson to pardon him. Rumor circulated that the educated, dashing "gentleman" had been driven to piracy by a shrewish, nagging wife. Colonel Rhett, who had promised Bonnet that he would seek clemency for him, volunteered to escort Bonnet to England for a new trial. But the governor remained adamant.

On December 10 Stede Bonnet, manacled and clutching a nosegay of wildflowers, was taken in a hurdle to the place of execution near White Point where the once bold pirate appeared terrified and near collapse. The executioner dropped the noose over this head and around his neck and then Bonnet was "swung off" the cart. He died the agonizing death of strangulation, the invention of a gallows that would break the victim's neck being years away. Forty-nine pirates had been executed within five weeks. After 1718 the few buccaneers who appeared off Charles Town did not linger.[59]

Leading citizens were prompt to point out that the people of Charles Town had saved themselves from Indians and pirates without much help from Proprietors or king. Increasingly the townspeople resented the men who tried to govern from thousands of miles away.

A Bloodless Revolution

In early 1719 the Proprietors disallowed certain import duties passed by the Assembly, prohibited further issuance of money, and ended the policy of granting land to settlers, claiming for themselves the vast lands taken from the Yamasees. The town's merchants particularly disliked the disallowance of the import duties, since any new taxes would have to be assessed now on real and personal properties. Next the Proprietors ordered the reorganization of the Council, which also alarmed the Carolinians, who reasoned that if one branch of their government could be changed by executive fiat so too could others. Then in July 1719, Governor Johnson at the Proprietors' request dissolved the Assembly and called for new elections.

When news arrived in Charles Town early in November that a Spanish armada was being readied to invade Carolina, alarmed residents worried about the town's fortifications, which had remained in ruins since the devastating hurricane of 1713. Influential citizens urged the English government to send regular troops and frigates to defend Charles Town. In mid-November one citizen noted that the "Substantial people" were "very uneasy" and predicted correctly that "they will endeavor to make themselves independent of the proprietors and get themselves under the King's government as the other Colonies in America are." Governor Johnson himself realized that some of the "Richest Inhabitants" had stirred up the masses and convinced them that only the Crown could protect them.

Convened at Charles Town on December 10, the Assembly declared itself "the government until His Majesty's pleasure be known." When Governor Johnson refused to accept the new government, the rebels elected as provisional governor General James Moore, Jr., who had led a very successful attack on the Tuscarora Indians and was the popular son of an unpopular governor. They chose December 21, a day previously set aside for a muster of the militia in Charles Town, to proclaim Moore governor. From his plantation home Belvidere, Governor Johnson rushed to town and ordered the militia to disperse, but Colonel Parris who commanded the troops ordered his men to level their muskets at Governor Johnson "and bid him stand off." General

Moore was inaugurated as governor and William Rhett, who had ardently supported Johnson and the Proprietors, went over to the rebels when he learned they would carry the day. Some months later the ever ambitious Rhett and the local Anglican rectors supported Johnson's attempt to regain control of the colony. When it failed, Johnson departed for England and without bloodshed the "Charles Town Revolution" had ended proprietary government in South Carolina.[60]

❦ 4. 1720–1730: Interim

Governor Nicholson and Commissary Garden

Rumors of a Spanish invasion still flew in Charles Town, and while Carolinians awaited the Crown's representative, the interim government rushed ahead with defensive preparations. By late 1720 one observer wrote that the town was now "regularly Fortified and hath about 100 Guns mounted on the Walls," but the Spanish fleet was wrecked in a storm off Providence Island and the feared invasion never came.

On May 22, 1721, leading citizens of Charles Town greeted South Carolina's first provisional governor appointed by the Crown, Francis Nicholson, whom they soon discovered to be "profane, passionate and headstrong." The sixty-six-year-old Nicholson, a zealous Anglican with a deep interest in science and education, had served in England's American colonies since 1686 as both professional soldier and governor.

The devastating Yamasee War, pirate raids, heavy taxation for defense, the issuing of paper money that caused soaring prices, and a severe drought in 1720 followed by heavy rains two years later, which destroyed about one-half of the rice crop, disrupted the economy of South Carolina. Governor Nicholson's insistence on additional issues of paper money in 1722 and 1723 precipitated more inflation and increased political bickering between creditors and debtors. Merchants led by Joseph and Samuel Wragg charged that the money bills would destroy the public credit, while small farmer-debtors championed the inflated currency. Long and bitter, this dispute soured relations between Charles Town's mercantile community and Nicholson.[61]

The governor's plans to create a government for Charles Town independent of the Assembly also brought sharp criticism.

The act "For the Better Government of Charles Town" passed the Assembly in June 1722. It changed the name of the town to Charles City and Port and specified that a mayor, six aldermen, and twelve councilmen would govern for life and elect their successors. Although New York and Philadelphia were already governed by similar systems, many Carolinians petitioned the Crown for relief, charging that the act was rushed through the Assembly in "a secret manner," that it would create "the completest Oligarchy . . . ever," and that so great would be the "grievances" that many would leave Charles Town. The Crown disallowed the act, and local government would not be established in Charles Town until after the American Revolution.

Nicholson attempted to exclude Dissenters from the Assembly and to prohibit their ministers from performing marriages. When three Presbyterian preachers arrived in Charles Town in the summer of 1724 Nicholson was outraged and he tried unsuccessfully to drive them away. He warned the bishop of London that Dissenters "infuse ante Monarchial Principles into the People and are Setting up for an Independt Government both in Church and State," and should be prohibited from coming into the colony.

Charles Town's Anglican clergy enthusiastically agreed with Governor Nicholson. Unpopular since 1721 when local rectors sided with the Proprietors and against the rebel government, the Anglican clergy looked to Nicholson to help them restore confidence in the church. The Reverend Alexander Garden, who held an M. A. degree from the University of Aberdeen, had been appointed by the bishop of London in 1720 to fill the pulpit at St. Philip's and serve as commissary to the colony. He was a strong personality, a vigorous supporter of the church and education, and perfect for the task facing him.

When he first arrived, Garden was informed by the clergy, who had long been disliked by the poor and uneducated because of their condescending attitude, that they now were insulted by both the rebel elite *and* the "inferior sort of People." Garden's likable personality and his vigorous leadership of St. Philip's and its 300 communicants soon began to dispel this local hostility toward Anglicanism. He and Governor Nicholson persuaded the Assembly to raise the salaries of ministers and to appropriate funds for the completion of St. Philip's Church and for the grammar school, which had been defunct for several years.[62]

When the Reverend Thomas Morritt was appointed headmaster by the SPGFP in early 1723, Nicholson prodded the Assembly into voting Morritt a salary of £100 pounds annually, and the Reverend Mr. Garden offered him the use of St. Philip's parsonage as a temporary lodging and a meeting place until a new school and master's house were built. Morritt began his job with great enthusiasm, teaching his pupils Latin, composition, geography, and classical history. His students sang at Sunday services at St. Philip's and afterward both Morritt and Garden catechized them. In this way the school was used as an agency to win young new communicants. A year after he arrived, the school enrolled forty-five boys, but by mid-1726, however, Morritt was becoming despondent. "There is no Library here," he complained, and both he and his wife were "fateagued" from running the school; the Assembly was bickering over where to build the new school house; and worried that his present dwelling would fall down, Morritt resigned in December 1726. The school continued under a succession of headmasters, with a curriculum less rigorously classical.[63]

By early 1721 repairs were underway at last on the structure that was to be the new St. Philip's Church, which had been so severely damaged by the hurricane eleven years before; and on Easter Day 1723, the first services were held in the new building. It was a massive, brick edifice of "lofty arches and massive pillars." An octagonal tower topped by a dome and a "quadrangular Lantern" and weathervane soared eighty feet above church and town and became a comforting symbol to those approaching by land or sea. Persons who worshiped there or visited the church described it as a "work of . . . Magnitude Regularity Beauty & not . . . paralleled in this majestys Dominions in America."

St. Philip's Church physically testified to the growing wealth and power of Anglicanism in Charles Town. In April 1724 the Reverend Alexander Garden enthusiastically reported to the bishop of London that no less then 400 parishioners attended Sunday services. By way of congratulation, the bishop sent an organ to be used in the church.[64]

Garden was distressed, however, by developments some twenty-five miles north of Charles Town in St. John's parish, where the Reverend Brian Hunt had fallen into debt and been accused by his vestry of drunkenness, quarreling, abusive language, and lying. To make money to satisfy his indebtedness, Hunt began marrying couples whom no other clergyman would join, and in 1727 he married a young teenager, Miss Gibbon Cawood, to Robert Wright in a secret midnight ceremony in Charles Town against the wishes of her guardians, Mr. Andrew Allen and Mr. Charles Hill, prominent local merchants. Garden and other clergymen condemned the marriage, since to do otherwise would produce "nasty repercussions." Charles Town merchants looked to the Anglican church to provide the foundations for an orderly, stable environment in which they could make money and if it failed to do so, they might question the need to support the church. Garden moved quickly. The Reverend Brian Hunt was jailed in Charles Town and persuaded to resign his parish post and return to England.

Commissary Garden next had to deal with the case of the Reverend John Winteley, who in the fall of 1728 was dismissed from his pulpit as a "whore monger and drunkard" by the vestry of Christ Church parish (in what is today Mount Pleasant). Winteley crossed the bay and took up residence in Charles Town, where he was seen in taverns and sometimes the streets "much in Liquor." Garden was shocked when he heard that Winteley had made "lewd attempts" against six women and supported Winteley's dismissal by his vestry, a power of the vestry unknown in England. Garden believed that ancient traditions had to give way to the wishes of well-to-do Carolinians and that disreputable clergymen like Winteley had to be removed for the good of the Anglican church. By 1729 he had arranged for Winteley to be sent to a church on the colony's frontier.[65]

Charles Town expanded beyond its original limits during the 1720s. The costly fortifications on the western side of the town were pulled down and the three principal east-west arteries, Tradd, Broad, and Dock streets were extended. The Assembly appropriated funds to build bridges "over the marsh from White Point" and north from Craven's Bastion, a room for the Assembly, and one for the Supreme Court. Shortages of brick and building stone often necessitated the use of cypress and mahogany in private dwellings, despite the danger of conflagrations. But a "water engine" had been purchased in England, making Charles Town the second town in America to own a fire engine.[66]

Margaret Kennett

In Barbadian fashion the residences that were being built had high-pitched roofs of tile and the rooms had high ceilings with large windows and wide piazzas to catch the cooling sea-breezes. Margaret Kennett in 1725 described houses "after the English Fashion" going up on the western side of Bay Street with stores on the ground floor where Mrs. Kennett herself, perhaps Charles Town's first business woman, ran a shop. Her father, a well-to-do Englishman, characterized his daughter as a "cheerful" and "industrious" person with "a Mind to see Strange places." Margaret and her husband had sailed for Charles Town in the early 1720s, and she soon wrote that "the whole Burthen" of the business "Lyes on my Shoulders." She discovered that as for items to sell "Variety . . . do best in this Country."

Margaret was very critical of the townspeople. They are "Trained up in Luxury and are the Greatest Debauchers in Nature," she wrote, but she did enjoy the wild game, "the finest fish," and the climate. Cold weather was short-lived while spring-like weather seemed to linger most of the year; however, in the "Hott Months" Margaret was "forc'd to use Pavilions made of Catgut Gause" for protection from "very Troublesome . . . Muschatoes."[67]

A "barbarous plott"

The Afro-American population of the colony rose sharply during the 1720s. Within the town, demands increased for skilled black labor; in the surrounding countryside the production of rice and naval stores required more and more gang laborers, and during the decade nearly 10,000 West Africans were brought in and sold. The ratio of black to white within Carolina was nearly 2 to 1. In Charles Town by 1725 the permanent population approached 5,000 and was about equally divided between black and white residents. As the number of slaves increased, so did reports of their various ways of resisting slavery. They continued to run away to Spanish Florida or west into Indian country and rumors of arson and poisoning by slaves become more frequent, but it was the threat of insurrections that caused the greatest fear.[68]

In June 1720 the first revelation of a serious conspiracy—"a wicked and barbarous plott"—terrified the white population. Blacks near Charles Town were said to have plotted "to destroy all the white people in the Country and then to take the town." Most of the Afro-Americans were caught and "burnt . . . hang'd [or] banish'd." A second slave conspiracy appears to have been uncovered in 1721 and the town watch was given additional power to deal with blacks. A well-armed, twenty-one-member force was to patrol the streets nightly to "Quell any . . . Designs . . . by Negroes." Blacks who refused to stop when so ordered could be shot. Also in 1721 the Assembly merged South Carolina's militiamen and the slave patrols. The main duty of the militia soon became "supervision" and "control" of slaves. In 1722 a new Negro Act passed the Assembly, which stipulated that slave conspirators found caching ammunition would be executed immediately as examples to other slaves. Despite such precautions, whites continued fearful of slave conspiracies, their anxieties fed by gruesome reports of revolts at sea and in the Caribbean islands.[69]

In February 1726 residents witnessed the first snowfall in the town's recorded history. That winter was the worst the colony had known, and the snow was the first most of the blacks had seen. In the twelve months that followed, the Crown's removal of the bounty on naval stores, heavy buying of slaves on credit, and increased taxes brought many small farmers to bankruptcy. These farmer-debtors formed an antitax association, held mass meetings, called for an expansion of the local currency, and physically prevented Charles Town creditors from collecting debts. When their leader was arrested for rebellious activities, an armed mob of some 300 small farmers marched on Charles Town in June 1727. The new, temporary governor, Arthur Middleton, a wealthy planter, called out the town militia only to see them join the mob. To avert violence, Middleton summoned the Commons House of Assembly to consider the demands of the debtors, but political wrangling between the Assembly and the Council continued into 1728, and the Assembly repeatedly refused to endorse the Council's tax bills until the Council approved measures for expanding the currency. The Assembly stopped meeting, taxes went uncollected, the judicial system collapsed, and mobs threatened violence. The colony seemed on the brink of anarchy.[70]

A prolonged drought occurred in the very hot summer of 1728. Ponds dried up, produce wilted, livestock perished, and in the midst of the drought yellow fever returned to Charles Town. "Multitudes" of both black and white residents died. Physicians prescribed the usual remedies of snakeroot, bleeding, and emetics but with little success. Backcountry farmers, fearing infection, refused to bring fresh produce to town. Food prices soared, people went hungry, and commerce ceased.

Then, while disease still raged, on the evening of Friday, August 13, gusting winds intensified and a "violent hurricane" swept in just to the south of town. Twenty-three ships riding in the harbor were heavily damaged, high waves smashed the wharves, walls, fortifications, and houses along Bay Street, littering the town with debris.[71]

As the Carolinians buried the several persons who perished in the storm and cleared away the wreckage, events in England were underway that would affect Charles Town dramatically. The Crown had been made aware of the internal divisions, the governmental crisis, and the natural disasters within the colony by the influential Charles Town merchant Samuel Wragg and the former governor Robert Johnson. Under their influence the Crown bought out the Proprietors' interests in Carolina, approved a plan to increase the numbers of whites in the colony, and endorsed a moderate expansion of the currency. In 1729 the Crown appointed Johnson as the first royal governor of South Carolina.[72]

II

The Royal Colony

❦ 1. 1730–1739:
"... the metropolis ... a neat pretty place"

Boom Times

An economic boom surged across the colony in the early
1730s, creating frantic times for Carolinians. The climate, the
evolving agricultural society, the institution of slavery, and Anglicanism were shaping in the hearts and minds of Charlestonians a
worldview different from that of Bostonians, New Yorkers, and
Philadelphians. White Charlestonians hungered after pleasure,
profits, property, and status, and a few lucky ones won it all. But
the decade began with a terrible scare.

In August 1730 black men on the neck of the peninsula were
overheard talking about murdering white people and taking
young, white females for their sexual partners. Suspects were apprehended and those thought to be withholding information
about the plot were tortured; those who appeared to be the leaders in it were executed. For years to come accounts of this
aborted black insurrection were furtively told and embellished.

The mood of the busy port swung from terrified despair to
joyous confidence. Since the early 1700s the British government
had permitted rice from Carolina to be exported only to Great
Britain and its colonies, but when these restrictions were removed in September 1730 vast new markets were open to Carolina rice and there were few white males who did not feel that
they had a good chance of soon becoming rich. And when the
new royal governor, Robert Johnson, arrived on December 15 a
happy colony greeted him as an old friend.

Lowcountry planters scrambled for more land and more
slaves to cultivate it and, while Charles Town waited for the rice
crop of 1731, exports of tar, pitch, turpentine, and deerskins began a steady increase that was to last several years. Then in August 1731 new legislation stabilized currency at £7 South
Carolina to £1 sterling and royal quitrents were established, putting landholding on a firm financial basis. This prompted a fren-

One of the best-known portrait painters of the 1730s, Bishop Roberts, painted this "View of Charles Town" in 1739, a year of war, insurrection, and disease.

zied pursuit of acreage throughout the lowcountry and in a few years 1 million acres were added to the tax books.[1]

The need for a public printer had become clear and by late 1731 Thomas Whitmarsh, who had worked for Benjamin Franklin in Philadelphia, was setting up a press in Charles Town. On January 8, 1732, he brought out the first issue of the *South Carolina Gazette*, which was for many years the most important newspaper in the South. Advertisers occupied so much space in the early *Gazette* that one wonders how business was transacted before it.

In July a catastrophic epidemic of yellow fever struck the port. Public and private business came to a standstill, and there were so many funerals every day that the tolling of bells was prohibited. From sun-up to sundown, St. Philip's rector, Dr. Alexander Garden, was in "the sick Chamber or Church Yard" consoling or burying his parishioners until he also fell victim to the fever. Although many of the well-to-do fled to plantations in the countryside, Governor Johnson believed it was his duty "not to quit the Town," and his wife, "the best of wives," a son, and three servants died. When cooler weather came it killed off the mosquitoes and the governor exclaimed in late September, "thank God it

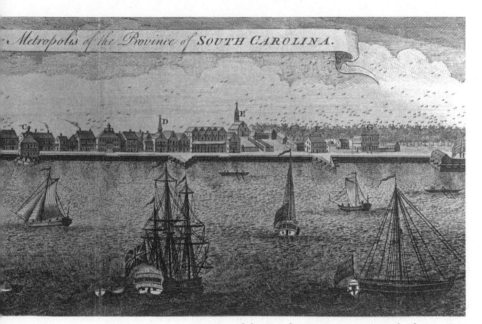

Courtesy of the Carolina Art Association, Charleston, S.C.

is now almost over." "One-hundred and thirty whites besides a great many slaves" succumbed, about 7 percent of the population of Charles Town.[2]

Business prosperity, briefly interrupted, quickly returned. In shallow boats, usually canoes or pettiaguas manned by black slaves, rice came down the Ashley, the Cooper, the Wando, and the Stono to the wharves. During the first five years of the 1730s more than 40,000 barrels of rice were exported annually, each barrel containing about 420 pounds, and the market value of the rice rose from 6 shillings sterling per 100 pounds in 1732 to over 10 shillings by 1738. At the same time Charles Town merchants continued their long-established trade in tar, pitch, turpentine, sole leather, deerskins, corn, peas, beef, and pork. The major exporters of these commodities were also major importers, bringing in English-made consumer items, West African slaves, and wine, sugar, molasses, and rum from the West Indies. About 134,000 gallons of rum, the Carolinian's favorite drink, were imported into Charles Town in 1735, but for the merchants the most profitable import was slaves. Besides laborers to cultivate more and more rice, planters needed carpenters to construct the casks and barrels in which it was shipped, and caulkers and boatmen to maintain and man the small crafts that were used for transporting rice down the rivers to Charles Town.

The slave trade required enormous capital outlays, so Charles Town merchants turned to their Caribbean and English connections for credit and made their profits by wharfside auctions of slaves to lowcountry planters, who usually paid in rice. The merchant took about 10 percent of the rice as his commission for negotiating the transaction and shipped the remaining rice to his English creditor. Out of his commission the merchant paid import duties on the slaves and the wages of the crew of the slave ship while in port. The import duty on slaves during the 1730s, £50 Carolina money for those over ten years of age and £5 for younger slaves, provided the colony with nearly half its operating revenues. British creditors insisted that Charles Town merchants assume the risk for bad debts on any credit extended to planters, but many local merchants willingly took the risk. Aggressively expanding their acreage and buying more slaves, planters mortgaged both to Charles Town merchants, who knew, as one Carolinian wrote in the 1730s, that "Negroes" were "the bait proper for Catching a Carolina Planter, as certain as Beef to catch a Shark."[3]

Easy credit was the road to ruin for some planters, such as Charles Lowndes, a well-connected member of the sugar-planting gentry of the island of St. Kitts, north of Barbados. Impoverished by his love of luxury, he came to Charles Town with his wife and children in 1730 in the hope of reversing his fortunes, bought 500 acres and a house on Goose Creek, and went into the rice-producing business. Two years later he was the nominal owner of 1,000 acres and thirty-eight slaves, but everything he owned was mortgaged to the hilt to his neighbors or to merchants a few miles down the river in Charles Town. Lowndes could not pay his debts because he was extravagant, and by 1735 no one in South Carolina or abroad would extend him credit. His wife left him and when Lowndes refused to provide separate maintenance for his family he was jailed. On the morning of Saturday, May 22, 1736, he arose early in his cell, dressed carefully, took a pistol, which as a gentleman he had been allowed to keep, and shot himself. Provost Marshal Robert Hall became the legal guardian of Lowndes's fourteen-year-old son, Rawlins, a youth who was later to play several roles in the history of Charles Town.[4]

1730–1739: " . . . the metropolis . . . a neat pretty place"

But for many South Carolina whites the 1730s were good years, and for about thirty of the merchants of Charles Town the profits were enormous. Sixty-eight merchants imported rum in 1735, but eleven of them brought in 70 percent of it. Of the fifty or so exporters of deerskins, nine paid 79 percent of the export duty. During the decade nearly 20,000 slaves were imported, most of them from Angola, and more than 30 percent were brought in by Joseph Wragg and Company, which handled far more slave cargoes than any other trading house.

The distinction between Dissenters and Anglicans was rapidly becoming less important, and there was no sharp division between the most successful merchants and the most successful planters. Several of these merchants bought land outside Charles Town, sometimes to grow rice on but in other cases purely as a speculative investment; some made an income as moneylenders. Opportunities to arrange marriages between offspring of the affluent led the prominent mercantile families of Charles Town to marry into prominent planter families. The most fundamental social division, of course, was between blacks and whites, but a second division was becoming increasingly important: those white males who by virtue of skill, luck, and good connections had accumulated a great deal of wealth and those who had not. A plutocracy was developing.[5]

Several hundred retailers, wholesalers, manufacturers, and craftsmen also were prospering even if they were not making fortunes. An amazing assortment of goods was advertised in the *Gazette*. From Bay Street shops small tradesmen sold Philadelphia and Bristol bottled beer, rum, butter, spices and Rhode Island cheese; Lisbon wines, Russian and Holland cloth, and "Cadiz diappers"; silk rugs, furniture, pewter, hats, and stockings; shoes, wig powder, ribbons, and curls; silver and gold necklaces, and knee garters. At Robert Pringle's store the dry goods that sold best included "coarse cloths, Linnen, Cotton, . . . Indian Trading guns & Gun Flints, Green plains for Negro Cloathing, Coarse Leather shoes, China Ware & Punch Bowls, Linseed Oyl, Cables, Hawsers & Running Rigging, pewter plates, Dishes & Spoons, Tobacco, Shortt Pypes, Writing paper, Salt." Broad Street merchants like Sarah and Lucy Weaver offered well-to-do ladies the latest London creations; shopkeepers on Lower Tradd Street sold cider, rum, and sugar. When Elliott Street, first called Middle Street, was opened between Broad and Tradd streets in the early

1730s, a number of small merchants relocated there to sell wine, rum, and lime juice. Prices of these imported goods remained high in Charles Town, one consumer complaining that prices were "400 or 500" percent higher than in Europe, but merchants frequently extended credit to their best customers—sometimes regretting it later.

If you had plenty of money or credit, Charles Town was one of the best places in North America to go shopping. Goldsmith Moreau Sarrazin, whose shop and home were on Broad Street, made enough money in a few years to acquire 500 acres on the Black River near Georgetown. Lucas Stoutenburg, a silversmith of Dutch ancestry, opened a shop in Tradd Street, prospered, and purchased a plantation and slaves on the Wando River. A silver tankard done by Stoutenburg can be seen today in the Charleston Museum. From his shop on Elliott Street, John Paul Grimké offered a stock of "Brillant Diamonds, Rubies, Emeralds, and Saphirs." He became well-to-do through his business and by marriage to Ann Grimball of the planter family of Edisto Island. Men could have their clothes fashioned by Broad Street tailors and, to keep them fresh and new looking, they patronized the cleaning and dyeing establishment of Mrs. Barbtram or of Edward Knight. Craftsmen on Church and Elliott streets advertised for sale "Teaboxes and . . . Clock Cases . . . made neat . . . and cheap." Josiah Claypoole, who came from Philadelphia, offered "Side-Boards and Waiters" at his shop in upper Broad Street and guaranteed his work for seven years "the ill usage of Careless Servants only excepted." Even after death Charles Town's gentlemen and ladies could surround themselves or families in luxurious "silver'd" burial coffins of red bay mahogany which could be purchased from William Hammett "at the sign of the Coffin and Chair." Samuel Holmes, a craftsman who may have been Charles Town's first professional architect, advertised in 1733 that he also "performes . . . Brickwork and Plastering." He prospered, for in a few years he owned a house on Tradd Street with "outhouses and Garden, well planted with Orange Trees and Grape Vines." White indentured servants and black slaves worked side by side as apprentices of the skilled artisans. After their period of indenture ended, some white men established businesses of their own, but Afro-Americans had very few opportunities to improve their circumstances.[6]

Slaves and Servants

Skilled slave apprentices often were sold by their owners for a substantial profit, and advertisements for the sale of black ship carpenters, caulkers, wheelwrights, smiths, and soapmakers appeared frequently in the *Gazette*. Owners also hired out their slaves for either public or private work by the week, month, or year, and some ambitious slaves contracted for work and pay without their owner's consent. Others concealed some of the cash they earned and invested it wisely. Charles Town blacks sometimes brought upcountry produce, for instance, and sold it in the vicinity of the town market. White merchants complained that they were hurt by these "hucksters" and persuaded the Assembly to prohibit slaves from selling near the market place without their owner's permission.

Demand remained high throughout the decade and into the 1740s for both black and white apprentices and common laborers. The St. Philip's vestry helped to meet this demand by binding out the young offspring of the white poor in their charge, and ship captains and local merchants did a lively trade in importing white indentures and selling them at wharfside. Most of the whites who entered South Carolina as indentured servants in the 1730s were either Lutherans or German-speaking peasants from Calvinist sections of Switzerland.

In affluent Charles Town households, there were many Afro-American or Indian female slaves serving as domestics, but few male slaves. Most of the men servants were indentured whites, black males being employed for the most part outside the house. Samuel Dyssli, a recent immigrant, wrote to his family and friends in Switzerland on December 3, 1737: "I am over here, thank God, hale and hearty, and doing at present quite nicely. I am working with an English master. He gives me every week . . . 50 shillings, and . . . plentiful . . . food and drink." Yet for one reason or another many white bondsmen and even greater numbers of black slaves ran away from their masters. Samuel Holmes, the architect, was so angry and frustrated by two of his servants who ran away and burned their indenture contracts, that when they were finally captured he declared that anyone who wanted to buy them "may have them cheap."[7]

" . . . a Negro Country . . . "

Astounded at the number of slaves, Samuel Dyssli wrote that "Carolina looks more like a Negro Country than like a Country settled by white people." White residents of Charles Town remained anxious about the large number of local slaves and those from the countryside who came in to town on Sundays to celebrate their day of rest. In 1734 a group of prominent merchants and craftsmen formally complained to the Assembly that the numbers of blacks gathering in the streets on Sunday "was endangering the safety of the Inhabitants." In March 1737 another curfew law was enacted. If any blacks appeared on the streets after sundown without a lantern and written permission from their master, white persons might apprehend them. They were to be taken to the Watch House, kept overnight, and whipped in the morning. Their owners could reclaim them after paying a fine.

Their bondsmen's fondness for drink disturbed some masters. Elizabeth Smith urged townspeople not to employ her "negro man Lancaster" in any sort of work because the money he earned "he loses either by Gaming or spends among the little Punch-Houses." In 1734 the Broad Street tailor Hugh Evans accused George Wyss and other Broad Street tavern-keepers of entertaining his slave apprentices with liquor and threatened legal action if it continued.

Most slave runaways were young-adult, male house servants or skilled artisans. Black males outnumbered females in the town and lowcountry by four to one during the 1730s and for years after. A few couples ran away together with their children. Many fled to Charles Town where they found anonymity among the crowds of blacks, friends who would hide them, and even a job. Here too they might escape aboard a vessel departing the port town. A typical runaway slave advertisement in the *Gazette* sought the return of Minos, Guam, and Flora, plantation slaves, suspected "to be lurking . . . about Charles Town." Diana, a half-breed who ran away from William Harvey on six occasions, may have set a record for the number of times a female slave fled her Charles Town master. The intelligence of their runaways worried some slaveholders. When two black carpenters fled their Charles Town owner, he believed that they were "crafty" enough to concoct a "plausible story that they are not runaways."

Runaways recaptured across the province and whose ownership could not be determined immediately were brought to Charles Town and confined. The warden of the town jail periodically posted pick-up notices in the *Gazette* listing the fugitive's name, if known, and describing his dress. If owners recognized their runaways from these advertisements, they could reclaim them. To help ensure the return of their property, some Charles Town slaveowners branded chronic runaways. A hot iron was used to burn the initials of the owner into the flesh on almost any portion of the body from forehead to buttocks.[8]

Particularly alarming to Carolinians were the rising numbers of "saucy" slaves who resisted recapture and defied the system by acts of violence or persistent theft. They were shocked in the summer of 1733 when an ax-wielding town slave murdered a white man. Whites hoped that public confessions and executions would cow the blacks. Shortly after "Caesar" fled his owner's house in Charles Town and attempted to escape to Spanish Florida, he was hanged publicly. The *Gazette* reported that he "made a very sensible speech to those of his own color," exhorting them to be "just, honest and virtuous." His body was "hung in chains at Hangman's Point opposite" Charles Town "in sight of all Negroes passing and repassing by Water."

Yet despite harsh, public punishments, escapes, violence, and larceny by slaves increased. When items disappeared, blacks were the first to be blamed, and the Charles Town Watch sometimes confiscated goods from slaves on the mere suspicion that they were stolen. A loosely organized crime ring appears to have operated in the town by 1735 and there was a growing market for stolen merchandise. One grand jury condemned the practice of "Negroes buying and selling wares in the streets . . . whereby stolen Goods may be concealed and afterwards vended undiscovered."

The fear of slave insurrections haunted whites. Wild rumors flew often during the Christmas season because whites believed that slaves on holidays had more time to scheme and act. In December 1732, amid rumors of a conspiracy, Governor Johnson ordered out extra detachments of militia and told them to "ride about to keep the Negroes in due order." Three years later during the Christmas season reports again reached Charlestonians that "the Negroes were going to rise." But before the alleged plot could get underway, a white man chanced upon a "great number of Negroes" and their cache of weapons and "the Wretches were . . . taken with all their Arms" and confined in Charles Town.

Rumors of slave plots sent periodic scares through Charles Town until the American Civil War. Some of the conspiracies were more imagined than real: garbled stories reported second or third hand, which reached whites nervous enough already over the lowcountry's black majority, or deliberate tales started by whites to justify making examples of blacks as a warning to slaves who might nurture thoughts of rebellion. Blacks themselves may have started rumors to avenge injustices by scaring whites. In a few cases the rumored conspiracies were well founded in fact and posed a real threat to the white population of Charles Town. Occasionally "good" Negroes, more loyal to the whites than their fellow slaves, betrayed both real and imagined plots.

By the end of the 1730s Charlestonians were becoming so apprehensive over their slaves that they were discussing how to allow only "a stated number . . . to inhabit among 'em." A Georgian observed: "Our Neighbors at Charles Town, I hear have their Belly-full of" blacks.

The well-known preachers Charles Wesley and George Whitefield recorded many instances of cruelty toward slaves, which they observed and heard about during their visits to Charles Town in the 1730s. Wesley noted that even white children had slaves of their own ages "to tyrannize over, to beat and abuse out of sport." Small wonder, he wrote, that upon growing up some whites treated their slaves in so brutal a fashion. Whitefield observed that for the "most trifling Provocation," Carolina slaves were whipped unmercifully. Some died from the punishment, and the backs of many were permanently scared by the lash. Runaway advertisements placed in the *Gazette* bear Whitefield out. Some slaves were described as "well marked . . . by whipping."[9]

An immigrant to Charles Town during these years was surprised to learn that "the whites mix with the blacks . . . and if a white man has a child by a black woman, nothing is done to him on account of it." The Reverend Johann Martin Bolzius observed that most Carolina slaves "live in Whoredom," and while visiting Charles Town the Reverend Henry Melchior Muhlenberg noted that "one . . . finds here many slaves who are only half black, the offspring of those white Sodomites who commit fornication with their black slave women."

Extramarital and interracial sex was discussed in the *Gazette*—sometimes gravely, sometimes superciliously, but nearly always candidly. As early as March 1732, the *Gazette* published a brief, anonymous poem entitled "The Cameleon Lover," which warned that whites with a "Taste" for "a Close Embrace With the *dark* Beauties of the Sable Race" might well become "Stain'd with the Tincture of the Sooty Sin." In the following issue "Albus" agreed, labeling miscegenation "an Evil" that was "spreading itself among us" like a "dreaded . . . *Epidemical Disease.*" He conjectured that any man would "fall into the utmost confusion to see the *Product* of *such* an *Amour,* the exact Features of his own Face sculking beneath the . . . thin disguise of a *tawny complexion.*" The writer who signed himself "Albus" evidently assumed that many of the readers of the *Gazette* would know that *albus* was the Latin word for "white." A different view was offered by a correspondent in the *Gazette* who wrote: "Kiss black or white, why need it trouble you? Of all things that make us truly blest, Is not that dear variety the best?" A writer in the *Gazette* in 1735 observed that mulattoes "are seldom well belov'd either by Whites or Blacks."

Whites were increasingly aware that the number of people in the category that we today call black or Afro-American constituted a majority of the population of Charles Town and the surrounding lowcountry—a majority they were by no means sure they could control. To offset the dramatic increase of Africans, Charlestonians encouraged the immigration of white Europeans. A steady stream of immigrants seeking work was lured to the Carolina boom town, which by the end of the 1730s with a population of over 6,000 persons, was the fourth largest city in British North America.[10]

"Paupers, vagrants, and . . . beggars"

Among the immigrants who came to Charles Town, the skilled and women fared best. Soon after his arrival in 1733 with 170 Swiss and German immigrants, Anthony Gordy wrote to his brother in Europe that "the artisans" were "getting along best of all." So too were the female immigrants, Gordy explained, as "all our single women . . . have been favorably married." But for the poor, unskilled male there was little work. In the late 1730s when a boatload of "Poor Protestants" arrived in Charles Town, one immigrant complained bitterly that most of those recently arriving had to live in shacks. They subsisted on "Indian corn" or potatoes and "see neither bread, meat, nor anything else." He declared angrily that slaves were often hired over white immigrants because they are "able to do . . . work . . . much cheaper."

In 1734 a Charles Town grand jury condemned the "common practice" of hiring out slaves who competed with white laborers for jobs. A few years later the Assembly prohibited slaves from being hired out as cart drivers, porters, or fishermen unless their owners paid a licensing fee, but apparently the regulations were not enforced rigorously. The continuing competition for jobs between whites and Afro-Americans contributed to the increasing numbers of poor whites. By the mid-1730s the inhabitants observed that the "Town is filled with people begging from Door to Door. . . . "[11]

Prominent officials, well-to-do merchants, and artisans formed social and benevolent organizations that extended some assistance to the indigent. One of the first was the St. Andrew's Society founded in 1729 by Scottish residents of Charles Town. Its principal aim was "to assist all people in Distress of Whatsoever Nation or Profession." Not to be outdone by the Scots, men of English origins founded the St. George's Society in 1733. Several years later artisans of French Huguenot descent renamed their "Two-Bitt" Club the South Carolina Society, which included among its goals "relieving the wants and miseries" of the poor. They believed also in "promoting the welfare and happiness of one another," which they did at their meeting places, first at Jacob Woolford's Broad Street Tavern and later at Joel Poinsett's Tavern on Elliott Street opposite Bedon's Alley. At each meeting the steward of the society was to see that no member was "disguised in liquor" and that the behavior of the members was "decent, peaceable."[12]

Taxes on real property remained the major source of money for charitable purposes. The vestry of St. Philip's Church collected these taxes and provided food, shelter, and medical attention for the elderly, the disabled, and the destitute. When indigents died, the vestry arranged for their burials. They reimbursed foster mothers 20 to 40 shillings a week for boarding very young orphans or abandoned children. As the numbers of whites increased during the 1730s, so did the demands on the vestry and the need for higher taxes. The vestry and churchwardens elected to care for the poor met with increasing frequency. "I have lately been elected into an office which is attended with some Trouble," wrote the merchant Robert Pringle after his election as a churchwarden.

By mid-decade, the vestry of St. Philip's was alarmed by "the number of idle, vagrant . . . people" who were "speedily reducing themselves to poverty and disease" by "drinking and . . . debauchery" and becoming a great financial burden on the parish of Charles Town. The churchmen also came to the conclusion that the private dwellings being rented as "Lodging . . . for Sick Persons" and paupers were inadequate, dilapidated, and too "extravagant" in price. Consequently, the parish officers petitioned the Assembly "to erect a Public Workhouse and Hospital." The Assembly responded by passing an "Act for the Better Relief and Employment of the Poor." It authorized the vestry to raise £2,000 immediately and £1,000 annually thereafter and to build a hospital for "Paupers, vagrants, and common beggars." Construction of the hospital began on an "acre of . . . Land called *the old Burying Ground*, lying on the back Part of Charles Town." It would face newly cut Mazyck Street. The crude frame structure was completed by 1738. Five "commissioners" were elected by the Assembly and a warden was appointed. The physician of St. Philip's parish who attended "sick Persons" throughout the town was obligated to visit and care for the poor at the hospital.

The "disorderly" Poor and Crime

The act of the Assembly creating the "hospital" stipulated that it was to serve also as "a Workhouse and House of Correction." The "lewd, idle, and disorderly" poor were to be lodged with the ill and indigent. The warden was authorized to use "fetters or shackles" on the inmates, "moderate whippings," and to deprive them of food if necessary to maintain order. He was permitted to supplement his own salary by hiring out the labor of the inmates and collecting their fees. True charity patients and "idle poor" lodged here now could be segregated from the hardened criminals who were confined in the "stifling" and filthy rooms of private dwellings.[13]

The numbers of fugitive slaves, "disorderly" poor whites, brawling sailors, sometimes drunken Indians, confidence men, and counterfeiters within the town alarmed some citizens. They believed that the lack of a well-built, escape-proof local jail was responsible for the breakdown in law and order. Prominent citizens repeatedly urged the Assembly to provide for an adequate prison but, after some debate, the cost-conscious members usually buried such demands in committees. Since there was no adequate jail, the Assembly authorized the provost marshal of the province to lease private dwellings to serve as jailhouses, where black and white criminals and debtors were herded together without adequate food or medical care. Confined in such facilities and often unguarded, criminals frequently escaped.

Petty thievery increased as Charles Town's population and wealth grew. An immigrant in 1737 observed that "crimes, especially Theft, are severely punished." When Alexander Forbes was convicted of "stealing Cloathes and other things" in March 1737 the Court of General Sessions for the province sentenced him to be whipped on the bare back "at the cart's tail through the Town." During the following few years the General Court sentenced Dorothy Holmes, who stole two silver waiters, to be burned on the hand with a hot iron. Sometimes horse thieves were ordered to stand in the public pillory with one ear nailed to the post. At the expiration of the sentence the ear was sliced off.

Particularly severe punishments were reserved for sex-related offenses and crimes against nature. Members of the General Court sitting at Charles Town in March 1738 found Sarah Chamberlain guilty of "the Murder of her Bastard Child" and sentenced her to death. Some months later the court sentenced John Perrins to death for bestiality.[14]

Sporting and Cultural Life

"Punch Houses" like the Two Brewers on Church Street and The Pig and the Whistle on Tradd Street served common laborers and sailors, while a few slightly more respectable public taverns catered to merchants, artisans, and planters. Here they were served salted fish, wild game, and rice-flour puddings with rum-based "slings," "flipps," and "toddies," wine, or molasses and persimmon beer to slake their thirst. For amusements the taverns offered cockfights, raffles, and other entertainments.

At the northern end of King Street just beyond the town's limits Mrs. Eldridge was the innkeeper of the Bowling Green House. In January 1735 she announced that a "saddle and Bridle" valued at £20 would "be run for . . . ." It was the first mention in the *Gazette* of horse racing, which soon became the most popular sport in the lowcountry. That same year the newly formed Jockey Club laid out a race track at the Quarter House near Charles Town. William Sterland, who ran a "house of entertainment" gave notice in December 1734 "to all Gentlemen that he had a fine new Billiard-Table with new sticks and balls at their service." Several years later the tavern-keeper, Mr. Laurans, advertised that at his place "Gentlemen may enjoy their Bowl and Bottle" over a game of "SHUFFLE BOARD."

The most popular tavern among the affluent was Charles Shepheard's place at the northeast corner of Church and Broad streets. Today it is the site of the Citizens and Southern Bank building. Shepheard's Tavern was so large that he rented out one of the rooms to the Assembly as a meeting place and another as a courtroom. The St. Andrew's Society held dinners described as "handsome entertainments" at Shepheard's, where also Charles Town's newly formed "Ancient and Honourable Society of Free and Accepted Masons" held its first meetings. Charles Shepheard also knew how to lure customers. In 1735 he placed an advertisement in the *Gazette* announcing that at his establishment the "muffled cock . . . BOUGRE DE SOT . . . will fight against any cock in the Province."[15]

That same year Shepheard rented his "long room" to a group of strolling players and local musicians who launched the town's first theatrical season on Friday evening, January 24, 1735. Charlestonians able to afford the 40 shillings for a ticket crowded in for the opening performance of Otway's *The Orphan, or the Unhappy Marriage*. The tragedy began with the first recorded prologue done in America. Composed by a local author, it recounted flatteringly the Carolinians' heroic triumph over the wilderness. *The Orphan* was given again on January 28 and twice more during February. In a new prologue and an epilogue the players announced to the audience that they had been "encouraged by your smiles," that unlike the "witch hanging" and "play abjuring" New Englanders, Charlestonians knew how "to blend amusement with life." The players next tried ballad-opera. Popular in England, the plots revolved around the life of the laboring classes and were spiced with social and political satire and slapstick comedy. The first advertised opera performed in America, Colley Cibber's *Flora or Hob in the Well*, opened at Shepheard's Tavern on the evening of February 18. Local musicians, organists and fiddlers, probably provided the accompaniment and sang the vocal parts.

Charles Town's first theatrical season was a grand success and a subscription drive was soon undertaken to raise money for the building of a permanent playhouse. The funds were subscribed remarkably quickly and the construction of a theater began on the south side of Queen Street just west of Church Street, about 100 yards from St. Philip's and the Huguenot church. The playhouse built here on Queen Street, which had been recently renamed from Dock Street, would be referred to by the townspeople out of force of habit as "The Dock Street Theatre." It featured box seats and pit and gallery benches, costing 30, 20, and 15 shillings respectively; it opened with Farquhar's bawdy comedy *The Recruiting Officer*, on February 12, 1736. The impressario Henry Holt probably was directing from the wings. The epilogue, written by the local physician, Dr. Thomas Dale, matched the coarse gaiety of the play. It was delivered by "Monima," the leading lady of the season before, who in *The Recruiting Officer* acted a role in men's clothing. The bawdy comedy was so well received by the Charles Town playgoers that it was presented twice more during the season.

Musicians such as the organist of St. Philip's Church, John Saltar, and the dancing master Henry Campbell led concerts of "vocal and instrumental Musick," and conducted dances for their prosperous patrons in the council chamber, a room overlooking the busy harbor above the Guard House at the foot of Broad Street. Saltar spent so much of his time arranging or performing in secular concerts that in 1735 the vestry reprimanded him for neglecting his duties to the church. But over time Shepheard's Tavern and the new playhouse became the site for such festivities. Charles Town was developing a colorful and varied cultural, artistic, and intellectual life.

For those who had little money to spend on entertainment there were occasional parades by the local militia or such public events as the day-long celebrations of George II's birthday, which began when the various units formed in Bay Street and to the "sounds of Kettle drums and Trumpets" marched round the town. In the evening, there were "great demonstrations of Pleasure" and "the town . . . was handsomely illuminated" with bonfires and candles. Sometimes exhibits were brought to town by enterprising impressarios who set ticket prices low enough to lure the poor. No doubt many people went to see the "Royal Waxwork"—representations of England's king, queen, and family— in August 1737, since tickets cost only 10 shillings at a time when carpenters in Charles Town were making 30 shillings a day.

Charles Town began attracting some of the most important performers in colonial America, among them Theodore

Pachelbel, a Prussian immigrant whose father had influenced J. S. Bach. In Charles Town, Pachelbel opened a singing school, married, and eventually succeeded John Saltar as organist at St. Philip's; at his death he was buried in the churchyard.[16]

When the founder of the *Gazette*, Thomas Whitmarsh, died suddenly in 1733, Lewis Timothy, another of Benjamin Franklin's trainees, succeeded him as Charles Town's leading printer, editor, and publisher. He moved the newspaper and printing house to newly cut Union Street, later renamed State, which ran parallel to upper Church Street. He joined in the social and civic life of the community, helping to organize the South Carolina Society and a subscription postal service for the town. When he died in 1738, his wife, Elizabeth, was caring for six small children and was pregnant with another, but she somehow managed to continue the *Gazette*, becoming the first woman in the American colonies to publish a newspaper and one of the most successful business women. By 1739 Elizabeth was running the printing and newspaper business from a dwelling on the western side of King Street just south of Broad Street. When her eldest son, Peter, reached his majority in the mid-1740s, Elizabeth turned the business over to him. She died some years later and left her surviving son and three daughters land, three houses, and five slaves, a substantial amount of worldly goods.

Besides ship clearings and arrivals, slave notices and advertisements, the *Gazette* published many literary pieces, encouraging contributions from readers by "assuring them that their Essays in Prose or Verse shall be kindly received." Subscribers responded with hundreds of poems and essays and frequently imitated or quoted British writers like Shakespeare, Addison, Pope, Swift, and Milton. Local contributors most often wrote about the morals and manners of their society. They usually used pseudonyms and their two favorite topics were religion and love. A writer in 1734 reflected the community's attitudes about one elderly gentleman's affair with a young lady: "In this our Town I've heard some Youngsters say, / That cold *December* does make Love to *May*. / This may be true, that warm'd by youthful charms. / He thinks of Spring, when melting in her arms. / As trees, when crown'd with blossoms white as snow / May feel the heat, and yet no life below . . . ." This poem may have been written by a woman, as females were frequent contributors. A few years later a poem entitled "The **LADIES** *Complaint*" obviously was submitted by a woman. It was among the first in Charles Town if not in the American colonies to condemn the double standard and to demand sexual equality, and read in part, "Then equal Laws let Custom Find, / And neither Sex oppress: / More Freedom give to Womankind, / Or to Mankind give less." The local verse and prose, and reprints from London journals, published in the *Gazette* indicate a growing intellectual maturity and sophistication among Charles Town's affluent. So too did the number of locally written pamphlets and books.[17]

As the public printer of the colony, the *Gazette* editor's first priority was to publish proclamations of the governor and militia, slave regulations, and other acts of the Assembly. A second consideration was to bring out what would sell. The editors discovered that "useful" publications on subjects of local interest sold quickly. Among these "how-to-do-it" best-sellers were books on horsemanship and military discipline. Lewis Timothy's two outstanding publications were Chief Justice Nicholas Trott's *Laws of the Province of South Carolina* (1736) and the first edition of John Wesley's *Choice Collection of Psalms and Hymns* (1737).

Books were offered for sale at the offices of the *Gazette*, and in 1735 Eleazer Phillips, Sr., opened the first bookstore. There were also frequent public auctions of books. The variety of titles offered and the number of sales indicate that the book-buying public was not limited to the well-to-do. A common characteristic of libraries of professional men was that the titles reflected their chosen occupations; however, nearly one-half of the titles held in private libraries and those advertised in the *Gazette* could be read for entertainment. As might be expected, the most widely read historical work was Paul de Rapin-Thoyras's *The History of England*. The travel book most Charlestonians turned to during their leisure hours was George Anson's *Voyage Round the World*.[18]

Drawing masters and mistresses and portrait painters came to the growing town seeking their fortunes. Bishop Roberts, who at first supported himself as a house painter, became the best known of them for a few years. In the maturing port on the edge of the Carolina wilderness an increasing number of Charlestonians became interested in education. To attract good teachers for the Free School, the Assembly in 1734 increased the salary of the headmaster, which came from the export duty on deerskins, from £100 to £500 and shortly thereafter authorized that "several necessary Repairs" be done to the school house. Benevolent societies and the St. Philip's vestry increased their support of the Free School by paying the tuition of poor scholars.

The master of the Free School continued to offer a modified classical curriculum grounded in Latin and Greek, but more than a dozen new teachers advertised instruction in what were considered more practical subjects such as geometry, surveying, navigation, bookkeeping, and astronomy, "whereby youth may be qualified to Business by Land or Sea." The parents of "Young Gentlemen" sent them to polish their French with John Fouguet or Peter Percour and to Thomas Buttler or James Vaughan for instruction in fencing. For the polite education of the "Young Ladies," Mrs. Phillippene Hennig offered French, English, and needlework; Henneriette Fisher taught dancing and writing. To some the port was rapidly becoming what young Eliza Lucas would call a few years later, "the metropolis . . . a neat pretty place."[19]

Growth and Expansion

From 1729 to 1739 the town spilled beyond the bounds of its fortifications, nearly doubling in size from its original eighty or so acres. Property values increased by more than 500 percent, and hundreds of private and public structures went up. Most were cheaply constructed frame dwellings, but the several that survive from this period on lower Church Street are of masonry construction. The dwelling at 71 Church is the oldest "single house" in the city and was the prototype for many others. The design was a concession to the local summers. The term "single house" refers to its width, that of a single room. Consisting of two rooms on each floor with a hall between containing the stair case, its gable-end faces the street. Piazzas run south or west, sheltering the dwelling from the heat of the sun and providing outdoor living room. The north walls are windowless to keep out the cold winds of winter.

By 1739 eight wharves jutted from Bay Street into the Cooper River to serve the sharply rising shipping trade. Middle Wharf was the largest and here were located shops, stores, and the Old Market. The other seven wharves were named after their owners or builders: Brewton's, Lloyd's, Pinckney's, Motte's, Elliot's, Rhett's, and Crockatt's. By mid-decade over 500 ocean-going ships and hundreds of smaller craft were loading or off-loading slaves, produce, and merchandise annually. To relieve traffic snarls around the wharves and to accommodate the rising numbers of vehicles on the streets, old ways were extended and enlarged and new streets developed. Bay Street was extended northward and three new streets were cut westward: Thomas, Ellery, and Pinckney streets. Numerous narrow passageways leading from the bay were widened, among them Unity Alley, Simmons Alley, and Wragg's Lane. Each intersected with newly cut and north-south-running Union Street, later State Street. The three principal east-west streets, Queen, Broad, and Tradd, were extended from the bay to the salt marshes of the Ashley River. New ways like Lamboll Street were opened westward. Church, Meeting, and King were extended southward to White Point, and a bridge was built over Vanderhorst Creek where today's Water Street intersects Church Street. By the end of the decade thirty-three principal streets conforming to the original gridiron plan criss-crossed the city.[20]

In the streets the excrement of horses, mules, people, pigs, dogs, and cattle mingled malodorously with animal fats from tallowmakers and offal from butcher shops. Only after repeated complaints from citizens did the Assembly appoint a special committee to investigate ways to clean the streets, which recommended that the town be divided into four districts with each electing "way wardens" annually who would oversee street-cleaning details composed of slaves. But the Assembly postponed acting on these recommendations until stinking semipermanent ponds finally made it almost impossible to move about in the town and by which time Charles Town had become paralyzed by the most feared scourge of eighteenth-century cities.[21]

Epidemics

The *Gazette* of May 4, 1738 reported that several slaves recently imported had "the Small Pox," and a proclamation promptly issued by the governor's office instructed citizens to "take all imaginable care to prevent" its spread. The editor of the *Gazette* rushed into print a variety of cures sent in by subscribers: bleeding, blistering, "Syrup of White Poppies," "liquid Laudanum," a mixture of cow's dung, milk, and bread to be taken internally, and doses of tar water. Townspeople gratefully accepted the extravagant claims of the prescriber of tar water as being both a preventive and an antidote until the author himself died of smallpox. After several years of prosperity and good health, the luck of the Carolinians had turned. On June 26 the royal governor proclaimed "a day of publick Fasting and Humiliation" because of the deaths from disease.

An epidemic of whooping cough seems to have accompanied the smallpox, but very few of the physicians in Charles Town were competent to distinguish clearly between the two as no major outbreaks of whooping cough had been reported up to that time in North America. As the epidemics spread, one of the ablest physicians in the colony, James Killpatrick, became the leading advocate of inoculation despite opposition on medical and moral grounds. It had been tried first in Boston in 1721 and remained controversial for a century.

The inoculators took pus from the sores of smallpox victims and inserted it into incisions made on the arms and legs of healthy people, who would then develop smallpox. Some of those inoculated died, but it is now known that Killpatrick and others were correct in their observation that smallpox spread by inoculation was a comparatively mild form of the disease, and those who survived were immune to it thereafter. Inoculation saved more lives than it took. This had not yet been clearly demonstrated, however. Some of the inoculators were charlatans, and others mistakenly believed that their incisions must be painfully deep if the inoculation was to be effective, and the resulting attack of smallpox was in the best circumstances both unpleasant and frightening, so there was a great deal of opposition to inoculation for a long time. Killpatrick's foremost medical antagonist was his Church Street neighbor, the notoriously belligerent Dr. Thomas Dale.

As the number of indigents stricken with smallpox increased and the "hospital and workhouse" became overcrowded, St. Philip's vestry rented a house to serve as a temporary hospital. In early September the merchant Robert Pringle lamented that the "Small Pox . . . has put an entire stop to all Trade," and the Assembly, meeting outside the town, prohibited further inoculations. About 10 percent of the town's population died of smallpox or whooping cough in 1738.

Eventually Dr. Killpatrick went to London and became famous throughout Europe as an inoculator, but before he left he saw yellow fever devastate the colony in the summer of 1739. As the sickness raged, the rector of St. Philip's conducted "4 to 12 Funerals a Day & as many sick to Visit." To quench "the violent thirst and Heat" and "to keep up the Spirits" of those infected, they were given "burnt Wine, hot Punch, and strong Juleps," but these prescriptions were of little help. In September schools closed, the *Gazette* ceased publication, the fall session of the Assembly was postponed, and at the height of the epidemic, a long-dreaded dispatch reached Charles Town. Hostilities between England and Spain had broken out again. What came to be called the War of Jenkin's Ear had begun.[22]

❦ 2. 1739–1749: "Calamitys and Misfortunes"

Charles Town had three good reasons to deplore the outbreak of war between England and Spain in 1739. In the first place, such a war was likely to interfere with the international commerce that was making some South Carolinians the richest men in North America. Second, the Spanish might launch another attack on Charles Town from Florida. The third reason was the probability of an insurrection of slaves either deliberately instigated by the Spanish or at least encouraged by the prospect of life in Florida, where the few Spanish colonists had less interest in black slave labor than the Carolinians.

The Stono Rebellion

The bloodiest slave revolt in colonial America began early Sunday morning, September 9, 1739, at the Stono River Bridge, about twenty miles south of Charles Town. Here a group of slaves murdered over a dozen whites, looted a store, burned houses, and set out toward Spanish Florida and freedom. Late Sunday afternoon they were intercepted near Jacksonborough Ferry by armed and mounted planters who cut down fourteen and took others, who were questioned briefly and then shot on the spot. But at least thirty of the black insurgents escaped into the woods. Charles Town was terrified. A hunt for the escaped rebels was launched by a militia whose ranks were thinned by yellow fever, and within a few weeks over forty suspects had been seized in the countryside and killed. A number of Indians and slaves who had helped suppress the insurrection were brought to Charles Town and rewarded with clothes and cash. The following year slaves near Goose Creek several miles north of Charles Town apparently made plans to seize the city. Betrayed by a fellow slave, Peter, sixty-seven alleged conspirators were brought to trial. Some were hanged "to intimidate other Negroes," some had their ears sliced off or were branded and whipped, and Peter also was commended and rewarded by a grateful Assembly.[23]

A New Negro Act

As long as merchants and planters felt they had a reasonable chance of making a good profit from slave labor they suppressed their fears of black insurrection, but whenever it became difficult to profit from slave labor the number of blacks in the colony distressed them. On April 5, 1740, therefore, the Assembly imposed prohibitively high import duties on slaves and the following year passed a new Negro Act, which was grounded on earlier legislation and remained the core of South Carolina's slave code through the Civil War. A major aim of the new act was to ensure that slaves "be kept in due subjection and obedience." Freedom of movement, action, and assembly were limited severely. No slave living or working in Charles Town was to be allowed to go beyond the town limits without written permission from his or her master. The sale of alcohol to slaves and teaching them to read or write was prohibited, and only the Assembly could grant a slave freedom. The dangers of enraging blacks were faced by specifying that any white person who "shall wilfully cut out the tongue, put out the eye, castrate or cruelly scald" a slave was liable to a fine. The patrol system was strengthened, and retailers of liquor were forbidden to serve rum or wine to slaves without permission of their owners, but innkeepers and proprietors of bawdy houses flagrantly disregarded the act. Blacks had the same needs for recreation and the company of friends as whites, and periodic attempts to control them usually proved futile.

In the late summer of 1740 the government at Charles Town believed that South Carolina faced a "dangerous Situation" and reported to His Majesty in London that the province had been "greatly reduced & weakened by a series of Calamitys and Misfortunes . . . Small Pox . . . Pestilential Fever . . . and Insurrection." The town remained "exposed to dangers from abroad" and "to Enemies very near."[24]

The "Great Fire" of 1740

Perhaps the most destructive fire that ever roared across Charles Town began "in a Sadler's House" at the corner of Broad and Church streets around two o'clock on Tuesday afternoon, November 18, 1740. A brisk wind fanned the flames and blew sparks across the southeastern section of the city. The weather had been fair for weeks and the roofs of tinder-dry, wooden dwellings, shops, and warehouses on Broad, Church, Elliott, Tradd, and Bay streets were quickly ignited. Here in the main trading district of the city vast stores of deerskins, rum, pitch, turpentine, and powder exploded and fed the conflagration. "Amidst the cries and shrieks of women and children," the sounds of roaring flames and collapsing buildings, and the confusion of men seeking safety for their families, the bucket brigades formed to fight the fire broke down.

Citizens watched in horror as their hard-won possessions went up in flames; some risked their lives to salvage what they could. At his store and residence on the bay between Tradd and Elliott streets, Robert Pringle tried to save merchandise on the first floor while Jane, his wife, remained upstairs attempting to save the family's personal belongings. She fled the doomed dwelling only after "her cloaths . . . catch'd fire." The carpenter John Bee labored "as much as in his Power to extinguish the . . . Fire" raging in buildings on the north side of Broad Street while being doused repeatedly with buckets of water. Afterward he claimed that his exertions brought on a "Distemper," which "threw him into violent Convulsions, and deprived him of the Use of his Limbs and Sight," causing "great Expense . . . in employing Physicians & . . . Loss of Business." The Assembly reimbursed him for his medical expenses.

Nearly 70 percent of the fire losses were sustained by merchants. James Reid was "burnt out" of his home and shop in Elliott Street as was John M'Call on Tradd Street and William Stone and Henry Williams on the bay along with dozens of others. For the merchant-investor William Pinckney the fire meant financial disaster. Just a few years before he had been a founder and investor in the first fire insurance company in America, the "Friendly Society for the Mutual Insuring of Homes against Fire at Charles Town." Both the company and Pinckney were reduced to bankruptcy.

In the late afternoon crews from British warships came ashore and blew up several houses on the corner of Tradd and Church streets to stop the conflagration from spreading, but not until the breeze died at dusk did the firefighters bring the fire under control. In four hours the fire had destroyed about 300 houses, many stores, some wharfs, and an enormous quantity of goods. The wooden gun carriages and platforms on the fortifications along the Cooper River were burned or scorched and many weapons became useless. Dazed and exhausted, Robert Pringle could not find the words to describe "the dismal . . . [scene] . . . the best part of . . . town being laid in Ashes."

Initially some citizens suspected that the fire had been set by black arsonists. Fresh in their minds was the burning and pillaging of the Stono rebels the year before and they now remained "apprehensive" of an insurrection and looting. Guards were posted day and night and a patrol roamed the burned-over section, but despite these precautions unburned goods in the streets and shops mysteriously disappeared.[25]

Evangels, "domestic enemies," and War

The dynamic, twenty-six-year-old English evangelist and reformer George Whitefield believed that the conflagration and other calamities recently visited upon the town were the judgments of a righteous God on a sinful people. Whitefield publicly declared that the Anglican clergy had become so preoccupied with their own material interests that they had allowed their congregations to go astray. The clergy themselves were but "Thieves and Robbers" who did not follow in "the Footsteps of Our True Sheperd," Whitefield and his recent convert Hugh Bryan wrote in the *Gazette* of January 8, 1741. Almost immediately Whitefield was clapped into a "prison-house" for libeling the Anglican church. But he soon raised bail money and departed for England.

Whitefield's evangelistic, "Methodist" principles, which he preached in Charles Town from time to time in the late 1730s, threatened the established Anglican church. As a leader of the religious revivalism, or "Great Awakening," sweeping America, Whitefield found attentive audiences. He preached to Dissenters at the Reverend Josiah Smith's Congregational Church on Meeting Street and the Reverend Timothy Millechamp's French Huguenot Church. With "burning zeal" Whitefield talked of a personal, redeeming God. He appealed to the people to give up their vices and criticized the Anglican clergy for failing to teach the slaves Christianity. Some who heard him "wept"; some told him that his preaching had helped them find the "everlasting righteousness of the Lord Jesus Christ"; still others sent him "little presents as tokens of their love."

Whitefield's religious principles, his popularity, and his attack on the Anglican clergy brought a furious response from the commissary of Carolina and rector of St. Philip's Church, the Reverend Alexander Garden, who said only the "Lower sort" ran to hear him, and denounced Whitefield as a "Pig," a "Pharisee," and a preacher of "Gibberish." In response to Whitefield's criticism of the clergy for neglecting the religious instruction of slaves, Commissary Garden raised the funds for books and the building of a Negro school near the parsonage of St. Philip's Church. He personally trained the teachers, two young teenage slaves, Harry and Andrew. Within a few years Harry, who was "of excellent Genius," assisted by Andrew, a "good natur'd & willing creature," were teaching more than seventy young slaves in the principles of Christianity. Adult slaves were being taught in the evening. Commissary Garden was delighted. The school succeeded beyond his highest expectations.[26]

During the winter of 1740–41, the Reverend Mr. Whitefield saw the "great Want and Distress" of many Charlestonians burned out by the fire. Destitute, hundreds turned for help to family, friends, and the church. The St. Philip's vestry received funds from the government for the support of those persons in dire need, and for weeks the dedicated, hard-working vestrymen doled out cash for the "present necessities" of poor families who had lost their homes and belongings. Charlestonians, Philadelphians, Bostonians, and Barbadians donated cash and food, and eventually the London government appropriated £20,000 sterling "for the relief of the Fire-Sufferers."

But there was little immediate respite from suffering during the long winter. Records kept by the first American meteorologist, Dr. John Lining of Charles Town, indicated that temperatures plunged to their coldest prolonged readings ever during the colonial period. A few days after Christmas Robert Pringle noted that "the Weather . . . Continues with hard frosts & Snow." The effects of the fire and the severe weather continued to hamper commerce and trade. In late January 1741, Pringle wrote: "The great Fire has . . . put . . . a stop to Business . . . ." Two weeks later he observed that "there are no Storehouses in Town for Rice, being all Consum'd in the Fire, so that it lyes all about the Streets & on the Wharfs."[27]

Slaves were immediately hired to pull down fire-gutted structures and to remove the rubble. The Assembly passed an act

in late December 1740 specifying that wooden shingles could be
used temporarily and frame buildings erected, but both had to be
replaced by fire-resistant materials after December 1745. The
fire commissioners were authorized to prohibit the business of
distilling, and candle- and soap-making, from those parts of town
judged "perilous in Respect of Fire." But over the years, despite
citizens' fears of another conflagration, these regulations often
were ignored.

Both the real and fancied fears of black arsonists continued to
prey on the minds of many white Charlestonians. Their anxieties
seemed justified when in the summer of 1741 an incendiary plot
was uncovered. A mulatto slave, Kate, was apprehended for attempting to set fire to a house on Union Street. Within forty-eight
hours she was tried, convicted, and sentenced to die. Just prior to
her execution, however, Kate was pardoned for naming a co-con-
spirator, the slave Boatswain. At his trial Boatswain confessed and
told his judges that he "looked upon every white Man he should
meet as his declared Enemy." On Friday, August 15, he was
burned alive. The *Gazette* reported that Boatswain "died like . . .
[the] impudent hardened Wretch . . . he was."[28]

Anxieties over "Domestick Trechery" were intensified by
the behavior of Hugh Bryan, one of George Whitefield's con-
verts, a wealthy, forty-one-year-old rice planter and militia officer
who lived some sixty miles south of Charles Town. Filled with
religious zeal and deeply disturbed by the death of his young
wife, Bryan began preaching to "great assemblies" of blacks to
convert them to Christianity; in early 1742 he was said to be
prophesying "the Destruction of Charles Town," which would be
"executed by . . . Negroes" with "fire and sword." A warrant
was issued for Bryan's arrest, but it was the failure of his pro-
phetic powers that made him seek public forgiveness and also
made him the "laughingstock" of the colony. First, like Moses, he
had tried to divide the waters of a river with a wand and, failing at
this, he tried to walk across and nearly drowned. Though their
terror turned to laughter, Bryan had briefly threatened both the
elite's Anglican establishment and the slave system. But with his
recantation, which indicated his willingness to support the local
political, social, and racial order, authorities in Charles Town
dropped charges against him and Bryan returned to his life as a
planter near Beaufort.[29]

Early in July 1742 a fleet of Spanish ships out of Havana

blasted their way past the harbor defenses at St. Simon's Island, Georgia, about 200 miles southwest of Charles Town, and began disembarking a powerful army. Lieutenant Governor William Bull reported the news to a shocked Assembly and warned that Carolina was "very much endangered." Appropriation bills were enacted quickly to pay troops, to hire slaves to dig entrenchments and repair the fortifications, and to finish building Fort Johnson. Colonel Othniel Beale, former member of the Assembly, land speculator, merchant, and sometime engineer, was placed in charge. In July Robert Pringle noted that "We now all in Arms and Preparing for a Vigorous Defense in case of Attack" and he was "much Fatigued in keeping guard Day & Night."

Then as suddenly as it had come the threat of an immediate attack passed. When the vanguard of the Spanish army was smashed by a force of Georgians and rumors spread that a British fleet was approaching, the invaders hastily sailed away. By the late summer fears of "outside" enemies had eased among the townspeople. They remained wary, however, that the lingering Spanish threat might encourage "domestic enemies," their slaves. On October 25, 1742, a visitor to Charles Town noted: "matters between the whites and the blacks here are such that one fears to be seen outside the house." Several months later citizens who "apprehended great danger from the evil designs of Slaves" urged the Assembly to post guards at the "Powder Magazine" where "several hundred barrels of powder" were stored.

Portions of the fortifications of the city and much of the business section remained in ruins from the "great fire" and the war between Spain and England was interfering with the trade in exports. Rice piled up on the wharves and prices dropped. Many Charlestonians would have agreed with Robert Pringle in the summer of 1742 when he wrote: "This province Seems to be a Subject to Series of Accidents and Missfortunes." Wild rumors swept the town in early 1743: another invasion from Havana was being planned and French forces were attacking Indians friendly to the English on Carolina's frontier. Word was sped to London from Charles Town that "the Inhabitants are in the greatest Apprehension of . . . danger." Though several English warships patrolled the coast and Charles Town's fortifications were being strengthened, some citizens believed that their defenses could offer "little resistence . . . against any . . . regular forces." Reinforcements arrived in the autumn. One British warship, the *Loo*, entered the harbor in October and another, the *Tartar*, carrying the new royal governor, James Glen, arrived on December 18. After surveying the conditions in the colony, Glen moaned that he found "Charles Town and this Province . . . in Ashes, Defenseless, Declining."[30]

In early 1744 Charlestonians received more bad news. France had declared war on England. The business community believed that this would further diminish trade and any lingering hopes merchants may have had of profiteering from the war were fast evaporating. Since the outbreak of King George's War merchants had sought to make quick profits from government contracts, but the Charles Town government distributed its purchases throughout the local mercantile community so no one merchant was able to make the kind of huge profits that John Hancock made at Boston. Some merchants profited from the many British officers and men who shopped and sipped in Charles Town's stores and taverns. Ship carpenters and caulkers did a lively business at Hobcaw on the eastern bank of the Wando River near Charles Town, the site of South Carolina's shipbuilding industry. Here good profits were made by hauling, scrubbing, and refitting His Majesty's ships.

A few merchants attempted to profiteer by illicit trade with the enemy. Some townspeople were outraged when they learned that the merchants Mathew Roche and John Colcock had received 9,000 Spanish dollars for smuggling provisions and goods aboard a Spanish flag-of-truce ship in the harbor. Other merchants, encouraged by the local government, formed partnerships to outfit vessels for preying on Spanish ships reported to be laden with gold and silver swarming off St. Augustine and Cuba. But most of these privateering schemes failed. Far more successful in taking Spanish prizes were the fighting ships of His Majesty's Navy.

Since the opening years of the war British warships were stationed at Charles Town to guard against invasion by sea, to convoy merchantmen, to prevent smuggling, and to harass Spanish shipping. Among the many British naval officers who sailed in and out of the port, none was a more dashing or romantic figure than Captain Thomas Frankland of HMS *Rose*. Cruising southward he scoured the Caribbean taking Spanish and French ships loaded with sugar, coffee, and gold and silver coins. He sailed these prizes into Charles Town where they were condemned by the courts and sold as spoils of war. Frankland and his crews shared the handsome profits while local merchants benefited from the business and the sorely needed gold and silver coins. For this stimulus to commerce, the merchants presented Captain Frankland with a silver bowl. Other citizens hungry for any victory at Spanish expense, praised Frankland with poetry in the *Gazette*: "Below our Bay you make their Vessels ride/stripp'd of their Riches, and all Spanish pride." Growing rich from his many prizes, Frankland bought a wharf, for mooring his captured vessels, and a home, which became the center of the social life of the city. In 1743 he married Sarah Rhett, "a beautiful and accomplish'd young Lady, with a large Fortune." She was the granddaughter of Charles Town's ambitious soldier-of-fortune and conqueror of the pirates, Colonel William Rhett.

Captain Frankland was not highly esteemed by all Charlestonians. There was a rising antipathy to him and other British naval officers stationed at Charles Town. Robert Pringle believed that "The Captains of Kings Ships have . . . Certainly too large a Share of Prizes . . . . The Prize money ought to be Limited."[31]

Complaints by Carolinians against the British Navy increased as the war progressed. Captains of locally owned merchantmen were harassed frequently by His Majesty's ships seeking to impress sailors to augment their crews. On one occasion Captain Townsend, commanding HMS *Tartar*, stopped the merchantman *Caesar* under Captain Francis Williams in the Charles Town harbor and sent an armed press gang aboard. The *Caesar*'s crew resisted and the leader of the British boarding party shot and killed one of the merchantman's sailors. Captain Williams brought the incident before the courts in Charles Town and a local jury returned a verdict of "Willful Murder" against the British sailor who had fired the fatal shot. But when the Charles Town government requested that Captain Townsend turn over the sailor to local authorities, he refused. The British sailor charged with the murder showed no remorse. He was quoted as saying he was only "sorry he had not kill'd Capt. Williams."

Such arrogance by the Royal Navy angered local merchants. Impressment also contributed to a scarcity of merchant seamen and drove up their wages. Faced with this dilemma and chronically short of hands, captains of local merchantmen encouraged British enlisted men to desert by luring them with cash bounties. But when British captains sought cooperation from the merchant-dominated local government in apprehending deserters hiding in Charles Town, they met with little success. By the mid-1740s relations had so deteriorated between the Royal Navy and the Charles Town government that local officials were reporting directly to London that the sea lanes were unsafe because "Many of the Commanders . . . of ships . . . stationed here . . . have layed up in harbor . . . instead of Cruizing for the Protection of Trade." By late 1744 Spanish privateers prowling off Charles Town brought trade to a near standstill and sent insurance and freight rates soaring. Speculators in rice acreage found few buyers, and the slave trade was virtually closed by high duties and the falling demand. The deerskin trade with the Indians declined as the threat of tribal wars hung over the backcountry.

Confronted by the economic depression and war, merchants and planters in the Assembly and the Council subordinated their sharp differences for cooperation and compromise. In both bodies the leadership was passing to the wealthy merchant- and rising lawyer-elite of Charles Town. Large planters, their social status assured, now found politics boring and no longer stood for election to the Assembly. Elected in their stead were prominent Charles Town merchants like Peter Taylor, Isaac Mazyck, John Dart, and Gabriel Manigault who were the leaders of the Assembly by the mid-1740s. The wealthy tradesman Edmond Atkins assumed a similar leadership role on the Council. Among these merchant-legislators were men whose descendants had long ago settled in Charles Town; others were more recent immigrants from England or Scotland. Most were related by marriage to the families of the planters. This merchant leadership sought remedies to the "decay of the rice trade." They urged the London government to provide more naval protection and to remove certain trade restrictions, but the Crown remained unresponsive. Exploring alternatives to trade, a few Charles Town merchants established distilleries, tanyards, and sawmills. However, for most merchants, trade in rice, deerskins, and other commodities was what they knew and they were reluctant to pursue new ventures.

In 1745 the price of rice on the Charles Town wharves dropped to its lowest point in years. The rice trade was the lifeblood of both city and lowcountry and without it many merchants and planters were reduced to poverty. The depression worsened and real and other property was seized by the colony's provost marshal, Rawlins Lowndes, and sold at public auctions to satisfy lawful debts. Lowndes, who had been orphaned when his own father fell into debt and committed suicide some fifteen years earlier, made a fortune in fees for seizing and selling debtors' properties. Houses, town lots, and buildings, including the playhouse on Queen Street, household and mercantile goods, and slaves were auctioned to the highest bidders. White and slave artisans competed fiercely in the depressed job market. Andrew Ruck, a shipwright, petitioned the Assembly for relief from the employment of slave carpenters because white carpenters could get "no work . . . and . . . they and their Families were thereby reduced to Poverty."[32]

Still facing the possibility of an invasion and upon the request of the new royal governor, James Glen, the Assembly appropriated some funds to strengthen the defenses. At the southwestern and southeastern corners of the city, new brick bastions were built and connected by a palisaded curtain line with the older works. Rusting guns and rotting carriages were remounted and repaired. Yet the governor and townspeople remained apprehensive when it was pointed out that enemy vessels could sail up the Cooper and disembark troops for an assault on the town from the landside. For a consultant on this problem Governor Glen and the Assembly hired Captain Peter Henry Bruce, His Majesty's engineer of the Bahama Islands, who arrived in Charles Town in early 1745. He first inspected Fort Johnson and its forty-two guns that guarded the southernmost approach to the harbor, finding the fortification "badly executed." After examining the works and weapons commanding the Ashley and Cooper rivers, Bruce advised the Assembly to build a battery of earth, mounting many guns at "Rhett's Point" near "Anson's House," once the home of Captain George Anson, a British naval officer on the South Carolina station. When a new suburb began being laid out nearby in 1746, it was named after him, Ansonborough. Captain Bruce also recommended that entrenchments be dug across the Neck from the salt marshes of the Cooper to those of the Ashley. At the center of these works would be built "a Fortress or Citadel."

The Assembly scaled down Captain Bruce's recommendations, eliminating his "Citadel" entirely, but offered to double his pay if he would remain in Charles Town to supervise the construction of the fortifications. Bruce, nevertheless, found members of the Assembly too "dilatory in their determinations" and departed the city in June 1745 after giving complete instructions to Colonel Othniel Beale under whose supervision works were begun to defend the city from the landside. A new powder magazine and brick barracks also were constructed. When the magazine was finished, Governor Glen called it "the finest . . . in America" and "bomb proof," and within a year the barracks were ready for occupancy by British regular troops.[33]

British soldiers and sailors on the Carolina station and mariners from American privateers and Spanish flag-of-truce ships out of a dozen foreign ports spent their liberties in Charles Town in search of gaming, liquor, and sex. Bawdy houses like The Bear and other grog shops sprang up in Roper's Alley and along the dark, narrow passageways opening near the wharves on the bay. Here crowds gathered in the evenings to gamble and drink the night away. Even pious women were attracted to the gaming tables, where they were said to mix "Religion and Cards." As the rowdiness of night life increased, robberies became more frequent. Prominent townspeople blamed the breakdown of law and order on the "Notorious Neglect" of the forty-eight-member night watch. A formal investigation confirmed their suspicions. It was charged that officers of the watch while on duty sold "Juggs of liquor" to "Seamen & Negroes." Some citizens attributed these problems to the watch's low pay and therefore its inability to attract "persons of good character." Governor Glen personally discovered that the watch did not know "how to behave upon . . . emergencies." On one occasion Glen rushed to the scene of a rapidly spreading fire to find members of the watch "instead of being useful" only adding "to the confusion." The governor attempted to bring the watch under his own personal supervision. Yet townspeople became resentful of what they called his "military rule," especially after Glen issued orders to apprehend on Sundays "all Loose and Idle Persons . . . going a Pleasuring during the Time of Divine Service."[34]

Prisons and Pest House

The increase in arrests and the imprisonment in Charles Town of prisoners-of-war strained the grossly inadequate prison facilities. Formal complaints again reached the Assembly pointing out the need for a good jail. The provost marshal and the warden of the workhouse informed the Assembly that "Vagrants and disorderly People of either Sex," prisoners-of-war, and debtors were confined "with the most notorious Criminals." During summer

1745 almost all the prisoners escaped from the main jail and subsequently a convict set the prison afire, burning it to the ground. Provost Marshal Lowndes asked the Assembly "that something be speedily done" to build a substantial structure, pointing out that South Carolina was Britain's only colony "that never had erected" an adequate prison. While the Assembly deliberated, thirteen prisoners who were awaiting trial on charges of murder escaped from their temporary lodgings. The governor again pleaded with the legislators to provide for a prison, "which all civilized Governments in the known World do always provide for at the Public Expense." But the Assembly was unresponsive and prisoners of both sexes continued to be lodged together and boarded on meager rations in the "close, stinking" rooms of private dwellings.[35]

The large numbers of transient ships and sailors made local authorities wary of the possibilities of "the Plague being brought among us." Members of the Assembly were concerned enough over the threat of epidemic disease to vote £1,000 for the construction of a "pest house" on Sullivan's Island in 1744. Captains of vessels from distant ports were required to send ashore to the pest house any "infected persons" before bringing their ships into Charles Town's harbor. By 1745 a structure was being built and a caretaker, Thomas Christie, was appointed. He took his family to the island to live, yet months later the pest house remained unfinished and Christie remained isolated and unpaid. He petitioned the Assembly for his salary and a boat, the lack of which was causing his family "great inconvenience and Misery," and he complained that the brick pest house was without doors and a ceiling. In sum, Christie concluded his masterfully understated petition, the pest house "is too airy for . . . Persons afflicted" with diseases. The ever fiscally conservative Assembly promptly rejected every line of Christie's petition, reasoning perhaps that the concept of the pest house had failed anyway, since various diseases were currently scourging the streets of Charles Town. One was the dreaded yellow fever.[36]

The *stegomyia fasciata*, or yellow-fever-carrying mosquitoes, probably were brought in again from the West Indies aboard warships during the summer of 1745. Dr. John Moultrie, Jr., believed that the cause of yellow fever was the excessive heats of the summer months. Likewise the young merchant Henry Laurens told a business associate that as "the Weather is extremely hot & the yellow fever in Town . . . I must . . . not Venture abroad in the Sun." The epidemic raged into the autumn. Within a few days of infection it proved fatal to many. Damaging the liver and kidneys of the victims, traces of blood appeared in their vomit and urine, and their skin took on a yellowish hue. In November one observer noted that the town was still "very much afflicted with . . . Yellow Feaver, in which . . . [persons] die suddenly." It appears that the mosquitoes remained to plague the city for several successive summers. Even after the coldest day of the eighteenth century in Charles Town, in February 1748, when the thermometer dropped to 10 degrees fahrenheit, yellow fever became epidemic again during the following summer. Evidently the infection remained endemic in the town. During the late 1740s mumps, measles, dysentery, "hooping cough," and possibly typhoid and pernicious malaria also reached epidemic proportions in Charles Town. A newly arrived immigrant, William Langhorne, found "prodigious Sickness," which "rages Fatally."

As the contagious diseases felled the citizens, the hospital or workhouse constructed some ten years before became crowded to capacity. Seeing the need and hoping to make money by caring for stricken black slaves, the "Apothecaries" Olyphant and Mackie opened a private "Hospital for sick negroes" in Church Street in 1747. "Sick sailors" sought lodging and care in several "old . . . little . . . rotton . . . punch houses" along the bay. Soon townspeople complained about the "noissome smells emitted from" these houses, which "proved very offensive and injurious to many in the neighborhood," and repeated complaints finally persuaded the usually frugal Assembly to designate funds "for a Public hospital for sick Sailors and other . . . transient persons." The vestry of St. Philip's Church was to oversee this expenditure and by the end of the decade the churchwardens had rented a house "distant from Charles Town" and hired a "discreet matron" to manage the hospital. Believing that earlier precautions had failed, the Assembly also tightened quarantine regulations. By the end of the decade no vessel would be allowed to enter the harbor until its captain took an oath that no one aboard was ill.[37]

Some Charlestonians complained to the Assembly that a greater threat to the health of the inhabitants was the filthy conditions of the streets and alleys. By the late 1740s the Assembly prohibited the dumping of "rubbish or filth" about the town and warned residents that all "goats and swine . . . found running at large" would be slaughtered and the meat distributed to the poor. The Assembly appointed another town scavenger and increased his powers and his pay, which was raised from taxes on private property. Commissioners of the streets were instructed to repair and sink or lay new drains. Alarmed at the rising numbers of horses and horse-drawn vehicles, the Assembly passed one of the first speeding ordinances for the town, which promised punishment for those "who shall drive . . . or ride their Horses in the Streets so fast as to endanger Persons passing and re-passing." Despite efforts to improve health conditions, Charles Town remained a disease-ridden community, and there were few adults who had not seen the death agonies of friends or relatives.[38]

Rumors and Fears

In the late 1740s citizens once more expressed to the Assembly their anxieties over the large numbers of slaves who flocked to Charles Town for holidays and fugitive slaves who found profit-minded businessmen willing to harbor and hire them. The townspeople worried especially about the "gatherings together" of "great numbers of Negroes" for "playing at Dice and other Games" and for burials. They were alarmed over the persistent sale of liquor to slaves by whites, despite its being prohibited, and the rising incidents of slave thefts. In May 1745 Governor Glen asked the London government for three companies of British regulars who "would give heart to our . . . people" and "prove usefull in preventing or suppressing any Insurrections of our Negroes." That December rumors of plots by slaves "to cut the throats of the White people of Charles Town in the Night time" terrified the citizens, but nothing came of it. About a year later further "alarms of insurrections of Negroes" prompted the government to pass an additional temporary import duty on slaves, which left little room for importing Africans for profit. Near the end of the decade, James Akin, a wealthy planter, and Agrippa, his slave, told local officials that slaves were plotting to seize Charles Town, set it "afire . . . Kill the white People," and flee in canoes for Spanish Florida. Governor Glen strengthened the night watch with British soldiers now stationed in the city, sent horse troops to patrol the Neck, and ordered the arrest of fifteen Afro-Americans and seven white men named as "ringleaders." After they were interrogated the governor announced that the "plot" was only a "Hellish Forgery . . . hatched and contrived" by the slaves. Nevertheless, Glen cautioned that "a careful and strict Eye" needed to be kept on the slave population.[39]

❦ 3. 1749–1763: Prosperity

The end of the war was proclaimed officially in Charles Town on June 12, 1749. Celebrations lasted throughout the day. British regular troops stationed in the city and the local militia paraded down Broad Street. Provost Marshal Rawlins Lowndes, wearing the ceremonial robes of his office and carrying the great sword of state, led the traditional procession of government officials to each of the four corners of the town where "His Majesty's Proclamation of Peace" was announced. That evening "Demonstrations of Joy," "sky-rockets," and other "illuminations" exploded over the city.

No one could have been happier over the signing of the peace treaty than the merchants. The nine years of war had disrupted severely the economy of the city and the lowcountry, but now the cost of freight and insurance was falling and the price of rice and indigo was rising. The indigo plant, introduced into South Carolina during the war years, was beginning to be cultivated extensively by lowcountry planters. The demand for the dye from the plant by England's fast-developing textile industry became so great by 1749 that Parliament began awarding bounties or price supports to planters for growing the crop. Indigo soon became the second of the two pillars of the lowcountry economy, rice still being the first crop. The sharp rise in the cultivation of these crops brought demands for more slaves. But unless the prohibitive duties were allowed to lapse, merchants could hope for little profit from the importing of slaves, and the whites of Charles Town had qualms about increasing the number of blacks in the colony.

" . . . this growing Evil"

The "detestable crime of poisoning" white people by blacks had reached such alarming proportions by 1749 that the Assembly passed an addition to the Negro Act, which decreed death for Afro-Americans who administered poison to any person or who "shall be privy" to such acts. About the same time the slave Caesar was freed and awarded £100 per year for life for his antidote to poison. "Caesar's Cure" was reprinted frequently in the *Gazette* and local almanacs for years.[40]

In February 1750 a committee of the Commons House of Assembly reported that because of an excessive number of slaves in the town, the "Quiet of the inhabitants is very much disturbed, and their Safety rendered precarious." The committee concluded that there were more than enough slaves to perform any tasks necessary and urged "that some . . . Restraint . . . be put to this growing Evil to reduce the present Number." The committee recommended that citizens give special preference to white persons "who will accept . . . servile labor" over blacks for such jobs as "Porters etc."; to prevent large gatherings of slaves at night for burials, the committee suggested that all slave cadavers be interred in the "negro burying-ground" to the west of the city limits "before Sun Set." That same month the Assembly defended the continuation of supplemental pay to British regular companies quartered in the town on the grounds that "our Slaves will be deterred from" insurrections "if they . . . see such a Body of Men ready to repel them in any of their evil Designs."

But merchants who remembered the boom years of the 1730s were sufficiently numerous and influential to stifle the community's fear of blacks for awhile: the duties on slave imports were sharply reduced by the Assembly and over the next few years thousands of newly enslaved West Africans, not yet able to understand English or where they were or what had happened to them, entered North America through Sullivan's Island.[41]

Economic Revival

Demand for white indentured servants also rose, leading ship captains and merchants again to exploit this very profitable trade by bringing in boatloads of German peasants. Business improved, established merchants expanded their operations, new commercial firms were opened, and new men came over from England and Scotland to embark on mercantile careers. The very small community of Sephardic Jews that had been in the port since the turn of the century had been augmented in the 1740s by Jewish immigrants from London and Amsterdam who knew the indigo trade, and in 1749 the Beth Elohim Synagogue was organized. The burned-out section of the town was being rebuilt, new suburbs were being laid out, and the colorful, pleasure-seeking social life of the 1730s began to reappear.

In 1751 the South Carolina Society was incorporated and the Assembly divided the parish of St. Philip's into two. The second parish was called St. Michael's, after a Barbadian parish named in honor of the archangel traditionally associated with ships and harbors, and the construction of a church for the new parish was authorized. An English visitor noted that silver serving dishes were beginning to show up on Charles Town sideboards and there was "scarce a tolerable house . . . that has not a chaise," a small, fashionable two-wheeled carriage. The Anglican church-sponsored school for black slaves was flourishing, and the Free School for whites was well attended.

But longstanding problems continued to plague the townspeople and torment the Assembly, which tended to regard taxes as a hellish invention of the Devil. Hospitals, jails, and law enforcement remained grossly underfunded and, despite the efforts of the new scavenger, the congested streets were often filthy, slimy, and stinking. Except in dire emergencies, the Assembly persisted in neglecting many of the needs of the townspeople.[42]

" . . . the great . . . hurricane"

A real and terrible threat to Charles Town suddenly arose in September 1752. For five months "violently hot" weather had enveloped the town. The dogs that usually wandered about the streets could only "lie panting with their tonges lolling out." Even the oldest inhabitants of the city could not recall such a prolonged and intense heat wave. Then in the early evening of Thursday, September 14, the prevailing southeasterly sea breeze died, a northeasterly breeze sprang up, and the sky over the city turned "wild and threatening." The wind velocity increased and by the early morning hours of September 15, objects not fastened down were being blown away. Rain mixed with the spray from waves crashing around the peninsula drenched the city. A brig was blown up Vanderhorst's Creek where Water Street runs today, ripping away a corner of the new Baptist Church, and coming to rest in Meeting Street. Dozens of small sailing craft were dashed to pieces against the wharves, sheds, and warehouses along the Cooper River. Huge waves undermined the brick curtain line and the three principal bastions along the bay and on White Point. The storm's debris was hurled against the houses and stores fronting Bay Street by both wind and waves. The "Negro School" near the parsonage of St. Philip's Church was blown "flat to the Ground and destroyed." Gable ends and chimneys toppled and slate and tile roofs tore away from even the most substantial brick houses. Seawater spilled over White Point and the settlement of poor people there abandoned their shacks and fled to higher ground. Torrents of water swirled across Queen, Broad, and Tradd streets and up Church, King, and Meeting streets. The waters cascaded through stores and homes terrifying the inhabitants. Realizing that the tide would not crest until one o'clock, some scrambled to the upper stories of their houses and contemplated death. The flood smashed into the dwelling occupied by the Bedon family, a few doors from where the Heyward-Washington House stands today at 87 Church Street. The Bedons were fleeing their home and Mrs. Bedon, her three children, two white servants, and five black slaves almost immediately were sucked under the rushing, swirling torrent and drowned. On James Island three persons perished when waters swept over it destroying the works at Fort Johnson. On Sullivan's Island the sea battered down the pest house and fifteen persons climbed atop its roof to save themselves, but only five still clung to the roof when it scraped high ground at Hobcaw. By eleven o'clock the entire city was under about nine feet of water when suddenly the winds veered and blew from the southwest. Thankfully, the terrified citizens watched, some prayed, as "the waters fell about 5 feet in the space of 10 minutes."

By three o'clock in the afternoon it was over. Townspeople emerged from their places of refuge and waded through the receding waters. One witness found the streets littered with the "ruins of houses, wrecks of boats, masts, yards, incredible quantities of all sorts of timber, barrels, staves, shingles, household and other goods." The fortifications around the city were so thoroughly destroyed that it appeared to Governor Glen "as if Mines" had been exploded under them. Scattered grotesquely among the debris where the surging waters had deposited them were the bodies of its victims. More than fifteen persons had perished in the city. To maintain order and to prevent looting, Governor Glen called out the militia and the town watch.[43]

Within a thirty-mile radius around Charles Town, the storm had flattened dwellings and devastated livestock and crops. The greatest financial disaster beyond the city for both plantation owners and Charles Town merchants was the loss of huge stands of trees, particularly pines. Thousands were bowled over like tenpins, uprooted and splintered. Exports of tar, pitch, and turpentine went into a sharp decline that lasted for years.

The September storm was perhaps "the greatest and most destructive hurricane that has ever taken place in Carolina" a contemporary wrote. During ensuing decades dozens of other storms skirted the western edges of the Bermuda High and thundered across or by the city. But 141 years would pass before another hurricane crashed into the Southern port that could be compared in ferocity to the blow of 1752.

With trees down across roads, bridges swept away, most small boats wrecked, and winds and rains continuing into late September, travel to or from Charles Town was hazardous if not impossible. Then on September 30 a second hurricane sideswiped the city, causing only minor flooding and "damaging the tops of some houses." Accompanying rain-squalls, however, inundated the countryside and further damaged crops. More than half the rice crop was destroyed. The government struggled for months to feed both the human and the animal populations, and the Assembly temporarily prohibited the exportation of food crops. Dozens of property owners asked the legislature to compensate them for their losses and many in the city and the countryside were forced into bankruptcy. Their tragedies increased the already considerable wealth of Provost Marshal Rawlins Lowndes, who was receiving more and more fees for seizing and selling debtors' properties.

The poor whites of the city suffered the most. Many applied for relief from St. Philip's, and the churchwardens responded by doling out cash, clothes, and blankets until their resources were exhausted. Yet as the "calamitys of the poor" continued to "call for immediate relief," the churchmen dipped into the "sacrement cash." They sent the injured and sick to the parish hospital and the homeless to the workhouse. Sarah Murray, who was living at White Point when the hurricane struck, lost all of her possessions. She was given £5 and clothes for herself and her three young children. But she never recovered from the shock of the storm and her losses. Sarah being incapable of supporting her children, the churchmen of St. Philip's bound out one "to learn to sew" and another "to be schooled" at the expense of the parish.[44]

Repairing the Old and Building the New

The hurricane disrupted temporarily the life of the port city. Under the direction of the commissioners of the streets, citizens cleared away the debris, repaired their dwellings, constructed new ones, and resumed the building of public works.

A systematic rebuilding of the defenses had been among Governor Glen's top priorities and the 1752 hurricane seemed to him to provide an opportunity to assert his authority over the commissioners of the fortifications. Glen believed that the commission system of government had usurped much of the power of the royal governor. He complained to officials in England that the administration of the "executive part of government . . . is by various Laws lodged in different sets of commissioners" appointed by the Assembly. "We have commissioners of the market, of the workhouse . . . and so on without number," he wrote. And since he as governor had "no power either to reprove them or remove them . . . little by little the People have got the whole administration into their hands, and the Crown is by various Laws despoiled." To him the governor of South Carolina was being "stripped naked of power." When Glen told the Assembly that the commissioners of fortifications infringed on the royal prerogative and asked for revision of the law, the Assembly, now led by merchants who had made or married money in the 1730s, not only refused to act, but objected to his remarks.

In early October the governor proposed plans for repairing and improving Charles Town's fortifications. He told the legislators that historically the town's defenses had been thrown up "piece-meal" with "too much haste" and too little funding. Therefore, Glen believed, "the first step to be taken" should be the hiring of a "regular Engineer" and one who would be "under the Eye and direction of the Governor and Council." For this, the governor concluded, "is the method prescribed by the British Constitution." The Assembly was opposed. The legislators had little regard for the British Constitution if it infringed on what they regarded as their own established legal prerogatives. They knew too that the engineer whom Glen had in mind was the German-born William De Brahm whose "versality of genius" included military fortifications, so the legislators offered the specious argument that no "Foreigner" should be allowed to make "Plans of our Works" or to "Sound our Channels." Their main concern, however, was that it was a prerogative established by law that the commissioners of the fortifications should direct the rebuilding of the works and not the governor.

Despite these objections, Governor Glen invited De Brahm to design a comprehensive plan for rebuilding the city's fortifications, and in late November 1752 De Brahm presented his plan to the governor and a bill for his services. Furious that Governor Glen had proceeded against their advice, the Assembly refused to pay De Brahm's fee, which Glen ended up paying out of his own pocket. The Assembly, whose members were beginning to enjoy defying the royal governor, then directed the commissioners of the fortifications to make minor repairs on the works.[45]

Carpenters, brick masons, and laborers were in short supply for several years, and private individuals, churchmen, and government officials competed for their services. Commissioners for building the new Anglican church, St. Michael's, at the southeastern corner of Broad and Meeting streets where the first St. Philip's had stood needed laborers as did the commissioners building a State House on the northwestern corner of Broad and Meeting streets. But money and manpower were directed first to repairing the fortifications and then to building the State House. Members of the Assembly were tired of meeting in rented quarters, and their impatience slowed the building of the new church for years.

In 1754, when Charles Town enjoyed its first theatrical season in seventeen years, the return of peace and prosperity seemed to be complete, but in 1755 came rumors that the rivalry between England and France was about to explode into war once more. Believing that the colony was in real danger of a French attack, the Assembly now reversed itself and, acting on a new request by Governor Glen, agreed to hire the man they had refused previously to employ, William De Brahm. But the legislators stressed that De Brahm would work under the direction of the commissioners of the fortifications, who drastically revised his original plan. The Assembly, alarmed over costs as usual, scrapped De Brahm's expensive scheme for defending the landside of the city, which like the earlier plan of Peter Henry Bruce called for a moat "from River to River" and a grandiose "Citadelle." The commissioners decided to concentrate the initial rebuilding of the defenses along the southeastern seaward-facing sides of the peninsula where De Brahm was instructed to construct a line of fortifications.[46]

The work began in July, and almost at once De Brahm encountered labor problems and differences of opinion between his foremen and the commissioners. Because of "boggy marshes" along the intended line of works, and especially near the mouth of Vanderhorst Creek, he had to use fill and construct a "grillage," or foundation, which could be laid only at low water. When the tide ebbed to its lowest level, black slaves and white laborers worked frantically to build the "grillage" of cedar posts, cypress planks, and fascines or faggots anchored by stakes and to cover it with layers of mud, lime, and oyster shells. De Brahm believed that the low wages appropriated by the Assembly, 7 shillings per day for whites and 5 shillings for black slaves, attracted too many "inferior characters." Then in early 1756 De Brahm's foreman hired a group of Acadians who were dumped onto Charles Town during the winter of 1755–56 and were a problem for several years. They were enemies, they were indigents who would have to be supported by the community, and they were Roman Catholics, "Papists . . . enemies to the laws and religion of" South Carolina. And there were more than 1,000 of them. The Assembly quickly enacted legislation to distribute most of the unfortunate farmers and fishermen throughout the lowcountry parishes. However, 137 men, women, and children remained in Charles Town, and the churchwardens of St. Philip's Church were charged with caring for them. It was these Acadians whom De Brahm referred to when he wrote that he found "too many French people" employed on the works. He bemoaned that "no body is able to make himself to be understood by them."[47]

By March 1756 the new State House was ready for use. It was the largest and most imposing structure in South Carolina. Shortly after it was built a prominent local physician and a visiting Philadelphia merchant described the State House as a two-story, "large, commodious Brick Building . . . of about 120 by 40 feet," the south front of which was "decorated with four . . . columns." The courtrooms and several offices were on the first floor, from which separate flights of stairs led to two large rooms above—one the governor's and council's chamber, which was decorated with elaborate "heavy pillars" and "carvings," the other the Assembly's chamber, which was "much plainer." The new State House attested to the craftsmanship of both black and white artisans.

Thirty-two years after it was first occupied, an accidental fire destroyed the building. The structure built on the same site to follow the lines of the original design became the Courthouse of Charleston County and retains that function to this day.[48]

De Brahm's work on the fortifications was finished by May 1756. In less than ten months, De Brahm's foreman and 300 laborers had built a continuous line of "Ramparts, forming regular Bastions, detach'd or joined with curtains." The defensive line connecting Granville's Bastion with Broughton's ran across the mouth of Vanderhorst Creek and continued around White Point. A writer for the *Gazette* observed that the new curtain line was four feet higher than the previous one and that "the sea is damn'd out."

About a month after De Brahm completed the works, on June 1, 1756, a short, slim, thirty-one-year-old man, well connected with England's aristocracy by birth and marriage, arrived at Charles Town aboard HMS *Winchelsea*. Crowds of leading citizens gathered to toast their new royal governor, William Henry Lyttelton. The wealthy merchant and influential member of the Assembly, Henry Laurens, expressed the feelings of many: "We are much in want of a new Governor. We mean a good one."

The French and Indian War

On July 2 news reached Charles Town that England had declared war on France. Fearing invasion by both land and sea, and enjoying a honeymoon with their new governor, the Assembly responded quickly and generously to Lyttelton's requests for funds for defense by raising the duties on rum, bread, and flour. The wealthy legislators purposely avoided increasing taxes on real and chattel property for "these parts of the people's property ought not to be further burthened."[49]

Governor Lyttelton hired the now highly respected William De Brahm to design plans for a fort in the backcountry for England's Indian allies, the Cherokees, and the expedition to build it soon departed Charles Town. Two British Army engineering officers were also hired to strengthen De Brahm's defenses at Fort Johnson on James Island and along the bay where they completed a third major bastion named Lyttelton's in honor of the new governor. On land purchased from prominent merchants, John Wragg and Peter Manigault, on the Neck and just north of where Boundary Street, later Calhoun, would be cut, a curtain line of tabby, lime, sand, and oyster shells was begun. Heavy weapons were mounted and within a year the defenses bristled with 119 cannons, which local militia were recruited and trained to use.

By early 1757 a French squadron was cruising the West Indies and the Assembly feared "that this Province is in great danger of being invaded." Merchants like Henry Laurens, remembering the economic depression caused by King George's War, worried that trade again might be curtailed. However, in this struggle between England and France for North America— the Seven Years' War to Europeans and the French and Indian War to the colonists—the main theaters of the fighting took place hundreds of miles from Charles Town. No French privateers appeared off the city to threaten shipping. Thus freight and insurance rates remained stable, as did the value of exports. Indigo production boomed, the demand for slaves increased, and many local merchants did a lively business in supplying the British Royal Forces in America.[50]

British fighting ships in the harbor—and the French prisoners they brought in—were a constant reminder of the war. During the opening years of the conflict, soldiers seemed to be everywhere in town. Militiamen and the "gentlemen volunteers" of the Charles Town artillery company who served at their own expense mingled in the streets and taverns with the blue-and-buff-clad Provincials, troops raised in South Carolina and paid by the Assembly, and the Independents, also recruited locally but paid by the English government

When many of the Acadians who had been sent to nearby parishes drifted back to Charles Town in 1757, the townspeople thought of the French prisoners-of-war (POWs) quartered in town and feared that the "discontented . . . naked and forlorn Acadians" might join the POWs or the black slaves in an insurrection. They added substantially to the number of welfare cases St. Philip's had to care for.

In British North America, Charles Town was by far the most important commercial center south of Philadelphia, and the British, fearing that the French would find it a tempting target, sent royal troops to defend it. During the summer of 1757 Provincials and Independents were joined by the First Royal Highland Battalion of over 1,000 officers and men from Ireland. Townspeople could easily distinguish the Highlanders because each wore "a plaid of good tartan cloth . . . and a Bonnet." By early September the town swarmed with more than 1,700 armed men under the command of the brash, thirty-eight-year-old British soldier-of-fortune, Lieutenant Colonel Henry Bouquet.[51]

Charles Town was not prepared for so many soldiers, and

Colonel Bouquet had to set up an encampment on the northwestern edge of the city. Exposed to the torrid summer sun or lashed by drenching rains, soldiers and horses fell ill. So in July, Bouquet urged Governor Lyttelton to provide temporary quarters for his troops in the town until new barracks were completed. The governor directed the colony's commissary general to use public funds to rent comfortable private rooms in the city for the senior officers while the enlisted men were assigned quarters in empty houses, "a half finished Church without windows" (apparently St. Michael's), and "in Damp Store Houses" where "most of the Men were obliged to ly upon the Ground without Straw or any sort of Covering." By October 500 men were unfit for duty, and by the end of November sixty had died. Bouquet blamed the outbreak of disease on the unhealthiness of the housing and the failure of the Assembly to provide adequate bedding. "There is no Danger that We shall fall in Love with South Carolina," he confided to a colleague. In late November the Assembly discontinued paying the rent for the officers who were quartered in private homes in Charles Town. Outraged, Bouquet ordered his senior officers not only to keep their rooms, but to refuse to pay their rents.

In early 1758 the pine-timber "New Barracks," constructed with funds appropriated by the Assembly, was completed, and by the end of February most of the soldiers occupied the new quarters located on a site that is now part of the campus of the College of Charleston. Only the question of who was to bear the expense of quartering the officers remained to be settled.

On February 28 Bouquet once more demanded that the Assembly pay the officers' rents, but the legislators again balked, claiming that the traditional rights of Englishmen to be free from having soldiers quartered in their homes without their consent had been violated. On March 18 the Assembly concurred with a report prepared by members of the Assembly, including the wealthy and politically powerful citizens Peter Manigault, Christopher Gadsden, Charles Pinckney, Henry Laurens, and Rawlins Lowndes. It denied Bouquet's request, declaring: *"Officers and Soldiers cannot, legally or constitutionally, be quarter'd in private Houses, without the special Consent of the Owners or Possessors of such Houses."* The legislators were determined to protect what they viewed as rights and privileges of the colonists as Englishmen.

A further confrontation between the Assembly and Bouquet

was avoided when he and his men were ordered north and the constitutional issue raised by the dispute remained unresolved. No one ever paid for the senior officers' rent. Colonel Bouquet departed Charles Town believing that it was the obligation of South Carolinians to bear the expense for supplying and quartering his officers and men and that the Assembly's financial support had been niggardly. He complained bitterly that townspeople were *"extremely pleased to have soldiers* to protect" them, "but will feel no inconveniences from them, making no great difference between a soldier and a Negro."[52]

One of the curiosities of Charles Town in 1758 was the rector of St. Philip's, Richard Clark, who grew a long beard and spent hours in the streets almost every day yelling, "Repent, Repent for the Kingdom of Heaven is at hand." There were people in the town who took him seriously as a prophet, but a greater number merely found him amusing and the vestry of St. Philip's were relieved when he resigned in 1759 and went back to England.

Meanwhile Governor Lyttelton's mind was focused on the foothills of the southern Appalachians, 200 miles northwest of the town, which were being settled by farmers from Pennsylvania and Virginia of Scottish, Irish, and Welsh extraction. When they found themselves at war with the local Indians, the Cherokees, Charles Town was the only place they could turn to for help. After news of a late summer uprising reached the port on the last day of September 1759 two cannons were fired three times, the alarm for a general muster of the militia. Troops of horse and foot poured into Charles Town, and militia across South Carolina prepared to move to a general rendezvous at the Congarees, near the present-day site of Columbia. Yet the Assembly, with the support of the Council, appropriated very little money for Lyttelton's dream of conquering the Cherokees and winning military glory, because of their customary reluctance to tax and spend, because white farmers on the frontier were not closely connected in Charles Town, and because lowcountry Carolinians usually thought of the slave-owning Cherokees as allies.

Despite the opposition to his plans, Governor Lyttelton rode out of Charles Town at the head of several hundred horse and foot soldiers in late October. Others joined the expedition along the way to bring the force to 1,300. Most of the soldiers were "miserably cloathed, and worse paid." By the time Lyttelton reached Fort St. George near the Cherokee Indian village of Keowee in early December, desertions and diseases had reduced the fighting strength of the expedition. When word reached the encampment that a smallpox epidemic was raging in the nearby Indian village, most of the remaining troops were ready to desert. Lyttelton hastily concluded a peace treaty with the Cherokees when smallpox broke out among his soldiers, many of whom fled from the terrifying disease. The governor and the hungry, tired remnants of his expeditionary force returned to Charles Town, and on January 9, 1760, local militia paraded down Broad Street and at noon cannons boomed a welcome to the returning soldiers. A few days later smallpox broke out in Charles Town, which had not experienced a major epidemic of the disease since 1738. The port was full of whites and blacks who had no immunity to it and what followed was the worst smallpox epidemic in the town's history.[53]

Most white adults who had not already had the disease wanted to be inoculated at once, and many demanded inoculation also for their children and slaves. There were about eighteen physicians in the town, of whom at least half had no medical training of any value. Young Dr. Alexander Garden, born and educated in Scotland, and of no relation to Commissary Alexander Garden, was the city's most respected physician and became Carolina's most celebrated scientific figure. For his writings on botanical and zoological subjects, Garden was elected to the prestigious Royal Society of England and the gardenia was named after him. He helped to inoculate between 2,400 and 2,800 persons within two weeks; by the late winter, in the city of some 8,000 black and white inhabitants, approximately 6,000 lay ill from infection by inoculation or "in the natural way." Because there were so many victims and so few physicians to care for them, Eliza Pinckney believed that "Many poor wretches . . . died for want of proper nursing." It was common practice among physicians to quarantine smallpox patients for a month in "closed rooms," and to "nail blankets over the shut windows," while the disease ran its course. During the period of quarantine physicians like Garden also prescribed "purges" by "vomits," "stools," and "bleedings." Some persons preferred to treat themselves with home remedies. One used to reduce high fever specified: "kill a fowle and split it [and] lay to the soles of [the] feet"; if at the same time the patient's throat began to swell, a mixture should be applied consisting of a "little Honey" and "Dry White Doggs Dung."

During the height of the epidemic, hundreds of townspeople

died. It appears that more blacks were stricken than whites. At the "Negro Burying Ground" just beyond the city limits there were twelve to eighteen burials a day. In mid-March 1760 Eliza Pinckney wrote that the smallpox "rages" so in the city that it "almost puts a stop to all business."

While smallpox ravaged the town, word arrived from the frontier in March 1760 that once again the Cherokees were on the warpath. Governor Lyttelton asked for additional troops and Colonel Archibald Montgomery arrived in Charles Town on April 1 with 1,200 Highlanders. Four days later Lyttelton departed to assume governorship of Jamaica and William Bull, Jr., became acting governor. Believing that God was punishing a sinful people through a visitation of smallpox and the uprising of the "barbarous Cherokees," he declared a "Day of Fasting . . . and Prayer." The smallpox epidemic ended in late June. More than 730 blacks and whites had succumbed in the six months, about 9 percent of the city's population.

After reaching the frontier Colonel Montgomery began burning Indian villages and in late June skirmished with Cherokees near present-day Franklin, North Carolina. Although he held the field, Montgomery took heavy casualties and promptly began a "strategic withdrawal" from the region and then the colony.[54]

Early in 1761, nearly ten years after the authorization for its construction, St. Michael's opened for public worship. The builder of the church, Samuel Cardy, may have based his plans on the designs of James Gibbs, an English architect whose *Book of Architecture* frequently was used by colonial American builders. St. Michael's, built and supported by public taxes, was one of the most impressive American churches constructed in the eighteenth century. Its steeple soared over 185 feet and was topped by a gilded ball and weathervane done by the local artist Jeremiah Theus. Soon a clock and bells were installed. Since the steeple could be seen from far offshore, it was a comforting sight to those arriving after a long sea voyage. It remains today the oldest steeple and one of the highest points in the city. Visitors to Charles Town in the early 1760s especially admired St. Michael's and St. Philip's, "large stone buildings with porticos with large pillars . . . ." They noted only briefly the six other "Meeting Houses" for "religious worship"—a Scotch Presbyterian, an Independent, a French, a German, and two Baptist "Meeting Houses." There was also an "assembly for Quakers and another for Jews." The

German church was St. John's Lutheran, later described as "a quaint wooden structure" and eventually replaced by the present handsome building.[55]

Retaliation against whites on the frontier by the Cherokees prompted Governor Bull to appoint the merchant-planter Thomas Middleton as colonel of a newly raised regiment to send against them and to request once more military assistance from the British. In January 1761 Scottish Lieutenant Colonel James Grant arrived in Charles Town with regular troops, which, combined with Middleton's Provincials, made a force of over 2,200. Under Grant this expedition reached the Carolina frontier in May, burned Cherokee villages, slaughtered numbers of Indians, and drove others into the mountains to starve. Having accomplished their mission, they returned to Charles Town where Colonel Grant expected a hero's welcome. Instead he found criticism. For a variety of reasons—especially personal jealousies increasingly common in relations between British regular officers and provincial officers—Colonel Middleton publicly accused Colonel Grant of poor tactics during the recent campaign. On December 17 the well-to-do merchant and hot-headed politico Christopher Gadsden charged in the *Gazette* that Grant failed to be aggressive enough toward the Indians, not permitting his men "to cut the throats of as many as they could have." Grant challenged Middleton to a duel and apparently could have killed him, but "gave him his life" and thereby rose in esteem among the Carolinians. In the midst of this inflammatory controversy, Thomas Boone, the new royal governor, arrived.[56]

The French and Indian War fueled the economy of Charles Town. It concentrated even greater wealth and power in the hands of a tiny elite at the top of society, but life deteriorated for many of those at the bottom. Contracts awarded by the Assembly for furnishing materials to complete the fortifications around Charles Town and for supplying goods to British and Provincial troops went to the leading exporters and importers in the city—Smith and Brewton, Austin and Laurens—and made them even richer. The colony underwrote these contracts with Carolina currency, which had an exchange rate of about 7 to 1 for sterling. The three wealthiest merchants in Charles Town, Henry Laurens, Gabriel Manigault, and Benjamin Smith, also made money by lending money.

These same merchants bought at bargain rates French vessels

taken as prizes by the British Navy and condemned and sold by the Vice-Admiralty Court at Charles Town and elsewhere. Henry Laurens alone became part-owner in nine vessels and with his wealthy merchant friends used these prizes to supply British forces sweeping the Caribbean. With the fall of Guadeloupe in 1759, and Martinique, St. Lucia, and Cuba in 1762, new markets opened for corn, peas, beef, and especially rice, and from Charles Town oceangoing ships hurried these commodities to distant ports under the protection of British warships. From the early winter through the spring the Cooper River appeared so choked with vessels that it resembled a "floating market." But the greatest profits for the export-import merchants continued to come from the importation and sale of slaves.[57]

Wartime scarcity in the late 1750s, coupled with the increased demand for rice and other commodities, sent the value of Carolina products soaring. Lowcountry planters, believing that a new era of prosperity was at hand, began a spree of reckless slave buying, thereby driving up the prices for slaves. Between 1757 and 1762, about 12,000 black Africans were imported into Charles Town, a 20 percent increase over the previous six years, and the purchase price of slaves rose about an equal percentage. In 1756 the average cost of a slave was £24.5 sterling and in 1762, £29.6 sterling.[58]

In these hurried, heady, prosperous war years, the gentry had time too for cultural activities. The elite founded a musical organization in 1762, the St. Cecilia Society. They commissioned Jeremiah Theus, the town's most fashionable artist, to paint their portraits. When his subjects are viewed today, they stare back, confident and self-important. Both the men and the women are dressed in richly embroidered silks and satins, the women with loops of pearls in their hair, the men sporting wigs or perukes.

In September 1762 another constitutional crisis suddenly emerged, disrupting the government at Charles Town. The opponents of Christopher Gadsden reported an irregularity in his election to the Commons House of Assembly, but the Assembly voted to seat him nonetheless. Governor Boone, however, refused to administer the oath of office to Gadsden and dissolved the legislature. This was the first time that a royal governor had so blatantly challenged the prerogative of the Commons House to determine the validity of the election of one of its members, and the Assembly censured Boone and refused to conduct any further business until he apologized for his act. Boone soon left for England. The outcome of the election controversy made the self-confident elite of the Assembly even more assertive in their relationship with British officials and more tenacious of their rights as Englishmen in America. Almost to the man members of the Commons House were closely connected merchants or planters.[59]

In late 1762 the dreaded smallpox returned. Dr. Garden and other physicians again began mass inoculations. But citizen reaction emerged again and once more physicians discontinued the practice.

In late August 1763 the end of the French and Indian War was proclaimed in Charles Town. But with peace came conflict in the form of a new British colonial policy, which ultimately contributed to a revolution in the relationship of the British government to its colonies in North America.[60]

III

Toward Independence

❦ 1. 1763–1774:
"Poor Sinful Charles Town"

Parvenu and Poor

Great Britain emerged from the Seven Years' War as the dominant power of Western Europe and North America. France relinquished Canada and the Mississippi Valley, and England acquired Florida from Spain, but the London government had incurred an enormous national debt. The great merchants of Charles Town, however, had accumulated vast wealth during the war and were now passionately interested in spending it. They built handsome houses, imported expensive silks and satins to wear, went to the theater and to concerts and balls, bought luxurious carriages, and dressed their slaves in grand and costly liveries.

In December 1763 the renowned David Douglass and his Company of Comedians appeared on the stage of the New Theatre on Queen Street, and well-to-do Charlestonians thronged to see them. They crowded into the house three nights a week for six months to enjoy performances of popular plays like *The Mourning Bride, The Jealous Wife, Romeo and Juliet,* and *King Lear.* Ann Manigault, wife of Gabriel, saw almost every performance. Dr. Garden, observing that Douglass had "met with all imaginable success" during his first tour in Charles Town, calculated that he collected "never under £90 sterling" at each performance.[1]

Like the actors, painters and drawing masters were attracted to Charles Town by its dazzling prosperity, but to turn a quick shilling many of them had to settle for painting or creating signs for new shops and taverns like the Tea Kettle & Lamp or Sign of the Bacchus. At least eight drawing schools opened during the 1760s. John and Hamilton Stevenson opened their drawing school because they realized "the great importance of this Art to Ladies and Gentlemen as a Branch of polite Education."

In the early 1760s a New England visitor who returned to

Charles Town after a twenty-year absence noted vast changes and the heady pace of the new prosperity: "The city is twice as big as when I was here" before; "one cannot go anywhere where one does not see new buildings and large and small houses . . . . To me who comes from poor, humble Rhode Island, it seems . . . a new world."[2]

But there was also desperate and increasingly widespread poverty in Charles Town. The Acadians who had been dumped there, homeless and penniless, in 1756 were only the first of many waves of poor people washed into the port. Similar to Boston, New York, and Philadelphia, a few grew wealthier while the number of indigent whites increased, alarming the propertied classes. The growing numbers of poor made Charles Town's upper classes more apprehensive than their counterparts in northern cities for several reasons: unrest of any sort might encourage slave conspirators, and the pool of white laborers, already embittered by having to compete with black slaves, would grow; additional indigents, who were especially vulnerable to disease, would amplify the town's reputation as an unhealthy place.[3]

In 1764, hoping to prevent smallpox from ever again reaching epidemic proportions in the city, the Assembly forbade mass inoculations except upon the royal governor's authority; if heads of households discovered an outbreak of the disease among their families or slaves, they were required to warn the public immediately by posting notices on their homes and at the State House. And for new immigrants, slaves or free, stricter quarantine procedures were specified for those suspected of carrying contagious diseases. The following year, on "a hot, sultry" June day, a visitor to the Sullivan's Island "Pest House" observed "2 or 300 Negroe's performing quarantine with the smallpox." But to him "the most moving sight was a poor white man performing quarantine alone in a boat at anchor ten rods from shore with an awning."

Perhaps due to the more rigorous enforcement of laws, there were no further outbreaks of smallpox in colonial Charles Town, but during 1765 whooping cough swept the city. Dysentery, "fevers," and mumps broke out among soldiers and recent immigrants during the late 1760s; a few years later there were severe outbreaks of diphtheria, scarlet fever, and measles.[4]

Besides the epidemical diseases, Charlestonians suffered almost year round from a wide variety of ailments. The diseases

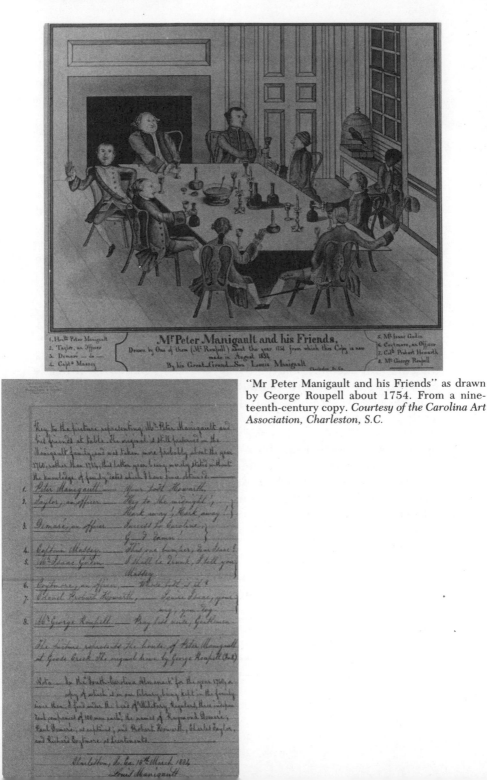

"Mr Peter Manigault and his Friends" as drawn by George Roupell about 1754. From a nineteenth-century copy. *Courtesy of the Carolina Art Association, Charleston, S.C.*

interrupted business and social life and sometimes proved fatal. Neither the rich nor the poor escaped them; for instance, the wealthy Charles Town merchant Henry Laurens and members of his family were bedridden for weeks by dysentery and "fevers." Shortly thereafter two of his infant children died, plunging his wife, Eleanor, weakened by childbirth, into deep grief. The births were "as usual once in the round of twelve Months," Laurens noted.[5]

The wealthy sometimes escaped Charles Town's epidemics and the "sickly season" of the year by trips to homes in the countryside or to Newport, Rhode Island, where they enjoyed the cooler, "salubrious" climate. Packet boats making regular runs between the two towns were crowded with passengers during the summer and fall months. Charlestonians usually departed their city in May and remained at Newport until October or November. The Motte, Izard, Wells, Rutledge, and Middleton families and others returned year after year. During the 1760s and early 1770s, so many Charlestonians spent the summers at Newport that the New England town became known as the "Carolina Hospital." Some of the wealthiest Charlestonians even traveled to England in an effort to restore their health and vitality and a few decided to remain there indefinitely, since they could not live in Charles Town due to a chronic "want of health."[6]

The poor whites and most of the blacks of Charles Town had to remain in the city; poor whites, crowded into "a low set of Wood Tenements, with walls little thicker than a Sheet of Brown Paper" along Meeting Street, were particularly susceptible to epidemics. Because of the high mortality rate among Charles Town's indigent, the average size of the port's poor white families was far smaller than the average number per household among the families in England's other North American colonies. Unable to afford private medical care, poor whites who were sick sought funds from St. Philip's Church or were treated by the parish physician. By the 1760s the demands on the parish physicians increased such that they asked for more pay. At least two town doctors set aside certain hours of the day to provide free medical service to the poor. And by the late 1760s members of the propertied class urged the construction of a new building to replace the pitifully overcrowded "Workhouse and Hospital" built years before on Mazyck Street.

Ranking fourth in population behind Philadelphia, New York,

and Boston, Charles Town ranked first in health problems. Both layperson and practitioner alike ascribed the sickliness of the port to its unique climate: the "violent heat" in summer which "caused perpetual perspiration . . . noxious vapours" and in winter "piercing cold nights and hot noon days" rendered "the human body . . . feeble and sickly." Others believed that the "narrowness [and] filthiness of the alleys" and the "nasty and stinking streets" were a "nursery for diseases."[7]

To meet the rapidly escalating costs of housing, feeding, clothing, and providing medical care for the poor, the churchmen of St. Philip's levied higher and higher taxes. Between the early 1750s and the 1770s taxes soared almost 700 percent. In addition to the funds raised in Charles Town, the Assembly gave the churchmen money from the general taxes raised across the province to meet the needs of the local poor.

Swelling the ranks of the town's poor during the early 1760s were physically crippled soldiers and sailors, and their wives, widows, orphans, and prostitutes who had come there during the Seven Years' War. From the 1730s through the early 1750s most of the people seeking relief in Charles Town had been the "ancient" and "infirm," but after 1756 the vast majority of those seeking relief were young women with small children. From 1751 to 1773 the requests of over 880 persons were granted by St. Philip's. These the vestry and churchwardens judged to be the "deserving poor" as the churchmen made a careful distinction between the "deserving" and the "disorderly poor."[8]

The churchwardens of St. Philip's determined the type and amount of relief granted the applicants, decided whether or not to place them under the care of other families, to institutionalize them in the hospital-workhouse or parish school, or to "bind-out" as apprentices their offspring. The churchmen willingly acted on requests for welfare from those who met their own set of values. Poor persons known to be "industrious" or "pious" always received aid. Inducements of both money and goods were offered to those indigents willing to leave the city. When applicants of questionable morals sought assistance, the churchmen sometimes granted them money in hopes of using it to reform them. Frances James applied for relief and was "promised 30 pence per month," but only as long as "she remains sober."

The most frequent appeals for aid came from the wives of servicemen who had deserted them. There was also a sharp increase in the number of wives deserting their husbands, which began during the social dislocations of the 1750s when the first reported cases of extramarital sex came before the churchwardens. Equally disturbing to the churchmen was the dramatic rise in premarital sex and bastardy.[9]

A very large proportion of the poor children maintained by St. Philip's Church were either reared by one parent, foster parents, or kept in institutions supported by the church. Solicitous over the health and care of these children from their earliest years, the churchmen sometimes placed them with "wet nurses" and occasionally ordered the children removed from the residences of their parents or immediate families and placed elsewhere. By the late 1750s some of the children supported at public expense were living in the "Orphan House," a structure rented by St. Philip's Church. But wherever the poor children resided, the churchmen expected them to attend the parish Free School upon reaching six years of age. Between 1751 and 1773 the churchmen bound out only twenty-two children of the approximately 618 under their care. In their early teens, these children were to serve until their eighteenth birthday. By apprenticing these youngsters the churchwardens of St. Philip's were able to reduce the "expenses of the parish" and to ensure that their wards learned a trade which they could use to become productive adults.[10]

For the parvenu Charlestonians who gave any thought to the best type of elementary education for their own sons, some favored a "practical" education while others favored one founded on the classics. The merchants Henry Laurens and George Austin, for example, questioned the value of a classical education in "a Commercial Country," while John Rutledge considered a thorough reading of Greek and Latin authors to be essential. But with the exception of the Provincial Free School supported by St. Philip's Church, no tax-supported grade school was established in Charles Town during the colonial period like those established in certain New England towns. Since the Free School by the 1760s had become primarily an institution for orphans and children of the poor, it bore the stigma of charity, and the well-to-do refused to enroll their offspring there. In 1763 Henry Laurens declared that children had to be sent abroad "even for A B C and a little Latin."

The absence of public schools lured private teachers. Between 1760 and 1775 over 100 of them offered instruction in arithmetic, fencing, French, Latin, drawing, dancing, music, needlework, bookkeeping, navigation, and surveying in Charles Town. The new rich remained indifferent or opposed to the establishment of an institution of higher learning in the city, and in the 1760s when citizens of moderate means revived earlier attempts to establish a college, they again failed.[11]

A few members of the elite like Christopher Gadsden and Henry Laurens passed along their ideas on politics to the literate public through Peter Timothy's *Gazette* and two other newspapers being published in Charles Town by the mid-1760s, one by Charles Crouch and the other by Robert Wells. After emigrating from Scotland to Charles Town during the 1750s, Wells also established a bookstore and bindery. Wells prospered and in 1766 he purchased a house at 71 Tradd Street next door to his "Printing Office, Bookseller's and Stationer's Shop." From this location, near the corner of Tradd and Meeting streets, a site occupied today by the First Scots Presbyterian Church, Wells boasted that he had the largest stock of books in America. He was indeed the largest bookseller and printer in the Southern colonies. Before the outbreak of the Revolution, Wells printed or reprinted ninety works ranging from the *Standing Regimental Orders for the IX Regiment of Foot* to the *Letters of Abelard and Eloise*. However, more than half of his titles were local sermons, the rules of local societies, and almanacs, publications enjoyed by eminently practical men.[12]

During the 1760s the dramatic increase in the "disorderly poor" alarmed local grand juries, which spoke of "vagrants, drunkards, and idle persons" roaming the streets "swearing and talking obscenely . . . insulting the inhabitants." Among them were unemployed sailors, deserters, "and notorious bawdes and strumpets." Concerned over the growing vice in the city, the grand jurors urged the Assembly to act to shut down houses of prostitution, and Mary McDowell of Pinckney Street and Mary Grant of another location were cited for keeping "a most notorious brothel" and for "harboring loose and idle women." The latter's establishment was closed, but only temporarily. She soon reopened her business elsewhere in the city. Grand jurors believed also that "the superabundance of licensed Taverns and Tippling Houses, . . . gaming houses and disorderly houses" were contributing to the ruin of the health and morals of the poor and the rising vice in the city. Until the end of the colonial period, grand juries continued to appeal to the Assembly to close those establishments where the "youth of the town are entertained and debauched."

For poor whites, jobs were hard to find, except in construction. Even educated transients like Thomas Anderson, by turns a sailor and a schoolmaster, could not find work in the city. He had been "about Town . . . four months trying all possible means to get a" position, but being unsuccessful he wrote, "I am not able to pay for my board and was obliged . . . to Dispose of one of my Jackets to get me a Pair of Shoes."[13]

The hiring out of slaves for public or private work was well entrenched in Charles Town by the 1760s. The slaves themselves were furnished a "ticket" indicating that they could be hired. The rented slaves were expected to feed and clothe themselves and to turn over to their masters most of their remaining earnings. Skilled black coopers, carpenters, wheelwrights, boatmen, and fishermen were hired out as were "house wenches" and a few male domestics like the "very orderly negro man that understands how to wait on a gentleman." Slave "porters" who were rented out for heavy physical "Labour in Ships at the Wharves" were paid 10 shillings daily. Those hired for "rolling of rice (barrels), or other common porterage" earned over 7 shillings. Some slaves hired themselves out without the knowledge of their owners. When Ishmael, a slave of Henry Laurens, earned £30 as a porter, Laurens reprimanded him for attempting to conceal his earnings. Ironically, the economic self-interest of both the owner and the employer of hired-out slaves encouraged the illegal entrepreneurial efforts of the slaves themselves. The practice of hiring out provided blacks the autonomy to seek jobs and make money for themselves. Employers did not scruple to hire unlicensed slaves without "tickets" despite the threat of heavy fines. One white Charlestonian observed that even runaways "who will work, may get employ."

Venturesome black apprentice chimney sweeps, slave porters, and black common laborers sought to manipulate the local economy by combining to fix the pay for their services during the 1760s. These were some of the first such labor actions in North America. In the late 1760s the *Gazette* noted that "the Negro JERRY," presumably a free black, "has just completed a WELL-BOAT, in order to supply the inhabitants of this town with LIVE FISH every day." About the same time a local official complained that blacks "at their pleasure . . . supply the town with fish or not" and set the prices for the seafood sold in the city. Despite restrictive regulations, Afro-Americans also came to "monopolize the market business" in Charles Town. Along the public streets and in the markets black "wenches and other slaves" sold "all sorts of Dry Goods, Fruit and Victuals."

Also limiting the job prospects for whites was the increasing identification of certain tasks like "cart driving" as "Negro work" and the refusal of unskilled whites to undertake such jobs. The owners of carts and wagons who wished to hire drivers found that "there is but very few white people who will follow that Employment in this Town."

Some of the gentry recognized the employment problems encountered by white laborers, and a correspondent in the *Gazette* charged that the failure to enforce the laws regulating slaves affected "poor white people in a greater degree than is generally imagined." By the late 1760s grand juries were recommending that the Assembly amend the Negro Act "so as to prevent idle slaves interfering with poor, honest white people supporting themselves and families amongst us." But many of the legislators habitually hired out their own slaves, and they were unwilling to amend laws from which they profited. As one Charlestonian observed, slaveholders who rent the labor of their slaves "care little how their slaves get money" as long as "they are paid." So, while the elite were alarmed by the growing number of welfare cases in the city and the resulting social "disorder," they failed to ease one of the problems causing the high rate of unemployment among the poor whites.[14]

In 1764 wealthy slaveholders recognized that further importations might have the "dangerous consequences" of "too great a disproportion of slaves to white inhabitants" and the Assembly imposed nearly prohibitive duties on all slaves brought in after January 1, 1766. That same year, 1764, the British Parliament passed a Currency Act aimed at decreasing the issue of paper currency in the colonies. The resulting shortages of money in Charles Town at a time when provisions were scarce and prices high were very hard on the poor whites. In February 1765 "A Tradesman" writing in the *Gazette* warned that more almshouses would soon be needed, for it is no doubt "that an industrious Man who does not earn more than Thirty or Forty Shillings in the Day (and few do that) cannot possibly pay House-Rent, Cloath and feed his Family." The "Tradesman" also accused the propertied class of buying up large quantities of commodities and driving up prices.[15]

The Stamp Act and Christopher Gadsden

In the following month Parliament passed the Stamp Act, which imposed a direct tax on such items as legal documents, newspaper advertisements, and playing cards; this alarmed Charles Town's *nouveaux riches*, who saw it as a threat to their power. Only the year before, the legislators had thwarted a challenge from the colony's royal governor, Thomas Boone, who questioned the right of the Assembly to determine the validity of the election of its members. Subsequently, the London government appointed Lieutenant Governor William Bull, Jr., a well-liked native Carolinian, as the acting Governor of the colony. Heartened by this victory the Assembly was determined to resist other threats to the powers it had arrogated to itself over the years, powers that included the levying of taxes and control of the budget.

The rich Charles Town factor Christopher Gadsden, who led the successful opposition to Governor Boone, now organized the fight against the Stamp Act. Gadsden had served as a member of the Assembly since 1757 and as captain of the Charles Town artillery company. Known for his relentless pursuit of wealth and power, he viewed royal officials and England's new schemes for raising money in the colonies as a threat to his ambitions. An acquaintance remarked that Gadsden "could not brook the encroachments of any man or body of men intrenching on his rights." At forty-one years of age, Gadsden was an extremist, impetuous, and intemperate in his language. Unique among members of the Assembly and Charles Town's elite, he had established a following among the city's laboring classes. Some of these artisans and mechanics were members of his artillery company, and he apparently convinced them that their "natural priviledges" and Charles Town's economy were being threatened. His politicking among the poor alarmed his conservative colleagues. Some found him "violent" and "wrongheaded"; others saw Gadsden as a "tribune of the People." In 1764 Henry Laurens privately called him a "rash headlong Gentleman who has been too long a ringleader of people engaged in popular quarrels." Lau-

rens, like other conservatives, believed that "the calamity of domestic broils . . . are more awful & more distressing than Fire,
Pestilence, or Foreign Wars."[16]

In leading the opposition to the Stamp Act in the Assembly,
Gadsden believed that the measure was inconsistent "with that
inherent right of every British subject, not to be taxed but by his
own consent, or that of his representatives." During the summer
of 1765 he urged the Assembly to answer the call of the Massachusetts government for representatives from each colony to
meet in New York in October to protest the act peacefully. The
South Carolina Assembly was the first to select its delegates for
the extralegal meeting and Gadsden was one of those chosen.
Thomas Lynch, the wealthy rice planter, and John Rutledge, the
young Charles Town lawyer, also were elected. On September 4
they sailed from Charles Town for the Stamp Act Congress where
Gadsden took a leading part. He served as chairman of the committee that drafted resolutions condemning the act and wrote the
cover letter transmitting them to the London government. But
while Gadsden used peaceful methods of protest in New York,
members of his artillery company and others in Charles Town,
calling themselves "Sons of Liberty," and probably following
Gadsden's instructions, used violence.

During the late summer of 1765 news arrived in Charles
Town that riotous mobs had taken to the streets in the northern
cities to protest the Stamp Act. Charlestonians themselves in public taverns and private homes raised many "hearty damns of the
. . . Act over bottles, bowls and glasses." Then, when on October
18 the *Planters Adventure* sailed into Charles Town's harbor carrying a consignment of stamps, royal officials worried about a
possible "disturbance" by "evil disposed" persons. The following
morning, a Saturday, a forty-foot-high gallows appeared at the
intersection of Broad and Church streets. Inscribed on it were the
words: "Liberty and No Stamp Act." Hanging from the structure
was an effigy of a stamp distributor. In the evening the gallows
was loaded on a horse-drawn wagon, and a crowd of about 2,000
persons marched beside it as the vehicle rolled eastward on Broad
Street toward the bay. Among the crowd were laboring-class artisans—themselves the architects of the gallows—sailors, and vagrants. Royal officials were powerless to maintain order. At the
home of George Saxby, the London-appointed inspector of
stamps, a mob rushed in and, upon finding no stamps, they ran-

sacked the dwelling. The mob then moved on to a field near the New Barracks, burned the effigy, and buried a coffin labeled "American Liberty." Some members ended their evening in local taverns drinking "Damnation to the Stamp Act." But the violence was just beginning. For eight days the city would be swept by disorder.[17]

Lieutenant Governor William Bull had transferred the stamps from the *Planters Adventure* to Fort Johnson on James Island, where they were kept under armed guard while the mob continued to roam the city searching for them. Henry Laurens denounced the "Sons of Liberty" who, he said, under the guise of "Patriotism . . . committed unbounded acts of Licentiousness & at length Burglary & Robbery." There was a rumor that Laurens himself was concealing the stamps, and late at night on October 23 an armed mob "heated with liquor" began banging on his door in Ansonborough, demanding to search the premises. Worried about his pregnant wife who was becoming hysterical, Laurens admitted the mob. They searched the house, "cursed me," Laurens recalled, "and threatened . . . to carry me away to some unknown place & punish me." But after he told the crowd that he was opposed to the Stamp Act, the mob departed and Laurens wrote, "Riot is in Fashion."

On October 26 leaders of the mob spread the news that the two local stamp agents George Saxby and Caleb Lloyd were at Fort Johnson, and for the next two days a mob surged through the streets threatening to murder them if they did not resign. Lieutenant Governor Bull lacked the forces to quell the rioting and on October 28 Saxby and Lloyd publicly announced that to "restore and preserve the peace," they would not enforce the act. Celebrating Sons of Liberty poured into the streets and unfurled a flag with the word "LIBERTY" sewn across it. An African-born slave, Olaudah Equiano, later recalled: "I saw the town illuminated, the guns were fired, and bonfires and other demonstrations of joy shown." After the events of October 1765, all Charlestonians, rich or poor, black or white, were acutely conscious of the power of violence as a political weapon. Benjamin Smith observed: "I am afraid some of the lower class who have been made men of consequence in the late comotions, will not readily endeavor to promote peace." Even those members of the propertied class like Peter Timothy and Christopher Gadsden, who were more sympathetic with "the lower class," worried for the future of peace and order.[18]

Lieutenant Governor William Bull charged that Peter Timothy's *Gazette* was the "Conduit Pipe" for northern propaganda, which had "poisoned" the minds of Charlestonians against the Stamp Act. Apparently alarmed over the excesses of the October riots, Timothy declined "to directly support and engage in the most violent Opposition." Gadsden, leader of the Sons of Liberty, sought to preserve order in Charles Town after he returned from Philadelphia by convincing the Assembly to endorse the methods of peaceful protest adopted by the Stamp Act Congress. The Sons of Liberty had prevented the issue of stamps. Lacking authority under the Stamp Act to do business without stamps, the civil courts and the Customs House closed down. The export trade ceased, since vessels could not leave port without legal clearances, and by December ships were stacked up in the harbor and barrels of rice jammed the wharves.

Hundreds of idle sailors thronged the "tippling houses" and roamed the streets, some of them harassing citizens and demanding "money of the People." This led Gadsden to call out the Sons of Liberty to control the mobs. One citizen observed that the "Liberty Boys . . . suppressed them instantly and committed the Ring-leaders to Gaol." Gadsden, like other members of the propertied class, was determined to preserve law and order in the city. As one local observer noted in the *Gazette*, "the richer folks were terrified at the spirit which themselves had conjured up."[19]

The Slave Trade

The streets swarmed with blacks as slave-traders brought in cargo after cargo before the import duties increased. Fabulous fortunes were reaped from black cargoes by merchants like Laurens who sometimes negotiated the sale of more than 700 slaves in a single year. These merchants knew that lowcountry planters and those from nearby colonies who purchased slaves in Charles Town preferred certain African tribes and certain characteristics. Laurens advised business associates abroad to "let your purchase be of the very best kind of slaves, . . . free from blemishes, young & well grown, the more Men the better, but not old. None sell better than Gambia Slaves . . . ." Of the 338 recorded cargoes of slaves arriving in Charles Town from Africa during the colonial period, more than one-third were brought in from either Gambia or Angola.

Following the sale of the slave cargoes, the putrid holds of the slavers, awash with excrement, urine, and vomit, would be "smoked" by the crews who plunged heated bullets into buckets of vinegar to clean the vessels for the loading of outward bound cargoes of commodities. Despite these efforts, sailors often refused to serve on slave ships after several voyages as the smells of the human cargoes seemed to permeate the timbers. As the common saying went: "You can smell a slaver five miles down wind on the open ocean." The masters of such ships, " Guinea Captains" as they were called, were "a rough set of people," one visitor to Charles Town observed. However, he discovered that they were "carressed" by the city's slave merchants "on account of the great profits of their commissions."[20]

Those Charles Town firms and merchants monopolizing the local export-import trade in commodities and consumer goods also brought in most of the slave cargoes and were linked by marriage, blood, and business. The firm of George Austin and Henry Laurens, later Austin, Laurens and Appleby when Austin's nephew George Appleby joined the business, handled sixty-one cargoes of slaves. Miles Brewton was associated with firms that handled approximately fifty cargoes of slaves, one of the first that Brewton joined being the prestigious company of Benjamin Smith whose wife was Brewton's half-sister. Marriages between the sons and daughters of these great merchants and the offspring of wealthy planters became so important that sometimes they were referred to as "alliances" between families. By their early teens the offspring of the propertied class recognized the importance of a proper match and most promised dutifully to cooperate with their family's wishes. Family connections through a proper marriage provided votes for church or government offices and economic opportunities through family contacts and inheritance. Such marriage patterns contributed to the continuing harmony and homogeneity of values among the Charles Town elite. Like the Virginia gentry, the gentry of lowcountry South Carolina became "one great tangled cousinry."

By the end of the 1760s the city's wealthiest merchants or their families were Benjamin Smith, Jacob Motte, Henry Laurens, and Gabriel Manigault, who were millionaires several times over—the latter two perhaps the wealthiest in the American colonies. They enjoyed yearly incomes of £2,500 to £3,000 sterling. By comparison, the city's physicians and attorneys of ability and connections might make £250 to £500 sterling a year. Dr. Garden, who had the largest medical practice in the port during the 1760s, earned £500 sterling per annum, which he found to be "a modicum to maintain and educate my young family." First-rate artisans made £100 to £150 sterling annually.[21]

By the 1760s Charles Town's elite families, grown wealthy in trade, land, moneylending, and slaves, linked by marriage and united in their values, constituted about 5 percent of the city's white population of approximately 5,000 persons. Most of them were members of St. Philip's or St. Michael's Church. Wealth was a prerequisite for election to the Commons House of Assembly. To stand for election the law required candidates to own 500 acres of land and ten slaves or lands, buildings, and town lots worth at least £1,000 currency. Voting requirements were not much easier. Free white males, twenty-one years of age or older, who professed the Christian religion and owned fifty acres or paid an annual tax of at least 20 shillings and were local residents for one year could appear at their parish churches to vote. These qualifications excluded perhaps 90 percent of Charles Town's adult population if women, indentured servants, free blacks, and slaves are included. In a city of some 10,000 persons, potential officeholders and their electorate numbered perhaps less than 500. The same men were returned again and again as vestrymen and churchwardens at St. Philip's and St. Michael's, and repeatedly they were elected to serve as members of the city's governing bodies: commissioners of the fortifications, markets, streets, workhouse, and on local grand juries. They served as justices of the peace, magistrates, constables, and headed militia outfits. Often serving simultaneously in local church, civic, and military offices and as members of the Assembly, these plutocrats controlled the politics of the city. One visitor observed: "If a few of the Leading Men are so disposed, 'tis enough to prevent the doing of anything," but with few exceptions they had modest beginnings. Henry Laurens, himself the son of a saddlemaker, declared that the Charles Town merchants "almost to a Man by means of their commissions and profits arising from . . . trade [have] risen from humble and moderate Fortunes to great affluence . . . ." Their hard work and good fortune had made them, as one visitor observed, "rich, haughty and arrogant." The monopoly of commerce by Charles Town's wealthy merchant-planters, Britain's trade policies, and the increasing scarcity of good lowcountry rice and indigo lands narrowed economic opportunities for the many.[22]

In December 1765 a rumor rippled across Charleston that

there was "a design of the Negroes to make a general insurrection & Massacre of the White People" on Christmas eve. Acting Governor Bull also received evidence of a plot from "two Negroes" living on nearby John's Island who came forward with their information because of their "friendship to the White People," and on December 17 Bull convened an emergency session of the Council. One hundred militia men were deployed to guard Charles Town during the holidays and Bull arranged with the captains of ships in the harbor to have sailors stand sentinel duty nightly on the wharves. Christmas Day dawned without incident, but Bull ordered night and day patrols to sweep Charles Town and its environs into the bitter cold weather of early January.

Henry Laurens thought that "there was Little or no cause for" alarm. He believed that the whole "disturbance" sprang from several slaves shouting out "Liberty" in the streets in imitation of "their betters" who had done the same during the Stamp Act riots in October. The whole affair ended with the "banishment of one fellow not because he was |an| . . . instigator of insurrection," but because "in the . . . course of his Life he had been a sad Dog." Laurens conjectured that, since the authorities had overreacted to the presumed plot, the slave was banished "to save appearances." But the Assembly and Bull continued to believe that a serious insurrection had been planned. In late January Bull reported to London authorities that any schemes of "a Negro Insurrection" had been defeated, but warned the Assembly that there was a lesson to be learned from the affair: "The cause of our danger is domestic." The Assembly immediately appointed a committee to determine if there had been "an intended Insurrection" and to devise "precautions as may effectually" prevent "the future . . . dangers of Insurrections."[23]

Violent opposition in the colonies and in England and the trade embargo prompted Parliament to repeal the Stamp Act in March 1766. When the news reached Charles Town, church bells rang, ships in the harbor unfurled their colors, cannons boomed, militia companies paraded, and toasts were drunk. Since Shepheard's Tavern no longer existed, Robert Dillon's Tavern on Queen Street now was the favorite tippling house of the gentry and here Gadsden led his Liberty Boys to celebrate. The Assembly sped their thanks to George III for the repeal and voted to erect a marble statue in Charles Town of William Pitt, who had so persistently advocated the concerns of the colonists in Parliament. For several years Masons, who were growing in numbers and influence, would meet on March 18 to mark the anniversary of the repeal of the hated Stamp Act. Freemasonry played an important role in Charles Town during the Revolutionary era because it brought together on common ground influential merchants and some of the most prosperous artisan leaders.

In 1766 leading artisans petitioned for the incorporation of the Fellowship Society, believing that, despite the efforts of several charitable agencies, there were still "poor distressed persons" who suffered from the lack of food, lodging, and a hospital. Edward Weyman the upholsterer, Daniel Cannon the carpenter and developer, and George Flagg the artist were among the first officers of the Fellowship Society. Closer to those at the "bottom" of society, they recognized and knew better the needs of the poor than the rich elite. They were prominent members of Gadsden's Liberty Boys, and like him they realized that the policy of "arbitrary governments . . . falls heaviest upon men who have little," men like artisans and common laborers who "depend . . . upon their daily labour . . . for the maintenance of themselves and families." The "circumstances" of the laboring classes are "low," Gadsden declared publicly in the late 1760s, and the "apprehension" of even less in the future causes among them "extreme uneasiness."

And the poor continued to arrive. During the late spring of 1767, 300 indigents "landed out of a ship from Ireland." Provided temporary lodgings at the "old Barracks," the Irish immigrants soon were "confined to their beds by a cruel Flux and Fever." Churchwardens of St. Philip's who visited them there "saw . . . corpses . . . many dying, some deprived of their senses . . . young children lying entirely naked . . . reduced by sickness . . . whose parents had expired." The churchmen posted notices about the town appealing for "monies or other things" for the survivors, and eventually some money was raised, but the churchmen reported that "the sum is too inconsiderable to afford these poor people the necessary relief."[24]

The Artisans

While catering to the rich, about a score of the artisans became wealthy themselves. Owning land, slaves, and rental property, and lending money at interest, they served as church officers at St. Philip's and St. Michael's, as commissioners in less prestigious local government posts, and on grand juries, but they rarely presumed to stand for election to the Assembly. John Rose the shipwright, who owned his own shipyard at Hobcaw Point, became one of the richest artisans in North America. The carpenter Edward Bullard, who amassed some wealth as a builder for the elite, acquired two homes in the city and seven slaves. Among the twenty to thirty cabinetmakers working in the city from the 1760s through the 1770s and meeting the demands of the new rich for chests, clothes presses, beds, desks, chairs, and tables, only Thomas Elfe accumulated substantial wealth. Emigrating from London in the 1740s, Elfe prospered quickly in the furniture-making business. A master craftsman whose creations are now eagerly sought by collectors, Elfe produced more than 1,500 pieces of furniture at his Broad Street shop from 1768 to 1776. Like other cabinetmakers in Charles Town, he copied the styles of the English master Chippendale, but also carved into some of his pieces rice leaves in homage to the crop from which the lowcountry gentry were reaping their fortunes. Among the most affluent artisans were the silversmiths Thomas You, Alexander Petrie, Moreau Sarrazin, and his son Jonathan, who bought "a large brick mansion" at the northern edge of town. Today this dwelling at 54 Hasell Street, originally built for Colonel William Rhett in 1712, is believed to be the oldest house in the city. Barrel-making was a particularly important occupation, given the extensive export trade. Daniel Saylor maintained a cooperage factory near the wharves and barrelmaker Gabriel Guignard became wealthy at his craft. Thomas Vardell, a cooper, was well paid by the great merchants to pack the country produce into barrels for shipment abroad.[25]

Approximately twenty chandlers supplied the local needs of candles and soap, and an equal number of tanners provided all types of leather goods; coachmakers met the demands of the new rich for "elegant" carriages, chariots, and riding chairs; there were gunsmiths, tobacconists, and tinsmiths. Edmund Egan, perhaps colonial Charles Town's most successful brewer, erected a "large and expensive Malt house" and adopted the slogan "Let the beer justify itself." The *Gazette* praised his product as "superior to most that is usually imported from the Northern Colonies." Blacksmiths like William Johnson, James Lingard, and John Cleaton shod horses, erected lightning rods, and did scroll work on railings for staircases. These artisans continued to employ

Bernard Elliott, Jr., by Jeremiah Theus. *Courtesy of the Carolina Art Association, Charleston, S.C.*

Henry Laurens (1724–92) by John Singleton Copley. One of the city's first millionaires through investments in trade, land, and slaves, and a president of the Continental Congress. *Courtesy of the National Portrait Gallery, Smithsonian Institution, Washington, D.C.*

white indentured servants as assistants on a temporary basis; how-ever, they preferred to purchase Africans, who, as slaves, served as assistants for their lifetimes. Some slave craftsmen became "no-tably proficient" in their trade.[26]

Still seeking a source of revenue to reduce the government's indebtedness, the British Parliament passed the Townshend Acts in 1767. Their effects, like those of the Currency Act and the Stamp Act, fell heaviest on laborers, debtors, and the poor. Im-posing an import duty on painters' colors, white lead, glass, and paper, the Acts affected the businesses of painters, cabinetmakers and builders, bookbinders and printers.

The grand jurors of Charles Town and the churchmen of St. Philip's again petitioned the Assembly during the mid-1760s for funds to enlarge the workhouse and hospital because it was "in-sufficient" in size and the "vagrants . . . and idle persons who might be there committed, reign and infest the . . . town." In De-cember 1766 the churchwardens of St. Philip's told the Assembly that due to the great numbers of "seamen and slaves" confined at the workhouse and hospital, the numerous poor could not be ac-commodated and they urged that the "New Barracks" be used as temporary quarters for the "deserving poor." Such persistent complaints finally led the Assembly to make an "inquiry" into the state of "the poor in Charles Town." In April 1767 the Assembly concluded that there were specific causes for "the greatly in-creased numbers of Poor": the ease by which indigents from neighboring colonies and immigrants from abroad could settle in Charles Town and obtain welfare; "the super-abundance Tippling Houses" which brought "the Ruin of their health"; the *many Women and Children*" abandoned by soldiers, and recent British policies, such as the Stamp Act, which had caused "a stagnation of Trade and business," leaving many jobless. The report did not cite the hiring out of slaves as a cause of unemployment among whites, perhaps because wealthy legislators profited from the practice.

In response to the "inquiry," the Assembly increased the res-idency requirements in Charles Town from three to twelve months for anyone seeking welfare at St. Philip's and in early 1768 passed an "Act for appropriating the present Work House for a place of Correction . . . and for building a Poor House and Hospital." These new brick facilities were built facing Mazyck Street on the four acres of public land bounded by Queen Street to the south, Magazine Street to the north, and the Ashley River marshes to the west. Within these bounds on the city's western fringe was already a public powder magazine, the "old Barracks," and the old poor house and hospital. When the new poor house and hospital were ready for occupancy in the spring of 1770, the older facilities were to be used solely as a place of confinement and correction for fugitive slaves, seamen, "vagrants and disorderly persons." Nevertheless, until the end of the colonial era grand juries continued to petition the Assembly for additional legislation "to prevent the *poor* and the Idle from . . . neighboring provinces . . . and other parts of the world" from coming to Charles Town.[27]

Private and public wharfs, bridges, a watch house, a jail, markets, drainage systems, and public wells were constructed throughout the rapidly expanding town. Architects, surveyors, and artisans were in great demand as the money and energy that had for so long gone into building and repairing the city's fortifications now went into civic improvements while the defenses of the city themselves fell into ruin. Peter Timothy wrote Benjamin Franklin, "all *White Point*, which for many years was almost a desolate Spot, is lately almost covered with Houses, many of them very elegant." Across Meeting Street from St. Michael's Church at the southwestern corner of Broad and Meeting streets, a "New Guard-House," or watch house, was completed in October 1769. One of the builders and possibly the architect was William Rigby Naylor, who for some years had practiced carpentry in the city. Naylor and another builder, James Brown, were awarded a contract by the Assembly to construct the building. An English traveler in the early 1770s admired the two-story structure, which had offices of the Public Treasury on the second level, as "a . . . good building . . . of brick inside and plaistered over . . . on the outside to imitate stone." he also liked the structures on two other corners at the intersection of Broad and Meeting streets— St. Michael's and the State House—but described the building on the fourth and northeastern corner as "a low dirty looking brick market house for beef." This crossroads at Broad and Meeting streets was considered to be the center of town by the 1760s. It was just to the east of the site of the moat and drawbridge, long since demolished and partially filled in.[28]

Petitions and arguments before the Assembly by Charles Town's wealthy merchants and investors prompted the government to pass an act in 1767 for the building of an "Exchange or Custom House." Designed by Naylor, the £40,935 contract for the construction of the "Exchange" was awarded to Peter and John Adam Horlbeck, master masons and recent immigrants from Germany. This contract led to many others for the Horlbeck brothers, who invested in real estate, married well, and died leaving sizable estates. The new Exchange was needed to accommodate the heavy export-import trade and as a place to conduct both public and private business. But the site, design, and construction of the building also symbolized the self-image of Charles Town's elite. And it was one of the first examples of local urban planning. The site chosen for the new Exchange at the foot of Broad Street was a symbolic point in the life of the city. It was the center of the waterfront, where streams of inland and maritime traffic long had converged, and the intersection of its first import thoroughfares. Since the city's beginnings major civic structures had occupied the site. The Half-Moon Battery had first been built here, later the "Court of Guard," and then the old Council chamber, which was razed between 1767 and 1768. The "siting" of the Exchange was an attempt "to harmoniously relate spaces and uses," the basis of modern-day urban planning; even adjacent street markets were moved because they were "indecorous." In late July 1768 the foundations of the new building were laid and construction began.[29]

The new civic consciousness and the persistent demands of Charles Town's well-to-do prompted the Assembly to authorize expenditures for new streets, bridges, and the filling of low-lying lands as the city spread to the southwest and the northwest. For the convenience of planters living along the Ashley and Stono rivers, a canal was dug from the western end of Broad Street through the marsh grass to the Ashley. Spoil from the canal was used to fill the marsh on each side of the cut, creating a commons for the townspeople.

During the 1760s Ansonborough, one of the town's first suburbs, became "thickly Inhabited." For the use and convenience of homeowners there, the Assembly in 1767 authorized the building of the "Governor's Bridge" across the wide creek at the north end of Bay Street near Craven's Bastion; at the same time Meeting Street and Old Church Street were extended northward to intersect with George Street. Two years later, just to the south of the city's landside defensive line, Boundary Street, later named

Calhoun Street, was laid out. It marked the northernmost limit of Ansonborough. Now the intersection of Boundary Street and the Broad Path, or King Street, just below the defenses and new town gate, was the main landward entrance to the city. By the late 1760s small businesses had sprung up along King Street catering to the wagoners transporting goods to and from Charles Town and it became the retail center of the city while Bay Street remained the focus of the wholesale trade.

Private developers undertook the laying out and promotion of various suburbs in the late 1760s through the early 1770s. To the northeast of Ansonborough and just to the south of Boundary Street, Henry Laurens laid out Laurens Square; just to the north, Christopher Gadsden developed Middlesex along the Cooper River. The street names that Gadsden selected for his development, Wilkes and Pitt, reflected Gadsden's political enthusiasms. A principal feature of Gadsden's suburb was a wharf extending into the Cooper River, which he promoted as "one of the most extensive in America . . . at which thirty Ships can be Loading at the Same time." The city also spread to the southwest when the wealthy silversmith Alexander Petrie subdivided into twelve building lots the old Orange Garden, a stand of orange trees just to the west of King Street. Here he opened up a new avenue, Orange Street, linking Broad and Tradd streets. Among the buyers of Petrie's lots was "Amy, a free woman of color." At about the same time William Gibbes and Edward Blake were filling in the low marshy ground at White Point, the very southwestern corner of Charles Town.[30]

In 1770 the northwestern edge of the city was approved for development by an act of the Assembly. Here according to the provisions of the will of John Harleston, a tract of land indented by Coming Creek, meandering streams, and marshy banks was surveyed and laid out into building lots by the architect William Rigby Naylor. It became known as Harleston Village. This large development is today bounded by Beaufain, Calhoun, Coming, and Ashley streets. Its east-west-running streets included Wentworth, Montague, and Bull; the north-south thoroughfares included Pitt, Smith, Rutledge, Lynch (later renamed Ashley), Gadsden, and Barre. The names of these streets, like those in Gadsden's Middlesex development, reflected the times. They were named in honor of British officials sympathetic to the rights of colonial Americans and local advocates of independence from

England. In 1770 the Assembly also permitted St. Philip's Church to subdivide its Glebe Lands into income-producing lots. A great part of this seventeen-acre tract bequeathed to the church in 1698 by Mrs. Affra Coming was carved into thirty-eight lots, each of which was quickly leased. Today these Glebe Lands are bounded by George, Coming, St. Philip's, and Beaufain streets.

The new streets, like the old ones, were cut and leveled with earth or mud and remained unpaved during the colonial period. Some effort was made to pave the footpaths that ran beside the principal streets with "bricks and mortar." However, due to the soaring city taxes, householders often strenuously objected to new expenditures. And as the human and animal population increased, the city scavenger and the commissioners of the streets faced an exasperating job of keeping the thoroughfares clean and in good repair. For despite heavy fines, citizens continued to feed their horses and cows in the streets and to dump garbage and night soil there too, which caused the persistence of soft, slimy, stinking roadways.

More than 200 private dwelling houses of wood and brick with balconies and piazzas went up during the building boom of the 1760s and early 1770s. Many of the larger homes constructed during the two decades before the Revolution were built on the "double house" plan, which presented two rooms to the street with an entrance between them that opened into a hallway running the length of the home. But the "single house" remained popular because it could fit on a narrower lot. Only the best yellow pine and cypress were used in the construction of the homes. These trees were felled in nearby forests during the winter months while the sap was down, cut into forty- to seventy-foot lengths by water- or wind-powered saws at mills located along the rivers, and then the lumber was floated or hauled to Charles Town. Cured in salt water and air-dried, it became nearly iron-hard and frequently turned white from the salt, which acted as a preventive of fungus growth and termite infestation. The lumber that was hammered into place by the artisans and laborers of Charles Town more than 200 years ago endures in many of the city's private dwellings.

A "double house" was constructed at 15 Meeting Street by the merchant John Edwards. Emigrating from England to South Carolina about 1750, Edwards amassed a fortune exporting commodities and importing slaves. When Edward's home of cypress built over a brick basement was completed in 1770, he staffed the residence with twelve slaves. In 1980 the asking price of the dwelling was $500,000. Up to that time only two previous sales of homes in the city's historic district had equaled or exceeded that price.[31]

Crime and the "Disorderly"

While the boom times concentrated greater wealth into a few hands, the poorer classes lost ground and the gentry became alarmed at the number of "disorderly" whites and slaves within Charles Town. They believed that plots against their property and perhaps their lives originated in the great numbers of "tippling or disorderly houses" which illegally sold "spirituous" liquors to sailors, idle and vagrant whites, and slaves. Repeatedly, grand juries concluded that the "tippling houses" were the "source from which many of the Evils . . . daily committed derive." Here fraternizing with runaways and other slaves, vagrant whites were "corrupting and seducing . . . Negroes to rob and steal" and to commit "other disorders." Nor could the rich depend on the town watch to control the growing "vice and Immorality" spawned by the "tippling houses." Some watchmen or their wives operated "dram shops" and encouraged "Negroes and others to frequent their houses." In 1763 there had been 66 "houses" licensed to sell "spirituous liquors," in 1769 there were 106, and by 1773 the number had risen to 115. There was a steady increase in the number of tippling houses on Bay, King, Union, Queen, and Meeting streets, while the number decreased on Broad and Tradd streets. Consistently, about half the licensees were women.[32]

Charlestonians became aware that more and more robberies and assaults were occurring in a city where the contrasts between wealth and poverty were more spectacular perhaps than in any other city in the American colonies. Thieves broke into the homes of Miles Brewton and Roger Pinckney and took silver spoons and bowls, clothes, and watches. Following a series of burglaries the *Gazette* warned readers "to be particularly on . . . guard against thefts at this time."

Townspeople urged the erection of lamps, additional stocks, and a substantial jail, the present public jail being "insufficient." During the late 1760s there were three mass breakouts from the notoriously inadequate facility near the corner of Tradd and King streets. In 1769 the Assembly finally passed a supplement to the Watch Act, which promised a reward for any citizen who apprehended "any white person or persons" who broke into a dwelling. It imposed the death sentence on anyone convicted of knowingly buying or receiving stolen goods or concealing a burglar. The Assembly also appropriated a limited amount of money for street lamps, public pillories, and a new jail. The Assembly awarded the contract for building the new jail to William Rigby Naylor and James Brown who had recently completed the construction of the city's new Guard House. Naylor, who drew the plans for the Exchange building, probably designed the new jail. By mid-1770 Naylor and Brown had broken ground for its construction near the new hospital and workhouse and the House of Correction.[33]

Criminal activity and disorder also increased in the South Carolina backcountry, and the murderers and thieves were sent to Charles Town for trial where the dockets soon became jammed. By the late 1760s the bewigged judges of the criminal court like Robert Pringle and Rawlins Lowndes were meeting three times a year. The sentences they handed down were severe and carried out in public in hopes of deterring the growing criminality.

Between 1769 and the mid-1770s over twenty-five white persons were convicted and sentenced for murder, arson, larceny, or receiving stolen goods. During these years Charlestonians witnessed at least five public hangings and numerous brandings, ear croppings, whippings, and confinements of persons to the public pillories. The harsh public punishments were inflicted on both male and female felons. Catherine Malone, convicted of larceny, received "25 lashes on the bare back," while Moses Thompson for the same offense was whipped thirty-nine times. However, when John Milner was convicted of "killing a Negro in a sudden heat of passion," he was merely fined.

The harshest punishments were inflicted on white felons who conspired with blacks. During the spring of 1770, three white men and four slaves seized a schooner near Charles Town and sailed south, but were apprehended and returned to town. Each of the three white men were sentenced to be hanged, but the fate of the blacks is unrecorded. Two years later the Court of General Sessions sentenced "a Negro" to be hanged for stealing money, and he named Jacob Ramos, a white man, as an accomplice. The court accepted the testimony of the black, fined Ramos £350, sentenced him to thirty-nine lashes and the public pillory, where, the *Gazette* reported, he "was severely and incessantly pelted by an enraged populace."

Soon after the street lamps were erected, some were "wantonly" and "maliciously" smashed. Breakouts continued even from the new jail, and leading citizens urged the Assembly to pass an act "for incorporating Charles Town" so that the "internal government of the city could be managed more successfully."

A Captain Martin of a British man-of-war, who apparently knew Charles Town well, put into verse a rather unflattering yet in some ways accurate description of the city in 1769: "Black and white all mix'd together/Inconstant, strange, unhealthful weather . . . /Agues plenty without doubt/Sores, boils, the prickling heat and gout/Musquitos on the skin make blotches/Centipedes and large cock-roaches . . . /Houses built on barren land/No lamps or lights, but streets of sand . . . /Every thing at a high price/But rum, hominy and rice."[34]

Resistance to British Policy

New royal customs officials who arrived in Charles Town in the late 1760s began to enforce long-ignored trade regulations. Some of them sought to enrich themselves, refusing to allow some vessels of the great merchants to sail and seizing others and demanding "gratuities" for their release. Infuriated, Gabriel Manigault and Henry Laurens instituted legal proceedings, but the crown-appointed judge of the Vice-Admiralty Court at Charles Town, Egerton Leigh, usually found in favor of the British customs officials. Laurens became so angry that he physically assaulted a royal official in the streets and launched a pamphlet war against Judge Leigh and "customs racketeering." Like Laurens the lowcountry elite faced a dilemma: either sacrifice basic, hard-won political prerogatives and remain within the safety of the British colonial system, which had provided them with ready markets, price supports, and the protection of the Royal Army and Navy, or openly challenge the British government.

No member of the elite saw the dilemma more clearly than Christopher Gadsden, who realized that successful resistance to Britain's policies depended on the recruitment of the laboring classes to the cause. But Gadsden also knew that resistance itself might unleash the masses and disorder. The resistance, then, must be carefully manipulated, otherwise it would threaten the "peace and good order." Consequently, as the popular leader of the laboring classes, Gadsden carefully orchestrated the public meetings he called at taverns and the "Liberty Tree," a huge oak on Isaac Mazyck's lands in the northeastern section of the city. A stirring, rousing orator, Gadsden told the crowds that they must continue their peaceful "vigilence" to England's conspiracies and "designs" that threatened their "Liberty and Property." As the adverse economic effects of the Townshend Acts rippled through Charles Town's economy, Gadsden exploited the accelerating hard times among the laboring classes. He met with the local artisans and mechanics to organize and ensure peaceful resistance to the act and they repeatedly returned him to the Assembly as a representative from the parish of St. Philip's. He led the successful effort in the Assembly to join with the other colonies in boycotting British goods to force repeal of the Townshend Acts.

To ensure local compliance with the nonimportation agreement with the other colonies, on July 22, 1769, the Assembly appointed a Committee of Thirty-Nine, which included an equal number of merchants, planters, and artisans, thus for the first time granting the laboring classes a significant voice in the government of South Carolina. The wealthy planter William Wragg fumed that now his "freedom" might be endangered. Another member of the lowcountry oligarchy, William Henry Drayton of Magnolia plantation near Charles Town, declared that men educated in the liberal arts should not have to "consult on public affairs with men who" knew only "how to Cut up a beast . . . Cobble an old shoe . . . or to build a necessary house." To him the laboring classes were the "profanus vulgus." Such men feared the growing political power of the lower orders and their threat to the deferential society that the elite had long enjoyed and profited from. Gadsden also recognized such a threat, but he believed that it was to his own interest and to that of his class to work with the laboring classes. For if political and economic resistance did evolve into revolution it was best that the laboring classes "see it out [come] what may" aligned with and led by the native rich. Henceforth men representing the laboring classes, and under the restraining influence of Gadsden, would serve on the various local committees and in the "town meetings" until the outbreak of the Revolution. With the Assembly deadlocked in disputes with royal officials, these extralegal organizations came to govern the colony and city.

On December 8, 1769, the South Carolina Assembly voted a gift of £1,500 sterling to a demagogic member of the English Parliament, John Wilkes, who had been charged with seditious libel for criticizing the king and clapped into a London prison. To the members of the Assembly, Wilkes's cause seemed to symbolize their own, yet Crown officials looked on the Assembly's actions as an insult to the king. The controversy embroiled Royal Governor Lord Charles Montague, recently returned to the colony, in a serious dispute with the Commons House when he attempted to strip the body of its rights to initiate action on money matters. Henry Laurens declared that at stake was "nothing less than the very Essence of pure liberty." When the Assembly refused to transact any business whatsoever, Governor Montague dissolved it repeatedly. When this ploy failed, Montague returned to England and resigned in disgrace. Now the Council, dominated by royal appointees, took up the struggle and demanded that the Assembly assent to the Crown's contention that it no longer was solely responsible for the appropriation of public funds. The Assembly refused and the situation became deadlocked. Little legislation was passed after 1771.[35]

Conservative members of the propertied class were becoming convinced that a conspiracy existed within the British government to undermine the Assembly's long-standing prerogatives in local matters. As the Wilkes Fund controversy dragged on, Crown officials in England directed that only men loyal to His Majesty's government would be appointed to the South Carolina bench. Native judges like Rawlins Lowndes were removed, and by the early 1770s "placemen," officials appointed by the Crown, were arriving in Charles Town to serve as judges and customs officers.

The lowcountry's indigenous oligarchy were obsessed with preserving the social, political, and racial system that guaranteed their personal independence and wealth. Having grown up with the institution of chattel slavery, they were especially sensitive to any challenge to their own liberty. They raised in their writings and speeches the awful specter of England's desire to reduce them to "abject slavery" in which England would "rule . . . with a Rod of Iron." "Liberty and Property" became one of their rallying cries.[36]

In May 1770 the *Sally George* carrying 345 African slaves

entered the port, but her captain was refused permission to land them. The nonimportation agreement of 1769 specifically outlawed the importation of slaves and it appears that the mechanics now used their influence to enforce the act. By now Parliament's repeal of the Townshend Acts—with the exception of the tax on tea—was known in Charles Town and this encouraged the artisans to congratulate themselves for their role in the successful boycott of British goods. In July Joseph Wilton's statue of Pitt was erected at the intersection of Broad and Meeting streets amid much celebration.

On December 13, 1770, a general meeting of the citizens of Charles Town was called to consider ending the local boycott. Merchants whose shops were empty and whose trade in slaves had dwindled to nothing were eager to lift the boycott. However, artisans, who had long resented the competition of British products and who during the boycott had crafted and sold a variety of consumer items from chairs to "Liberty Umbrellas," wished to continue it. Despite Gadsden's eloquence as their spokesman, the artisans were outvoted by a coalition of merchants and planters, and the local boycott was lifted except on tea and luxury items.

Trade Revival and Building Boom

Trade revived quickly and before the spring of 1771 had turned to summer the stores held a vast array of imported consumer goods. Sales were brisk. The price of the barrels of rice rolling across Charles Town's wharves for shipment abroad doubled within two years. As usual during boom times planters plunged their huge profits into the purchase of slaves rushed to the city by the few great merchants. In 1772 and 1773 sixty-five vessels, their holds jammed with more than 10,000 black Africans, tied off Charles Town's wharves. More slaves were auctioned off in the city than in any two previous years and at unprecedented prices. The great Charles Town merchants and lowcountry planters rapidly added to their already considerable fortunes, one of the merchants remarking in April 1772: "The desires of the planters increase faster than their riches." By the early 1770s more than 800 vessels were entering and clearing Charles Town annually including 140 British-owned ships employed in the carrying trade between the port town and England. When one visitor sailed into Charles Town at the height of the shipping season, in the early 1770s, he observed that "about 350 sail lay off the town." He was amazed at the number of vessels, writing that "the number of shipping far surpasses all I had seen in Boston."[37]

Indeed, the annual export-import trade at Charles Town exceeded even the tonnage through New York's port, though the population was only half as large. The reason for this, historian Jacob Price argues, is that Charles Town was a "shipping point," its trade based on the immediate hinterland, while northern ports were "commercial centers" supporting an indigenous business community, great shipyards with large numbers of workers, insurance brokers, and a manufacturing population to process goods in transit. Charles Town's commercial life, however, was "colonial," controlled by businessmen in Britain who raised the capital and chartered and insured the ships for the Carolina trade. Nevertheless, vessels owned by Charlestonians also plied the export-import trade routes each year. Their names through midcentury indicate the owners' pursuit of wealth and status—*Merchants Adventure, Good Hope, Enterprize, Success,* and *Endeavor.* By the 1760s and after, however, the names given to vessels out of Charles Town reflected the growing nationalism and desire for economic and political independence. Keels were laid for the *Fair America* and *Heart of Oak,* and after 1764 nine ships were christened *Liberty.*[38]

During 1771–72 the Exchange building, Palladian in its symmetrical design, went up at the foot of Broad Street. The Horlbeck brothers imported shiploads of cut, dressed, and beveled Portland stone for the Exchange's façade. In design and construction materials it was unique. Only two notable colonial American buildings preceded it, Philadelphia's Town Hall and Boston's Faneuil Hall. Yet neither of these structures matched the architectural distinction of Charles Town's new Customs House, or Exchange.

While the Exchange was going up at the eastern end of the "full half mile long" Broad Street, a poor house, hospital, and jail went up near the western end of the street. The new three-story brick jail, which faced Magazine Street and cost £7,500, was finished in 1771. Nearby, the land that is today bounded by Queen, Franklin, Logan, and Magazine streets was set aside as a cemetery for "strangers and transients."

During the building boom Colonel John Stuart, the superintendent of Indian affairs for the Southern District of the American colonies, was building a house at the corner of Orange and Tradd streets. Born in Scotland, Stuart immigrated to Charles Town, became a merchant and slave-trader, and was elected to the Assembly. Following his appointment as superintendent of Indian affairs in 1762 at a salary of £1,000 sterling per year, Stuart was one of the wealthiest and most important officials in the colony. He owned over 15,000 acres of land worked by some 200 slaves. His handsome three-story house constructed of black cypress with heart pine timbers and flooring was completed in 1772 and cost £2,350 sterling. It still stands today at 106 Tradd Street. Private dwellings also were being built on the far southwestern fringe of the town, along South Bay, today South Battery, where low, marshy land was being filled with shells and mud. William Gibbes was building here by 1772. A member of the Assembly, a shipowner, and a merchant, Gibbes constructed a wharf that extended from near the entrance of his home 800 feet across the marsh grasses and into the Ashley River. Through the windows of his mansion he could watch trading vessels tie off his wharf to load or unload. Visitors approaching the city by sea must have been impressed by the grand, white Georgian dwelling on the southwesternmost edge of the city.

Lord Adam Gordon marveled that the private residences of Charles Town were "large and handsome, having all the conveniences one sees at home." Costly East Indian silk or satin curtains graced the windows, Dutch linens covered dining tables set with imported china, and silver goblets, teapots, and bowls gleamed on handsome sideboards.[39]

Society and Thought

The entertainments and dinners given in these homes, where guests were served by black slaves in livery, were extravagant affairs. The Bostonian Josiah Quincy was awed by what he saw when he dined at the new residence of one of the richest men in South Carolina, Miles Brewton. Upon entering Brewton's home at 27 King Street, Quincy found "the grandest hall I ever beheld," gilted wallpaper, and "most elegant pictures, excessive grand and costly looking glasses." When the large company sat for dinner Quincy found "a most elegant table." Three courses were offered and the wine, he observed, was "the richest I ever tasted." Following the dinner "two sorts of nuts, almonds, raisins, three sorts of olives, apples, oranges" were served. Perhaps most amazing to Quincy was the "vastly pretty" bird that "kept familiarly playing over the room, under our Chairs and the table, picking up the Crumbs, and perching on the window, sideboard and Chairs."

At public taverns and private clubs, horse races, foxhunts, and cockfights, many of the wealthy pursued pleasure and amusement. Their favorite tavern in the 1770s belonged to William Holliday who had taken over Robert Dillon's establishment on Queen Street. Whether patronizing Holliday's Tavern or attending gala affairs at private clubs such as the Monday Night Club, the Smoking Club, the Hellfire Club, the Friday Night Club, the Fellowship Society, the Bachelor's Society or the "New Market Races" on the Neck, "cards, dice, the bottle and horses engross[ed] prodigious portions of [the] time and attention" of the affluent. What conversations there were, a northern visitor observed, turned on "land, Negroes, and rice." And at their hunt clubs following the morning chase, the afternoons usually were "spent very merry, after killing foxes."[40]

White men frequently entered into liaisons with young, black slave women. The Pennsylvania-born, geographer-historian Ebenezer Hazard, who visited Charles Town, heard about "balls given by Negro and Mulatto women to which they invite the white gentlemen." Hazard observed that the mulatto women "dress elegantly and have no small acquaintance with polite behavior." Josiah Quincy wrote: "The enjoyment of a negro or mulatto woman is spoken of as quite a common thing . . . . It is far from being uncommon to see a gentleman at dinner, and his reputed offspring a slave to the master of the table." And it was not unusual for a member of the elite at his death to manumit a "favorite" slave woman. The wealthy Charles Town merchant Hopkin Price, who never remarried after his wife's death in 1754, freed his mulatto woman Sylvia upon his death in 1781, settling on her a handsome yearly income of £143 sterling.[41]

Each year from January through early spring, the families of merchants and planters were at one ball, concert, or theatrical performance after another in Charles Town. The women particularly looked forward to the busy social season. The vivacious Eliza Wilkinson wrote of her excitement in preparing for a ball: "The important day arrived, and there was such powdering! And frizzing and curling! And dancing." Even politics was subordinated to dancing. During one social season, one sober member of the propertied class, Henry Laurens, observed disgustedly that sessions of the Assembly were shortened "in favor of the ball."

The love of dancing and music among the female elite of Charles Town and the lowcountry was unparalleled in colonial America. Many of the wives of the new rich sought musical instruction for themselves and for their daughters, and by the early 1770s more than twenty-three music, singing, and dancing masters offered lessons in Charles Town. The most successful of these music teachers was Thomas Pike, who also taught dancing. Instruction was available in violin, harpsichord, oboe, bassoon, flute, French horn, mandolin, and guitar. The first female music teacher in the city and perhaps in the American colonies, Ann Windsor, announced in the *Gazette* in 1774 that she specialized in teaching "young ladies upon the Harpsichord." The musicians frequently gave concerts during Charles Town's annual social season at the new theater on Queen Street and Thomas Pike's "Long Room" located on the western side of Church Street between Elliott and Tradd streets. Here in 1773 Josiah Quincy attended a meeting of America's first musical society, the St. Cecilia, and he found the music excellent. He also noted that there were "upwards of two-hundred-fifty ladies" in the audience, the wives of the well-to-do who were passionately fond of music. Otherwise an "English Traveller" described them as having "a disagreeable drawling way of speaking," and a Virginia visitor was surprised to find that lowcountry gentlewomen "talk like Negroes." But not "given to the great intemperance of the men," a contemporary observed, the Carolina women usually lived longer.[42]

The port's reputation for being wealthy and unhealthy attracted physicians, who used to say "Carolina is in the spring a paradise, in the summer a hell, and in the Autumn a hospital." Peter Fayssoux, who returned to Charles Town after receiving his medical degree from Edinburgh University in the late 1760s, found to his disgust that "it is sufficient for a man to call himself a Doctor, and he immediately becomes one, & finds fools to employ him." However, among the thirty-five to forty physicians practicing in the city, Fayssoux also found "respectable . . . Men of Letters & Candour" like John Moultrie, Sr., Lionel Chalmers, and Alexander Garden, all Scottish-born and educated. Moultrie was the first physician in the port and among the first in America to specialize in obstetrics, and at his death in 1771 the ladies of

Charles Town went into mourning. Chalmers undertook studies of tetanus and meteorology, and his *Essays on the Weather and Diseases of South Carolina*, published in 1776, was colonial America's major contribution to general medicine. Besides his medical practice, Dr. Garden was an indefatigable collector of botanical specimens and a member of the most distinguished scientific societies in America and Europe.

These few Charles Town physicians and naturalists, born and educated abroad, provided the intellectual leadership within the city. Active in the Charles Town Library Society, they sponsored scientific experiments and were among the first to urge the founding of a natural history museum. Very few of them became wealthy. Competition from other doctors and the slowness of patients to pay fees drove many into debt or out of the profession. Even those with excellent medical credentials like Bermudian-born Thomas Tudor Tucker who was educated at Edinburgh University and settled in Charles Town in the 1770s could not earn enough to support his family. His mother blamed his patients who, she believed, were "the meaner sort of People that are not able to pay him." His debts accumulated and a few years later he told his family: "I scarcely know how to keep myself out of jail." Eventually he left the medical profession.[43]

Patronized by the wealthier classes, painters continued to do a good business. Soon after he arrived from England in 1773, Thomas Leitch began painting "A View from Charles Town" and requested money through the *Gazette* to underwrite the return of the work to London for engraving, promising that it "will be so exact a Portrait of the Town as it appears from the Water that every House in View will be distinctly known." He got his money.

In the early 1770s a bill for establishing a local college was introduced into the Assembly, but the new rich opposed it because they believed that "learning would become cheap and too common, and every man would be for giving his son an education." A contemporary wrote that the bill failed because men of moderate means "had not influence enough to carry it through, and the rich did not need it." Unlike Boston, Philadelphia, and New York, Charles Town had no institution of higher learning until after the Revolution. Higher education was available only to sons of the lowcountry elite. Those who traveled to England for their education usually studied law at the Inns of Court. On the

"A View of Charles-Town, the Capital of South Carolina, From an Original Picture Painted at Charlestown in the Year 1774, painted by Thomas Leitch, engraved by Samuel Smith, published June 3, 1776 by S. Smith, London." *Courtesy of the Museum of Early Southern Decorative Arts, Winston-Salem, N.C.*

eve of the Revolution less than twenty lowcountry Carolinians held college or university degrees.

During a visit to Charles Town the Pennsylvanian Ebenezer Hazard inquired as to the education of the daughters of the parvenu and was told that most were "put to a boarding school for a year" and therefore "*their* education in particular is scandalously neglected." A correspondent in the *Gazette* in the early 1770s observed that the young ladies of the town are trained "in no Professions at all, except Music and Dancing," and therefore they "make . . . very agreeable Companions, but . . . expensive wives." And among both sexes companions were not sought "for their wit or learning . . . but for Rank." Even at parties with "the *best company* . . . little is said, and less attended to."

The wealthy men of Charles Town spent their energies in getting and consuming, and in their scramble for quick fortunes and status most did not live to see sixty; for many, old age had set in at thirty. The Reverend Alexander Hewatt of Charles Town observed that "men are distinguished more by their external than internal accomplishments. They are known by the number of their slaves, the value of their annual produce or extent of their landed estate." One astute observer of the local scene concluded that wealth and status were the goals of the elite and of those who aspired to join them: "Their whole Lives are one continual Race: in which everyone is endeavoring to distance all behind him; and to overtake or pass by all before him; everyone is flying from his inferiors in Pursuit of his Superiors."

During his visit in the early 1770s, Josiah Quincy found that "Many people express great fears of an insurrection." He believed that "the brutality used toward the slaves" was intended to ensure their servility and that such treatment debased the whites themselves, especially the children. Ebenezer Hazard, also visiting the city about the same time, reached similar conclusions. When he inquired of the slaveholding gentry why the Negroes were treated with such "severity," Hazard was told "that it is necessary in order to break their spirits, and thereby prevent insurrection." "Accustomed to tyrannize from their infancy," Hazard wrote, the gentry "carry with them a disposition to treat all mankind in the same manner they have been used to treat their Negroes."

Clergymen joined with physicians in the intellectual life of the port as members of the Library Society and as leaders of the group that organized the natural history museum in 1773, the first of its kind in the American colonies. However, as in London and Paris at the time, the gentry of Charles Town were staying away from church in large numbers. When Josiah Quincy attended services at St. Philip's, he was surprised to see so "very few present." He was shocked by the sermon of less than twenty minutes during which he observed "gentlemen conversing together in prayer as well as sermon-time." The sabbath in Charles Town, Quincy noted, "is a day of visiting and mirth with the rich." An Anglican minister noted that there were "very few Communicants in any Congregation." The pastor of the Huguenot Church in Charles Town bemoaned "the great Decay and almost utter Dissolution" of his congregation, and the Baptist divine, the Reverend Oliver Hart, frequently fretted over "poor sinful Charles Town."[44]

The renewed importations of slaves coupled with the hiring out of slaves created severe competition for the laboring classes. The city's carpenters and coopers complained bitterly. The continuing dispute between Assembly and royal officials also jeopardized the livelihood of the artisans. Since the Assembly refused to pass a tax bill and appropriate public funds, artisans who were to be reimbursed for public works went unpaid. In growing numbers angry, young, white artisans and common laborers joined the already swollen ranks of the city's unemployed poor.

By the early 1770s the city's permanent and transient population reached approximately 12,000 persons. Of this number there were at least 6,000 black "domestics and mechanics" and transient slaves; white indigents maintained by the church, vagrants, and the laboring poor numbered roughly 3,000 souls, while those whites who owned some property and the small elite included a like number. Approximately three-quarters of the city's population were either black slaves or poor whites. Vastly outnumbered, the propertied classes, who constituted 8 to 9 percent of the total population, but owned approximately 75 percent of the wealth of the city, remained uneasy.

During 1773 and 1774 Charles Town's grand jurors in their petitions to the Assembly reflected the anxieties of the wealthy. Because of the "great number of disorderly and idle persons" who "beg about the streets and insult the inhabitants," the grand jurors urged the Assembly to pass a "vagrant law" and provide more public stocks in the city in which to confine slaves to put a stop to their "insolence . . . in . . . talking obscenely in the streets." The grand jurors believed that the "negroes" in the city had become so "superfluous in their Numbers . . . so wanton mischievous . . . [and] disorderly" that "it calls for the immediate Attention of the Legislature." Because "the Town is greatly extended and increased in its inhabitants," the grand jurors believed that "the public watchmen are insufficient in numbers."Once again the Assembly was urged to incorporate the city, so that "the internal police . . . may be more easily regulated and better managed," but the legislators were preoccupied by their struggle with the governor for their traditional rights and had no time for merely local problems. An act by the English Parliament also distracted the Assembly and reopened old wounds.[45]

The Tea Act

To serve powerful financial interests in England, Parliament passed an act giving the East India Company a virtual monopoly on tea trade to America. Subject to a duty of only threepence per pound and consigned directly to a few favored importers, the East

India Company's tea could be sold to consumers at a lower price than most American merchants could and still realize a profit. This plan neatly coincided with the Crown's interest. By taxing the tea imported into America, the British government could reassert its authority so rudely challenged by the colonists—the right of Parliament to tax the colonists. But once again, the Americans viewed the duty on imported tea, like the duties under the Stamp and Townshend acts, as a tax designed to raise revenue and one levied without their consent. Their personal independence, property, and the power of their Assembly were again threatened.

In the autumn of 1773 seven ships dropped down the Thames and into the open sea carrying East India Company tea consigned to merchants in Boston, New York, Philadelphia, and Charles Town, and the captain of the *London* carrying 257 chests of tea steered for the Southern port. Seven weeks later, on December 2, 1773, the ship anchored in the harbor at Charles Town. A crisis was at hand. If the tea was landed and the three-pence-per-pound duty collected as authorized by Parliament, it would be an admission that the power of taxation lay with the distant English government rather than South Carolina's Assembly. Christopher Gadsden again assumed the leadership in resisting British policy.

On the day the *London* arrived, the Liberty Boys circulated handbills and posted notices along Broad Street inviting "all the inhabitants" to a meeting the next day in the Great Hall over the Exchange building, where "the sense of the people" would be taken on what to do about the tea.

At the meeting a presiding officer was elected, resolutions were drafted to prevent the landing of the tea, and a committee was appointed to obtain signatures to the agreement. The membership of the committee reflected the two principal groups attending: Charles Pinckney, his cousin, Charles Cotesworth Pinckney, and Thomas Ferguson represented the planters, while Gadsden and Daniel Cannon represented the interests of the artisans. This committee hoped to enlist the support of the merchants, but many of them already had quantities of tea on hand or on order, and three of the city's most important merchants, John Savage, Miles Brewton, and David Deas, organized the Charles Town Chamber of Commerce to coordinate opposition to boycotts.

Detail from Thomas Leitch's View of Charles-Town of the Exchange. *Courtesy of the Museum of Early Southern Decorative Arts, Winston-Salem, N.C.*

In late December the captain of the *London* received anonymous warnings that unless he moved his ship into deeper water it would be burned. Mob action was averted when armed royal officials seized and stored the tea in the basement of the Exchange, but the city remained sharply divided over the question of a boycott.[46]

At this time David Douglass and his Company of Comedians launched the most brilliant season in the history of the colonial American theater. During the summer of 1773 a wooden and brick theater had been constructed on the western side of Church Street between Elliott and Tradd streets, next to Pike's Long Room. Here Douglass opened his third season in Charles Town, which ran from late December 1773 to late May 1774. Seventy-seven different plays, mostly farces and operas, were given during 118 performances. Plays by Shakespeare were among the most frequently performed. The New York *Gazette* raved that Douglass's new, "elegantly furnished" Church Street Theatre was the largest "on the continent." And on opening night, the northern paper observed, the scenes, dresses, music, and "disposition of the lights contributed to the satisfaction of the audience who expressed the highest approbation of their entertainment." Several local critics, however, sounded sour notes. An anonymous writer in the *Gazette* using the pen name "Cleopatra" denounced the new playhouse as the "Devil's Synagogue."[47]

In December 1773 Bostonians dressed as Indians dumped English tea into their harbor, and at New York and Philadelphia mobs turned back tea-laden ships. In Charles Town Gadsden carefully managed meetings of his Liberty Boys so as to maintain the tea boycott without violence. Then in June 1774 the news arrived that king and Parliament, outraged by the criminal acts of the colonists who opposed the landing of the English tea, had closed the port of Boston and placed the government of Massachusetts under strict royal control.

Gadsden and other members of his class saw in the "hostile acts of Parliament against Boston" threats to their own control of Charles Town and summoned the "Inhabitants of the Colony" to a general meeting at the Exchange building in July "to consider . . . such steps as are necessary." The three-day meeting, beginning on July 6, drew over 100 "gentlemen" from across the colony. Resolutions condemning the recent British legislation were adopted quickly, but in the process of selecting delegates to a general congress to meet in Philadelphia in September to formulate a plan of nonintercourse against Great Britain, spokesmen for merchants who opposed a general boycott wrangled bitterly with Gadsden who with others spoke for the artisans. A compromise was reached when instructions to the delegates were worded to satisfy all factions and Henry Middleton and John Rutledge, nominated by every interest group, were elected along with Gadsden, Thomas Lynch, and Edward Rutledge. Colonel Charles Pinckney, a member of the merchant faction, was elected chairman of a General Committee, which included fifteen merchants and fifteen artisans representing Charles Town and sixty-nine planters representing the rest of the province. This General Committee became the temporary government of the city and colony.

In late June more tea had arrived in Charles Town aboard the ship *Magna Carta*. The captain, Richard Maitland, quickly promised local officials charged with enforcing the boycott that he would return the tea to England, but in early July rumors that he planned to renege on his promise angered many of the hungry, unemployed men in the port. A mob boarded the *Magna Carta* from one side, and Captain Maitland went off the other to take refuge aboard a British man-of-war.

Several weeks later the Reverend John Bullman of St. Michael's Church lamented from his pulpit the lack of peaceableness in the city, which he blamed on the "idle and illiterate" laboring classes who no longer kept to their "own place." The vestry, under pressure from the city's laboring classes, dismissed Bullman and until he departed for England he was "threatened with violence to his person."

In October 1774 the Continental Congress in Philadelphia resolved that until relations between the British government and the American colonies returned to normal, all Americans should abstain from public amusements. Nowhere in North America could one have found another group as fond of public entertainment as wealthy Charlestonians, but they obeyed, and David Douglass's upcoming theatrical season was canceled. When the *Britannia* entered the harbor in November carrying tea consigned to local merchants, the General Committee, in order to avert mob violence, instructed the consignees to dump the tea into the Cooper River, and the merchants did as they were told. Forced finally to choose between British authorities, however remote and unrealistic, and the white laborers, artisans, and shopkeepers of Charles Town, however coarse and disorderly, the merchants had chosen an uneasy alliance with the white workers on their doorsteps.

David Douglass never came back to Charles Town.[48]

❦ 2. 1775–1782:
Charles Town's Second Revolution

"Men of Property" and "the Herd"

After the return of the South Carolina delegation from the First Continental Congress at Philadelphia, the General Committee called for elected delegates from across the colony to a meeting in Charles Town in January 1775. The delegates were to form a government for the colony and were to be elected by the free, white males who paid annual taxes of 20 shillings, about 65 cents. Each parish in South Carolina would elect six delegates, while Charles Town's two parishes, St. Philip's and St. Michael's, were allowed thirty delegates between them, apparently since thirty representatives from the city served on the General Committee. Thus began the custom of treating the city as a separate political entity, a practice that continued until after the Civil War when it was merged into and came to dominate the county.

The 184 elected delegates met in Charles Town at the Long Room of Pike's Church Street Tavern in early January. Among the delegates were about forty of the gentry who served also in the now nearly moribund forty-eight-member Commons House of Assembly, and thirteen of the thirty delegates representing Charles Town were prominent artisans. The meeting transformed itself into the First Provincial Congress and the delegates moved their meeting place to the Assembly's room in the State House, where they endorsed the nonimportation and nonexportation agreements concluded at the First Continental Congress, and elected local committees of Safety and Observation to enforce this boycott of British goods.

In March Robert Smythe, a South Carolina merchant, returning from England aboard the *Proteus* requested the landing of furniture and horses for his own personal use. The local committeemen charged with enforcing nonimportation voted to allow him to bring the goods ashore, but the port's artisans vowed to prevent the unloading of Smythe's goods at all costs. A crowd gathered along Bay Street where they could see the heads of the horses above the deckrail of the *Proteus*. The armed men in the streets threatened to kill the animals if they were brought ashore. When the committee assembled to reconsider their vote a mob invaded their meeting, and Christopher Gadsden urged the committee to reverse itself, as did William Henry Drayton, who told the committee to respect the "will of the people." John and Edward Rutledge and Rawlins Lowndes, representing the conservative merchants, urged the committee to abide by its original vote and not be swayed by the crowd, but when Edward Rutledge denounced mob rule he was shouted down; finally, by a narrow vote, the committee reversed itself. The freight was not permitted to land, but "Much ill blood was occasioned . . . by the terms of Contempt" used by both sides against the other. The merchants were losing patience with the boycott because it was cutting sharply into their profits, but once more the artisans and other members of the laboring classes had demonstrated that they would resort to violence to ensure the continuance of policies in their interest. A few days after the "Smythe Horses Affair," Lieutenant Governor William Bull wrote to officials in London that in Charles Town a "torrent of popular prejudices . . . have been increasing near ten years." And now "The Men of Property begin at length to see that the many headed power of the People, who have hitherto been obediently made use of by their numbers and occasional riots to support the claims set up in America, have discovered their own strength and importance, and are not now so easily governed by their former Leaders."

On April 14, 1775, news reached the port that the British Parliament was dispatching more troops to enforce British policies in the colonies. This news prompted the Secret Committee of Five created by the Provincial Congress to act. Headed by the recent convert to the people's cause, William Henry Drayton, the committee—which included Edward Weyman, the respected artisan, other prominent citizens, and members of the laboring class—seized the arms and powder in the local magazines on the night of April 26. These military supplies were carefully hidden in homes about the city.[49]

Relations between England and the colonies rapidly deteriorated following the clash between British regulars and Massachusetts militiamen, news of which reached Charles Town in early May. At about the same time rumors swept the city that the British government was planning to incite Indian attacks and slave rebellions across South Carolina. The rumors linked the Indian agent at Charles Town, John Stuart, with the alleged British counterinsurgency plans and he fled his Orange Street mansion in late May. The rumors revived the old fears of a slave revolt. "Massacres and Instigated Insurrections, were words in the mouth of every Child," a royal official at Charles Town reported. To quiet these fears and to meet the rumored threats, the Provincial government ordered 100 militia men "to mount Guard . . . every evening with a Patrol of Horsemen." The passions of the townspeople were rising to a frenzy. One royal official observed that "the King's Friends . . . are . . . expecting every moment to be drove from their Occupations, and Homes, and plundered of all they have."

In this anxious atmosphere the extralegal Provincial Congress convened in Charles Town in early June. Most of the 172 delegates believed that the British shots fired at Lexington constituted a declaration of war on America and a vigorous response was necessary, but few entertained any thought of independence. Henry

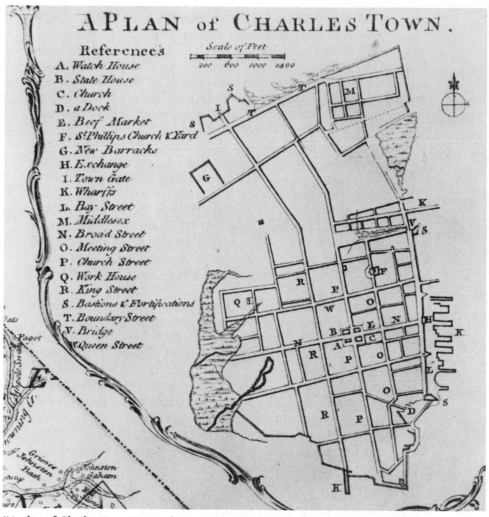

"A plan of Charles Town." Inset from "A Map of the Province of South Carolina . . ." by James Cook (London, 1773). *Courtesy of the South Caroliniana Library, University of South Carolina, Columbia, S.C.*

Laurens, who had long feared that the growing revolutionary sentiment was bestowing upon "persons not possessed of any visible Estates" the power to decide the fate of "Men of property, Rank and respectable character," was elected presiding officer. As the Provincial Congress opened, a royal official observed that "the Opulent and Sensible" representatives "wish to avoid . . . desperate measures . . . but they are powerfully opposed by a numerous body of the Low and Ignorant, led by a few desperate Incendarys, who have nothing to lose, and some hot headed Young Men of fortune." Included among the latter was the political chameleon William Henry Drayton, and during the first days of June these radicals captured control of the Provincial Congress and drafted a document known as the "Association" wherein they agreed to "sacrifice lives and fortunes against every foe" in defense of "liberty." Citizens who refused to sign the "Association" were to be treated as enemies of their country. The Provincial Congress also ordered the raising of three regiments, authorized funds for the defense of South Carolina, and elected a thirteen-member Council of Safety vested with extraordinary powers to function as the executive body of the colony following adjournment of the Congress. The president of this council, Henry Laurens, described the members as follows: "Some are Red-Hot and foolishly talk of arms and there is another extreme who say that implicit Obedience is the Surest Road to redress of Grievances, the great majority of members lie between, and are men of wealth and consideration."

The Council of Safety immediately issued warnings against "instigated insurrections by our negroes" and created a special committee "to secure the Province against an insurrection of slaves or counter-Revolutionary moves." The Provincial Congress also recommended that when the citizens of Charles Town attended church services they should "take with them their Fire-Arms & Ammunition."

While the Provincial Congress met in Charles Town, it was reported to the Secret Committee of Five that two Crown loyalists, Laughlin Martin, a small merchant, and one James Dealy, had publicly cheered the rumor that blacks, Catholics, and Indians were to receive British arms. Martin and Dealy were seized and on June 8 they were stripped naked, "tarred, feathered, and carted through the streets of Charles Town." The spectacle excited the city mob, which spilled into the streets to jeer the "two poor wretches." To Alexander Innes, a royal official who witnessed and reported the tarring and feathering to his London government, law and order was breaking down and a class struggle was emerging. Moderate leaders no longer were able to control *"the Herd* which has been led on from one step to another and now . . . there is no drawing back as they have gone so far." The citizens were at the mercy "of a set of Lawless vindictive Ruffians," Innes wrote. Among them were "desperate" men, "the Violent, who are in general the needy, drove at desperate measures . . . might in the struggle mend their situation." His views on the emerging class struggle in the city, Innes reported, were shared by "Mr. [Henry] Laurens . . . Mr. [Rawlins] Lowndes, Mr. [Miles] Brewton and several other men of fortune [who] tremble at the lengths already gone and strive now to check the torrent."[50]

Thomas Jeremiah

To prevent future spectacles that might excite the city mob, members of the conservative elite stopped further committee-directed violence. A resident later recalled that leading merchants, planters, and lawyers feared "that the mob would take the matter out of their hands unless immediately restrained." Following the tarring and feathering of Martin and Dealy, the Provincial government ordered the imprisonment of a number of blacks upon suspicion of planning an insurrection, but after a rigorous interrogation most of them were released for lack of evidence. However, one black, Thomas Jeremiah, was detained under suspicion. He was a successful free black who owned property of over £1,000 sterling, "had several slaves of his own, who he employed in fishing," and was "one of the best" of the small group of skilled and licensed black harbor pilots. The new royal governor, Lord William Campbell, described Jeremiah as "a fellow in affluent circumstances." He was the type of free black who would arouse jealousy and resentment among the many poor laboring-class whites of the city. Both the governor and the conservative elite realized that some of the poor whites of Charles Town were jealous of him. Gabriel Manigault wrote to his son in early July: "We have been alarmed by idle reports that the Negroes intended to rise, which on examination proved to be of less consequence than was expected."

Meanwhile, authorities continued to build a case against Jeremiah based on the testimony of two slaves, Sambo and Jemmy.

Sambo, also a harbor pilot, testified that some months before, Jeremiah had told him that a "great war" was coming "to help the Poor Negroes." When the war came he was to set his schooner afire and to "jump on shore, and join the soldiers." The testimony of the slave Jemmy, the brother-in-law of Jeremiah, was even more damaging. In a deposition taken on June 16, Jemmy declared that some weeks before, he was approached by Jeremiah who asked him "to take a few guns" to Dewar, a runaway slave. The weapons were "to be placed in Negroes hands to fight against the inhabitants of this Province;" furthermore "Jeremiah was to have the Chief Command of the Negroes; he . . . believed he had Powder enough already, but that he wanted more Arms . . . [and] he would try to get as many as he could."

Governor Campbell believed that Jeremiah was innocent. Any man in such a "thriving" situation would be incapable of "so wild a scheme as to instigate an insurrection"; and he believed also that the testimonies of Sambo and Jemmy had been extracted under duress: the two slaves "terrified at the recollection of former cruelties were easily induced to accuse themselves and others."

Although all evidence against Jeremiah was in by mid-June, the conservative, antiwar Council of Safety did not begin the trial until August, when merchants and artisans were bitterly contesting the selection of candidates for the upcoming elections to the Provincial Congress.

On Friday, August 11, Thomas Jeremiah stood trial in Charles Town before two justices and five freeholders. Tried under the provisions of the Negro Act of 1740 and on the basis of the depositions taken from the two slaves, Sambo and Jemmy, he was sentenced "to be hanged, and then burned to ashes, on Friday the 18th." When Governor Campbell learned on what grounds the court "had doomed a fellow creature to death," he wrote, "My blood ran cold."

On August 12 a mob seized a British soldier "for some insolent speech he had made," gave him a "Tarring & Feathering," and "putting him in a cart paraded through the Town . . . using him very cruelly all the time." By late afternoon, the mob, grown to some 400 persons, stopped before the home of each suspected Crown sympathizer to demonstrate what their fate might be. Frightened Loyalists made arrangements to leave the city.

Alarmed at the continuing threats of violence to citizens loyal to England, Royal Governor Campbell nevertheless focused his energies on attempting to save the life of Thomas Jeremiah, but when he suggested a pardon the Provincial government officials "declared [that] if I granted the man a pardon they would hang him at my door," Campbell wrote. A wealthy citizen warned Campbell that his intervention "would raise a flame all the water in the Cooper River would not extinguish."

The day before the scheduled execution, the slave Jemmy, whose deposition had been the most damaging to Jeremiah, retracted his testimony and declared that Jeremiah was innocent. Nevertheless, on Friday, August 18, Thomas Jeremiah was taken to the place of execution and hanged and then burned to ashes. Governor Campbell wrote that Jeremiah "asserted his innocence to the last" and "behaved with the greatest intrepidity." He believed that Jeremiah was the innocent victim of a hysterical public and the political machinations of local leaders. The royal attorney general for South Carolina agreed. He wrote: "The story of this horrid Conspiracy, which . . . [n]ever had any foundation in fact, was industriously propagated, by the Designing, & was credited by and terrified the Weak."

Henry Laurens, the president of the Provincial Congress, took the opposite view. Ten years earlier, in 1765, he had privately criticized local officials for overreacting when the rumors of a slave revolt swept the city, but in 1775, explaining the recent events to his son in London, he wrote that there had been "a design and attempt to encourage our Negroes to Rebellion. . . ." Laurens thought Jeremiah was guilty, yet he was painfully aware of the weakness of the evidence and the severity of the sentence. He hoped there would be no reflection on the emerging leaders of South Carolina whose "mad conduct, will appear glaring enough." Other members of the gentry also sought to justify and distance themselves from the trial and execution of Jeremiah. When Governor Campbell protested to the Assembly the tarring of a British soldier and Jeremiah's severe sentence, the Assembly declared: "It is not in our power in such cases to prescribe limits to Popular Fury."

Indeed, Thomas Jeremiah may have sought to organize a black revolt at a time of grave external threats and white unrest. Other black insurrectionists had plotted or acted under like circumstances earlier in the century; or he may have been the scapegoat of a scheme developed by the political elite who hoped to divert the attention of the laboring classes by playing on their deepest fears. With the pro-war, politically ambitious laboring classes so preoccupied, the wealthy elite could continue their control of the new, emerging political machinery and seek a settlement short of war with England; or Thomas Jeremiah may simply have been a victim of white paranoia, sacrificed as an example to other blacks. It had been done before and would be done again in the future. If, however, the latter conjecture is correct, at least one slave overlooked the message. Less than three months after Jeremiah's execution, the owner of the slave Limus placed a runaway notice in the local *Gazette*. It read: "Limus is well known in Charles Town for his saucy and impudent tongue . . . he has the audacity to tell me he will be free, that he will serve no Man."[51]

The Opening Shots

Tensions remained high in the city throughout the late summer. When new rumors swept Charles Town in early September that Royal Governor William Campbell planned to arm and march backcountry loyalists to subdue the lowcountry, laboring-class leaders called for his arrest. Fearing for his safety, Campbell fled to a warship, HMS *Tamar*, in the harbor. That same day the Council of Safety ordered the seizure of Fort Johnson guarding the southeastern approach to the city. It was occupied on September 15 by a hastily recruited force under Colonel William Moultrie.

On November 1 the Second Provincial Congress convened in Charles Town. Conservatives who hoped to avoid war with England elected William Henry Drayton as president in hopes of silencing him, but their scheme backfired. Drayton, the acknowledged leader of the laboring classes while Christopher Gadsden was attending the Second Continental Congress in Philadelphia, used the presidency to push for more violent measures. On November 11 he personally supervised the scuttling of hulks in the mouth of the Cooper River to prevent a possible cannonading of the city by British warships. Drayton's purposely provocative actions drew fire from the British vessels *Tamar* and *Cherokee* and Drayton ordered his ship to respond. The first shots of the Revolutionary War in South Carolina had been fired.

Fears of a British bombardment or invasion continued to send tremors through the city. Many well-to-do fled to the countryside. In late November, Eliza Pinckney wrote that a "heavy cloud hangs over us . . . almost all the Women, and many Hundred *Men* have left town." Henry Laurens wrote to his son: "I am . . . sitting in a House stripped of its furniture & in danger of being knocked down . . . by Cannon Ball."[52]

Work was rushed forward on the physical defenses of the city. The laboring classes "went cheerfully to work" to repair bastions, to mount guns on several wharves, and to throw up earthworks around the city and to erect barricades in several streets. The Council of Safety ordered that "all able-bodied negro men be taken into the public service . . . and employed without arms for the defense of . . . Charles Town." Some were furnished hoses, axes, ropes, and ladders and assigned to strategic points to extinguish any fires begun by bombardments. Those masters who hired out the services of their slaves were compensated. To defend the channel and harbor to the north of the city a fortification of "Mud & Sand, faced with Palmetto Tree" was begun on Sullivan's Island. Schooners were outfitted for coastal defense, and provisions and arms were collected. Troops were recruited, drilled, and rushed to Charles Town. Well-to-do Loyalists and members of the city's wealthiest class continued to leave Charles Town. By early 1776 "half the best Houses were empty." And as the raw recruits streamed into Charles Town from the countryside, they moved into the unoccupied dwellings and "destroyed & even burnt as firewood such furniture as remained." Charles Town came to resemble an armed camp.

In early 1776 the Provincial Congress met in Charles Town to consider the recommendations of the Continental Congress at Philadelphia that local constitutional governments be established, but when the two laboring-class leaders, Gadsden and Drayton, called for absolute independence from England, it shocked most of the representatives. Henry Laurens branded their proposal "indecent" and John Rutledge thought the idea treasonable. Most of the city's wealthiest classes would have agreed with Edward Rutledge who warned that a struggle for independence would bring "those levelling Principles which Men without Character and without Fortune in general possess, which are so Captivating to the lower class of Mankind, and which will occasion such a fluctuation of Property as to introduce the greatest disorder." Hence the proposals for independence by Gadsden and Drayton were buried in committee and a temporary constitution was adopted until an accommodation could be reached with England. It was a conservative document avoiding change and keeping power where it was.[53]

In early 1776, Admiral Sir Peter Parker and General Sir Henry Clinton decided to seize and hold Sullivan's Island and establish there a base of operations, which would encourage British Loyalists in the South. When the armada of fighting ships carrying 3,000 British regulars appeared off the bar in May, panic swept the city. Believing that Charles Town was the British objective, militia were summoned and defenses strengthened. Efforts were redoubled to complete the 20-foot-high, double-walled fort of Palmetto logs on the southern tip of Sullivan's Island, which guarded the harbor's northern entrance.

Major General Charles Lee, the American commander-in-chief of the Southern Department, who soon arrived from North Carolina with 200 Continentals, assumed command of the local forces now grown to over 6,000 and helped bolster morale. Lee ordered the streets barricaded and buildings razed along the Cooper River to permit the newly mounted cannon a wider angle of fire. He urged the president of the Provincial Congress, John Rutledge, and the ranking local military officer, Colonel William Moultrie, to evacuate the unfinished fort on Sullivan's Island, which Lee characterized as "a slaughter pen." When they refused, Lee tried to make the best of what he believed to be a desperate situation by personally supervising slaves working on the fort and sending 780 riflemen to protect its northern flank and 400 defenders. Already General Clinton was ashore on Long Island, today the Isle of Palms, massing 2,000 British troops for an amphibious assault across Breach inlet.

On the morning of June 28 before a favorable breeze and on a rising tide, Admiral Parker ordered his ships into action. General Clinton launched a simultaneous attack across Breach Inlet, but his force was stymied by tides, channel depths, and fire from American forces. Almost immediately three of Parker's frigates ran aground and became "sitting ducks" for gunners in the fort. The remaining ships continued to fire on the fort, and although the spongy, freshly cut palmettos absorbed many of the shot—the palmetto tree later became a state symbol—numerous rounds fell among the defenders. "A mulatto waiting boy" was hit, Lieutenant Thomas Hall's cheek was smashed by a splinter, Sergeant McDaniel fell mortally wounded, "his stomach and bowels shot away by a cannon ball." When a ball toppled the flagstaff over the fort, Sergeant William Jasper, shouting, "Don't let us fight without a color," grabbed a cannon swab, hastily tied the flag to it, leaped atop the bastion, and stuck the staff into the battlements. The garrison cheered. Enveloped by dense smoke, the "blaze and roar" of cannons in their ears, the defenders paused to swill the grog ordered passed among them by Colonel Moultrie. All the while he called on his gunners to aim carefully, which they did, for by nightfall when the firing ceased, the British ships were badly battered, the dead and dying littering their decks. "Thus," a British officer wrote, was "the Invincible British Navy defeated by a Battery which it was supposed would not have stood one Broadside." After reembarking General Clinton's regulars from Long Island, Admiral Parker and his mauled fleet soon departed for New York.[54]

The British attack on Sullivan's Island played into the hands of laboring-class leaders who sought separation from England, but it dashed the hopes of the lowcountry gentry who had sought reconciliation. On August 5 news arrived in Charles Town that the Declaration of Independence had been adopted in Philadelphia; it was signed by lowcountry Carolinians Arthur Middleton, Edward Rutledge, Thomas Lynch, Jr., and Thomas Heyward, Jr. In September the government at Charles Town approved the Declaration of Independence. Like other reluctant revolutionaries of his class, Henry Laurens mused: "God only knows what sort of world it will be."

The Elite and the Rank and File

South Carolina became an independent state. The temporary constitution was revised and another adopted, but only after months of debate. Most of the propertied class sought to continue their domination of the government, while the city's laboring-class leaders and backcountry representatives demanded more equitable representation in the legislature, better local government, and separation of church and state. The movement for the separation of church and state was led by the Reverend William Tennant of Charles Town's Independent Church. Tennant argued that established churches were oppressive and "an infringement of religious liberty." Despite strong opposition from Anglicans in the legislature, the church was disestablished under the new constitution. No longer were persons required to support financially a church where they did not worship. It was the major change in the new constitution.

Property qualifications for voting were lowered in the new instrument of government, but high property qualifications for holding office were continued. The legislature also continued to elect the governor and the lieutenant governor—first called president and vice president—and most other officers of the state. Although four-fifths of South Carolina's white population lived in the backcountry, apportionment to the legislature was weighted heavily in favor of Charles Town and the lowcountry, which held nearly three-quarters of the seats. The new state government remained all-powerful, while local governments remained weak and subordinate. The new constitution perpetuated the concentration of political power in a lowcountry oligarchy.[55]

Rawlins Lowndes, the orphan who became among the most conservative of Charles Town's elite, was elected the first president under the new state constitution and Christopher Gadsden vice president in March 1778. That same month the legislature passed an act requiring every free male inhabitant over sixteen years of age to take an oath of loyalty to the state. Unwilling to swear such allegiance, several dozen prominent Loyalists made plans to leave the city. However, a group calling themselves the "Friends of the British Government" refused either to leave or to take the test oath. When Lowndes issued a proclamation extending the date for taking the pledge, a riot erupted in the city. Already distrustful of Lowndes "the procrastinator" and full of anti-British zeal, the laboring classes believed that the government was being too lenient with the British Loyalists. Vice President Gadsden rushed to the scene of the riot. He discovered a mob led by Dr. John Budd, Henry Peronneau, and the young lawyer Joshua Ward. In defending Lowndes's proclamation, Gadsden came close to blows with Ward. A few days later Gadsden wrote: "I am afraid we have too many amongst us [who] want to be running . . . to . . . the Liberty Tree, a Disease amongst us far more dangerous than anything that can arise from the whole present herd of Contemptible, exportable Tories."

Gadsden's support of President Lowndes "displeased the people & made him very unpopular," one citizen wrote. For years Gadsden had tried to manipulate the city mob to his own interests and to those of his class. Now laboring-class leaders were emerging who sought far-reaching social, economic, and political

changes that alarmed Gadsden. He feared class conflict and anarchy. Like other members of the elite, he realized that now more
than ever the revolutionary movement had to be carefully managed lest the "licentiousness" of the masses rush out of control.[56]

Efforts of the lowcountry's propertied classes to control the
course of the revolution and to maintain the status quo internally,
and the social tensions and conflicts within the society itself, are
reflected in the composition of South Carolina's military organizations and the attitudes and relationships of the officers and men.
For "armies are but the projections of the societies from which
they spring." In early 1776 the government of South Carolina ordered the raising of six regiments. Both the field-grade and com-
pany-grade soldiers were selected by the legislators. They choose
men like themselves, "gentlemen" of fortune and family, who had
"a stake in society." Of the twelve officers appointed by the legislature who rose to the rank of colonel or general in the six regiments, ten were members of the Provincial Congress and the
remaining two were younger men from prominent families. Likewise, a majority of the men elected to a captaincy were men much
like their superiors. Now the elite officer corps had raised an army.

Scouring the backcountry for recruits in July 1775, Captain
Bernard Elliott found the type of men the officers wanted—
"young men [who] . . . have little, and some no property," yet he
met with very limited success in recruiting. Three years later the
regiments remained at only half-strength and one Charles Town
resident complained: "It is difficult to fill them when the inhabitants don't incline to enlist for Soldiers. But we are in hopes to fill
them up by a Vagrant Act," which passed the South Carolina
legislature in March 1778, ordering the immediate enlistment of
all "idle men, beggars, strolling or straggling persons." Though
persons volunteering were promised land and sizable bounties,
troop strength remained down. A French official at Charles Town
in late 1778 observed that the garrison numbered only 600 men
and these were "recruited with . . . difficulty."[57]

The enlisted men came under a disciplinary system initially
tempered with paternalism. During the early months of 1776, the
lowcountry officer elite admonished their troops to behave like
soldiers, and their lectures on Christian habits often carried a
strong puritanical strain and an ultra-patriotic theme. But when
the recruits showed little disposition to behave as their superiors
admonished them to do, swift and severe disciplinary action was

meted out. Despite direct orders to cut their hair, shave, and "to touch" their caps to officers, the soldiers showed little inclination to obey.

Perhaps rankling the enlisted men were the visible signs of the great social cleavage between themselves and the elite officer corps. An English traveler in South Carolina described the officers as "people of property [who] cutt a pretty good regular appearance having handsome uniforms," but the enlisted men, "if possible, make a worse figure than the Train Bands of London." The common soldiers also noted the great inequities in lodging, food, and leisure. It became apparent to the enlisted men that while they were neither well quartered nor well cared for, their officers lived high and well. This intensified their hostility toward their officers and may account for the continuing assaults on the property of the officers.

Regimental records abound with accounts of enlisted men stealing their officer's silk stockings and linen shirts; of rioting and drunkenness. There is ample evidence of more serious offenses like refusing to obey a direct order, threatening an officer, desertion, and treason. It was for these and other offenses that courts-martial were convened with astounding frequency in South Carolina's six regiments. For all offenses, the punishment most frequently prescribed was flogging. The maximum number of lashes authorized by the Continental Congress was 100, but the number frequently exceeded the offense in the South Carolina units and some sentences were cruel and unusual punishments.[58]

In 1777 three of four men of the second regiment were sentenced to 100 lashes "on the bare back" for disrespect to their officers. However, the fourth, James Orange, received 200 lashes "because of the atrociousness of his crime," attacking Lieutenant Preveaux "with a knife" and "repeatedly damn[ing] the Continental Congress . . . saying he . . . would support the cause of Great Britain to his last." The Reverend Oliver Hart, a Baptist minister at Charles Town, attended an execution for desertion and watched as a Sergeant Malcolm was blindfolded, made to drop to his knees, and then shot, "which was thrice repeated before he was quite dead."

In military units raised in the northern states, it has been argued, middle-class officers commanded sturdy yeomen or "embattled farmers" united in a "people's war of political independence." The officers fraternized with the men and avoided the lash, and a leveling spirit prevailed. But in South Carolina units social tensions and class conflict seemed endemic. Deep-seated antagonisms over common values and goals spawned the epidemic of rebelliousness and hostility of the rank and file toward the "glorious cause" and their officers. Indeed, the elite came to fear the threat of disorder from enlisted men as much as they feared Charles Town's mob or slave insurrections.[59]

Throughout the war years, Charlestonians worried that their slaves were collaborating with the British. When Scipio Handley, a free, black Charleston fisherman, who may have known Thomas Jeremiah, was caught carrying messages to the British, he was condemned to death as a spy. Handley escaped execution by sawing his way out of the notoriously inadequate Charles Town jail. After the British promised runaway slaves their freedom for carrying intelligence, Governor John Rutledge ordered officers operating around Charles Town to make "severe examples . . . of all negroes who . . . aid or assist . . . the enemy; all such negroes shall suffer death." One military officer believed that the manpower shortages in military units resulted from "the great proportion of the citizens necessary to remain at home to prevent insurrection among the negroes, and to prevent the desertion of them to the enemy."

Small wonder, then, that South Carolina's legislators greeted any proposals to enlist and arm slaves with horror. Even though threatened by invasion, their military units grossly under strength, and the Continental Congress recommending the enlistment of slaves, the South Carolina legislature refused. Christopher Gadsden wrote, "We are much disgusted here at the Congress recommending us to arm our Slaves, it was received with great resentment as a very dangerous and impolitic Step." Henry Laurens believed that the scheme was defeated because of the refusal of "Rich men to part willingly with the very source of their wealth," their slaves, as well as "rooted habits and prejudices." Laurens himself soon departed Charles Town on a diplomatic mission abroad, but was taken prisoner by the British on the high seas and imprisoned in the Tower of London. The legislature continued to draft or hire black slaves to perform the manual labor of the armies and to build the defenses around Charles Town, but the South Carolinians continued to refuse to consider blacks as soldiers.[60]

1775–1782: Charles Town's Second Revolution

Following the abortive attack on Sullivan's Island in June 1776, the British concentrated their war efforts in the northeastern states. With trade through Boston, New York, and Philadelphia interrupted, the export-import trade flourished at Charles Town despite the embargoes on agricultural products by the Continental Congress to prevent the loss of provisions for the American armies. The lucrative, sometimes illicit, wartime profiteering produced fortunes for a few. In less than a year one group of investors grossed over $60,000 in gold and silver. Other wealthy investors established the Bank of Charles Town and two insurance companies. Such profiteering led one patriot at Charles Town to remark that "A spirit of money-making has eaten up our patriotism. Our morals are more depreciated than our currency."

The paper bills issued by the Continental Congress and the state government at Charles Town to finance the war effort rapidly depreciated in value and, combined with soaring prices and the scarcity of food, caused rampant inflation. An item selling for a shilling in the city in 1777 might cost 61 shillings two years later. Inflation fell heaviest on the laboring classes and the poor. Some citizens blamed speculators for buying and hoarding corn "to keep up the price in town." Sharp class divisions and anger surfaced when craftsmen publicly complained that they were being exploited by a "set of monopolizers and extortioners . . . Villains and Sharpers." Soaring costs and the scarcities of materials and tools forced artisans out of business.[61]

The city's indigent, mainly women and children made rootless and homeless by the war, continued to seek relief at the doors of St. Philip's Church. After 1775, however, the churchwardens themselves faced a chronic shortage of funds with which to relieve the poor and sick. The new government at Charles Town neither permitted the churchmen to collect poor taxes nor appropriated money for the indigent. To raise funds the churchmen now had to borrow money at interest from individuals. But despite their efforts to feed, clothe, maintain, and provide medical services, the scarcity of goods coupled with rampant inflation left many of the city poor hungry and ill. To maintain the city's indigent during 1778 and to pay off earlier loans, the churchwardens had to borrow $25,000. Two years later they had to borrow an even larger sum to supplement the allowances of the poor because of "the very extravagant prices of every necessary of life." Indeed, some of the poor were seen "begging their daily bread from door to door." And the parish physician declared that he could no longer provide adequate care on his salary for the growing numbers of the indigent ill because of the "extravagant prices of medicines."

Also swelling Charles Town's population were soldiers and mixed-national sailors. Over 1,000 soldiers and an equal number of mixed-national sailors were stationed near the city or aboard ships in the harbor. The officers of these young, undisciplined, sometimes riotous men coordinated their efforts with committees of the legislature and the night watch in an attempt to preserve order. The officers told their troops to avoid the "Dissipation and Seduction" of Charles Town's grog shops, but despite such admonitions soldiers thronged the local tippling houses in the dark alleys running to the Cooper River. Here they mingled, drank, gambled with foreign sailors, and found female companionship. Fights and riots frequently erupted among them and the South Carolina government responded quickly. When a "great riot" broke out between French and American sailors carrying "canes and small arms," Governor Lowndes called out the militia, regular troops, and "artillery." The rioters were quickly "pacified," one observer wrote. Even more disruptive to the life of the city was fire.[62]

The Fire of 1778

Repeatedly the town firemasters and other prominent citizens appealed unsuccessfully to the Assembly for additional public wells and pumps to supply water for the city's fire engines. Despite laws prohibiting "the throwing of Fire-Works," occasionally the roof of a home was "set on Fire by a Sky Rocket"; despite protests, jerry-built structures went up on the wharves; and despite the threat of heavy fines, some residents neglected to keep fire buckets and ladders on their premises or to keep their chimneys clean. The propertied classes also worried over the negligence of slaves employed nights to tend the ovens of bakers and candle- and soap-makers; they believed that the carelessness of household slaves with lighted candles put "the Town . . . in continual Danger." Prominent citizens also were haunted by the fear that the town could be fired at any time by "some hellish Incendiary."

To prevent "disorder" if fire did break out, heavy penalties were to be imposed on any resident who refused to obey the orders of the firemasters: stiff fines were levied on white men and twenty lashes were meted out to slaves. Persons detected carrying away property other than their own from the site of a fire were to be "pilloried" and "to have their Ears cut off." Arsonists received the death penalty. Before the end of the colonial period two "Negro Wenches" were "examined, tried, and convicted" in Charles Town of willfully setting fires. For their criminal acts, they were "burnt" to death.[63]

On the night of January 15, 1778, either in a bake-house or "in a kitchen hired out to some negroes" near the intersection of Queen Street and Union, now State Street, a fire broke out. A northerly wind blew "fiery flakes" from one rooftop to another. The flames engulfed house after house along Queen Street; it spread down Union Street to Broad Street, to Elliott Street and Bedon's Alley; down the east side of Church Street to Stoll's Alley, and it swept "the whole of Tradd Street" to the east of Church Street. Eyewitnesses described "a sea of flame" and dazed, "wandering . . . half dressed matrons . . . and children" in the streets; "the crackling of flames . . . the shrieks of the . . . sufferers" and the "horror . . . in every countenance." The following day citizens looked upon "the smoking ruins, and the constant falling of walls and chimneys" where once had been the "trading port" of the city.

The fire destroyed the Charles Town Library, the museum, about 250 homes, and countless other outhouses and structures. The losses exceeded $3 million. Rumors that incendiaries, British Loyalists or Tories, had set fire to the city both frightened and infuriated the residents. A year later with a British Army threatening to overrun the city, another conflagration broke out. Two British sympathizers were arrested and charged with attempting "to fire the town." Both suspects were tried and convicted as arsonists and executed by hanging.[64]

The Siege of Charles Town

Savannah and most of Georgia already had fallen to the British Army that threatened Charles Town in early 1779. Unable to win a decisive battle over Washington's armies in the northern states and with France entering the war as America's ally, the British hoped that an invasion of the South would interdict trade through the port cities, encourage Loyalists, and turn the tide of war in their favor. By May the British Army of several thousand under General Augustine Prevost had reached the outskirts of Charles Town. There was a "Great uneasiness" and "confusion" among the inhabitants and they heard "Much firing." The Reverend Oliver Hart observed that "everybody expected (and many wished) the attack would be made." Like others, the Reverend Hart was aware of the strong Loyalist sentiments of some Charlestonians. The British withdrew with the approach of a several-thousand-man army under Massachusetts-born General Benjamin Lincoln, now commander of the American forces in the South. As General Prevost's army retreated south toward Savannah, British marauders, camp followers, and deserters "ravaged" and "plundered" the homes of the planters. The Bull family's Ashley Hall plantation was looted. At Belmont, the plantation of Eliza Lucas Pinckney, the furnishings were smashed; at Major Thomas Pinckney's home on the Ashepoo, the marauders carried off nineteen slaves and the best horses, sheep, and poultry, "drank the liquors," then burned the dwelling house. The wanton plundering embittered many of the wealthy landowners.

Warned in late 1779 of the possibility of yet another attack on Charles Town, General Benjamin Lincoln continued to be plagued by shortages of military equipment, the soaring costs of food, and an insufficient number of well-disciplined soldiers. He was disturbed by the number of troops he saw "strolling about the streets" or asleep at their posts when they were supposed to be on duty. Like South Carolina's officer corps, Lincoln remained doubtful of the quality and loyalty of his troops. Few seemed motivated, Lincoln wrote, by "Patriotism . . . love of Country, and concern for . . . freedom and independence." Believing that he lacked forces to defend the city, General Lincoln repeatedly appealed to the American Congress for troops. Finally, in December 1779, General Washington ordered 1,400 Continentals to join Lincoln in the South, and the Continental Congress dispatched supplies and four armed naval frigates under Commodore Abraham Whipple. Using gangs of black slaves, Lincoln repaired and armed the fort on Sullivan's Island, known as Fort Moultrie following the British attack of 1776, Fort Johnson on James Island, and batteries at Haddrell's Point in Mount Pleasant. With these fortifications and Commodore Whipple's squadron guarding the harbor, General Lincoln assumed that any attack would have to come from the northwestern, or land, side of Charles Town and he ordered the building of earthworks on the Neck. Here just to the north of Boundary Street (now Calhoun Street), gangs of slaves dug a line of trenches and built and mounted cannons on a series of oyster-shell and mortar redoubts linking the marshes and rivers to the east and west of the peninsula. The main redoubt stood in the center of the lines near the intersection of King and Boundary streets. Known as the Citadel, its remnants remain there today. To the front of these works a network of abatis—sharpened stakes embedded at an angle—was implanted. Beyond these a deep, wide ditch was excavated and flooded with water. Now, General Lincoln believed, the city was "pretty safe." However, by early 1780 the entire army of South Carolina, some 5,000 soldiers, were walled up in Charles Town without an adequate escape route. General Lincoln himself recognized the risk if "besieged" by a numerically superior army. And during the winter of 1779–80 a massive combined sea and land expedition under Vice Admiral Arbuthnot, Sir Henry Clinton, and Lord Cornwallis bore down on Charles Town.[65]

During February 1780 reports reached the city that an armada of British transports and warships were disembarking thousands of troops on the sea islands to the south. From the steeple of St. Michael's, the editor of the *Gazette*, Peter Timothy, with spyglass to eye saw the smoke rise from a thousand campfires as the British regulars moved slowly up the coast. Southeast to seaward he saw the first ships of the supporting fleet paralleling the line of march. By the end of the month the British troops occupied James Island and in late March and early April the warships swept past the forts guarding the harbor entrance and anchored within broadside range of the city. Commodore Whipple withdrew his squadron up the Cooper River after scuttling some vessels near the mouth to obstruct it. By early April the British Army had crossed the Ashley River unopposed. On the Neck they began constructing a line of breastworks just 1,800 yards north of the defensive works of Charles Town. The classic siege plan of encirclement by land and sea was complete.

The British Army under General Clinton brought up heavy guns and daily dug their way closer to the city. The batteries of both armies exchanged cannonades. During a heavy bombardment in early April, a Hessian officer serving with the British, Captain Johann Ewald, heard "A terrible clamor . . . among the inhabitants" and the "loud wailing of female voices." On the

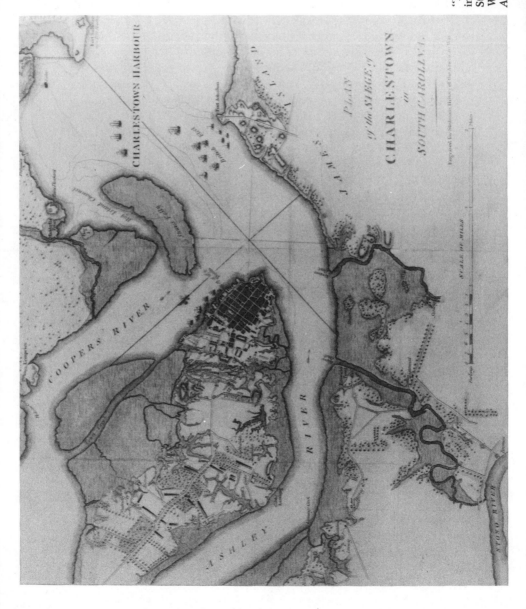

morning of April 13 British batteries opened a two-hour barrage of round shot and incendiary bombs. Fires broke out in the town, which in part remained in ruins from the fire of 1778, and several civilians were killed. To escape the destructive bombardment some residents huddled in their basements. That same day the governor of the state, John Rutledge, and his aides, on the advice of General Lincoln, evacuated the city. Food and military supplies were becoming exhausted. Whole families fled "out of fear of famine." Packs of dogs roamed the empty streets. Soldiers were ordered to patrol and "kill all the dogs they shall find . . . in any way whatever, saving that of shooting." By mid-April the British cut the last escape route when they killed or captured members of an American cavalry unit in a bloody encounter at Monck's Corner.

The British before Charles Town slowly inched their lines forward. In late April they drained the canal paralleling the American entrenchments, crossed it, and began building redoubts at the edge of the abatis. Within the town food supplies were dangerously low. One defender wrote: "Our rations of meat reduced to six ounces; coffee and sugar allowed only to the soldiers." Also desperately short of ammunition, the defenders had to fire "ragged Pieces of Iron, broken Bottles, Old Axes, Gun Barrels, Tomaw Hawks."

Under these grim conditions, General Lincoln and most of his officers believed that further resistance was hopeless and negotiations for surrender were opened with the British. However, Lieutenant Governor Christopher Gadsden, the ranking civilian official in the city, Colonel Charles Cotesworth Pinckney, and members of the Governor's Council damned "any thought of capitulation," so negotiations for surrender broke down and the British renewed their attack. On May 7 Fort Moultrie fell before an amphibious assault by British seamen; and two days later General Clinton ordered his 200 artillery pieces that encircled Charles Town to open a bombardment. Throughout the night and into the next day and the next, "musket fire, grape-shot, bombs, and red-hot cannon balls" crashed and exploded within the city. Twenty houses were hit and set afire. Bucket brigades of slaves raced from one blaze to another. General William Moultrie recalled that the bombardment "was incessant, cannon balls whizzing and shells hissing continually amongst us; ammunition chests and temporary magazines blowing up; great guns bursting and wounded men groaning along the lines." A British cannonball ricocheted off St. Michael's Church and tore off the right arm of the town's highly prized statue of William Pitt.

Surrender and Occupation

On May 12 after a forty-two-day siege, General Lincoln surrendered America's last open seaport and the only army in the Southern theater of the war: 5,500 officers and men and their military stores. It was the greatest victory of the war for the British. One British officer who watched the surrender of the men and arms near the city's main redoubt, or Citadel, noted that the defenders were "the most ragged rabble I ever beheld." A Hessian officer who entered Charles Town that same day observed that "the . . . people looked greatly starved," the houses "were full of wounded," while the homes of some of the well-to-do were "empty and locked." These, "however, were now opened and occupied by the garrison."[66]

A few days later as the British stored the captured arms in a magazine on what is today Magazine Street, which ran between Archdale and Mazyck streets, a rifle discharged accidentally, causing a violent explosion and fire. An eyewitness described the scene as "horrible." Some "sixty people . . . burnt beyond recognition, half-dead and writhing like worms" lay scattered about. "Mutilated bodies" and "limbs" were hanging on nearby houses; the explosion blew one man against the steeple of the new Independent Church with such force that the imprint of his body remained for several days. Over 200 people were killed and fires started by the blast destroyed six houses, including a brothel. More people were injured or killed by the explosion than during the siege; and now both the eastern and western edges of the city and portions between were in ruins.

The British confined General Lincoln, his officers, and the Continental troops in barracks in Charles Town and near Mount Pleasant, and on British transports in the harbor. Most would be exchanged within a year. The South Carolina militia and local citizens were treated as prisoners on parole.

General Sir Henry Clinton established his headquarters in Miles Brewton's house on lower King Street and issued a proclamation promising a pardon of all "treasonable offenses" to citizens who took an oath of allegiance to the British government.

Loyalists from across the state streamed to Charles Town to join them. On June 3, 1780, 110 of the "principal and most respectable inhabitants of Charles Town" pledged their loyalty to England. They offered General Clinton their "warmest congratulations on the Restoration of this Capital and Province to their political connection with the crown and Government of Great Britain." Over the next several months hundreds of the inhabitants declared themselves to be "true and faithful subjects to His Majesty the King of Great Britain" and among those who pledged their allegiance to the new government were Henry Middleton and Charles Pinckney, formerly president of the South Carolina Assembly; Rawlins Lowndes, the former governor of the state; Gabriel Manigault, the city's wealthiest inhabitant; Daniel Cannon, the prominent artisan; Daniel Huger, aide to Governor John Rutledge; and Colonel Isaac Hayne.[67]

The small merchants of Charles Town, other businessmen who flocked there, and many among the laboring class also pledged their allegiance to the king. Some were opportunists who shifted their allegiances to take advantage of the huge profits to be made in the export-import trade; others did so out of political conviction; still others out of financial necessity, since eventually those who refused to pledge their loyalty were labeled as "rebels" and were excluded from participation in business. Dr. George Carter took the oath of loyalty out of financial necessity so that he could continue practicing medicine to feed his family. Though he often invited British officers to his home, he remained sympathetic to the Patriot cause. On one occasion he entertained a few of his friends who shared his feelings and several British officers at a seated dinner. Toward the end of the evening, as the party began to break up, he glanced around the table, and thinking that all but his close friends had left, Dr. Carter proposed a toast. Raising his glass, he shouted: "To the American Congress." As he prepared to toss off the drink, a voice from a far dark corner of the room rasped: "What is that you say? Do you mean to insult us with such a toast?" Realizing that at least one royal officer remained, Dr. Carter quickly and shrewdly responded: "My dear friend hear me out. I meant to add, "may they all be hanged." The British officer, now satisfied, raised his own glass and drank down the toast.

Still others later maintained that they were frightened into taking the pledge. For instance, both Patrick Hinds, the shoemaker, and Thomas Elfe, the cabinetmaker, insisted that they were "intimidated" into taking the oath by Tories. Others testified that suspected "rebels" were repeatedly subjected to "threats and Menaces." Feelings of hatred and vindictiveness of one citizen for another persisted in the city for years. Often families were divided when they chose different sides. Dr. Alexander Garden, the physician-botanist, was a Loyalist, his son a Patriot.[68]

The British established civil government in Charles Town with the appointment of a commandant of the city and a Board of Police. Loyalists served as firemasters and as commissioners of the streets. The new government encountered many of the same problems that long had plagued the city. For instance, the Board of Police remained chronically short of funds to relieve the city's numerous poor. Repeatedly the churchwardens of St. Philip's Church petitioned the Board of Police to provide both provisions and funds for the maintenance of the indigent. To raise funds the Board of Police taxed the licenses of the retailers of "spirituous liquors" and auctioneers. But due to the steady and alarming rise of food prices, money raised to relieve the poor depreciated faster than it was collected. The Poor House remained "much out of repair" and by the winter of 1781 there was neither "a stick of wood" available to the poor nor a doctor to attend them.

The great numbers of runaway slaves who flocked to the city for safety and "to join the King's Army" also posed problems for British officials. Fearing that they might become "dangerous to the community," the officials ordered the arrest of many blacks. They were confined in the "large Sugar House" located near the western terminus of Broad Street on the Ashley River, the property of the slave-trader William Savage. These slaves were used frequently to repair the fortifications and to clean the streets, which, despite their efforts and huge expenditures by the British, remained "exceedingly filthy," and "detrimental to the health of the Inhabitants."

The health of the slaves themselves who were kept in the "Sugar House" was jeopardized by their "long and close confinement." Due to the frequency of deaths among these slaves and others in the occupied city, blacks were quickly buried in "different lots" around Charles Town. A newly opened "Negro burying ground" in Church Street became so "extremely noxious" to the inhabitants that they complained to British authorities. The "Strangers and Transients" Cemetery and other white burial grounds also filled up when smallpox and dysentery swept through the prison ships in the harbor.

While the British grappled unsuccessfully with many of the city's long-standing problems, some of their actions, and one of their administrators particularly, the commandant of Charles Town, Lieutenant Colonel Nisbet Balfour, outraged a few Charlestonians. General William Moultrie would later characterize Balfour as "tyrannical" and "insolent." Balfour angered over sixty of the city's most politically influential inhabitants and their families when he charged them with "seditious activities" and exiled them to St. Augustine. Among them were laboring-class leaders who first advocated independence from England: Christopher Gadsden; Edward Weyman, the upholsterer; William Johnson, blacksmith; James Brown, carpenter; and George Flagg, the painter. Also under Balfour's orders suspected rebel spies were seized and imprisoned in the basement of the Exchange building or in the fever-ridden ships in the harbor. Residents who persisted in refusing to take an oath of loyalty to the Crown were prohibited from appearing before the Board of Police to bring suit against debtors. However, Loyalists could summon "rebels" to answer similar charges. Suspected rebel ministers and schoolmasters were removed from their posts and replaced by Crown sympathizers. The South Carolina *Gazette* was shut down and its politically active patriot and editor, Peter Timothy, exiled, only to perish at sea. Loyalists like Robert Wells, publisher of the *South Carolina and American General Gazette*, flourished; appointed official printer to the king, Wells changed the name of his paper to the *Royal Gazette* in 1781. Legend has it that one citizen so despised Balfour that he dressed a pet baboon in an exact replica of his uniform and addressed the animal as Colonel Balfour.

During the occupation British officers commandeered the homes of some of the city's wealthy and helped themselves to the "luxuries of the [wine] cellars." Here they sponsored lavish balls and concerts and invited the local Tories, their ladies, and single women. One "rebel" lady recalled that those women who became "too fond of the British officers" were ostracized by good "patriots." Occasionally these officers invited black females. At one elegant affair in February 1782 slave women "dressed up in the richest silks" and British officers danced away the evening.[69]

Perhaps the single act that caused the most bitterness and a desire for revenge against the British "oppressors" and their Tory supporters was the execution of Colonel Isaac Hayne. Colonel Hayne of the South Carolina militia, who had surrendered with the fall of Charles Town and pledged his allegiance to the king, had subsequently taken up arms again against England. Then in July 1781 he was captured by the British near Charles Town. Having broken his oath and suspected of committing atrocities against Loyalists in the ruthless civil war raging beyond the city, British officials hoped to make an example of him. Hayne was hanged just outside the lines of Charles Town on August 4, 1781. For years local poets would romanticize the life and death of Colonel Hayne, "Patriot and Martyr."

During the same summer of 1781 the American counterattack to retake South Carolina scored significant successes. One by one British outposts in the state fell to the army of the Rhode Island-born, fighting Quaker, General Nathanael Greene. Coordinating his efforts with partisan bands operating out of lowcountry swamps, General Greene moved his army within fifteen miles of Charles Town by the winter of 1782. Now the British garrison was in danger of being encircled by Americans.

To restore civil government to South Carolina and to suppress widespread plundering, murder, and anarchy, Governor John Rutledge called a meeting of the legislature in early 1782 at Jacksonborough. Here in this tiny village to the south of Charles Town and under the protection of General Greene's army, the legislators assembled in late January. They included members of the state's officer corps and ten prominent Charlestonians previously exiled to St. Augustine. The composition of the Assembly resembled the prewar legislatures, which were dominated and controlled by the lowcountry's wealthy planter-merchant-lawyer oligarchy.[70]

A spirit of vindictiveness spawned by several years of occupation, plunder, and persecution of "rebels" by the British and their followers pervaded the Jacksonborough Assembly. One member wrote that "the very females talk as familiarly of shedding blood & destroying the [Tories] as the men do." An "enemies list" mentality was emerging. A committee of the Assembly began drafting an act of confiscation, banishment, and amercement to punish Tories, to raise revenue, and to serve their own self-interest. One legislator observed that everyone on the committee offered his own list of the state's enemies, and "the Enquiry is not so much what he has done, as what Estate he has." Members of the Assembly themselves became speculators in the confiscated lands.

The welcoming addresses of Charles Town's residents to the British in 1780 provided the Jacksonborough Assembly with the names of British sympathizers. The legislators published a list of 425 families who either were to be banished from the state and their property confiscated or were to have their property amerced. Approximately 90 percent were residents of Charles Town or the surrounding lowcountry. These acts of the Jacksonborough Assembly, motivated by revenge, retaliation, and self-interest, affected the political life of Charles Town for years.

After the news of the surrender of Lord General Cornwallis's army at Yorktown reached London in late 1781, Parliament resolved to bring the war to an end. On December 31, 1781, Henry Laurens was released from the Tower of London in exchange for the release of Cornwallis by the Americans. During the summer of 1782 the British commander at Charles Town, General Alexander Leslie, received orders from his government to evacuate the city. General Greene moved his forces to the western bank of the Ashley River where they watched and waited. Governor John Mathews, recently elected by the South Carolina legislature, opened negotiations with the British for an orderly evacuation. By the early fall an agreement had been worked out between the British and Governor Mathews and his advisers, Benjamin Guerard and Edward Rutledge, prominent Charles Town attorneys. The British pledged to restore property seized and held by them, including all slaves who had not sought to join the British; in turn Mathews pledged that the state would neither pass additional legislation for the confiscation of Loyalist property nor interfere with the collection of debts owed to British subjects; also British merchants were permitted to remain in Charles Town for six months to collect outstanding debts. Laboring-class leaders were shocked by these agreements. They came to believe that the attorneys had drafted a document to serve only the local elite: large slave-owners and those planters who wished to export their fall crops through the city's well-connected British merchants.

On October 27 a convoy of forty ships departed Charles Town carrying most of the British Army. With them were over 3,700 white civilians, many of whom were South Carolina Loyalists. Despite their pledge the British carried off more than 5,000 slaves, large quantities of indigo, shipping seized in port, and the spoils of petty looting, including the bells of St. Michael's Church. The remaining troops evacuated the city, embarking from Gadsden's famous wharf on December 14. By 11:00 A.M. that same day, General Greene's army took possession of Charles Town. After two and one-half years of British rule, Charles Town was once more in the control of Carolinians.[71]

IV

The Antebellum City

Incorporation: "Engine of Oppression"

When the South Carolina legislature convened in Charles Town in early 1783, it was dominated by merchants, lawyers, and lowcountry planters for whom survival of the import-export trade was the highest priority. They acted favorably on the petitions of British merchants and returning Loyalists seeking permanent residence and citizenship, some of whom came back from East Florida when it reverted to Spain under the treaty of 1783. But the city's small merchants deeply resented legislation benefiting their prominent, capital-rich competitors, and the artisans were angered by the renewed importation of British crafts. It seemed to the mechanics and small shopkeepers that their former enemies stood to profit handsomely by the acts of the affluent legislators while those who had fought and bled in the Revolution were ignored, and they turned to violence.

Assaults on Loyalists became commonplace. By June four men had been murdered. Dr. David Ramsay observed that "A spirit has gone forth among the lower Class of people to drive away certain persons whom they call Tories." The new governor, Charlestonian Benjamin Guerard, a lawyer and planter who had been a prisoner of the British during the Revolution, issued a proclamation calling on all good citizens to assist in curbing the disorder. During July, public meetings of the laboring classes called for the expulsion of the British merchants and Tories. When the legislature reconvened in the steamy heat of early August, it ignored these requests and, instead, in an act considered "indispensably necessary . . . for the preservation of peace and good order," incorporated the City of Charleston. Charles Town may have been changed to Charleston to reflect more accurately the local pronunciation of the port, "CHAHLston," or as a way to announce dramatically the city's new independence of the British Crown. A seal of the city was authorized in August and the first

One of the first printed representations of the Seal of the City of Charleston.
Courtesy of the South Carolina Historical Society, Charleston, S.C.

known representation of the seal appeared in 1789. In the fore-
ground a female figure holds a staff in her left hand; a waterview
of the eighteenth-century city and a ship under full sail are in the
background; beneath in Latin, in Roman capitals, are the words
THE BODY POLITIC and above SHE GUARDS HER BUILDINGS, CUSTOMS
AND LAWS. Over time several seals have appeared, each differing
slightly from the one before.[1]

The city was divided into thirteen wards with a warden
elected from each by the free, white, male residents who paid 3
shillings a year in taxes. These voters chose the city's chief executive officer, called the intendant, from among the thirteen
wardens.

On September 1, 1783, Richard Hutson was elected as
Charleston's first intendant through the support of the local oligarchy. Born near Beaufort and educated at Princeton, Hutson
had practiced law in Charleston and served in the legislature. At
thirty-six years of age he owned over 2,000 acres of lowcountry
land and seventeen slaves. His opponents came to call him Richard I. Two artisans were elected to the City Council, but the
government of Charleston remained firmly in the hands of the

propertied classes whose immediate aim was to restore good order. One of the first ordinances passed by the city government required all sailors to return to their ships an hour before sundown; another established a thirty-man, armed City Guard to enforce the laws of the City Corporation, especially those relating to drunken behavior among slaves and sailors.

In September Dr. Ramsay described the quickening pace of the economy: " . . . partnerships . . . are daily forming. The infamous African trade . . . will among other branches of business be resumed." Native-born and British merchants once again extended easy credit to planters, who pledged the coming season's crops toward their purchases of luxuries and slaves to replace those lost in the plundering during the war. In a year more than 6,000 Africans had been purchased locally at £50 sterling on the average, and other merchandise poured into the state reaching an incredible figure of over £1 million sterling. The city's social life also recovered quickly. The rich resumed meetings of their hunt clubs, musical and dancing assemblies, smoking clubs, and ugly clubs where their consumption of Spanish wines and Jamaican rum soon assumed its legendary proportions.[2]

Diatribes against Tories gave way to attacks on the legislature and City Corporation by late 1783, and there were enough newspapers to accommodate most political opinions. The *South Carolina Weekly Gazette* began publication in 1783, and three years later, the daily *City Gazette*. The paper that Benjamin Franklin helped found and Peter Timothy last edited, the *South Carolina Gazette*, resumed publication as the *South Carolina State Gazette* under the direction of Benjamin Franklin Timothy. One writer who defended members of the City Council as men of rank in the local press was answered by another who declared that indeed they were men of rank—*"rank cowards . . . rank upstarts . . . rank idiots."*

The most influential organization formed to oppose the oligarchy controlling the state and city governments was the Marine Anti-Britannic Society. Its officers included Alexander Gillon who had been exiled to St. Augustine by the British and, though he died impoverished, upon returning to Charleston made a quick fortune speculating in confiscated property, and Dr. James Fallon, a Roman Catholic, denounced by his enemies as "A Jesuit and disturber of all good Government"; several others joined them who harbored personal and financial grievances against the city government. To Charleston's affluent, they were "artful, designing and turbulent men" whose followers were "of the lower and rougher class."

Into early 1784 fires set by arsonists and "tumults" broke out, probably encouraged by officers of the Anti-Britannic Society. In April, Captain William Thompson, a local tavern-keeper and advocate of "social equality" for all except wealthy Tories, had angry words with John Rutledge, who was then a member of the South Carolina House of Representatives. Briefly imprisoned for contempt of the legislature, Thompson roared that he did not consider it a breach of the privileges of the House "for a common citizen to dispute with a *John Rutledge*, or any of the NABOB tribe" and insisted he had been punished simply because *"the great John Rutledge* was individually offended by *a plebeian."*[3]

On the evening of July 8 about twenty opponents of the city government and some sailors unfurled an American flag and began marching through the streets. An eyewitness and ally of Intendant Hutson described them as a "daring set of ... bandetti, who seemed determined . . . to destroy" the city government and to introduce anarchy for their "own selfish purposes," and Hutson ordered out the militia to disperse them. Later Hutson's enemies charged that his own "mob" drove his opponents "through the streets at the *point of a bayonet.*" Officers of the Anti-Britannic Society were arrested and brought before Hutson for refusing to take up arms against the "rioters." They were acquitted, defending themselves by charging that the intendant and his "Tory . . . adherents" wielded such extensive powers that they could legally massacre the citizens under the pretext of preventing riots.

During the late summer a bitter contest for the annual elections of intendant and wardens began. Alexander Gillon and his followers ran against the incumbent and his council. During the vituperative newspaper campaign, the one-time hero of the artisans, Christopher Gadsden, condemned Gillon as a "ring leader" of the "Mob" and questioned his patriotism during the Revolution. Gillon replied that Gadsden was a profiteer at public expense and the spokesman for a few "aristocratic" families who opposed democratic government. Just before the election, the City Council resolved that anyone could vote who kept a house in Charleston or resided there for three months in the year preceding the election and satisfied citizenship requirements. This permitted some lowcountry planters to vote in the elections and Gadsden's newspaper articles led many artisans to support the incumbents. Ten of the thirteen incumbent wardens were returned to office and Hutson trounced Gillon by a vote of 387 to 260. It was an overwhelming victory for the "Nabobs." Following elections to the legislature in November the city's laboring class believed that at both city and state level "a few ambitious, avaricious, and designing families" have "wriggle[ed] themselves into power."[4]

The bitter class antagonisms in Charleston did not end with the elections of 1784. A few years later over 170 inhabitants of Charleston asked the state Senate to repeal the act of incorporation, since the city government had become "an Engine of Oppression . . . in the hands of *a Potent few*" who resembled "that garbage of Monarchy . . . which the republican Freemen of this State have but lately shaken off." The legislature never seriously considered these demands, but the "aristocrats" were uneasy. Both Edward Rutledge and Christopher Gadsden believed that the persistent, hostile criticisms of their class were inspired by those many men who after the Revolution refused to "fall back in ranks."[5]

Postwar Depression

The false economic boom ended for Charleston by 1785 as a postwar depression spread across the new nation. Locally, a drought one year followed by heavy rains the next drastically cut the indigo and rice crops. The traditional markets for South Carolina rice were also closing and Britain's restrictions on trade to the West Indies, the decline of the Indian fur trade, and the lack of specie all fed the widening economic downturn. Planters were unable to repay their loans, the price of African slaves dropped sharply, and imported merchandise piled up unbought in the stores. A few of the most powerful attorneys, planters, and merchants, like William Smith, Ralph Izard, Henry Laurens, Gabriel Manigault, and Christopher Gadsden, continued to live comfortably and even made money during the depression, but most of Charleston's merchants and lowcountry planters remained heavily in debt to their British creditors. The Chamber of Commerce first organized in 1773 was revived by the city's merchants on August 4, 1785, following which a public meeting was called and recommendations for increasing trade were drafted and sent to the legislature. A few months later Ralph Izard and other prominent lowcountry planters and businessmen petitioned the legislature for a charter to dig a canal joining the Santee and Cooper rivers to bring backcountry produce to Charleston more speedily. Their request was granted with the incorporation of "the Company for the Inland Navigation from Santee to Cooper River." Construction of the canal soon began but would take years to complete and cost many times the original estimate. Daniel Cannon introduced water-powered sawmills to the city during the depression years. By impounding a branch of Coming's Creek that ran behind where Roper Hospital stands today, he powered the machinery of three mills located near the western end of Boundary Street (now Calhoun).

In late summer 1785, Arnoldus Vanderhorst, a factor and lowcountry planter who owned 2,350 acres on Kiawah Island, a large wharf, three tenements, and other property in Charleston, was elected as the city's second intendant. He was a member of St. Michael's Church. Control of the city government remained in the hands of the lawyer-planter-merchant, usually Episcopalian, oligarchy until after the Civil War.

Governor William Moultrie called a special session of the legislature in September 1785 to deal with the spreading economic catastrophe. Attempting to minimize the financial losses of planters, the legislature passed the Sheriff's Sales Act, which permitted debtors to repay creditors with any property, like near worthless "pine barren lands," and it hurt Charleston merchants. The legislature also authorized the creation of £100,000 sterling in paper money to be offered as loans secured by land. The act passed quickly because of the unique cooperation among laboring-class leaders, debt-ridden planters, and the backcountry men who were growing in numbers and influence.[6]

The depression, disease, and a continuous flow of new immigrants increased the numbers of poor in Charleston. The newly incorporated city relieved St. Philip's Church of the responsibility for these indigents, and the legislature made its first grant of money to the city to assist the transient poor in 1784. But the next year when the economy worsened and the treasury became empty, one Charlestonian remarked on the decline of city services: "the streets are unlighted and the poor are left to their fate." Nevertheless, some 100 inmates were receiving food, clothes, and lodging in Charleston's Poor House.

The poor remained especially susceptible to disease in the notoriously crowded and dirty city. During the 1780s over 16,000 people lived on the narrow peninsula south of Boundary Street, many of them in tenements and shacks on narrow streets and alleys. From street drains and thousands of privies human waste seeped into the sand, mud, and shell-strewn streets to mingle with other refuse, which remained until collected at irregular intervals by the city scavenger. Cow yards and hog pens abounded, adding to the city's filth and odors. In the spring of 1785 one visitor counted forty-two dogs, fifteen cats, and as many rats lying dead in the city's streets, "all in a state of putrifying effevetence [sic] . . . offending the sight and smell." He would count himself "fortunate" if he departed "before some putrid disorder rages." Repeatedly, citizens urged the city government to drain the low-lying lots of "stagnated waters" to control the "stench" in the city as it "must be highly injurious to the health of the inhabitants."[7]

Despite the unstable economy, big speculators continued to lay out new suburbs and the city grew up the Neck. To the west Daniel Cannon developed Cannonsborough just north of Harleston Village, joined to the city by Cannon's Bridge, and in 1786 about midway between the Ashley and the Cooper, Radcliffeborough was surveyed for Thomas Radcliffe. To the east of Meeting Street, Mazyckborough was surveyed for Alexander Mazyck. Somewhat later John Wragg created Wraggsborough and laid out two malls also on the east side of Meeting Street. With their businesses in the doldrums, Scottish merchants found time to organize the South Carolina Golf Club on September 29, 1786, and soon began playing the game on Harleston's Green. At this time a few Irishmen formed the tiny nucleus of a community of Roman Catholics that was to evolve into an important element in Charleston. The first Latin Mass known to have been celebrated in the city was said in 1786 in a private home, "an humble abode," by an Italian chaplain from a ship bound for South America.

Following the war traveling players had used the Exchange as a temporary theater since the New Theatre in Church Street had burned, but in 1786 two itinerant actors opened Harmony Hall, the city's first permanent post-Revolutionary playhouse, located just "without the city" on the northeast corner of King and Boundary streets. During its first season "a riot took place . . .

owing to a disappointment which the audience received in their expectations"; they "threw . . . bottles upon the stage, one of which was returned" by a performer. After a brief second season the playhouse closed, perhaps due to both bad theater and the worsening economy.[8]

Ratifying the Constitution

Over the vigorous opposition of the lowcountry's delegation, South Carolina legislators by a narrow margin voted in 1786 to move the state capital inland to a site that was eventually named Columbia and was much more accessible to the backcountry. Essential state offices were duplicated in Charleston, and for years some Charlestonians pretended that the new capital did not exist. But the lowcountry oligarchy continued to dominate the government. During the fall 1786 campaign for the legislature, which would elect delegates to the Constitutional Convention at Philadelphia, the intendant and wardens of Charleston used intimidation and fraud to ensure the election of pro-federal government legislators. Subsequently, the legislature elected Charlestonians John Rutledge, General Charles Cotesworth Pinckney, Charles Pinckney, and Pierce Butler (three lawyers and a planter) to represent the state in Philadelphia. Here these men, favoring "an aristocratic republic" based on property interests, and convinced that only an increase in trade could revive commerce, and that only a strong central government could help accomplish this, voted for the new Constitution. They led the fight for the insertion of a fugitive-slave clause and for the continuation of the importation of slaves to 1808.

But in the South Carolina legislature, with the lowcountry delegation almost evenly divided, an act passed on March 28, 1787, prohibiting the slave trade from any source for three years under penalty of fine. During the course of the hot debate on the issue Dr. Ramsay joked that on the Sunday preceding the vote "every man who went to church . . . and said his prayers was bound by a spiritual obligation to refuse the importation of slaves. They had devoutly prayed not to be led into temptation, and negroes were a temptation too great to be resisted." The legislation banning the trade in slaves was renewed every two or three years and officially the slave trade remained closed, though there were apparently numerous violations of the act.

On February 5, 1788, the former State House at Broad and

Meeting streets burned and three months later, from May 12–23, the state convention to ratify the new federal Constitution had to convene in the Exchange. The local legal establishment argued for it and with little opposition the Constitution was approved "by a great majority." Charleston remained a Federalist stronghold for a long time. Two years later upcountry demands led to the drafting of a new state constitution in which the lowcountry gentry so apportioned the legislature to ensure their dominance, required sizable property holdings for those standing for office, and restricted the franchise to adult, white males owning fifty acres of land or its equivalent. The new instrument of government reflected the elite's desire for an aristocratic republic. In Charleston the two decades of disorder and revolution had altered little the social and political relationships among Charleston's white classes.[9]

Gardens and Gardeners

For years Charleston had been noted for its gardens. With the help of his many business contacts abroad, Henry Laurens kept a "useful and ornamental" garden, introducing locally "olives, capers, limes, ginger, guinea grass, the alpine strawberry, red raspberrys, blue grapes; apples, pears, plums, and vines which bore abundantly of the choice white eating grapes called Chasselates blancs." Assisting Laurens was John Watson, "a complete English gardener," who also established the first nursery garden in the state on a large lot extending from King to Meeting streets.

Another local horticulturist, Robert Squibb, established a large garden on the south side of Tradd Street, between present-day Legare and Logan streets where he carried on experiments that led to the publication of his *Gardener's Calendar* (1787), only the second work on gardening brought out in America. New seeds and bulbs for flowering trees and plants were introduced to the city when the Chamber of Commerce enlisted the aid of Alexander Gillon and Thomas Jefferson to help revive the local economy by increasing trade with Holland and France. André Michaux, a French botanist, purchased land about ten miles up the Neck, where he established an extensive garden to produce seeds, trees, shrubs, and plants for the royal palaces in France. Through his French Botanic Garden, or French Garden as it became known, Michaux introduced the camellia japonica, the ginkgo tree, the candleberry tree, and became the premier importer of new flowers; upon his advice local planters transformed their plantations into show places of color in the spring.[10]

Returning Prosperity

By 1789 the ruins of the old State House were being cleared away and a new building similar in design was rising, which serves as the courthouse to the present day. In December the records of the state were moved to Columbia. The first federal census in 1790 revealed that Charleston County had a population of 11,801 whites and 34,846 blacks. Within the city the black to white ratio was 8,831 Afro-Americans to 8,089 whites. Fourth in population among urban centers, Charleston had by far a denser concentration of Afro-Americans than the other three combined—New York, Philadelphia, and Boston.

Exports of rice and indigo were rising, and a ravenous market for cotton was developing. Sea-island cotton was a very fine, strong cotton that came to be grown near the coast from Florida to Georgetown, South Carolina. Although susceptible to damage by spring frost and autumn fog, it was grown successfully and shipped abroad through Charleston, Beaufort, and Savannah until the boll weevil ruined the crop in the early twentieth century. Short-staple, or "upland cotton," more difficult to weave in mechanical looms, was neither as strong nor felt as luxurious as sea-island cotton, and therefore never commanded as high a price. Methods of extracting seed from long-staple, or sea-island, cotton had been perfected earlier, but short-staple cotton remained of no commercial value until the new ginning technology introduced in the early 1790s by Eli Whitney. Thereafter, since short-staple cotton could be grown in a far wider region than the sea-island cotton, it spread, and slavery with it, across the backcountry to make money for both backcountry farmers and lowcountry merchants. This agricultural revolution also silenced backcountry opposition to slavery and blunted lowcountry hostility toward the backcountry. For years the upland cotton was exported almost exclusively through Charleston, making the local merchants less dependent on lowcountry planters for exports. Both the long- and short-staple cotton crops were planted in the spring, picked from September to October, ginned and compressed during October and November, and then carried to local ports for shipment to English and European manufacturing centers.[11]

New Institutions

The unique pluralism of Charleston was reflected in the continuing growth in the numbers of various religious groups, especially Lutherans, Jews, and Catholics in that order. On February 19, 1791, the congregation of St. Mary's was incorporated as the Roman Catholic Church of Charleston, and the Jewish Congregation of Beth Elohim also was incorporated under articles of the newly adopted state constitution permitting the practice of religion without discrimination. Within a few years Charleston had the largest community of Jews in the United States and the Catholics had founded the Hibernian Society, an organization concerned with the welfare and social life of Roman Catholics.

Other new institutions emerged as prosperity returned. In 1790 the College of Charleston, incorporated five years earlier as a private institution, opened its doors to students. Its grounds were bounded on the west by Coming Street, on the east by St. Philip's Street, to the south by George Street, and on the north by Boundary Street. For a variety of reasons the college struggled along for years as primarily a grammar school with few students and many debts.[12]

When the president of the new nation, George Washington, visited Charleston for the first and only time, from May 2–9, 1791, he commended the city for its commitment to institutional care of the city's orphans. Annually the City Council inducted a board of twelve commissioners who were to oversee the construction and operation of the Orphan House. By the mid-1790s a large four-story brick orphanage designed by Thomas Bennett was completed and in the 1850s enlarged along the lines of the then popular Italian Style. Gabriel Manigault drew the plans for the separate chapel for the Orphan House, which was built in the front of the orphanage between 1801–2 and faced south on Boundary Street. Carved above the entranceway to the chapel was the text: "The Poor Shall have the Gospel preached unto them."

In 1792 a branch of the First Bank of the United States opened in Charleston and the "Charleston Theatre" was being constructed on the edge of Savage's Green, at the triangular Corner where Middleton (later New) Street intersected Broad Street. Promoted by two experienced London theater managers, it was modeled after London opera houses and could seat 1,200 persons. That same year the lowcountry gentry organized another

The Charleston Orphan House, topped by the figure of "Charity," 1790s–1950s. *Courtesy of the Charleston Museum, Charleston, S.C.*

formal form of recreation when the fourth South Carolina Jockey Club ran its first race on February 15, 1793, at its recently acquired Washington race course. Race week became the highlight of the social season as the lowcountry planters and their families flocked to the city for rounds of parties and balls. John Randolph, the Virginian, who was not easily impressed, visited the gaily decorated race course in February 1796 and enjoyed "the display of beautiful women, gallant fellows, and elegant equipages . . . ." By the early 1790s Vanderhorst Creek had been drained and filled, the resulting land being named Water Street, and the creek slicing westward into the city off the Cooper and flowing under Governor's Bridge was filled in for a market place.[13]

England vs. France

The outbreak of war between England and Revolutionary France on February 1, 1793, fueled the recovery. Officially America remained neutral and the trade in raw materials and foodstuffs was reopened with France and the French West Indies and subsequently with England. It brought to a few Charlestonians—Nathaniel Russell, William Blacklock, Josiah Smith, Thomas Radcliffe, and Adam Tunno especially—the last great wealth amassed in the carrying trade, and they displayed it in the grand mansions they built. More homes constructed during this Federal period, an era of great prosperity that lasted until the Embargo of 1807, still stand in the city today than from any other period.

Edmond Charles Genet, the French minister to the United States, arrived in Charleston in April to organize privateering against England, and Jean Bouteille and his ship *La Sans Pareille* arrived in July to launch raids on English shipping. Republican societies and Jacobin clubs were organized and mainly supported by the lesser tradesmen, but the strong attachment of the great merchants to England and the love of the propertied classes for an ordered society made many feel closer to England.

By late 1793 compressed bales of short-staple cotton crowded Charleston's wharfs. After the collapse of the indigo market in the late 1790s because of the competition from British India, the local export trade was based primarily on rice and cotton. In 1791, South Carolina grew 1,500,000 pounds of cotton, a decade later, 20 million, and production doubled again within the next ten years. The pulse of the city beat regularly again to the rhythms of the agricultural seasons: with the harvest peaking in

October, boats and schooners came down the rivers and along the coast carrying bales of cotton and rough rice for milling and shipment, commercial life boomed along the wharves, and country shoppers flocked into King Street stores until business slowed just before Christmas, reviving again from January to April as ocean-going vessels jammed the harbor competing for freight runs to Liverpool or Le Havre. By June the harbor had nearly emptied, and those who could afford it left Charleston as a hot and steamy summer enveloped the now quiet waterfront.

Lowcountry planters came to look down on those in trade, probably because British merchants tainted as Tories came to monopolize commerce in Charleston. From the mid-1790s until about 1820 only one of the twenty-one foremost trading houses in the city was owned or managed by a native Carolinian. The *City Gazette* observed that by the 1790s "the aristocracy" thought it "disreputable to attend to business of almost any kind." Over a decade later Henry Gourdin took a position in a Charleston export firm and his brother remarked that he was the first planter's son "to embark in a business on which the elite of the community looked down." This new hostility to business as a career may have resulted from the growing attitude that the retailing trade was the occupation of "Yankees" and Jews, as by the 1790s a number of Jewish families were emerging as prosperous retailers. Other observers reasoned simply that Charlestonians avoided the "tedious course of business" and manufacturing because they were lazy.[14]

Immigrants, Anxieties, and Culture

While the economic prospects of many Charlestonians brightened, black and white refugees fleeing from French Santo Domingo in 1791 told dark tales of rape, "murder . . . blood and flames." The slave rebellion there was the most successful in the Western world, and it haunted Charleston for three generations. Local officials searched incoming vessels from Santo Domingo to prevent blacks immigrating from there, and in September 1793 a mob stormed the home of a prominent free black looking for weapons. The following year the state legislature prohibited entry into the state of Afro-Americans either free or bond and required all able-bodied white males between the ages of eighteen and forty-five to enroll in a militia company. If the local police were inadequate to suppress a disorder or insurrection, the gov-

1783–1800 " . . . the public weal . . . at stake"

"View of Broad Street," circa 1796, from a Charles Fraser Sketch Book on deposit at the South Carolina Historical Society, showing the William Pitt statue at the intersection of Broad and Meeting streets, St. Michael's on the right, the Exchange at the foot of Broad, and the recently completed courthouse on the site of the old State House to the left. It was used as a backdrop for a theater in Charleston in 1796. *Courtesy of the Estate of Maud Winthrop Gibbon, South Carolina Historical Society, Charleston, S.C.*

ernor was authorized to call out the militia. The Militia Act was greeted enthusiastically in the lowcountry where there was the long-held conviction that public displays of men in arms were necessary for social order.[15]

The new prosperity attracted a record number of cabinet-makers to Charleston—over sixty-three by the early 1790s—and new silversmiths whose output reached a peak at the end of the decade. John Trumbull, who was commissioned by the City Council to paint a portrait of Washington, visited the city in 1791, and artists from the French West Indies and refugees from revolutions flocked to Charleston. In 1794 the accomplished entrepreneur, Paris-born ballet dancer and pantomimist Alexander Placide, established a French-language playhouse with a company of come-

dians and pantomimists in a brick building on the west side of
Church Street between St. Michael's Alley and Tradd Street.
Known as the "City," "Church Street," or "French Theatre,"
it became a rival of the Charleston Theatre, which was known
as the Federalist's or pro-English playhouse. Patronized by the
well-to-do, both houses enjoyed great success during the last
years of the eighteenth century. When the Charleston Theatre
installed an air pump in June 1794 for the benefit of patrons,
its rival, the French playhouse, six days later boasted of "a
Fan" which provides "a pleasing coolness" for theater-goers.
Placide, like his players, was involved in several scandals, eventually closed his French Theatre, and took over the management of the Charleston Theatre. To keep and attract well-to-do
Charleston audiences, Placide added such novelties as tum-
bling, bird calls, and tight-rope walking.

With the arrival of the French, the quality of musical performances improved and an amazing number of musical organizations emerged. In the 1790s there was a symphony orchestra, two
theater orchestras, a chorus for the opera, and frequent public
and private concerts. This influx of foreigners, especially vulnerable to local fevers and recurring epidemics, the persistence of
unsanitary conditions, and demands by influential citizens led to
the creation of the city's first Board of Health in 1796. Subsequent boards were selected by the City Council and dominated
by the local Medical Society, which had been incorporated two
years before.

The French immigrants took jobs as dressmakers, musicians,
and teachers, started a newspaper, *Le Patriote Français*, and
added to the growing Catholic congregation on Hasell Street.
Sarah Rutledge's *The Carolina Housewife*, first published in 1847,
reflects the substantial influence of French cuisine in Charleston.
The French refugees from Santo Domingo also brought their fears
of slave insurrections, and the chronic local anxieties quickened
when a group of twenty-three itinerant Methodist ministers met
in Charleston in January 1795 and issued a call for the immediate
emancipation of slaves.[16]

On June 13 a fire began in Lodge Alley, swept out of control
and burned along Queen, Union (later State), and Church streets,
destroying every house on Queen Street from Bay to Church
streets, the Huguenot Church, and threatened St. Philip's
Church. When still other fires broke out, arson suspects were

clapped into jail. Some citizens believed that both local and "French Negroes . . . intended to make a St. Domingo business of it." Yet, at least one prominent Charlestonian thought "that these suspicions arose rather from the affrighted imaginations of the people . . . than from any real grounds of suspicion."[17]

On November 14, 1797, several "French Negroes" were charged with plotting to murder white people and "fire . . . the town . . . ." On the testimony of slave witnesses, two slaves were banished and three were sentenced to death by hanging for treason against the state. On December 2 they went to their deaths protesting their innocence. A few days later the city's elite petitioned the state legislature to establish a permanent "Guard" composed of infantry and cavalry in Charleston, as "conspiracies of Negroes . . . may there by fire . . . effect . . . disasters in a short time." One white transient was tried and found guilty of "having talked wildly in the moment of intoxication about conspiracy and house burning." Unable to pay a fine of $10,000, he was sentenced to two years in prison.

South Carolina legislators renewed the prohibitions against the importation of slaves from 1792 to 1803. Yet white Charlestonians continued to believe it would take only the slightest encouragement for conspirators to "lay the firebrand to our houses and the daggers to our throats." The Mutual Insurance Company for protection against fire and the Charleston Insurance Company for marine insurance were incorporated in 1797, the first incorporated in the state.[18]

With the outbreak of the undeclared naval war between the United States and France in 1797, a fortification on Shute's Folly, a shoal in the harbor a short distance from the tip of the peninsula, was rushed to completion with the aid of federal appropriations. It was named Castle Pinckney after the locally prominent family. The fear of invasion prompted a mass meeting in St. Michael's Church in May 1798, and in July Governor Pinckney asked the state's legislators to meet in Charleston to discuss actions for defending the state. The next year a public subscription was used to build the sloop-of-war *John Adams*, named after the Federalist president, but by this time diplomatic efforts brought an end to the quasi-war with France.

During December 1799 the city's first public utility, the Charleston Water Company, was chartered to pump water from Goose Creek, and the indomitable Alexander Placide opened an extensive garden, or Vaux Hall, on the northeast corner of Broad and Friend (later Legare) streets. Although the concert and social season ran from November to May, Placide hoped to continue outdoor musical entertainments in the evening during the summer months. For a small fee patrons could enjoy instrumental music and vocalists, refreshments, fireworks, strolls through the gardens, public baths, and even elephants! In 1800 a branch office of the First Bank of the United States, designed by Gabriel Manigault, went up on the northeast corner of Broad and

This is *Plate 231: Long-billed Curlew* in *Birds of America* by John James Audubon, who completed it in November 1831. *Courtesy of the Charleston Museum, Charleston, S.C.*

Meeting streets where the Market House had burned four years earlier. The imposing, magnificent building eventually became City Hall. The Santee Canal also opened that year, the second important canal in the United States, and, with the rivers and wagon paths, forged another link between Charleston and the interior. It became a primary carrier of the new boom crop, cotton.[19]

Charleston in the year 1800 with a population of 10,104 blacks, both slave and free, and 8,820 whites, had slipped to fifth in size, behind New York, 60,515, Philadelphia, 40,220, Baltimore, 26,514, and Boston, 24,937. The Methodist bishop Francis

Asbury visited the Orphan House on February 5, 1800, and praised it as unequaled in America, but he repeatedly denounced Charleston for its wicked and frivolous ways. That same year long-smoldering fears of the possible threat of slave revolts suddenly exploded: two white Methodist ministers, apparently colleagues of Bishop Asbury suspected of preaching insurrection to local slaves, were seized by mobs and driven out of the city. In a private letter Charlestonian Jacob Read summarized the view of the elite: "violence" is justified "when the public weal is at stake." It is a recurrent theme in Charleston's history: the use of violence in the name of the social order was no crime.

Lotteries were frequently used to raise funds for charities and public works in Charleston, and in 1800 a remarkably intelligent slave called Denmark bought a chance in the East Bay Lottery. In his early thirties, he could read, write, and speak several languages and belonged to Captain Joseph Vesey. Black folklore has it that he came from the island of St. Thomas in the Danish West Indies. His name is one of the best known in Charleston, but Denmark Vesey remains an enigmatic and controversial figure. Captain Vesey employed him on a ship that traded regularly between St. Thomas, Santo Domingo, and Charleston, where he probably picked up the name Denmark as an anglicization of Telemaque, his original name, one influenced by the Danish heritage of St. Thomas. He won $1,500 in the lottery and promptly bought his freedom for $600. He set himself up in business as a carpenter and became a skilled and prosperous craftsman, amassing several thousand dollars' worth of property, including a home at 20 Bull Street, took several wives, and was an active participant in the African Church of Charleston founded in 1818. Vesey was well known among the city slaves and by those on lowcountry plantations. But his growing wealth, powerful personality, sophistication, and quick mind brought him enemies as well as friends.[20]

❧ 2. 1801–1819:
Black Slaves, White Cotton

Boom Times

The rapid expansion of rice- and cotton-growing and the fabulous prices commanded by these commodities fueled Charleston's longest boom. Lowcountry planters, speculators, and would-be slave-traders, mindful of the enormous profits made before the Revolution, demanded that the state reopen the slave trade. With the lowcountry delegation split, the South Carolina legislature voted by a narrow margin to reopen the foreign traffic in slaves, which resumed on December 17, 1803, and continued until prohibited by the United States Constitution on January 1, 1808. Overnight, one Charleston businessman wrote, "Vessels were fitted out in numbers for the coast of Africa, and as fast as they returned, their cargoes were bought up with avidity." Over the next several years nearly 40,000 slaves were brought into Charleston and shipowners, ship captains and crews, and merchants profited handsomely. As in past boom times, the export-import merchants plowed their new wealth into land; planters, too, taking advantage of low interest rates and an inflated currency, mortgaged their estates for more land, slaves, and luxuries.[21]

Auctions of both foreign and domestic slaves were held publicly in the streets near the Exchange, like Vendue Range, and this vicinity remained a favorite location of slave-traders throughout the antebellum period, though auctions were conducted elsewhere in the city. The Englishwoman Harriet Martineau was deeply disturbed at a slave auction in Charleston where she witnessed the sale of "a mulatto . . . woman . . . with two children, one at breast, and another holding by her apron." She believed that "the jocose zeal of the auctioneer . . . was the most infernal sight I ever beheld." Advertisements of slave auctions were placed in both the Republican and Federalist papers, the *City Gazette* and the Charleston *Courier*; the latter first began publication on January 10, 1803, and continues today as the *News and Courier*.[22]

The resumption of the African trade brought changes observed by Ebenezer S. Thomas, one of the four book dealers in Charleston, who remarked that the planters became so absorbed in buying slaves that they had neither time nor money for anything else. And while opposition to slavery was rising in England and France and was beginning to be heard in New England, the influx of new Africans made Charlestonians increasingly sensitive to any criticism of the institution. In July 1804 John James Negrin, an immigrant printer, was arrested for selling the pamphlet, *A Declaration of Independence of the French Colony of Santo Domingo by Dessalines*. Charged with intending "to excite domestic insurrection and disturbing the peace of the community," Negrin spent eight months in confinement, during which city authorities permitted the sale of his means of livelihood, his printing presses. Upon release Negrin was destitute and his health impaired. Such violent responses by the local oligarchy represented a historic continuum of their efforts to wall off the city from people and ideas perceived as threatening to slavery.[23]

In 1804 a hurricane roared in during the late summer with destructive winds, torrential rains, and on a rising tide. Eyewitnesses recalled that the storm put "a great part of Charleston under water . . . in some places breast deep." Since many Charlestonians relied on shallow wells and cisterns for water, such storms undoubtedly mixed privy wastes and drinking water, partly explaining the outbreaks of cholera, diarrhea, and dysentery.

The Board of Health and city officials kept mortality records, promoted Jennerian vaccination against smallpox, and tried to keep the city clean. It was widely believed that the miasma created by "warmth and moisture on the filthy drains and cellars," and sometimes impure westerly winds, caused disease, and citizens were instructed to dump quick lime in coffins upon burial and in privies once a month. Goats and swine were prohibited within the city limits, privately owned low-lying lots were to be drained or filled, cellars ventilated and pumped dry, and people were prohibited from dumping garbage and trash within the city. The commissioners of the streets and lamps and the city marshal were empowered to enforce these regulations, and state and city officials were authorized to declare maritime quarantines. Two city garbage collectors accompanied by three blacks with horse-drawn carts "painted red, numbered, and marked with the words 'Scavenger's Cart,' " were to patrol the city daily to dispose of "all the rubbish . . . and to keep drains open." The City Council also allocated money to pave and enlarge the streets, to wash down the wharves and market, and to plant trees for "pure and vital air." Yet the council was unwilling to tax or spend enough to fund these projects fully.

Efforts to clean up Charleston did little to stem the outbreak of epidemical disease. Yellow fever and malaria were the major killers. Between 1800 and 1860 there were twenty-five epidemics of the former. Dosages of thirty or more grains of calomel usually prescribed by physicians, and purging, vomiting, and sweating the patient probably did more harm than good. Sporadically, the epidemics of influenza, dengue fever, smallpox, scarlet fever, diphtheria, cholera, measles, and tuberculosis also scourged the antebellum city. John C. Calhoun sniffed in 1807 that the prevalence of the fever in Charleston was simply "a curse for their intemperance and debaucharies."[24]

The reopening of the slave trade brought thousands of recently enslaved Africans into Charleston, and the City Council in 1806 enacted a strict ordinance regarding "negroes." Slaves and people of color, under threat of whippings and fines, were prohibited from assembling in numbers greater than seven except for funerals or in the presence of a white person; nor could they gather for "dancing or merriment" without permission; they were prohibited from selling most articles and from employment unless they possessed a license or displayed a badge purchased from the city; they were prohibited from "whooping or holloring" in the streets, from smoking a "pipe or segar," and from walking with a "cane, club, or other stick" unless "blind or infirm."

Also in 1806 the City Council replaced the elected police force, which consisted of two constables in each ward, and increased the City Guard to about seventy members who were paid a monthly salary for preventing disorder and enforcing the new "Negro" law. They were to protect the streets and alleys at night, "to apprehend . . . all disturbers of the public peace . . . ," and to arrest all "persons of colour . . . who after the beating of the tattoo," the nine o'clock curfew, were in the streets unlawfully. In case of fire they sounded the alarm by cries or rattles they carried and assisted the volunteer firefighters. Designed as a para-military force to awe criminals and blacks, members of the City Guard carried muskets and bayonets and wore a uniform of "buff and blue." They were drilled daily before their Guard House on the southeastern corner of Meeting and Broad streets. From here they sallied forth in random patrols of twenty to thirty men to keep law and order.[25]

Dueling

The gentry enjoyed uniforms, arms, and fine horses, symbols and prerogatives of their class and proof of their manliness, as was the duel. The rules specified pistols at thirty feet and were adhered to closely. The local elite came to regard this *code duello*, "the affair of honor," as the method for seeking satisfaction of real or imagined insults or disputes. The Washington Race Course was a favorite site of the combatants. One traveler from the North observed: "To fight a duel in the New England states would, under almost any circumstances, be disgraceful. To refuse a challenge, to tolerate even an insinuation derogatory from personal honour, would be considered equally so in the South." Ralph Waldo Emerson, who attended Harvard with Charlestonians and visited the city in the early 1800s, later wrote of "the shooting complexion," the Southern penchant for violence—he believed that Charleston represented the epitome of the trait.

One of the first antidueling petitions to reach the new state legislature was sent by the Charleston Baptist Association in 1805. Two years later, following the dueling deaths of three young men of prominent local families, newspapers condemned the so-called affairs of honor. The Reverend Nathaniel D. Bowen of St. Michael's Church preached a sermon urging his congregation to strip dueling "of the respectability it has borrowed from illustrious names, and consign it to the contempt" it deserved, but a member of the prominent lowcountry Ball family noted that despite "the fine sermons on duelling, it is still in vogue among our young Bucks." The older, wiser heads among the city's elite denounced dueling because they recognized its potential threat to their class and the social order. Especially, it set a bad example for the lesser classes in that it subordinated law and authority to personal gratification where "the bowie knife, the pistol and the sword, [became] the only standards of right and wrong." This was something to take note of in a city teeming with a large transient, seafaring, and slave population. Five years after the three tragic deaths, the continuing public outcry resulted in the passage by the state legislature of "an Act to Prevent the Pernicious Practice of Duelling." Parties to a duel could be imprisoned, fined, barred from professions and, if a death occurred during a duel, the survivors could be tried for homicide. Now more of the sons of the oligarchy sought satisfaction to remedy real or imagined insults in the courtroom rather than on the "field of honor."[26]

Era of the War of 1812

As the Napoleonic wars raged in Europe and on the high seas, the American Congress in an attempt to find a way to prevent the country from being sucked into the maelstrom passed the Trade Embargo Act of 1807, which went into effect in December and closed U.S. ports to the export-import trade. The following month, on January 1, 1808, further slave importations were prohibited by the Constitution. Planters, merchants, mariners, slave-auctioneers, professional people, and artisans all felt the economic effects of the trade restrictions. As cotton bales piled up in the idled port, several entrepreneurs laid the cornerstone for the Charleston Homespun Company at the west end of Wentworth Street in October 1808. Two months later it was the first manufacturing company to be incorporated in South Carolina. This cotton mill was among the first of numerous industries, but like the others locating in the city and in accord with the wishes of the wealthy planters who owned homes there, it was built on the periphery of Charleston. The Homespun mill failed by 1815.

In December 1808 lowcountry legislators agreed to a compromise that amended the state constitution to give the upcountry more representation, and in 1809 the City Council consolidated Charleston's thirteen wards into four larger and more manageable ones.

One of the indirect effects of the trade embargo and the end of the slave trade was the closing of the Vaux Hall gardens in 1809 even though the promotional efforts of Alexander Placide had been spectacular. The failures of subsequent, similar enterprises also signaled a deeper malaise: the "carriage trade," the 7 percent of the population who could afford such entertainment, had stopped growing. Only the open-air concerts given during the summers in White Point Gardens and partially subsidized by the City Council remained ever popular.[27]

In early October 1812 a catastrophic fire roared along Church to Queen Street and into Broad Street, destroying nearly 200 houses. The City Council once more sought ways to control fires, but were distracted when the United States declared war against Great Britain in 1812 and Charlestonians again enthusiastically plunged into the privateering business. The *Saucy Jack* of 170 tons and 130 men and the *Decatur* of 240 tons, both constructed by the local boatbuilders Pritchard and Shrewsbury, were the most successful of the dozen or so privateers out of Charleston that eluded the British blockading fleet to take British and Spanish merchantmen as prizes. Forts Moultrie and Johnson and Castle Pinckney were garrisoned and armed with federal funds; the Battery got its name during the war when fifteen guns of large caliber were mounted there and aimed toward the open harbor.

With enemy ships hovering off the coast in May 1813 Governor Joseph Alston sent word to the Charleston militia to guard the local powder magazines, but members of the four companies refused, foreseeing no emergency and unwilling to leave their own occupations for even temporary guard duty. In August Governor Alston attempted to prosecute the militiamen for mutiny, but the courts dismissed the suit. On August 27–28 a great hurricane slammed into the coast near Charleston, wreaking devastation only slightly less than the earlier one of 1752 and the later one of 1893. The following year, when the nation's capital fell to the British, the government at Charleston began issuing paper money, but it was disallowed by the legislature. Charlestonians found it difficult to accept governance from Columbia even when the governor was a lowcountry Carolinian. Fearing a landside invasion in August 1814, the city again built a line of fortifications across the Neck, which followed the course of today's appropriately named Line Street, and the specie in the city banks was rushed to Columbia for safekeeping. Amid these tensions, a fire broke out and "Sally, a mulatto girl about 15 years old," was arrested for arson. Tried and convicted for "setting her master's house afire," she was summarily executed.[28]

During the war the number of inmates increased dramatically in the three-story brick building completed in 1771 near the corner of Mazyck Street (Logan Street today) and Magazine Street, which still served as the city's Poor House. Those inmates certified by the Poor House physician as physically and mentally able were expected to work. Like those charged with overseeing the care of the indigent in Northern cities, Charleston's commissioners of the poor believed that the best way to preserve "the peace . . . correct . . . the public morals and prevent . . . the spread of Pauperism is to compel those to labor whose sufferings proceed from Idleness and Intemperance." Hence the inmates usually were kept busy at a variety of jobs. Those who were "refractory" were placed in solitary confinement on bread and water. The hospital ward of the Poor House served as a medical laboratory for the city physicians, and the "lunatics," who "filled the house with their unearthly whoopings and hallooings," usually were kept in the basement cells. One of these insane whom the historian and physician David Ramsay committed, but who remained at large, fatally shot Ramsay in the streets of Charleston in 1815. Also that year, in its issue of February 14, the Charleston *Courier* announced the end of the war and the signing of the Treaty of Ghent.[29]

The Postwar Boom in Rice and Cotton

Soon after the hostilities ended, the renovated Charleston Theatre reopened under the direction of an experienced British-born actor-manager. The remodeling of the theater made the seats in the pit and those in the two tiers of boxes partially encircling it the best in the house. A third tier, or gallery, was reserved for the "lesser social classes." Following an act of 1818, "Persons of color whether bond or free" were "not admitted to any part of the house." Throughout the antebellum years there were few affordable, legitimate entertainments for the laboring classes besides occasional public fireworks, balloon ascents, or traveling menageries that included lions, leopards, giraffes, and monkeys.[30]

Planters on the sea islands to the south of Charleston enjoyed postwar boom prices for their long-staple cotton from 1815 to 1819 as demand in Europe soared. On February 20, 1817, the *Courier* reported that exports from South Carolina in 1816, valued at $10,849,409, mainly cotton, were second only to the exports of New York, which were valued at $19,690,031. Planters of short-staple cotton were enjoying an equal bonanza and in 1818 its price hit a record of 35 cents per pound, the peak of cotton prices during the antebellum period. The planters invested some of their enormous profits in the Second Bank of the United States (1816), whose charter was written by John C. Calhoun, and some they spent conspicuously on sea-island mansions and summer homes in the city. These spacious town houses with ample piazzas went up in Wraggsborough, Mazyckborough, and Radcliffeborough. Most of the summer residents, planters and their families, like the city's merchant and professional elite, were Episcopalians, and a third Episcopal church, St. Paul's, was built between 1810 and 1815 in the parish of Radcliffeborough on Coming Street, just to the north of Boundary Street. This spacious brick and rough-cast church was the largest in the city. Over the next several decades other congregations were organized. Each was dominated by the first families of the city and county and included communicants from the lesser classes.

Rice planters were enjoying big profits too. The first steam-powered rice mill for pounding of threshed rice to remove the husks and to polish the grains was established by the skilled laborers of the Jonathan Lucas family and was a booming enterprise by 1817. That summer a virulent outbreak of yellow fever brought commerce to a standstill, but in late November Thomas Weyman wrote to his brother: "Business now begins to make its appearance & everything once more appears lively." The statue of William Pitt at the busy intersection of Broad and Meeting streets had become a traffic hazard and was removed in 1818 and placed in the courtyard of the Orphan House.[31]

Capital of the Plantations

To the great rice and cotton planters, many with familiar eighteenth-century lowcountry names—Alston, Coffin, Deas, Heyward, Horry, Izard, Legarè, Lowndes, Manigault, Middleton, Pinckney, Pringle, Rutledge, and Vanderhorst—Charleston was the social and cultural capital of the plantations. From late January through March they brought their families and their household slaves into the city for the annual season of horse races, balls, concerts, and theatrical performances. Some stayed in hotels or with family and friends while others took up residence in their summer homes to which they returned in May and remained until the first frosts of fall to escape the so-called sickly season on the plantations. Both laypersons and physicians believed that the miasma rising nightly from the lowcountry swamps caused malaria ("the country fever").[32]

Despite the risks of epidemics in Charleston during the summer months, the planters welcomed the refreshing sea breezes that swept the city. Here too the planters and their families could escape the isolation of their plantations, socialize with the wealthy professional and merchant families, and through their offspring continue the pattern of intermarriages or alliances established in the eighteenth century. When the young William Gilmore Simms returned to his native city of Charleston to study law, his planter-father in Mississippi advised against it: "Why . . . return . . . where you can never succeed in any profession, where you need what you have not, friends, family, and fortune?"

The emphasis of the planters on family connections, landed wealth, agreeable manners, sociability, and conspicuous leisure influenced Charleston far in excess of the actual representation of planters in the governing circles of City Hall. Visitors noticed this and one remarked that there is "a class of . . . closely associated" wealthy citizens who "think and act precisely as do the nobility in other countries." Indeed, the importance of family and ancestry to the lowcountry gentry is dramatized in the antebellum doggerel: "I thank thee Lord on bended knee I'm half Porcher and half Huger . . . . For other blessings thank thee too—My grandpa was a Petigru."[33]

The young architect and native Charlestonian Robert Mills also described the "exclusiveness" of the elite after he returned in 1817 to the city where years before he had launched the Classical Revival Style with his pantheon-like Congregational Church (1806). He would soon begin the First Baptist Church (1819–22) and somewhat later the Fireproof Building (1822–27), home today to the South Carolina Historical Society. Mills attended the Jockey Club Ball, a highlight of the annual social season, and found "none but the higher classes attending." At the annual Jockey Club races in February, while a crowd of several thousand encircled the mile of track to watch, wager bets, and cheer on the horses, the choice seats in the tiny grandstand were limited to the members and friends of the exclusive Jockey Club.

During the annual social season the festivities were both exhilarating and exhausting. One participant wrote: "We have had one month of incessant gaiety. Ball has succeeded to Ball, dinner to dinner, concert to concert, & Masquerade to Masquerade." It was a time for marriages between elite, which Charleston's premier antebellum raconteur, William Gilmore Simms, believed sapped the vigor of the ruling elite. He told the tale of the lowcountry "colonel" who married three cousins one after another and the "natural consequence was physical and moral imbecility."[34]

A dissolute lifestyle contributed to the wild behavior of supposedly "well bred" young gentlemen during gala gatherings. The insistence of the great lowcountry planters on the subordination of their sons and the latter's dependence on inheritance undermined the personal industry and motivation of the sons and encouraged idleness. A contemporary recalled that there was a whole "class of young men from Charleston . . . whose parents were . . . wealthy planters, who, after school or college . . . spent many years before marriage, in perfect idleness." A Scottish visitor who mingled with the well-to-do males observed that at their clubs "day light often surprises them at the gambling table exhausted with fatigue & tortured with unsuccess." The women, he noted, "frequently expatiate with regret on the vices of their countrymen who they say are fonder of their Cards and Brandy and Segars than their Company."[35]

Samuel Morse came to Charleston during the social season of 1818 to paint the wealthy and he was introduced to Charleston's "people of fashion" and promptly was overwhelmed with commissions. Morse created portraits of the wealthiest and most influential men in Carolina—General Charles Cotesworth Pinckney, the Honorable John Ashe Alston, Dr. Alexander Baron, Judge Henry DeSaussure, Major Simeon Theus, and Colonel William Drayton. By the end of his first season in May 1818 he had begun more than sixty portraits and earned over $4,000. He returned in November 1818 to find thirteen other painters in the city including the ever popular Charles Fraser, whose career as a miniaturist in Charleston spanned the years from 1815 to 1850; but despite the competition Morse remained in great demand and earned over $5,000. He returned to Charleston for a third social season in 1819, but Morse observed that patronage of the arts by "the fashionable few" had declined. That same year the New England Society of Charleston was organized at the Carolina Coffee House at the corner of Tradd Street and Bedon's Alley by Northern cloth manufacturers who had been coming to Charleston to buy cotton for their new mills.

In spring 1819 overproduction led to a worldwide collapse of cotton prices, which lasted for years; also the opening of the vast, fertile lands of the Southwest lured away upcountry South Carolina cotton planters, and the port cities of Mobile and New Orleans rapidly emerged as the major depots for the new "Cotton Kingdom." Navigational improvements on South Carolina's waterways and the advent of the steamboat provided upcountry cotton planters a faster and less expensive means than the horse-drawn wagon of getting their crops to Charleston. The hundreds of wagoners who annually brought the crop to the city fell by three-quarters over the next several years. The small retailers in upper King Street, the heart of Charleston's economy, who formerly bartered goods for the wagoner's cotton, and the skilled artisans who repaired the wagoner's equipment were ruined financially. As new market towns sprang up farmers hauled their cotton there to sell and less of the staple came to Charleston. The city also was losing its century-long preeminence among American port cities. Steam-powered vessels no longer had to follow the trade winds into Southern ports, and more direct, financially rewarding routes were opening between England and the fast-growing Northern cities.[36]

The city's booms and busts were getting longer. After nearly twenty-five years of prosperity, a long period of economic stagnation and a mood close to despair were setting in.

❧ 3. 1820–1836: "... this once flourishing city"

In May 1820 Congress designated Charleston as one of the eight Atlantic ports where foreign armed vessels were permitted to enter. Although this act did not save the deteriorating economy, it seems to have brought business to local brothels. After repeated complaints of grand juries, the City Council in 1821 forbade dance halls "where women notoriously of ill fame are entertained for the purpose of dancing with . . . persons as visit such places," but city officials got into the habit of ignoring this prohibition.

During the social season of 1821 Samuel Morse joined with local art patrons to organize the Carolina Academy of Fine Arts and to oversee the construction of a small temple in the Greek Revival Style on Broad Street to house its collection. After 1821 Morse and many other talented artists never returned to the city and the academy, which raised little money locally and failed to get state support, eventually closed.

The influence of the city in the state capital was slowly ebbing—fewer and fewer governors would hail from Charleston—but the process was very gradual. Indeed, the consecration of John England as the first Roman Catholic bishop of South Carolina in 1821 brought Charleston recognition as the capital of Catholicism in both the Carolinas and Georgia. England became a dynamic activist bishop, involving himself in the affairs of the community, until his death over twenty years later.[37]

Women and Slavery

In May 1821 Sarah Grimké, the eldest daughter of Charleston's eminent jurist John F. Grimké, sailed for Philadelphia where she would be strongly influenced by the abolitionist movement. Eventually Sarah and her sister Angelina, repulsed by the local cruelty to slaves would leave Charleston permanently for the North where they themselves became abolitionists and advocates of women's rights. They were remarkable women. While growing up Sarah discovered that some of the most diabolical punishments of slaves occurred at the hands of the "first families of Charleston." On one occasion a female friend told her "that she had the ears of her waiting maid slit for some petty theft."

As in the lowcountry of the eighteenth century, miscegenation was not uncommon during the antebellum years. Unlike the Grimké sisters who opposed slavery on humanitarian grounds, some women of the slaveholding class quietly opposed it for the immorality that slavery fostered and the opportunities it offered their husbands for interracial sex. Mary Boykin Chesnut, who knew the lowcountry so well, wrote: "Like the patriarchs of old, our men live all in one house with their wives and their concubines; and the mulattoes one sees in every family partly resemble the white children. Any lady is ready to tell you who the father is of all the mulatto children in everybody's household but her own." Well-to-do white, male Charlestonians sometimes provided for their slave mistresses in their wills or petitioned the legislature for the freedom of their offspring, since after 1820 no slave was to be freed in South Carolina without the special consent of the legislature. In 1821 Philippe Noisette, a Charleston botanist, asked the legislature to emancipate his six children "begotten upon his faithful slave . . . Celestine." When antislavery writers denounced Southern slaveholders for sexual promiscuity with slave women, lowcountry Carolinians defended the practice, William Gilmore Simms arguing that "The negro and the colored woman in the South supply the place, which at the north is usually filled with factory and serving girls."[38]

The Brown Elite

Unlike other Southern states, South Carolina did not prohibit interracial marriage until after the Civil War and in Charleston there were occasional marriages between mulattoes and well-regarded whites. Among Charleston's brown elite were approximately 500 free mulattoes laced together by intermarriage within a free Afro-American population of more than 3,000, many of whom were slaveholders themselves. Rivaled in numbers only by those of New Orleans, Charleston's brown elite was an aristocracy of status, color, and wealth. One of them astutely reflected: "An amalgamation of the races produced us" and the hostility of both black and white is "the whirlpool which threatens to swallow us up." The brown elite generally looked down on blacks and many identified more closely with their white patrons than they did with blacks.[39]

Denmark Vesey

Emotionally charged debates in Congress from 1818 to 1821 over whether or not to admit Missouri as a slave state revealed to Charlestonians the extent of Northern hostility to slaveownership. Charles Pinckney, a member of the wealthy lowcountry oligarchy and a member of Congress, spoke for most white Charlestonians in his eloquent defense of slavery and attack on the North. Pinckney was one of the first to articulate publicly the extreme Southern sectionalism that more and more white Southerners came to embrace.

By 1820 some 58 percent of the population of Charleston was black, and whites were alarmed by rumors that, contrary to state law, blacks were being taught to read and write by Northerners sent to the city by abolitionist societies. Also there were repeated clashes between the City Council and free black leaders like the Reverend Morris Brown, pastor of the African Methodist Episcopal (A.M.E.) Church on Reid and Hanover streets, who had been briefly jailed in 1818 and remained in touch with leaders of the new A.M.E. Church of Philadelphia. White Charlestonians believed that the local A.M.E. Church harbored abolitionists and that it had been built with funds from Northern antislavery societies. In 1821 city authorities ordered the church closed and its nearly 3,000 black worshipers reluctantly joined the white Methodist churches of the city. By 1821 Charlestonians more than ever were convinced that free blacks were "a bad example to our Domestics & a growing evil to our State."[40]

On May 25, 1822, two slaves, William Paul and Peter Desverneys, met on a wharf near the fish market and before long

Paul was telling Desverneys that some white people were going to be killed by their slaves who were plotting to seize their freedom by armed force. Desverneys later told William Penceel, a free mulatto slaveowner, about this conversation. Penceel urged him to tell his "master," Colonel J. C. Prioleau, and on May 30 the intendant of Charleston was officially informed. William Paul was quietly arrested and after several days of solitary confinement in the "black hole" of the workhouse be began to babble about a murderous uprising of slaves. He named Mingo Harth and Peter Poyas as leading conspirators and Gullah Jack, a conjurer who empowered parched corn, ground nuts, and crab claws to protect those joining the conspiracy. But William Paul's incredible story left city officials skeptical. Nevertheless, city authorities dispatched a trusted slave, George Wilson, to spy on the people and places Paul had mentioned. When Wilson reported on June 14 the alarming news that there was a rebellion planned for June 16, militia units were called out, guards were posted around the city, and mounted patrols searched for weapons and rounded up suspects. Some 2,500 armed men patrolled the city on the night of June 16 and few white citizens slept as the horror of insurrection was on their minds. On June 17 and 18, ten blacks were arrested, including Peter Poyas and Mingo Harth, and a Magistrates and Freeholders Court of seven men began hearing testimony in the oppressive summer heat of a closed, guarded courtroom in the workhouse on Magazine Street. A white Charlestonian observed that a "feeling of alarm and anxiety . . . pervaded the community." On June 22 Denmark Vesey, having been named as a conspirator, was arrested after a three-day search of the city. He and Peter Poyas denied any knowledge of a conspiracy, but on July 2, with four other blacks who were regarded as insolent, they were hanged along the once fortified lines north of Boundary Street. Their bodies were left hanging for hours and then turned over to physicians for dissection.

The remaining prisoners at once bore witness to all sorts of remarks they had heard various blacks make about what they would like to do to this or that white person. Slave after terrified slave was called in for questioning, and the court records are replete with absurd contradictions. There was talk of an Afro-American army of 9,000, of hundreds of weapons being manufactured and stored in secret places, of midnights of July 16, of June 16, of Emmanuel Church, and of July 4; of ships, troops, and arms being sent from England and France, of allies in Santo Domingo, of couriers connecting the plantations to Charleston; and of repeated references to Joshua 6:21, which in the King James Version reads as follows: "And they utterly destroyed all that was in the city, both man and woman, young and old, and ox, and sheep, and ass, with the edge of the sword." One theme that gradually emerged was that many of those who were most interested in the sustained pursuit of freedom for themselves and for other blacks were leading members of the African Methodist Episcopal Church at Reid and Hanover streets. William Paul in particular came back to testify again and again, and before his memory and his tongue had exhausted themselves, 131 blacks had been arrested. But it was Monday Gell, a slave who ran his own carpenter's shop on Anson Street in competition with Denmark Vesey, who first named Vesey, a prominent, active, and articulate member of the African Methodist congregation, as the ringleader.

Governor Bennett and Justice William Johnson expressed their disapproval of the proceedings, but their unpopular protests were ignored. Most white Charlestonians were convinced there had been a widespread and well-organized conspiracy and that it had been master-minded by Denmark Vesey. A total of thirty-five blacks were eventually hanged, thirty-one were banished, thirty-eight were discharged after questioning, and twenty-seven were tried and acquitted. How much truth there was in the testimony, or how much the belief in the conspiracy was the result of anxiety and overreaction to remarks misunderstood or taken out of context will probably never be known.

In August a court gave Morris Brown, the pastor of the now notorious African Methodist Episcopal Church, fifteen days to get out of South Carolina, and soon after he had left, the City Council had the church building demolished. Peter Desverneys and George Wilson were freed by the state legislature and given an annual pension of $50. Desverneys married into the mulatto elite of Charleston and became a slaveowner himself. William Penceel was exempted from the free Negro capitation tax and was awarded $1,000.[41]

"The Maintenance of Public Order"

Alarmed by perhaps the most elaborate slave conspiracy in American history, the state legislature passed a law on December 1, 1822, requiring all free black males over fifteen years of age either to take a white guardian or to be sold into slavery; free Afro-Americans who left South Carolina and returned could be enslaved. On December 21 Charleston's City Council established a municipal force of 150 men and petitioned the legislature for an arsenal or "a Citadel" "to protect and preserve the public property . . . and safety . . . ." The temporary arsenal and a guard house were set up in the tobacco inspection warehouse, no longer in use since tobacco was no longer a backcountry staple. Also in December at the prodding of Charlestonians the legislature enacted the first Negro Seaman Act, which provided that all black sailors whose ships entered the port of Charleston be locked up ashore until their vessels departed. If their captains failed to pay the cost of board and lodgings, the black sailors could be sold into slavery. The following year, when the act was suspended and then declared unconstitutional by a federal court, the city's well-to-do formed the South Carolina Association, and for over the next forty years this and similar extralegal organizations assisted local authorities in policing Charleston's blacks. In 1823 the association successfully lobbied the legislature for a second Negro Seaman Act, for Charlestonians feared free blacks who may "corrupt our . . . slave population."[42]

Other methods of racial control instituted by the city authorities following the Vesey affair included a treadmill that was installed in the workhouse, or House of Correction, on the southwest corner of Magazine and Mazyck streets just east of the city jail where slaves were sent for "a little sugar," which meant they were flogged by the keeper of the workhouse upon payment of a small fee by the slave's owner. City officials hoped that the new treadmill at the "Sugar House," as the workhouse was sometimes called, would offer "a better prospect of reclaiming a criminal and of making him useful." But Sarah Grimké described the treadmill as an instrument of torture. With the arms of the slaves, both men and women, fastened to a rail above their heads, those unable to keep up suffered a constant hitting of their legs and knees against the steps of the treadmill while "drivers" flogged them with a "cat o' nine tails" for failing to keep up. In 1823 the City Guard was reorganized. A "beat" system was started and mounted couriers kept in touch with men at their posts and officers at the Guard House on the southeastern corner of Broad and

Meeting streets. From this organization Charleston's modern police force steadily evolved.[43]

Throughout the antebellum years thousands of black slaves and free people of color were members of the white churches. Most belonged to the Methodist or Baptist congregations, but the Presbyterian, Congregational, and Episcopal churches included some blacks and a few belonged to the Lutheran and Catholic churches or the Jewish congregation of Beth Elohim, where in 1824 modern Reform Judaism was launched when members organized the Reformed Society of Israelites. Black watchmen or preachers presided over all-black Sunday school classes preceding the main services, for which blacks took their seats in the galleries or on the main floor toward the rear of the sanctuary, where some free blacks owned pews. With the white members they sang, took communion, and participated in baptisms. When a Northern minister preached in the Congregational Church on Meeting Street he observed that a "wide gallery is . . . provided for blacks and is pretty well filled"; some of the "colored gentry were handsome in their manners & rather luxurious in dress."[44]

No Southern city could boast of a more sophisticated, cosmopolitan, or scholarly clergy than antebellum Charleston, but they were ardent defenders of the status quo. Indeed, the Reverend John Bachman of St. John's Lutheran Church has been called the "chief religious spokesman for slavery." Many were good and kind men who in a paternalistic way were genuinely concerned for the spiritual life of blacks. The Reverend John Adger in a sermon at the Second Presbyterian Church clearly expressed the ideal of compassion and kindness toward the slave: "Our mothers confide us, when infants, to their arms, and sometimes to the very milk of their breasts . . . a race distinct from us, . . . yet they are not more truly ours than we are theirs; . . . children of our God and Father; dear to our Saviour; to the like to whom he died, and to the least of whom every act of Christian compassion and kindness we show he will consider as shown also to himself." At the same time Bishop Gadsden, grandson of the Revolutionary leader and rector of St. Philip's Church from 1814 to 1852, frequently reminded blacks that they should "fear God, obey the civil authority . . . , be subject unto their own masters, and be contented in that state of life to which God hath called them . . . ." Likewise, Theodore Dehon, rector of St. Michael's Church, told his mixed congregation that St. Paul urged fugitive slaves to return to their masters. But slaves more often took their problems to practitioners of voodoo, "conjurers," or slave preachers of Afro-American Christianity than to white preachers or to their masters. The fact was that the spiritual life of most slaves remained hidden from white observation.[45]

The legislature answered the local plea for an arsenal, or "Citadel," and by 1825 it was under construction near the former site of the tobacco inspection warehouse, between the lines dug during the Revolutionary War and the War of 1812, and near the location of the gallows where the Vesey conspirators swung to their deaths. The newly created municipal guard was assigned to oversee the care and disposition of the arms and ammunition stored there. When the Marquis de Lafayette visited the city in March 1825 he was welcomed with a succession of balls, dinners, fireworks displays, and military parades. He praised officers of Charleston's military organizations for their discipline and uniforms. In turn they responded: "We could not have chosen a more honorable [profession] . . . . It constantly reminds us that [among] the first duties of a citizen are the maintenance of public order."[46]

Debtors, the disorderly poor, and desperate criminals were locked up in the Charleston District Jail on which the City Council was as reluctant to spend money as the Assembly had been in colonial days. Grand juries repeatedly petitioned the state and city government about conditions at the old jail that were "injurious to the health of the prisoners." Finally in 1802 funds were appropriated for construction of a new Charleston District Jail on the site of the eighteenth-century facility. Located at the corner of Magazine Street and Back Street (Franklin Street today), the three-story brick building adjoined the workhouse for Afro-Americans. However, in the early 1820s the sheriff of the Charleston District told the council that the only secure cells remaining were those in the attic where all classes of criminals were confined to prevent escapes, which meant that "Negroes are frequently associated with the white prisoners, the state of things obviously repugnant." Funds were appropriated in the mid-1820s for a four-story brick wing of solitary cells for hardened criminals.[47]

Beginning on Christmas eve 1825 and for the first several months of 1826 fires broke out almost nightly. On January 20 a businessman in Charleston wrote his daughter in Connecticut:

"The frequent attempts of incendiaries . . . has caused much alarm. The citizens patrol the streets at night to prevent the city being burned." The City Council offered a $1,000 reward for the capture of the arsonists. Furious mobs attempted to lynch suspected incendiaries, and several Negroes were convicted and apparently executed.

No year passed in antebellum Charleston without reports of attempts by arsonists to fire the city. Of 204 fires reported in the *Courier* between 1825 and 1858, the editors labeled 91 as arson. The evidence of arson was often, by modern standards, extremely flimsy, but it was a rare occasion when, in 1840, the *Courier* observed: "The prevailing disposition to attribute every fire to incendiaries is becoming too common, and we can see no good result in so doing."

The rash of fires in 1826 prompted the City Council to assign six horses to the City Guard. Mounted patrols covered more territory. This force and the uniformed and armed men who comprised the municipal guard attached to the Citadel were expected to keep the city's Afro-Americans "compleatly subordinate." From a new, main Guard House at the southwest corner of Broad and Meeting streets, the site of the Post Office today, the guard enforced the city's "Negro" law. Over a decade later the Englishwoman Fanny Kemble observed that in the evening there is "a most ominous . . . beating of drums . . . and the guard set . . . every night" out of "dread of . . . domestic insurrection." She preferred a society where she could go "to sleep without the apprehension of my servants' cutting my throat in my bed." During the day a salaried marshal in each ward and two dozen constables patrolled the city to enforce the peace, receiving a commission on all fines they levied.[48]

" . . . *this once flourishing city*"

In 1828 the city shipped its greatest rice crop and the second largest cotton export ever, 214,000 bales, but that same year the Chamber of Commerce reported: "Charleston has for several years past retrograded . . . . Her landed estate has within eight years depreciated in value one half. Industry and business talent . . . have sought employment elsewhere. Many of her houses are tenantless and the grass grows uninterrupted in some of her chief business streets." Hugh Swinton Legaré wondered in the first issue of the *Southern Review*, published in 1828, if the decline of

Venice offered any lesson for Charleston, "this once flourishing city."

Despite the especially hard times for both small retailers and skilled laborers, many of the planter-merchant elite prospered. The price of rice declined only slightly less than the cost of living; and unlike upland cotton, the price of luxury sea-island cotton dropped only slightly. Nor did the city's institutions completely atrophy. The Medical College of South Carolina authorized by the state opened in 1824 as the South's first school of medicine and was chartered by the legislature as the state's medical college seven years later. The College of Charleston attained collegiate rank in 1824, but continued to attract few students. From 1828–29 William Strickland's Greek Revival building went up on the campus of the College of Charleston and the free black Daniel A. Payne, who later became a bishop in the African Methodist Episcopal Church, opened a school for black children.

During the attacks on slavery and its defense by Charles Pinckney on the floor of Congress in the early 1820s, the state moved away from nationalism and toward extreme sectionalism, opposing internal improvements and protective tariffs that were beneficial to the Northern and Western states, but economically harmful to South Carolina. In 1827 the wealthy planter-lawyer Robert J. Turnbull in a series of articles in the Charleston *Mercury* elaborated on the growing rift between South Carolina and the federal government. His writings made the word "disunion" familiar across the state. Turnbull had carefully crafted the whole concept of the right of a state to nullify an act of the federal government that was not acceptable to the state. Another Charlestonian, James Hamilton, Jr., former intendant and soon to be governor, coined the term "nullification" when from the stump he opposed the federal tariff of 1828, a "tariff of abominations." Indeed, he predicted that continued protectionist policies would lead to the dissolution of the Union. On December 19, 1828, the legislature of the state adopted *Exposition and Protest*, secretly written by the then vice president of the United States, John C. Calhoun, who like Turnbull argued the unconstitutionality of the protective tariff.

The American Colonization Society for the transportation of free blacks to Africa, endorsed early in the century by leading Charlestonians, was now condemned as a scheme of the abolitionists. Rather, planters championed conversion of slaves to Christianity, which was endorsed and undertaken by local churchmen like the Methodist minister the Reverend William Capers.[49]

The Federal Board of Engineers for Fortifications, responsible for defense of the national frontiers, received appropriations for work on the defenses around Charleston, and in 1829 work began under Lieutenant Henry Brewerton, U.S. Army Engineers. A sea wall was built around Castle Pinckney and defensive works were begun on a shoal opposite Fort Moultrie, which, with Fort Johnson and Castle Pinckney, could close the harbor to any attacking force. This new fortification was Fort Sumter.

During the late 1820s Charlestonians saw an answer to their economic problems in the building of a railroad that would intercept the cotton that was going by water from Augusta to Savannah. The South Carolina Canal and Railroad Company, chartered in 1827, turned to the Army Corps of Engineers to build a rail line. After surveys the Corps suggested a route between Hamburg and Charleston covering 136 miles. The government of Charleston, banks, insurance companies, and local individuals supplied all of the working capital. Two locomotives capable of speeds of twenty miles per hour on straightaways were purchased, and on December 25, 1830, the first steam locomotive to be used in a business venture in the United States, *The Best Friend*, was put into service. One of the first riders in the open cars recalled that "People did not wear their best clothes . . . on account of the sparks and cinders." Three years later the railroad was completed. It was the world's longest under one management, but prominent Charlestonians would not let the company lay tracks to the wharves, insisting that the rails stop at Line Street where freight had to be transferred to wagons and hauled to dockside at a high surcharge. The advantage of intercepting the Savannah trade was thus lost in a city that remained "a summer home for planters" and, by the end of the decade, due to soaring maintenance costs, a poor return on investment, and its failure to increase Charleston's trade, the railroad was held in "ill repute."[50]

Elections and Politics

During the 1830 legislative contest 2,562 votes were cast in Charleston, slightly more than two-thirds of the city's eligible voters. Suffrage was restricted to adult white males over the age of twenty-one. By now property qualifications for voting had been eliminated although property requirements for officehold-ing remained on the books for some years following the Civil War.

On April 13 that year in the nation's capital at the Thomas Jefferson birthday celebration, President Andrew Jackson and John C. Calhoun clashed. Jackson toasted "our Federal Union—It must be preserved," but the South Carolinian replied, "The Union—Next to our liberties most dear." In Charleston during the next several years partisan contests between Unionists and Nullifiers reflected the statewide and national debate. Influenc-ing the politics of the day was the publication on January 1, 1831, in Boston of William Lloyd Garrison's newspaper, the *Liberator*, which called for the immediate abolition of slavery. In June Nat Turner, a slave in Southampton County, Virginia, led the bloodi-est slave revolt in North American history. These events sent shock waves of anger and fear across Charleston and the South, reminding Southerners anew that their "peculiar institution" re-mained under attack and rekindling old fears of servile revolt. The Charleston *Mercury*, soon to become the South's premier newspaper advocating secession, presaged the end of free speech in the South on the issue of the pros and cons of slavery when it condemned the Virginia legislature's public discussion of slavery in 1831 and 1832.

The talent and wealth of Charleston was divided between Unionists and Nullifiers and the two factions competed furiously for votes. During the elections they locked up qualified voters and voted unqualified ones like paupers, transients, and deceased persons—sometimes at more than one polling place; members of the City Guard were instructed to vote or not to vote if they wished to keep their jobs; others were bribed with money and liquor; and ballot boxes were stuffed or stolen.[51]

Perhaps the most furiously contested election in the antebel-lum city came at the height of the nullification controversy in the 1832 legislative race. The Nullifier party threatened secession over high protective tariffs imposed by the federal Congress and Northern antislavery agitation. The Union party counseled mod-eration. Tension was high on the eve of the election and fistfights broke out. Transients and the working classes supported those who offered the most grog. Both parties used strong-armed tactics to recruit voters while intimidating the opposition, but the con-test also served as a form of recreation for the participants.

The Nullifiers swept to victory in Charleston and across the state and the new legislature convened in Columbia in November and issued an ordinance that declared the tariff acts of 1828 and 1832 null and void. On December 10 President Jackson condemned the Act of Nullification as treason and warned that he would use force to prevent it. The legislature first promised to meet force with force, but on January 21, 1833, a convention of Nullifiers assembled in Charleston to postpone the date on which nullification was to go into effect, February 1, 1833. By this time other Southern states were condemning South Carolina's course as "alarming" and "reckless." Seeking compromise, President Jackson on March 2 signed a lower tariff bill and the Force Act to compel South Carolina's compliance with the law. Sixteen days later the South Carolina legislature repealed the Ordinance of Nullification, but nullified the Force Act. A compromise had been reached temporarily, but the principle of nullification was still very much alive in South Carolina. For a few short years tensions between Nullifiers and Unionists persisted on Charleston's City Council until both factions subordinated their feud for the sake of harmony and unity.

William Grayson, writing of the city's antebellum political factions, observed that "there was little difference between them. They differed on no important principles or purposes . . . . The only matter in dispute was whether one or the other should control the power and emoluments of the city government." Indeed politics was primarily entertainment. The gentry rarely permitted politics to disrupt their closely knit personal relationships for long. While the politics of Northern cities became increasingly divisive, Charleston's became more homogeneous. The political harmony of the eighteenth-century elite reappeared on a broader social scale. The city became an anomaly in a furiously partisan Jacksonian America; more than anything, abolitionism united the upper class. In 1833 especially they were shocked to learn that the American Anti-Slavery Society was organized in Philadelphia and that the English Parliament had ended slavery in the British West Indies.[52]

Economic Hard Times

The anemic local economy contributed to the failure of the *Southern Review* in 1832 and to the final curtain call a year later at the Charleston Theatre. It soon was sold to the Medical College of South Carolina, which used the building as a School of Anatomy, causing the Irish comedian Tyrone Power to say of it in 1834 that "cutting up is still the order of the day." Three years later a writer in the *Mercury* accused "the refined of the city" of neglecting "to foster and encourage the fine arts." Nevertheless, the artist John James Audubon raved about the local hospitality while visiting Charleston in the 1830s where he began a long friendship with John Bachman based on their mutual interests as naturalists.

Charleston had endured its first epidemic of Asiatic cholera in 1832 brought in by the *Amelia* out of New York, and the following year the author of a widely read travel book wrote: "The people of Charleston pass their lives in endeavoring to escape from . . . the . . . fever. This continual dodging with death strikes me as very disagreeable." In 1835 a lazaretto was built on James Island to provide a more effective quarantine, but despite this precaution a cholera epidemic ravaged the city the next year and nearly 400 people died. A state-owned pest house was constructed on Morris Island in 1838.

Some of Charleston's leaders blamed the city's declining trade on "the want of confidence which foreigners have in the health of this place," but what Charleston lacked was rail connections to the West, a harbor deep enough to accommodate large steamships, a broader range of crops and products to export, and a growing pool of free, educated, and ambitious workers. Most of all Charleston needed leaders to meet these problems head-on. For when the city's decisionmakers at the turn of the century had promoted upland cotton and reopened the slave trade, in the long run they had backed the wrong horses. As it moved West, cotton left behind exhausted soils and crowds of slaves whose labor it was often impossible to employ profitably. Charlestonians increasingly came to embrace Calhoun because of his compulsive willingness to provide them with a neat theoretical underpinning and justification for their society.[53]

During the economic hard times of the 1830s, about 260 children were placed in the Orphan House, usually by their mothers. As the depression worsened there was a corresponding rise in alcoholism; by the mid-1830s approximately 20 percent of all inmates of the Poor House were alcoholics. Even while confined there the inmates found ways to get their hands on booze. On one occasion even the cell-keeper of the Poor House, John

Innis, and Agnes Todd, the nurse of the "Maniac Department," were found "under the influence of liquor."

The nationwide temperance crusade made little headway in Charleston or the South. For one thing it was antithetical to the elite's habits of "conspicious consumption" and social conviviality. On occasion visiting temperance lecturers found platforms in the Baptist and Methodist churches of the city, and local temperance societies held public meetings at "the old theatre in Broad Street" and "the Depository in Chalmers Street," but during one such meeting of the Charleston Temperance Society, the suggestion that the legislature enact laws to enforce temperance nearly disrupted the gathering.

Indigent women sometimes turned to prostitution. They found a steady stream of clients among sailors who were frequent customers of brothels in French Alley running between Meeting and Anson streets, and many mariners were admitted to the Poor House with syphilis. The Charleston Port Society for Promoting the Gospel among Seamen aimed to rescue sailors from "the haunts of dissipation and vice" and to persuade them that there were "pleasures above the brothel."[54]

It was in Cornel June's sailors' boardinghouse, a brothel "of the very lowest and degraded character," at the corner of State and Linguard streets that a fire broke out on a blustery February night in 1835. Wind-blown flames swept down State and Church streets consuming over sixty structures occupied by poor blacks and whites; this time St. Philip's Church did not escape. Spectators watched as sparks set the steeple afire and saw it glow like a torch against the night sky until it crashed into the sanctuary below. Shocked and saddened by the losses, Charlestonians nevertheless launched an immediate rebuilding of the area affected and St. Philip's Church, the church building that stands today.

Before the city recovered from the February fire another conflagration destroyed a portion of Charleston on June 6, this time to the north of the previous fires. Beginning on the west side of Meeting Street, near Hasell Street, it spread across eight blocks leveling between 125 and 300 structures, most of them the businesses and homes of citizens of modest means.[55]

" . . . utmost vigilance"

In July 1835 when it became known that antislavery tracts were in the federal Post Office destined for distribution across the

South, Jacob Schirmer wrote that "a Mob broke open the P.O.
. . . and took out the Incendiary Papers and Pamphlets . . . and
on the Evg. of the 30th a bonfire was made on the Parade ground
and also burnt in Effigy the leading . . . [abolitionists] of the
North viz., Garrison, Cox, and Tappan." The Charleston intendant, newspaper editor, and later congressman, Henry Laurens
Pinckney, publicly condemned antislavery activities, charging
that the abolitionist "whets the knife . . . and lights the torch of
insurrection." On August 10 Pinckney and members of the
lowcountry elite, Robert Y. Hayne, Thomas Lowndes, Nathaniel
Heyward, Henry A. DeSaussure, Edward R. Laurens, and others,
met at City Hall and called for the state legislature to legalize the
seizure and destruction of "all incendiary publications . . . calculated to excite domestic insurrection." They further requested
that city officials employ the "utmost vigilance" in "detecting
and bringing to punishment" all persons engaged locally "in the
dangerous schemes of the Anti-Slavery Society." Before adjourn-
ing they affirmed that they were determined to "DEFEND OUR
PROPERTY AGAINST ALL ATTACKS—BE THE CONSE-
QUENCES WHAT THEY MAY." The following day the City
Council posted a $1,000 reward for the arrest and conviction of
anyone distributing abolitionist literature. Elias Vanderhorst told
his wife in September 1835: "As regards the Abolitionists & their
infernal cut throat schemes, if the South . . . will separate from
their Northern Brethren we will be safe enough. . . . we can do
much better without them than with them."

That same year, fearful that abolitionist literature might fall
into the hands of Afro-Americans, the state legislature passed a
law prohibiting slaves from being taught how to read or write. In
Charleston pressure groups like the Lynch Club forced the closing of the Catholic school conducted for blacks, but only after the
tough-minded Bishop England, who suspected religious prejudice, reached an agreement that similar schools also shut down.[56]

❦ 4. 1836–1860:
"Queen City of the South"

A *Sputtering Economy*

In 1836 the title "intendant" was dropped and Robert Y.
Hayne, former governor and champion of nullification in the famous Hayne-Daniel Webster debate on the floor of the U.S. Sen-

ate, became the first officer of the city of Charleston to be called "mayor." Like the intendants before them, the mayors continued for the most part to be affluent Episcopalians, more likely to be planters or lawyers than merchants. In May, Henry Laurens Pinckney, now a member of the U.S. House of Representatives, introduced the so-called gag resolution, which became law: all antislavery petitions sent to Congress were to be tabled.

Although the port never recovered the prosperity or the extraordinary combination of complacency and ambition with which it had entered the nineteenth century, Charleston was beginning to find some of its old self-confidence, and in 1837 John C. Calhoun defended slavery on the floor of the U.S. Senate as "a positive good." Sales were brisk along King Street, the business of professional men increased, demand for Carolina rice in Europe was up, and the reviving economy put Charlestonians in an ebullient and speculative mood. Construction was going on all over the city: the rookeries gutted in the fire of 1835 in Philadelphia Alley and Cock Lane and buildings along Ellery Street were demolished and new structures were going up, five new stores were being constructed at the corner of State and Market streets, City Hall was undergoing a face lift, and land along the Battery was being transformed into a city park. A group of local citizens raised $60,000 to build the New Charleston Theatre on the west side of Meeting Street between Market Street and Horlbeck Alley in 1837. Greek Revival in design, it was a large and imposing structure that could accommodate 1,200 persons. When it opened under the management of yet another experienced English impresario, William Abbott, the *Courier* predicted a theatrical renaissance.[57]

The Apprentices' Library Society was sponsoring public lecturers in the late 1830s, by which time its holdings included nearly 2,000 books on religion, and biographies and novels with themes of moral uplift. One prominent Charlestonian claimed such institutions helpful in "the absolute extinction of *the mob*, so . . . dreaded wherever it is found." It was probably for similar reasons that the Charleston Port Society in 1837 appointed a committee to solicit books and money to create "floating libraries" for mariners on vessels belonging to the port of Charleston. It was not until 1858 that the New York Seamen's Friend Society inaugurated such a plan.

Other than lectures and lending libraries, however, there were in the late 1830s few educational opportunities for children of the city's laboring class. Those lucky enough to win scholarships might attend church and charity schools or the High School of Charleston, established by the city in 1839, which charged an annual tuition of $40. The city Orphan House also conducted a school and some of the city's poor attended the state-supported "free school" near Charleston. By this time black children had hardly any opportunities for a formal education.

Successful white merchants, planters, and professionals sent their sons to the private boardingschool conducted in the city from 1820 to 1850 by the Englishman Christopher Coates. To give their daughters the polish necessary to make a good match they enrolled them in one of Charleston's private "female academies" or sent them to dancing masters and music teachers. The daughters of the oligarchy were educated more for the pedestal than the demanding daily routines of managing large and complex households.[58]

Charleston's finest and most expensive female finishing school, one of the most exclusive in the southeast, was Madam Ann Marsan Talvande's French School for Young Ladies, where young women from wealthy families studied the arts and sciences and received instruction in dancing, piano, guitar, and singing. Located near the corner of Legare and Tradd streets, the school was surrounded by a high brick wall topped with broken glass, and to one boarding student it seemed "a Convent in its seclusion."

More and more of the lowcountry elite were keeping their sons within the state for their higher education. Many went to South Carolina College in Columbia where the lowcountry and upcountry gentry, educated together, began to form a single South Carolina mentality. The College of Charleston was slowly collapsing under the presidency of Jasper Adams, an Episcopal clergyman from New England whose dour personality and abrasive manner alienated both townspeople and faculty. By 1836 only three students remained, and the following year trustees closed the school and began to work quietly with the city government to gain permanent municipal support. Realizing that the school's reputation as the "alma mater of the wealthy and high born" had first to be overcome, trustees, editors, and City Council members began saying that in the future "all classes of our citizens" would have an equal opportunity to attend the college, and the school reopened in 1838 as a city-supported institution.[59]

Well-to-do visitors to Charleston in the early 1830s took lodgings at the Carolina Coffee House, 20 Tradd Street, the Planter's Hotel on the southwestern corner of Church and Queen streets (formerly the site of the Dock Street Theatre), and Jones' Hotel operated by Jehu Jones, "a free person of color." Jones had purchased the William Burrow's mansion on Broad Street next to St. Michael's Church for $13,000 and converted it into a hotel. The Englishman Thomas Hamilton always stayed there "because . . . the apartments are good . . . . The pleasure of . . . clean tablecloths and silver—of exchanging salt pork and greasy corn cakes for a table furnished with luxuries of all sorts—was very great . . . ." But following Jones's death both the service and the accommodations deteriorated, and merchant-boosters hoping that Charleston would become "to the South what New York is to the Union" invited Charles F. Reichardt, one of the country's leading architects, to design a hotel to match their vision of Charleston as "the Queen of the South." Built in the Greek Revival Style, the four-story Charleston Hotel featured an imposing colonnade of fourteen Corinthian columns across its front facing Meeting Street, and a second-floor piazza enclosed by iron railings. The hotel, which could accommodate 300 lodgers, was completed in March 1838 but was destroyed a month later in a catastrophic fire. The blaze broke out around 9:00 P.M. in a small fruit store near the corner of Beresford and King streets and spread quickly east and north. Throughout the long night the screams of people fleeing a fire-storm of "sparks borne on the increasing wind" mingled with the sounds of tolling church bells and the deafening roar of buildings being blown up. Ansonborough was obliterated. Seven hundred acres of the heart of the city were "blackened walls and smoking ruins." Some 560 dwellings and 600 outbuildings had been consumed, an estimated loss of $3 million.

The 700-member fire department had been unable to control the blaze. The department consisted of sixteen engines manned by black slaves and five companies of proud white volunteers directed by a Board of Firemasters appointed from the city's well-to-do. It was a force divided by both class and caste. The volunteers, artisans, and clerks, viewed their work as both dangerous and glamorous and they had little in common with their supervisors, and even less with black slaves who were dragooned into service during fires. Indeed, the white volunteers of the Aetna

Fire Company believed that there were among "the black population few . . . who . . . feel any interest in saving the property of the citizens and many . . . who . . . we fear would rather increase than extinguish fires."

After the terrible April conflagration, twenty-five arson attempts were reported in May and June. After each fire the "domestics on the premises" were arrested and interrogated, but apparently none was convicted. As fears mounted in the devastated city, the *Courier* counseled: "We caution our fellow citizens not to give credence to every idle story that may be told, and thus create a panic in the community."[60]

During the spring and summer following the fire, yellow fever scourged the city. It seemed that Charleston was living up to its reputation as "a city of *disasters*." During the yellow fever epidemic, city officials had a revealing close look at the living arrangements of the city's poorest white classes living in rented tenements along the alleyways near the Cooper River waterfront "where great numbers were stowed into places of small dimensions." Mayor Pinckney and other city officials also attributed the high death rates of the poor in epidemics to "the . . . vice of intemperance, and the . . . vicious and destructive habits . . . connected with it," and therefore they called for "regulating the houses which . . . are . . . hotbeds of infections." Furthermore, Pinckney lamented, because of the city's marshy location and its many cemeteries, Charlestonians drank a decoction "not only [of] the soluble filth, and excretion of men and animals, but the very mortal remains of our citizens." He concluded that "unless our city be improved in healthiness, vain will be all its natural and commercial advantages, all our plans . . . to re-establish its prosperity." Between 1838 and 1839 ten low lots whose "stagnant waters" were "corrupting the atmosphere" were filled; twenty-five public drains were built, cleaned, or repaired; 1,500 nuisances, like potholes, were eliminated; the city pavements were swept twice weekly, and the number of scavenger carts was increased. Steps were taken to prohibit future burials in Charleston when the City Council purchased land along the Ashley River for use as a cemetery, but proposals to the council for a city water system got nowhere.[61]

A request reached the City Council for the installation of a treadmill in the Poor House, but it was turned down on the grounds that it was a "punishment for slaves and other colored persons and the committee are unwilling to break down any of the distinctions between that class of persons and the white population by subjecting them to a common mode of punishment." Likewise, the commissioners of the Poor House refused to admit blacks except for those certifiably insane. They preferred to go to the expense of building separate facilities at the workhouse.

The Charleston Hotel was quickly rebuilt and opened again in July 1839. One visitor described it in terms of "Large columns outside—tough steak inside," but the proprietor, Daniel Mixer, was praised by "Charleston epicureans . . . for his capacity at the conception and concoction of good things, solid and liquid.[62]

The Charleston Hotel was built in the Greek Revival Style, completed in March 1838 and destroyed by the fire of April and immediately rebuilt, opening in July 1839. It was destroyed again by the wrecker's ball in March 1960. *Courtesy of the Library of Congress, Washington, D.C.*

The city's economy was sputtering again by 1840. Jonathan Lucas III built the West Point Mill near the western end of Boundary Street on the Ashley River, the largest rice mill in South Carolina, but from October 1839 to July 1840 the city's banks suspended specie payments to avoid being drained by Northern financial institutions. The Charleston merchant R. C. Carson wrote on April 14, 1840: "Times are wretched here . . . . We are compelled to sell to our friends on time and unless we get money from the country we cannot pay our debts. Several wealthy houses have failed lately."

Though the city's musical and theatrical life was vigorous, the New Charleston Theatre was not a financial success and in 1841 Abbott resigned as manager. None of his successors was able to make the theater financially viable either. The actor Louis Fitzgerald Tasistro observed that theater managers "lavish upon [the gentry] . . . every species of *extra* civility . . . and the comfort of everybody else was forgotten in the . . . desire to please and accommodate them."

Besides the new playhouse, the largest and most popular auditoriums in the city were South Carolina Institute Hall on Meeting Street, Military Hall on Wentworth Street, and Hibernian Hall, which was constructed on the west side of Meeting Street in 1841. Greek Revival in design, the building was described upon opening as "one of the chief architectural ornaments of our city." The St. Cecilia Society, which by now had evolved into a social cotillion, began holding its balls at Hibernian Hall and a contemporary remarked that "its membership remains exclusive and its affairs somewhat secret."[63]

After persistent urging from Charlestonians, the state legislature chartered the South Carolina Military Academy, or Citadel, in 1842. A corps of young men like those who had been formed locally as a municipal guard would be permitted to enroll in the Citadel for "a broad and practical education." On the site of the Arsenal, bounded by Boundary, King, Meeting, and Inspection streets, an imposing, two-story brick, fortresslike building with turrets went up. Over time two additional stories and wings were added. The highly visible, heavily armed cadets who drilled on the parade ground before the institution were intended to be conducive to the "public order." One Charlestonian observed: "The nature of our institutions of domestic slavery and its exposure of us to hostile machinations . . . render it doubly incumbent on us, . . . to cherish a military spirit and to diffuse military science among our people." The Citadel also reflected the lowcountry elite's love for military trappings and ceremony and it provided the training for an officer class.[64]

The planters, part-time residents of the city, had kept railroads from entering Charleston and restricted the building of steam-powered mills to its periphery. Many of the city's professionals and merchants agreed that commercial and industrial establishments threatened both the ambience and the social order of the city. Slave laborers accounted for 60 percent of Charleston's work force, most of whom were engaged in domestic service, and were viewed by upper-class Charlestonians as servants, not as an industrial work force. Additional concentrations of slave laborers in industry within the city would jeopardize the social safety of the community. Industry would also attract free white laborers who were looked upon by Carolina's elite as "a species of labor . . . which is antagonistic to our institutions." The great lowcountry planters also worried over the possible emergence of a powerful commercial class within the city.

In 1844 local opponents of industrialization were surprised by a series of articles in the *Courier* by William Gregg, a Pennsylvanian who had come South in 1824. Having accumulated a fortune in Columbia and Charleston as a jewelry craftsman, Gregg founded the premier cotton mill in the state in Graniteville and became the chief promoter of large-scale cotton manufacturing in the South. In his articles entitled "Domestic Industry," Gregg argued that the South must encourage manufacturing if it wished to enjoy general prosperity. He wrote that Charleston especially was behind the times, for where else is it except Charleston that a carpenter "is prohibited in the use of a small steam engine . . . to enable him to compete with others in supplying us with ready made doors, blinds, sashes, shutters, etc.?" Gregg concluded that "This power is withheld lest the smoke of an engine should disturb the delicate nerves of an agriculturist; or the noise of the mechanic's hammer should break in upon the slumber of a real estate holder, or an importing merchant, while he is indulging in fanciful dreams of building on paper, the *Queen City of the South.*"[65]

The Entrepreneurs

Even before the appearance of Gregg's articles, a handful of merchant-parvenus, both immigrants and native-born, were waging an uphill battle to revive commerce in Charleston: among them the Irish investor James Adger; the Bank of Charleston president, Ker Boyce, whose humble beginnings led political opponents to call him "the cur of Newberry"; John F. Blacklock, a partner in the city's largest rice commission business; Henry W. Conner, member of a leading mercantile firm, and the self-made wholesale grocer, George W. Williams, both natives of North Carolina; Charleston native James Hamilton, Jr., a cotton merchant and former mayor; and George Alfred Trenholm, a native Charlestonian. Characterized by historian Frederic Jaher as being of "undistinguished ancestry," Trenholm was the city's most highly regarded antebellum business leader and one of America's richest men. Ker Boyce and Henry Conner jointly built a string of wholesale houses along Hayne Street, which became the center of the city's growing jobbing trade. But the commercial heart of the city within a few years radiated from the intersection of Broad and East Bay streets. Clustered here within several blocks were the city's nine banks and most of the commission merchants, brokerage houses, importers, and auctioneers. Lawyers' offices were concentrated along Broad Street, nearby Law Range, and behind the courthouse. King Street developed into a ribbon of retail specialty shops, particularly for clothing and food. Similar shops dotted Tradd, Queen, Meeting, Broad, and East Bay streets.

The new businessmen again wanted to make Charleston a major regional distribution center serving an agricultural hinterland, and they formed partnerships with local politicians and some of the more patrician merchants to manage banks, railroads, and shipping. These networks resembled the interlocking directorates that dominated banking in New York and Boston but were more conservative and less specialized and did not have as much capital. The Bank of Charleston, founded in 1834, became the largest financial institution in antebellum South Carolina and the only one to survive the Civil War.[66]

Nouveaux riches entrepreneurs were among the founders, presidents, or directors of the six major railroad projects undertaken in the antebellum city, including the first, the Charleston to Hamburg Line; and also the Louisville, Cincinnati, and Charleston Railroad, the Blue Ridge Railroad, the 755-mile Memphis and Charleston Railroad, and the Charleston and Savannah Line, which was completed near the end of the antebellum era along a coastal route of some 107 miles across seven rivers and in some places through dense swamps.

The great lowcountry planters, content with things as they were, viewed the railroads as antithetical to their interests and some actively tried to thwart their construction. The City Council, however, as mercantile interests became increasingly dominant, appropriated more funds for building rail lines each year and Charleston soon became the hub of a network of railroads that fanned out to the hinterlands of the state and beyond. These lines brought into Charleston increasing amounts of cotton, flour, grain, naval stores, and livestock. In 1835 rail shipments of cotton to Charleston totaled 34,796 bales, in 1840 they reached 58,496 bales, and in 1845 they were 197,657 bales. The railroads funneled off much of the traffic on the Santee Canal, especially after the "Camden Branch" line went into operation in the late 1840s. Nevertheless, about 60 percent of South Carolina's exports and 80 percent of its imports traveled overseas through New York, Boston, Philadelphia, and Baltimore. To recapture this trade and reverse Charleston's decline as a port, businessmen like George Trenholm, Henry Conner, and James Hamilton, Jr., founded six transatlantic lines. But all eventually failed due to national or local economic panics and depressions, management problems, and lack of financial support from the great planters.

The entrepreneurs were more successful in reviving the city's merchant marine. By the 1840s local shipowners included Trenholm; Henry Gourdin; James Adger; John Fraser; Moses Mordecai; Hugh Vincent, a real estate speculator; and Thaddeus Street, whose descendants remained in the shipping business into the late twentieth century. Such individuals or firms owned twenty to twenty-five vessels, a fleet of some 65,000 tons. By comparison, the shipping tonnage owned and operated out of New York in the late antebellum period reached 1,400,000; out of Boston, 464,000; and out of Philadelphia, 241,000 tons.

Strolling near the wharves jutting into the Cooper River and paralleling East Bay Street one visitor observed the hustle and bustle, finding himself "alongside of vessels from all parts of the world, loading and unloading their cargoes." On one wharf, "abreast of a vessel just come from Havannah," he saw "a great pile of unripe bananas . . . a pyramid of cocoa nuts . . . oblong boxes of sugar; . . . great bales of cotton, . . . barrels of rice, . . ."

Local entrepreneurs recognized that deepening of the harbor and improvement of the port's facilities were crucial to the revival of trade and they hoped to receive federal assistance to remove the sandbar blocking the main channels by having Charleston designated a naval depot. When these efforts failed, James Adger and other businessmen had a steam tug built to pull larger vessels over the bar. The political influence of these businessmen was dramatized when in the mid-1840s the city government repealed the law prohibiting steam engines within the city. Shortly thereafter a group of local investors organized the Charleston Cotton Manufacturing Company, built a three-story brick building in Hampstead, a Charleston suburb, and installed machinery bought in Rhode Island. When the machinery roared into operation driving 3,165 spindles and 100 looms, it was the third largest cotton factory in antebellum South Carolina and the only one powered by steam. There was a big turnout to watch the lighting of the building by gas, which was a novelty and its first use in Charleston. But the cotton factory had too few spindles to meet its overhead and within a few years it failed and the building was acquired by the city as an almshouse.

The city's entrepreneur-boosters exerted a powerful influence on the local press to manipulate or repress information about health conditions in the city. During the 1840s, despite severe outbreaks of yellow fever, the *Courier* announced that Charleston enjoyed a "state of health . . . unparalleled in any city of the union of equal population."

With the best rice and cotton lands already under cultivation and the professions glutted, some planters pushed their sons toward business as a career. Within a few years more than 30 percent of the sons residing in the households of their planter-fathers in Charleston were employed in commercial concerns. But a dislike of business and business people among some of the great planter families persisted into the late twentieth century.[67]

Amid the city's commercial revival the issues of human slavery, tariffs, and the efficacy of secession continued to intrude. In the presidential election year 1844 the Methodist church split into Northern and Southern branches over the question of whether or not a bishop might own slaves. John C. Calhoun, now secretary of state in President John Tyler's cabinet and supported by the *Courier* and the *Mercury*, used his influence for moderation and the election of the Democrat James K. Polk, after which Judge Samuel Hoar of Massachusetts arrived in Charleston to institute a suit for the release of imprisoned free Afro-American seamen. City officials immediately advised him that he "was in great danger" and that he should leave, which he soon did. It came to the point, he wrote, as to "whether I should walk to a carriage or be dragged to it." The incident was another example of Charleston's long-standing "intellectual blockade"—raising questions touching slavery met with a violent response. The next year the Baptist church split nationally into Northern and Southern wings over the issue of slavery.[68]

Literati and Scientists

A high-water mark for Charleston's literati came in the autumn of 1844 with the publication of *The Charleston Book: A Miscellany in Prose and Verse.* Ambitious to foster a cultural renaissance like that in the Northeast, which had produced Emerson, Thoreau, Hawthorne, and Melville, antebellum Charleston's most famous literary figure, William Gilmore Simms, edited the book, which included representative works by local writers. The New York *Morning News* gave the book a lukewarm review, while the Charleston press ignored it. Simms, whose book *The Yemassee: A Romance of Carolina*, a romantic tale about the conflict between early settlers and the Indians, published in New York a decade before when he was only twenty-five, enjoyed great success, but Simms would remain forever unhappy with the treatment accorded his works in Charleston and the local attitude toward the intellectual life. The male members of the lowcountry elite preferred other pursuits and had little time for reading. One Charleston belle, Anna Hayes Johnson, cautioned a female friend to suppress any interest in books if she hoped to be popular with the "beaux of this most enlightened city." Literary topics, she warned "make them run from you as if you had the plague." Simms believed that the fertility of the soil and the institution of slavery nurtured that local intellectual laziness. The planter, Simms wrote, preferred "to hunt, to ride, to lounge, and to sleep . . . ."[69]

Heirs of eighteenth-century gentry famous for agreeing with one another, the nineteenth-century elite cultivated a soft, smooth style in language, manner, and bearing that minimized fractious public debate and counteracted the violence that sometimes flashed across the city like summer lightning. It was a society that placed a premium on good looks, good companionship, bright conversation, and a rounded personality. It embraced the sparkling dilettante, avoided the solitary thinker. A visitor observed that in Charleston the "young fellow of fashion looks down . . . upon the man of study with . . . pity and contempt." Harriet Martineau, the Englishwoman, heard only "lively talk about . . . gay society" while in Charleston, which to her seemed "a place of great activity without much intellectual result."

Writers and the few merchants, planters, physicians, lawyers, and clergymen who were interested in ideas met at Russell's Book Store on the east side of King Street between Wentworth and Hasell streets. Here Simms dominated the conversation among a group that also included the young poets Henry Timrod and Paul Hamilton Hayne. The Antiquarian Society of Charleston founded in the early 1800s was soon reorganized as the Literary and Philosophical Society of South Carolina embracing all areas of knowledge from fine arts to mechanics. Stephen Elliott, the first president of the society, was a Yale graduate, banker, and gentleman botanist who wrote a solid two-volume work, *Sketch of the Botany of South Carolina and Georgia*, and established a museum of natural history for the society on Chalmers Street, which was open to the public, few of whom attended. Following Elliott's death, interest and membership in the society fell sharply until revived by local gentlemen of literary tastes who began meeting weekly in the homes of its members. But the local gentlemanly amateurism frustrated Simms, who grew increasingly bitter. In 1847 he exploded: "The South don't care a d—n, for literature or art." The city became a graveyard for his magazines and for those of others. The poet Paul Hayne, born to wealth and status in Charleston, shared Simms's assessment, writing that Charlestonians "are intensely provincial . . . . Literature they despise."[70]

The most intellectual member of the Charleston bar by the end of the antebellum era was not a local native but one recently arrived from North Carolina, Johnston J. Pettigrew. Among the ministers only the transplanted Northerners like Unitarian Samuel Gilman and Lutheran John Bachman, the foreign-born Catholic bishop John England, and the Presbyterian Thomas Smyth were recognized nationally for their intellectual abilities. Most local clergymen were, in the words of Frederick Porcher, "respectable rather from their character than their talents."[71]

It was the city's physicians and naturalists who made the greatest contributions to the antebellum city's intellectual life. Primarily lowcountry natives, they trained in Northern colleges, returned to Charleston to practice medicine, and carried on an extensive correspondence with scientists in both Philadelphia and Boston. Whereas generally the city's elite had little appreciation of the local literati, they had a high regard for the local physicians who were perceived as useful men. The Reverend Dr. John Bachman, by avocation a competent zoologist, helped establish the Horticultural Society in 1830; Francis S. Holmes, a science professor at the College of Charleston and curator of the Charleston Museum, which was located at the college by 1850, helped found the Elliott Society of Natural History in 1853. A few years later Dr. Lewis R. Gibbes, a nationally known scientist, was elected president. One historian recently accorded Gibbes "a distinctive role in the advancement of scientific activity . . . in Charleston, which was clearly the center for such pursuits in the southeast before the Civil War." His scholarship also helped resuscitate the College of Charleston. The new Medical College enjoyed a sustained growth in enrollments into the 1840s, while members of the faculty and other scientists in the city enjoyed a period of intense productivity. Several of their works won international recognition: the Reverend John Bachman's *Viviparous Quadrupeds of North America* (3 vols., 1845–48) which he co-authored with James J. Audubon; John E. Holbrook's *The Ichthyology of South Carolina* (1855); and Edmund Ravenel's *Fungi Caroliniani Exsiccati* (5 vols., 1853–60).

Charleston's naturalists also promoted scientific understanding locally. In the 1840s they felt obliged to view and expose the "Feejee Mermaid" exhibited by an agent of "that great master of humbuggery, P. T. Barnum," who charged 50 cents a peek. They published their findings in the Charleston press, charging that Barnum, playing on the gullibility of the public, had glued together the head, arms, and upper torso of a monkey and the abdomen and tail of a fish, and they deplored "the exhibition of such a deformity" as "an injury to natural science." But some of the best physician-naturalists in the city succumbed to the city's mentality. Edmund Ravenel, who won international recognition as a conchologist, resigned his professorship at the Medical College at the age of thirty-eight to become a planter and, in the words of historians Jane and William Pease, "live the life of a gentleman amateur in the land of rounded edges."[72]

Charleston's reviving economy of the 1840s attracted portraitists and art teachers, but they seem to have been less talented than those who had worked the city during the opening decades of the century. When daguerreotypes became the rage among the city's well-to-do, artists seeking to both please and win patronage promised "portrait painting" as well as "whole length likenesses in Daguerreotype." One enterprising photographer advertised: "Sick and deceased persons taken at the shortest notice."[73]

". . . public peace and order"

For the first time since the early years of the century, the city was again attracting Irish and German immigrants, but some Charlestonians distrusted these working-class immigrants who, they believed, were "a worthless, unprincipled class . . . enemies to our peculiar institution [slavery] . . . and ever ready to form combinations against . . . the peace of the commonwealth." Many white working-class women competed with black women for jobs as maids, and white male workers repeatedly complained that the city government failed to enforce laws prohibiting slaves hiring themselves out. They were angry that the "opulent inhabitants . . . leave it to their Domestics to employ what workmen they please, [and] it universally happens that those Domestics prefer men of their own color . . . ." The competition between recent immigrants and blacks for work sometimes became vicious and on one occasion an Irish drayman "knock[ed] out the eye of a slave, his competitor."[74]

America's desire for territorial expansion and the Texas boundary dispute were among the reasons for Congress declaring war on Mexico in May 1846. Several months later a Pennsylvania congressman offered a resolution banning slavery from any territory acquired during the war, igniting a fiery debate between Northern and Southern representatives. It once more injected the issue of slavery into the political arena.

In July 1848 Charleston was connected with the country's main telegraph lines by a line that ran up the Neck to Columbia. Samuel F. B. Morse's patents were making him wealthier than his paintings ever did. About a year later messages tapped out of

Charleston in Morse Code probably pertained to a melee at the workhouse on July 13, 1849, when thirty-six black inmates escaped. Most were immediately recaptured and tried the following day, and the ringleaders and two others were sentenced to death by hanging. But several escapees remained at large and hysteria swept the city. A mob gathered before Calvary Church, a nearly completed Afro-American church on Beaufain Street that white Episcopalians in the city were assisting in building. Some among the mob called it the "nigger church" and they wanted to destroy it. Urging on "the rabble of the city" were prominent citizens who sought, one observer noted, "to arouse the fears of a community which had not forgotten the events of 1822." They worried that as a meeting place for both free blacks and slaves, Calvary Church might come to threaten the "public peace and order." Once more a mob was poised to use violence for race control and the social order. But the local attorney, James Louis Petigru, one of the persistent voices of reason among Charleston's elite, faced down the mob and called them "damned fools . . . ." His pleadings for calm and those of several city officials finally turned the mob away.[75]

Calhoun's Funeral and Charleston in the 1850s

Charleston was draped in mourning on April 25–26, 1850, for the funeral of John C. Calhoun, perhaps the most elaborate ceremony of its kind the city ever witnessed. Federal and state troops assembled in Marion Square in front of the Citadel to lead the funeral car, modeled on Napoleon's, which was flanked by a guard of honor and accompanied by distinguished pallbearers like Jefferson Davis as it moved through the streets to City Hall. Here the body lay in state for a day until interred in St. Philip's Cemetery. Boundary Street was soon renamed Calhoun. Admirers in Charleston raised $27,000 to pay off Calhoun's debts, enabling his lowcountry-born wife to keep their upcountry plantation.[76]

In 1850 the city limits of Charleston reached northward to the Neck, southward to the Battery, eastward to the Cooper, and westward to the Ashley. The population had grown to nearly 43,000. With the prime residential and recreation areas in the hands of the elite, the remaining population fitted in where they could. Sometimes modest houses and even shacks stood on the same streets as elegant mansions behind which were their slave yards and kitchens. But most often the poorer residents, free blacks, whites, and some slaves whose owners permitted them to "live out," resided in the crowded alleyways near the wharves or were pushed north of Calhoun Street to the center of the Neck where "bilious . . . or Neck fever" supposedly was epidemic. The city's upper classes believed "that to sleep on the Neck between the first of June and frost was . . . tantamount to ordering one's coffin."

In preempting the choice residential sites in the city, Charleston's well-to-do clustered together on the lower peninsula. Others built homes on the flanks of the peninsula, especially along Rutledge, Pitt, and Lynch (later Ashley) streets, which bisected the suburbs on the city's western edge, Harleston, Cannonsborough, and Radcliffeborough. Here the antebellum elite could enjoy "salubrious" sea breezes, proximity to social institutions, and distance from the perceived unhealthy areas. When the planter Thomas Aston Coffin built his Charleston mansion in 1850 at One East Battery, he took the most coveted site in the city. His modified "single house" of three stories with three tiers of piazzas offered a magnificent view of both the Ashley and Cooper rivers and the harbor. Visitors in the spring found these homes "screened, by the beautiful foliage of evergreen shrubs" and the air "perfumed with the blossoms of the orange and jessamine."

The city's upper class also appropriated to themselves the most choice spot for their outdoor activities, the filled land on the southern tip of the peninsula. Called Oyster Point by the first settlers, then White Point, city officials had authorized the planting of gardens here in the 1830s and the building of "beautiful pagodas" and "broad and serpentine walks" along the Battery. When Frances Kemble went for a walk she found the Battery "a most delightful promenade" with the Ashley River on one side and on the other "large and picturesque old houses . . . ." During the 1840s the City Council prohibited blacks from using the gardens and Battery between five and ten in the evenings.[77]

The city's grand mansions were the sites of ostentatious parties and balls during the annual social season. In the social season of 1850–51, Jenny Lind, "the Swedish Nightingale," presented her forty-sixth grand concert in America and first in Charleston, and the *Courier* raved that from her lips came "the richest musical treat . . . ever . . . offered in our city." In February Mrs. Charles Alston gave what may have been the most splendid ball the city ever knew. Approximately 200 guests used 18 dozen plates, 14 dozen knives, 28 dozen spoons, 6 dozen champagne glasses, and consumed 4 turkeys, 4 hams, 50 partridges, 12

"Charleston, 1851: View from the Ashley River at White Point Gardens," by William Hill. *Courtesy of the South Carolina Historical Society, Charleston, S.C.*

pheasants, 22 ducks, 10 quarts of oysters, 4 pyramids of crystallized fruit and coconut, and "immense quantities" of bonbons, cakes, creams, and jellies.

Visitors to Charleston during the annual season found accommodations at the older Planter's Hotel on Queen Street, the Charleston Hotel on Meeting Street, or newer hotels on the same street—the Mills House, a five-storied structure at the southwestern corner of Meeting and Queen streets, and the Pavilion Hotel, a four-storied building at the northwestern corner of Meeting and Hasell streets. William Gilmore Simms described the Mills House, famed for its wine cellar and cuisine, as "costly in furniture, rich in decoration" and favored by "all the fashionable gentry," while the Pavilion Hotel was "less ornate." Besides these noteworthy Meeting Street hostelries, visitors and Charlestonians could lodge or dine at three King Street hotels, the American on the southwestern corner of King and George streets, the Merchant's Hotel at the northwestern corner of King and Society streets, and the Victoria near the southwestern corner of Market and King streets.[78]

In Washington the determination of some Northern politicians to restrict and eventually abolish slavery was increasingly troublesome to senators and representatives from South Carolina, where the state legislature began to talk of secession and war in December 1850. An election was held in February 1851 for members to attend a state convention to consider action separate from other Southern states if necessary. Fiery advocates of this persuasion, like Robert Barnwell Rhett and other members of the South Carolina Southern Rights Association, convened in Charleston from May 5 to May 8. Here also in July and again in September the state's Cooperationists met—politicos desiring secession only if other slaveholding states seceded too. In October the Cooperationists triumphed when in a statewide election South Carolinians voted against seceding separately. The plantation districts where black slaves were heavily concentrated returned large numbers of Separatist votes, but most of the voters in Charleston and the upcountry showed themselves to be Cooperationists. By the time the convention met in Columbia in April 1852 support for independent secession was lacking and South Carolina remained in the Union because the rest of the South was not yet willing to leave it.

The year 1852 saw the publication of two books that profoundly influenced public opinion in both the North and the South: *Uncle Tom's Cabin* and *The Pro-Slavery Argument*. The former was the classic attack on slavery and the latter its classic defense. *The Pro-Slavery Argument* contained essays by prominent Southerners quoting Aristotle, the Bible, and purportedly scientific evidence proving that blacks were inherently inferior. The book was published in Charleston.[79]

The Manufacturing Center of South Carolina

Leading Charleston businessmen and the local press advocated the development of manufacturing in the city during the decades of the 1840s and 1850s, boosted the commercial conventions held there in 1839 and 1854, and helped organize the "South Carolina Institute for the Promotion of Art, Mechanical Ingenuity and Industry" through an annual fair, the first being held in 1849. In 1852 the legislature appropriated $10,000 to enable the South Carolina Institute to build a hall to exhibit products at its fair.

By this time Charleston had become the manufacturing center of South Carolina. There were fourteen grist mills, six rice mills, six iron foundries (including the Phoenix Iron Works whose annual productivity was surpassed only by foundries located in New Orleans, Louisiana; Richmond, Virginia; and Nashville, Tennessee), six turpentine distilleries, a railroad machine shop and depot, and numerous sawmills. There were six blind, sash, and door factories located near the western ends of Tradd, Broad, and Beaufain streets where, with easy access to vessels in the Ashley River, they continued to operate into the twentieth century. The manufacturing enterprises included two umbrella factories; a cordage factory; a hatmaker; manufacturers of organs, stained glass, silverware, railway cars, paper, crockery, and furniture; a friction-match shop; several carriage and wagon shops, saddleries, brickyards, and tinware shops; eleven boat-builders; and several sail-making and rigging concerns. In accord with local ordinances and planters' wishes, the industries were located on the edge of the city.

In the early 1850s Henry Conner, Henry Gourdin, and George Trenholm successfully lobbied city, state, and national governments for harbor improvements, and over $120,000 was appropriated for the dredging of a suitable channel for large merchantmen. These businessmen achieved another major goal when Congress approved the construction of a new customs house, and by 1861 over $2 million had been spent to build it. Though construction was interrupted by the Civil War, the building stands today on East Bay Street near the intersection with Market Street.[80]

Fueling the city's economic boom of the early 1850s were the railroads in which a merchant-dominated city government had invested over $3,500,000. This municipal debt became a grim burden on four generations of Charlestonians. Planter interests, which had so long blocked the extension of the rail lines to the wharves, were neutralized by the City Council, which permitted the Charleston and Savannah and the Northeastern railroads to extend their tracks there during the 1850s. By 1850 rail lines brought into the city 284,935 bales of cotton, and in 1855 as much as 449,554 bales. To console those who thought that the new commercial boom might adversely affect the city's integrity, the *Courier* told Charlestonians that they need not "fear the loss of character." Strongly influenced by the attitudes of the great planters, Charleston may have been the first important American city to have a strong sense of its own character as something to be preserved.[81]

Beginning in 1853 the members of the City Council were elected for two-year terms instead of annually. In that year Leonidas W. Spratt of the Charleston *Southern Standard* advocated reopening the African slave trade because he was concerned that Charleston's growing white proletariat increasingly competed with slave labor, "creating a condition dangerous . . . to slavery as a living system at the South." Although there was some local support for Spratt's views, the movement to reopen the slave trade failed because wealthy slaveholders wished to protect the value of their slave property.

William J. Grayson, whose commitment to Unionism isolated him in Charleston and made it difficult for him to continue as the port's collector of customs, retired to his plantation in 1853 and began writing *The Hireling and the Slave* in which he contrasted the lives of British laborers with those of slaves in South Carolina. The vivid but old-fashioned couplets of this extraordinary poem, published in the city in 1854, reveal how intensely the lowcountry planters believed in the wisdom and benevolence of slavery as they thought they knew it.

In the summer of 1854 a hurricane lashed through the city, flooding the streets, and yellow-fever-carrying mosquitoes returned bringing a virulent epidemic. While the disease raged in the city during the late summer, the Charleston press advised that "no real dangers exist" and charged that newspapers in rival ports like Savannah were exaggerating the severity of the epidemic, but from mid-August to mid-November 627 persons died.

In 1855 Governor James H. Adams doubted the need for keeping the Negro Seaman Acts on the books, since they were likely to foster antislavery sentiment, but the laws were not changed. Offering a $2,000 reward for information about suspected arsonists, Charleston's City Council was in no mood to welcome more free black strangers.[82]

One of the earliest daguerreotypes taken by the Charleston photographer, George S. Cook, in 1857 shows Charlotte Helen Middleton about three years of age in the lap of her nursemaid and family slave, Lydia. *Courtesy of the Black Charleston Photo Collection, College of Charleston Library, Charleston, S.C.*

A City "of the past"

After the mid-1850s Charleston's economy was in jeopardy again. Competing railroads out of Savannah, Mobile, and New Orleans were siphoning off rail traffic, and Charleston's export trade was falling. Six and one-half percent of the population worked in manufacturing in 1848, but only 2.1 percent did so twelve years later. The city had failed to diversify its economy and was the least industrialized of the nation's major population centers. Also, as Allan Pred has shown, Charleston failed to develop economic linkages within a Southern regional system of cities and it became a "colonial" outlier of the Northeastern regional system. Furthermore, Charleston's hinterland interdependencies, among them Beaufort, Cheraw, and Greenville, were too small and too few to promote the city's growth. They offered only limited markets for Charleston's wholesalers and produced few manufactured products to be sold and shipped abroad from the port city. Travelers observed that the pace of life in Charleston did not compare with the hustle and bustle of other North American ports. To the Britisher Charles Rosenberg, Charleston appeared to be a city "of the past . . . ."[83]

The economic downturn coupled with the steady stream of immigrants, sailors, and vagrants who straggled into the city seeking work caused growing unemployment. By the mid-1850s approximately 40 percent of the white population of nearly 9,000 were recent Irish or German immigrants. From 1850 to 1856 the number of inmates in the city's Poor House rose from 691 to 1,363 and the ratio of foreign-born to native reached seven to one. Class divisions became as obvious as racial divisions. Economically most whites living in the city had more in common with blacks than with the white elite.

Prostitution flourished, and at least one brothel appears to have enjoyed special favors from the leading citizens. Located at 11 Beresford Street, the imposing three-story brick structure was owned in the 1850s by Grace Peixotto. One writer who knew her described Grace as "a notorious woman who kept the worst kind of a brothel for years, where harlots of all shades and importations break the quietude of night with their polluted songs." He concluded that her business was "openly tolerated . . . by leading men" of the city. Slaves also sought out brothels and prostitutes. The wealthy planter John Berkeley Grimball had his slave Josey placed in solitary confinement for running away to "the house of two white women of bad repute."

In September 1855 the City Council was convinced that the "evils which arise from a too underrestricted sale of spiritous liquors [to] the white and colored population" resulted in the increasing number of robberies. The *Courier* saw new threats to the city from thieves and "idle persons who have been turned upon us from the northern cities." The number of homicides was also rising dramatically. Contributing to the uneasiness of the city's elite was the rising Northern antislavery rhetoric, which they believed encouraged slave conspiracies. An English traveler in Charleston observed the constant patrols moving about the city and was informed that such surveillance was necessary because "a great many desperate men" congregate in port cities. All these factors prompted a reevaluation of the city's agencies of social control. Seaports in the Northeast faced similar problems of social fragmentation and instability and launched their own moral reformation and search for order, but Charleston's problems were compounded by its large slave population, for which there existed several separate agencies of control.[84]

Agencies of Social Control

During the decade of the 1850s the outmigration of slaves and the immigration of whites transformed Charleston from a city that was 53 percent black to 58 percent white; from a city dominated by a skilled black labor force to one where two-fifths of the working class was white and of whom 60 percent were foreign-born by 1860. Like Leonidas Spratt earlier, Christopher G. Memminger was thinking of the rising numbers of white laborers when he began promoting a public school system in the 1850s: "The ignorant and uneducated are always the first to engage in outrage and violence . . . and measures hostile to our institutions . . . ." Orphaned at an early age, Memminger was adopted by the Charleston merchant Thomas Bennett, given all the educational and social advantages of great wealth, and now was championing educational ideas whose purpose was to improve and safeguard Southern society. He believed that the greatest danger to Southern institutions came from the white proletariat who "could be marshalled against the Planters, upon the idea that they were fighting against the aristocracy." Memminger urged "bringing together the children of rich and poor" in the same classroom so as to "benefit both by removing from one any disposition to arrogance and self-will, and from the other the spirit of envy and jealousy." In the late 1850s his ideas came to fruition with the opening of a handsome three-story structure on St. Philip's Street, Charleston High and Normal School, South Carolina's first free public school, later renamed Memminger. Bostonian Frederick A. Sawyer, a man of character and ability who was hired as superintendent of the city's schools in 1856, and nine northern teachers trained in the most recent pedagogical methods assisted local officials in transforming Charleston's school system, which they modeled after New York's, into the best in South Carolina by the end of the decade.[85]

The Poor House, looked on by the city's well-to-do "not only as a place of refuge for the victims of misfortune, but as a . . . House of Correction" was jammed with paupers and criminals. The commissioners of the poor urged the city government to find other quarters because the needy poor refused to apply to the old Poor House because of its reputation "as a place of punishment for the unworthy." In 1856 the indigents were transferred from the old Poor House at the corner of Mazyck and Magazine streets to a larger brick building, the defunct Charleston Manufacturing Company on Columbus Street, between Drake and Court streets. Renamed the Almshouse, later the Charleston Home, it admitted only worthy paupers, and the city government believed the institution had been "relieved" of its former bad reputation. Besides the more than 200 indigents maintained there by the late 1850s, approximately 900 "pensioners," most of them native Charlestonians, received outdoor relief in the form of rations of bread, beef, and grits.

After extensive remodeling and additions, the Orphan House contained 130 dormitory rooms, large play, school, and dining rooms, and a hospital ward, all heated by steam. It was the largest building in the city, and by the end of the decade some 360 orphans were housed there. The towering cupola supported a statue of Charity and held the city's massive fire-alarm bell. The commissioners of the Orphan House expected the orphans to follow the moral code they demanded of their families and slaves. Between 1790 and the 1850s the commissioners rescued nearly 2,000 children from abuse and neglect, providing them with a good diet, a basic education, strict supervision, and safe areas for recreation. Over the years former inmates wrote that they appreciated the commissioners "acting the part of fathers" and numerous former inmates became successful. The orphanage's reputation as an institution that reflected the citizens' generosity and social conscience became increasingly important to an elite that was being denounced for the cruelties of slavery.[86]

Charleston's police force doubled in size from the 1830s to the 1850s and maintenance costs soared fivefold. Policemen, enlisted from the laboring class and usually Irish, were poorly paid. While the common laborers might receive $1.00 a day, members of the police force earned 60 cents for a night's work. Sometimes the city's mayors made appointments to the force because they "voted on the right side." Occasionally policemen were charged with drunkenness, dereliction of duty, and corrupt practices. A citizen wrote to the *Courier* that there were instances "when amounts of money are paid . . . to the police as a reward for shutting their eyes, and closing their lips."

The police force of 250 members by the mid-1850s was reorganized following the election of William Porcher Miles as mayor. Salaries were increased, the office of chief of police was created, four detectives were appointed, a "rogues" file of daguerreotypes was expanded, and a corps of horsemen was initiated to patrol the suburbs. Mayor Miles appointed John Harleston, a graduate of West Point and a colonel in the militia, as the first chief of police. Joining him were eight other officers, six of whom were graduates of the Citadel. The new organization soon won grudging respect among the city's rougher classes, who took to calling the policemen "Paddy Miles' Bull Dogs." By 1857 this new, professional police force numbered 197, including 25 horsemen, and cost city taxpayers nearly $100,000 annually.

The courts of the General Sessions and the City Court tried only white persons by juries for crimes and misdemeanors. The Magistrates' Court of usually five slaveholders tried only slaves and free blacks. A Mayor's Court tried both whites and blacks for "riotous and disorderly" conduct.[87]

Public whippings continued to be used for both black and white, male and female, until Charleston's first citizens became concerned that public whippings of white persons threatened white supremacy. A grand jury declared that when whites were taken to the whipping post there is an "evil arising from this public exposure," for there was usually a "crowd of our colored population . . . attendant . . . who" may feel "self gratulation in the degradation of the white by the same punishment to their own level." Public hangings, usually advertised weeks before the scheduled date and attracting large, often unruly crowds, continued to serve as the ultimate solution in the maintenance of the social order.

The City Jail by the 1850s had become to City Council members, in "both size and security," inadequate for "the welfare of the city." One visitor to the prison found in one room "nine or ten persons . . . and such was the morbid stench . . . that we were compelled to put our handkerchiefs to our faces." A successful appeal for state funds and local appropriations promised enough money by 1855 to raze an earlier wing, add a four-story brick octagonal wing and the presently existing front portion of the building with its façade in the Romanesque Revival Style.[88]

The End of an Era

In 1855 members of Charleston's small community of intellectuals, especially James Petigru, Frederick Porcher, and Mitchell King, founded the South Carolina Historical Society, and in the following year "Russell's Bookstore Group" initiated *Russell's Magazine*, the last of the Old South's literary publications. It first appeared in April 1857 and included writings by Simms, William Grayson, Henry Timrod, and Paul Hamilton Hayne. That year Charles Fraser, South Carolina's greatest miniaturist, exhibited in Charleston 313 of his miniatures, 139 landscapes, and also large portraits. The Carolina Art Association was founded in 1858 and sponsored a show featuring Emanuel Leutze's "Jasper Rescuing the Flag at Fort Moultrie."

For some years Charleston's boosters had believed that cleanliness, healthiness, and business prosperity were linked, and by the late 1850s the city was spending about $70,000 annually to clean, repair, and drain the streets. The principal burial ground for white Charlestonians, Magnolia Cemetery, was located several miles up the Neck along the west bank of the Cooper River. Cow stalls kept by citizens now were required to have paved or wooden flooring. But for their water Charlestonians still relied on cisterns and shallow wells, and the liquid remained "for the most part undrinkable, . . . hardly fit for washing . . . ." New sidewalks of brick, stone curbing, and guttering were laid. The south end of East Bay Street on the Battery was filled in and covered over with sawdust and shell, and the western ends of Calhoun and Beaufain streets were extended by filling in marshland. Hundreds of planks were laid along Rutledge Street and a wooden bridge built across the pond bounded by Rutledge, Beaufain, Lynch (later Ashley) and Broad streets, which was fenced in and sidewalks built around it. During these efforts to clean and beautify Charleston, yellow fever once again scourged the city in 1858. More than 700 persons succumbed. William Gilmore Simms buried two of his sons "in one grave, within twelve hours of each other." Only after the pestilence subsided did the newspapers acknowledge that an epidemic had occurred. But efforts to suppress information about the port's unhealthiness were futile. In 1860 Frederick Law Olmstead publicly characterized Charleston as having "the worst climate for unacclimated whites of any town in the United States.[89]

The inequality in the distribution of wealth in the city was enormous by comparison to Northern cities: some 155 white persons or just over 3 percent of the 4,644 free heads of households controlled property ranging from $54,000 to $104,000 and owned approximately half of the wealth in Charleston. They were at the top of the pyramid of wealth in the city, state, and nation. Most Charlestonians owned neither land nor slaves, and James Stirling, an English visitor strolling through the city in the 1850s, noticed there seemed to be "no middle class; only rich and poor." At the end of the decade a "master mechanic" wrote in the *Courier* addressing the city's slaveholders: "In placing the negro in competition with white mechanics . . . you drag the latter down . . . . This breed[s] discontent and hatred and make[s] . . . the white mechanic . . . an enemy of . . . slavery." But Charleston's aristocrats remained unresponsive to concerns of the white laboring class, whom they regarded almost as a separate species. One Charlestonian described poor whites as "mean, thieving, sneaking, ... They teach our negroes to steal, sell them liquor, do everything to corrupt and demoralize them . . . they ought to be slaves themselves . . . . I almost wish we might have a war with the Yankees: we should get some of them killed off, then!" But the gentry did support the Charleston Marine School, which was established in May

1859. The students were "boys who had . . . been wandering about the streets of Charleston" and it was the first "floating" school of its kind. In seeking state support for the institution, local boosters agreed that the school would help replace Northern seamen with Southern sailors and "our peculiar Institutions [would] be protected from their [the Northerners'] evil communication with our negroes."[90]

With a population of 40,522 in 1859—it had declined about 2,500 since the beginning of the decade—the city of Charleston ranked twenty-second in the nation, although in manufacturing it ranked only eighty-fifth. The most populous of the South Atlantic ports and the major distribution center for the state, Charleston more closely resembled a modern police state than any other city in the nation. Frederick Olmstead observed that "the cannon in position on the parade ground, the citadel, . . . with its martial ceremonies, the frequent parades of militia . . . the numerous armed police, might lead one to imagine that the town was in a state of siege or revolution."

Repeatedly, Charleston's most respected civic leaders denounced Northern abolitionists, defended slavery as a positive good, and urged secession from the Union. In March 1859 the *Southern Episcopalian* of Charleston editorialized: "Slavery [is] a necessary element towards the composition of a high and stable civilization—as a thing good in itself, . . . in short the best mode in which labor and capital can stand associated."

In October the antislavery fanatic John Brown and his small band of followers attacked the federal arsenal at Harper's Ferry, Virginia. The South panicked. The editor of the *Courier* put on display one of Brown's fierce-looking pikes, and Robert Barnwell Rhett, editor of the *Mercury* and the South's leading disunionist, drew parallels between Brown's foray and Nat Turner's massacre of white Virginians some thirty years before. Local papers reported "incendiary attempts" within the city and Charlestonians again approved extreme, extralegal methods. A new Charleston Vigilance Association was formed to monitor the activities of slaves, free blacks, and "traitorous" whites. A British consul at Charleston wrote: "Persons are torn away from their residences and pursuits, sometimes tarred and feathered; 'ridden upon rails,' or cruelly whipped."

In April 1860 the city was a blaze of color. The fragrance of flowers filled the air as hundreds of Northern and Southern delegates arrived for the Democratic National Convention at South Carolina Institute Hall on the east side of Meeting Street, just north of Queen Street. A contemporary observed that "there was a Fourth of July feeling in the public sentiment of the city. It was overwhelmingly in favor of the seceders." In a few days the convention split into Northern and Southern wings and disbanded. Rhett's *Mercury* proclaimed: "The last party, pretending to be a national party, is broken up, and the antagonism of the two sections of the Union has nothing to arrest its fierce collisions."

When the National Republican Party nominated Abraham Lincoln for president, lawyer Edward McCrady, businessmen Robert and Henry Gourdin, and lowcountry planter John Townsend formed the "1860 Association," which soon became the South's leading publisher of pamphlets calling for secession, and military and psychological preparedness for disunion. In pamphlets like *The Doom of Slavery in the Union and Its Safety Out of It*, Southerners were urged "to defend their honor, their properties, and their families" or else suffer the "beastly horrors of the . . . Revolution in St. Domingo . . . ."[91]

In August the Charleston police began a systematic door-to-door search and interrogation of the free black community. Some were rich; some were desperately poor. In 1860 there were 3,237 free blacks in Charleston and 122 of these owned slaves themselves. Poor free blacks unable to produce absolute proof of their emancipated status were reenslaved and even the city's slaveowning mulatto aristocracy was terrorized. Previously, families like the William Ellisons, who owned sixty-three slaves, the Johnsons, the Derefs, and the Westons had escaped police harassment because of their relationships with the white elite, but as the secession crisis worsened, the white guardians of the brown aristocracy were silent.

For nearly 200 years Charleston's white laboring class had resented especially the brown elite's close relationship with the city's white upper class. Now in the summer of 1860 two successful and slaveowning white mechanics, James M. Eason, a foundry owner, and Henry T. Peake, superintendent of shops of the South Carolina Railroad, launched a movement to protect the white laborer from the competition of free blacks and "slaves hiring their own time." In campaigning for election to the state legislature they attacked both the white and the brown elite, and both Eason and Peake were elected by a large turnout of the white working class who lived north of Calhoun Street. Once in the legislature Eason sponsored a bill that would have made it illegal for free blacks to take any jobs except as day laborers or domestic servants, but more urgent business prevented his bill from coming up for consideration.

Many of the brown aristocracy considered emigrating from the city but felt that they could not leave successful careers, take enormous losses through sale of their real estate, or even get safe passage out of South Carolina. But hundreds of less prosperous free blacks—carpenters, masons, shoemakers, tailors, and their families—sold what they could, packed what they could carry, and fled. Some sold their property at huge losses and felt cheated by white persons who took advantage of their predicament.[92]

When the news of Lincoln's election reached the city on November 7, the foreman of the grand jury in the federal court in Charleston, Robert Gourdin, refused to conduct any further business as the North "through the ballot box . . . has swept away the last hope for the permanence . . . of the Federal government of these sovereign States"; Judge Andrew G. Magrath rose and divested himself of his robes of office; United States District Attorney James Conner, and William Colcock, the collector of the port, also resigned. Secessionist sentiment flourished and the leaders likened themselves to earlier American or French revolutionaries: the Palmetto and Lone Star flags were hoisted, "liberty poles" were erected, and many citizens affixed a blue cockade to their lapels—a gold badge with the palmetto tree, a lone star, and a coiled rattlesnake superimposed upon a plain blue silk ribbon.

"—our honor—aye and our very lives"

A huge public rally was held at Institute Hall on the evening of November 9. One participant wrote that the speakers called for "in burning phrases . . . immediate secession." In response "the multitudes . . . waved their hats in the air, and thundered forth resounding cheers." A delegation from the rally took the next train to Columbia to call for disunion. Several days later the president of the Senate, William D. Porcher, remarked that "Charleston . . . is clamorous for secession" and "in the state I think no one can resist the current." Visitors to the city were impressed by its unanimity. In November and December patrols prowled Charleston's street as rumors of black unrest circulated. Among the few Unionists remaining in the lowcountry was James Petigru, who, addressing a group of secessionists, remarked that "South Carolina is too small to be a Republic, and too large to be an insane asylum."

On December 17 more than 160 delegates elected from across South Carolina convened in Columbia to decide whether the state would secede. The twenty-three representatives from Charleston comprised the largest single delegation and, like the others, they were primarily a wealthy, middle-aged, native-born, slaveholding elite of planters and lawyers. Following an outbreak of smallpox in Columbia, the convention reassembled in Charleston, where on December 20 in St. Andrew's Hall the delegates unanimously adopted the Ordinance of Secession from the Union. In the evening they signed it at Institute Hall. The news "spread through the city like wild-fire," the *Mercury* reported. "The church bells rang . . . artillery salutes were soon . . . thundering . . . union flags were . . . thrown to the breeze. . . . volunteers . . . donned their uniforms . . . ." An Englishman in Charleston described two young women of Charleston's upper class as "ardent secessionists" who, when asked what would happen if the federal government encouraged slave revolts, answered: "If the slaves rose, we should kill them like so many snakes." Eighty-two brown aristocrats dispatched a message to the mayor of Charleston: "We are by birth citizens of South Carolina, in our veins is the blood of the white race in some half, in others much more, our attachments are with you."

In their enthusiasm for secession, the gentry were living up to their tradition of resorting to violence when threatened. In 1776 British authorities, in the early nineteenth century outside agitators and local arsonists, in 1822 Denmark Vesey, and by 1860 Northern abolitionists—all threatened the hegemony of the elite and a social order of deferential whites and servile blacks. John Brown's Raid and the election of Lincoln led planters, merchants, lawyers, scientists, physicians, clergy, and writers to forget their considerable differences and unite. To Charleston's gentry secession meant the possibility of war and social dislocation, but remaining in the Union posed even greater threats from a federal government controlled by abolitionists who raised more terrible specters. As one young member of Charleston's planter-elite put it: " . . . we are oppressed and are contending for all that we hold most dear—our property—our institutions—our honor—aye and our very lives!"[93]

Major Robert Anderson, a slender, graying combat veteran of the Mexican-American War commanding the U.S. garrison at Fort Moultrie, received orders " . . . to hold possession of the forts in this harbor, and if attacked . . . defend yourself to the last extremity." The walls of Fort Moultrie, built in 1811 near the site of the Revolutionary fort, were cracked, and sand had drifted high enough to permit cows to wander over the parapets and into the fort to graze. Castle Pinckney, less than a mile east of Charles-

A rare photograph of the officers of the Phoenix Fire Engine Company, January 18, 1861, one of the many proud volunteer fire-fighting companies in antebellum Charleston, which were kept busy fighting fires. *Courtesy of the Charleston Museum, Charleston, S.C.*

ton's downtown residential area, had not been garrisoned since 1836, but Major Anderson believed it was needed "to keep command of this harbor" and promptly ordered a work party to repair it. Anderson knew, however, that the key to controlling the port was Fort Sumter, begun in 1829 near the mouth of the harbor and not yet completed. Its sixty-foot walls rose steeply from the waters that surrounded it and the three tiers of guns could command the shipping channel and fire on the city. His engineers hurriedly prepared the fort for a long siege and then, in the late afternoon of December 26, his troops spiked the guns of Fort Moultrie and rowed out to Fort Sumter. Major Anderson and his force of eighty-two men now occupied the strongest and most strategic fortification in Charleston's harbor.

The news spread quickly, Anderson's military superiors in Washington applauding the maneuver while President James Buchanan and his cabinet viewed it as a "calamity." Surprised and angry, the secessionists believed Anderson had violated an unwritten agreement to maintain the status quo. "Major Robert Anderson, U.S.A.," said the *Courier*, "has achieved the unenviable distinction of opening civil war between American citizens by an act of gross breach of faith."

There were only about a dozen United State soldiers holding Castle Pinckney, Fort Moultrie, and the federal Arsenal in the city and they offered no resistance when, in the first military encounter of the war, South Carolina troops seized all three points and hauled down the Stars and Stripes. By December 30, 1860, the only flag that fluttered over the Arsenal, Castle Pinckney, and Fort Moultrie showed a new moon and a palmetto tree, both in white, on a dark blue background. It was the South Carolina flag.[94]

V

War and Peace

❦ 1. 1861–1865:
Civil War

" . . . The opening ball of the Revolution"

Expecting the federal government to attempt to reinforce
Fort Sumter, Governor Francis W. Pickens sent a guard boat to
patrol off the bar and ordered a battery of four howitzers posi-
tioned on Morris Island to rake the main ship channel. On January
7 Charlestonians heard that the *Star of the West,* jammed with
armed troops, had departed New York for their city. The vivacious Emma Holmes recorded in her diary that "the city seemed
suddenly turned into a camp. Nothing was heard but preparations
for war." Three days later the *Star of the West* appeared off
Charleston.

Near daylight the sidewheeler steamed up the main ship
channel paralleling Morris Island and toward Fort Sumter. Concealed among the sand dunes on the island, Citadel cadets and
their officers waited until the vessel came opposite their howitzers, then fired. Hit by shots near the rudder and bow, the *Star of
the West* came about, recrossed the bar, and steamed north to
return to New York. The following day the *Mercury* boasted:
"Yesterday morning was the opening ball of the Revolution. We
are proud that our harbor has been so honored."

Citizens and soldiers were eager to storm Fort Sumter. Governor Pickens ordered additional batteries built on Sullivan's,
Morris, and James islands, dispatched two more guard boats to
patrol the harbor, and hulks were sunk in the main channel to
prevent the resupplying of Fort Sumter. By February nearly
7,000 troops were camped in and around Charleston.

One of Charleston's elite observed that in the city "Every
body apprehends that the *crisis* is approaching." Emma Holmes
reflected soberly on the "terrors of a civil war," but also eagerly
looked forward to attending the growing numbers of military parades and balls in the city. Also in a holiday mood, Susan Smythe
celebrated Washington's birthday by going shopping, buying silk

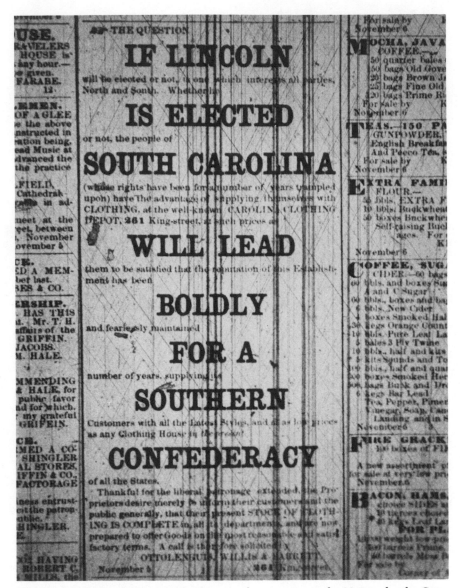

This blunt message was superimposed on an advertisement in the *Mercury* by the Carolina Clothing Depot on the eve of the presidential election of 1860. *Courtesy of the South Caroliniana Library of the University of South Carolina, Columbia, S.C.*

dresses, and visiting "the floating battery, which she thought would soon be launched to attack Fort Sumter.[1]

Following the formation of the Confederate States of America (CSA), at Montgomery, Alabama, President Jefferson Davis ordered Brigadier General Pierre G. T. Beauregard "to take charge" of the volatile situation at Charleston. Beauregard arrived on March 3. A West Point graduate of Creole extraction, he was a landed aristocrat from south Louisiana with an olive complexion, a cropped mustache, and a protruding chin. Courteous, often grave in manner, he spoke with a trace of a French accent, and Charleston went wild over him. A skilled engineering and artillery officer, Beauregard immediately, but tactfully, rearranged the growing ring of fortifications and batteries around Fort Sumter.

The day after General Beauregard arrived in Charleston, Abraham Lincoln took the oath of office in Washington as president of the United States, promising to use the power conferred on him to "hold, occupy, and possess the property and places belonging to the government." Charlestonians knew this meant Fort Sumter. Emma Holmes observed that Lincoln's "speech was just what was expected of him, stupid, . . . and insolent, and is everywhere considered as a virtual declaration of war."

On March 21 President Lincoln sent his trusted friend Ward H. Lamon "on a confidential mission" to Charleston where he met with one of the city's last Unionists, James Petigru, who told him that "peaceable secession or war was inevitable." He also met with Governor Pickens who informed him that any attempt to resupply Fort Sumter meant war. Lamon returned quickly to Washington, and on March 29 Lincoln ordered a naval expedition to reprovision the fort in Charleston harbor. When Major Anderson and General Beauregard learned of this, both prepared for war.

In his own hand on April 6 Lincoln drafted a message to Governor Pickens, which was read to him and General Beauregard two days later, promising that if resupply was neither resisted nor the fort attacked, no attempt would be made "to throw in men, arms, or ammunition . . . ."

Mary Boykin Chesnut, who in quieter times had studied at Madame Talvande's School on Legare Street, wrote in her diary: "Any minute . . . cannon may open on us, the fleet come in. . . . The air is red-hot with rumors." On April 9 word swept through

the city that "seven vessels were . . . off the bar" and cannons
were fired and the bells of St. Michael's rung as signals for troops
to report to their stations. Throughout a night punctuated by
downpours of rain Emma Holmes listened to "the tramp of armed
men . . . marching to the boats" along streets " . . . thronged and
bustling with the preparation for war . . . ."

Beauregard received his orders on April 10: request Major
Anderson to surrender Fort Sumter or Confederate guns will
begin firing on it. In the afternoon three of Beauregard's staff,
including Colonel James Chesnut, husband of Mary Boykin Chesnut, delivered this message to Major Anderson. Spectators
thronged the Battery day and night, Emma Holmes wrote, "anx-
iously watching and awaiting . . . cannon opening on the fort or
on the fleet off the bar." Dining with friends that same evening
Mary Boykin Chesnut enjoyed the "merriest, maddest dinner we
have had yet . . . . We had an unspoken foreboding it was to be
our last pleasant meeting."

On April 11 and again in the early morning hours of April 12
Major Anderson refused to surrender. Therefore, at about 3:20
A.M. Colonel Chesnut handed Anderson the following note and
departed: " . . . General Beauregard . . . will open the fire of his
batteries on Fort Sumter in one hour from this time." Colonel
Chesnut and his party were rowed away in the darkness toward
the torches and campfires of Fort Johnson on James Island. Meanwhile, Mary Boykin Chesnut lay awake in the Mills House unable
to sleep knowing that her husband was "somewhere in that dark
bay" and that if Anderson did not surrender "at four—the orders
are—he shall be fired upon." She recorded in her diary that at
"four—St. Michael chimes. I begin to hope." But at half-past four
she heard "the heavy booming of cannon" and "sprang out of
bed, and on my knees—prostrate—I prayed as I never prayed
before."

By 5:00 A.M. forty-three batteries and mortars around the
harbor were bombarding Fort Sumter. The cannons shook the
city awake and Charlestonians rushed to the Battery, the
wharves, and to housetops for a view of the pyrotechnics. Mary
Boykin Chesnut joined a crowd of people on the roof of the Mills
House. "The women were wild there . . . . Prayers from the
women and imprecations from the men, and then a shell would
light up the scene."

A steady drizzle fell all day on the crowds watching the bombardment. By nightfall 2,500 shot and shell had been fired into Fort Sumter. Major Anderson returned the fire, but the Confederates were beyond his range. Before retiring that evening, Jacob Schirmer noted in his diary: "a day ever to be remembered, war has commenced in earnest."

The following "morning rose clear and brilliantly beautiful," and the bombardment began again. Around 8:00 A.M. crowds of soldiers and civilians watching around the harbor broke into cheers: Fort Sumter was on fire. A "hot shot" had crashed into the barracks and started the blaze. Inside the fort Private John Thompson of the First United States Artillery found the "heat and smoke . . . awful. Our magazine was becoming enveloped in flames, and our own shell were constantly bursting around us." The blaze was nearly out of control and after thirty-four hours of almost continuous bombardment, at about 2:30 in the afternoon of April 13, Anderson surrendered.

Phoebe Townsend remembered that when the news reached observers on the Battery a great shout went up. Across the city, church bells rang and batteries fired off salvos. Mary Boykin Chesnut saw her husband, Colonel Chesnut, a party to the surrender negotiations, "carried by a mob to tell Gen. Beauregard the news." Among the soldiers there was "shaking of hands, . . . tossing of hats . . . screams, . . . hugging." Some got drunk.[2]

Parties and celebrations continued for days. William Howard Russell, an English correspondent, observed that the streets "present some such aspect of those in Paris in the last revolution. Secession flags waved out of all the windows . . . ." Militia companies appeared constantly on parade with "drummers beating calls and ruffles." Russell described the soldiers as "young and old some with the air of gentlemen; others coarse, long-haired fellows, without any semblance of military bearing" who were "full of fight, and burning with enthusiasm." Also "groups of grinning Negros delighted in the glory and glitter of a holiday." One female resident later recalled the "joy and exultation of the times: "Victory was ours . . . and the . . . [Confederate] flag the 'Stars and Bars' . . . floated beside the Palmetto from the battered walls of Sumter."

Lincoln's call for 75,000 volunteers from the loyal states on the day following the fall of Fort Sumter and his blockade of Southern ports fed the patriotic fervor sweeping Charleston. Talk around military messes turned to invading the North, and a young

Confederate soldier in Charleston wrote, "it is firmly believed that we will have Washington in less than a month."

While the frugal Charleston lawyer Christopher G. Memminger, recently appointed secretary of the treasury of the Confederacy, organized his new department in April and May, General Beauregard resumed work on the coastal defenses around Charleston. Fort Sumter was put in fighting order and batteries went up on islands to the north and south of the city, but the defenses he had so carefully planned were only partially built when he was reassigned to Virginia in late spring and Colonel Richard H. Anderson assumed command at Charleston.

The USS *Niagara*, the first ship of what soon became a formidable Union flotilla, arrived off Charleston on May 9. By mid-July eleven warships of the Atlantic Blockading Squadron were cruising off Savannah, Charleston, and the North Carolina coast.

On August 21 Brigadier General Roswell S. Ripley, CSA, took charge of the troops in and around the city and immediately turned to strengthening the fortifications. Then on November 7, the day after General Robert E. Lee arrived to assume command of the newly created Military Department of South Carolina, Georgia, and East Florida, a federal fleet swept into Port Royal Sound fifty miles to the south of Charleston and launched a successful amphibious assault. Hilton Head Island, Port Royal, and Beaufort, summer home to many wealthy sea-island planters, fell quickly, giving the Union coaling stations for the blockading fleet, huge stores of cotton, and a base from which to attack Charleston and Savannah.[3]

The occupation of the sea islands shocked Charleston. Rumors spread of fifth columnists in the city and Union soldiers and gunboats rushing there. On November 11 John Berkley Grimball observed that "there is great Panic . . . and many men have removed their families to the interior." James Petigru found "nothing . . . more common than to hear people gravely talk of setting fire to the city if they can not defend it."

Planters abandoning their homes on the sea islands were profoundly shocked to see their slaves fleeing into enemy lines. The wealthy planter Louis Manigault wrote: "This war has taught the perfect impossibility of placing the least confidence in any negro." By early December the sea-island planters were refugees throughout the state. Henry William Ravenel observed that many were "reduced to poverty," forced to flee federal "thieves and murderers." Some planters took refuge in Charleston with those of their slaves they "saved." Once more fears surfaced about the number of blacks in the city and the possibility of insurrections now encouraged by the proximity of enemy troops. When six Confederate enlisted men serving as pickets some seventy miles south of the city were captured in December, they told the Union officers that "the common people had been led into the war by the leaders."[4]

"The Great Fire"

December 11 had been a clear, mild, and windless day. Around 8:30 P.M., after completing an inspection of the city's defenses, General Robert E. Lee dined at the Mills House. He soon heard cries of "fire" and the ringing of alarm bells.

Slave refugees in the city had started a campfire perhaps for warmth or cooking purposes near the sash and blind factory at the foot of Hasell Street just east of East Bay. But it got out of control and spread to the factory and to Cameron's Foundry next door, and rising winds blew it southwesterly to Market Street where sparks set ablaze wooden tenements. Quickly the fire roared into neighboring streets; within minutes the Gas Works was engulfed and exploded into flames. The conflagration swept down both sides of Meeting Street destroying the Circular Congregational Church, the Institute Hall where the Ordinance of Secession was signed, the Art Association, the Apprentices' Library, and the Charleston Theatre. At Queen and Meeting streets the Mills House was saved, but the fire roared westward down Queen Street where fourteen homes were blown up to save the Marine and Roper hospitals, the Medical College, and the Roman Catholic Orphan House. Nearby the magnificent Cathedral of St. John and St. Finbar at the corner of Queen and Friend streets burned to the ground. Emma Holmes and her family heard the approaching fire, "the roaring and crackling of the flames, the cracking of roofs falling in," and before the inferno destroyed their home they fled with all the valuables they could carry. Other terrified Charlestonians crouched in the streets with their belongings piled high about them.

The gale-force winds swept the fire down Friend Street burning homes and a new public school and on to Tradd Street destroying its north side to the foot. On lower Broad Street it set ablaze St. Andrew's Hall; on lower King Street, the Quaker Meet-

The fire of 1861 swept down Meeting Street destroying most structures in its path like the Circular Congregational Church, the ruins of which are on the left, midway down the street. *Courtesy of the South Carolina Historical Society, Charleston, S.C.*

ing House; and then on to one dwelling after another along Limehouse, Mazyck, Logan, Franklin, Greenhill, Savage, New, and Council streets. By late morning, December 12, the fire had burned itself out. James Petigru, whose home was destroyed, found the city "one smoking ruin" from the "front of Hasell Street . . . to a point between Tradd and Gibbes Street." The fire burned over 540 acres and 575 private homes, among them splendid Revolutionary-era dwellings, numerous businesses and public buildings, and five churches. The property losses ranged between $5 million and $8 million. Surprisingly, there were no deaths, but many people, both rich and poor, were destitute and homeless, and were taken in by friends and relatives and assisted by legislative appropriations from several states and private contributions in cash and services of about $1 million. The destruction from "The Great Fire" was the most devastating of all the city's many fires, and throughout the war and for years afterward, a wide scar of "bare and blackened walls" stretched diagonally across Charleston from the Ashley to the Cooper.[5]

Defenders and Social Life

Suspicions lingered over slave arsonists in the city and the general fidelity of the slave population. Most Charlestonians, however, did not question the loyalty of the free black population. In the opening years of the war members of the free brown elite pledged their "allegiance . . . to South Carolina and promised to . . . offer up our lives . . . in her defense"; 150 volunteered to help erect the defenses around Charleston; others "contributed $450 to sustain the cause of the South" and to local relief agencies. The City Council showed great trust in the city's free blacks when they enrolled them in the city's fire-fighting companies in 1862. Through their close association with the well-to-do, some free blacks made handsome profits during the war. But Charlestonians continued to wonder about the loyalty of their slaves. One newspaper reporter observed that "slaves . . . pretend to be faithful, but some have told me how they said to their masters and mistresses . . . , 'The Yankees will be whipped, Massa and Missus,' but . . . prayed and believed otherwise."

In late February 1862 Charleston-born Captain Duncan H. Ingraham, formerly of the U.S. Navy, and now the ranking naval officer at Charleston, was empowered by the Confederate government to complete the building of an ironclad for harbor defense. He recruited unskilled black laborers, and highly skilled, free Afro-American ship carpenters, and construction was soon underway on a 150-foot vessel, which would be launched as the *Palmetto State*. The government of South Carolina also authorized the politician and foundry-owner James M. Eason to build a second ironclad, and in March he laid its keel on the waterfront behind the Exchange. Commissioned as the *Chicora*, she sported 500 tons of iron armor over a wooden hull and mounted six guns. Eason later built another ironclad, the last of the armored vessels constructed in the city during the war, and it was named the *Charleston*.[6]

When General Lee was reassigned in early March 1862 he was succeeded by Major General John C. Pemberton. Within the year Charleston had changed dramatically. The stores were closed and the streets were almost deserted except for soldiers and prostitutes. In the port city already notorious for its brothels, "free colored street walkers" and white "loose women impudently accosted passers-by, and filled the hotels with their presence," one observer commented. Houses of prostitution were located in the area of West and Princess streets. Some Charlestonians became concerned over the possible spread of venereal disease and the police arrested numbers of prostitutes, incarcerating them in the already crowded city jail. Eventually black and white prisoners were "living in tents in the [jail] yard, many without shelter, and . . . with short rations."

"Gambling saloons were opened and drove a thriving business," one resident noted, and "both officers and men were swept away by the same current of dissoluteness and vice." Because Confederate officers who were supposed to be defending the city were "infesting" the bars and gambling dens, the City Council passed a law "closing all bar rooms in which liquor is retailed" in late February 1862. In May state and local officials agreed to place Charleston under martial law because of the growing disorder from the concentration of troops there and the threat of imminent attack. Colonel Johnson Hagood was ordered to establish a military police to prohibit "all distillation . . . and sale of spirituous liquors," and violators could be sentenced to a month at hard labor. In August 1862, after fear of a Union assault passed, martial law was lifted and the bars reopened to a booming business.

Drunk and disorderly soldiers and deserters plagued the local police. Sometimes soldiers prowled about the city in groups. On one Sunday morning nine apparently drunk marines attacked a saloon while on another occasion a young naval officer was killed by bricks tossed by a gang of soldiers.

Despite police attempts to enforce an ordinance of 1806 banning the unauthorized use of firearms, soldiers repeatedly fired off their guns needlessly, sometimes at each other, and occasionally with fatal results. Planters on James and John's islands were infuriated by the "infamous" conduct "of our own troops" who carried away or used for firewood furniture from homes temporarily vacated. Also "pictures served as targets for pistol shots or objects for bayonet practice," William Grayson, the poet, declared. He concluded that "no destruction of Lincoln's men could be more complete or unsparing" and condemned the "characteristics of a democratic soldiery who elect their own officers, crack

jokes together and slap each other on the back in a hearty way."
The mayor of Charleston repeatedly urged military officials to
stop the "wanton destruction in property," but the depredations
and thievery of common soldiers increased. As the war continued,
morale declined, and desertions and crimes soared.[7]

During the early years of the war, social life for many of the
officers in the city revolved around garden and dinner parties,
weddings, military balls, and informal picnics and supper dances
at Forts Moultrie, Sumter, and Pemberton. They enjoyed the
company of the well-to-do young women of the city who were
swept up in the heady atmosphere of the times and dazzled by
the glamour of uniforms. The young spinster Emma Holmes particularly enjoyed the "many parties" and she lunched in the field
with officers on "fruit cake and champagne, . . . turkey, ham, and
lobster" and at balls enjoyed dancing the polka. One "moonlight"
evening Emma's officer friends awakened her near midnight below her window singing, "Let Me Kiss Him for His Mother" and
other songs and she found the serenade "an exquisite pleasure."
Emma concluded, in describing an upcoming wedding in the city,
"The war seems . . . an incentive to love . . . ." As late as the
Christmas season of 1862 there were "grand parties" in the city.

But to some young women and older inhabitants, the parties
in Charleston were shocking. Upon hearing that the officers of
Beauregard's staff danced the "CanCan" at their quarters for a
group of young ladies, the thirtyish spinster Susan Middleton told
her cousin Harriott that having seen the "CanCan" in Paris she
had "been trying ever since to forget that I ever did see anything
so purely disgusting." Harriott, also thirtyish and a spinster, was
equally mortified by the new "very vulgar set of men in Charleston and the . . . dreadful fast set of girls."

Many of the city's female elite continued to appear in expensive clothes despite the increasing effectiveness of the Union
blockade, which drove up prices and caused scarcities. Everyday
articles of clothing, like shoes, became unobtainable in the stores.
The young midshipman James Morris Morgan, stationed in the
city during 1862, was "amazed" that the "old blue bloods" had
been so little affected by the war. He saw "handsome equipages,
with coachmen and livery on the box, driving through the town,"
and at a ball in the city in January 1863, a Mrs. Rhett wore a dress
costing $800.

Yet women of all classes contributed to the war effort, some undertaking work they had never done before. They formed the Ladies' Relief Association, the Ladies Christian Auxiliary Association, the Ladies' Clothing Association, and the Soldiers Relief Association. Emma Holmes joined the Ladies Volunteer Aid Society, learned to use a sewing machine, and in August delighted in telling her friends that she had finished "my first pair of 'drawers'" for the soldiers. The women helped organize money-raising concerts on the Battery, in private homes, and at balls in Hibernian Hall. At a concert in March 1862 to raise money for "the gunboat fund," young women of the city sang "the Marseillaise and My Maryland" while "The French Consul's wife let fly a white pigeon decked with Confederate colors . . . ." Women also eagerly volunteered to assist in the growing number of hospitals around the city.[8]

The First Attack

On the evening of May 12, 1862, the three white officers aboard the armed Confederate steamer *Planter* moored the vessel at the Southern Wharf, today East Battery near the Shrine Temple, and went ashore. Robert Smalls, a short, stocky, slave in his early twenties, who had navigated Charleston waters for a decade, remained aboard in charge of a black crew of eight. Around 3 A.M. he brought his wife and children aboard while the crew fired up the boilers, whereupon the steamer quietly slipped into the dark harbor. At sunrise he ran up a white flag and turned the *Planter* over to the blockading Union fleet. Smalls was financially rewarded for his daring feat, commissioned as a second lieutenant in the Thirty-Third Regiment of the United States Colored Troops, and given command of the *Planter*. In Charleston both civilian and military authorities were stunned. The white officers of the *Planter* were arrested and court-martialed for neglect of duty.

Robert Smalls also provided Union forces with valuable military intelligence for their first attempt to capture Charleston, which began on June 2 when a large body of federal troops were landed on James Island just southeast of the city. Panic swept Charleston. "People are moving in crowds from the city. Carts are passing at all hours filled with furniture," one observer remarked. The bells of St. Michael's Church, which had been taken by British troops upon their evacuation of the city in 1782 and later returned by a sympathetic English merchant, were now sent to Columbia for safe-keeping. The attack came at a place near Secessionville on James Island at 4 A.M. on June 15. Over 6,000 massed Union troops launched an assault across a narrow peninsula against a small breastworks on the seaward side of James Island opposite Lighthouse Inlet where some 500 Confederate soldiers with cannons waited. After three assaults and two and one-half hours of fierce, bloody hand-to-hand fighting, the blue-clad troops retreated. They suffered almost 700 casualties; the Confederates about 200.

Bitterness toward Yankees mounted with the number of casualties and the closer the Union forces came to the city. Many "Charleston boys" who were in the thick of the fight at Secessionville were killed or wounded, and James Petigru observed that "the war begins to make itself felt very near us." Within a year Petigru himself died, a victim of heart disease and anxiety over the war. He was buried in St. Michael's Churchyard.[9]

The first attempt to take Charleston had failed. But the continued presence of the Yankee blockading fleet off Charleston, the example of Robert Smalls, and President Lincoln's preliminary Emancipation Proclamation in September continued to encourage slaves to run away to the enemy.

Alarm over "domestic enemies" prompted Charleston officials to prohibit slaves from fishing in certain parts of the harbor, since they might attempt to join the enemy fleet, to enforce rigorously the curfew, and to require passports for anyone wishing to get in or out of the city. Members of Charleston's ruling class believed that a vigorous ministry among the city's "Colored population" of 20,000 would keep them "quiet and loyal." The Reverend John Wightman, pastor of Trinity Methodist Church, which included 2,000 Afro-American communicants among its large white congregation, believed that Christianity could "check insubordination . . . should [slaves] be . . . inflamed with false hopes of liberation." But planter refugees living in the city and local masters became embittered and felt betrayed when their slaves continued to run away to join the Yankees. The paternalistic veneers of the owner-slave relationships were cracking and some masters became so angry at the loss of their property that they sought reprisals. When a slave belonging to William Middleton ran away to join the "Yankees," Middleton hoped to see him "hang."[10]

General Beauregard returned to Charleston in September

1862 as commander of the Department of South Carolina and Georgia. He received a hero's welcome from Charleston's elite, who were delighted that the Louisianian was replacing the Northern-born Pemberton, perceived by them as "too . . . domineering" and "wanting in polish." Beauregard immediately requested that General Ripley, who had assisted him initially with the city's defenses, be reassigned to his command, and promptly Ripely was appointed as commander of the First Military District, South Carolina, Headquarters, Charleston.

Convinced that it was only a matter of time before Union forces attacked Charleston, Beauregard with characteristic zeal completed his defensive works. To guard against a naval attack he increased the number of guns in the "circle of fire" around the harbor to seventy-seven, and the main channels of the harbor were thickly sown with torpedoes, similar to mines. An obstruction of hemp and logs designed to foul the propellers of enemy ships was stretched across the main channel between Fort Moultrie and Fort Sumter, and pilings were driven in the shallower parts of the rivers and harbor. At strategic points along the city's waterfront, batteries went up that could fire on any enemy vessels breaking through the outer harbor defenses. Large earthworks were dug at White Point, which soon "bristled with heavy guns," and gun batteries were built at the foot of Laurens and Calhoun streets. To guard against an attack on the city from the landside, entrenchments were dug across the Neck from the Ashley to the Cooper rivers as had been done during the Revolution and the War of 1812. Indeed, by late 1862 one officer observed that the entire "city is enveloped with earthworks, most handsomely constructed." The slaves who built these fortifications sometimes had to be impressed by military authorities when planters in the countryside refused to provide slaves as requested. They also complained that the military failed to return their slaves when promised. In March 1863 Beauregard wrote: "The want of sufficient number of negros . . . has materially crippled the artificial defenses of Charleston."

By early 1863 the number of troops encamped in and around the city rose to over 10,000. Tents blossomed under the oak trees on White Point and along the Battery to the west of Church Street, on the Laurens Street Wharf, the Citadel green, and the Washington Race Course. While the military buildup was underway, the number of people who could not afford to feed, clothe, or house themselves had exceeded the capacity of the private charitable agencies to help them, so a remarkable Free Market was established, and with public taxes and private donations an Executive Committee of prominent citizens purchased food that the Free Market carefully distributed to "the deserving poor." By early 1863 about 2,000 indigents were receiving food, but Miss Fannie DeSaussure feared that "the sufferings of the poor this winter will be very great . . . from the high price of all supplies."[11]

Blockade-Running

Union forces remained determined to seize Charleston. The city was a hated symbol of rebellion, "the Cradle of Secession," and military strategists wanted to stop the manufacture of ammunition and vessels and to interdict the flow of shipping. The steam-powered workshops of the former United States Arsenal located on the western edge of the city now produced thousands of cartridges daily for the Confederacy. In 1863 the three iron-clad gunboats that had been launched earlier in the year came under the command of Captain John Randolph Tucker who replaced Ingraham as the ranking Confederate naval officer at Charleston. Both Tucker and Beauregard found the locally built ironclads ineffective for harbor defense and urged the secretary of the Confederate Navy to rush into production what they considered to be better weapons, torpedo boats like the *David* and the *Hunley*.

During the first two years of the war, blockade-runners had regularly slipped through the Union blockading fleet off Charleston. Sometimes they brought in goods purchased in Bermuda that were manufactured in the North, but disguised by "London" or "Paris" labels put there by Yankee merchants whose conscience remained untroubled by trading with the enemy, yet who knew that Southerners would resist buying Northern-made items.

Blockade-running was a big business. The Importing and Exporting Company of South Carolina, whose stockholders included William Bee, Theodore P. Jervey, William P. Ravenel, and Benjamin Mordecai, was one of the most successful. Its six ships ran out of Charleston from 1863 to 1865 with some 25,000 bales of cotton, which were sold for about U.S. $8 million paid in gold. At Liverpool, Bermuda, and Nassau the ships took aboard military and medical supplies, dry goods, groceries, and occasionally luxury items for the return trip. Approximately 80 percent of the blockade-runners eluded capture off Charleston, and the captains, crew, and especially the investors reaped huge profits. George A. Trenholm was a major partner in the Charleston firm of Fraser and Company, which also made enormous sums from the blockade-running business. In July 1863 the chief of Confederate Ordnance, Joseph Gorgas, observed: "The sins of the people of Charleston may cause that city to fall; it is full of rottenness, every one being engaged in speculations."[12]

The Second Attack

A second attempt to take the city was made on the afternoon of April 7, 1863. On smooth waters and under clear skies Admiral Samuel F. DuPont's nine ironclads steamed into the harbor and attacked Fort Sumter. Confederate gunners there and in Fort Moultrie opened a heavy and concentrated fire. Riddled, the Union ships withdrew. Five were severely damaged. But a primary factor in the failure of the initial federal naval attack on the city and subsequent ones was the threat of the "thickly sewn" mines, or submarine torpedoes, a naval weapon developed by the Confederate Torpedo Bureau that inaugurated a new era in naval warfare.

In the face of the renewed Union thrusts at Charleston in early 1863, the rapidly increasing desertion rates in the Confederate ranks alarmed military authorities. William Garland, a young Confederate soldier stationed on James Island, told his father that "there has been 20 men gone over to the enemy from this Regt. within the last month," adding that he "did not blame them for we are not treated right by our officers. We are compaired [sic] to niggers . . . and they are taking to bucking and gagging the men for hardly any offense at all." In May, when a deserter was executed by a firing squad at the Washington Race Course, the Charleston *Courier* expressed the hope that "this severe lesson will not be lost" on his fellow soldiers.

The Third Attack

Following the aborted attack in April, Union officers concluded that it would take a combined military operation of the U.S. Army and Navy to take the city. Begun in July this attempt called for the army, under volunteer Brigadier General Quincy A. Gillmore, to reduce Fort Sumter and nearby Battery Wagner on Morris Island, so that the navy, under Admiral John A. Dahlgren, could then steam into the harbor and demand the surrender of the city. On July 10, the same day that he was promoted to major general, Gillmore occupied most of Morris Island with 6,000 troops, including a black regiment under white command, and then attacked Battery Wagner.

The use of Afro-American troops in combat by the United States Army especially outraged Charlestonians. To them, slaves in arms as Union soldiers were engaging in insurrection, a criminal offense. In the fighting on Morris Island the black soldiers suffered heavy casualties. During the engagement Charleston civilians heard that "it had been an understood thing among our men that no negro prisoners were to be taken." Nevertheless, thirteen were captured and "made to double-quick ½ a mile to the rear before a squad of cavalry . . . and when they flagged . . . prick[ed] with a sword or bayonet." The black soldiers were imprisoned in Castle Pinckney with thirty-three other black Union soldiers and sailors, where they remained "in close confinement"

Looking across Meeting Street west from the ruins of the Congregational Church, 1865. *Courtesy of the Library of Congress, Washington, D.C.*

on "corn bread and water" until they were transferred from Charleston late in the war.

When two fierce and costly assaults on Battery Wagner failed to dislodge the entrenched Confederates, Gillmore dug in, constructed batteries, and trained his rifled, long-range guns on Fort Sumter. One 200-pounder Parrott rifle gun was aimed at Charleston some four miles distant.

The Citadel closed in July 1863 as did the College of Charleston and the Medical College after most faculty and students marched off into Confederate service.[13]

During the summer of 1863 in battles around the city and at Gettysburg, Charlestonians were killed or wounded by the scores. Susan Middleton wrote her cousin: "Troubles are falling thick upon our people." Military funerals occurred with alarming regularity and one resident observed that it had become "a sad sight" to "see the number of persons wearing mourning." The torrent of casualties strained the resources and personnel of the city's hospitals. Dr. Robert Lebby of Wayside Hospital at King and Cannon streets repeatedly asked military authorities for adequate supplies of blankets and towels and construction of a "more commodious privy," since the old one by late 1863 was "in such condition to exclude occupancy."

Charlestonians began characterizing Union soldiers in the press and in private conversations as "fiends" and "vandals" who commit a "million atrocities daily." The Charleston poet Paul Hamilton Hayne advised his son, stationed at Fort Sumter, to "Always despise . . . Yankees for they are bad, wicked, deceitful people," and Emma Holmes hoped Charleston would "become one grand funeral pyre before her soil is polluted by Yankee tread."[14]

Besieged

On August 21 General Gillmore sent a message to General Beauregard demanding "the immediate evacuation of Morris Island and Fort Sumter . . . within four hours . . . [or] . . . I shall open fire on the city of Charleston." When the note arrived at Beauregard's headquarters he was away inspecting the city's defenses and as the precious minutes passed there was little time to reply before the bombardment was scheduled to begin. When at last Beauregard received the message, he angrily dashed off a response charging that in failing to give "timely notice" Gillmore was committing "an act of inexcusable barbarity."

In the early morning hours of August 22 a reporter for the British press lay awake in his hot, mosquito-infested room at the Charleston Hotel. Around 1:30 A.M. he heard a shrieking sound, a deafening explosion, and was thrown from his bed. The bombardment had begun and would continue for the next 587 days. Charlestonians were angry and frightened. During the next several days one observer noted that "the streets were crowded with carts and carriages . . . and trains," which departed regularly with those affluent enough to flee to safer communities such as Columbia, Camden, and Flat Rock. "The poorer class seek refuge on the race course and other open squares," one witness observed. The Post Office, banks, and hospitals were moved north of Calhoun Street, beyond the range of the Union artillery, and the city's orphans were evacuated to Orangeburg. In Charleston the parties were over. Jacob Schirmer wrote in his diary on August 31, 1863, "our prospects are darker and darker every day."[15]

As the blockade tightened and Union land forces inched closer to the city, Confederate money depreciated and prices soared in Charleston. In 1861 beef had sold for 15 cents per pound on Market Street; three years later it cost $3 per pound. A bushel of corn cost $225 by late 1863 and it was costing the city $10,000 per month to feed about 3,000 poor people. Before long the Executive Committee cut the rations in half. A few speculators made huge profits while maimed and destitute soldiers and sailors and widows and orphans swelled the ranks of the city's poor.

Farmers balked at bringing produce into a city under constant bombardment and eventually even families of the local elite like the Manigaults faced "penury and want." To meet this emergency the Charleston government again used public funds, creating a Subsistence Committee that sent agents into the countryside to barter or buy produce. With the cooperation of military authorities the city government also contracted with the railroads to bring into Charleston thousands of pounds of rice, meal, peas, potatoes, and firewood, which was sold in the stores for a fraction of what the costs would have been otherwise. These entrepreneurial ventures by the local government prevented wholesale deaths among the destitute.

Daring military actions boosted spirits only briefly. On the evening of October 5, 1863, the CSN *David*, the first combat submarine, a fifty-foot, cigar-shaped vessel manned by a crew of four, left wharfside at Charleston, a torpedo attached to a ten-foot rod extending from its bow. Proceeding unobserved through the blockading fleet, it struck the large frigate *New Ironsides,* blowing a hole in its bottom and disabling the vessel for months. The *David* ran a gauntlet of fire before returning safely to port.

On November 2 Jefferson Davis arrived in Charleston by train and was met at the depot by General Beauregard and members of the City Council. Admiring citizens and a military escort took him to City Hall through streets thronged with people wanting a glimpse of their president. At the corner of Bee and Rutledge streets Davis saw a pyramid of artillery shells produced at the local Confederate States Arsenal and on each side stood "the sturdy artisans of the Arsenal, with their aprons on, their hats off, their tools in their hands . . . ." A garland of laurels stretched from City Hall to the Courthouse welcoming the president, who gave a stirring and patriotic speech at City Hall. He closed by invoking prayers "for the sacred soil of Charleston." But Davis and Beauregard disliked each other, and Davis said little in his speech of the remarkable siege of Charleston or its equally remarkable defense. The *Mercury* reported the visit by President Davis, refraining briefly from its persistent criticism of his military strategy and centralization of authority.[16]

In early 1864 the Confederate submarine *Hunley* sank the Union sloop-or-war *Housatonic* in Charleston harbor, but in so doing it also went down with all hands. The *Hunley* was the first submarine to sink an enemy vessel. By this time Confederate ironclads could no longer patrol the inner harbor nightly due to the lack of coal, and the construction of additional ironclads at Charleston was slowed because of the tardiness of the Confederate Treasury in providing funds.

The Union bombardment from Morris Island was sporadic until late 1863 when the shelling commenced with regularity for the duration of the war. During nine days in January 1864, some 1,500 shells were fired into Charleston; occasionally they started fires. St. Philip's Church was hit repeatedly and its interior wrecked. City Hall and the Guard House were punctured with shell fragments, but because the city below Market Street was deserted, few people were killed during the bombardment. A visitor in early 1864 observed that "the whole life and business of Charleston had been crammed into a few squares above Calhoun Street and along the Ashley, where the . . . shells did not reach

. . . . To pass from this bustling, crowded scene to the lower part of the town was . . . like going from life to death."

With many of the city's firemen and police doing soldier duty, city services began to break down. Robberies increased dramatically. A former resident noted that "houses in the lower part of town are constantly . . . plundered" and a volunteer fireman wrote: "I seldom step out late at night and when I do I have a weapon about me." Declines in student enrollments and the bombardment severely impaired classroom instruction in the city's public schools.

General Beauregard was ordered by the Richmond government to report to North Carolina in mid-April and Major General Samuel Jones assumed command of the defenses of Charleston.

In July the city's most esteemed businessman, George Trenholm, replaced Charlestonian Christopher Memminger as the secretary of the treasury of the Confederacy. By this time thousands of Union troops had overrun and occupied all of Morris Island, and their artillery was pounding Fort Sumter into "a pile of ruins." Throughout the summer Union forces probed for weaknesses in the defenses around the city, and fierce skirmishes frequently broke out on John's Island and James Island. Union artillery stepped up their bombardment of the city and during the fall several civilians were killed. Two of the worst days of the bombardment were September 30 and October 10 when 110 and 165 shells, respectively, fell into the city.

Lieutenant General William J. Hardee, replacing Jones, arrived in Charleston in early October 1864 to take command of the remnants of the Department of South Carolina, Georgia, and Florida, and about 12,500 soldiers concentrated around Savannah and Charleston. Hardee discovered that some were "absolutely barefoot" while many others were poorly trained, armed, and fed. In mid-November, leaving the defense of Charleston to Major General Robert Ransom, Hardee took hundreds of his troops to meet General William Tecumseh Sherman who was marching through Georgia toward Savannah with 60,000 battle-hardened soldiers.

Confederate forces evacuated Savannah on December 21 and the following day Sherman occupied the city. The garrison retreated into South Carolina, where Hardee established new lines of defense along the Combahee and Salkahatchie rivers fifty miles south of Charleston. He also reorganized and redeployed 16,000 troops around the city, for it was generally supposed that Sherman planned to attack Charleston next. In late December General Henry W. Halleck told Sherman that if he captured Charleston, "I hope that by *some* accident the place may be destroyed" and if salt were sown there "it may prevent the growth of future crops of nullification and secession."

In early 1865 Sherman crossed the Savannah River and invaded South Carolina, which he called "the Hellhole of Secession." His numerically superior and faster moving force quickly outflanked Hardee's defenders. Continuing his policy of total war, Sherman's army cut a swath into the state. Homes of well-to-do, lowcountry planters, churches, even whole villages went up in flames. "Bummers" looted the countryside. A soldier stationed near Charleston wrote: "Almost every one here is in a perfect panic." But Sherman told his officers that the city was "a mere desolated wreck . . . hardly worth the time it would take to starve it out." Moving vaguely north, he sometimes feinted eastward, as if his destination were Charleston, sometimes to the northwest, as if he were aiming at Columbia, thus keeping the defenders of both cities from coming to each other's aid. His actual destination was Columbia, for he realized that without a hinterland the once great port was of no importance. For nearly two centuries Charleston had been the most important city in the vast territory of the Carolinas and Georgia. South Carolina had been largely controlled by Charlestonians, and from about 1837 to 1862 Southern policies had been largely determined by South Carolina, but in three years the city lost forever both its wealth and its influence.[17]

By mid-January rumors were rife that Charleston like Savannah might have to be abandoned. Edmund Rhett wrote from Charleston on February 3, "Our troops are fighting here in the worst way." Demoralized, they deserted "at every opportunity" and "the men cry when their names are called out to go on picket." Less than two weeks later General Hardee concluded that it was no longer militarily feasible to defend Charleston. Sherman's troops were threatening the state capital and Charleston's supply lines. Amphibious assaults on the city's defenses increased, Union shells were falling onto the Neck north of Calhoun Street, and a strong Union force was preparing to come ashore at Bull's Bay just twenty miles to the north.

During the night of February 17–18 the soldiers and most of the few remaining well-to-do evacuated the city and its defenses, some 10,000 troops retreating northward up the peninsula to cross the Santee River headed toward Cheraw. A prisoner-of-war saw some of the departing Confederates getting "drunk and crazed" on "turpentine whiskey." The three ironclads were blown up, huge stores of cotton and rice and the shipyard set afire, and, to slow the Union advance, the Ashley River Bridge was set ablaze.

In the upper part of the city that same morning of February 18 small boys found gunpowder stored with other provisions in the Northeastern Railroad Depot and began throwing handfuls of it into a roaring cotton fire. Unwittingly, they left a trail of powder in the larger cache and around 8:00 A.M. it ignited. A tremendous explosion and fire ripped through the depot, maiming, burning, and killing several hundred poor whites and blacks who were there seeking food. It became a scene of "indescribable terror." The fire spread quickly to nearby residences, destroying nearly all the buildings on Chapel, Alexander, Washington, and Charlotte streets. About twenty separate fires were burning furiously from the Ashley to the Cooper when Union troops landed at the foot of Broad Street around 10:00 A.M. That day a Charlestonian wrote: "Total ruin is staring us in the face."[18]

2. 1865–1869: ". . . the utter topsy-turveying of all our institutions"

Occupation

Lieutenant Colonel Augustus G. Bennett and about twenty-five white soldiers from the 52nd Pennsylvania Volunteers and the Third Rhode Island Artillery cautiously entered the rubble-strewn city near the intersection of Broad and East Bay streets. They were met by City Councilman George W. Williams who handed Colonel Bennett a note from Mayor Charles Macbeth that read: "The military authorities of the Confederate States have evacuated the City. I have remained to enforce law and preserve order until you take such steps as you think best."

Bennett's troop impressed blacks to extinguish the fires, and when units of his 21st United States Colored Regiment arrived, he marched them through the city to Marion Square and established his headquarters at the Citadel. He ordered the Stars and Stripes raised over all public buildings and fortifications and declared martial law. "And thus," remarked one of Admiral Dahlgren's officers, "after a siege which will rank among the most famous in history, Charleston becomes ours." By 5:00 P.M. the rest of Bennett's command of black soldiers arrived to take over as the provost guard of the city. Their white officers observed that "nearly all the inhabitants remaining in the city belong to the poorer classes."

Colonel Bennett immediately appointed a committee of prominent citizens headed by George W. Williams to distribute the rice, grist, and salt seized by the army, and soon hundreds of blacks and whites were standing in line together at various food distribution points. One Charlestonian observed that they were "utterly destitute, undernourished, and near starvation; some of them unable to restrain themselves at the sight of food, snatched mouthfuls of the raw grain and began eating even while it was being measured into their receptacles." George Williams recognized one of the women receiving a dole of rice as a person who before the war had been worth "half a million dollars and lived in a mansion on the Battery."

On Saturday, February 19, a 100-gun salute fired by the Union fleet off the harbor and a 38-gun salute from a land battery celebrated the capture of Charleston, while photographers who had accompanied the Union troops were taking pictures of ruins all over the peninsula.[19]

For months remnants of the congregations of three Episcopal churches damaged by the bombardment, St. Philip's, St. Michael's, and Grace, had been sharing in the services at St. Paul's, where on Sunday, February 20, the Reverend Mr. Howe refused Colonel Bennett's order to say the prayer for the president of the United States. That afternoon, on Bennett's instructions, the offices and equipment of the *Courier* were turned over to George Wittemore and George W. Johnson, correspondents of Northern journals who arrived with the army and were "authorized to issue a loyal Union newspaper." During the week that followed the 127th New York Volunteers and the 21st U.S. Colored Troops were assigned to garrison Charleston under Brigadier General Alexander Schimmelfennig, who had been commanding the troops on Morris Island, and he quickly set up his headquarters at 27 King Street, the Miles Brewton House. By this time the unoccupied homes of the elite who had fled the city had been looted by black soldiers and their white officers. Union commanders moved quickly to stop such depredations, but the stealing of priceless heirlooms heightened the local hatred for the invaders, and the thefts would be recounted and sometimes embellished far into the twentieth century.

On Sunday, February 27, Episcopalians found St. Paul's Church closed by order of General Schimmelfennig and, on February 28, General Order Number Eight called on the citizens of Charleston to take the Oath of Allegiance to the United States and declared that passes and favors would be withheld from those who refused. No guards were to be placed on private property, but anyone robbing or damaging a house that displayed the U.S. flag would be punished.

Unlike the whites, black Charlestonians welcomed the occupying forces. On March 3 an enormous crowd of blacks in Marion Square watched a carefully planned ceremony in which thirteen black women, elegantly dressed to symbolize the original thirteen

Photographers accompanying the Union troops triumphantly entering Charleston in February 1865 took this photograph, which shows the Mills House in the background, one of the few buildings on Meeting Street near the great fire of 1861 to escape the conflagration. *Courtesy of the Library of Congress, Washington, D.C.*

states, presented the Union garrison with a flag, a bouquet of flowers, and a fan for Mrs. Lincoln.

James Redpath, a fiery abolitionist, was appointed superintendent of city schools, and in early March he opened the Morris Street School to some 1,000 black and 200 white children who were separated on different floors by race. Seven schools were open by April enrolling over 3,100 children and taught by 83 teachers of whom 74 were "loyal Charlestonians of both races."

Thousands of former slaves, deserting the lowcountry plantations, streamed into Charleston to celebrate their new freedom, to find families, and to enlist. The official *Daily Courier* reported that "the recruiting officers in Charleston are head over heel in business. The colored men are flocking to the . . . Flag . . . ." Within a few years there were 4,000 more blacks than whites in Charleston, and many of the freedmen crowded into "filthy . . . miserable shanties" along the waterfront. Some occupied the deserted homes of the well-to-do, and Robert Smalls, who returned with Union troops and soon piloted the *Planter* back into Charleston harbor, bought the house of his former master, Henry McKee, at a tax sale.

On March 29 black Charlestonians celebrated their emancipation with the largest and grandest parade held in the city since the funeral of John C. Calhoun. Marshals in red, white, and blue sashes on horseback, a band, and the 21st Regiment United States Colored Troops led through the city a two-and-one-half-mile procession of 4,000 black artisans and tradesmen all proudly carrying the tools of their trade. A "Car of Liberty" bearing thirteen young girls dressed in white rolled along the line of the parade route, while 1,800 school children followed carrying placards bearing the words "We know no caste or color," "The Heroes of the War: Grant, Sherman, Sheridan," and "Slavery is Dead."

The sudden increase in the numbers of blacks in the city, and the sight of armed black soldiers in the streets, frightened and angered whites, who were also astonished to find that blacks were refusing to worship with them and were with remarkable determination establishing their own churches.

Shortly after Grace Church reopened on March 19, its rector was ordered to pray for the president, and a squad of soldiers stood at attention in the middle aisle until the conclusion of the services. There is a story that the rector said: "I will gladly obey your order. I know of no one who needs praying for more than the President of the United States."

Shortly after Lee surrendered to Grant in Virginia on April 9, ex-Confederate soldiers, maimed in body and spirit, began to straggle into the city. On April 14 the country's leading abolitionists, Henry Ward Beecher and William Lloyd Garrison, and 3,000 Afro-Americans, including Robert Smalls and the son of Denmark Vesey, assembled on the pile of rubble that had been Fort Sumter to watch Major General Robert Anderson hoist the same flag that he had lowered precisely four years earlier to the day. Beecher delivered a speech blaming the war on "the cultured . . . and wholly unprincipled ruling aristocracy who wanted to keep power." That evening while the celebrants enjoyed a ball, a supper, and a fireworks display, around 10:00 P.M. in Washington D.C. President Lincoln was fatally wounded by an assassin. In Charleston, most blacks mourned for days, but the white rector of St. John's Episcopal Church refused to conduct services for the dead president.[20]

With the spring life quickened in the city. The theater resumed soon after two New York producers arrived in Charleston with sixteen players and German Artillery Hall on Wentworth Street was repaired and refurbished. It opened on April 12 with *The Honeymoon*, a comedy that played to a packed and enthusiastic house of Union soldiers, freedmen, and native Charlestonians night after night for nearly three months. Other productions followed, yet by fall 1865 legitimate drama gave way to minstrels, burlesques, serenaders, trombonists, and "bone players." Lodging and board for visitors became available again when the Mansion House on Broad Street reopened in May to offer its guests grand viands and drinks, as before the war, and the Mills House Hotel on the southeast corner of Meeting and Queen streets resumed business in December. A second newspaper the *Charleston Daily News*, founded in early 1865 at 18 Hayne Street, quickly became a successful enterprise.

In May General Sherman visited Charleston on an inspection tour and called on the widow of James Petigru. He wrote: "Anyone who is not satisfied with war should go and see Charleston, and he will pray louder and deeper than ever that the country may in the long future be spared any more war."[21]

As the white elite trickled back to the city, some saw in the freedmen a new assertiveness and even "insolence." Henry William Ravenel found "Negroes shoving white persons off the walk," while members of his family lived "in a dreadful state of apprehension of insurrection." Some Charlestonians formed para-military organizations to combat possible uprisings. Yet A. T. Smythe remarked that those blacks he met were "civil and humble as ever . . . and greet me enthusiastically as 'Mass Gus.'"

The older order had demanded deference from the Afro-American, and Charleston's antebellum free brown elite found it in their interest to continue this deferential relationship. They "are exceedingly respectful to Charleston gentlemen, taking their hats off and expressing their pleasure at seeing them again," Emma Holmes wrote in May 1865, adding that this "respectable class of free negroes . . . won't associate at all with the parvenue free."

By June the committee headed by George Williams, having distributed food to 20,000 persons, ran out of supplies. The *Daily Courier* reported that the suffering and starvation among the poor in the city was widespread: "Hundreds . . . are perishing around us," despite the efforts of the Freedmen's Bureau, a relief agency created by Congress to distribute rations and clothing and to assist in the education of ex-slaves.

Black refugees were among the first victims when smallpox and dengue, or "break-bone fever," swept through the city in 1865. Late that year, with the cooperation of the Freedmen's Bureau, the City Council created what may have been the first full-time health department in the United States. Organized to prevent disease, to treat the sick, and to establish hospitals for "*all* the destitute poor and suffering in our city," the Health Department cared for 4,141 whites and 4,953 "blacks and colored" in 1866.[22]

Some whites deeply resented the educational opportunities the federal government provided the illiterate ex-slaves through the local Freedmen's Bureau, Jacob Schirmer declaring "the little *nigger race*" was being prepared "to enter college, whilest our poor white children are growing up in ignorance." One Yankee teacher believed that the Northern teachers who came to teach the freedmen were so despised "we should none of us be surprised if they made a bonfire of us some dark night." Eliza Fludd, who had been robbed by Union soldiers, denounced the Freedmen's Bureau for distributing rations, believing such practices and the preachings of immigrant abolitionists made "the negroes . . . a pack of *lazy, insolent thieves . . . .*"

Some Charlestonians who before the war had rarely used the term "nigger" now did so frequently. A female member of the Porcher family wrote that "we rarely go out, the streets are so niggery and Yankees so numerous." A contemporary found it galling because "every mulatto is your equal and every 'Nigger' is your superior." Blacks strolling on the Battery, a place reserved for whites before the war, became a "nauseating sight" to Henry Raymond, who lived nearby, and a woman complained that "one cannot go out without being jostled by flaunting mulattoes with their soldier beaux . . . or . . . having . . . songs shouted in your face . . . as . . . 'Hang Jeff Davis on the sour apple tree' . . . ."

The losses of the elite were enormous. John Berkely Grimball did not exaggerate when he declared "the war has ruined us." William Middleton told his sister in Philadelphia that no one could imagine "the utter topsy-turveying of all our institutions." Richard H. Anderson, who had taken charge of the city's defense in the summer of 1861 and later rose to the rank of lieutenant general in the Confederate Army, now worked in the city railroad yards. The James Heyward family took in sewing. Some reopened their mansions to take in boarders while others became tellers in banks.[23]

In late July 1865 Union General Carl Schurz passed through Charleston's nearly deserted harbor and tied off "a decaying pier constructed of palmetto-logs." Schurz saw no human activity, but "the crests of the roofs and chimneys were covered with turkey buzzards . . . ." Two months later a Northern reporter, Sidney Andrews, toured Charleston and described it as "A city of ruins, of desolation, of vacant homes, of widowed women, . . . of deserted warehouses, of weed-wild gardens, of miles of grass-grown streets . . . ."

The occupation forces continued to clean up and police the city. Fifty teams and 200 laborers were hired to remove debris from the streets, and by June 25 about 30,000 cartloads of garbage had been dumped into the marshes or used as fill. Colonel William Gurney, who was temporarily in command of the troops at Charleston, warned the freedmen there that if they did not return to the farms in the countryside, he would arrest those found loitering and put them to work. In July when riots erupted between black troops and local whites, weapons were seized and white soldiers armed with clubs were detailed to keep order among the Afro-American troops.

Major General Daniel Edgar Sickles became the military commander of South Carolina in September and established his headquarters in a fine house on Charlotte Street. The next month Sickles permitted civil government to resume in Charleston and on November 3 elections were held for the two-year terms of mayor and aldermen. Colonel Peter C. Gaillard, a well-to-do factor and commission merchant for the firm of Gaillard and Minot, was elected mayor by the city's white voters, since Afro-Americans remained disfranchised. Born in Charleston County, Gaillard had graduated from West Point in 1835 and soon afterward entered the cotton factorage business. He served in the Confederate Army as a colonel and lost an arm defending Battery Wagner on Morris Island. Gaillard and his council set out to restore white rule and the system of antebellum race relations. By this time the Charleston *Courier* had become an independent paper again and was edited by a signer of the Ordinance of Secession, Thomas Y. Simons.

The all-white state legislature in Columbia, composed of the same socioeconomic class as before the war, was enacting a Black Code similar to the ones being passed by other Southern legislatures defining the status of the new freedmen, making them unequal to whites before the law. At the same time a remarkable group of educated and articulate Afro-American leaders was converging on Charleston. All of them had been free before the war, but none of them belonged to the city's antebellum free brown elite.[24]

Black Politicos

Blacks came for personal and professional reasons. Francis Louis Cardozo, whose father was a Sephardic Jew and whose mother was half Indian and half black, matriculated abroad, became a Presbyterian minister, and returned to the city of his birth from New Haven, Connecticut, in 1865 to help James Redpath establish schools. The Reverends E. J. Adams and Jonathan C. Gibbs, the latter a Dartmouth graduate and both Presbyterians, left Philadelphia to minister to Charleston freedmen. Benjamin Franklin Randolph, a Methodist minister educated at Oberlin, came south as chaplain to the 26th U.S. Colored Infantry as did Bishop Daniel Alexander Payne, a mulatto leader of the African Methodist Episcopal Church who was born in Charleston but had moved to Pennsylvania in the 1830s. Richard H. Cain, also a minister of the A.M.E. Church and educated at Wilberforce, came to Charleston from Brooklyn. Major Martin Delany, one of the few Afro-Americans to receive a commission, was stationed in Charleston with the U.S. Army and became a nationally known figure. Before the war he had attended Harvard Medical School and traveled abroad. These Afro-American newcomers to the city joined prominent local black leaders like the young tailor, Robert C. De Large, the city's most enthusiastic and ambitious black politico, and Alonzo J. Ransier, a mulatto and native-born Charlestonian who worked as a shipping clerk before the war.

It was a group of predominantly local Afro-American artisans, eight mulattoes and nine blacks, who petitioned the all-white Constitutional Convention meeting in Columbia to remember in any documents produced the "equality of all men *before the law.*" When their formal request was tabled without further debate, Robert De Large urged blacks in the first issue of the *South Carolina Leader*, October 7, 1865, one of many Northern-sponsored Republican journals now being published in Charleston, to continue to assert themselves. About this time Francis Cardozo wrote privately that "the feeling of hate and revenge toward the colored people seems to me fiendish."

In early November the Colored Peoples' Convention of South Carolina opened at the Zion Presbyterian Church. Charleston's black and mulatto artisans who had the most to lose economically under the new Black Code had organized the convention and composed nearly half of those attending. Guests of the convention included Major Delany and the Reverends F. L. Cardozo, R. H. Cain, and J. C. Gibbs. Within a week the conventioneers hammered out "An Address to the Legislature of the State of South Carolina" asking for the right to vote, the right to testify in court, and the repeal of the Black Code. To calm white fears, they promised to remain "law abiding citizens." But the state legislature and the white press ignored them.

Angry with the conservative *South Carolina Leader*, which had admonished preachers to stay out of politics, Cardozo and Benjamin Randolph publicly criticized the paper. De Large called for an end to the *Leader* and the inauguration of a "colored paper with a colored editor, . . . read only by the colored people." Subsequently the white owner, Timothy Hurley, a Bostonian, turned over the editorship of the *Leader* to Richard Cain and Alonzo Ransier. Under their leadership the paper vigorously defended blacks against racial slurs and urged the acquisition of land as a way for blacks to achieve financial security. Randolph and E. J. Adams founded a second black newspaper, the *Charleston Journal*, which was soon absorbed by the *Charleston Advocate*, a weekly newspaper backed by Boston Methodists.

In November 1865 the Medical College of South Carolina

In occupied Charleston, Union troops stand guard in front of City Hall at the corner of Broad and Meeting streets, looking toward the Exchange. Photographed in 1865, apparently by an official photographer. *Courtesy of the Library of Congress, Washington, D.C.*

reopened and two months later the College of Charleston began classes with seven students, but both colleges continued as white-only institutions.

General Sickles, a cigar-chomping, womanizing, military hero, who had lost his right leg at Gettysburg to a cannonball and a surgeon's saw and now the military commander of the state, was at first magnanimous in his dealings with white Charlestonians. The prewar Democrat, congressman, and crony of Southern leaders was moved by the local suffering and devastation. When General Ulysses S. Grant visited Charleston in December 1865, Sickles held a grand dinner in his honor, inviting some of the state's former rebel leaders. Grant found them cordial and cooperative, but one of his aides observed that while riding "through the city . . . several . . . ladies made faces at . . . us . . . they express openly what their husbands and brothers feel but do not show."

Because Sickles saw his job as protecting the rights of the freedmen, preserving order, and curbing disloyalty, on January 1, 1866, he declared South Carolina's Black Code null and void. The legislature responded by modifying parts of the code and on April 2 President Andrew Johnson proclaimed the rebellion at an end in South Carolina and other ex-Confederate states. The laws of these states were now to be enforced by the civil authorities, and over the next several months Sickles's command was reduced from 7,408 to 2,747 troops. But on April 5, over Johnson's veto, Congress passed the Civil Rights Act guaranteeing the races equality before the law, as did the Fourteenth Amendment, which Congress submitted to the states in June. South Carolina and every ex-Confederate state except Tennessee rejected it, angering congressional radicals who then planned their own Reconstruction of the South. During that same month, June 1866, Sickles was given command of the Department of the Carolinas, which increased his responsibilities while the number of his soldiers continued to decrease.

During a clash on Tradd Street in June, a white man, Richard M. Brantford, was attacked and killed by a mob of blacks hurling bricks and brandishing knives. Scipio Fraser, a black ex-soldier, bragged throughout the city that he had "killed the rebel son of a bitch, and he is not . . . the last I will kill." Outbreaks of violence continued for a week, and the *Courier* expressed alarm over "gangs . . . infesting the city." Shortly after the end of the war a visiting Bostonian had astutely observed "the growth of a bitter and hostile spirit between blacks and whites—a gap opening between the races."

The Morris Street Baptist Church was a significant black church in the city and state, but under the evangelical leadership of the Reverend Mr. Cain the African Methodist Episcopal Church soon became the largest black denomination. For $10,000 he reorganized and rebuilt on Calhoun Street the Emanuel Church that city officials had dismantled in 1822 and he organized other A.M.E. churches on Morris and Glebe streets. The black churches became the most important institutions within the Afro-American community, nurturing black leadership, providing a refuge from white hostility, prescribing public and personal morality, and supporting private, separate black education.

In 1866 the white Episcopal minister E. Toomer Porter solicited money from Northern Episcopalians to open the Franklin Street School for blacks, and with the permission of federal authorities he opened another for black children in the United States Marine Hospital, where a visitor found "the teachers all but one are Charleston ladies." The American Missionary Association established Avery Normal Institute for black teachers in Charleston, and the Shaw Memorial School was supported by the New England Freedmen's Aid Society. But Francis Cardozo observed that "colored people would prefer separate schools, particularly until some of the present prejudice against their race is removed."

At the occasional social gatherings attended by both blacks and whites, the races tended to separate themselves, though whites sometimes attended Afro-American churches, and there were, of course, genuine examples of friendship and mutual respect, especially between skilled black men and upper-class white men. When the well-known black barber Tom Brown died he was eulogized as "very civil and polite . . . faithful to his white friends throughout the late war." Interracial marriage was discouraged, but the vows of black women to white men were solemnized in the churches. The most integrated places in the city were the brothels, which for the next thirty years were staffed by black and white women who served customers of all races.[25]

Economic Stirrings

In 1866 President Andrew Johnson appointed Dr. Albert G. Mackey, a white Republican who had grown up in South Carolina, as Charleston's collector of customs. A Board of Trade was organized to promote commerce, and over fifty businessmen signed an address "To the Merchants of the South" announcing that connections to the city by land and sea had been restored and that the city was ready to do business. They envisioned the city soon becoming "the center of Southern trade." The boosters' apparent interest in Southern rather than nationwide trade squared with the observation of General Sickles that white Charlestonians refused to celebrate the national holiday, July 4. He told the secretary of war in July 1866 that he had never seen a Carolinian raise an American flag and if one were ever hoisted "over a Dwelling, or a Hotel, or a Shop, the population would avoid the place as they would shun a pest house filled with lepers . . . ."

Post-Civil War activity on Charleston's wharves. *Courtesy of the South Carolina Historical Society, Charleston, S.C.*

However, some whites learned quickly how to make the best of the changed circumstances; others never did. William Gilmore Simms, almost penniless, spoke for many in December 1866 when he wrote from Charleston: "Everything is gloomy here. The prostration is complete."

But there were glimmers of economic recovery. That same December a street railway was completed, and not long afterward the Charleston to Savannah Railroad, whose bridges and track were destroyed by Sherman, had been rebuilt as far as the Coosawhatchie about halfway between the two ports. The Northeast Line linking Charleston to Florence and the South Carolina Rail Road, backed by Charlestonians George Trenholm, Edward Frost, Henry Gourdin, and William A. Courtenay, stretching from the port city to Hamburg, were also in operation, but the passenger cars were described as filthy and the trains were agonizingly slow.[26]

Additional economic stimulus came in 1866 when the City Council passed "an ordinance to aid in rebuilding the Burnt District and Waste places of the city of Charleston" by providing low-interest loans for citizens who agreed to build in brick. Building construction was also financed by a few men whose fortunes survived the war, and between 1865 and 1872 approximately $4,510,000 was spent on projects throughout the city. George Williams cleared away ruins and demolished older structures along Church, Pinckney, Anson, and East Bay streets and built fifteen large cotton warehouses at a cost of about $100,000. The city banks clustered along Broad Street near the intersection with East Bay were renovated, but much of the activity focused on King Street, especially where the fire of 1861 had gutted buildings. The city's Episcopalians welcomed the return of the bells of St. Michael's, which had been sent to Columbia for safe-keeping. Upon surviving the fire there of 1865 they were sent to England for recasting in their original molds and then recrossed the Atlantic to be placed in St. Michael's steeple in 1866.[27]

The idea conceived by two scientists, Dr. Francis S. Holmes of the College of Charleston and Dr. Nathaniel S. Pratt, that money could be made by mining phosphate deposits along the banks and in the beds of local rivers for use in the manufacture of fertilizer had a profound economic impact locally. Failing to raise funds in Charleston in 1867 they went to Philadelphia, where after several days investors put up $1 million to found the Charleston Mining and Manufacturing Company. When this news spread a speculative mania swept the lowcountry as investors rushed to form companies and plantation owners quickly leased their lands along the rivers. Both of the former Confederate treasury secretaries, Christopher Memminger, who received presidential amnesty and returned to the city in 1867 to practice law, and George A. Trenholm, invested in phosphate mining. Memminger became president of the Etiwan Phosphate Company, while Trenholm and Son became the largest firm in Charleston doing a general commission business chiefly in fertilizer and phosphate rock. As a leading member of the Chamber of Commerce and the new Board of Trade, the younger Trenholm became a featured speaker at events to promote the city and, like other boosters, he argued that the best way to ensure the commercial prosperity of Charleston would be to improve local transportation facilities and woo trade from abroad.[28]

The Poor

By early 1866 the orphans, who had been evacuated during the war, were returned to the Orphan House, just to the north of Calhoun Street and west of King Street. The Board of Commissioners asked Miss Agnes K. Irving, a thirty-eight-year-old New York native and a teacher and principal of the Orphan House since 1854, to assume the duties of steward and matron.

The Almshouse continued to care for elderly whites, while "aged and infirm colored people" were maintained at the Ashley River Asylum at the end of Mount Street after it opened in 1867. Also that year a parochial school of the Episcopal Church of the Holy Communion at Cannon and Ashley streets was established by the Reverend A. Toomer Porter to accommodate "the children of our fellow citizens who may have been reduced by the war from wealth to poverty."

In August a group of prominent women met to arrange for the care of the destitute female relations of Confederate soldiers, and two months later the Confederate Home at 62 Broad Street opened its doors. Within a short time there were 70 "permanent inmates," who were provided soap three times weekly and paid a room rent of $1 monthly when they could.[29]

Social Life

Those of the elite whose health and fortunes survived the war were soon enjoying the city's famous social life again. They

danced away the evenings at the annual St. Cecilia Society Ball
and the Cotillion Club, attended weddings, teas, dinners, debutante and card parties, and enjoyed walks in the public pleasure
grounds like the Battery promenade, White Point Gardens, and
around the Rutledge Avenue Pond. Elizabeth Allston Pringle attended the St. Cecilia Ball in 1867 wearing an expensive gown of
"silk, . . . white kid slippers . . . and kid gloves." On St. Patrick's
Day 1868 the Irish of Charleston and some 200 distinguished
citizens from across the state assembled at Hibernian Hall on
Meeting Street "in old fashioned dress" to enjoy a twelve-course
feast where the drinking was so spirited, the press reported, that
"the salutary detonations of Champagne reminded one of a mimic
engagement on a bloodless field."

Emancipation Day parades and July 4 celebrations were the
principal annual outings for Charleston's Afro-Americans. On
New Year's Day, the day the Emancipation Proclamation had
taken effect in 1863, blacks heard orations from their ministers
and turned out to watch black militia and their bands parade
through the city. Jacob Schirmer repeatedly condemned black
Independence Day festivities, writing in his diary on July 4, 1868:
"The day now belongs to the 'Nigger,' very few whites moving
about." It would be thirty years before many white Charlestonians felt like celebrating Independence Day.

Horse racing sponsored by the Jockey Club resumed soon
after the war at the Washington Race Course, attracting both the
well-to-do and the general public during the social season. Separate black and white baseball teams were organized in the spring
of 1867 and the game played on the Citadel green quickly became a popular spectator sport.[30]

" . . . *military tyranny*"

In March 1867 the United States Congress gave black males
in the South the right to vote, prohibited whites who had supported the Confederacy from voting, and required ex-Confederate states to draft new constitutions before being readmitted to
the Union. The ex-Confederate states were divided into five military districts, and military commanders were appointed to oversee the Reconstruction of the South. North and South Carolina
constituted the Second Military District, and General Sickles was
appointed military commander, formally assuming the office on
March 21, 1867, at his headquarters in Charleston. Although

nominal state governments existed in Raleigh and Columbia, for fifteen months the de-facto government of both the Carolinas was in Charleston. On March 26 about 2,000 Afro-Americans gathered on the Citadel green to organize a local Republican party, the party of Lincoln and emancipation. As the meeting ended dozens of black men inspired by speakers who urged them to unite and to demand equal rights, boarded the horse-drawn streetcars of the Charleston City Railway Company, whose unwritten company rules prohibited blacks from riding inside the cars. The black riders were arrested and removed by local police and federal troops, but following a second "sit-down," on April 1, the president of the railway company ended the white-only policy.

General Sickles remained concerned over the growing bitterness of Southerners whose loyalty to the United States was a "reluctant . . . sullen . . . allegiance." In late April, as Charleston fire companies prepared for the annual parade during which they traditionally carried only their own colors, he ordered that a United States flag and an honor guard of firemen lead the seven hand engines and the seven steamers. Under protest the firemen carried the national banner, but when one of them removed a star from a flag to indicate that South Carolina wanted no part of the Union, Sickles slapped him into prison for a month.

South Carolina blacks held the first state convention of the Union Republican party in Charleston on May 7, 1867, but due to a slim attendance the delegates reconvened in Columbia where they established a Central Committee and agreed to organize Union Leagues across the state.

White Charlestonians came to dislike Sickles and revealed how they felt about him in a story they circulated that was almost certainly apocryphal: upon entering one of the city's horse cars with a cigar, Sickles was informed by the conductor that smoking was prohibited. "'Ah, indeed,'" the commander was said to have replied, taking out his pocket watch. "'Then you shall consider the rules suspended for the next half hour.'" When Sickles was removed from command by presidential order on August 31, 1867, the *Mercury*, now edited by Robert Barnwell Rhett, Jr., the son of the fiery abolitionist, exulted: "Here in the city there was an universal feeling of relief."

He was succeeded by General R. S. Canby, who in October canceled the municipal elections and removed Mayor Gaillard and his thirteen white aldermen from office—apparently because they refused to take the new, "iron clad" oath that they had neither voluntarily fought against the Union nor aided the Confederacy. Canby appointed General W. W. Burns to serve as mayor, and six Caucasians and seven Afro-Americans to serve as aldermen. The Afro-Americans were mostly selected from the antebellum free brown elite. The whites included a thirty-eight-year-old Tennessee native, George I. Cunningham, who had moved to Charleston in 1852, become a partner in a slaughterhouse, and bought up real estate. It was Cunningham's first political post, but not his last. White Charlestonians complained that these removals and appointments were "the hardest thing yet done to us" by the "military tyranny."

In November 1867, in the first elections in the state in which Afro-Americans fully participated, voters across South Carolina chose delegates to write a new state constitution. From Charleston, Cardozo, Ransier, De Large, Cain, and Randolph were among the blacks elected, and Christopher Columbus Bowen and Dr. Albert G. Mackey were among the whites. A total of 124 men (76 black, 48 white) were elected and the overwhelming majority of them were Republicans. The State House in Columbia was without a roof, and Canby's troops were concentrated in the lowcountry, so to the horror of Charleston he instructed the delegates to assemble in the port city on January 14, 1868.[31]

A New Constitution

Meeting at the Charleston Club, the delegates elected Dr. Mackey as their president and spent the next seven weeks working out the details of a constitution that guaranteed the civil rights of males over the age of twenty-one without regard to race, except that whites who had supported the Confederacy were to remain disfranchised until the United States Congress decided otherwise. The local press observed that "the best men . . . are the colored members" while a correspondent for the *New York Times* wrote that, of the white delegates, there was "scarcely . . . a man . . . whose character would keep him out of the penitentiary." One delegate, Christopher Columbus Bowen, was a Rhode Islander who had moved to Georgia before the war. Though he served in the Confederate Army, he had been court-martialed for instigating the murder of his commanding officer so he was no longer categorized as disloyal to the United States. J. J. Pringle

Smith, one of Charleston's elite, told a friend: "The Negro Convention is . . . our daily humiliation." Robert Barnwell Rhett, Jr., stormed in the *Mercury* that the purpose of "the negro constitution is to establish negro rule." Within several months the *Mercury* ceased publication forever and in April a state legislature was elected under the new constitution.

General Burns had been reassigned earlier in the year and the *News*, in saluting his departure, conceded that he had improved the city's finances, punished "the bellicose Negro," and put "the dubious woman" to work cleaning the streets. Colonel Milton Cogswell served as mayor until General Canby appointed George W. Clark, a prosperous wholesale grocer who had come South with Union troops.

In June a coalition of black and white Republicans selected Gilbert Pillsbury as their mayoral candidate. The Democratic party chose Henry D. Lesesne, a former legislator and a well-connected local attorney. Pillsbury, a fifty-five-year-old Massachusetts native, Dartmouth College graduate, and former abolitionist, had come to Charleston with the Freedmen's Bureau and was resented by the white patricians. The press of the city branded him "a fanatic" who is "here to pull down the whole framework of society." During the mayoral race it was rumored that he and other Republicans were marked for assassination. By now Southern whites referred to Northerners who came South during this tense period as "carpetbaggers" and native whites who collaborated with them were labeled "scalawags."

South Carolina was readmitted to the Union in June 1868 and again permitted to send a delegation to Congress. The state legislature elected Thomas J. Robertson, a prosperous merchant, and Frederick A. Sawyer, the schoolman, both from Charleston, as U.S. senators. General Canby remitted his authority to the government at Columbia on July 9. Military districts 2 and 3 became the Department of the South. Stretching from North Carolina to Alabama, the department came under the command of General George Gordon Meade. By October there remained only 881 troops in all of South Carolina, a small number of whom occupied the lowcountry's seacoast fortifications.

During the month of October the Reverend Benjamin Randolph, chairman of the Republican State Central Committee, was assassinated while canvassing the upcountry, sending a wave of shock and fear through Charleston's Afro-American community. By now the city's black state senator, Richard H. Cain, who distrusted the Northern white Republicans, joined the mulatto aristocracy in supporting the Democratic candidate, Lesesne. Meanwhile, Pillsbury was promising free schools for all, a police force that would ensure equal justice, and employment for the city's many indigents. To ensure victory, the Republicans imported large numbers of black voters from the sea islands. On election day, November 10, the city was tense. In addition to the Union soldiers who were rushed to Charleston, forty-two blacks were deputised by the county sheriff to keep order at the polls.

Pillsbury beat Lesesne by twenty-two votes, 5,065 to 5,043, but Democrats charged that the Republicans had used "violence and intimidation" to prevent the "Democratic colored" from voting. Incumbent Mayor George W. Clark and the City Council immediately investigated the election and a week later declared it invalid. Thereupon Charleston's white state senator, D. T. Corbin, introduced a bill in the legislature to validate the election of Pillsbury and his aldermen. Senator Cain fought this bill, which nevertheless became law on March 1, 1869, but Mayor Clark refused to step down and Pillsbury, as mayor-elect, had him arrested. Clark posted bond and resumed his duties as mayor while his supporters had the legislation validating the election declared unconstitutional by Republican Judge Robert B. Carpenter. Pillsbury loyalists promptly appealed to the State Supreme Court in Columbia, which overruled Carpenter's decision and declared that Gilbert Pillsbury had indeed been elected mayor of Charleston.[32]

❧ 3. 1869–1877: Reconstructions

Mayor Pillsbury

In May 1869, six months after election, Gilbert Pillsbury finally took office. At the first meeting of the City Council a faction led by Thomas Jefferson Mackey, a Freedmen's Bureau agent and brother of Albert Mackey, president of the Constitutional Convention, bitterly disagreed with Mayor Pillsbury over the division of the spoils of office. At this and subsequent council meetings Mackey refused to allow business to be conducted by using tactics ranging from dominating debate to firing off several rounds from his pistol as aldermen dived for cover. Police had to be brought in to keep order. The mayor described Mackey as "unreliable, impracticable, dangerous," and orderly meetings of the council became possible only after the two factions agreed to divide the patronage equally.

Charleston's first Republican government was bitterly criticized by many white citizens. The City Council's proceedings were characterized as scenes "which would have disgraced a brothel," and the city government was called a "sink [of] villains, bribery, . . . corruption." At the state level there were eighty blacks and forty-four whites in the House of Representatives, eleven blacks and twenty whites in the Senate, and Charlestonians told a visiting Englishman, Robert Somers, that they were under "nigger rule." Confirming this view to some was the successful strike for higher wages by the black Longshoremen's Union of Charleston, in the fall of 1869. Over the next seven years more blacks than whites were elected to public office from Charleston. White Charlestonians were particularly irritated that Afro-Americans had unrestricted access to theaters, saloons, and restaurants under the new state antidiscrimination law, but Charlestonians seemed to be permanently infatuated with the theater and not even the embarrassing proximity of a former slave—or master—could keep them away.[33]

The Academy of Music

Touring opera, ballet, and dramatic companies had been performing in Hibernian Hall for several years, but it was too small and its sets and stage equipment antiquated. "The merchants of Charleston cannot afford to allow the city to become . . . shunned on account of a lack of . . . refined amusements," the *Courier* declared. At a cost of $35,000 the Adger Building, a wholesale establishment at the northwest corner of King and Market streets, was remodeled by Irish immigrant John Henry Devereux. The new theater could accommodate 1,200 people and its frescoed ceiling and red plush velvet seats were like those of the nation's grandest theaters. Renamed the Academy of Music, it formally opened on December 1, 1869, with the nationally acclaimed comedy, *School*. The following morning a reviewer for the *Courier* was effusive in praise of the production, noting that a "large . . . enthusiastic, and . . . brilliant assemblage of ladies and gentlemen" attended. The academy made Charleston one of the theatrical centers of the New South. Into the 1930s international stars like Laura Keene, Edwin Forest, Fanny Davenport, Ellen Terry, John Drew, and Sarah Bernhardt performed on its stage where touring opera troupes and orchestras were also heard.[34]

Transportation, Business, and Rebuilding

The steamship line connecting Charleston and New York was revived and such vessels as the *Manhattan,* the *Charleston,* and the *James Adger* were taking passengers and freight between the two cities by the late 1860s. Efforts to remove the Confederate blockade-runners and Union gunboats that went down in Charleston's main channels during the war and posed hazards to navigation were begun, and in June 1868 Captain George Purce discovered both the *Housatonic* and the submarine that sank it. In the early 1870s the *Housatonic* and others were finally brought up and cleared away.

The major railroad serving Charleston, the South Carolina Rail Road and its feeders, connected the upcountry and Macon, Georgia, to the city. By 1870 two other lines had been repaired, the Northeastern and the Savannah and Charleston, which reunited "the two sister ports," and served as links in the shortest New York-to-Florida route. These railroads were hauling phosphate fertilizers away from the city and bringing in cotton and rice, naval stores, and lumber in increasing quantities for export. Yearly hundreds of oceangoing steamers, side-wheelers, barks, brigs, and schooners entered from or cleared for European and coastal ports.

Transportation about the city improved more slowly. An English visitor found the city streets following a rain storm such "a vast bath of mud . . . that it seemed . . . impossible for the horse to drag the omnibus from the hotel to the station"; the city sidewalks were described as "dangerous to life and limb." But by the end of the 1860s the city's 222 streets and lanes were lighted by 290 lamps at an operating cost of $23,460 per year.

As business revived, Charleston's Board of Trade, organized to boost commerce, attracted more of the older families of the city and its members developed a greater interest in its amenities as a club than in promoting trade, and as an organization it expired in 1872. That year the Exchange Club was founded, but it also soon failed.

The carpentry and contracting firms of the city were busy

repairing, renovating, and constructing public buildings and both black and white churches. In the area of Meeting Street so devastated by the fire of 1861, the Circular Congregational Parish Hall went up in 1870, and the rebuilding of the Circular Church, a project that was to take twenty years to complete, began. Work on the U.S. Customs House resumed and went on for many years. St. Mathew's German Lutheran Church on King Street, designed by John Henry Devereux, was an imposing Gothic Revival structure with a tower and spire that soared 297 feet, the highest in the city. It was completed in 1872. The Freundschaftsbund, or Friendly Alliance, a social club for German immigrants, was the most significant structure of its kind built after the war. Designed in the Gothic Revival style by the architectural firm of Abrahams and Seyle, ground was broken on January 21, 1870, at the corner of George and Meeting streets; somewhat less than a year later the building was completed.

But hardly any capital was going into the construction of private homes, and along the west side of Bay Street between Elliott and Tradd streets the once handsome eighteenth-century residences and prosperous shops became barrooms, bordellos, tenements, and boardinghouses. Drunkenness, brawling, gambling, and stabbings became common in this neighborhood, which the local press described in the early 1870s as "the filthiest and . . . wickedest" in Charleston. Here and elsewhere in the city blacks and whites lived in close proximity. One writer observed that in Charleston "the magnificent and the mean jostle each other very closely in all quarters of the city; tumble-down rookeries are side by side with superb houses."[35]

Politics Again

In the fall of 1870 Governor Robert K. Scott was reelected, Alonzo Ransier was elected lieutenant governor, and Christopher Columbus Bowen was elected to Congress from Charleston. Convicted of bigamy the following year, he received a pardon from President Ulysses S. Grant.

In the summer of 1871 when the Republicans nominated Mayor Pillsbury for a second term of office with a slate of nine black and nine white aldermen they were still quarreling among themselves, and the Democrats beat them at the game of what we might today call "ethnic politics." For mayor the Democrats nominated the well-to-do president of a local insurance company, fifty-six-year-old John A. Wagener, former state commissioner of immigration, and himself a German immigrant. He settled in Charleston in 1833, entered the retail business, founded a German-language newspaper, helped organize St. Matthew's Lutheran Church, and emerged as the leader of the city's large German community, which controlled about $6 million of some $30 million worth of real estate in Charleston. To broaden Wagener's appeal to the ethnic vote, the Democrats ran him on a ticket that included Irish, German, and black council candidates. The Greeks who were trickling into Charleston's grocery business, soon to be followed by Syrians, Lebanese, and Italians, were not yet voting in significant numbers, but there were some 5,000 Afro-Americans registered to vote in Charleston and the Democrats solicited their support citing their common backgrounds. Blacks remained doubtful, however, unfurling a campaign banner on one occasion that read: "We have played together you say, but were we ever whipped together?" Some blacks wanted to have as little to do with white people as possible. At this time the Reverend Richard Cain was organizing a small, entirely black community near Charleston that he named Lincolnville.

Both before and during the mayoralty race the Republicans charged that the local Democrats were dominated by the "Broad Street clique." Charleston's *Daily Republican* characterized these Conservatives, or Democrats, as professionals, men of great wealth, whose offices were in the heart of the city's financial and legal district, who had a grandfather with a voice in local affairs "no matter how big an ass he was." The charge that attorneys and bankers controlled party affairs persisted in the twentieth century with much basis in fact.

As election day approached each party accused the other of planning to use violence. Urging Democrats to vote, the Charleston *News* declared: "This fair city cannot be surrendered to the lasting rule of thieves, fanatics, and black barbarians." Federal troops were called in from seacoast fortifications to help maintain order. On election day, August 3, 1871, Wagener narrowly defeated Pillsbury by 777 votes of 10,395 cast, and the Democratic press proclaimed a heroic victory over "brute ignorance and personal and public corruption," advising employers to fire anyone who voted Republican.

Shortly after the election, there were reports of yellow fever in the city. Since its cause and cure were still unknown, officials minimized its prevalence to avoid arousing hysteria. But when the disease reached epidemic proportions in late August, terrifying the populace, the *News* blamed it on the recently defeated Republican administration, especially Mayor Pillsbury and Joseph Jenks, his stepson, the city inspector, who was accused of permitting unsanitary conditions to develop. Later there were rumors that some doctors had participated in the coverup of the prevalence of the yellow fever, hoping that Republicans would be infected.

Hundreds were felled by the disease and the life of the city came to a halt. Then, on August 25 a hurricane swept across Charleston, inundating all of Sullivan's Island where some had fled to escape the yellow fever. Not until the cold weather of November did the epidemic end, having killed sixty-eight Charlestonians, sixty-six of whom were white persons. [36]

Mayor Wagener

Inaugurated in late 1871, Mayor Wagener proclaimed that the city enjoyed a position in the commercial markets of the world that would bring it "riches and power," and then like the Republicans before them the Democrats distributed the spoils of office. Dozens of Republicans were ousted in favor of Democrats as city policemen and appraisers. Several appointees were members of the antebellum, black elite. The city restored its annual appropriation for the College of Charleston, but the Wagener administration overspent its revenues by $258,189, and the Democrats were roundly condemned when it was publicized that meat for the city's Almshouse was being purchased from a party supporter for 6 cents per pound when it could be bought elsewhere for 4 cents per pound. But state government and most municipal governments in South Carolina were controlled by the Republican party, and it was the Republicans who acquired a long-lasting reputation for corruption and extravagance. In 1872 when Alonzo Ransier addressed a large gathering of Republicans in the city, he called on them to clean up their party and to elect men, black or white, "who are above suspicion." That year Ransier himself was elected to the Congress of the United States.

The economic shortcomings of the Wagener administration and the mayor's alienation of his closest advisers demoralized the Democratic party as the campaign for municipal officers got underway in 1873, and some disgruntled Democrats joined the Republican party. George I. Cunningham, who had been appointed to the City Council by military authorities in 1868, was the unanimous choice of the Republicans for mayor.

The gradually recovering economy was suddenly affected by a worldwide deflation that lasted until 1896. Capital in the city's banks, which had totaled almost $12 million in 1860, declined to less than $4 million by election day, and some thirty-eight firms collapsed in 1873. Financially it was a grim year. Three of the city's four state banks suspended payments. Physical devastation also ripped across the city on October 15 when a fierce hurricane destroyed the Southeastern Railroad Depot and caused several deaths and extensive damage.[37]

The entire Republican ticket was swept into office, Cunningham outpolling Wagener 6,706 votes to 5,391. Democrats again charged that the Republicans had bought votes for 75 cents, stuffed ballot boxes, and moved polling places during the election. The *News and Courier*, a product of the recent merger of the *News* and the *Courier*, edited by the ex-Britisher and ex-Confederate officer Frank Dawson, led a formal protest to the local elec-

Francis Warrington Dawson and the staff of the *News and Courier*. Dawson is fourth from the left, back row. *Courtesy of the South Caroliniana Library of the University of South Carolina, Columbia, S.C.*

tion commission, but the five Republican members of the commission declared the election valid and in mid-November the city's second Republican administration took office.

Mayor Cunningham

To meet the debt left by the Democrats, Cunningham and his council cut costs, raised taxes, issued bonds to redeem past-due city stock, and reorganized the Board of Health. Hoping to prevent the recurrence of yellow fever, the mayor stressed the need to keep the city clean.

In 1874 sixty businesses in Charleston collapsed, and the Broad Street office of the National Freedmen's Savings Bank closed its doors when the parent bank in Washington, D.C., failed. Approximately 5,300 Afro-Americans and 200 whites had deposits in the bank. None of them got their money back.

In July it was alleged that members of the City Council were taking meals at the Almshouse and some indigents were drawing rations and exchanging them for liquor. A committee of the City Council recommended several management changes. Originally built as a cotton factory, it "was never suitable" for an Almshouse an investigating committee once concluded. The rambling, dark, poorly ventilated structure was located on Columbus Street just off Hampstead Mall. Under crowded conditions it could accommodate 260 white inmates. Most were "old and infirm" and without means of support, though some were young paupers or recent immigrants. The master and matron were expected to live on the premises, to lead the inmates in prayer before meals, and to supervise their behavior. Those who repeatedly disobeyed the rules were confined to cells within the Almshouse. During Cunningham's administration the Chamber of Commerce charged that the Almshouse had been "converted into a huge machine for the manufacture of paupers" and that its management was "a disgrace to a civilized community."

There were numerous private, benevolent relief societies that catered to various social classes and religious groups within the community by the 1870s. The Jewish congregation and the Catholic church maintained orphan houses, and the City Council appropriated a modest amount of money annually to the latter, since it relieved some of the pressures on the Charleston Orphan House. The Episcopal church established a "House of Rest" on Ashley Street in 1874 for the elderly, the young children of working parents, and the "reclamation of fallen women." A Sailor's home was maintained at 16 Market Street; the Ladies Mutual Aid Society and the Ladies Garment Society were active, providing work for and selling "the work of poor needle-women of both races"; and the Ladies Fuel Society helped relieve "suffering and want among the destitute."[38]

In 1874 Charleston's export trade reached prewar levels, but the import trade did not catch up until 1903, and the city never regained its percentage of the prewar tonnage of ships either entering or clearing American seaports. The city inherited a huge bonded debt from the antebellum years that was almost as large as the state's public debt, and Charleston had to spend more than 25 percent of its budget on debt retirement for many years. Nevertheless, the shipping channels desperately needed dredging and on July 8, 1874, the City Council, urged by Cunningham, appropriated $56,000 to dredge the harbor to a depth of twenty-two feet. The black Longshoremen's Protective Association of Charleston, originally the Longshoremen's Union, by 1875 numbered 800 members who closely watched the export-import trade levels. The *News and Courier* in December 1875 called the Union "the most powerful organization of the colored laboring class in South Carolina."

Despite difficulties, between 1870 and 1880 the city's municipal debt actually decreased by about 9 percent. This remarkable drop is partly to be accounted for by the widespread deflation that made it possible to refinance the debt at advantageous interest rates, but much of the credit for it must also go to George Cunningham's intelligent and flexible thriftiness.

On September 8, 1874, the state convention of the Republican party meeting in Columbia nominated for governor the Harvard Law School graduate, former Union officer of black cavalry and attorney general of South Carolina, Daniel H. Chamberlain, and for lieutenant governor, R. Howell Gleaves, a black man. On October 2 in Charleston the Independent Republicans nominated Judge John T. Green of Sumter for governor and Major Martin Delany of Charleston for lieutenant governor. Democrats in the city supported this ticket, but statewide Chamberlain won the race.

The Charleston police force was reorganized several times during the Reconstruction era by various mayors, but its membership remained about one-half black, including George Shrewsbury, chief of detectives. Blacks and whites were also fighting the city's fires together. Afro-American volunteer companies were incorporated into the city fire department, and by the late 1870s over 500 black firemen served in eight companies but maintained their equipment separate from the white volunteers.[39]

Members of the city's antebellum free mulatto elite like the Weston, Holloway, Noisette, De Reef, and McKinlay families segregated themselves from the new freedmen and resumed their prewar connections with the white upper class, which helped them keep up a standard of living comparable to the city's most affluent families. A Northern visitor to Charleston in the early 1870s spent an evening with a "colored" family "whose house was furnished with every modern improvement whose table was supplied with choice meats and rare wines." The socially prominent Afro-Americans, many of whom attended small Presbyterian churches or Centenary Methodist on Wentworth Street, asked Louis J. Barbot to design a new church, St. Mark's Protestant Episcopal Church. In 1875 the Devereux brothers began building the wooden structure in the Greek Revival Style at the corner of Thomas and Warren streets in Radcliffsborough and completed it three years later. The predominately mulatto congregation of St. Mark's chose a white rector of the old order and let it be known that "no black nigger" was welcome. This brown elite of craftsmen, professionals, and proprietors continues to exist, but has never been more than about 2 percent of the city's Afro-American population.

Persistent complaints about the city's streets during Cunningham's term of office prompted the City Council to investigate conditions and afterward remind citizens that because of "our poverty" little has been done to the streets except "patch-up and repair." Nor was there much progress in improving sanitary conditions within the city. In 1875 Dr. Robert Lebby, the city registrar, complained about the clogged street drains, which were little more than "lines of cesspools" that received "the sewage of houses and privies."

Frank Dawson and the News and Courier

That summer Christopher Columbus Bowen, who had been elected sheriff of Charleston County in 1872, challenged Mayor Cunningham's leadership at ward meetings across the city. Finding that he could not dislodge Cunningham, Bowen and some prominent black Republicans joined the Democrats, forming a coalition headed by former Mayor John A. Wagener. Conservative Democrats, disgusted at the takeover of the party by the Bowen-Wagener faction, joined the Independent Republicans and fashioned a coalition headed by Mayor Cunningham. During the race for mayor, Frank Dawson's *News and Courier* praised the Cunningham administration while describing Wagener's mayorship as "highly unsatisfactory." Cunningham and his ticket were reelected by a wide margin. When this third and last Republican administration took office with a coalition council, patronage was dispensed on a bipartisan basis. In these final years of Reconstruction, the city's experience was not at all typical of the rest of South Carolina. In Charleston, Caucasians and Afro-Americans, Democrats and Republicans, Southerners and Yankees who respected the values and manners of the upper-middle classes united in their determination to control those whose values and manners were different. The perennial patricians concocted a brand of Republicanism-with-racial-integration they could live with, whereas in Columbia the Republican state government, despite genuine achievements, was so unstable and corrupt that the number of white South Carolinians who could not endure it much longer was rapidly increasing. Dawson was such a close political confidant of the educated and cultured Republican Governor Chamberlain that the governor cautioned him privately in June 1875: "You know we must not be *too good* friends."

A persistent optimist, Frank Dawson was a tireless warrior for the reestablishment of the port's prosperity, and hyperbole was one of his favorite weapons. As the nationwide depression settled over Charleston in 1875, he declared that nothing would hinder "the steady march forward of this old city to the heights of mercantile supremacy in the South." Through the *News and Courier*, which because of the rapid distribution made possible by railroads was becoming the first truly statewide newspaper in South Carolina, Dawson and Trenholm, Gourdin, Courtenay, George Williams, and a few others kept alive the antebellum dream of linking Charleston with the Middle West by rail. He also argued for the location of the textile industry in Charleston and is said to have coined the phrase "Bring the Cotton Mills to the Cotton."

The most serious fire in the city since 1861 broke out near the intersection of King and Columbus streets on the morning of March 20, 1876, and high winds blew the blaze up King Street, westward to St. Philip's Street, and eastward to Railroad Avenue. These streets became "a smoldering mass of ruins, with nothing standing but the naked chimneys" of over 100 houses occupied by the poorest families, now "homeless and helpless upon the streets."[40]

Political Violence

As the race for governor got underway, a bloody and tragic incident at Hamburg, South Carolina, on July 8–9, 1876, rocked the state and the nation. While disarmed and under guard, six black men were murdered by local rifle clubs. Racially and politically the state was polarized, and the Democrats, determined to establish white supremacy, nominated General Wade Hampton for governor. Born into the Carolina elite at the Rhett House on Hasell Street, Hampton became a cotton planter with vast properties in South Carolina and Mississippi. When war came the broad-shouldered, barrel-chested Hampton raised troops at his own expense, was twice wounded, and rose to lieutenant general, the highest-ranking officer from South Carolina to serve in the Confederacy. The Republicans nominated the incumbent, Governor Daniel H. Chamberlain.

During the late summer "Hampton's Red Shirts" organized across the state. In Charleston, as elsewhere, these mounted men paraded and brandished weapons to intimidate blacks and keep them from the polls on election day. It was a strategy that had rid Mississippi of Republican government, and Martin Gary of Edgefield was touting it across the state as a similar remedy for South Carolina.

On the evening of September 6 black Democrats who were supporting Hampton held a political rally in Archer's Hall at the corner of King and George streets and characterized Republicans as thieves. Afterward a mob of black Republicans attacked the black Democrats and their white escorts near the Citadel green. Guns were drawn, shots fired, and a riot erupted. For several days blacks roamed upper King Street "from midnight until sunrise, breaking windows, robbing stores, and attacking and beating indiscriminately every white man who showed his face," the *New York Times* reported. Before order was restored about 100 persons were hurt, one white man was accidentally shot and killed, and a black man died of injuries. For the next several months the twenty local rifle clubs, some recently reorganized from antebellum militia units, used the riots as a pretext to patrol the city on horseback.

On the eve of the November gubernatorial election Martin Gary urged Democrats to vote early and often. Blacks and whites, Republicans and Democrats, heavily armed, remained tense. Martin Delany campaigned for Hampton, who received more support from blacks in the city than elsewhere in the state. Three companies of U.S. troops managed to keep the peace in Charleston on election day, but the following day a fight broke out among the crowd of persons who were awaiting the election returns in front of the offices of the *News and Courier* on Broad Street amid rumors that a Republican leader had been shot. Armed men rushed to the scene. Gunfire exploded and bullets criss-crossed Broad and Meeting streets. Black policemen poured from the stationhouse at the southwest corner of Meeting and Broad streets and took up positions behind tree boxes and on the steps of City Hall and began firing at the rioters. A white man fell dead, then a black man was mortally wounded. Black policemen were accused later by whites of shooting at whites almost exclusively. Only the intervention of federal troops restored order. Besides the dead in the streets, at least another dozen men suffered gunshot wounds, including the newspaper's editor, Frank Dawson.

In this presidential election year, the Republican ticket of Hayes for president, incumbent Chamberlain for governor, and seventeen local candidates for the South Carolina House beat the Democratic ticket by over 6,000 votes in Charleston and Charleston County, but across the state Hampton and Chamberlain seemed to have received approximately the same number of votes. Both sides claimed victory and for five extraordinary months South Carolina had two governors and two legislatures. "The people have elected me Governor," Wade Hampton declared, "and, by the Eternal God, I will be Governor or we shall have a military Governor."

Eventually Chamberlain resigned, the remaining 683 federal troops were withdrawn from their ten posts across the state, and a State House controlled by Democrats declared the seats of the Charleston Republican delegation vacant and ordered new elections. Three blacks were elected by the Democrats along with fourteen whites to serve as the new seventeen-member delegation. The three Afro-Americans were twice returned. For his support of Democratic candidates in the gubernatorial race of 1876,

Martin Delany was appointed a magistrate by Governor Hampton.

Mayor Sale

As the 1877 mayoral election approached, Major William W. Sale began to win support at ward meetings across the city, and in November the Democratic convention unanimously nominated him as its candidate. Dawson and the Broad Street Ring, or clique, were chagrined. White supremacy was something they took for granted, and they were embarrassed by the vehemence of Sale's hatred of blacks. They would also have preferred a native Charlestonian. Sale had been born within the state and acquired administrative experience as a mayor of Hamburg, South Carolina, but had lived in Charleston only twenty years.

The Broad Street Ring hastily formed an Independent Democratic party and endorsed D. F. Fleming as their candidate, but on election day Sale, perceived as a defender of ordinary men against the powerful, beat Fleming by nearly 5 to 1: 5,288 to 1,924 votes cast by the 9,586 registered voters. On December 17 Sale and his aldermen were installed at the mayor's office in City Hall.

Having achieved stable, prudent government in which both blacks and whites, Democrats and Republicans participated, Charleston gave it up to participate in the statewide campaign to return to power the white Democrats. By 1877 the city's future was controlled by the federal government, the state government in Columbia, and the upcountry.[41]

❦ 4. 1877–1889:
Redemption and the Charleston Style

After 1877 white Democrats controlled state and local government and claimed to have redeemed South Carolina from the Republicans; neither black nor white Republicans were elected to Charleston's City Council or the state legislature for decades. The local white Democratic "Redeemers," or ex-Confederates, now controlling the election machinery prohibited blacks previously supporting the Republicans from voting in municipal elections. Haunted by the potential political power of the black majority, whites depicted Reconstruction as black-dominated, corrupt, inefficient, and barbaric government that must never be allowed to recur. Nevertheless, federal patronage positions for blacks, such as those with the United States Postal Service, continued into the twentieth century. Black men like Francis Cardozo were forced out of politics after 1876. Cardozo had fought fraud for years as a state officer, but now was prosecuted by the Democratic administration and himself convicted along with Robert Smalls for corruption during the term of Governor Chamberlain. Both avoided jail only because of a reciprocal agreement with the federal government to drop charges against Democrats for acts of violence and electoral fraud during the election of 1876. Cardozo moved to Washington, D.C., where he worked for the postal department and then became the principal of a black high school. After returning to his home town of Beaufort, Smalls was elected to Congress.

Federal Money

In 1878 federal money finally was appropriated for the modernization of the harbor, and Frank Dawson was delighted, prophesying that "the commercial effect will . . . [make] Charleston . . . the receiving and distributing point for a vast section of the country." The United States Corps of Engineers, commanded by the same Quincy A. Gillmore who had ordered the bombardment of the city in 1863, constructed two rock jetties, one running out from Sullivan's Island on the north and the other from Morris Island on the south, so that the outgoing tide, concentrated between the jetties, would keep a broad channel scoured of sediment. Eventually the depth of the main channel at low water was thus increased from twelve to more than twenty feet, but federal funding waxed and waned and the modernization of the harbor took nearly two decades.

The Customs House begun in 1849 at the corner of East Bay and Market streets, which had been damaged by Union shelling during the bombardment, was completed with federal funds in 1879.

In the first hours of that year the four presses and warehouses of the Union Cotton Press and Wharf Company, crammed with 10,161 bales of cotton, burst into flames, which so illuminated the sky that the glow could be seen miles away. But the fire was contained and extinguished by daylight. Charleston was at last beginning to learn how to fight fires.

The First Telephones

On August 26, 1879, the first telephone exchange in South Carolina, one of only eleven in the nation, opened for business in a second-story room at 135 East Bay Street with eighty-four sub-scribers. But Charlestonians regarded the prediction that the telephone would soon be in wide use as "extravagant and exaggerated."[42]

Politics, 1879 Style

Earlier that year the City Council amended Charleston's charter, extending the terms of mayor and aldermen to four years. The effect made it easier for Conservative Democrats to control the political process.

Opposed to the style and populist political tactics of the up-country man and Charleston mayor, William W. Sale, the *News and Courier* and the Broad Street Ring were determined not to be caught unawares again by the kind of vigorous grassroots campaign that had first elected him.

At the city's Democratic convention in October both Sale and Captain William Ashmead Courtenay were put forward as mayoral candidates, but the convention unanimously endorsed Courtenay, a forty-eight-year-old Charleston native who, after serving as a captain in the Confederate Army, had established a successful shipping and commission business. He was the candidate of the powerful Broad Street financial and legal community, and the *News and Courier* repeatedly praised him as a "capable, experienced businessman" who is "devoted" to the city. Sale ran, as did an Independent Democrat, W. J. Gayer, and Courtenay received 4,463 votes, Gayer, 2,191, and Sale, 1,660. On December 15 Mayor Courtenay and his council were installed at City Hall.

Mayor Courtenay: Retrenchment and Reform

Just at the time when other municipalities were beginning to spend tax dollars to promote commerce, Charleston paid a terri-ble price for having done so in the 1850s. The dream of linking Charleston by rail with the Midwest had failed, and in 1880 the South Carolina Rail Road defaulted on interest payments on bonds worth $6 million. Most of the bonds were held by Charles-tonians or the city government, which was obliged to make penny-pinching a priority. The council enacted a measure prohib-iting the city from borrowing money unless the loans were ap-proved by two-thirds of the council and by voters at a special election.

War and Peace

In 1881 the South Carolina Rail Road was reorganized as the South Carolina Railway Company, which soon built a modern waterfront terminal and at long last rails were extended across the streets of Charleston to dockside.

By the late 1870s Charleston had 53.5 miles of streets. Just over one-third were paved, and those with a variety of materials—stone blocks, wood, or shells—and approximately thirty-five miles of streets remained dirt. Upon taking office in 1879 Mayor Courtenay remarked that he was amazed that Charlestonians tolerated such primitive streets and sidewalks and he launched a systematic program under which miles of shell and plank roads were replaced by "Belgian blocks," small blocks of granite. From 1880 to 1883 some 94,000 square yards were laid in the principal streets of the city, primarily those south of Calhoun, and flagstone sidewalks and curbing replaced those of shell. Also city scavengers now made their rounds daily collecting "night soil" from the privies, and garbage and animal carcasses from the streets, and dumping them into the marshes around the peninsula or using the refuse as fill for road-building on the Neck.[43]

Drains in the lower city were broken, clogged, and filthy, and pools of water left standing and stagnating were believed to cause "fevers . . . catarrh, pneumonia," but the city's most notorious sanitation problem was the lack of a water-conducted sewage system. About 50,000 Charlestonians were living on 3,300 acres, using some 7,000 privies, and depositing into them every twenty-four hours approximately 100,000 pounds of solid and fluid excreta. Since the privy-vaults were not watertight, Mayor Courtenay lamented, they leached into the soil. A nationally circulated report, *Social Statistics of the Cities*, based on the 1880 census, stated that in Charleston "nearly five-sixths of the drinking water from the wells is . . . contaminated by privy-vaults." Citing data from such progressive cities as Boston and London, Courtenay declared that the privy system of waste disposal caused "filth maladies"—scarlet fever and diphtheria—and contributed to the city's high death rate. He called for the abolition of the privy-vault system and its replacement by city sewers, well-paved streets, and good drains. Insisting that *the only proper way to deal with excrement is to carry it as fast and as far away from human dwellings as possible*," he reorganized the Board of Health in early 1880 and, in a move that proved grandly propitious, appointed the forty-one-year-old Dr. Henry B. Horlbeck as the city's chief health officer. Born in Charleston into a physician's family, Horlbeck had graduated from the Medical College of South Carolina and served as a surgeon for the Confederate Army. An energetic bachelor, he campaigned tirelessly for a modern sewage system.[44]

During Courtenay's years in office a mix of public and private agencies provided only the barest minimum in the way of lodging, food, and health care for some of the city's many poor, primarily white, very young or old and ill. The city expended about 10 percent of its annual budget on their maintenance, and the aims of the agencies reflected the historic interests and values of the board members, the city's upper class: to uplift the "worthy" poor, to inculcate middle-class manners and morals, and to maintain social control. One of the motivations in providing free medical care for the poor was the hope of reducing the threat of epidemic disease. Vaccinations and medicines were given to outpatients, while the aged and chronically ill were hospitalized. The Shirras Dispensary in Society Street near Meeting Street, established by a bequest in 1810, also distributed drugs to the sick poor, and one city official observed that "the deserving poor have learned to appreciate its value."

Municipal-supported hospitals serving the sick indigent included a portion of the old workhouse on Mazyck Street, a former mansion in Hampstead, Roper Hospital on Queen Street, and the Marine Hospital on Franklin Street. Physicians of the city's health districts and at these hospitals between 1871 and 1880 treated about 2,500 white and 8,500 black indigents annually, but after seeing the accommodations for the poor, Courtenay declared that "beds, bedding, the commonest necessities were lamentably deficient."

Courtenay slashed the costs of operating the Almshouse. In 1876 expenses were nearly $12,000, but during Courtenay's first years in office costs were reduced by about 40 percent. The mayor cut the number of "transportation passes" given to the poor to leave the city, and after investigation of the claims of inmates and outdoor pensioners, many of whom received $75 annually to support foundlings, Courtenay curtailed expenditures on this program in 1883, declaring that "all the foundlings have grown up." Operating costs and the numbers of inmates continued to decrease while the number of outdoors pensioners, who were less costly to maintain, increased.[45]

The police force remained the largest single item in the city's budget. Per capita, Charleston had more police than New York City. The police department, which numbered about 100 men in the late 1870s, one-third of whom were black, included a regular uniformed force and plainclothes detectives. In winter months the regulars wore black helmets, white gloves, and dark blue military frockcoats with brass buttons emblazoned with the city crest and the words "Charleston Police," and in the summer they changed to blue flannel suits, sack coats, and Panama hats. Each man carried a rosewood club and handgun, a five-pointed star, and rattles and whistles. When new policemen were hired, they usually came from white, working-class families of German or Irish extraction, and there were always plenty of applicants, since police work paid better than comparable jobs. In 1880 industrial workers in Charleston earned about $300 annually, while patrolmen and sergeants earned twice as much, lieutenants $900 and the chief of police $1,800, the highest paid in the cities of the ex-Confederate states with the exception of New Orleans. The chief usually had some military experience and was expected to run a well-disciplined force organized along military lines. It was a political appointment and politics was also a factor in the appointment of lieutenants and the rank and file.

Policemen learned their jobs on their beats. The city government hoped they would be physically fit, disciplined, sober, and honest. Often they were not. Annually patrolmen were punished for causes ranging from intoxication to neglect of duty.

Shortly after his first election to office Mayor Courtenay publicly observed that despite high local tax support, the public schools were meeting the needs of only one-half of the city's children. "We need outside help," he declared. "We need . . . the help of the National Government." The city was trying to educate twice the number of children with one-half the amount of money as before the Civil War. An all-white Board of School Commissioners, six elected locally and four appointed by the governor, presided over the city's schools, two for blacks and five for whites. Since the school enrollments were nearly equal, about 2,000 black and 2,000 white children, "the colored schools" were "very crowded."

Although a public institution, the High School of Charleston at the northeast corner of George and Meeting streets charged a tuition and maintained the standards of a private, preparatory school for the white, college-bound sons of the well-to-do, and the Charleston Female Seminary at 151 Wentworth Street was a similar institution for women. The publicly supported Memminger Normal School, on St. Philip's Street between Beaufain and Wentworth streets, trained the female teachers for the city's schools, and there were several private schools for blacks and several for whites, most of them church-related. Dr. Porter's school moved into the old federal Arsenal, where military training was introduced, and became Porter Academy, a predecessor of today's Porter-Gaud School.[46]

Emerging Economic and Institutional Segregation

Economic stagnation preserved the prewar pattern of integrated neighborhoods. No new industries forced people out of their neighborhoods, but some of the unhealthiest sections of the city were becoming exclusively black because blacks could not as readily afford to move from deteriorating neighborhoods as whites. One such area in the upper city east of King Street had been reclaimed from marsh by filling with garbage and, due to inadequate drains, it became submerged during heavy rains. Such conditions raised mortality rates among blacks to twice the white rate by the 1880s.

The residences of two-thirds of white Charleston's professional classes were clustered in the lower of the city's twelve wards. South of Broad Street, along Meeting Street, as in the antebellum years, were the homes of the city's most prominent families: Smyth, DeSaussure, Adger, Ravenel, Jervey and Trenholm. Other desirable neighborhoods developed north of Beaufain Street, another around Hampstead Mall between Meeting and East Bay; and another in West End, between Calhoun and Spring streets, along and west of Rutledge Avenue, a broad tree-edged street and, like those nearby, lined with imposing residences with large yards.

The pace of discrimination and the enforced institutional separation of the races quickened at the end of the 1870s. By 1880 the insane of both races were strictly segregated at Roper Hospital. Even unto death the races were separated. Depending on the color of the corpse, interments were made in either the black or the city white cemetery. The complexion of Charleston's City

Council became whiter. Only three black aldermen served between 1877 and 1883: Democrats C. H. Holloway, a drayman; John R. Dourant, a carpenter; and Clarence B. Nell, a barber—who represented wards 4, 5, and 6 respectively. The black leaders of the Reconstruction era were getting out of politics, leaving the state or dying. The Reverend Richard "Daddy" Cain completed his final term as a member of the United States House of Representatives in 1879 and then was elected bishop of the African Methodist Episcopal Church and assigned to Louisiana and Texas where he became president of Paul Quinn College in Waco. Alonzo Ransier fell on hard times and ended his days as a street cleaner in Charleston, dying there in 1882. That December Charleston's City Council increased its already near lily-white membership when the state legislature acting on the council's request divided the city into twelve wards and provided for the election of two aldermen from each. Seventy-three years passed before the number of representatives to the City Council was changed again.

When Mayor Courtenay's budget cuts made it necessary to reduce the number of policemen in the 1880s it was nearly always blacks whose services were dispensed with. Likewise, following major retrenchments and the merger by the City Council of Charleston's volunteer companies into a paid city fire department in 1882, only a few black firemen were retained. The merger did bring a certain professionalism to local fire-fighting, ending such antics as those of the white volunteers of the Washington Fire Company who at one fire were observed "playing water upon persons passing . . . indiscriminately."

The new fire department was composed of about 100 officers and men, nine steam engines, and three hook-and-ladder trucks carrying 10,900 feet of hose and pulled by twenty-eight horses. A Board of Fire Masters governed the department and a chief and assistant directed its operations.[47]

The Economy

The year 1883 was the best year the city's economy had known since before the Civil War. There were in or near the city 273 industrial establishments employing over 8,000 persons. The local mining operations alone employed over 3,000 blacks who dug the phosphates to supply the eleven processing plants on the Neck where another 1,000 laborers dried and pulverized the rocks and nodules and added sulfuric acid and ammonia to produce fertilizer. It was Charleston's largest industry, and prominent planters and cotton factors—J. H. C. Claussen, Elias Horry Frost, Theodore D. Jervey—served as officers of the fertilizer companies. In 1883 the local factories produced 350,000 tons of phosphates with sales of about $14 million. Some 400 hands operated twelve local sawmills, and over 700 persons worked in the cotton factory at 106 Drake Street, a bagging plant (now the Chicco Apartments on Meeting Street), and four cotton presses. Other manufacturing operations employing over ten people included iron foundries, printing firms, a cigar factory, harness shops, shipyards, and sheet-metal works, but little was produced for export. The value of manufacturing in and near Charleston reached $17,200,000 in 1883, about two-thirds of the value of agricultural products sold there.

A few merchants had made fortunes out of blockade-running and speculation during the Civil War and through cooperation with the U.S. Army, and state and federal governments afterward. Some members of the old "rice aristocracy," like Charles H. Drayton, built new wealth on phosphate-mining. These men financed the building boom from 1881 to 1885 of over 1,000 structures, many of them residential, which went up north of Line, Cannon, and Amherst streets. Drayton himself built a home on the ruins of another at the choice site 25 East Battery, in the "Queen Anne" style, recently devised as a reaction to neo-Gothic by the British architect Richard Norman Shaw, and Charleston embraced the style because it blended with nearby eighteenth-century buildings. The construction binge increased the value of Charleston real estate from $15 million to $17 million, but despite appearances there was much less construction going on in Charleston than in Atlanta, Charlotte, Greenville, Spartanburg, Nashville, Memphis, and Jacksonville, and no comparison at all with the building booms in Boston, Philadelphia, New York, Chicago, and St. Louis. Here the metropolitan areas were expanding explosively and thousands of vaguely neo-Gothic and neo-Romanesque buildings were being erected by recent Irish and Italian immigrants, but Charleston was too poor to demolish its antebellum buildings and to Victorianize itself.

Progress and good profits were made in both the crab and shrimp "industry" and truck-farming. During the season some 100 boats put out daily and with baited nets caught 50,000 crabs.

The *News and Courier* noted that this equaled one for each city inhabitant. Most were sold to restaurants, while others were boiled and sold on the streets by "peripatetic crab merchants." Charlestonians also consumed $1,200 worth of shrimp daily at their breakfast tables, providing work for dozens of black fishermen. On the northern Neck of the city, near the fertilizer factories, truck-farming, especially in cabbages and potatoes, made "handsome profits" for a few black and white farmers. In 1882 the value of vegetables and fruits grown near Charleston and shipped to Northern markets exceeded $1 million.

Charleston remained South Carolina's major port, its rail and trade center, and its largest city. With a population of over 50,000 it was the largest port south of Baltimore. The wharves could accommodate the cargo of 200 vessels and the city's warehouses could store 500,000 bales of cotton at one time. About 10 percent of the nation's cotton crop was being shipped through Charleston, and the number of barrels of rice and the broad feet of lumber and naval stores were increasing in 1883, when the value of exports reached $20,100,000, almost double the 1873 average, and approximately 2.5 percent of the nation's total exports.

Times were good. Courtenay was a popular mayor and in 1883 he was reelected without opposition. All members of the City Council now belonged to the Democratic party, and after 1883 no black man was elected to the council until 1967. After 1882 George Mears was the only Afro-American to serve in the South Carolina legislature and he would be returned for six consecutive terms but, according to one historian, Mears was "almost a totally silent member." Gerrymandering by the state legislature, complicated voting procedures, intimidation, and fraud were used to eliminate black participation in government. This factor and the end of the local two-party system accounts for the absence of a volatile political atmosphere in late nineteenth-century Charleston so characteristic of city politics during Reconstruction. There was, however, an undercurrent of resentment among the city's white working class toward a group of prominent attorneys and businessmen who controlled the city's politics, the Broad Street Ring.[48]

The prosperity of the early 1880s was illusionary. Despite the building boom, the high employment, the profits of Charleston's industrial, wholesale, and retail establishments, and the rising export trade, the economy was in a relative decline, particularly by comparison with other New South urban centers. Near the end of the decade the South Carolina Railway Company again faced bankruptcy. The anemic local economy was due in part to the city's aging business leadership.

The Charleston Style

Eighty percent of the pre-Civil War business executives provided the leadership in postwar Charleston. In 1880 about 40 percent were sixty years of age and most of the rest were in their fifties. Their family names attested to the continuity of this elite—DeSaussure, Gibbes, Huger, Middleton, Pinckney, Ravenel, Rhett—all having roots in the city's distant past. Few were "new" men like those emerging in Atlanta, Nashville, and Charlotte. Charleston's economic leaders, having made their fortunes in the export staples of the Old South were neither flexible enough to meet new economic challenges nor willing to welcome people who might undermine their own entrenched positions. A common saying put it that in Boston a man was assessed on the basis of his intellect, in New York on how much money he had, and in Charleston on "who was his grandfather."

The lifestyle that had characterized the city before the war, a style that emphasized conviviality over diligence, dilettantism over specialization, and leisure over work, persisted. Professionals and businessmen opened their offices and stores around nine o'clock, took a long midmorning coffee break, and departed for home at the sound of dinner bells around two o'clock. After a leisurely meal of several courses, including liquor and wine, they returned to work by four and left for the day between five and six o'clock. Such habits differed sharply from the daily regimens of businessmen in the growing cities of the New South.

Among the city's economic elite there lingered the aristocratic disdain for trade. A strong Chamber of Commerce might have overcome such an antibusiness bias, and members debated local commercial policies and petitioned the government on matters touching trade from time to time, but like the social clubs the Chamber of Commerce was dominated by merchants who carefully selected for membership people like themselves. In such a chummy atmosphere their club room, well-stocked with liquor and wine, became a prime attraction where even on Sundays members could mix, dine, and drink. In 1884 the "ancient Chamber of Commerce" celebrated its centennial with testimonials praising the colonial era as the golden age of prosperity.

Charleston's conservative businessmen remained tied to old business practices, which they passed down from one generation to another, and no local business school emerged to offer courses in new business techniques. William L. Trenholm and Frank Dawson worried that the business leaders were too enmeshed in the old ways of doing things ever to join the American success story, and Mayor Courtenay, who invested in upstate cotton mills rather than in Charleston, regretted that the "dominant thought" of recent years "has been to have Charleston a nice quiet place to live in, and not to allow it to expand into an influential and wealthy metropolis."

It was the vision of these men of what Charleston could be that prompted the Chamber of Commerce in 1884 to hire a "Yankee" and professional booster, Jonathan Land, to improve the city's image and to attract capital. With much hyperbole and in purple prose, he characterized the city in *Charleston: Her Trade, Commerce and Industries, 1883–1884* as a dynamic urban center of the "New South."[49]

Social clubs like the Huguenot Society, the St. Andrew's Society, the St. Cecilia Society, the Charleston Club (reorganized in 1881), and the Carolina Yacht Club (first organized in 1883) perpetuated a social structure founded on race, class, and family. The names of the persistent old elite who controlled the social, economic, and political life of the city predominated among the charter members of the Charleston Club: Alston, DeSaussure, Frost, Grimball, Heyward, Huger, Jervey, Laurens, Manigault, McCrady, Middleton, Pringle, Ravenel, Rutledge, Simonds, Simons, and Vanderhorst. The club rooms were located at 3 Meeting Street in a dwelling whose two broad piazzas overlooked a well-cared-for garden.

The younger athletically inclined organized the Charleston Sailing Club and the Palmetto Boat Club, which held annual sailing and rowing regattas in the harbor during the late spring and summer months, and members of this same set formed a tennis club in the mid-1880s.

The less prominent in the white community could choose to join a variety of organizations such as the Deutscher Freundschafts Bund on George Street, the Emerald Social Club, the E. G.

The High Battery looking north over a forest of schooner masts in the 1880s.
Courtesy of the South Carolina Historical Society, Charleston, S.C.

Social Club at the northwest corner of Broad and East Bay, the Harmony Social Club, the Queen City Club, and the Annex Club.

For upper- and middle-class blacks the church was the most important social institution, but fraternal societies like the Odd Fellows, Good Samaritans, Good Templars, Masonic Lodges, and social clubs like the Attucks Club and the Mystic Club at 61 Hasell Street held parties and balls, and organized excursions beyond the city.

The participation of fathers and brothers in military organizations, the presence of the Citadel, which had reopened in 1882 under a strict military regimen with a corps of 185 uniformed cadets, made youngsters of the city "think a deal more of dressing up their bodies in . . . gaudy uniforms than in drilling their minds," one Charlestonian observed. The military air that pervaded antebellum Charleston persisted, and leading politicians and ex-Confederate officers formed and commanded local militia units and gun clubs. These organizations met frequently for drills, shooting contests, tournaments, and "Grand Military" balls during the annual social season. Members of these outfits enthusiastically participated in parades and celebrations on George Washington's birthday, Carolina Day (the anniversary of the Battle of Fort Moultrie on June 28, 1776), and St. Patrick's Day.

Commemorations for veterans and the Confederate dead became increasingly popular ceremonial events. On Confederate Memorial Day, May 9, white Charlestonians gathered to strew flowers over the graves of the Confederate soldiers and sailors at Magnolia Cemetery, to make "stirring speeches," and to enjoy military music. In 1882 a monument to the Confederate dead was unveiled there, and four years later a statue of John C. Calhoun went up in Marion Square. July 4 continued to be a day of Afro-American celebrations and parades in which infantry and calvary companies of the First Colored Regiment of the National Guard of South Carolina, participated, but a day whites continued to ignore.[50]

During the 1880s local authors like Colonel Edward McCrady, Jr., began publishing articles in the local newspapers that nostalgically recalled the Old South as the best of times. McCrady was born into a well-to-do family in Charleston in 1838, educated at the College of Charleston, and admitted to the local bar in 1855. During the Civil War he rose to the rank of lieutenant colonel and was severely wounded at the Second Battle of Manassas. Following the war he built a highly regarded legal practice, won election to the state House of Representatives from Charleston County, and in 1882 wrote and introduced legislation at the state level that upon adoption became known as the Eight Box Law, a complicated voting process designed to confuse voters, especially Afro-Americans. Well-connected by family, church, politics, and the military with South Carolina's "master class," McCrady devoted more and more time to justifying "the Lost Cause" in speeches and writings, condemning the selfishness and aggressiveness of the North on the eve of the Civil War and justifying the South's secession. Like others of his generation, especially the ex-Confederate officer class who enjoyed a worshipful following, McCrady glorified the pre-Civil War South.[51]

Hurricane and Earthquake

Just after dawn on August 25, 1885, dark clouds scudded across Charleston at house-top level. Soon they were releasing blinding torrents of rain. The wind reached about 125 miles per hour, tearing thousands of slates from roofs and hurling them along the streets. Tin roofs were rolled up and blown away, doors and windows blown in, fences flattened, and trees uprooted. A huge tidal surge crashed over the Battery submerging White Point Gardens, smashing windows of nearby homes and flooding their first floors with three to six feet of seawater. Along the Cooper River waterfront, piers, wharves, offices, and vessels were smashed to pieces. When the storm began to subside at noon, it had killed twenty-one people in the city. Ninety percent of the private homes were damaged or destroyed, about one-quarter of the houses were unroofed; churches and other public buildings were heavily damaged. Estimates of the destruction exceeded $2 million, not including shipping in the harbor or the railroads serving the city. In the week following the storm more than 10,000 cartloads of leaves, limbs, and trees alone were hauled away. It took days to restore the 1,200 gas lamps, which alone cost the city $19,000 to illuminate its streets and public buildings in 1885. Other cities were busily adopting electricity to meet urban needs, but the City Council continued its contract with the Charleston Gas Light Company, which counted more investors locally than its competitors in electricity.

The same year of the hurricane and for the following six years the frugality of the city government was dramatized by its withholding from the College of Charleston its annual appropriation for $2,000.

At 9:15 on the hot, sultry evening of Tuesday, August 31, 1886, after many Charlestonians had gone to bed, a roar swept across the peninsula city. Ellen W. Hard described the sound as "the bellowing of . . . wild animals, the grinding of immense rocks." Thrown against the wall of her house, she clung to a banister to keep from falling when the second shock hit. To another Charlestonian the first shock "was terrific," coming "without any warning . . . and the smashing and falling of buildings made a tremendous noise." People rushed into the streets. Buildings swayed and some collapsed, killing or maiming the people inside. Telegraph poles and wires fell into great tangled masses. Shock followed shock in the darkness. The citizens were terrified and cries of "God help us!" filled the hot night air. René Jervey, who tried to rush his family to safety in the northern part of the city, found the streets filled with debris, the maimed and the dead, and the air "so thick with dust and smoke as to be almost suffocating."

Eleven minor quakes had jolted the city since 1698, but never had there been anything comparable to this one. At first light Charlestonians began to comprehend what had happened to their city. About 2,000 buildings were substantially damaged and more than 12,000 chimneys had been sheared off at the roof-line. Damages reached about $6 million in a city whose buildings were valued at approximately $24 million. Twenty blacks and seven whites died during the quake. Over the next few weeks more than 100 buildings were declared unsafe and pulled down, and eighty-three more people died from injuries and diseases connected with the earthquake.

Hundreds were without housing, and makeshift shelters made of carpets, blankets, shawls, and sheets went up in the open spaces of the city. Ellen Hard observed that "In some camps the people were in a pitiful state, in others there was constant card playing and drinking—men and women drinking to excess who had never done so before."

A nine-member Executive Relief Committee chaired by Jo-

Earthquake! Corner of Cumberland and East Bay streets, 1886. *Courtesy of the Black Charleston Photo Collection, College of Charleston Library, Charleston, S.C.*

seph W. Barnwell but dominated by Dawson and Courtenay collected and distributed over $646,000 to the disaster victims, and donations from church and civic groups brought in nearly $400,000 more. A portion of this money, in addition to over $2,500,000 in privately borrowed funds, went into repairing 6,956 buildings and erecting 271 new ones. In 1887 the number of carpentry and building firms in Charleston increased to forty-one.[52]

Extensively damaged, Roper Hospital and the Mazyck Street facility were abandoned, and by 1888 a new city hospital, Memorial, had been built at Barre and Calhoun streets. Damaged fire stations were demolished and three modern two-story fire stations of Carolina gray brick were built at Meeting and Wentworth streets, Cannon near King Street, and at Meeting near Queen Street. The upper stories of these new buildings were the living and sleeping quarters of the firemen. Each station house was equipped with a Silsbee heating unit, which kept the building warm in winter and steam in the boilers of the engines day and night so that the engine could be powered at a moment's notice. Telegraph and later telephone lines were linked to the station houses, and when an alarm came in an automatic gong sounded and mechanical systems dropped the guardrails around the horses, turned up the gas lights, recorded the exact moment the alarm came in, and indicated the number of the box in the city sounding the alarm. Hearing the gong, the firefighters on the second floor slid down a brass pole to reach the engines and horses below.

Second only to police protection in the city's budget, the cost of firefighting went up sharply in the final decades of the century, but Charleston willingly paid for vastly improved protection. As one promoter of the new force put it, the professional firefighters learned rapidly the new "science of putting out fires," and the city never again experienced the devastating conflagrations that sometimes had burned out-of-control for days.

Battered by the hurricane, St. Michael's was seriously damaged by the earthquake, and the restoration was almost complete when, at St. Philip's Church, on May 13, 1887, two blacks were allowed to vote in the Diocesan Convention. Delegates from St. Michael's withdrew in horror. When the repairs were completed in June, St. Michael's reopened as a church that used an Anglican prayerbook but was not formally affiliated with the Protestant

Episcopal Church of the United States of America. It was also the year of the fiftieth anniversary of Queen Victoria's reign, and though the city was more inclined to the temperament of its namesake, the hedonistic Charles II, than to Victoria's, the famous bells of St. Michael's were pealed to mark the Queen's Jubilee.

In 1887 the police department moved into its new quarters and jail at the corner of King and Hutson streets. The following year telephone call boxes and a patrol wagon were put into operation to keep the patrolmen in closer touch with headquarters and to assist them in arrests. By this time only sixteen black policemen remained on the force.

Within a year of the disastrous quake of 1886 the perennial boosters were proclaiming: "Strangers who visit the city have to hunt up traces of the earthquake, very few of which remain. Charleston has once more risen from her ashes." Among the boosters was George Williams, who, until his death in 1903, did more to promote the city than anyone in his generation. Iron rods were run through the interiors of many buildings and fastened to the exterior walls with large bolts of various shapes to prevent the collapse of the structures in future quakes. These round and star-shaped bolts are visible on many homes and commercial buildings today. Much of what attracts the modern tourists in the city is what a visitor would have seen in spring 1887, a few months after the earthquake. Many blocks on the peninsula have changed very little since then, and the secret of Charleston's charm is the peculiar combination of antebellum wealth and postbellum poverty.

In October 1887 Gala Week, celebrating the city's recovery from the earthquake, opened the autumn season. Stores and businesses were decorated, flags flew, and merchants paraded through the streets advertising their wares. A torchlight procession at night illuminated men in masks, some wearing wigs and bustles, impersonating women. The sounds of Roman candles and skyrockets filled the air at the Rutledge Avenue Pond. On King Street, where vendors hawked balloons, cotton candy, walking sticks, "and bird whistles that . . . trilled when water was put into them," bearded ladies, freak animals, and snake charmers occupied sideshows. Gala Week attracted people from across the state and became an annual event, promoted by shopkeepers for the next twenty-two years.[53]

Democratic Divisions

Near the end of his second term of office, in 1887, Mayor
Courtenay resigned, acknowledging that directing the affairs of
the city and his own private business had become too stressful
and he was experiencing "nervous strain" due to "overwork."
The once warm relationship between Courtenay and the Broad
Street Ring had cooled. He resented Frank Dawson's criticisms of
his refusal to increase the city debt, and when his son was dismissed from the Citadel for what he believed were unjust causes
he was disappointed by the failure of a Board of Visitors dominated by the local elite to reinstate him. Courtenay later became
the major financial backer of the *Charleston World*, a newspaper
that opposed the *News and Courier* and "ring rule."

Christopher S. Gadsden, great-grandson of the famous eighteenth-century Charlestonian, was mayor pro-tem when, in early
October, about 200 working men, both black and white, met to
form the United Labor party of Charleston. They endorsed the
single-tax schemes of the economist Henry George, charging that
Democrats and Republicans were out of touch with the issues of
the day, and invited citizens of all social classes to support their
candidate in the upcoming municipal elections. The few local
Republicans also chose a candidate for the race, and in early November the city's Democrats nominated a member of the Broad
Street clique, the forty-two-year-old son of a highly regarded
United States district judge, Attorney George D. Bryan. Educated
at the College of Charleston and the Naval Academy, he had risen
to the rank of captain in the Confederate Navy. A member of the
Washington Light Infantry, Bryan had been president of the Re-
gatta Association of South Carolina and a warden of St. Michael's
Episcopal Church, and was corporation counsel of the City of
Charleston for almost ten years.

During the campaign Frank Dawson warned that divisions
among whites could lead to Republican and "Negro" rule. The
Laborites retorted that this was a dead issue and both blacks and
whites had joined together to form a new party "to guarantee
equal rights to all." But on December 7, 1887, Captain Bryan
received 4,962 votes, the Independent and United Labor party
candidate 442, and the Republican candidate, 316.

The Democratic party in Charleston, however, could not remain united for long. The city's Roman Catholics, who were laying the foundations for a massive Cathedral of St. John the Baptist

at Broad and Legare streets, aware of the powerful Irish-American Democratic machines in Boston, Philadelphia, and New York, were developing a taste for political power. The friends of Sale and Courtenay, much as those two mayors had disliked each other, now shared resentment of the influence of the Broad Street Ring. Some businessmen had lost patience with the city's faltering economy and hoped that livelier politicians would rejuvenate it, and some malcontents were simply tired of standing at the outer edges of the Broad Street Ring, waiting to be noticed, and were beginning to think of ways of promoting their own interests.

A farmer from Edgefield County, Benjamin R. Tillman, whose diatribes against blacks were among the most vicious in the state's history, had been attracting a great deal of attention in the upcountry with raucous attacks on the bankers and aristocrats who, he claimed, were running the state. In 1888 a group of Charleston's Democrats who felt excluded from crucial political decisions invited Tillman to speak in Charleston. Describing the *News and Courier* as a "powerful influence" in fostering the local "political combination," they asked him to help them get "a full, free and fair party vote" and to bring an end to "ring rule."

Frank Dawson rebuked the dissident Democrats for questioning the integrity of the Simonds, Jerveys, McCradys, Lesesnes, and other honorable men who had served Charleston so well. The Englishman who had for more than twenty years earned a good living as the articulate representative of the city's affluent upper-middle classes was especially upset that the petitioners had sought counsel from an outsider like Tillman, whom he described as a "professional agitator."

In August, under an evening sky, Ben Tillman, who loathed Charleston and liked to refer to the Citadel as "the dude factory," addressed a crowd of several thousand from the steps of City Hall while distant thunder rolled and lightning occasionally flashed. Standing within a stone's throw of the offices of the *News and Courier* and glancing at the recently repaired spire of St. Michael's, he told the crowd that they were "arrant . . . cowards" for submitting to the "tyranny" of elite rule. Encouraged by cheers, laughter, and applause, he observed that "Dawsonism is the domination of that old, effete aristocratic element that clings to power with the grip of the octopod." The next day Frank Dawson in the *News and Courier* summed up the attitudes of the local political establishment toward Tillman and his

movement in scorching language, dramatizing the divisions between upcountry farmers and lowcountry gentry and blasting
Tillman as "the leader of the adullamites, a people who carry
pistols in their hip pockets, who expectorate upon the floor,
who have no tooth brushes and comb their hair with their fin-
gers." Courtenay's *World*, however, backed Tillman and his local friend and politico John F. Ficken. The chief clerk of
General Beauregard during the Civil War, Ficken was president
of a company that built a much-needed wooden toll drawbridge
across the Ashley in 1889, replacing the one that had been
burned in 1865.[54]

The Murder of Frank Dawson

On the morning of March 12, 1889, Frank Dawson received
two police reports feeding his suspicions that Dr. Thomas Ballard
McDow, a physician with many black patients, had seduced
the Dawsons' young and beautiful governess, Hélène Marie
Burdayron. That afternoon Dawson carried a walking cane to Dr.
McDow's office located on the ground floor of his home, today
101 Rutledge Avenue. The McDow residence could actually be
seen from the rear piazzas of the Dawson home, today 99 Bull
Street. The two men exchanged angry words and, apparently
when Dawson attempted to cane McDow, the doctor shot and
killed him and then turned himself in.

When word of Dawson's death reached the City Council
meeting that evening Mayor Bryan collapsed into sobs. On the
day of the funeral a reporter observed that "the very heavens
wept" for Dawson as people lined the city streets to catch a
glimpse of his funeral cortege; there had not been such a mass
outpouring of grief in Charleston since the funeral of John C.
Calhoun. But Dawson, having recently written an editorial arguing that a white rapist of a black woman should be treated more
leniently than a black rapist of a white woman, had been disliked
by many blacks and by those whites who were most extreme in
their racial prejudices.

Dr. McDow's trial began on June 24 in the Charleston
County Courthouse, which was filled to overflowing. The former
judge and Civil War governor of South Carolina Andrew Gordon
Magrath, together with Asher D. Cohen—two of the best trial
lawyers in the state—represented Dr. McDow. The solicitor of
the First Circuit, William St. Julian Jervey, and Dawson's friends

Henry Augustus Middleton Smith and Major Julian Mitchell were the prosecution team.

Medical witnesses for the defense indicated that Dawson had been shot from behind, and the voluptuous Miss Burdayron was a spectacular witness whose story set Charleston tongues wagging. But the defense discredited the medical testimony, depicted Miss Burdayron as a temptress, and emphasized McDow's claims of self-defense within his own home, while contrasting the large 200-pounder Dawson with the mere "pygmy" McDow.

Seven of the jurors were black, and one of the five white jurors was Dawson's bitter political opponent, A. McCobb, Jr., with whom Dawson had quarreled over control of the party machinery in Ward 4 and whose efforts to win federal patronage had been thwarted by Dawson. When this jury found Dr. McDow not guilty, a cheer swept the packed courtroom.[55]

VI

An Old Southern City

❦ 1. 1890–1908:
"Reform" and "the Dawn of a New Era"

Upcountrians and the Lowcountry

Upcountrian Ben Robertson in *Red Hills and Cotton*(1942) wrote that Charleston had been "hard on us for a hundred and ten years, and we have been hard on it for the past eighty." The rest of the state "looked down upon" Charleston, he observed, as "a worldly place, a sea city trading with . . . Canton in heathen China. It had silks and a theater and artists came there to paint the portraits of the Rutledges and Ravenels . . . . Charleston was . . . sumptuous, with the wicked walking on every side." In South Carolina demagogues built their careers on such resentments, blaming virtually any problem on the lowcountry's effete aristocrats. "Charleston's reply was feeble and futile," William Watts Ball wrote, and "After 1890 it accepted the verdict. Its leaders scattered and returned to their tents." Knowing they could not succeed in statewide politics, Charlestonians focused on local contests, which were, Ball noted, "of a heat seldom observed elsewhere . . . outsiders gaze upon a Charleston election with wonderment, sometimes with merriment."[1]

After winning the governorship in 1890 Ben Tillman encouraged and supported his long-time state House colleague, John F. Ficken, in his campaign for the office of mayor of Charleston. John Ficken was born in Charleston, a descendant of German immigrants, took his A.B. degree at the College of Charleston, served in the Confederate Army, studied law at the University of Berlin in 1868, and was admitted to the Charleston bar. From 1876 to 1891, Ficken was elected eight times as a member of the South Carolina House of Representatives. He belonged to St. John's Lutheran Church and was a member of the local political establishment, as were his lieutenants: Frederick Von Kolnitz, whose ancestors also had immigrated from Germany, and who was married to a descendant of one of Charleston's earliest settlers; George Legaré, a future United States Representative; the brothers Daniel and Hugh Sinkler; and Turner W. Logan, a young attorney and yachting enthusiast. Together they built a coalition of the uptown working-class wards and labor groups, exploiting the long-simmering hostility toward the Broad Street clique by styling themselves the "reform" wing of the local Democratic party. At the Democratic convention in late October 1891 Ficken was nominated over incumbent Mayor Bryan by the narrow margin of 1,715 to 1,558, and during a light turnout of voters on election day, December 9, Ficken and his ticket were elected. He brought in as chief of police an upcountry friend of Governor Tillman, J. Elmore Martin, who became the mayor's closest aide. An editor of the *News and Courier* later described Chief Martin as "a clean and likeable man who preferred good company to bad and would rather the public affairs be well managed and in good hands. But his one aim and object in politics was to keep himself in office . . . ."[2]

Society, Thought, and Recreation

The most vigorous intellectual organization in late nineteenth-century Charleston was the Timrod Chautauqua Literary and Scientific Circle, which consisted of fifteen young men and women who met weekly. One member, Oliver J. Bond, a young professor and future commandant at the Citadel, noted that in spring 1890 the members were researching, writing, and presenting essays on Southern authors.

In the late 1880s J. F. O'Neill renovated the Hall of the Agricultural Society on Meeting Street as a theater with over 1,500 seats and renamed it the Opera House. Illuminated by gas, heated by hot air, its scenery designed by a Chicago firm and boasting a drop curtain adorned with scenes of Venice, the Opera House offered patrons minstrels, comedies, and operas by Gilbert and Sullivan. It was destroyed by fire on January 1, 1894.

The Charleston Amusement Association sponsored concerts in order to "cultivate the tastes of the Charleston public" one reporter noted. Churches occasionally hosted concerts of sacred music, and operettas were performed at Hibernian Hall. Concerts moved outdoors in the summer, local bands performing on Saturday afternoons and evenings before large crowds at the Battery and the Rutledge Street Pond. Charleston's Afro-Americans also formed minstrel troupes and bands that gave concerts, usually for Charleston's black citizens. Recreational parkland, primarily for the upper class, continued to be acquired by the city, increasing from 33 to 449 acres during the final two decades of the century.

White Charlestonians began again to celebrate July 4 with gusto in the 1890s, giving the day over to excursions, bicycle races, and fishing tournaments. The city's whites also persisted in remembering nostalgically the "Lost Cause." In July 1891 "imposing ceremonies" were held in Washington Square to unveil a memorial shaft to Charlestonians who died at the First Battle of Manassas.

In 1892 a group of prominent young men organized the Charleston Road Club with the object of encouraging bicycle-riding for pleasure and exercise. The enthusiasm for cycling spread rapidly and a cinder track in upper Meeting Street attracted some of the best competitive riders from across the country. The *News and Courier* noted that whereas a few years before it had been "uncommon to see a lady in this strict old city on a wheel, today girls in their shortest skirts are spinning over the principal streets."

The city restored its annual appropriation to the College of Charleston in 1892, which was limping along on an income of less than $11,000 from an endowment that had to cover the costs of maintaining the physical plant and paying the five professors who taught about twenty-seven students. There was no librarian and the library of 7,000 volumes was, as the historian of the college wrote, "fifty years out of date." But the college was fielding a baseball team that on one occasion lost an exhibition game to the New York Giants, 31–1. The city also had a professional baseball club, the Charleston Sea Gulls, that entertained teams like the Baltimore Orioles.

In 1891 "Ladies Day" was introduced into the elite Charleston Club, but "was abolished one year later without opposition," the club historian noted, "on a resolution ungallantly proposed by a member whose name shall not here be divulged." With a membership of about 120 during the 1890s, "the club-rooms were crowded of an evening and the bottle was passed freely," the club scribe recorded.

Governor Tillman's Dispensary system, a state-owned state-wide liquor monopoly that went into effect on July 1, 1893, was intended to close down forever all saloons and liquor wholesalers and restrict the retail sale of alcoholic beverages to state-operated dispensaries. Charlestonians, who for generations had enjoyed beer, wine, rum, and whiskey in congenial public bars and restaurants, were shocked and they simply ignored the law. Illegal bars, called "blind tigers," sprang up across the city, and prominent citizens engaged in illicit liquor traffic. Governor Tillman spoke of "raising hell on Chicco Street," referring to the notorious bootlegger and member of the City Council, Vincent Chicco. Mayor Ficken and Chief Martin cooperated with Tillman in repeated ingenious, hard-nosed, but futile attempts to enforce the law, which contributed to the defeat of the Ficken administration in the next municipal election.[3]

A Soft Economy

A few new buildings incorporating new technology in gas chandeliers, ducted hot air, steam radiators, and even electric light were going up. The few merchants who could afford opulent new townhouses continued to prefer the so-called Queen Anne Style, but the stuccoed bricks of the new African Methodist Episcopal Church at 108 Calhoun Street kept the neo-Gothic tradition alive, the new Post Office at Broad and Meeting streets was Charleston's grandest gesture to the Renaissance Revival, and the M. Marks & Son Department Store at King and Calhoun conspicuously reflected the latest fashion in American architecture, Romanesque Revival. King Street remained the center of Charleston's retail trade and upper King, north of Calhoun, was sometimes referred to as "New Jerusalem" because many of the proprietors of the numerous small clothing, dry-goods, fruit, drug, and second-hand furniture stores were Jewish.

About 5 million had been invested in manufacturing and mining in or near Charleston where at least 2,500 blacks were digging phosphates with pick and shovel from early light to last for $1 a day. For almost twenty years a few firms operating close to the city had nearly monopolized the American agricultural fertilizer industry, and Governor Tillman, growling about conservative aristocrats in "the greedy old city of Charleston," raised the state royalty on phosphates.[4]

In the late afternoon of August 27, 1893, a hurricane slammed into Charleston. Its winds reached a velocity of 120 miles per hour by midnight, terrifying the citizens and causing vast damages. Roofs were ripped off homes, wharves smashed, most of the Battery promenade demolished, and the new bridge across the Ashley River was destroyed. Four hurricane-related deaths occurred in Charleston and property damage reached $1,160,000, but south of the city a huge wave had swept over the islands from Hilton Head to John's Island, drowning about 2,000 blacks, many of whom worked in phosphate mining. Mayor Ficken's private company immediately rebuilt the Ashley River Bridge and it remained a toll bridge until the first quarter of the twentieth century.

The machinery and facilities of the phosphate-mining operations were damaged so extensively by the hurricane that some companies never fully recovered. Phosphate prices tumbled as more accessible phosphate deposits were discovered in Florida and Tennessee, and northern capitalists were consolidating the industry. By the early 1900s there were only three independent fertilizer manufacturers near Charleston, none of which were owned locally, and two land mining companies, and most of the profits made in the fertilizer business flowed out to Northern investors.[5]

Northern syndicates also bought the South Carolina Railway Company and other bankrupt railroads within the state and incorporated them into the north-south system of the Atlantic Coast Line, Southern Railway, and Seaboard Air Line. Consolidation and higher freight rates to ports south of Cape Hatteras caused trains that had previously carried exports from upcountry South Carolina to Charleston to take them to Norfolk and points north. While Atlanta, Augusta, Columbia, Charlotte, and northeastern cities, all growing in size, were linked in the 1890s by a new southwest-northeast rail axis, Charleston became a commercial backwater, and by 1900 its exports were only 2 percent of the national total. Goods that once had been hauled to Charleston for ocean transportation were going to other ports. Although the number of upstate textile mills was increasing dramatically, their yarn and cloth were carried out of state by rail rather than through Charleston, and the price of cotton kept falling. Nor could rice save Charleston as its price dropped due to the enormous amounts now being grown in the Mississippi Valley. Also fewer blacks were willing to work in the rice fields and planters were having trouble raising the money to maintain their unique systems of dikes and sluice-gates.

The volume of trade through the harbor fell from $98.5 million in 1890–91 to $29.5 million a decade later as Charleston's share of the total United States export trade dropped below 1 percent. The taxable value of Charleston real estate declined from $25 million in 1895 to $19 million in 1904 and the city's population relative to other American cities continued to decline: in 1870 it ranked twenty-sixth among urban centers, in 1890, fifty-third, and by 1910, ninety-first. During the last decade of the century, the city's population increased by a mere 1,000, while Savannah and Jacksonville each grew by 10,000, Augusta by 6,000, and Atlanta by nearly 25,000.

Two hotels had been refurbished by October 1894 to attract the tourist trade, but by this time local capitalists regarded Charleston enterprises as too risky. Both the old money and the new wealth made in phosphates by the Smyth, Pelzer, Jervey, Frost, Bee, and Chisholm families were being invested in upcountry textile mills, Alabama iron foundries, and street railways and utilities in cities like Nashville and Atlanta. At the same time ambitious and capable young men with prominent, local family names like Hayne, Barnwell, Rhett, Smith, and Huger were leaving Charleston for southern cities that offered them more opportunities. The city's younger generation of businessmen had become so unhappy with the Chamber of Commerce that they founded a Young Men's Business League in October 1894, its prime concern being "the mercantile welfare of the city." And though the harbor was modernized by the mid-1890s, making it accessible to the largest vessels afloat, there was not enough business in Charleston to attract the ships.[6]

Institutions and Services

Complaints that the costs of maintaining some 200 children in the Orphan House were too high led its chief executive officer, Agnes Irving, to cut expenditures per child from $155 to $106 annually. The boys kept the grounds, chopped firewood, and carried coal, while the girls made all the clothing and did all the washing and ironing. City officials were delighted with the cost reductions and the operation of the institution during Miss Irving's administration. A speaker at the centennial celebration of the Orphan House on November 6, 1890, observed that the orphanage had inculcated "habits of order, industry, health, thrift, honor, and emulation of excellence." A few black orphans were cared for from time to time at the city's "Old Folk's Home" for Afro-Americans, and though Mayor Ficken requested funds to establish a black orphanage, the City Council did not respond.

Troubled over the number of vagrants in the city, affluent citizens organized the Associated Charities Society of Charleston to monitor and coordinate both public and private almsgiving. Former Mayor Courtenay, who had rooted out "unworthy" recipients of charity at the city Almshouse, was elected the first president, and a future mayor, J. Adger Smyth, served on its first Board of Directors. A secretary who managed the office became the society's investigator and distinguished between "worthy" and "unworthy" applicants. The society planned to reduce "vagrancy and pauperism" and to "elevate the home-life, health, and habits of the poor" and professed no desire "to meddle with . . . one's politics or religion," but, at the request of Charleston's police chief, provided Bibles for boys sentenced to reform school. Despite its efforts, the society's annual report of 1900 acknowledged that "beggars . . . are still with us." The number of indigent patients and the costs of providing medical care for them at Memorial Hospital also rose. In 1890 there were 764 patients treated without cost, while in 1900 there were 1,101; total costs for operating the hospital increased from $21,922 to $38,382 during the same period.

Most charity was directed to "deserving" whites by whites. William Enston, who wished "to make old age comfortable," bequeathed funds to the city, and nineteen cottages were constructed and furnished on upper King Street for whites "advanced in life." The Ladies Benevolent Society, which included Charleston's prominent matrons, did not extend its charity north of Calhoun Street until the mid-1890s.[7]

J. Adger Smyth

The nearly complete legal disfranchisement of the Afro-American in South Carolina came with the new Tillmanite state constitution of 1895. In order to vote persons now were required to pay a poll tax, a property tax, and demonstrate an understanding of the state's constitution, which also prohibited interracial marriage.

J. Adger Smyth, the candidate of the Broad Street establishment, easily won the city's Democratic primary in November 1895. A prosperous fifty-eight-year-old cotton factor and commission merchant who had been born in the city and educated at the college, Smyth campaigned against Tillmanism, for home rule, and for local rather than state regulation of liquor. His ticket swept to victory in the general election by a few thousand votes. Apathy hung heavy in a stagnating city where white Republicans and Afro-Americans were virtually excluded from politics. One of Mayor Smyth's first acts was to fire Chief of Police Martin, but a Tillmanite governor quickly placed Charleston under a special metropolitan police force and reinstated Martin.

Beginning in the mid-1890s the flagstone sidewalks and curbing installed primarily in those streets south of Calhoun Street were replaced by concrete. By this time Calhoun, a major east-west corridor, had been extended to the Ashley River; two years later, a major north-south thoroughfare paved in "cement gravel" extended from the Rutledge Street Pond to the city boundary and was described as "a beautiful boulevard." With the exception primarily of some forty acres of marsh and mudflats on the southeastern side of the city, the principal streets of the city were in place by 1900.

Businessmen complained bitterly about the quality and quantity of the city's water supply, and the city sued the Charleston Waterworks Company in 1898, but the state Supreme Court decided in favor of the company. Angry, Mayor Smyth declared that "representatives of the people" should control the water supply and he vowed to continue the fight for a clean and ample supply of water, an "essential necessity to all city growth and prosperity."[8]

Dr. Henry Horlbeck

The city's chief health officer, Dr. Henry Horlbeck, a bachelor and an indefatigable sanitarian, was elected president of the American Public Health Association in the mid-1890s. He helped launch the United States Quarantine Service and promoted research into yellow fever that led eventually to the discovery that bites of certain mosquitoes, not miasmas, caused the disease. With a flush toilet in his living room, at a time when even in Boston and Paris people considered the indoor privy unsanitary, Horlbeck persistently reminded the City Council that the city's 10,000 privy-vaults were "horrible receptacles" that made "our sub-soil . . . dangerous to human life." He eventually convinced the city government to install a modern sanitation system, but only a small portion of the city south of Broad Street received a sewer installation with the Shone pneumatic pressure system. As the sewer pipes began to be laid, Charlestonians worried over their exposure to miasmas, so to calm their fears Dr. Horlbeck had lime thrown into the excavations. When this became too expensive, he quietly substituted spoiled flour, which he was able to purchase cheaply, and nobody noticed the difference.

Dr. Horlbeck continued his crusade. At the end of the 1890s an increase in the number of deaths from typhoid fever, which he considered "a preventable disease" caused by polluted waters, especially alarmed him and his new aide, bacteriologist Dr. Robert Wilson, Jr. In his last *Annual Report,* in 1900, Dr. Horlbeck once more called on the city government to put an end to the "privy vaults polluting our soil, poisoning our cisterns and wells," and causing "odors . . . at times in the summer simply unbearable . . . ." For years, however, the neighborhoods of poor whites and especially poor blacks, who were not represented politically, remained almost untouched by sanitary improvements.

Dr. Horlbeck also urged the city government to pass laws for food inspection and called for an end to the city's "primitive slaughter houses" and the establishment of a modern abattoir. The lack of such laws, Horlbeck declared, caused the persistently high rate of deaths in Charleston from "diarrheal diseases," which between 1865 and 1897 reached 5,274, second only to deaths from consumption, 6,972; the particularly high death rate among the city's blacks may have resulted from eating tainted meats, uninspected and purchased cheaply, Horlbeck noted. But as the years went by and the City Council failed to act on his advice, Horlbeck told them: "I cannot forgo the expression of my disappointment at the apathy and indifference of our community in the large health matters of sewage, . . . and the establishment of a thorough system of inspection for . . . meat."

Charleston continued to be thought of as sickly, but good luck and the efforts of Dr. Horlbeck saved the city from catastrophic outbreaks of disease. Several small epidemics of typhoid fever between 1865 and 1897 caused 1,418 deaths; malarial fevers, diphtheria, and whooping cough exacted their tolls, and during 1891–92 about eighty persons died from a fast-spreading influenza, but there were no major epidemics comparable to the yellow fever outbreaks that scourged Memphis in 1878 and New Orleans in 1897. Horlbeck launched a strict quarantine policy and disinfection system, and the officers of the quarantine station at Fort Johnson on James Island cleaned and fumigated hundreds of ships and their cargoes, using the latest method of steam fumigation. From May to October Dr. Horlbeck presided over the disinfection of the principal drains, market places, and privy-vaults. A "zealous and efficient" city health detective, Mr. F. Nipson, and four sanitary inspectors roamed the city investigating, cleaning, and fumigating hundreds of premises annually.[9]

In 1897 Charlestonians turned out by the hundreds to pay tribute to "the last commander of Fort Sumter," General Thomas A. Huguenin, for years the city's superintendent of streets. Nostalgically, Mayor Smyth described his funeral: "battle-scarred Confederate flags . . . were placed over his sleeping form," and those attending "bedew his grave with tears." The following year 2,000 Confederate veterans came to Charleston for a reunion and were welcomed with bands and parades. Businessmen hoped they would help the city's failing economy.

On June 26, 1897, the Charleston City Railway Company operated the first electric trolley in the city. The first urban trolley had appeared in Richmond, Virginia, about a decade earlier. In 1898 the Charleston Consolidated Railway, Gas and Electric Company took over the operation of all the electric railways, gas, and electric properties within the city. The major investors and officers of the company lived in Baltimore, but well-to-do Charlestonians Andrew Simonds, George W. Williams, Jr., George A. Wagner, and William M. Bird were investors and members of the Board of Directors. By the late 1890s the City Council authorized private companies to erect the first telephone poles in the city along Church Street, and on January 24, 1899, a crew from Southern Bell began installing the first long-distance lines, linking Charleston with Augusta.[10]

Crime

As the nineteenth century neared its end, assaults, robberies, illegal traffic in whiskey, gambling, and prostitution increased. Fights and stabbings were commonplace in saloons along Market Street from Archdale Street to East Bay. On nearby Anson Street a "low Negro dive," the Eden Hotel, owned by the wealthy businessman George W. Williams, Jr., was declared "to be a den of iniquity and vice" and in violation of city ordinances. Judith, Ann, Princess, Charlotte, and Elizabeth streets and nearby Gabeau's Row became notorious for the incidence of crime. Cumberland Street near Church Street gained notoriety when there was a "brutal murder . . . in a house of ill favor" there. The fact was that when pork cost 12 cents a pound, eggs 20 cents a dozen, and a brass bed $10, some blacks preferred robbery, bootlegging, selling cocaine, gambling, and prostitution to working for 10 cents an hour. The victims of black crime were usually black and they no longer had any political power. Repeatedly requesting police protection, Afro-American taxpayers who lived near Nassau and Columbus streets complained that they were reluctant to leave their homes "for even an hour unprotected" for fear they would be robbed.

One police chief after another appealed to City Hall for better facilities and weapons, more money, and additional policemen. Chief William Boyle told city authorities: "The yearly increase of the negro population, with attending increase of turbulency and crime, together with other demands of the department render it a physical impossibility to cover a territory of 69 miles of streets with about 65 patrolmen for daily duty." By this time Afro-Americans exceeded 56 percent of Charleston's population of some 55,000 persons, the highest black-to-white ratio of any major Southern city. Arrests of whites for public drunkenness exceeded black arrests by a 3-to-1 ratio, but arrest of blacks for larceny exceeded white arrests by 15 to 1 in the 1880s and subsequently soared much higher. In the last twenty years of the nineteenth century there were eight arrests in the city daily, while in the final decade the annual homicide rate averaged slightly over 20 per 100,000 population; Atlanta's rate was 24, Boston's 6, and Philadelphia's 2.45. While Southern cities such as Charleston and Atlanta had much more murder and mayhem annually than those of the Northeast, they had much less than Western communities like Dodge City, Kansas, where the murder rate exceeded 71 per 100,000 inhabitants in 1885.

The police regularly swept the streets of vagrants, especially Market Street and its vicinity. These "loafers" were sent to the city's new, predominantly black, notorious chain gang. Here the inmates were shackled, worked hard under close supervision, and whipped for the least provocation. Policemen frequently used what today would be considered grossly excessive force, primarily against blacks. In 1898 blacks convened at the Morris Brown A.M.E. Church to protest the shooting of an Afro-American, William Chisholm, by a white policeman. Public confessions and hangings of convicted black murderers were also used to deter crime, and the *News and Courier* cooperated by reporting the events in graphic details. Policemen sometimes spent so much time controlling black crime that white crime was ignored.

The police force was the largest agency in the city and the chief the highest-paid official. In 1900 the city spent $52,500 on its fire department, $74,307 for the salaries of teachers and principals and the maintenance of the public schools, and $79,500 for police protection. In the new century Charleston rewarded the police by building a new station house for $42,000 at the corner of St. Philip's and Vanderhorst streets.

Fear of black crime helped a black Baptist minister, Daniel J. Jenkins, persuade the City Council to support the orphanage he had recently founded. The ingenious Reverend Mr. Jenkins argued that he was keeping potential juvenile offenders off the streets and making "breadwinners out of beggars and loafers," and in 1897 the City Council voted $250 to support the fifty-four "colored orphans" lodged at the Jenkins Orphanage. The *News and Courier* believed he would provide a place where "the small . . . thieves, crap shooters, and razor pushers could . . . learn an honest trade," and annually the city government continued to support the orphanage.[11]

In 1898 Charleston's Chief of Police J. Elmore Martin stepped down and successfully ran for sheriff of Charleston County, from which post he controlled county politics for the next twenty years. Other members of Mayor Ficken's "reform" wing of the Democratic party won county and district offices, but Tillmanites never again captured Charleston.

Elections at the state and local levels were conducted through an all-white Democratic primary operated like a private club that effectively blocked black participation in the electoral process. Charleston's municipal elections were held every four years. In the year preceding presidential elections a mayor and twenty-four councilmen were chosen. The campaign usually began in April and ended with the Democratic primary, it being a foregone conclusion that the winner of the primary would win the general election in December. The faction controlling the local Democratic Executive Committee could usually determine the election. Chosen by the city or county convention some six months before the election, the committee named poll managers who would oversee registration proceedings, voting, and the counting of ballots. The committee was supposed to purge the rolls of Democratic voters who had died, moved, or registered

Board of Stewards, Charleston's Centenary Methodist Episcopal Church, circa 1900. *Courtesy of the Black Charleston Photo Collection, College of Charleston Library, Charleston, S.C.*

The Reverend Daniel J. Jenkins, founder of Jenkins Orphanage. *Courtesy of the Black Charleston Photo Collection, College of Charleston Library, Charleston, S.C.*

improperly, and was required to rule on postelection challenges, but the system was readily corrupted. In 1899 J. Adger Smyth and the Broad Street clique of the party were reelected without opposition.

In the summer of 1899 a gasoline-powered automobile, probably the first in South Carolina, was shipped by boat from Boston to Charleston for Captain Ernest O. Patterson, an engineer who took only a few spins along the Battery before city authorities banned the contraption as a public nuisance.[12]

Segregation

A number of new laws were enacted from 1898 to 1906 providing for segregation on railroads, streetcars, ferries, restaurants, and steamboats. For instance, Charleston blacks were prohibited from riding the city's new electrified trolley cars shortly after they were put into operation. The *News and Courier* opposed these new laws, editorializing " . . . we have no . . . need for a Jim Crow car system." But by 1900 WHITE ONLY and COLORED signs were being posted on restrooms, drinking fountains, doctors' waiting rooms, schools, hotels, restaurants, parks, and playgrounds. An unwritten and unposted law banned Afro-Americans from the Battery and its benches.

The *News and Courier* also opposed lynching as firmly as it earlier denounced dueling, and although there were some seventy-three lynchings of Afro-Americans in South Carolina in the last eighteen years of the nineteenth century, there were none in Charleston. Nevertheless, as the late 1860s had been the worst of times for white Charlestonians, so the years around the turn of the century were the worst of times for black Charlestonians. A few Charleston blacks continued to hold federal offices. George Washington Murray, for instance, was inspector of customs and Benjamin Boseman was postmaster. By the early twentieth century there were no black teachers in Charleston's public schools.

Despite the enthusiasm for education by black Charlestonians, black illiteracy remained high. This was due in part to "the prevailing poverty of the colored people," which forced many to drop out of school. In 1900 there were 4,229 "colored" and 4,211 whites between five and twenty years of age in Charleston schools. Yet there were 7,462 "colored" and only 301 whites over ten years of age who were illiterate.

Some black residential enclaves had emerged, but Afro-

The Charleston Light Dragoons near White Point Gardens, circa 1895. *Courtesy of the South Carolina Historical Society, Charleston, S.C.*

The docks in Charleston in the era of the Spanish-American War, circa 1898. *Courtesy of the Library of Congress, Washington, D.C.*

Americans continued to live throughout the city. In Ward 3, one of the most prestigious in the city, there were 917 blacks and 1,542 whites at the turn of the century. This was the highest white-to-black ratio in the city's twelve wards. The ratio was reversed in Ward 11 where 2,591 whites lived among 5,921 blacks. The shift of the Afro-American population from the lower to the upper wards would accelerate in the twentieth century. The decline of employment of black domestics who lived near their employers, the preservation movement, and the advent of public housing all contributed to this phenomenon and the eventual residential segregation of the races.[13]

Federal Money

The new construction and weaponry installed at Fort Moultrie and Fort Sumter were a part of the federal government's national coastal defense plans, which brought a permanent army garrison to the Charleston area. At about the same time, the federal government completed the building of the Charleston jetties and the dredging of the channel, which vastly improved the har-

An alleyway in downtown Charleston before "gentrification" in the late nineteenth or early twentieth century. *Courtesy of the South Caroliniana Library of the University of South Carolina, Columbia, S.C.*

bor. The improvements were promoted in Washington by Charleston officials like Mayor Smyth and former governor and now United States Senator Benjamin Tillman, chairman of the Naval Affairs Committee. Despite his distaste for what he called "self-idolatrous" Charlestonians, Tillman helped local boosters lobby successfully for the transfer of the naval base at Port Royal to Charleston in 1900. The Navy Department agreed to the relocation primarily because of the deeper, wider harbor. The site for the new Navy Yard was purchased in 1901. The federal government paid $110,207 for 2,250 acres of marsh and high land on the west bank of the Cooper River about six miles north of the Customs House. Mayor Smyth congratulated Tillman, the perennial foe of Charleston "aristocrats," whom Smyth earlier had bitterly opposed, for his "wise and efficient counsel." The land was carved from four former rice plantations; here within six years the United States government spent over $7 million at the Charleston Navy Yard, most of it for a dry-dock, which was the largest on the East Coast.

The leadership of the faction of the Democratic party backed by the Broad Street Ring had been gradually passing from ailing Mayor Smyth to his mayor pro-tem, R. Goodwyn Rhett. President of the People's National Bank, the city's largest and oldest bank, Rhett was an Episcopalian who belonged to the St. Cecilia Society and the Charleston Yacht Club. He had been born in the state capital in 1862, but his ancestors had come from Charleston.[14]

The "Ivory City"

In 1900 Charleston's economy was moribund. Some leading citizens, however, continued to try to develop and improve Charleston through expositions, festivals, conventions, and a national advertising campaign. With some funds appropriated by the state and with the backing of Mayor Smyth and the City Council, an Exposition Company was formed and incorporated, but few of Charleston's wealthy and socially prominent elite endorsed it. Captain Frederick W. Wagener, a German immigrant and wealthy wholesale grocer, was elected chairman of the board, and with a few progressive young businessmen, he organized the South Carolina Interstate and West Indian Exposition, which opened in December 1901. By attracting worldwide attention to Charleston, the organizers hoped to revive the stagnating economy, especially the city's trade with the Caribbean.

The exposition's "ivory-city" was built around an artificial lake on a 250-acre site, once the Washington Race Course. The alabaster buildings displayed the most recent technology in machinery, commerce, transportation, and agriculture, and there were exhibits of mining, forestry, and livestock. There was a "Negro Building," as in most such expositions of the age. Over 3 million feet of lumber went into building a court of great "palaces" that faced sunken gardens planted in rare tropical foliage still visible today. The grounds were adorned with statuary and criss-crossed by wide asphalt walks, which were lined with thousands of roses, azaleas, rhododendrons, camellias, and oleanders. A zoo, an administration building, and an auditorium with a seating capacity of 6,000 also went up and here on December 2 the exposition opened with much hoopla. As part of the celebration two battleships were stationed off Charleston, Philadelphia sent the Liberty Bell, and President Theodore Roosevelt and Mark Twain came to the city in April.

More than 500,000 persons visited the exposition and spent millions of dollars in the winter and spring of 1902, but in May it closed. Failing to act as a long-term stimulus for Charleston's economy or to attract investment capital, the exposition was a

The South Carolina Interstate and West Indian Exposition, 1902. *Courtesy of the Charleston Museum, Charleston, S.C.*

picturesque disaster. The buildings were dismantled and sold to satisfy debts, the legend being that the materials were used in the building of houses in the vicinity for the people who moved into the area after the exposition, especially the neighborhood just to the south of Hampton Park, so named after the exposition to honor General Wade Hampton. By the end of 1902 little remained of "the Ivory City."[15]

R. Goodwyn Rhett

On August 6, 1902, a bright, energetic Charleston lawyer launched a campaign for the state Senate, the first bid for public office by John Patrick Grace. He was born in 1874 in Charleston on Factory Hill, where County Hall stands today, into a second-generation Irish-Catholic family and grew up in a home on Society Street. His father, a graduate of the local college, was a bookkeeper, but died suddenly when Grace was nine years old. His mother began a small dairy to sell milk to neighbors. Several years later Grace left for New York to work as a clerk and later as a book salesman in the midwest where he heard socialists and populists advocate government ownership of public services. In 1896 Grace returned to Charleston and shortly thereafter accepted a staff position with lowcountry Congressman William Elliott, which also offered him an opportunity to study law at Georgetown University. In 1902 the twenty-eight-year-old Grace returned to Charleston with a law degree, established a practice, and immediately became embroiled in the city's politics.

The three-way race for the state Senate among Grace, incumbent George Von Kolnitz, and T. Moultrie Mordecai was marred by irregularities on election day, August 27, but Grace piled up a huge vote total in Ward 5 and a runoff was necessary between him and Von Kolnitz. The Broad Street Ring backed the incumbent, while Grace appealed to the Irish, German, and labor vote, telling his followers that "the vote of the little man counts just as much as the vote of the banker on Broad Street." There were complaints of interference by the city police during the runoff election, September 9, and though Grace was defeated the returns showed that he had received support from both Tillmanites and dissident members of the Broad Street clique. Grace almost pulled off a miracle in local politics and in doing so attracted the attention of Charleston's politicos.

Endorsed by Grace and the Broad Street Ring, Goodwyn

Rhett offered for mayor in 1903. When his supporters took control of the city Democratic convention at Hibernian Hall in April, Grace was rewarded with the position of secretary of the convention, and the candidate of the Charleston County machine, Sheriff J. Elmore Martin, withdrew from the race. In the Democratic primary in November and in the general election the following month, Rhett was unopposed. Voters swept him and his slate of aldermen into City Hall by a margin of 1,797 ballots. The light turnout dramatized the disfranchisement of large numbers of white and especially black voters. In the late 1870s, 5,497 whites and 5,949 blacks had been registered to vote, but now there were only 726 Afro-Americans and several thousand white Charlestonians registered.

Local attitudes toward Afro-Americans were highlighted when President Theodore Roosevelt decided to appoint William Demosthenes Crum, a black physician, as collector of the port at Charleston and the "best people" opposed the appointment. Major James Calvin Hemphill, editor of the *News and Courier*, asserted in early 1904 that the mere fact that Crum was black was sufficient "to bar him from public office." Also in the first years of the new century, Aaron Prioleau, a Charleston black and a perennial and unsuccessful candidate for Congress, was referred to by the *News and Courier* as a "cheeky Negro." Mayor Rhett embraced these white attitudes, viewing blacks as racially inferior but believing in the improvability of all through education. A progressive Democrat, Rhett entered politics out of a sense of duty and he was determined to adapt the latest business practices to city government.[16]

Between 1903 and 1910, Rhett and some of the city's younger businessmen founded the Commercial Club, the Charleston Manufacturing, Jobbers, and Banking Association, and the Real Estate Exchange, and reorganized the Chamber of Commerce. Even the dream of linking Charleston by rail with the West raised its tired head once more. Local boosters persuaded the Southern Railroad to build new facilities in Charleston between 1905 and 1911 and also to lower freight rates, but cotton shipments through the port continued to decline. While the railroads pumped fortunes into Savannah and Norfolk for the construction of facilities to export coal, cotton, and tobacco, Charleston's trade remained limited by its antiquated facilities. The Charleston Terminal Company, which held a franchise from the city to operate 70 percent of the wharves and warehouses along the Cooper River, permitted them to become "rotting piles of decaying timbers," and the city government charged that the company's failure to maintain the property hurt the local economy.

The statewide industrial and agricultural boom and the promotion of Charleston as the state's premier port by Governor Duncan Clinch Heyward (1903–07), a lowcountry rice planter, was reflected in the sharp rise in property values and trade.

Part of the Mosquito Fleet which sailed miles off Charleston to fish at Cantini's Wharf, Tradd Street, foot of Rutledge, 1903. *Courtesy of the Charleston Museum, Charleston, S.C.*

Charleston real estate increased by 50 percent between 1904 and 1911, and exports jumped about 2,000 percent.

When Rhett became mayor some 12,000 privy-vaults remained the primary means of human waste disposal, their contents leeching into the soil and their smells befouling the air. Health Department officials observed that citizens preferred water drawn from wells next to privies rather than drinking water piped to the city from Goose Creek reservoirs. Hogs wallowed in low-lying lots and the meat of slaughtered animals was often exposed to all sorts of contamination before it was sold. The few health inspectors were not adequately trained and Charleston was "a *dumping ground for all the condemned meat* turned away from other cities." Dozens of cows were kept locally for milk for private consumption and sale. Citizens protested efforts to banish the cows by arguing that warm milk was needed for their babies and milk sales provided an income for poor widows. Mosquitoes swarmed through the city and there was no program for the medical examination or vaccination of school children. Streets were filthy, but citizens often opposed new methods of garbage collection. One Charlestonian blamed the city's unsanitary conditions on "dirty politics," free-spending politicians, and "TOO MUCH TALK AND TOO LITTLE . . . WORK."

By 1905 Dr. J. Mercier Green was Charleston's new health officer. Another "fighting . . . sanitarian," a Northern urban reformer called him, Charleston was indeed fortunate to have the scholarly looking Dr. Green replace Dr. Horlbeck. Green reported that most of the city's Afro-American population was "huddled together in unfit and dilapidated structures"; the lanes and alleys where they lived were little more than open sewers. The sickness and mortality statistics, especially for blacks, dramatized the unsanitary conditions. Deaths among them from consumption and typhoid exceeded those of whites and were many times greater for smallpox and pellagra. A yellow fever epidemic in 1905, an outbreak of typhoid the next year, which resulted in forty-four deaths, led the City Council to enact new milk and meat inspection ordinances at the urging of Dr. Green.[17]

Charleston remained a patchwork of mostly unpaved and unconnected streets, lanes, and alleys. Over half of the fifty-eight miles of roadways were dirt, about one-third were paved in granite, brick, or asphalt, while the rest were gravel, oyster shells, cinders, or cobblestones. Mayor Rhett immediately substituted

Fire! 1890s–early 1900s. *Courtesy of the Charleston Museum, Charleston, S.C.*

long-range planning for the haphazard approach to the paving, maintenance, and cleaning of the streets by establishing the Board of Public Works in 1903. To finance this systematic approach, taxes were raised twice between 1904 and 1911. He also encouraged private developers to cooperate with the city in reclaiming land along the Ashley River and in building a boulevard and sea wall from White Point Gardens to Chisolm's Mill at the western terminus of Tradd Street. The sale of residential lots along the roadway, named after Charleston philanthropist Andrew B. Murray, helped finance the beautification project. Reared in the Orphan House, Murray accumulated a large fortune in local business ventures, then gave part of it away for civic improvements.

Determined to unseat the Tillmanite sheriff of Charleston County, J. Elmore Martin, Mayor Rhett pledged to support John P. Grace if he ran against Martin in 1904. It was a long shot at best in that Martin controlled most of the rural precincts where he could count on a 4-to-1 voting margin and there were no new substantive issues. Grace did win some votes for attacking Tillman and the Dispensary Act and promising Charleston voters home rule, but on election day Sheriff Martin was reelected by a margin of 4,000 votes, winning big in the county and in the strongholds of the Broad Street Ring, Wards 2, 4, and 6, as members of Rhett's faction refused to follow his instructions to vote for the young upstart, John Grace. Nevertheless, in his unsuccessful bids for public office Grace had attracted a broad following. Turner Logan, the reform-minded "aristocrat," became Grace's law partner and together they built a political machine. Eventually, other defectors from the Broad Street Ring like Daniel Sinkler joined Grace's inner circle. They helped select ward bosses and organize rallies and ward meetings, which were crucial to winning control of the local Democratic Executive Committee. The patronage system was the oil of the machine.

For most of the twentieth century the Republican party in Charleston was a joke. It was known locally as the party of the black man and federal patronage. In an election to the House of Representatives in 1906, the local Republican candidate received one vote. Aspiring Charleston politicians avoided any association with the Republican party. It was a one-party political system.

In the early 1900s the communicants of St. John's Lutheran Church on Archdale Street complained about prostitutes strolling near their church, but most of the time Charleston tolerated an extraordinary abundance of flagrant vice, reinforcing the belief in the rest of the state that Charleston was another Gomorrah. The city's open drinking, gambling, and brothels offended religious fundamentalists, and in 1907 a Baptist minister compared Charleston to a Western frontier town.

Accustomed to drinking liquor in their favorite taverns, restaurants, or private clubs, Charlestonians did not patronize the official dispensaries, which became the wholesale suppliers for the more than 300 "blind tigers" in the city. Of the 297 liquor licenses granted by the federal government in 1906 in South Carolina, 213 were issued in Charleston where "blind tigers" operated flagrantly. Fifteen were located around City Hall and nineteen operated near St. Philip's Church. Gambling at cards, dice, and by slot machines also flourished.

Always in chronic need of revenue, Charleston officials instituted a virtual licensing system in 1903 when the city began fining the "blind tigers" $25 every three months, or six times higher if any of them hindered the public revenues by obtaining their liquor from sources other than the state Dispensary system. "On these terms," historian David Duncan Wallace wrote, "the tiger and the law lay down together." The income was significant for the city, and local juries winked at the Dispensary Act by dismissing the obligation of the taking of oaths for testimony given in court by Charlestonians brought to trial for violating the state liquor laws. When the legislature repealed the Dispensary Act in 1907 and each county had to choose between total prohibition and establishing its own Dispensary system, there was never any doubt as to which way Charleston County would vote.

In 1907 in a quiet election Mayor Rhett was returned to office unopposed, but this would be the last amicable contest for mayor for years.[18]

❧ 2.1908–1923:
Sin and "The Revolution of 1911"

Factions

Four political groups contended for control of Charleston's City Hall in the twentieth century. The most important faction was the Progressive Capitalists. Few of them were rich by the standards of New York, Boston, or Philadelphia, but by the standards of Charleston in 1908 they were affluent. Among them were Presbyterians and Methodists, some Episcopalians, and a few Baptists and Lutherans. They could get along with politicians who spoke for the white working classes if they had to, but their Progressivism was usually for whites only. Among the mayors of Charleston, Smyth, Rhett, and later Maybank, Lockwood, and Wehman were of this persuasion. They had good social connections and, as conservative managers of the city's money, could generally count on the support of the *News and Courier*. Thought of as part of the Broad Street Ring, they sought new industries, welcomed federal funds, and enjoyed good relations with the more progressive governors in the state capital, such as Richard I. Manning; they winked at prostitution, gambling, and whiskey sales, which they wished to control, viewing any attempt to eradicate these traditional vices as hopelessly quixotic.

Another group, who might be called neo-Tories, or reactionaries, opposed any new industries and regarded federal funds with suspicion. Episcopalian and Anglophile, they tended to view the United States north of Alexandria, Virginia, south of Jacksonville, Florida, and west of the Appalachians as foreign territory, and they found it difficult to take seriously the government at Columbia. Distrusting democracy and disliking the twentieth century, they often withdrew from the political process in disgust, but when they ran for office in Charleston they were welcomed warmly by the *News and Courier* and grudgingly by members of the Broad Street Ring, some of whom they intimidated. They inherited land and beautiful old houses, but often their families had lost their capital in the Civil War.

A third faction, the Protestant Populists, were heirs of the artisans of the Revolutionary era. These members of various Fundamentalist and Pentecostal sects, Baptists, Presbyterians, and Lutherans—about 30 percent of the city's white population was German and some Lutheran services were conducted in German well into the new century—favored enforcement of laws against drinking, gambling, and prostitution. Isolationist in foreign affairs, vehemently anti-aristocrat, anti-Catholic, and antiblack, they were led by John Ficken and then by J. Elmore Martin and were in touch with rural populists across South Carolina, but were limited in numbers in Charleston because of their cultural bias, which was more agricultural than urban. Workers at the Navy Yard north of the city usually voted for Protestant Populists.

The fourth and newest faction in the city, Catholic Populists, had no equivalent elsewhere in the state, was urban in orientation, favored industrial development, and tolerated drinking, gambling, and prostitution. Italian or Irish in ancestry—the latter constituting between 10 to 15 percent of the white population of the city—the Catholic Populists were isolationist or anti-British in foreign affairs, bitterly anti-aristocrat, and somewhat milder than the Protestant Populists in their racism. Of these four groups, the Progressive Capitalists, who usually simply ignored blacks, were probably the least racist.

Wards 3 and 5, 7 and 9, north of Broad Street and east of King Street and bordering the Cooper River, were strongholds of the Grace machine. These working-class neighborhoods included sizable populations of first- and second-generation Irish and Italian immigrants, especially along Reid, Hasell, and State streets. Vincent Chicco, "king of the tigers," was the most important supporter of the machine in Ward 3. In Wards 7 and 9, H. Frank "Rumpty Rattles" Hogan typified the Grace leadership. A baseball player, boxer, and sometime dock foreman, he opened a "blind tiger" at 16 Blake Street, the Mexican Roost and Robbers

Inn, which was renowned for its homemade soup cooked in a fifty-gallon lard tin. In the late 1920s Hogan was shot and killed from ambush on Market Street.

In 1908 Grace tested the strength of his machine by plunging into a race for the Senate of the United States. Injecting into the campaign the personality issues that South Carolina voters enjoyed, he called Rhett "a Republican in disguise," a tool of monopoly, and falsely accused him of having supported the appointment of the Afro-American Dr. Crum as collector of customs. Ellison D. "Cotton Ed" Smith finished first in the race for the Senate, Tillmanite John Gary Evans was second, Rhett third, and Grace finished a distant fourth, but he had established his machine as something to be reckoned with.[19]

Education, Recreation, and Boosterism

The Charleston Orphan House continued to be the pride of the city's upper classes. When President William Howard Taft visited Charleston in 1909, city officials decided that a tour of the orphanage would be a high point of his visit. It took place at night and the orphanage was bathed in gas and electric lights from cupola to basement. The 200 children were arranged on the grounds in tiers, the boys in gray suits and the girls in blue dresses and white aprons. Each waved a tiny American flag while "singing one of the national airs in clear and lusty tones" and President Taft was impressed.

Support for public education by the city government in the opening years of the twentieth century continued lukewarm at best and even less so for black schooling. The prevailing notion held that the education of Afro-Americans, other than the most rudimentary or vocational, might undermine society. A board of white commissioners presided over the city's public school system, which included three white and two black grammar schools and Memminger Normal School for white girls. A private Board of Trustees ran Charleston High School, where white males only could pursue a classical or commercial course of studies. Funds for the schools were provided by the state, county, and city, and approximately 10,000 children, nearly equally divided between black and white, attended for a nine-month term.

In 1907 the principal of the Memminger School shocked civic leaders by blasting local public education as a disgrace to Charleston's cultural heritage. He averred that the city spent less per capita on schooling than any city of comparable size in the nation; that the teachers taught an estimated 50 percent more students than the maximum for effective instruction; that only the city's maintenance personnel made less than the city's teachers, who earned $35 per month; and that of the city's total budget, approximately 10 percent went to education compared to a national average of 30 percent. Stung by such criticism and with an educational revival sweeping the South and the state, Mayor Rhett and progressive civic leaders sought to improve the city's image. A new school for whites was built in the northwestern section of the city, a new building was constructed at Memminger School, and additional teachers were added.

The College of Charleston had a faculty of seven professors who taught approximately seventy students. About one-third of the city's physicians and attorneys received their undergraduate degrees there. Its president from 1897 to 1942, Harrison Randolph, repeatedly complained about gross underfunding, reporting in 1912 that the college's budget of $16,000 a year represented about two-thirds of the appropriations for the poorest funded of its

Charleston from St. Michael's steeple in the early 1900s. *Courtesy of the Library of Congress, Washington, D.C.*

peer institutions. Harrison pointed out that the school's library lacked the books needed for up-to-date instruction.

Paul M. Rea, a native of Massachusetts and professor of biology, also directed the college's museum, which had inherited the scanty funds of the Charleston Museum and the remains of its collections after the 1778 fire. Rea envisioned a museum separate from the college that would enrich the local cultural life through publications, lectures, and exhibits for both children and adults. He persuaded the City Council to fund the museum and move the exhibits from the college to Thomson Auditorium, a structure hastily built at 121 Rutledge Avenue in 1899 for a reunion of Confederate veterans.

The two major recreational sites were the Battery and Hampton Park. Here the lawns, paths, flower- and azalea-beds were maintained by the city, but for a group of civic-minded women this was not enough and in 1910 the City Council established the Municipal Playground Commission to explore the creation of recreational areas for directed, "systematic play." Within several years Mitchell, Mall, and Marion Square playgrounds were established.[20]

In the face of a still languishing economy, the *News and Courier* kept up a steady barrage of boosterism. On January 1, 1910, J. C. Hemphill printed a "Jubilee Edition" of fifty pages promoting Charleston as a city on the move. Mayor Rhett had it published in book form for wider distribution as *Charleston: Business, Trade, Growth, Opportunity* , and the next year, Philip Gadsden, a local entrepreneur with an old lowcountry name, led local businessmen on a cross-state tour to promote Charleston.

In 1909 the City Council appropriated $340,000 to build and maintain new sewer lines, but when sewer pipes were laid over the next few years during the summer months, the Health Department was severely criticized. To the amazement of Dr. J. Mercier Green, many Charlestonians still believed that "digging up the soil in the summer time . . . spread disease." By 1910 thirty-five miles of sewer drains were laid and below Broad Street privy-vaults were disappearing. But for decades privy-vaults would continue in use in black neighborhoods whose slumlords opposed "sewering." The city's last severe smallpox epidemic, which occurred in 1910, helped spur Dr. Green's crusade to clean up Charleston and provide medical examinations and vaccinations for all school children.

A hurricane swept northeastward off the South Carolina coast October 19–20, 1910, causing some damage to shipping. The historic pattern of these fierce storms continued—hurricanes striking the South Carolina coast for several years in a row and then smashing into the Gulf Coast for several consecutive years.[21]

John P. Grace and "the Revolution of 1911"

As the Charleston reform wing of the Democratic party had come to the mayor's office in 1891 on the coattails of Governor Benjamin Tillman, so too was John P. Grace aided by the victory of the racist demagogue Coleman L. Blease. The registered voters in Charleston voted overwhelmingly for the Newberry lawyer who won the governorship in 1910. Since Blease was soft on prostitution, gambling, and whiskey sales, it was easier for many Charlestonians to tolerate him than Tillman. Launching his campaign for mayor the following year, Grace's rhetoric sounded similar to Blease's. Taking as his theme the old slogan, "Equal rights for all—special privileges for none," he attacked Mayor Rhett as a representative of the elite and the electric utility "monopoly," the Consolidated Company. When the Broad Street Ring and Sheriff Martin's faction endorsed businessman Tristram T. Hyde, Grace charged that Hyde as chairman of the Democratic Executive Committee fraudulently added 1,500 names to the voting rolls. The Broad Street Ring quickly wrested control of the Democratic party machinery by electing one of their own, M. Rutledge Rivers, chairman of the Executive Committee, but the Grace machine responded by registering 800 new voters and securing an injunction to prevent the Executive Committee from purging them.

A severe hurricane crashed ashore south of the city on August 28, 1911, causing a "night of terror" for Charlestonians. Two people were killed and property losses exceeded $1 million. The winds drove salt water into the lowcountry rice fields and, after more than 200 years, ended forever most of the local cultivation of rice.

The *News and Courier* provided little coverage of Grace's campaign but gave maximum exposure to Hyde's, urging people to prevent dishonesty with their ballots by voting for Hyde and business prosperity. But Grace's opponents underestimated the extent of the anti-Broad Street feelings in the white working-class wards. The Rhett administration had made a beginning in reviv-

The August hurricane of 1911 looking north from the High Battery. *Courtesy of the South Carolina Historical Society, Charleston, S.C.*

ing the economic life of the city, yet provided few improvements in municipal service for most Charlestonians. This, plus the image of the city government as a businessman's administration and its rigid control of liquor sales, fostered working-class resentment— and John P. Grace capitalized on it.

Election-day excitement swept the city on the day of the Democratic primary, November 7, 1911. While Hyde remained cloistered at his headquarters, Grace moved from polling place to polling place shaking hands. The police arrested a Grace supporter for perjury and fistfights broke out in several wards. Grace received 2,999 votes to 2,805 for Hyde, and was unopposed in the general election on December 12. Calling his victory "the Revolution of 1911," Grace later boasted that "the Aristocratic class who had so considered itself divinely appointed to govern . . . us went into deep mourning." He immediately launched a broader and more aggressive brand of progressivism.

Grace's abrasive style made enemies. He called opponents "perjurers," "thieves," "aristocratic phonies," and "blue bloods" and twice while mayor he got into fistfights. He was not proud of Charleston's role in secession: "And notoriously it was here," he once observed, "that . . . the first shot of the Civil War was fired." But Grace was first of all a booster, luring conventions to Charleston and promoting business and tourism.

In 1912 a *New Guide to Modern Charleston* touted the port as "the city of destiny" and the Grace administration sponsored Fleet Week, which recognized the economic significance of the recent relocation of a naval base to Charleston. Eleven battleships of the Atlantic Fleet steamed up the Cooper River and dropped anchor on November 17, 1912, and remained for the next seven days, the largest naval force ever gathered in a Southern port. There was a huge military parade and a reception for the men of the fleet, and in his first annual report Mayor Grace observed that Fleet Week was the "greatest event in the history of Charleston." He could not resist remarking that there was little support from the business community "because of a sullen attitude against the administration."

Believing he had a mandate to modernize the city, Grace abolished the Board of Public Works as too political and then proceeded to appoint his own men to the City Council's Committee on the Streets, which authorized paving in Grace strongholds only. His program received a tremendous economic boost by a state law in 1913 that permitted the city to assess property owners one-half the costs of street improvements abutting their property. Suddenly thousands of dollars went into paving, new sidewalks, curbs, and drains. The major thoroughfares were covered with asphaltic concrete, which helped minimize the wear and tear on automobiles, more and more of which were appearing in the city.

In 1912 the City Council banned dairies from the city and established a public abattoir, which continued in use until 1949. But because the council refused to act, individuals continued to keep cows in the city. Restaurant inspections began in 1914 and the following year the Health Department's laboratory was established under the guidance of Dr. G. F. Mood and Mr. Leon Banov. The old city pest house was closed and patients for isolation were sent to the federally funded Public Health Quarantine Station.[22]

As in earlier years the mix of private and public charities barely met the needs of the city's indigent, usually the very young or the old and infirm. A sizable dependent Afro-American population influenced the attitude toward charity of the white well-to-do. The Jenkins Orphanage for black children remained woefully underfunded by the city, while the two white orphanages were generously supported. During the opening decades of the century the Jenkins Orphanage cared for more than 200 orphans in the old Marine Hospital on Franklin Street and another fifty, many of whom had committed petty crimes, at its Industrial Farm and Reformatory outside the city. Although it cost $16,000 to $20,000 a year to maintain and educate these several hundred abandoned and destitute children, the city for years appropriated annually only $1,000. Donations from Northern friends and the earnings of the Jenkins Orphanage Band exceeded the city's contribution by ten times in 1912.

The city continued to maintain two homes for its aged paupers, one black and one white, each with a Board of Commissioners elected by the City Council. Both homes received a small sum of money from the city, the black Almshouse receiving less than the white, and there was a weekly distribution of rations to white outside pensioners, but no similar distribution to blacks. Mrs. Ann Walker, director of the privately sponsored Associated Charities Society, "warned out" of the city "unworthy" paupers and sent "worthy" ones to the almshouses. The Shirras Dispensary also provided drugs and limited medical services to the poor on an outpatient basis, but the major treatment center for the indigent was the new city facility that had been built to incorporate a part of Memorial Hospital and opened in 1906 as Roper Hospital. Within a few years the local Federation of Women's Clubs charged that the hospital was dilapidated and poorly managed, and "colored" patients neglected. Mayor Grace, who pursued a more generous policy toward public charities than his predecessors, increased funding and negotiated a contract for the Medical College to provide care for the poor at Roper.

The local educational revival persisted into the first administration of Mayor Grace when local taxes were increased and remodeling of white schools continued, but vast inequalities existed between black and white schooling. Although a vocational school for blacks was constructed in 1910, there were only two Afro-American teachers of the 130 in the city schools that year. Additional black teachers were hired in the 1920s after persistent complaints by local blacks. Salaries for Afro-American teachers and expenditures for black schools in the city during the first half of the twentieth century were about one-quarter to one-third the expenditure for white schools.

During Grace's first term Paul Rea realized his goal for separation of the museum from the College of Charleston when the City Council approved the incorporation of "the Charleston Museum" under a Board of Trustees and Rea became the first full-time director. He launched membership drives, took traveling exhibits to the schools, and promoted research in natural history. The museum was chronically underfunded, and Rea spent much of his time pleading for financial support from the City Council and the museum's membership.[23]

In the opening years of the twentieth century Charlestonians celebrated their region's past in filiopietistic histories and nostalgic memoirs. Perhaps the most valuable work of the period was written by Miss Alice R. Huger Smith and her father, *The Dwelling Houses of Charleston* (1917). Following the death of George Hubert Sass in 1908, Charleston was without a significant poet. By World War I imaginative literature was dead.

The Academy of Music at King and Market streets continued to be one of the South's major playhouses for traveling troupes. The interior of the Italianate-style building was extensively renovated in 1911. Melodramas, musical comedies, minstrels, light and grand opera were sometimes booked directly from New York, and John Drew and Sarah Bernhardt played here to full houses. A second "splendid modern theatre," the Victory, located on Society Street between King and Meeting streets and devoted solely to vaudeville performances opened early in the century. It was owned by the Pastime Amusement Company, which was organized in 1908 by Albert Sottile, a young Sicilian who arrived in Charleston in the 1890s. Recognizing the potential of a new medium of entertainment, Sottile soon opened two "moving picture theatres," the Wonderland on King opposite Hasell Street and the Majestic, on King just above George Street. In 1912 the price of admission to each was 5 cents.[24]

Mayor Grace like Mayor Rhett made only a gesture of enforcing the state Dispensary law. Periodic fines of the hundreds of operators continued to provide a steady source of income for the city's usually empty treasury. Of far greater threats to "blind tigers" were the raids of state agents, who therefore had to be paid protection money, estimated to be as much as $50,000 monthly. Only under pressure from the governor did Charleston's mayors approve police raids, but usually just "for the record." Both Mayors Rhett and Grace believed that the "blind tigers" were "too much a part of the web of life" in Charleston to close them down. The well-known Vincent Chicco, "the state's most notorious liquor dealer," who was a close friend of Mayor Grace, served on the City Council for four consecutive terms and sat on a grand jury investigating local liquor violations. Another prosperous bootlegger was W. J. Cantwell, the brother of Charleston's chief of police!

Grace modernized the local police force and, like his predecessors and those mayors who followed, he cultivated policemen for their political support. A Cadillac patrol car was purchased in 1912, women matrons were hired to handle female prisoners in 1914, and a photography unit was added in 1915.[25]

Some Charlestonians believed that the availability of brothels protected the "respectable ladies of the city" and most mayors of Charleston thought it politically inexpedient to end prostitution. Brothels were clustered in the quasi-official "segregated district" just off lower King Street on Clifford, Beresford, and Princess streets, and along nearby West, Archdale, Beaufain, and Mazyck streets. One observer noted that sometimes on steamy afternoons "Clifford Street so resounded with ribaldry flung from open window to window by out-leaning women that shoppers on King Street stopped and looked." In 1913 a local Law and Order League attacked prostitution as a "social evil," urging Mayor Grace to clean up the district because of its proximity to Memminger Normal School and because prostitution transmitted disease, violated the laws of the state, and besmirched the honor of the city. Grace replied that he believed the role of the government was to prevent crime not sin.

Discriminatory freight rates contributed to Charleston's lingering economic malaise. It still cost almost twice as much to ship third class from Charleston to Chicago as from New York to Chicago. By 1913 a second railroad was serving the city, the Charleston Northern Railway, which eventually became part of the Seaboard Air Line system. That year a new lighthouse began operating and 145 manufacturing establishments in and around Charleston employed 10,000 persons at annual wages of $4,500,000. Only in 1915 did the Southern Railroad build a coal terminal there. Most significantly, however, the new, growing Navy Yard employed 10 percent of all the workers and paid 20 percent of all wages in the area.[26]

As the mayoral race of 1915 approached, the city's anemic economy persisted despite Grace's boosterism. Indeed, that same year a local newspaperman vexed local promoters by submitting as his entry in a contest to select a slogan for the city: PLEASE GO 'WAY AND LET ME SLEEP. To one visiting New Englander, the city was an anachronism. She wrote: "Charleston has . . . resisted the modern with fiery determination . . . . Charleston is caught in a dream of the romantic past."[27]

At the city Democratic convention in April 1915 the combined factions of Charleston County Sheriff Martin and the Broad Street Ring narrowly won control of the Executive Committee. The following month Grace received another setback when the new, progressive governor, Richard I. Manning, whom Grace had opposed, turned local law enforcement over to Sheriff Martin because the mayor had defied state law by permitting "blind tigers" to do business. Grace's opponent was again Tristram T. Hyde whose supporters aligned themselves with the governor and organized a whispering campaign that accused the mayor of graft. Sheriff Martin also circulated anti-Catholic literature that eroded some of Grace's labor support. The *News and Courier* praised Hyde while characterizing the Grace administration as four years "of turmoil." Grace responded by calling his opponents broken-down social climbers and members of the St. Cecilia Society. Tensions were high and the editor of the newspaper told a friend: "We shall be voting or rioting." Governor Manning dispatched militia units to Charleston to keep order on the eve of the election, but October 12 passed peacefully, Hyde receiving 2,790 votes to 2,776 for Grace.

The mayor demanded a recount and representatives of both factions guarded the sealed ballot boxes in a small room at the corner of King and George streets until the city's Democratic Executive Committee met at noon on October 15. Police were present to keep order, but as the meeting began Hyde and Grace partisans packing concealed weapons pushed into the room. Shots rang out and Sidney J. Cohen, a reporter for the *News and Courier*, fell mortally wounded. Three other men received gunshot wounds and two ballot boxes were hurled into the street and their contents scattered. Only the arrival of sheriff's deputies and the Washington Light Infantry prevented further violence. Militia patrolled the streets and both candidates called for calm. The next day the Executive Committee certified Hyde and his slate as the official Democratic candidates for mayor and the City Council by a final count of 3,109 to 3,081.

" . . . The moral tone of . . . photoplays"

Mayor Hyde took office at fifty-three years of age. Like his political ally, former Mayor Rhett, Hyde was born in Columbia in 1862. He attended the High School of Charleston, made money in real estate, was an officer in the Sumter Guards, and served as superintendent of the Sunday school at the Citadel Square Baptist Church for thirty years. One political analyst observed that Hyde was quite capable of leading "a Sunday School delegation in a parade [while] countenancing an alliance with bootleggers . . . ." Obsessed with lowering taxes and enforcing the law, Hyde's policies resulted in a budget surplus but a lower level of municipal services. Hyde courted the police department, and for the employment and training of the patrolmen he added to the station house a bowling alley and a firing range and purchased new motorized patrol wagons and motorcycles. During World War I the police force employed its first female member and the city and the federal government cooperated in areas related to national defense, which resulted in an image of Hyde as a reform-minded mayor.[28]

One of the first problems that Mayor Hyde was called upon to solve stemmed from the complaints by an old and distinguished citizen about a new, local medium of entertainment, motion pictures. Thomas R. F. Heyward wrote the mayor in 1916 in behalf of the city's parents urging Hyde to prevent the showing of motion pictures like those playing recently, which Heyward called "filthy." Other complaints prompted Mayor Hyde to warn the proprietors of the theaters and the National Board of Review of Motion Pictures in New York City that unless they kept up "the moral tone of . . . photoplays," movies would be censored locally. That same year the Colored Civic League of Charleston, forerunner of the local National Association for the Advancement of Colored People, appealed to the mayor to prohibit the showing of *The Birth of a Nation* as it misrepresented the Afro-American, "depicting him . . . in a manner that will cause new race hatred." But the "photoplay" was shown and the *News and Courier* called it a "remarkable picture" that would bring "enlightenment . . . to many people of the North."[29]

The Economic Stimulus of War

When World War I erupted in Europe in 1914, the Navy Yard was employing 1,240 civilian personnel and had an annual payroll of $883,945. It brought an enormous expansion of the yard and the military in the lowcountry and boom times. An Irish nationalist, John P. Grace opposed United States aid to England in its war with Germany. His pro-German and anti-President Woodrow Wilson editorials in the *Charleston American*, a paper he founded as an antidote to the *News and Courier*, resulted in the revocation of his paper's second-class mailing privileges.

On the morning of February 1, 1917, Charlestonians were surprised to see the German merchant steamer *Liebenfels*, which had taken refuge in Charleston harbor in 1914, lying on its side in the main shipping channel. Scuttled a day ahead of orders by her crew, the sinking alerted American officials to seize other German ships, thereby preventing the blocking of other harbors. The United States Navy raised the *Liebenfels* on March 14 and converted it to a troop transport.

Twenty-nine Afro-Americans, mostly professional people, established the Charleston branch of the National Association for the Advancement of Colored People (NAACP) on February 23, 1917, under the leadership of Edwin "Teddy" Harleston. A thirty-five-year-old Charlestonian who was a graduate of Avery Institute and Atlanta University and a fine artist, Harleston studied at the Boston Museum of Fine Arts and then returned to Charleston in 1913 to enter his father's undertaking business. During March the black scholar and leader W. E. B. DuBois came to Charleston and stayed at the Hametic, the city's only black-owned hotel, on Drake Street at East Bay near the Cooper River. DuBois was "hard on blacks, but it woke us up," Mamie Garvin Fields recalled, telling us to take pride in our accomplishments and "to strive to do more."

Also during March the War Department designated Charleston as the headquarters of the newly created Southeastern Military District, General Leonard Wood of Spanish American War fame commanding, and the mission of the local United States Army Corps of Engineers was expanded to include overseeing the readiness and maintenance of the coastal defenses. Chief S.M. Duncan of the State Constabulary Force privately moaned in March that he was unable to control the flow of liquor into Charleston by small speed boats that landed at isolated spots along the coast where they were met by fast cars, which then sped the whiskey into the city and to sailors at the Navy Yard. Duncan was worried because "The Secretary of the Navy is raising almighty hell and is threatening to close down the Navy Yard unless something is done."[30]

When America entered the war in April, the Navy Yard went on a war footing and became the headquarters of the Sixth Naval District. Rear Admiral Frank E. Beatty and a staff that eventually numbered 335 officers and 7,000 enlisted men supervised the training of 25,000 recruits. Civilian employment at the Navy Yard jumped to 5,000, many of whom were employed building two docks and eighteen vessels, including the destroyer USS *Tillman*. Civilians also worked in the yard's clothing factory, the only one of its kind in the country. Of the thousand or so females employed, 300 were black, hired only because black leaders of the Charleston branch of the National Association for the Advancement of Colored People demanded it. Production at the clothing factory leaped dramatically from 90,000 garments in 1914 to 2.7 million in 1918. Near the end of the year the combined military and civilian payroll of the Navy Yard exceeded $9 million annually. Charleston's economy also benefited from a flood of military construction projects. An animal embarkation corral that could accommodate 10,000 horses and mules, and a sprawling Army Port Terminal that alone cost $16,500,000, encompassed thirty-two acres of storage space, and included a 2,840-foot dock went up near the Navy Yard.

Thousands of laborers crowded into the area to work on these projects and prostitution flourished in the "segregated district," on street corners, and in rented rooms. Viewing prostitution as a menace to service personnel, the federal government enlisted assistance from the state government and eventually Mayor Hyde in cleaning up the city. During 1917 Charleston police and federal agents arrested fifty-four "fornicators" and closed eight brothels. By October the "segregated district" was so quiet that property owners began to complain that the antivice campaign had been too successful.

In 1915 the state legislature prohibited the sale of alcoholic beverages, and except during World War I when "blind tigers" were harassed by Mayor Hyde, Charleston officials generally ignored state and later federal prohibition laws. As one observer has noted, Charleston during prohibition was "wringing, sopping, dripping wet" and vigorously opposed to any restrictions on the sale of alcoholic beverages.[31]

In 1917 the City Council appropriated $2,500 to the Jenkins

Orphanage, recognizing that the black children there would otherwise "become a burden and menace to the community," but the institution's operating costs in 1917 exceeded $28,000. Its band alone, which was yearly on tour, performing up and down the East Coast and abroad until the 1950s, brought in over $10,000. The amazingly talented jazz musicians of the orphan bands later played with nationally recognized groups like Duke Ellington, "Jelly Roll" Morton, Count Basie, and Lionel Hampton.

In 1918 Louisa B. Poppenheim, who believed that organized play made better citizens and helped prevent crime, urged the creation of playgrounds for "colored children" and informed the City Council that "caring for this race is a part of our civic responsibility," especially in view of the "praiseworthy service" rendered by Afro-Americans during the war. There was no city agency to attend to the "suffering and neglect" of numerous "defective and delinquent" white or black children until the establishment in April 1919 of the Juvenile Welfare Commission, which Mayor Hyde hailed as both a rehabilitation measure *and* a money-saver. The salaried director and the voluntary chairperson were women. In 1923 a case-worker for "colored" children was added, but for years the work of the commission was "sadly handicapped" due to "inadequate financial support . . . by the city government."

More humane treatment of both white and black criminals also was slowly evolving in Charleston. When electrocution superseded public hanging as South Carolina's capital punishment in 1908, it was thought of as merciful, being both quicker and more private. Whipping was abolished as a chain-gang punishment in 1918.

The high costs of materials and labor brought on by the war and Mayor Hyde's fiscal conservatism threatened the street improvement program launched by Mayor Grace as new residents in the new suburbs began demanding paved streets. A new garbage incinerator was acquired, but it was never sufficient to the task. Street litter and garbage continued to be hauled to the marshes, used as fill, or taken to the city dump, which gave off "nauseating odors" and was described as a place where hogs roam and mosquitoes "breed in millions and rats and roaches are found in hordes." The United States Public Health Service opened an auxiliary health center near City Hall to assist the local health department, launching an antimalarial campaign in 1918 and opening a venereal disease clinic. That September the great worldwide Spanish influenza epidemic struck Charleston. The city's health officer wrote: "whole families were stricken, with no one to look after them, they suffered from lack of food, medicine, and clothing." Fear of infection swept the city. Schools, churches, theaters were shut down and all social gatherings were banned. The prime antidote, whiskey, was legalized and prescribed to fight the disease, but before it ran its course in November, the month the war in Europe ended, 18,500 Charlestonians were stricken and 450 died. A year later fear of a bubonic-plague outbreak led to the city's "great rat survey." It was estimated that there was a local rat population of 70,000, one for every person in the city, but no evidence of plague was discovered.[32]

Post-War Black-White Relations

In a pool hall at the corner of Beaufain and Charles streets on the night of May 10, 1919, a scuffle broke out between a black man and two sailors during which one sailor was wounded and the Afro-American killed. Rioters, hundreds of white sailors and civilians, poured down Market Street and onto Queen and King streets, ransacking black-owned businesses, assaulting blacks on the streets and pulling them from trolley cars. Blacks armed themselves, and the police called on the U.S. Navy for help. Marines arrived promptly in battle dress to sweep the streets and arrest rioters. By 3:00 A.M. on May 11 order had been restored, but the violence left three blacks dead and seventeen seriously injured. Seven sailors also were severely injured and thirty-five persons suffered minor bruises and cuts. The local branch of the NAACP asked the navy to punish the sailors involved and to compensate black businessmen for damages. Charleston's Afro-American leaders sent resolutions to Mayor Hyde saying that the black community had been "victims of the mob" and asked for protection from "the mob spirit in the future." They called for the hiring of black policemen, improvements in housing and sanitation, educational opportunities for blacks, and the creation of an interracial committee to help ensure "social justice." The navy concluded that six sailors were responsible for the riot and all were convicted and punished. The city reimbursed the owners of Freddie's Central Shaving Parlor, a black barber shop catering to whites, for damages sustained during the riot.

In late 1919 the local NAACP called for volunteers to assist in a canvass for signatures on a petition asking for the employment of black teachers in black schools, and a twenty-one-year-old Afro-American, Septima Clark, volunteered. Born in a white neighborhood in a dilapidated house at 105 Wentworth Street of a father who had been a slave and a mother of "free issue," Septima Clark grew up on Henrietta Street and was educated at local private and public schools and Avery Institute. In 1916 she took her first teaching post on remote John's Island at $35 a month and during the canvass of 1919 helped fill a croaker sack with over 10,000 signatures, which were presented to the legislature. The following year the state permitted black "maiden" women to be hired to teach in the city's black schools. Although the war had changed little in the way most white and black Charlestonians related to one another, an Interracial Committee was founded through the YWCA in the early 1920s. Mamie Garvin Fields, a black teacher and civic leader, recalled that Mrs. Celia P. McGowan, a white "aristocrat" headed it, and told the members of the committee, "'we must be friends and we must all work together . . . .'"[33]

Grace Again

Proud of his record and backed by the Broad Street Ring, Mayor Hyde ran for reelection in 1919. But supporters of John P. Grace narrowly captured control of the Democratic Executive Committee, elected Grace's law partner, Turner Logan, as chairman, and set the Democratic primary for August knowing that many of Hyde's affluent supporters would be vacationing in the mountains. As the campaign heated up, Grace blasted the Hyde mayoralty as a disaster, while Hyde partisans asserted that the election of Grace, a traitor during the war, would disgrace Charleston nationally and lead to the closing of the Navy Yard. Grace countered by pledging his loyalty to his country and attacking his opponents as profiteers. He averred that Hyde and Rhett convinced the federal government to locate installations along the Cooper River north of Charleston because they owned the land, which they sold to the government at inflated prices. Grace maintained that the real issue was progress under him or stagnation under Hyde.

It was the closest mayoralty contest in Charleston's history. Grace's slate of aldermen was overwhelmingly elected, but Hyde won the race for mayor by one vote: 3,421 to 3,420. However, thirty-six votes were challenged and the Grace-controlled Executive Committee was no fairer to Hyde in 1919 than the Hyde-controlled committee had been to Grace in 1915 and most of the challenged votes were awarded to Grace. Unopposed in the general election, Grace took the oath of office in the City Council chambers in December. Calling for the resignation of all city officials who had opposed him, he told a rowdy crowd of partisans: "Let us therefore fill the jobs and distribute the patronage." His support again had come from the city's working and middle classes: Jewish, first- or second-generation Irish Catholics and German Lutherans, liquor dealers, and a few "aristocrats." The German Lutherans sometimes voted with Baptists, but on occasion, as the descendants of non-English immigrants who were not accepted as equals by old Charleston, they voted with the Irish against the city's Anglophiles. Much of the importance of the Lutherans in Charleston's politics, from the 1850s to the 1950s and 1960s, when Ernest F. Hollings began his career, came from their ability to relate to both Protestant and Catholic populists. In 1919 many of them voted for Grace. [34]

That same year some 90 percent of the sea-island cotton crop was destroyed by the boll weevil, which had first appeared in the lowcountry just two years before. But despite huge losses among the planters, the boom stimulated by the war lasted another two years. Federal dollars continued to flow into the city, demand for farm goods remained high, the Standard Oil Company opened a new refinery in former Navy Yard facilities, and a new asbestos plant employing 1,000 workers began operations in the north area, as the region six miles up the Neck was referred to. Jobs went almost exclusively to whites, and carefully segregated mill villages sprang up around the plants. By 1920 Charleston and its suburbs reached nearly 100,000 in population and builders started new subdivisions and projects that totaled $3,900,000 compared to $900,000 the year before. There were 3,462 automobiles registered within the city, their numbers reflecting the local prosperity. The value of Charleston's ocean-borne trade reached $154,454,542 in 1921—a figure that would be unsurpassed until World War II—and the city bought the rotting, neglected docks from the railroads for $2,500,000.

During his second term Mayor Grace convinced the City Council to construct a new building for the High School of

Charleston on Rutledge Avenue, to increase teachers' salaries, and to end tuition charges at both the High School and the College of Charleston. Mayor Grace allowed the brothels of the segregated district to reopen, and in the early 1920s naval officials complained that the incidence of venereal disease was two to three times higher among sailors stationed in Charleston than elsewhere, but the city continued in its easygoing attitude to such matters, although medical examination of prostitutes was inaugurated.

Following the tradition of Charleston health officers, Dr. J. Mercier Green crusaded for closing all privy-vaults and extending sewer lines and water mains, especially to black residential areas. He warned city officials that the many "overcrowded, unsanitary houses and quarters occupied by the negroes and poorer classes of whites" posed a threat to the city's health, which nevertheless improved in the early 1920s. It was reflected in the declining death rates, which remained "shockingly high," especially for blacks whose death rates were more than twice those of whites: 25.1 versus 10.9 per 1,000. This vast disparity highlighted the bias in a political process that unevenly distributed the city's resources for health and sanitation.[35]

Preservationists, Poets, and "The Charleston"

Miss Susan Pringle Frost, a young, progressive-minded real-estate broker launched Charleston's modern-day preservation movement. The immediate cause of the preservation impulse was the destruction or dismantling of historic structures, the threat of street widenings to accommodate automobiles, and the efforts of Standard Oil Company to locate gasoline filling stations on the lower peninsula. Miss Frost arranged for a meeting of thirty-two of the city's elite on April 21, 1920, at 20 South Battery, the home of Mr. and Mrs. Ernest Pringle. Here the group resolved to save the Adams-style Joseph Manigault House (c. 1803), which was slated for demolition, and other historic homes some of which were "unfit for human habitation." They were prepared to do battle for dwellings that represented to them "the graceful way of life that had existed before the Civil War." They founded the Charleston Society for the Preservation of Old Dwellings, later renamed the Preservation Society of Charleston, the first of its kind in the southeast, and elected Susan Frost as its first president.[36]

Shortly after the war two young aspiring poets, DuBose Heyward, an insurance broker with a distinguished lowcountry name, but of limited education and in frail health, and Hervey Allen, a Philadelphia native, university graduate, and local high school teacher, were meeting at the home of their mentor, John Bennett, on Legare Street. A native of Ohio and author of the children's classic *Master Skylark* (1896), Bennett had settled in the city after marrying Susan Smythe. Around the corner on Gibbes Street, Laura Bragg, the director of the Charleston Museum, was meeting frequently to discuss poetry with several young poetesses, among them the talented Josephine Pinckney. The two groups soon merged and in the summer of 1920 they formed an organization to stimulate an interest in poetry throughout the city, the Poetry Society of South Carolina. Invitations were extended and at one of its first meetings at South Carolina Hall, one wag remarked that the members "appeared to be one-tenth poetry and nine-tenths society." Calling for "a genuine South-wide poetic renaissance," the society issued its first yearbook in 1921, invited well-known poets to the city for readings, sponsored prize contests for aspiring poets, and encouraged the development of similar organizations in other Southern cities.

Except for Josephine Pinckney's, the verse produced in Charleston was conservative and provincial, and when Carl Sandburg came and read his work in 1921 most members decided it was not poetry. Two years later the courtly John Bennett was afraid that the society's existence would be threatened if members discovered that Jean Toomer, recognized nationally for the novel *Cane* and who had been admitted as a member by mail, was an Afro-American!

In 1922 the Citadel was relocated in the northwestern section of the city along the banks of the Ashley River. The architectural models for the new buildings were those of the old. That same summer Ludwig Lewisohn (1883–1955) published an article about Charleston in *The Nation*. Born in Berlin, Germany, he grew up in Charleston and graduated from the college in 1901, the same year that he was rejected for the Chair of English in a local Episcopal academy "on account of his race," Lewisohn later wrote. He took an M.A. degree from Columbia University (1903), subsequently taught at leading Northern universities, and was a prolific author. In his article, Lewisohn wrote: "A tiny tongue of land extending from Broad Street to the . . . confluence of the

Ashley and the Cooper . . . is all of South Carolina that has counted in the past; the memories that cling to the little peninsula are all that count today. . . . new men control the state . . . . Quiet has stolen into the old houses and the lower city . . . ." But many who lacked Lewisohn's perspective and had never seen or even heard about the city first became aware of it after October 29, 1923, when the musical *Runnin' Wild* introduced "The Charleston" in New York City. It had been written by James P. Johnson to entertain blacks who had come from Charleston, but it soon became popular among whites all over the country.

Mayor Grace continued to boost business and tourism. In 1923 construction began on the third bridge and first concrete structure that was to span the Ashley River. That same year the city donated land on the Battery where a tourist hotel was completed in 1923. The city also supported the construction of the Francis Marion Hotel on the northwest corner of King and Calhoun streets; when completed in February 1924, just in time for the spring tourist season, it was the largest hotel in the Carolinas.

With the approach of the 1923 mayoral contest, Mayor Grace was confident of victory. Sheriff Martin was dead, the Broad Street Ring was in disarray, and Grace controlled a large block of city employees loyal to him, especially the police force. His law partner, Turner Logan, had won election to the United States Congress. An ally, John I. Cosgrove, was the city's corporation counsel, and reelection of Grace seemed assured when his machine captured control of the Democratic Executive Committee. However, Grace had raised taxes and added about $3.5 million to the municipal debt, and the city was finding it difficult to pay its bills. And he had not counted on the sudden entry into the race of Thomas P. Stoney.[37]

❦ 3. 1923–1938: "America's most historic city" and the New Deal

Thomas P. Stoney

Born at Back River plantation in 1889, Thomas Stoney was a lawyer whose ancestors were among some of the earliest colonists and included some of the wealthiest eighteenth-century merchants and planters like the Gaillard, Jenkins, and Porcher families. He was a Mason and an Episcopalian. With support from the Broad Street Ring, Stoney launched a whirlwind campaign in

Before the Jenkins Orphanage at 20 Franklin Street, the Marine Hospital, flappers are "doin' the Charleston" in 1923 to the accompaniment of the Jenkins Orphanage Band. *Courtesy of the Black Charleston Photo Collection, College of Charleston Library, Charleston, S.C.*

June 1923 aimed at winning the Democratic primary in August. He appealed to female voters by asking two women to run on his slate for City Council. The conservative *News and Courier* welcomed his run for the mayoralty, calling it a movement "for clean politics and efficient government," but the race became a matter of personalities rather than issues.

Stoney had a keen sense of humor and, unlike previous candidates of the Broad Street Ring, he was a good speaker. On one occasion Stoney observed that he did not know whether Grace was a steer or a heifer, but he sure was full of bull. Stoney defused the class issue injected by Grace partisans, who publicized Stoney's membership in the St. Cecilia Society, when he pointed out that he was now inactive, unlike Turner Logan and Daniel Sinkler, political confidants of Grace.

Toward the end of the campaign, the contest turned bitter. During a series of stump debates between the two candidates, Grace linked Stoney with the revived and historically anti-Catholic Ku Klux Klan. Stoney responded by characterizing Grace as a corrupt political boss who was hated throughout the state and therefore could never win recognition for Charleston as the port of South Carolina. Years later Stoney recalled that the acrimony engendered during the race led him to arrange for armed men to guard his home and family. Two days before the election and upon the request of Stoney partisans, Governor Thomas G. Mc-Leod ordered the National Guard into Charleston to relieve the local police in keeping order at the polls. This darkened any hopes for a Grace victory and he was outraged, calling the use of soldiers "military despotism." Stoney won by 6,725 to 5,992 votes. The wide appeal of the young, dynamic Stoney, the women's vote, and the concern of Charlestonians over the city's finances—all were factors in his victory. Within a month Grace's newspaper, the *Charleston American*, ceased publication, and the *News and Courier* and the *Evening Post* became the only daily newspapers published in Charleston. The following year Turner Logan lost his congressional seat, but Grace and his fanatically devoted followers remained active in political and civic affairs.

At thirty-four years of age Thomas P. Stoney became the youngest mayor in the city's history. He quickly replaced Grace's machine with his own by distributing city jobs to his supporters; Stoney and his law partners now wielded enormous influence: they could promise any bootlegger willing to pay their fees virtual immunity from prosecution.

The region's postwar prosperity was ending. The price of cotton dropped sharply; the resumption of operations by European factories led to layoffs at the state's textile mills; civilian employment at the Navy Yard was cut to 2,100, then chopped again to under 500 by 1924. Living costs and taxes rose in Charleston and job opportunities declined. Between 1920 and 1930 the city's population decreased by over 4,000 and, like Grace, in expanding municipal services, Mayor Stoney also increased the city's debt.[38]

Institutions and City Services

Stoney continued the successful but costly street-paving program, installing more than thirty-five miles in asphalt. During his administration the 1,733-foot Ashley River Bridge was completed and opened to traffic on May 5, 1926 at a cost of $1,250,000. It was dedicated as a memorial to those South Carolinians who "gave their lives in the World War." The usual balance between paying and indigent patients at Roper Hospital fell with the local economic downturn and became yet another drain on city finances.

In 1924 officials and friends of the Orphan House were stung by sharp criticism of their beloved institution. Dr. Carl E. Mc-Combs writing in a national journal charged that although the health and nourishment of the children at the orphanage was excellent, the instruction they received was "perfunctory and elementary." Indeed, "the bare . . . floors . . . the bleak, colorless . . . classrooms . . . were reflected in the apathetic . . . bearing of the children." Charlestonians have failed to acknowledge, Mc-Combs concluded, "that the methods of child caring of a century ago are not the approved methods of today." Progressive cities now placed children in suitable foster homes where they were able to interact with the larger society. Charleston's governing officials would nevertheless wait years before changing their methods of caring for the city's orphans, and then primarily for reasons of economy.

Charleston women like Susan Frost, the preservationist, and private women's organizations like the Ladies Benevolent Society and the Junior League of Charleston were in the forefront of advocating care for the city's children. Organized in 1923 by Anne Montague Stoney and eleven of her debutante friends, the Junior League established a Milk Station two years later for undernourished children; it distributed books and magazines in the children's wards at Roper Hospital, beginning regular distribution to the black wards in 1931. Under Mayor Stoney's administration a plan for the coordination of all public charity under a new Social Welfare Department of the Bureau of Health and Welfare was only partially successful. A new initiative, in tune with the nationwide approach, by Mrs. Ashley Halsey, secretary of the Board of Health, would end dependency by eliminating rations to outside pensioners, grown to some 4,000, and stress rehabilitation for self-support. Hundreds of families now came under the board's purview.[39]

When Dr. Leon Banov succeeded Dr. Green in 1926 the administration of both the city and the county departments of health was combined. Charleston was for the third time extraordinarily lucky in its choice of a chief health officer. Like his predecessors, Dr. Banov had to put up with the meddling of various mayors who wished to use Health Department jobs as rewards to party loyalists and he inherited an underfunded and poorly equipped department, but his energy and enthusiasm were inexhaustible. He campaigned to extend the sewer and water mains, stepped up the mosquito control program, introduced health education programs, and vigorously enforced the pasteurization of milk. Stoney himself called for the elimination of "filthy, overcrowded tenement houses . . . where . . . one toilet serves the purposes . . . for innumerable families" who pay "exorbitant rents." Such conditions, Stoney concluded, "are now unpardonable in any real city of the 20th century," but city officials were not interested in improving slums where landlords sometimes refused to pay for sewer or water-main connections and tenants had no political or social influence.

The county agreed to provide some financial support for the Charleston Museum and when Paul Rea resigned to undertake the organization of the Cleveland Museum of Natural History, Miss Laura Bragg, also a native of Massachusetts, became the new director. Miss Bragg encouraged blacks to attend the museum and in 1927 arranged for the traveling exhibits systematically to tour the county's black schools. Raising funds to fix the museum's perennially leaking roof and crumbling foundations also occupied much of her time. In 1930 when a grant of $80,000 from the Julius Rosenwald Fund helped the county establish in Charleston its first free library, Miss Bragg became its first librarian. A native Charlestonian, E. Milby Burton, succeeded her as director of the museum and emphasized the history and artifacts of the region. The following year a group of prominent Charlestonians took a nostalgic look at the past in a series of essays that were published as *The Carolina Low-Country.* One historian has recently observed that these writers tended to imagine antebellum Charleston and the Old South "as a harmonious and hierarchial society of pure, self-sacrificing women . . . brilliant cavaliers . . . and grateful, docile slaves. Reaffirmation of old ways necessarily entailed condemnation of modern times."

Mayor Stoney, who believed that "there is nothing more invigorating than wholesome, clean athletics . . . for the community as a whole," organized a drive for recreational areas for blacks. A city dump on the northwestern side of Charleston was cleared and with a grant from the W. E. Harmon Foundation of New York, and donations from black Charlestonians for playground equipment, Harmon Field playground opened in the late 1920s. During his administrations a municipal golf course was built and in cooperation with the local armed services, the city sponsored boxing matches that evolved into Golden Glove Tournaments; in addition to baseball and basketball, the city playgrounds sponsored football in the 1920s and on October 15, 1927, the Citadel played Oglethorpe University in football at the dedication of Johnson Hagood Stadium, an imposing brick stadium and athletic field where the community could enjoy athletic contests. Some council members had wished to name it after Mayor Stoney, who, however, urged that it be named after General Hagood, "one of the most distinguished officers of the Confederacy." Eventually too costly for the city to maintain, Johnson-Hagood Stadium was sold to the Citadel in the 1960s.[40]

From the 1920s to the early 1940s, the police and the madams of the various brothels in the city had an understanding that they would post bonds of $100 monthly at police headquarters for illegally maintaining houses of prostitution. Of course, the bonds were forfeited and the money flowed into the city treasury. The police also ensured that the "ladies of the night" had weekly medical exams and kept their health certificates up-to-date. The women themselves, clients remembered, wore everything from evening gowns to outfits resembling waitress uniforms. They were mostly Southern, neither beautiful nor plain, "some tough, others gentle," and both black and white. The city's Law and Order League reported in outraged tones that many of the city's "assignation houses . . . are run by negro women for use of white men and women." Nationwide, the report concluded, "Charleston alone bears this unenviable reputation." In the 1920s, before the area underwent "gentrification," the city administration received numerous requests for police intervention on "Tradd Street . . . [which] . . . is infested with negro dives of the lowest kind whose . . . orgies keep up all night." Complaints by voters about police corruption or their interference in elections led Mayor Stoney to secure passage of a state law establishing a three-man police commission elected by the voters, but it too became controlled by the faction in power.

As Charleston's economy deteriorated, Stoney and the Chamber of Commerce worked to develop the tourist trade. Describing Charleston as "America's most historic city," the mayor told Charlestonians "we have to sell the city . . . to the outside world." Knowing the elite's aversion to change, he added: "all we need is the right mental attitude." Tourism became the city's biggest industry. By the late 1920s over 47,000 visitors were coming to the city annually and spending $4 million, but William Watts Ball told a friend: "Nothing is more dreadful than tourists, whether grasshoppers, boll weevils, or money-bagged bipeds. They will make Charleston rich and ruin her."[41]

Cultural Life

The city's literary set were spokespersons for the opponents of growth and change. DuBose Heyward begged city planners, whom he characterized as thoughtless destroyers, to preserve "the beautiful city that time had forgotten before it destroyed." Katherine B. Ripley described the new Cooper River Bridge as a "complicated spider-web of steel . . . dwarfing the old town, throwing the solid brick buildings out of scale." In *The Dwelling Houses of Charleston*, the authors warned that the greatest threat to the old city would be new "incongruous" buildings. Such expressions were the intellectual foundations of the preservation movement.

Under the vigorous leadership of Susan Frost, "Miss Sue" as she was known, the Preservation Society raised money and found buyers to restore dwellings on Cabbage (later Rainbow) Row, in St. Michael's Alley, and the famous Heyward-Washington House (c. 1770). Also a remarkably complete work on the city's early architecture by Albert Simons and Samuel Lapham, Jr., published by the American Institute of Architects in 1927, made Charlestonians aware that their heritage of quirky, humane, and handsome buildings was attracting international attention.[42]

In the 1920s native Charlestonians and "outsiders" who settled there and were captivated by the mellowing old city remained driven by a desire to preserve Charleston's sounds, colors, and legends. Young white people living in Charleston and on nearby plantations began collecting the words and melodies of songs they heard blacks singing. They organized the Society for the Preservation of Spirituals and they sang up and down the East Coast, usually before segregated audiences. The Gibbes Art Gallery on Meeting Street, completed in 1905 with a private bequest, exhibited local artists such as Alice R. Huger Smith and Elizabeth O'Neill Verner, who celebrated Charleston and the lowcountry in charcoal, oil, ink, and watercolors. Alfred Hutty, an etcher from New York who was invited by the Carolina Art Association to serve as an instructor at the Gibbes, settled in the city and won international recognition, but for years the Art Gallery, like the Charleston Museum, struggled for existence. About 1930 one commentator observed that the gallery was "a dismal little . . . outfit with a membership of six and no activities." The collection was "hung from ceiling to floor without selectivity. An aging . . . lady . . . answer[ed] the phone, if it ever rang . . . nobody ever came in." But a new era began in 1932 when Robert S. N. Whitelaw, a Charleston native with extensive museum experience elsewhere, was hired as director. He brought a vigor and enthusiasm that won grants, new members, and important exhibits.

Private organizations like the Musical Art Club and the Philharmonic Society sponsored choirs and concerts at Hibernian Hall, German Artillery Hall, and the Freundschaft Bund Hall. Occasional private recitals of sacred music were given at the Huguenot Church, and the Christmas play in music and song presented annually by the young women of the private finishing school Ashley Hall, which required most to perform in male attire, inaugurated the holiday season. In 1924 the Philharmonic Symphony Orchestra of Charleston launched its first series of concerts and the Charleston Community Concert Association sponsored several concerts annually. The musical seasons began in November and ended in April, like the social seasons of antebellum Charleston.

DuBose Heyward, Hervey Allen, and Josephine Pinckney, the best writers among the founders of the Poetry Society, all turned to prose and left Charleston to pursue their careers elsewhere. But Heyward never forgot what he called "the negro life of the city" that he had known when he worked at a cotton warehouse on the waterfront, and his pungent, tragic novel *Porgy* (1925), reflecting his close observations, earned him a lasting international reputation. Heyward's wife, Dorothy, wrote a dramatization of the book that was produced by the Theatre Guild on Broadway to much acclaim in 1927, and George Gershwin's opera *Porgy and Bess*, produced in New York in 1935, was based on it. *Po' Buckra* (1930), an ambitious novel by Gertrude Matthews Shelby and Samuel Gaillard Stoney, the mayor's cousin, sensitively depicted relations between poor whites and the old Huguenot aristocracy north of Charleston. But the lowcountry produced little fiction or poetry of any merit thereafter until the 1970s.[43]

Stoney Reelected

Mayor Stoney's machine thoroughly controlled the electoral process in the mayoralty contest of 1927, but the candidate of the Grace faction, Daniel L. Sinkler, turned the primary into the kind of heated contest, filled with personal attacks and counterattacks, for which Charleston was noted. Grace charged that prostitution and bootlegging were flourishing under Stoney and that members of the City Council ran crap games. Sinkler criticized the high taxes, the city's finances, and the sweetheart arrangement for Stoney's friend, J. Ross Hanahan, who had profited from city street-paving contracts. Stoney retorted that Sinkler himself had profited handsomely by writing city insurance policies while an alderman during Grace's administration. The Stoney machine beat Sinkler by nearly two to one, Grace's candidate failing to carry any of the twelve wards.

Grace now turned his still considerable energies to promoting completion of the Cooper River Bridge and the paving of Route 40 to the North Carolina line. When completed it was the third largest cantilevered bridge in the world and at its festive dedication ceremonies in August 1929 public officials hailed Grace for his accomplishment and Grace loyalists sang "John P. Grace, the Champion of the Poor," which concluded, "He fought the people's battle until the fight was won/So let us give three rousing cheers for Charleston's favorite son."

At the outset of his second term Stoney persisted in expressing his displeasure with the "Colored Old Folks Home" located near the new Johnson-Hagood Stadium at the western end of Congress Street, calling it "a horrible and dilapidated building . . . [and] a disgrace to the city," and in 1930 it was razed. The black inmates moved into a new modern structure on city land near the Navy Yard and the number of inmates dwindled to eighteen by 1937. However, Stoney could not close down the white Almshouse at 63 Columbus Street, which he thought "looked like a jail," because the City Council was afraid that, like his predecessor, he was spending too much money.[44]

After the great Stock Market crash of October 1929 the northern capital so essential to Charleston's tourist trade and the truck-farming industry evaporated. Its economy heavily dependent on bulk cargo, primarily local in origin, the tonnage through the Port of Charleston dropped 16 percent from 1931 to 1941 and the harbor traffic consisted mainly of tramp steamers and sailing ships as the Great Depression settled over the land.

1923–1938: "America's most historic city" and the New Deal

In 1929 Mayor Stoney and the Preservation Society pushed through the City Council the first zoning ordinance to protect the historic district. But a year later the antebellum structure on Wentworth Street, German Artillery Hall, was razed and, in 1931 the mayor sponsored a measure that set aside twenty-three square blocks of the peninsula city as Old and Historic Charleston. It limited owners in what they could do with their property, established a Board of Architectural Review, and made provisions for prosecuting violators. The society's successes became the models for historic districts across the nation.

On May 9, 1930, the city's first radio station, WCSC, officially went on the air featuring an address by Mayor Stoney, music by the Charleston High School band, and a program of singing by the Society for the Preservation of Spirituals.[45]

Burnet Rhett Maybank and the Great Depression

The depression complicated the financial problems of Mayor Stoney's second administration. Between 1900 and 1930 the municipal debt increased from $3,798,200 to $10,683,406, the city budget rose from $596,786 to $1,472,750, and interest payments

A photograph of the members of the Society for the Preservation of Spirituals taken in 1925 in the yard of Herbert R. Sass on Legare Street. *Courtesy of the Black Charleston Photo Collection, College of Charleston Library, Charleston, S.C.*

on the bonded debt increased from \$155,793 to \$246,776. Approximately 18 percent of the city budget went each year to pay interest on the city's bonded debt. By 1931 the city teetered on the verge of bankruptcy. Early that year a group of prominent businessmen, including Andrew J. Geer, R. Goodwyn Rhett, and T. Wilbur Thornhill, met for lunch at the Francis Marion Hotel to discuss the coming mayoralty contest. They agreed that the fierce partisanship of past campaigns harmed the city and must be avoided in the future, and that a respected businessman unaligned with any factions should be the next mayor. They expanded the membership of the Citizens Committee, presented their ideas publicly, and appointed a steering committee that endorsed Burnet Rhett Maybank as a compromise candidate.

Maybank's ancestors were among the earliest settlers in Charleston and he was related to five governors of South Carolina. A graduate of the College of Charleston, an Episcopalian, and a member of the St. Cecilia Society, Maybank was the Charleston aristocrat par excellence, but he earned his living as an exporter of cotton and was respected for his abilities in the management of money and people. His brogue, influenced by Gullah-speaking childhood nurses, was an asset to an aspiring politician in the lowcountry, but upcountrymen had a difficult time following his exuberant staccato-style delivery. Years later at his funeral a colleague remarked: "We all knew Burnet. We all loved Burnet. We all wanted to do what Burnet wanted us to do—if we could just have understood what that was." In 1927 Stoney, needing someone from Ward 2, had invited Maybank to run on his slate, and in 1930 Maybank had been elected mayor pro-tem.

In 1931 Stoney quickly endorsed Maybank for mayor, and Grace did so after visiting with him and apparently reaching an understanding that he would have a strong voice in the Maybank administration. But Grace and Maybank soon quarreled and Grace then withdrew his support, backed Lawrence M. Pinckney for mayor, and offered himself as a candidate in Ward 4. The usual intemperate personal charges punctuated the campaign: Maybank was called a "drunken sot," while voters were reminded that Pinckney was divorced. Election day was quiet, however, and Maybank's victory was of landslide proportions: 9,630 votes to 5,030. Grace lost his bid for the City Council by nearly 4,000 votes.

Both Stoney and Maybank, members of the long-entrenched

upper classes of Charleston and the lowcountry and heirs to the old elite, reflected the restoration of the self-confidence and flexibility of their class. Like their predecessors in the 1770s and the 1870s, they were now willing to compromise with less affluent whites, and Grace had taught them how to run a modern American Democratic machine, one that included all classes. They had learned how to deflect the charge that they were aristocrats and they also understood the recent involvement of women in politics and the need to find new solutions to old social problems. And when political disagreements arose between Protestants and Catholics it was often advantageous in Charleston to be an Episcopalian. Sometimes Episcopalians were perceived as selfish snobs and were disliked as such, but at other times Baptists and Presbyterians saw them as fellow Protestants while Roman Catholics saw Episcopalians professing a religion that was much closer to Catholicism than the other Protestant sects. When this happened, an Episcopalian could get things done.

The city's debt was more than $11 million when the People's National Bank collapsed on the first day of the new year, 1932, carrying with it the city's payroll. Like many other American municipalities caught in the same quandary, Charleston resorted to scrip to meet expenses, but within two years of taking office Mayor Maybank returned the city to a cash basis by cutting operating budgets and the salaries of employees, refinancing the debt, and launching a vigorous drive to collect all the money owed the city.

There were approximately 65,000 men, women, and children in the city and about 6,500 of them willing and able to work, could not find jobs. The city's work relief programs were overwhelmed with applicants, and hundreds of sick people were turned away from Roper Hospital because they could not pay for treatment. Appropriations by the city to the black orphanage ended and only after repeated, desperate appeals by the Reverend Mr. Jenkins to Mayor Maybank for assistance did the City Council agree to provide $50 monthly. When a fire severely damaged the Franklin Street orphanage in 1933, Jenkins asked the city to rebuild it, but white opponents who long had opposed its location delayed any action for five years.

On April 7, 1933, Congress repealed prohibition and Charleston merchants offered 3.2 beer for sale the following day, which violated state law, but no one tried to stop it. Mayor Maybank announced that it did not matter whether or not the state legalized the sale of alcohol, since tourists wanted it and Charleston wanted tourists and "we will give . . . liquor . . . to them whether it be legal or illegal." The state soon permitted beer sales and in 1934 the legislature established state-licensed, privately owned package stores for the retail sale of liquor. Nevertheless, for years afterwards "blind tigers" continued to do a flourishing business outside the law in Charleston and with the consent of the city administrations.[46]

Maybank enthusiastically greeted the inauguration of President Franklin D. Roosevelt's federal relief program, which he took as a grand opportunity to improve the city he loved. Archconservatives like William Watts Ball, editor of the News and Courier, attacked the programs as "socialism," and Grace and Stoney, suddenly finding themselves outsiders, agreed with him. Maybank's friendship and political loyalty to South Carolina's junior U.S. senator and presidential confidant, Jimmy Byrnes, and Harry Hopkins, first director of the Federal Emergency Relief Administration (FERA) and later the Works Progress Administration (WPA), helped him obtain federal funds. Between 1933 and 1936, the alphabet agencies of the New Deal spent $34,780,966 in Charleston and the county and pumped 6.6 million additional federal dollars into the Navy Yard between 1933 and 1939, thereby saving the county's economy from collapse. Funds from the FERA permitted the city to hire hundreds of out-of-work Charlestonians who opened new streets and upgraded old ones. A group of Charleston women led by Mrs. Celia McGowan and Mrs. John P. Tiedman were instrumental in obtaining funds from the FERA and the WPA, which were used to plant thousands of azaleas, oaks, and palmetto trees in Charleston, to illuminate softball fields, to improve the city's nine segregated playgrounds, and to build two swimming pools, one for blacks and one for whites. In the 1930s more and more residential areas and recreational facilities developed that were exclusively white or exclusively black.

Over $200,000 in funds from federal agencies helped renovate buildings and build a new gymnasium at the College of Charleston and provide money for fifty students, which permitted them to continue their education. With a grant of $542,000, the Citadel built a mess hall, quarters for the faculty, and a chapel.

To revive tourism, Maybank encouraged the founding of the Azalea Festival, first celebrated in April 1934; this became an annual event attracting thousands to the city. Maybank's administration also promoted Charleston as a beautiful historic city and a resort through highway signs, brochures, and advertisements in national newspapers.

With federal moneys to disburse, Maybank's machine polled 90 percent of the vote in some county elections, and he won city wards by the same margin. He brought city employees more directly under his control by instituting a policy of annual appointments, and Edmund Grice, Jr., his closest friend and political ally, as the director of local federal programs controlled hundreds of jobs. In 1934 Maybank candidates Cotesworth Pinckney Means and Robert McCormick Figg crushed Graceites, J. C. Long and A. Russell McGowan for state and local offices.[47]

A federal survey that year described Charleston's housing as the worst of any city under study. Of 22,369 housing units, 21.7 percent had no running water, 48.9 percent had no indoor toilets, and 25.8 percent were without electricity. For these same categories the national averages were 5.0, 17.9, and 8.1 percent respectively. Mamie Fields, a leader in the Charleston Federation of the South Carolina Federation of Colored Women's Clubs, who assisted in the survey for the U.S. Regional Housing Authority in Atlanta, later recalled her experiences: "The conditions inside of Charleston's slums were worse than they looked from outside . . . . The fathers would tell us about the extra 'fees' that the landlords demanded, on top of the rent for indescribable property. They showed us rats big as rabbits."

In 1935 for the first time in twenty-eight years Charleston was spared an acrimonious contest for City Hall as Maybank was reelected unopposed. The following year he announced that the Public Works Administration (PWA) had made several million dollars available for building two separate housing projects in the northeastern section of the city, one for blacks and one for whites. The sites were chosen from the survey by the Federated Women two years earlier. With these federal funds the city government of Charleston began its first "slum clearance" program. In 1938 when the area around the fire-gutted Jenkins Orphanage was marked for demolition, the City Council agreed to build a facility north of the city to the delight of whites who wanted to rid the city of the black orphanage. To recoup the cost of the new building, the city sold the old Marine Hospital to the City of Charleston Housing Authority. Federal funds also provided an answer to the city health officer's long campaign for an incinerator when the Civil Works Administration (CWA) provided $240,000 to build a municipal garbage "destructor" on the Neck just off East Bay Street. A fleet of trucks now collected garbage directly from the yards to minimize street litter and hauled it to the incinerator. The departments of health of the city and the county were merged as one county health department in 1936, and Dr. Banov continued as the chief administrator.

During the presidential election year of 1936 Mayor Maybank threw the support of his machine behind Roosevelt and Senator Jimmy Byrnes whose opponent in the senatorial race was Maybank's former political ally, Thomas Stoney. As the campaign got underway Stoney injected the issue of race, criticizing the New Deal "for courting the Negro vote" and linking Byrnes with Roosevelt's "orgy of over-government, over-regulation, and over-taxation . . . ." But on August 25 Byrnes swept the state with 257,247 votes to 25,672 for Stoney, who also lost locally, which indicated the lowcountry's enthusiasm for the New Deal and the strength of Maybank's machine.

To embarrass Maybank for political reasons, Governor Olin Johnston sent in an election-day observer who subsequently issued a report critical of the city's election procedures: policemen and deputy sheriffs representing the Maybank machine were stationed at the polling places to campaign for Byrnes, "repeaters" were permitted to vote again and again in the same precinct, and "floaters" went from one precinct to another, casting ballots at each. Despite such alleged election chicanery, the Maybank machine seemed impregnable and the mayor's loyalty to Roosevelt was rewarded handsomely.

In 1937 Mayor Maybank announced that the city was granted $900,000 by the United States Housing Authority to promote public health measures among the "colored population, living in great part in congested and unsanitary surroundings, and often in dire poverty." By the late 1930s death rates remained above the national average for both blacks and whites in Charleston. Yet Dr. Banov, who continued to serve city and county until the 1960s, had reason for optimism. Infant mortality, the highest in the United States in the 1920s, was on the decline; where once the northwestern section of the city had been the "endemic focus of the infection" nationwide of the filaria parasite, it had disappeared as a result of the Health Department's efforts to fill in cisterns and other breeding grounds of mosquitoes. Dr. Banov also reported that the local health conditions were tracking those of the nation; while deaths from typhoid fever, diarrhea, malaria, tuberculosis, and pellagra were declining, deaths from cancer, cardiovascular disease, and automobile accidents were rising.[48]

After sixty-seven years of hosting some of the finest performances in the South, the final curtain fell at the Academy of Music in 1936. The Pastime Amusement Company purchased the building in 1920, giving the Sottile family a virtual monopoly of the theater business locally, but by the 1930s audiences were increasingly turning to movies for spectacle and to radio for music. Nevertheless, the Charleston String Symphony started its first concert season in 1936.

Maybank was a pioneer in the use of federal funds to preserve historic buildings, transforming a flophouse—the once elegant nineteenth-century Planters' Hotel at the corner of Queen and Church streets and site of an eighteenth-century playhouse—with city funds and $350,000 from the WPA. Built inside the shell of the Planters' Hotel was a replica of a 1730s London theater, the façade, entrance, and balcony being part of the pre–Civil War hotel and portions of the interior taken from old homes in the city. When completed, Harry Hopkins, administrator of the WPA, formally presented the key of the Dock Street Theatre to his good friend Burnet Maybank. The theater infused new life into local dramatic associations like the Footlight Players, who before a packed house on November 26, 1937, performed the same play, *The Recruiting Officer*, that had opened the original Dock Street Theatre in 1736. Reinvigorated, the Players presented twenty-eight different productions over the next four years.

By the late 1930s Charleston's only radio station, WCSC, which was operating from the twelfth floor of the Francis Marion Hotel, was losing money, and its owner, a Columbia insurance executive, was looking for a buyer. He opened negotiations with a native Charlestonian and graduate of the college and the University of Pennsylvania, John M. Rivers, a thirty-five-year-old investment banker. Subsequently Rivers purchased WCSC, taking over the operation, which was affiliated with the Columbia Broadcasting System, on January 1, 1938.

Around 8:00 A.M. on September 28, 1938, several violent tornadoes touched down in Charleston and its vicinity smashing buildings into kindling, killing thirty-two persons, injuring over 300 others, and causing more than $2 million in damages. A three-story brick building belonging to the Charleston Paper Company near East Bay and Market streets was totally demolished and some of the city's historic landmarks, including the famous statue of William Pitt, sustained heavy damage. It was the worst disaster for the city since the earthquake of 1886. Harry Hopkins returned to Charleston to survey the damages and immediately made money available to the city. The WPA provided $500,000 to repair landmarks like the City Market and City Hall. Maybank also succeeded in obtaining federal funds to preserve the Marine Hospital designed by Robert Mills.

In an election in 1938 the police simply took over the polls in Ward 10, one officer marking ballots for voters while others hauled the opposition's poll watchers to jail. An old saying went that Charleston did not report its votes until the rest of the state did, so that the local Democratic machine could see "how many votes were needed." To keep control of the police, Maybank induced the state legislature to pass a new police commission law that permitted the mayor to appoint the police commissioner!

Charleston's Azalea Parade, 1938. Seated in front, Vice President John Nance Garner and chauffeur; in the rear, left to right, Governor Olin D. Johnston, Mayor Burnet R. Maybank, and the Hon. James F. Byrnes. *Courtesy of the Charleston Museum, Charleston, S.C.*

Maybank was elected governor of South Carolina in 1938, the first governor from Charleston since Magrath (1865), and the first Charlestonian to be popularly elected to the Governor's Mansion in Columbia, the earlier governors from Charleston having been elected by the legislature. He had brought the city through the depression with flair, and his remarkably durable political machine, the most efficient the city has ever known, continued to run Charleston for ten years after he left it.[49]

Charleston had often been at odds with the rest of South Carolina and was almost used to being out of step with the federal government, but for fifteen years, from 1932 to 1947, the city enjoyed extraordinarily harmonious relations with the county, the state, and the nation. In part this was because the Great Depression and World War II tended to bring the country together. President Roosevelt, Harry Hopkins, Jimmy Byrnes, Bernard Baruch, and others deserve some of the credit for the harmony that proved so profitable for Charleston, but it was largely the achievement of an affable, skilled politico, Burnet Maybank.

❦ 4. 1938–1947:
" . . . buzzard town" and World War II

" . . . marked by poverty and neglect"

The City Council elected Alderman Henry W. Lockwood in 1938 to serve out the mayor's unexpired term. Lockwood was a trusted Maybank lieutenant and a wealthy Lutheran who had captained a tugboat in the harbor during the 1920s. In 1939 the Maybank machine elected Lockwood to a four-year term. With the enthusiastic support of the gentry, he followed a traditional Charleston policy of curtailing spending, opposing new taxes and bond issues, refinancing old loans, and reducing the city's debt.

On January 28, 1939, J. C. Long, a powerful county politician whose wife was a Sottile, bought the first ticket at the Riviera, a new cinema on the site of the Academy of Music at the northwest corner of King and Market streets. The feature film on opening day was *Secrets of a Nurse.* Cooled by fans blowing air across large blocks of ice, the Riviera seated 1,193 people and remains the city's most outstanding example of Art Deco architecture. Also that year the city's second radio station, WTMA, began operating on June 14 in Wagener Terrace at the north end of 10th Street. It was founded by J. W. Orvin and Y. W. Scarborough, but within four months was bought by the *News and Courier* and the *Evening Post*, and the studios were moved into the newsplant at 134 Meeting Street to become affiliated with the National Broadcasting Company in 1940. Charlestonian and State Senator Cotesworth Pinckney Means soon was warning publicly of "the harm . . . done by combination of two papers . . . and one radio station owned by one person."

In 1939 more than 300,000 tourists visited Charleston and one visitor accurately observed that "the tourists were welcomed but not wanted." That year the South Carolina Public Service Authority, chaired by Burnet Maybank, authorized the clearing of land for building the Santee-Cooper hydro-electric project which eventually helped rejuvenate Charleston's economy.

By the late 1930s Charleston's homicide rate was twice that of Chicago and four times that of New York City. Murder rates remained high for the region, reaching twice the national average in 1970. The sheer number of homicides in Charleston early in the new century bred a certain callousness toward murder. For instance, in 1904 there were twenty murders but no convictions. From January to November 1939 there were twenty-two homicides but only two defendants brought to trial. The city gained a certain notoriety on the eve of World War II when a writer in a national magazine observed that "slashings and cuttings" usually with "ice picks . . . open-blade razors, jagged broken bottles . . . are everyday occurrences. In Charleston," he concluded," it is commonplace for a man to lose his life over a woman, a jest, a string of catfish, or a dime."[50]

Almost immediately after the outbreak of World War II in September 1939 there was a demand for more ships and the Charleston Navy Yard was authorized to enlarge its industrial facilities. The following year all channels of the 210 miles of the Intracoastal Waterway within the state were opened, which facilitated the movement of commodities to the coast, but a British blockade of European shipping and the threat of German submarine attacks cut oceangoing traffic at Charleston by one-third, and the lowcountry was still far from prosperous.

The processing of rotten fish and chemicals in the fertilizer plants of the north area contributed to the stench that sometimes enveloped downtown Charleston. A former South Carolinian then living in New York, who visited there in May 1940, regretted leaving "the dear old city—only the smell reconciling us to the departure." She added, "strange that a city of its size would tolerate it." Others complained of the unsightly city dump and referred to Charleston as "buzzard town" because of the numbers of vultures they saw hovering over it. That year another visitor described the city as "marked by poverty and neglect," and appearances were not improved by the hurricane of August 11, which flooded streets and bowled over trees and telephone poles.

Governor Maybank appointed a legislative committee "to investigate the shrinkage of waterborne commerce through the state ports," and following a thorough study and hearings aimed at winning upcountry support, the legislature created a "Ports Authority" to develop South Carolina's ports. It was the first agency of its type in the nation.

The War on the Homefront

The war revived Charleston's moribund economy. In 1941 the federal defense program poured money into the South, and South Carolina received $136.8 million, 80 percent of which went into the Charleston area. At the Navy Yard twelve new destroyers slipped down the ways, shipbuilding facilities and the power plant were improved, and an ammunition depot and housing units constructed. The weaponry at Forts Moultrie and Sumter was upgraded, airfields enlarged, and a thirty-foot channel dredged in Shipyard River. Highway connections with the rest of the state were improved, school buildings renovated, and teacher's salaries raised in the federal defense-impacted area. Payrolls at the Charleston Navy Yard topped $400,000 *weekly* by October 1941. In South Carolina per-capita income averaged $301, but in Charleston it averaged $856.60, and by late 1941 the Charleston Navy Yard had supplanted tourism as the lowcountry's largest industry. It was the third largest industry in the entire state.[51]

When news of the Japanese attack on the American base at Pearl Harbor reached Mayor Lockwood in December, he placed all city departments on a war footing and ordered the police to apprehend for questioning any Japanese in order to prevent "any possible sabotage to the Navy Yard and other defense points." The closest Japanese family lived in Holly Hill, fifty miles away. The United States was now at war with Japan, Italy, and Germany. The Junior League and the Girl Scouts volunteered their services to the Red Cross and to Roper Hospital, and members of the Rotary Club became air-raid wardens. The Red Cross organized a meeting, to raise money to aid bomb victims in Europe, at County Hall on December 14 and over $6,680 was subscribed. The city's Afro-Americans launched their own Red Cross drive under Dr. E. B. Burroughs for the same cause at the same place a week later and raised $2,000. There was no isolationist opposition to the war that had been a noisy part of the city's intellectual life in World War I.

Civilian personnel at the Navy Yard, most of them white, increased from 6,000 in 1941 to over 28,000 two years later. They built some 230 destroyers or amphibious craft, converted vessels to military use, and repaired war-damaged submarines and allied surface vessels. The addition of a Naval Air Station at the Yard in 1942, the establishment of the Coast Guard Base at the west end of Calhoun Street, the army airfield, and the port as a point of embarkation brought in additional thousands of military and civilian personnel. To one of them, Ensign John Fitzgerald Kennedy, being stationed in Charleston in early 1942 and away from the action, was, he told friends, like being in "Siberia." In February the turbines of the hydro-electric plant of the Santee-Cooper project fifty miles north of Charleston on the shores of newly created Lake Moultrie roared into operation for the first time. Annually it would produce 450 million kilowatt hours of electricity supplying vitally needed power to the Navy Yard and defense plants across the Southeast during the war and stimulating industrial expansion afterward.[52]

The Charleston area swarmed with construction workers, sailors, soldiers, fliers, bookkeepers, and secretaries; and the population of the old peninsula city itself reached 71,000 in 1940, the largest in its history, and grew modestly over the next four years. But the population of metropolitan Charleston—the city and that part of Charleston County encircling the city, the southwestern tip of Berkeley County, and the southeastern corner of Dorchester County—exploded, reaching 225,000 by 1944; 15,000 new housing units were built by 1943 and the 6 million passengers using Charleston buses in 1940 increased to 25 million on 109 buses three years later; like eighteen other American cities, Charleston was designated "a congested production area." Retail sales soared 40 percent in just two years; contractors, landlords, merchants, taxi drivers, restaurants, bars, and brothels enjoyed the boom times. Three railroads, three national airlines, and eight motor freight companies now served the city, and Mayor Lockwood said that World War II brought to Charleston "sacrifice and inconvenience but . . . also national recognition as an important military and industrial center."

Early in the war German submarines waited off Charleston where no enemy vessels had been since 1865. These U-boats laid mines in the harbor approaches on three occasions and beach patrols were organized to prevent them from landing saboteurs on the nearby barrier islands. In June 1942 antisubmarine nets were laid in the harbor and aircraft patrolled the coast to help protect the transports and freighters carrying men and supplies out of Charleston for Europe. By mid-1943 the U-boat threat had been neutralized.

Among the well-to-do the usual rounds of balls, "hops," debutante teas, and receptions went on uninterrupted. The St. Cecilia Ball was held on schedule in January 1942 and that spring dances were sponsored by the Junior League, the Cotillion Club, the Carolina Yacht Club, and the Charleston Rifle Club; and the Charleston Garden Club held its annual Camellia Show. The Charleston Symphony Orchestra directed by J. Albert Fracht held its annual season throughout the war and the Charleston Community Concerts Association presented as usual four concerts a year with guest soloists, Enzio Pinza performing in February 1944. Vernon Weston conducted annual performances of Handel's *Messiah*, the Ashley Hall Christmas plays went on uninterrupted, and on Sunday evenings in summer military bands played on the Battery. The Footlight Players and the Dock Street Theatre offered a full complement of plays each season. An exhibit at the Gibbes Art Gallery in 1943 featured paintings of "Britain at War" and "America in the War." By this time there were seven motion-picture theaters in the city: the Gloria and the Riviera offered first-run movies while the Garden, Victory, Majestic, American, and Palace offered "B-grade" fare. Evening performances cost 55 cents, while seats in the gallery for blacks, referred to by them as "buzzard's roost," cost 28 cents.

County Hall was taken over for use by the U.S. Army, the Calhoun Mansion boarded army and navy personnel, and the Fort Sumter Hotel served as Sixth Naval District Headquarters. The city's street-car rails were removed by the federal government and yielded 1,800 tons of steel for the war effort. Beginning in

1943, gasoline, tires, sugar, shoes, meat, coffee, and fuel oil were rationed throughout the United States, and perfume, whiskey, and women's hose became scarce and expensive. As elsewhere in the nation, campaigns were launched for waste paper, scrap metal, books, scrap rubber, clothes for Russia, war bonds, and waste fat. A local slogan was *sock' em with your skillet*. More than 500 German and Italian prisoners-of-war incarcerated near Charleston were employed in farm work or at the paper mill and fertilizer plant in the north area.

The huge and sudden increase in population sorely tested Charleston's public services, and one local government employee, a New Yorker, writing under a pseudonym in *The Nation*, reported in November 1943 that the "land-proud, tradition bound" Charlestonians were fighting to preserve their way of life with "exorbitant rents . . . for bad . . . housing, hotel-dining-room prices for hash-house meals, and . . . lack of recreation . . . except for a few theaters with fuzzy acoustics."

The state Highway Department became responsible for maintenance of arterial traffic routes within the city in 1941 and the federal government continued to provide funds for asphalt-paving projects. Soaring revenues from local liquor and admission taxes enabled the city to expand its upkeep of the streets, although it was not until 1945 that the predominately black northwestern section of the city was paved. Street litter and garbage increased enormously and prisoners from the chain gang collected the refuse and hauled it to the city's incinerator, which twice was enlarged with federal funds and replaced the city dump.[53]

The local rat population rose sharply and an outbreak of typhus led to several deaths, causing Dr. Banov and the U.S. Public Health Service to launch a program of rat control. Volunteers helped manufacture and distribute 250,000 rat "torpedoes," dabs of food sprinkled with poison and wrapped in small squares of paper. To increase public awareness about their use, socially prominent women gave afternoon teas, dubbed "rat teas." Billboards advertised the campaign and the *News and Courier* urged Charlestonians to "Kill Rats Like Japs." The rodent extermination program worked and by the end of the war typhus had just about disappeared.

The war brought boom times again to the prostitutes of the "segregated district," which the police had protected for years.

Military officers and some Charlestonians, however, viewed venereal disease as a threat to the health of servicemen and the city
equal to that of typhus and called on the local government to
eradicate prostitution. When Mayor Lockwood and the city police proved unresponsive, Admiral W. G. Allen, commandant of
the Navy Yard and the Sixth Naval District, declared twenty-
seven beer parlors, mostly on King and Market streets, off limits
to navy personnel and he threatened to curtail all leaves in
Charleston, observing that "prostitution . . . the open and illegal
sale of whiskey, gambling and the sale of 'dope' are now permitted without restriction." Finally Mayor Lockwood acted. In late
1941 he shut down the segregated district permanently. The
prostitutes, however, moved their operations to "waterfront
dives, beer parlors, juke box resorts" and into taxicabs. In October 1942 the U.S. Army shocked Charleston by declaring the city
off limits. This led prominent local businessmen, politicians, and
clergymen, working with health and military officials, to organize
the Charleston Social Protective League to repress prostitution
and resist "the possibility of official indifference on the one hand,
and hurtful fanaticism on the other." City officials quickly ordered the police to undertake a vigorous campaign "against pro-
curers, pimps . . . and disorderly establishments." From
November 1942 to August 1943, the local police with the cooperation of the naval shore patrol arrested and detained for medical examination 626 suspected female prostitutes, 346 white and
280 "colored." Nearly half were found to be infected with venereal disease and sent to camps operated by the federal government for treatment and rehabilitation. Nevertheless, the number
of teenage girls working the streets and bars increased and, despite cooperation of the city and military police, federal investigators charged that five brothels operated openly, "call girls" were
obtainable at two hotels, and "Negro commercialized prostitution
[was] . . . flagrantly carried on." Until the end of the war federal
records listed Charleston among fifteen cities where vice conditions "remain unsatisfactory."

Reelected unopposed in 1943, Mayor Lockwood died suddenly the following year and the City Council elected E. Edward
Wehman, another Lutheran and Maybank supporter, to complete
his term of office. Socially prominent, Wehman had been president of the Carolina Mutual Insurance Company, the oldest fire
insurance company in the state, with offices at 37 Broad Street.[54]

At 3:00 A.M., June 6, 1944, Radio Station WTMA announced that Allied Forces based in England had invaded France and the bells of St. Michael's peeled into the afternoon for the greatest amphibious landing in history. Nearly a year later the war in Europe ended and the city quietly observed V–E Day, but on August 14, when news arrived that Japan had surrendered, frenzied celebrations erupted, church bells rang, sirens and horns sounded, and flares and searchlights punctured the sky over the harbor and city.

The old peninsula city was now surrounded by instant suburbs, but World War II had not impeded the implacable preservationists who in 1944 had published *This Is Charleston*, the nation's first citywide architectural survey. After the war whites came home to a Charleston that was more affluent than it had ever been, a beautiful port city that did not resemble any other urban center in the world. Black soldiers, having fought for freedom alongside whites in Africa, Europe, and the Orient, came home to a community that expected them to ride in the back of the bus, to avoid using the same toilet facilities as whites or eating at the same tables, and above all to refrain from even thinking about voting. Many blacks knew they could not endure such discrimination much longer. Very few Southern whites, however, had any inkling in 1945 of the profound changes that were about to sweep the South, and all that most white Charlestonians could see before them for the moment was economic opportunity and the resumption of their prewar lives.

In September 1945 navy officials in Washington created the U.S. Naval Base, Charleston, which was to coordinate all the shore activities of the navy in the area, including the Marine Barracks, the Naval Ammunition Depot, Hospital, and Degaussing Station. By the late fall the U.S. Navy Yard officially became a component of the now sprawling naval base and was renamed the U.S. Naval Shipyard, and the commandant of the Sixth Naval District became commander of the U. S. Naval Base.

A new banana-handling dock was completed on the Cooper River by the Southern Railroad Company on February 11, 1946, to replace the one destroyed by fire over a year before. Nearby on February 24 the *Nicaraguan Victory* slipped her moorings during a fierce storm and drifted into the Cooper River Bridge severing a section and causing an automobile to tumble through the break carrying a family of five to their deaths. The bridge had been owned by the state of South Carolina since the early 1940s and the tolls were lifted in a public ceremony on June 29, 1946. State Senator O. T. Wallace paid the last 50-cent toll and soon introduced a bill naming the bridge after John P. Grace.

In September the Atlantic Mine Warfare Command was relocated from Norfolk, Virginia, to downtown Charleston, along Lockwood Boulevard recently named in honor of the former mayor. During early February 1947 President Harry Truman signed over the Army Port of Embarkation in the north area to its original owners, the city of Charleston, which promptly transferred the property and the rotting docks in downtown Charleston to the State Ports Authority (SPA). Several months later the SPA formally assumed operation of properties of the Port Utilities Commission that had operated Charleston's waterfront facilities since 1922 and inaugurated aggressive efforts to attract trade to South Carolina's ports.

That spring, when the legendary azaleas bloomed, tourists whom the war had prevented from visiting the city for five years began to reappear.[55]

VII

Modern Charleston

❧ 1. 1947–1959: Voting Rights

J. Waties Waring

On July 12, 1947, Judge J. Waties Waring, presiding over the federal court of the Eastern District of South Carolina in Columbia, decided for the plaintiff in the case of *Elmore v. Rice*. George Elmore, a black man, was not permitted to vote in the Richland County Democratic primary and a suit had been brought in his name against the County Democratic Executive Committee by an Afro-American Citizens' Committee and the NAACP. During the hearings William Watts Ball, editor of the *News and Courier*, told his readers that in South Carolina the primary functioned much like a private organization, "a state-wide collection of white-skinned clubs." But in his decision Judge Waring reminded South Carolina Democrats that "private clubs . . . do not vote and elect a president . . . Senators and members of the House of Representatives," concluding: "It is time for South Carolina to rejoin the Union . . . [and] adopt the American way of conducting elections."

Black leaders were jubilant, but many whites in South Carolina were angry. The *News and Courier* editorialized that if the decision was upheld then South Carolinians should drop "the name of Democratic party . . . and reestablish white . . . political clubs under a new title. . . . for . . . white[s] . . . the court rulings mean changes . . . but not in their determination to maintain separation of white and colored peoples." Mayor Wehman predicted "the end of the Democratic party . . . as we have known it" unless the decision was reversed and Senator Burnet Maybank pledged to keep "the white Democratic party of South Carolina safe . . . from this new effort to overturn it." Judge Waring remembered that shortly after his decision in *Elmore v. Rice* a group of his relatives "waited until two thirty one morning to call and say hello and tell me that they didn't think it wise to see me anymore."

Seven generations of Warings had lived in the lowcountry. Born in Charleston in 1880, Waties Waring attended local private schools, graduated from the College of Charleston in 1900, read law, passed the bar exam, and began his practice in Charleston where as a bachelor he won a reputation as the city's foremost womanizer. An Episcopalian, he married Annie Gammell, herself a seventh-generation Charlestonian, and belonged to the best clubs, including the Charleston Club, the St. Cecilia Society, and the Charleston Light Dragoons. He was an assistant United States attorney for the Eastern District of South Carolina from 1916 to 1921, after which he returned to private practice and earned both a good reputation as an attorney and a good income. In 1931 Waring became the legal adviser to his friend Burnet Maybank during his successful bid for mayor and subsequently served as corporation counsel for the city of Charleston, on one occasion indicating that he embraced local racial customs when he restricted the U.S. Army's use of Stoney Field to white soldiers. In 1938 he assisted Maybank in his successful campaign for governor, and then at the age of fifty-eight Waring returned to private practice.

In December 1941 the state's senior U.S. senator, "Cotton" Ed Smith, an avowed white supremacist, and the new junior senator, Burnet Maybank, nominated Waties Waring to the post of U.S. district judge for the Eastern District of South Carolina. Within two years of his appointment Judge Waring handed down the first of two decisions, which helped eventually to end the racial inequities in the pay schedules of public school teachers in South Carolina. These decisions appeared to mark the beginning of Judge Waring's departure from the racial views he had held since childhood.[1]

As bridge partners Judge Waring and his wife enjoyed frequent card parties at the homes of their friends or in their own home, 61 Meeting Street. Joining this exclusive set in the early 1940s were the Hoffmans, a well-to-do Detroit couple who spent their winters in Charleston, and soon a strong, mutual, romantic attraction developed between the once-divorced, vivacious Elizabeth Avery Hoffman and the distinguished, stern, even gruff Judge Waring. Those who knew Elizabeth described her as "Strikingly attractive . . . tall and well shaped, very intelligent . . . animated, and . . . very tweedy." Opinionated and aggressive, she was a modern woman—a sharp contrast to the domestic and submissive Annie Waring. Still known as a "ladies' man" who occasionally made overtures to young legal secretaries, Judge Waring became romantically involved with Elizabeth and on a fall evening in 1944 he told Annie he wanted a divorce. Annie obediently followed Waties's instructions and left for Jacksonville, Florida, to establish residency for a divorce, which at the time was illegal in South Carolina.

During the graduation exercises of the College of Charleston on May 29, 1945, Judge Waring was one of the two Charlestonians who received honorary doctorates. Several days later Waring asked his nephew, Tom Waring, to come to his office. Born in Charleston in 1907 as a ninth-generation Charlestonian, he was educated at the University of the South and served briefly as a reporter for the *New York Herald* from 1929 to 1931 before joining the *News and Courier*, whose editor, the conservative curmudgeon William Watts Ball, was another of Tom Waring's uncles. Judge Waring told Tom about the imminent divorce and asked him to write a brief article announcing it in the local press. When the younger Waring questioned his uncle's judgment, suggesting that the divorce would "rock" Charleston society, the judge replied, "Let 'em rock."

On June 8 the divorce was granted in Jacksonville and the next day a brief announcement appeared in the *News and Courier* stating that Anne Gammell Waring was granted a divorce from Judge Waring and a property settlement concluded. Waties Waring purchased 61 Meeting Street from Annie and she moved around the corner to Tradd Street. About the time the notice of the Warings' divorce appeared, Elizabeth Hoffman was in Reno, Nevada, getting her second divorce, after which she traveled to New York, met Judge Waring, and sent her most recent husband a telegram informing him that they were no longer married. In the *News and Courier* of June 19, 1945, was the brief notice of an event that Tom Waring had read about in the *New York Herald Tribune* of June 18: "Judge Waring Weds Mrs. Hoffman at Greenwich, Conn."

When Waties Waring and his new bride returned to live at 61 Meeting Street, rumors were rife. There were tales of how they first became romantically involved and of intimate bridge games where the judge and Elizabeth played footsie under the table. Later Tom Waring and others would insist that the attitudes and actions of Charlestonians toward the Warings after the judge's landmark civil rights decisions were due primarily to the circumstances surrounding his divorce and quick remarriage to Elizabeth Hoffman.[2]

After Mayor Wehman decided not to run in 1947, former Mayor Tom Stoney seized the opportunity to reestablish his political dominance locally. He had a score to settle. Stoney blamed his one-time ally Burnet Maybank for his defeat by Jimmy Byrnes in the 1934 United States Senate race. He worked out a temporary alliance with the powerful county landowner and politician J. C. Long, and surrounded himself with a group of politically talented young men. Some of them were recently returned veterans of the war like Gedney M. Howe, Jr., who had run for city solicitor with Stoney's endorsement in 1946. Together they handpicked the city's next mayor, William McGillivray Morrison.

Born near Charleston in McClellanville in 1903, Morrison attended Clemson University, took a law degree at the University of South Carolina, became corporation counsel for the city in 1930 and then master-in-equity. Gedney Howe remembered Bill Morrison as "a good raconteur and likeable . . . with a good sense of humor . . . [without] any real meanness in him and the canniness . . . of a lowcountry man. [But] Bill was lazy." With Stoney's support, Morrison and his slate of aldermen scored an easy victory in both the Democratic primary and the general election in December 1947. The old Stoney faction had returned to power.

In late December the United States Circuit Court of Appeals upheld Judge Waring's decision in *Elmore v. Rice* and in early 1948 the Supreme Court refused to review it. South Carolina Democrats responded by adopting a set of rules that excluded blacks from party rolls but permitted qualified blacks to vote in the primary if they took an oath that included the words: "I believe in and will support the social and educational separation of the races." David Brown, a black resident of Beaufort, promptly brought suit in federal court against the Democratic party of South Carolina because the names of thirty-four Afro-Americans were stricken from the party rolls in Beaufort County. The case of *Brown v. Baskin* reached Judge Waring in Charleston on July 16, 1948. Thurgood Marshall represented the plaintiff, and the distinguished local attorney Robert McCormick Figg, Jr., represented the defendants. By now Judge Waring had ended the practice of segregated seating in his courtroom and instructed courtroom personnel to address blacks by their titles. The efforts of the state Democratic party to subvert his earlier ruling had angered Judge Waring and he told William P. Baskin, chairman of the party and defendant: "It is a pity and a shame when a Federal Judge has to tell you how to act like an American Citizen." Then turning to David Brown, the plaintiff, Waring exclaimed: "It is a disgrace and shame when you must come into court and ask a judge to tell you you are an American."

Rather than a formally written opinion Judge Waring issued a court order that provided for "books [to] be opened to all parties irrespective of race, color, creed or condition . . . ," adding that all those things should be there "because . . . next time they may exclude . . . Jews, or Roman Catholics . . . ." He concluded by warning that "any disobedience to the letter and spirit" of his ruling would result in imprisonment.

Politicians like Representative L. Mendel Rivers of Charleston responded immediately from the floor of Congress, calling Waring a "monster" and another South Carolina congressman, William Jennings Bryan Dorn, introduced impeachment resolutions. Senator Maybank, involved in a tight reelection campaign, told the *News and Courier* that "the actions of Judge Waring . . . are deplorable"; Maybank's opponent, Alan Johnstone, declared that Waring had "gone berserk." But across South Carolina Democratic books were opened and three days after Waring's court order 4,360 Afro-Americans and forty whites had been added to the voting rolls in Charleston County. The all-white Democratic primary was dead. In the August statewide primary, 30,000 Afro-Americans voted, the greatest number to go to the polls since their disfranchisement in the 1890s.

Judge Waring received letters from some individuals praising his actions. Charleston attorneys Edward K. Pritchard and Joseph Fromberg publicly endorsed Waring until, for social or economic reasons, both trimmed their support. The local Athenian Club rebuked editor William Watts Ball for escalating racial tensions by his editorial remarks about the decision. But Waring received numerous "vicious" and "obscene" letters and phone calls and later observed that he encountered "a stone wall of unpleasantness everywhere I went." In the August 23, 1948, issue of *Time* magazine Judge Waring was referred to as "the man they love to hate" in South Carolina. He told Rebecca West that he had attempted to "see over the fog of prejudice which has engulfed this land of ours since the fall of the Confederacy . . . . I have tried to do what little has come my way to see that the Negro receives justice in the court where I preside."

Like other white Southerners, most white Charlestonians were horrified when President Harry Truman recommended a civil rights program to Congress which included the protection of citizens' right to vote, the end of racial segregation on interstate buses and trains, and a federal antilynching statute. In mid-October 1948 Judge Waring attended a luncheon in his honor by the New York chapter of the Lawyers Guild and in his address remarked that "the South should not be left alone to deal with its racial problems in its own way." The *News and Courier* promptly observed that all judges should refrain from making political speeches. Then immediately after being reelected, President Truman invited Waring to the White House and told him that he "wish[ed] we had more Federal Judges like you on the bench."[3]

Mayor Morrison's First Administration

Despite the extraordinary political and social storm rolling across the South and Charleston in 1948, Mayor Morrison continued the city's pragmatic approach to slum clearance. He was motivated to raze tenements and extend sewage lines into black slums because socially prominent housewives expressed their fears to him that their "servants . . . lived in unsanitary areas." Morrison had the City Council view a fourteen-minute motion picture of slum conditions, after which, Morrison reported, the "members . . . expressed themselves as feeling disgraced that such conditions existed in Charleston." The city aldermen soon passed an ordinance "Regulating the Repair, Closing and Demolition of Dwelling Units Unfit for Human Habitation" and established an Office of Public Safety and Housing. Tenements were condemned and the inhabitants moved into properties financed by the Federal Housing Administration. By the early 1950s the city administration could report that over 900 buildings had been repaired and over 350 demolished with federal money. Morrison proudly announced in 1951: "Charleston's slum areas are fast being erased, resulting in greatly improved sanitary and health conditions throughout the city."

Mayor Morrison continued the draining and reclamation of marshlands and the improvement of the streets. The city stopped using the incinerator and, to cut costs, garbage again was used as landfill. In 1949 East Bay Street was opened from Calhoun Street to the Cooper River Bridge and subsequently to the city limits. It provided an urgently needed north-south artery, and Lockwood Boulevard was completed over reclaimed marshlands in 1951, providing a corridor for traffic moving east to west.

The city continued to boost tourism and the Azalea Festival, which had been revived in 1947 at the urging of the business community. Once more visitors returned to see Charleston's prime attractions—the flower gardens in the early spring, the historic forts, churches, and homes—and by 1948 over 475,000 tourists were spending $5.8 million annually. The city also promoted preservation, which continued to be funded primarily with private local money. The Historic Charleston Foundation, founded in the mid-1940s, assumed the lead in the movement by raising a sizable corpus of money to buy up deteriorating historic homes for renovation or resale, something the Preservation Society had been unable to do. In 1947 the foundation inaugurated its famous house tours, and when a dynamic young businesswoman, Frances Ravenel Edmunds, was selected to head the tours in 1949 they made a profit for the first time.[4]

The Junior League of Charleston established a speech correction school in 1947, but there was less demand on the city for charitable funds as outside agencies became increasingly important sources. The number of inmates at the City Almshouse dropped to under twenty and their average age was seventy by 1949. The City Council concluded that state and federal programs for the elderly would soon make the home obsolete. In December the Columbus Street institution closed its doors forever and the inmates were sent to private homes or to Baker Hospital.

In the late 1940s the Orphan House building was condemned by the Charleston County Health Department, and the Board of Commissioners sought advice from the Child Welfare League of America. The Welfare League suggested abandoning the building and the local centuries-old philosophy of institutionalized child care (recommending instead cottage-type housing beyond the city and emphasizing foster family and adoption services) and replacing the present staff with trained professionals who could deal with children with emotional and behavioral problems. The Board of Commissioners implemented these recommendations. In 1951 the 156 children in the Orphan House moved to a new five-cottage facility on thirty-one acres about eight miles from

Charleston, the Oak Grove Child Care Center. The new facility was built with the $350,000 the city received from the sale of the eighteenth-century Orphan House and its nearby "ancient orphanage chapel" to Sears and Roebuck Company despite the protests of preservationists. Two years later these historic structures were demolished and a retail store and parking lot built on the sites.[5]

" . . . the lonesomest man in town"

By early 1950 the bitterness was growing between white Charlestonians and Waties and Elizabeth Waring because of their own actions and public statements. Mrs. Waring cultivated and visited local black friends like civil rights activist Septima Clark and Arthur J. Clement, Jr., president of the Charleston Chapter of the NAACP and manager of the local office of a black-owned insurance company. With other blacks like Corinne and Harry Guenveur, the Waring's mailman, and Ruby and A. T. Cornwell, a local dentist, Elizabeth Waring invited them to her Meeting Street home. The Warings were the first couple in Charleston in modern memory to entertain blacks in their residence and by so doing they broke the ancient Southern social code. At the same time Charlestonians were warily watching civil rights cases like the Texas school desegregation suit, which was expected to reach the Supreme Court soon. On January 2, 1950, the *News and Courier* observed that a court decision unfavorable to the South "would precipitate a greater upheaval in the . . . life of the region than anything since Reconstruction . . . ." That month the all-black Coming Street YWCA (Young Women's Christian Association) invited Elizabeth Waring to address the organization, but when the white YWCA and the local Central Board heard of it they privately pressured "Y" officer Septima Clark to withdraw the invitation. She refused and on January 16 Elizabeth Waring spoke before the members of the Coming Street YWCA telling them that they were brave to come because "the 'white powers that be' have done everything to keep me from speaking to you . . . . They are afraid we will . . . destroy their selfish and savage white supremacy way of life . . . . And . . . that is exactly what the Judge and I are doing . . . ." Indeed, she continued, " . . . a new day is dawning . . . and you must make the final push now . . . ." Already, she concluded, "You negro people" have taken "the torch of culture and achievement from the whites . . . a sick

. . . and decadent people . . . full of pride and complacency, . . . morally weak . . . so self-centered that they have not considered themselves as a part of the country since the Civil War." Her address shocked many in the predominantly black audience and white Charlestonians the following day when they read it in the *News and Courier.* They had not heard such words hurled against their way of life since the era of the Civil War. Septima Clark described the evening as "exciting, challenging," but her mother was so overcome by the speech that she had to be carried from the room.[6]

After reading Elizabeth Waring's remarks, state Representative Joseph F. Wise of Charleston told the *News and Courier:* "We need no words . . . from a Damnyankee." Congressman Rivers encouraged T. C. Phillips, who headed a newly formed group of citizens, the Southern Association for the Advancement of White People, to begin a statewide petition drive to impeach Judge Waring.

On February 11 Elizabeth Waring appeared on NBC's "Meet the Press" and during the interview declared that other Southern states had made progress in race relations but not South Carolina, which remained "an exact replica of Russia." She also spoke "in favor of the complete breakdown of separation of the races in the South and intermarriage among whites and negroes" if they so desired. The following Monday a resolution was offered in the South Carolina House of Representatives to appropriate funds to purchase one-way tickets for Judge Waring and his wife to any place they desired provided that they never return to the state and "to erect a suitable plaque to [them] . . . in the mule barn" at Clemson College. Within twenty-four hours the resolution was taken up, read three times, passed, and sent to the Senate. While this was going on Judge Waring was in New York where he continued to fuel the feud, telling a church group: "We don't have a Negro problem in the South; we have a white problem. The white men . . . are obsessed" with white supremacy. The elderly Charleston banker C. Norwood Hastie wrote Senator Maybank that Charleston was "seething" and he should use his influence to get the Warings "out of town." By this time Maybank himself was telling friends that Waring was "crazy and should be in an institution."

In early March a cross was burned in front of the Waring home. The judge told the *News and Courier* that it was "no work of pranksters," since there were "400 or 500 Klansmen" in the city and the cross-burning was "an exhibition typical of the savagery of . . . white supremacists." The official police department report called it "nothing more than a prank."

The Warings realized they had become social pariahs and Waties Waring relinquished his membership in the St. Cecilia Society, resigned his captaincy in the elite Charleston Light Dragoons, and ended his affiliation with the local Episcopal church. In April *Colliers* magazine published an article on Judge Waring that called him "the lonesomest man in town." When Elizabeth Waring took her daily walk, the children of the well-to-do living south of Broad would call after her epithets like "witch" or "prostitute" and occasionally she was jostled on the sidewalks. On Monday night, October 9, as the Warings sat at home they suddenly were startled by what they described as three pistol shots close by and then a "big lump of concrete" came smashing through the window. In an interview with the *News and Courier* Judge Waring said that the attack was intended to intimidate him and that "South Carolina and aristocratic Charleston show sentiments against . . . the American creed . . . ." Historically sensitive to outside criticism and long anti-Klan, the paper criticized the Warings for making so much of the incident—assuming "the role of martyrs"—but also urged that every effort be made to find the "hoodlums" who tarnish "South Carolina's reputation for law and order." Two days after the event city and county policy considered the case closed, but the attorney general of the United States, J. Howard McGrath, ordered federal marshals to maintain round-the-clock protection for Judge Waring and to continue the investigation. Congressman Rivers declared that Waring had become the "most expensive luxury on the federal payroll" and that by November 10 his guards, who "even accompany Waring when he goes to visit his negro friends to play canasta . . . had been paid $1,103.81." The local Federal Bureau of Investigation (FBI) agents suspected neighborhood youths as the culprits in the incident, but their investigation was hampered when the judge of Charleston's Domestic Relations Court told them that his records did not show the names of anyone below Broad Street inasmuch as the "children residing . . . [there] were the sons and daughters of very . . . wealthy and politically powerful families and as such were not molested by the police but allowed to do much as they pleased . . . ."

To cheer up the Warings, friends organized a "pilgrimage" to Charleston in late November of 100 black and twenty-five white NAACP officials from seven Southern states, whom Judge Waring entertained at his home. They praised him for moving the country toward "true equality." Waring responded and was quoted in the local press as saying: "We do not live in darkest Africa, we live in darkest South Carolina."

By now Judge Waring was convinced that there could be little progress toward equal rights until segregation in the public schools ended and he encouraged Thurgood Marshall to enlarge a suit seeking equal facilities in Clarendon County to challenge the legality of segregated schools. In spring 1951 the Clarendon County suit, which was broadened and now known as *Briggs v. Elliott,* reached the Federal District Court and came before three judges, one of whom was Waring. While they deliberated, the *News and Courier* excoriated the NAACP and its liberal white friends who perpetuated the "utterly false contention that Southern colored people have not been well treated"; rather, "Southern Negroes have been generously treated since they were brought to North America out of SAVAGERY AND SLAVERY in Africa."

In *Briggs v. Elliott* a 2 to 1 decision upheld the "separate but equal doctrine" with Judge Waring dissenting. He offered a lengthy opinion based on a wide reading of history and sociology, concluding that "Segregation is *per se* inequality . . . and . . . when this [14th] Amendment was adopted, it was intended to do away with discrimination between our citizens." Tom Waring, now responsible for the editorial page of the *News and Courier,* called his uncle's dissent "a treatise on race relations" that raised the specter of "the exterminat[ion] of the white race" and was not a genuine "legal pronouncement." But black leaders like Arthur Clement, Jr., the Reverend Morris Glover of the Morris Brown A.M.E. Church, and several white Southerners privately praised Waring for his "courage and decency." A survey by the *News and Courier* of blacks in rural Clarendon County suggested that they favored keeping the schools as they were, but the newspaper also published a letter from Arthur Clement asserting that "Any local system that denies me the opportunity to participate in a cultural benefit at Dock Street Theatre, that denies me the aesthetic exposure at the Gibbes Art Gallery or keeps me out of a restroom at a city owned building on Marion Square is doomed to failure."[7]

Morrison, Blacks, and the Korean War

Comfortable around Afro-Americans, Mayor Morrison quickly realized they had again become an important force in Charleston politics. Blacks were added to the police force, he appointed some to other city jobs, and when country blacks displaced by mechanization moved into Charleston's eastside Wards 9 through 12 and white flight to the suburbs accelerated, Morrison carefully cultivated these potential new voters. In the 1951 mayoral contest it was suggested that the mayor fostered black support by winking at black gambling, liquor, and prostitution rackets, and Morrison's critics within the Democratic party sang: "Wild whiskey Bill of McClellanville . . . . Never worked and never will." It also was alleged that Morrison and his cronies were using public funds and property for personal aggrandizement, but with the help of black voters, Tom Stoney, and the *News and Courier*—a baroque coalition of supporters—he was reelected and began his second term in December.

On January 29, 1952, Judge Waring announced his retirement from the federal bench to the delight of most white South Carolinians. Waties and Elizabeth Waring immediately left for New York and returned to Charleston only once again.

The rising influence of Congressman Rivers on the House Armed Forces Committee and the outbreak of the Korean conflict were beginning to affect the economy of the Charleston area profoundly. The Naval Shipyard became a submarine repair yard and also assumed a major role in modernizing World War II surface craft. After an expenditure of $20 million, the Charleston Air Force Base in the north area was reactivated. Dedicated in November 1953, it became a vital link in the Military Air Transport Service (MATS), home base to thirty C–5 transports, the world's largest aircraft. The following January the U.S. Navy acquired a 5,219-acre tract for expansion of the Naval Ammunition Depot.[8]

In the early 1950s for the first time in Charleston's history the prospective clients of prostitutes were rigidly segregated: of some twenty-two dives located primarily along Market Street, seventeen catered to white men while five catered only to black males. The number of prostitutes, the openness with which they practiced their profession and the rising venereal-disease rate alarmed navy officials, and federal investigators once more charged that city officials were soft on vice. Embarrassed, the easygoing Morrison cooperated with military officials and gradually drove the prostitutes out of downtown Charleston into the more tolerant atmosphere of the county and the north area where they were closer to the naval facilities.

Mayor Morrison continued the Charleston tradition of enthusiastically supporting public playgrounds, believing they reduced juvenile delinquency. A member of the National Recreation Society observed: "The recreational program in the city of Charleston is one of the finest . . . in the entire southeast."

People who were not Southerners—especially Midwesterners who had made a lot of money during World War II—were buying restored houses below Calhoun Street, and the proportion of the population below Calhoun who were not native Charlestonians began to increase. At first such people were a tiny minority, but their numbers steadily increased for thirty-five years: they were often people who were used to voting Republican.

In 1951 the inexpensive and efficient window air conditioner came on the market, and on June 19, 1953, Charleston's first television station, WCSC–TV, established by John M. Rivers, broadcast its initial program when at 6:30 P.M. announcer Charlie Hall spoke the words: "Channel Five is now alive." Cotesworth Pinckney Means served as master of ceremonies and there were appearances by former Mayor Stoney and the Society for the Preservation of Spirituals, some of the same persons who had hosted the show when WCSC–Radio first went on the air twenty-three years earlier. Now these Charlestonians living south of Calhoun Street could enjoy cool air in their antebellum drawing rooms while viewing the flickering images on their newly acquired television sets, which also were contributing to the homogenization and privatization of American life.

Through the University of South Carolina Press, the Charleston Museum published one of the first American state ornithologies, and one of the most comprehensive, *South Carolina Bird Life* (1949) by Alexander Sprunt, Jr., and E. Burnham Chamberlain. The director of the museum, E. Milby Burton, was the author of important studies of the work of the city's antebellum cabinetmakers and silversmiths, and in the 1950s the Charleston Museum acquired for maintenance and exhibit the Heyward-Washington House and the Joseph Manigault House. But the museum like the Gibbes Art Gallery remained grossly underfunded. Only when the Carolina Art Association closed the gallery in 1953 and threatened to haul off its private collection did the city assume some maintenance costs and the physical upkeep of the building. Competition for city revenues persisted during the mid-1950s. Cost for the care of the city's indigent ill was lessened when the Medical College of South Carolina, which through federal grants was enjoying tremendous growth and soon achieved university status, assumed the medical care of the poor.[9]

In 1954 there was an effort to produce *Porgy* in Charleston, but local blacks, led by Mrs. R. L. Fields and Arthur Clement, Jr., refused to perform for a segregated audience and the show was canceled. During the month of May the U.S. Supreme Court reversed the decision in *Briggs v. Elliott* and accepted Judge Waring's learned dissent in the case as the basis for their unanimous opinion in *Brown v. the Board of Education of Topeka*, which declared that separate but equal facilities were inherently unequal. In the *News and Courier* Tom Waring bitterly assailed the *Brown* decision:"It can be carried out only by an army, dispatched into South Carolina from the outside." Both Governor Byrnes and his predecessor George Bell Timmerman, Jr., adopted a policy of massive resistance to the first *Brown* decision and *Brown II* (May 31, 1955).

Early in November 1954 more than 500 members of the NAACP gathered at a black elementary school in Charleston for a testimonial dinner honoring Judge and Mrs. Waring who, while in the city, stayed with Ruby and A. T. Cornwell. After the banquet Waring left South Carolina forever.[10]

Congressman Rivers was in Charleston on April 11, 1955, for the dedication ceremonies of yet another military installation, a $3 million Electric-Electronics building at the shipyard, the first major construction project there since 1945. With the recent addition of various transport, carrier, and fighter wings and squadrons, the Charleston Air Force Base was nearing its maximum capacity. But also that year, on June 15, a multi-million-dollar fire destroyed the Tidewater Terminals on Concord Street and two persons perished; in October the creosote tanker *Fort Fetterman* sideswiped the western bascule of the Ashley River Bridge knocking the twisted span into the channel and blocking what was then "the state's busiest traffic artery."

Mayor Morrison was elected to an unprecedented third term in 1955, in a contest "notable for its lethargy," one commentator observed. Charges of financial mismanagement and criticism of Morrison as a "do-nothing" mayor continued to plague the administration despite the fact that during his years in office the position of mayor became a full-time job. As in other urban areas of the state, the number of aldermen was reduced and Charleston's twenty-four City Council members were cut to twelve at-large aldermen. This was important for keeping the Broad Street establishment in power in view of the continuing white flight to the suburbs and the increasing political assertiveness of a black population approaching 50 percent within the city. At-large aldermen represented the various city wards but did not necessarily have to reside in those wards. Henceforth the mayor could hand-pick his slate of candidates and if half lived below Broad Street and none came from the primarily black areas of the city, this was perfectly legal.

The mayor promoted tourism and city beautification with the support of a highly regarded alderman, Alfred Halsey, and was instrumental in developing the multi-million-dollar Bushy Park project in Charleston County, which subsequently developed into a major industrial center. Morrison worked closely with the State Ports Authority (SPA) which began vigorously touting South Carolina's import-export facilities in the mid-1950s and making port improvements at Charleston, Georgetown, and Port Royal. After the legislature voted the agency $21 million in February 1957, the SPA purchased for $1,500,000 from the Southern Railway 137 acres of waterfront property in Charleston along the Cooper River, which included a banana pier leased by the United Fruit Company and a coal tipple with trackage. Another twenty-five acres adjacent to the Columbus Street Terminal were acquired for $622,235 from the Atlantic Coast Line Railroad. In March the SPA purchased Castle Pinckney from the U.S. General Services Administration for the bargain price of $12,026, and in September the agency bought seventeen acres of land, dock, and dockside trackage from the Seaboard Air Line Rail Road for $147,975.[11]

By the late 1950s no racial integration had taken place in the public schools of South Carolina despite the decision of the Supreme Court in *Brown v. the Board of Education of Topeka* and *Brown II.* The *News and Courier* persisted in its bitter denunciation of the decisions and the NAACP, which was pushing for implementation of the rulings. The paper's editor, Tom Waring, was now assisted by Anthony Harrigan, grandson of a well-known Irish vaudevillian of the New York stage, and Frank Gilbreth, also of New York and author of *Cheaper by the Dozen,* who was married to publisher Peter Manigault's sister. Gilbreth wrote for the *News and Courier* under the nom de plume Ashley Cooper.

In June 1956 Septima Clark was fired from her teaching post in the Charleston public schools. Now in her late fifties, Ms. Clark lost not only her job but also her retirement pension from the public school system of South Carolina after teaching in it for nearly four decades. Both whites and blacks had resented her interracial activities as an officer in the local NAACP, the YWCA, and other civic agencies, and this was a major factor in her dismissal. Almost immediately following her termination, she volunteered to conduct workshops and citizenship schools and programs for adult illiterates on John's Island. The following March, Tom Waring editorialized: "We see Red when the NAACP is mentioned . . . because we know of the long Red-front records of [its] leaders" who are in "cahoots" with the federal government "to put across ideals as foreign to American principles as Marxism . . . or Hitler's doctrines." Waring told the Reverend John B. Morris that if pushed too far by integrationists he would fight: "If it were necessary to use machine guns, I'd use them." In the *News and Courier* of September 27, 1957, Waring hinted at disunion as a solution: ". . . the day may not be far away" when "homemade bombs may be hurled in the streets" because "the spirit of rebellion never dies." Waring's views received national notoriety when, in *An Epitaph for Dixie,* Harry Ashmore wrote that the *News and Courier* under the editorial direction of Tom Waring "naturally has no scruples about rejecting a decision of the United States Supreme Court, or an act of Congress; it believes, as it always has, in aristocracy not democracy, and it has no apologies to offer for the incident at Fort Sumter."[12]

J. Palmer Gaillard

In 1957 the *News and Courier,* which had supported Mayor Morrison for over a decade, released audits that revealed that the city ran deficits in 1955 and 1956 of $304,000 and $493,000 and that the mayor had put persons on the municipal payroll for whom the City Council had not budgeted. City employees began to come forward complaining that their equipment was antiquated or inadequate. One joke circulated that a city policeman witnessed a mugging and went after the culprit in a patrol car, but the mugger outran the automobile! The fiscal condition of the city alarmed some businessmen and politicians, especially Alderman J. Palmer Gaillard, whose grandfather had been mayor of Charleston nearly a hundred years before. On Thanksgiving weekend, 1958, he received a call from Tom Stoney, who still wielded considerable power in Charleston politics: "If you'll get in that Mayor's race I'll support you," Stoney told him. Gaillard, who served as a navy pilot in World War II and afterward established a lumber business, entered politics as a Morrison supporter. An Episcopalian, he belonged to the best clubs, including the St. Cecilia Society.

It was an important decision for Gaillard and he consulted other politicos, businessmen, and attorneys like Kenneth Rentiers, Henry Smyth, Allen Legare, local millionaire Huger Sinkler, and Gedney Howe, who had served as city solicitor from 1946 to 1956. Howe was unique as a white champion of labor causes and racial equality, and because of his influence with Charleston's black and white leaders he remained a powerful figure in city politics until his death in the early 1980s. These "movers and shakers" convinced Gaillard that, with their support and Stoney's, he could win and he formally entered the race for mayor in January 1959. Mayor Morrison and the other alderman gave Gaillard "the cold shoulder" at City Council meetings for the next six months where he felt like "the bastard at the family reunion."

The local military-industrial complex grew with Congressman Rivers's seniority on the Armed Services Committee. The Berkeley County native and local resident, elected first to Congress in 1940, was subsequently returned sixteen times. In January 1959 the Mine Warfare School was transferred from Yorktown to Charleston and the new berths for twenty-five ships and twenty smaller craft and piers and shore facilities for the Atlantic Mine Force were dedicated at the Naval Base. Work also got underway near Goose Creek on a $10 million Naval Weapons Annex soon to be the sole facility on the East Coast for assembling, repairing, and maintaining for quick access Polaris missiles for the navy's new ballistic missile submarines.

By the spring Gaillard put together an all-white ticket of new faces—young and old, male and female—and launched an aggressive, well-financed race, the first in the city's history to exploit television. Using the slogan "We Need a Change," he charged Morrison with financial mismanagement and a dictatorial style that had permitted the city and its physical facilities to deteriorate, and several days before the election, asking where Morrison had been during World War II, Gaillard responded: "down at city hall working one-half day and drinking the best bourbon in the city."

Morrison, who was ill, ran a lackluster campaign, relying on a heavy turnout of black voters and simply contending that the city's finances were better than they had ever been.

Two days before the June 9 primary the *News and Courier* declared that "it was time for a change" and threw its support to Gaillard. Besides Stoney, ex-Mayor Edward Wehman also endorsed Gaillard, who won the primary by 445 votes, but most of the black vote went to Morrison. Ten members of his City Council slate were elected with him; the two "Morrison-men" elected, Vincent Sottile and Robert E. Hollings, soon became part of the Gaillard "team."

A month to the day after the mayoral primary, on July 9, Hurricane Cindy, a storm of barely hurricane intensity, came ashore some twenty-eight miles north of Charleston near McClellanville, felling trees, damaging roofs, and knocking out power. On September 29 Hurricane Gracie, with winds up to 140 miles per hour, lashed the South Carolina lowcountry from Beaufort to Charleston, causing eleven deaths and millions of dollars in damages.

Palmer Gaillard faced no opposition in the general election in November and he took the oath of mayor of Charleston in December 1959.[13]

❦ 2. 1959–1975: " . . . the smell of the Low Country"

Desegregation

At the beginning of the decade of the 1960s Charleston was a city of thoroughly segregated neighborhoods, transportation systems, public schools, colleges and parks, churches, theaters, restaurants, and even shopping districts. Afro-Americans were expected to shop on King Street north of Calhoun Street, while whites shopped to the south. Even when the city's brown elite occasionally patronized the better stores south of Calhoun, they were not permitted to try on shoes and certain articles of clothing. Then in early 1960 the Carolina Student Movement Association led by Afro-American students at Claflin College and South Carolina State College launched sit-ins across South Carolina. Through the *News and Courier* Tom Waring advised law officers to use "the whip, the rope, the knout, gun or anything else" to protect private property and to preserve the public order against these integrationists who were part of "a worldwide conspiracy." But already legal challenges to Charleston's segregated society were in the courts and others soon followed.

The first desegregation suit to reach Mayor Gaillard's desk was initiated during the previous administration by J. Arthur Brown, president of the local NAACP. It asked for integration of the city's golf course. Some members of the white community warned Gaillard that a decision for the black plaintiffs would ignite a "powder keg," but after talking with city attorneys Gaillard concluded "that the only legally acceptable thing . . . to do was to integrate," and during the latter part of 1960 the Charleston Municipal Golf Course was officially opened to both blacks and whites. It was the first integrated municipal facility in South Carolina. In the late fall of 1960 the courts ended the segregated waiting room of Charleston's airport terminal and the following year desegregated bus and train depots, parks, playgrounds, library, and restaurants, while Tom Waring blasted integrationists as "the apostles of race mongrelization and socialism."[14]

Economic Growth

For the second year in a row a hurricane threatened Charleston when Donna passed northeastward off the South Carolina coast on September 11. A tornado was spotted around 2:00 P.M. at the Ben Sawyer Bridge over the intracoastal waterway and it moved westward for about eight miles, demolishing several buildings until disappearing at the St. Andrews Shopping Center.

Appropriations for a federal interstate highway system during the administration of President Eisenhower answered the city's long-held dream of a corridor linking it to the west when I-26 terminated at Charleston. The flow of traffic into the city over the East Coast's major north-south route, Highway 17, was facilitated by the opening of the new eastbound bridge over the Ashley River on New Year's Day 1961, and five years later with the completion of the second Cooper River Bridge, which was twice as wide as the older Grace Memorial Bridge. These new arteries into Charleston nourished the growing business of tourism, which in turn spurred the local tradition of the open sale of whiskey and gin despite state legislation prohibiting it. The celebration of the Civil War Centennial locally—the "firing" on the *Star of the West* once more by Citadel cadets in April 1961 and the issuing of a postage stamp at Charleston commemorating the bombardment of Fort Sumter—drew national attention and visitors. The future of primary tourist attractions like Forts Moultrie and Sumter was assured when the state transferred over fourteen acres of Fort Moultrie on Sullivan's Island to the National Park Service to establish a headquarters to oversee both fortifications. In 1962 about 1.7 million visitors spent $25 million locally.

During the early 1960s the State Ports Authority received an appropriation of $22 million and continued to purchase additional waterfront property and to enlarge its berthing and storage facilities at the Columbus Street Terminal, the Union Pier Terminal, and the North Charleston Terminal. At year's end 1963 the SPA announced that the cargo handled at state docks had increased from 47,825 tons in 1947 to 1,057,020 tons in 1963 and that Charleston was linked to 100 major ports worldwide by eighty-eight steamship lines. The civilian and military traffic through the port was an "industry" in itself, channeling $600 million annually into the state's economy, which represented 12 percent of the net state product. To provide a navigational guide for the growing harbor traffic, a fifteen-story, 165-foot-high lighthouse was built on Sullivan's Island at a cost of $276,000. When the 70-million-candlepower light was put into operation on June 15, 1962, it was the most powerful lighthouse in the Western hemisphere.[15]

The Charleston Movement

Despite the desegregation of public facilities, Afro-American leaders in Charleston believed that the city's blacks still lacked equal opportunities and fair treatment in public and private employment. Meanwhile the *News and Courier* continued its denunciation of integrationists although editors, newspaper men, and civil rights activists locally and nationwide criticized Tom Waring's fulminations. Charles Viele, a reporter for the *News and Courier*, described Waring in December 1961 as "totally out of touch . . . with reality" and interested only in "the preservation of all things from old houses to the racial status quo." Mrs. Alice Spearman, director of the South Carolina Council on Human Relations, asserted that Waring and his paper had a chilling effect on free expression, and Harold Fleming, an executive director of the Southern Regional Council, characterized Waring's editorials as "mean spirited and punitive." But in September 1962 when Andrew McDowd Secrest, the white editor and publisher of the liberal weekly in Cheraw, South Carolina, the *Chronicle,* attended a civil rights committee meeting in Charleston, he concluded that the racial situation there was "much better than its newspaper would indicate." He found that the police force employed Afro-Americans and that the public facilities were desegregated, "though custom still largely keeps the races apart," and recently merchants on King Street had hired blacks in laboring as well as white-collar jobs.

In January 1963 outgoing Governor Ernest F. Hollings, a Charlestonian who initially vigorously opposed school desegregation, helped smooth the way for the admittance to Clemson College of Harvey B. Gantt, the nineteen-year-old son of a black employee at the Charleston Naval Yard whose attorney was the Afro-American and Charlestonian J. Arthur Brown. On January 28 Gantt entered Clemson, the first time a black had attended a previously all-white institution in South Carolina since the era of Reconstruction.

Gantt's victory encouraged leaders of "the Charleston Movement," civil rights activists like the Reverend James G. Blake, Marjorie Amos, Herbert Fielding, the Reverend I. D. Newman, the Reverend B. J. Glover, the Reverend Fred Dawson, Esau Jenkins, J. Arthur Brown, Bernice Robinson, and Septima Clark, and in June and July 1963 they led hundreds of local blacks and members of the Carolina Student Movement Association into the streets of Charleston. Septima Clark later recalled "in '63 the NAACP spent about $10,000 for two months that summer getting young people to march . . . and . . . sing . . . . They wanted jobs." They marched to integrate lunch counters, boycotted retailers who would not serve them, demonstrated for equal employment opportunities—and Martin Luther King, Jr., came to Charleston to lead a sit-in.

Mayor Gaillard remembered 1963 as an especially "tough" year for him. "Our biggest problems were not with the blacks . . . but . . . with whites." The owner of the local theaters and a powerful politico demanded an ordinance prohibiting blacks from attending; one caller simply told Gaillard, "shoot the bastards." On

A Charleston policeman oversees orderly demonstrators during the sit-ins and boycotts of 1963. *Courtesy of the Black Charleston Photo Collection, College of Charleston Library, Charleston, S.C.*

the other hand, a member of the old elite who lived on South Battery, Mrs. Eleanor Pringle Hart, argued in the *News and Courier* in early June that Charleston should "once again lead the South in a matter of principle," this time by lowering racial barriers, and she concluded that blacks were justified in their quest "for self-determination."

Despite harassment of the demonstrators by die-hard segregationists, the peaceful protests continued. Black leaders acknowledged that Police Chief William F. Kelly was courteous and restrained in maintaining law and order in the streets and in making arrests. Tough-minded but legalistic, Mayor Gaillard at first saw "no need" for a biracial committee as the demonstrations continued. But by early July racial tensions had escalated to the point where Gaillard and members of the City Council believed that further "demonstrations . . . could lead to a serious situation" and on July 5 they were granted a court order temporarily restraining black leaders from directing disorderly demonstrations. The defendants in the court action were the NAACP, I. DeQuincy Newman, state field secretary; a white divinity student, Douglas Parks; and twelve black leaders: J. Arthur Brown, state president of the NAACP; F. O. Pharr, president of the Charleston chapter, NAACP; James G. Black, national youth director, NAACP; also F. D. Dawson, B. J. Cooper, Herbert U. Fielding, Esau Jenkins, N. E. Blake, Robert A. Taylor, Jr., Christopher Gadsden Jr., George Kline, and B. J. Glover. A hearing was set for July 16 before the judge of the Ninth Circuit Court.

The number of incidents increased. On July 12 twenty-eight young blacks were arrested when some of them participated in a "wade-in" at the all-white pool on George Street during which the pool manager and policewoman Lois Ray suffered minor injuries; others were apprehended for using facilities at Hampton Park, and several days later black youths staged a "play-in" at three city playgrounds that were reserved for whites only. Then, suddenly, like heat lightning, violence flashed across the city.

On Tuesday, July 16, around 11:00 P.M. some 500 black demonstrators singing freedom songs marched from King Street into Columbus Street where they assembled before the *News and Courier* building to protest the editorial policies of the paper and to support the Charleston Movement. Squads of city and county police arrived and began quietly arresting the demonstrators, who went peaceably until a brick struck a police officer knocking him to his knees. Several other officers were hit by rocks, demonstrators scuffled with police, and one black man was hauled away shouting, "I'll kill you, I'll kill you." Two city fire engines quickly arrived, which threatened the use of fire hoses, and the crowd dispersed. Rioting charges were filed against sixty-eight of those arrested.

At the request of Mayor Gaillard, Governor Donald S. Russell rushed a force of 130 highway patrolmen to the city to assist the local police. Despite the threat from some 1,000 blacks who crowded into the Tabernacle Baptist Church on St. Philip's Street on July 17 vowing to continue demonstrations against racial segregation, the city remained quiet, tense, and well policed. For several days Mayor Gaillard had been huddling frequently with the city's white business leaders seeking ways to defuse the potentially explosive situation. Antisegregation marches continued on July 19 as Gaillard met with representatives of the black community, after which a local leader of the NAACP and the Charleston Movement, the Reverend Benjamin J. Glover, reported that the "atmosphere seemed favorable for some settlement." Within a few days eighty-seven small businessmen promised to provide equal employment opportunities, to desegregate customer services, to use courtesy titles in conversation with black customers and employees and in business correspondence, to serve each customer in turn regardless of race, to allow Afro-American customers to try on articles of clothing, to require the same wearing attire for both black and white sales personnel, and to provide equal pay for equal work for all employees. This announcement prompted leaders of the Charleston Movement to call off further demonstrations and to end the local boycotts, and in September Mayor Gaillard supported the formation of a biracial committee.

One of the first acts of the committee was to appeal to Tom Waring to stop publishing his inflamatory editorials while city officials and civil rights leaders were trying to settle sensitive racial issues. But he refused, and during that long, hot summer when Martin Luther King, Jr., led a march on Washington, D.C., in support of pending civil rights legislation, Waring kept up his criticism of the Charleston Movement and King himself, whom he called an organizer of "demonstrations in terror tactics . . . ."

During the summer Bishop Francis R. Reb of Charleston announced that the local Catholic schools would integrate in September, and discussions got underway between local public school officials on the same matter after the federal courts ordered the public schools of the peninsula city to admit blacks. In September 1963, without violence or publicity, Charleston's Rivers High became the first integrated public high school in South Carolina. Shortly thereafter the city's two undergraduate colleges, the private College of Charleston and the state-supported Citadel, admitted blacks for the first time. Heretofore, Afro-Americans had to attend college in Denmark, Orangeburg, Sumter, and Columbia, or go out-of-state. The first black cadet graduated from the Citadel in 1970, the same year that the College of Charleston became part of the state system of higher education and a massive infusion of state money and subsequently federal dollars ended the institution's chronic financial difficulties.[16]

On September 20, 1963, the Church of St. Luke and St. Paul, Radcliffeborough, became the Cathedral Church of the Diocese of South Carolina as the result of a written agreement between the bishop and the parish. Now the Anglicans finally had a cathedral. The church, which had a seating capacity of 1,200, the largest in the diocese, became the official church of the diocese and the See for the bishop of the diocese, Gray Temple at the time, who made it clear that blacks were welcome at his cathedral.

J. Palmer Gaillard was reelected unopposed in 1963 and soon had the pleasure of announcing that on January 1, 1964, the city made the final payment on its once enormous bonded debt.

Septima Clark, who was said to have had a strong philosophical influence on Martin Luther King, Jr., accompanied him at his request to Oslo, Norway, in 1964 where he received the Nobel Peace Prize. She continued to reside in Charleston, declaring that she loved her "old house" at number 17 Henrietta Street and "I love Charleston, too . . . . How can anyone born and brought up in Charleston not love that wonderful old city," she observed; "how can anyone who has been brought up with the smell of the Low Country in his nostrils ever stay away from it long?"

The Military-Industrial Complex

Charleston's defense industry continued to track the rising political influence of Congressman Mendel Rivers. During the early 1960s the secretary of the navy authorized the establishment of the U.S. Navy Fleet Ballistic Missile Submarine Training Center (FBMSTC) at the Charleston Naval Base, and on September 24, 1963, the FBMSTC was dedicated there. The following April a $16,500,000 dry dock for Polaris submarines and other nuclear-powered ships was completed at the Charleston Naval Ship Yard. Between 1960 and 1966 the number of military personnel stationed in or near Charleston increased from 13,500 to 21,500 and the number of civilians employed by the Armed Forces jumped from 6,500 to 11,500.

Rivers assumed the chairmanship of the House Armed Services Committee in 1965, and the defense buildup for the Vietnam War made him one of the most powerful men in Washington, D.C. During 1965 alone five ships were commissioned at the Charleston Naval Ship Yard; by early 1966 ten C–141 Starlifters were located at the Charleston Air Force Base in support of the escalation of the war for which Rivers became an outspoken advocate. The tall, white-maned, rough-talking, hard-driving, and hard-drinking lawmaker, who liked to pack a pearl-handled derringer while in Washington, was an unabashed champion of the Armed Forces, especially for the First Congressional District. His slogan was "Rivers Delivers" and by the late 1960s the Charleston area was a microcosm of what President Eisenhower had called the military-industrial complex. Because of the number of Armed Services installations in and around Charleston, one congressman quipped: "If Rivers puts anything else [down there] the whole place will sink . . . ."

Eighty-six commissioned ships with complements of 19,738 officers and men called Charleston home port by 1969; supporting them were more than 11,000 civilian employees. A substantial symbiotic community of industries were attracted to Charleston, like a Dupont plant that manufactured nuclear weapons or parts, Lockheed, McDonnell-Douglas, and General Electric. By the 1970s this military-industrial complex had an annual payroll of $318 million, about 40 percent of the payroll of the Charleston area, and piped about $200 million yearly into local businesses. The new, well-paying jobs created by the burgeoning military and civilian sectors were unavailable to many blacks, due in part to traditional white social attitudes, but also because of their lack of education. Pockets of poverty and high crime rates persisted in black neighborhoods. Like some of his predecessors Mayor Gaillard called the problem of the city's slums one of the "most serious [and] most difficult facing the city." During his administration the city upgraded housing standards and codes and obtained federal funds to build over 350 units for low-income families, but at the same time the crime rate soared. In Charleston and Berkeley counties in 1965, for instance, there were 1,710 offenses per 100,000 persons, substantially higher than the rate for South Carolina or the nation.[17]

" . . . a new spirit is abroad"

After the passage of the Federal Voting Rights Act of 1965, black Charlestonians registered to vote in even greater numbers, and when Gaillard decided to run for a third term in 1967 he selected several blacks to run on his slate for City Council. The local Republican party put forward its first candidate since the era of Reconstruction and the first woman ever to run for the office, Julia Ravenel Daugherty. Like Gaillard, she was an "old Charlestonian," which meant that she could trace her local ancestry to the eighteenth century, lived in a "blue-stocking ward," and be-

longed to the Episcopal church. But Gaillard swept the general
election with 5,558 ballots to Daugherty's 794. Most of his slate
was victorious, which included a hand-picked black candidate, St.
Julian Devine, the first black since Reconstruction to sit on the
City Council. Members of the white and black community, however, were divided on the election of Devine, a successful businessman and member of the local Afro-American elite.

Gaillard believed that his greatest accomplishment as mayor
during his first three terms was more than tripling the size of the
city. From 1849 to 1959 the city boundaries remained the same,
but from 1959 to 1969 Charleston grew from five to eighteen
square miles through mergers and annexations that encompassed
the burgeoning suburbs and growing shopping malls west of the
Ashley River. Already heavily populated by white ethnic groups
who had left the city for the countryside years before, the area
was adding people daily who were new to the region and employed in the expanding north area. Through such an annexation
program Gaillard added thousands of white voters loyal to the
city administration—thereby diminishing the effect of black vot-

Mayor J. Palmer Gaillard, seated center, with members of the City Council, including St. Julian Devine, the first Afro-American elected to the council since the
era of Reconstruction. *Courtesy of the City Council of Charleston, Collection of City
Hall, Charleston, S.C.*

ers in municipal elections—while he "packed" the City Council with friendly black aldermen under the at-large system.

For CBS News, Charles Kuralt reported from Charleston on the funeral of Waties Waring at Magnolia Cemetery, January 17, 1968, observing: "There are few white mourners here today. Many people have paid a price for their civil rights advocacy, a United States District Judge among them." Ruby Cornwell in a letter to the *News and Courier* wrote: "The Judge comes home . . . . We love you. We are honored to have you rest in our midst." Less than a dozen whites attended the funeral, but some 200 blacks were present at graveside.

When the black power movement led by young, more aggressive-minded blacks who had broken with the moderate approach of the Southern Christian Leadership Conference (SCLC) began sweeping sections of the country, Martin Luther King, Jr., returned to Charleston and addressed the city's Afro-American leadership at County Hall. He spoke for peaceful demonstrations and against the violence sanctioned by Stokely Carmichael and Rap Brown, calling on Charleston's black activists to help build the community rather than tear it down.[18]

On the surface, black-white relations in Charleston appeared good, and local boosters called race relations in the city "the best in the United States." Then suddenly, in March 1969, slightly less than a year after King's assassination, some 400 predominantly black female workers at the Medical College Hospital and the Charleston County Hospital struck for better working conditions and wages, which they wanted raised to $1.30 per hour, promotion of more blacks, recognition of their union, and bargaining through its leaders. The strike began when Mary Moultrie, president of Local 1199B of the Hospital and Nursing Home Workers of the AFL–CIO, and eleven other union leaders were fired by the Medical College. The Southern Christian Leadership Conference announced support for the strike. Mayor Gaillard, who was asked by union leaders to intervene, urged moderation and an early end to the dispute. Picket lines went up and the mayor ordered the police to keep order. The *New York Times* observed: "the strike of hospital workers in Charleston has become the country's tensest civil rights struggle" and the newspaper praised the coalition supporting the strike as "rightly angered by the systematic exploitation public agencies were practicing against underpaid black workers."

The new Police Chief John F. Conroy, an ex-Marine major with graduate work in criminology, earned the name "Mr. Cool" for his skill in handling the potentially explosive strike. In April Governor Robert E. McNair dispatched 5,000 heavily armed National Guard troops to Charleston and a curfew began.

Negotiations floundered and an already tense situation worsened. Local black clergymen like the Reverend Henry Grant and white Catholic priests took to the streets with thousands of black Charlestonians to demonstrate support for the strikers. Joining them were Ralph Abernathy and Andrew Young of the SCLC and Coretta Scott King, widow of the slain civil rights leader, who addressed a capacity crowd at the Emmanuel A.M.E. Church. The morale and resolve of the workers remained high. At "Union Hall, a frame building near the waterfront," one reporter observed, "there was constant activity, the smell of soul food, the sound of soul music, women waiting patiently . . . and children sleeping on benches." Over 900 demonstrators were arrested, including Ralph Abernathy who violated the prohibition against night marches. His detention touched off the most violent incident of the more than 100-day strike, a bottle- and rock-throwing barrage that injured several policemen.

As the dispute continued it gave South Carolina a bad image nationally and threatened its credit rating. The guardsmen and the curfew cost the state over $500,000 monthly. Meanwhile, negotiations continued between the governor's office, Mayor Gaillard, and the Medical College, and William Saunders, a local, militant black leader. While in the army Saunders fought in some of the bloodiest battles in Korea and later remembered angrily that upon discharge he returned home on a segregated bus. A settlement was reached in July, but only after high officials in the White House intervened. Federal mediators worked out the details, which were beneficial to the workers. A representative of the hospital employees observed: "We gained recognition as human beings . . . . It accomplished a lot for the poor people of the city . . . ."

The strike had divided the white community. There had been fear abroad in Charleston during the dark nights of the curfew. Some were reminded of a much earlier era. The Charleston poetess Alice Cabiness wrote: "merchants lounging in doorways cursing ease, grouping angrily . . . / patrolling windows, counting guardsmen going by / Denmark Vesey smiles with pleasure from another century / black shadows on the empty streets undo the handshakes of my friends."

The Charleston *Evening Post* on July 21, 1969, summarized the significance of the events: "Important lessons have been learned this summer. The most important is . . . the growing power of [those] who have hitherto been . . . voiceless. . . . a new spirit is abroad, which has the power to disturb . . . institutions and customs which have remained on dead center for so long that most people have come to take them for granted."

Less than a year later, on Sunday, April 5, 1970, worship services in churches across the state marked the beginning of South Carolina's Tricentennial celebration. Speaking in Charleston in St. Philip's Church on April 18, Bishop Temple observed: "We meet in our 180th Convention of the Diocese of South Carolina in the 'Mother Church' of the Anglican Communion in South Carolina. St. Philip's Parish is celebrating its 300th Anniversary along with the Tricentennial of our State. . . . the Lord Bishop of London has come to us. I think it is the first time in our history we have had an official visit from London." In the evening a reception was held for the Right Reverend and Right Honourable Robert Wright Stopford, the Lord Bishop of London, and was followed by a diocesan dinner at the Sheraton-Fort Sumter Hotel in Charleston.[19]

In June the state funded as part of the Tricentennial a production of *Porgy and Bess,* which was performed by an almost exclusively black cast on the stage of the new Gaillard Auditorium accompanied by almost exclusively white musicians. The singers were local blacks, and their relatives turned out in large numbers to see and hear them. Audiences were completely integrated.

The civil rights movement during Mayor Gaillard's first three terms of office ended legal segregation, brought better jobs and working conditions, and partially integrated the city's public schools. As across the rest of the South, only the federal courts and federal dollars ended the inequities in black and white education in Charleston. The city's public schools, like those of most communities in South Carolina, were desegregated quietly and peacefully, yet by the 1970s Charleston's once all-white inner-city schools had become all-black. This was due, of course, to white flight to the suburbs and the historic penchant of the city's upper classes to send their offspring to private schools. In 1970 Charlestonian Herbert Fielding became the first Afro-American to be elected to the state House of Representatives since the 1880s and Lonnie Hamilton became the first black elected to the County Council. Yet for all the social, political, and economic gains by blacks, many still lacked equal opportunities for jobs and education and decent housing.

Gaillard's Fourth Term

When Mayor Gaillard ran for reelection in 1971 many Afro-Americans refused to support him. They believed that he represented the elite, white Broad Street establishment, which hand-picked for political office those blacks who were loyal to them and used tokenism to preserve the status quo. But Gaillard thought that his opponent in the Democratic primary, lawyer and developer William Ackerman, "Turned the blacks against me." It was a "nasty campaign," Gaillard recalled. The bitterness engendered between the two Democratic factions persisted for years. Charges and countercharges of vote buying and stealing reverberated on election day. The election results gave Gaillard a narrow victory of 7,655 to 7,564 votes, a difference of 91 ballots. After a recount reminiscent of the Grace-Stoney era, the local Democratic Executive Committee named Gaillard the winner.

The general election was also hotly contested. Arthur Ravenel, a well-to-do Republican and "old Charlestonian," put together a coalition ticket and ran on a former Gaillard slogan, "It's time for a change." The usual mud-slinging accompanied the race. Gaillard again won, this time by a 9,046-to-8,221 vote count, because the Democratic party was better organized and he had the endorsement of leading state and local politicos. In December, Gaillard began a fourth and unprecedented term as mayor.[20]

Even though Mendel Rivers, the architect of the military-industrial complex in the north area, died in 1970, the region continued to expand. That year five vessels were commissioned by the Charleston Naval Ship Yard, and activity at the Army Depot in support of the Vietnam War continued at a record pace. The phenomenal growth of the north area led the Gaillard administration on one occasion to attempt to annex it, but the effort failed when the Charleston government was rebuffed by residents and received little support from the downtown elite, one matron among them remarking, "They wouldn't even know who I was up there." In 1972 the city of North Charleston was incorporated, having a population initially of 21,500 and an area of 7.6 square miles. Within two years there were 11,566 civilians employed at the Naval Base and over 20,200 military personnel stationed there, drawing a combined annual gross payroll of $309,842,521.

Port activity also expanded rapidly and by 1971 Charleston had become the number-one containership port on the East Coast. A state-funded capital improvements program launched in 1971 and continuing through 1975 enabled the State Ports Authority to increase its handling of high-value cargo. Between 1967 and 1973, for instance, cargo volume jumped from 2,000,000 to 2,700,000 tons, an increase of 35 percent. By 1973 Charleston ranked twelfth in the nation in the value of general cargo handled. Local and state officials seeking to increase cruise-ship traffic through the port opened a $1,200,000 facility in October at the Union Pier Terminal to accommodate up to 800 passengers per cruise vessel.

Charleston's tourist industry boomed. Between 1970 and 1976 the number of visitors to Charleston increased 60 percent. By the mid-1970s over 3,400,000 tourists were spending $50 million locally. The aging, travel-minded, and affluent generation who had enjoyed the post-World War II prosperity came to see the refurbished forts, Moultrie and Sumter, the hundreds of houses restored by the Historic Charleston Foundation, and the restoration of the buildings of the college done through the dynamic leadership of its president, Theodore Stern. Turning from neighborhood to commercial restoration, the foundation helped sponsor the beautification of Broad Street and the rehabilitation of seedy and dingy downtown streets like East Bay and Market, the last of which in the 1960s was described as a street where "in one block in half an hour, and for less than $10 you could get a bowl of chili, a tattoo, and a social disease." By the early 1970s dives on these streets were being replaced by boutiques, restaurants, and inns. The old city was becoming something it had never been before—freshly painted, clean, and well-preserved, although the preservation movement itself fragmented in 1973 when the Save Charleston Foundation was formed to prevent the demolition of nineteenth-century warehouses on Meeting Street. The tourists came also to see the site of the original settlement at Albemarle Point, which the state purchased for $4.9 million from the Waring family in 1970, made into a state park, and named Charles Towne Landing.

Coretta Scott King praying with the demonstrators during the Hospital Strike, 1969. *Courtesy of the Black Charleston Photo Collection, College of Charleston Library, Charleston, S.C.*

The resort industry lured thousands more to the islands to the north of Charleston, Sullivan's Island and the Isle of Palms, and especially to the sea islands to the south of the city. In August 1971 an exclusive development got underway on Seabrook Island, which was to be patterned after Hilton Head, and in early 1974 the Kuwait Sheikdom bought Kiawah Island and planned a similar resort type of development of single-family dwellings, condominiums, tennis courts, and golf courses, a few of the amenities for vacation and retirement living.

Known as a penny-pincher, "Pamma" Gaillard nevertheless during his fourth term of office helped the city acquire Cypress Gardens, Charles Towne Landing, a new police station, and a sewer treatment system. By the early 1970s raw sewage no longer was dumped into the Ashley River. During Gaillard's terms in office the Medical University and, beginning in the mid-1960s, the Charleston County Hospital provided health care for the indigent. By the 1970s the city was served by eight hospitals with over 1,900 beds. Additional funds provided by the county government, bequests, and an expanded membership by the 1970s also finally provided the city with an art gallery appropriate to Charleston's cultural heritage in portrait painting and scenes from natural life.

The annexations during Gaillard's terms of office brought miles of new streets to maintain. By the mid-1970s the city had over 162 miles of streets, 160 paved, and fifteen square miles of roadway under construction. Now with black Charlestonians once again politically enfranchised and with substantial representation on the City Council, the streets of black neighborhoods became better maintained than ever before.

Gaillard resigned as mayor in August 1975 and soon accepted the position of deputy assistant secretary for the U.S. Navy for reserve affairs, an appointment arranged by the state's powerful Republican senator, Strom Thurmond. After sixteen years in office, longer than any previous mayor, Gaillard recognized that it was time for him to step down in favor of "someone . . . young . . . with a fresh approach." The City Council promptly elected council member Arthur B. Schirmer as interim mayor.[21]

Gaillard left the city in far better fiscal shape than he found it, but a city decreasing in population and in business activity; indeed, by 1970 Charleston was no longer the largest metropolitan area in the state. Whereas in 1940 there had been 71,275 persons living in the old peninsula city, by the late 1970s only 40,000 resided there, about the same number as in 1850, and businesses followed the white flight to the suburbs. In 1940, for instance, 89 percent of the retail sales in Charleston County took place within the city of Charleston, but by 1976 such sales had fallen more than half, to 40 percent.

During the Morrison administration Charleston's Afro-Americans once again gained the right to vote, and during Gaillard's years in office they ended segregation in shops, schools, restaurants, theaters, transportation, and lodging. Thereafter their struggle was to be for equality without separation in social, economic, and political life.

❦ ## 3. 1975–1988: Integration

Joseph P. Riley, Jr.

After Gaillard resigned, influential Broad Street attorneys and businessmen like Gedney Howe and Hugh Lane, the bank executive, decided on a mayoral candidate who would bring the local Democratic party together, Joseph P. Riley, Jr. Riley also had support within the black community. He was genuinely concerned about the role of blacks in Charleston and they trusted him. Riley was quoted in the local press: "In the city of Charleston . . . black people have never had a piece of the action." He hoped to overcome their "alienation" from government and to involve young blacks, who "see most vividly the cruel contrast of our dual society."

Riley was born in Charleston in 1943 and attended local Catholic schools. His father, a wealthy real estate broker, was well connected with local politicos. Riley graduated from the Citadel and the University of South Carolina School of Law. In 1968 he was elected to the state legislature and then in 1975 a coalition of Gaillard and Ackerman lieutenants and key black leaders backed Riley for mayor. Winning broad support among Democrats in the primary, Riley faced Nancy Hawk, a serious candidate of the local Republican party, which had enjoyed a rebirth during the Goldwater presidential campaign of 1964, and two other contenders in the general election of December 9, 1975. Since the federal government had recently declared that Charleston's at-large-member plan for electing the City Council was illegal, it was the first municipal election in several decades in which city aldermen, now to be referred to as "councilmembers," would be elected according to the single-member plan. Now the citizens of predominately black districts in the city could elect their own representatives to the City Council, as could the burgeoning white population west of the Ashley, and therefore Riley was the first mayoral candidate in over twenty years to run without a formal "ticket" or slate. He captured 51 percent of the entire vote and 75 percent of the Afro-American ballots, beating his closest rival, Nancy Hawk, by 7,485 votes to 4,855. His good friend and raconteur Bill Regan, who became the city of Charleston corporation counsel, tells the story of the bishop of Charleston handing Riley an old envelope addressed to "The Next Irish Mayor." Inside was a message, written by the city's last Irish-Catholic mayor, John P. Grace. The message consisted of three words: "Get the Stoneys." Riley, however, avoided those bitter denunciations of the gentry, which once were the trademark of both Protestant and Catholic populists. He was not intimidated by the old aristocracy, but he was willing to compromise with them.

Only thirty-two years of age, Riley was the city's youngest mayor ever. In his inaugural address the five-foot-nine-inch-tall, boyish-looking mayor told Charlestonians that there would "be more blacks and more women in positions of authority," that his administration would fight crime, continue a vigorous annexation policy, preserve the Historic District, and rejuvenate business in downtown Charleston. He asked all Charlestonians to join with him "in a new age of tolerance, harmony, and creativity." Taking office with Riley were six black and six white, male and female councilmembers, a phenomenon resulting from the newly mandated single-member districts, which created an entirely new city politically.[22]

Mayor Riley moved quickly to heal centuries-old wounds by making Charleston's Afro-Americans feel that they were very much a part of the community. The city commissioned a portrait of Denmark Vesey and, since no likeness of him has survived, the artist painted Vesey facing an audience of blacks, his back to the contemporary viewer. In 1976 the portrait was hung in the Gaillard Municipal Auditorium and during the ceremony the mayor told the assemblage of 250 black and white citizens and city officials: "[T]his is . . . part of the effort . . . of the administration to see that parts of history heretofore forgotten are remembered . . . ." He asked his audience to remember Vesey as "a man of love . . . of compassion . . . "; and to treat the ceremony itself as a great victory for white and black Charlestonians "when we can come together so soon after a time of such great difficulty and look back to a very dark past and see someone as a hero, who gave his life so that men may be free." Bishop Frank M. Reid, Jr., of the A.M.E. Church responded in the same conciliatory spirit while subtly affirming Vesey's revolutionary aims: "We know who Denmark Vesey was and we know who we are. We know what he intended to do to them and we know what they did to him . . . . I say this is a creative moment for it recognizes that Vesey was . . . a liberator whom God had sent to set the people free from oppression."

Some white Charlestonians did not share the conciliatory spirit of Riley and Reid. Frank Gilbreth, the *News and Courier* columnist writing under the nom de plume Ashley Cooper, observed: "If black leaders in Charleston had searched for a thousand years, they could not have found a local black whose portrait would have been more offensive to many white people." Several letters-to-the-editor criticized the mayor and one person, apparently white, asserted: "If Vesey qualifies for such an honor, we should also hang the portraits of Hitler, Attila the Hun, Herod the murderer of babies . . . ." However, there were now Afro-American reporters on the staff of the *News and Courier,* and one of them put the matter in perspective: "Blacks—and understanding whites—are not honoring Vesey to upset their white neighbors. Most of us are interested in giving long overdue recognition to a man who is a true black hero. Many whites cannot appreciate black sentiments in this regard because of their tunneled vision of history, which to them has only white heroes . . . ." Shortly thereafter Vesey's house at 56 Bull Street, number 20 in his lifetime, was designated a National Historic Landmark, but efforts to name a public school after him failed.

During the mayoral campaign Riley promised to reverse the flow of businesses from downtown Charleston to the suburban shopping malls by revitalizing the central business district. To do this he planned to attract more tourists for longer periods of time by special events and to channel them downtown. In the tradition of Frank Dawson and George Williams, and of Mayors Courtenay, Grace, Stoney, and Maybank, Mayor Riley became one of Charleston's most determined boosters. At the heart of his plan for economic rejuvenation was the construction of a convention center and hotel complex of twelve stories, 431 rooms, 114 feet in height, costing $50 million, and financed by both public and private funds. It was to be located on a vacant lot in the central business district and in an area bounded by King, Beaufain, Meeting, and Hasell streets. The project called for the partial demolition of thirty-three deteriorating historic buildings, and the preservation and restoration of their façades. To Riley progress and preservation should march hand in hand.

The Historic Charleston Foundation supported Riley's concept, hoping it would rehabilitate King Street, which Francis Edmunds called the "weak, sick spine of Charleston," and approved the project with certain reservations. But the venerable Preservation Society, the Charleston Neighborhood Association, the Harleston Village Association, and the Save Historic Charleston Foundation, formed specifically to fight Riley's plans, launched a propaganda blitz and legal assault on the project. These preservationist groups condemned the proposed center as "incongruous" with the city's historic "ambience," destructive of valuable historic buildings, and they worried over the impact of growing numbers of tourists. Others simply resented the tourists and wished to return to quieter times and fewer visitors.[23]

Riley, however, vigorously pursued his plans to attract more tourists. In 1977 he helped bring both the Miss USA Pageant and Gian Carlo Menotti to Charleston. Menotti, the brilliant impresario who had founded the Festival of Two Worlds in Spoleto, Italy, in 1957, came to Charleston in the mid-1970s at the instigation of Countess Alicia Paolozzi, who had a home in Charleston and was a benefactor of the city. The Italian-born maestro was charmed by the eighteenth- and nineteenth-century dwellings and the atmosphere of the old city and wanted to bring the festival to Charleston. After negotiations between Menotti and a local coordinating committee broke down over arrangements and finances, Mayor Riley asked Theodore S. Stern, the energetic former president of the College of Charleston, to work out matters with Menotti, and in May 1977 the first Spoleto, USA, Festival was launched in Charleston, bringing to the city performing artists from around the world. "This bill of fare," *Newsweek* raved, "is like nothing else on the international scene, and Charleston is proud of it." The magazine also called the city a "Sleeping Beauty" and quoted Mayor Riley who "sees the Spoleto Festival as a chance to restore the city to its status in the 18th and 19th centuries . . . ."

This sister-celebration to the original Spoleto Festival supported by private and public funds is the most successful enterprise ever to boost the city and the arts. For two-and-one-half weeks in the late spring the city teems with established and emerging musicians, ballet dancers, actors and actresses, critics, hangers-on, and even royalty. One writer has observed: "The strains of Bach and Brahms waft over rooftops; street musicians perform spontaneously in public spaces; la dolce vita reigns after hours in bistros and at private parties."

After a black councilmember was excluded from the Hibernian Society's annual St. Patrick's Day bash in 1978, Riley refused to attend. The following year he personally escorted there the retired black insurance company executive and local civil rights leader, Arthur Clement, Jr. Once a Progressive Democrat and now a Republican, Clement wrote occasionally for the *News and Courier* and was the first black member of the Charleston Rotary Club, his sponsor being Tom Waring!

During the late 1970s Riley and the City Council bowed to complaints of downtown residents about the horse droppings in the streets, the result of horse-drawn tourist carriages, and required leather diapers for the animals. Otherwise, one local politico observed, strolling the streets of downtown Charleston was like walking through a minefield seeded with horse dung.

In April 1978 the cornerstone of the new Charleston Museum was lifted into place. The approximately 80,000-square-foot building, costing about $6 million to build and made possible by a bond issue approved by the voters, was under construction at the corner of John and Meeting streets. The following April, Museum staffers delighted in vacating their barnlike, leaky, deteriorating, drafty quarters on Rutledge Avenue for the handsome new building. The museum building burned a few years later and only its Corinthian columns stand today.

On September 5 Hurricane David brushed the South Carolina coast, causing about $10 million in damages, and two years later the Charleston area was again lucky when tropical storm Dennis turned inland before reaching the city.[24]

Joe Riley, Jr., was reelected unopposed in 1979 and he asked the aging Septima Clark to administer the oath of office at his second inauguration. The year before, the College of Charleston awarded her an honorary doctorate, the first Afro-American ever so honored. "The thing I'm proudest of," Riley has said, "is bringing together the black and white communities of Charleston." Those few white Charlestonians who found his policies toward blacks too accommodating nicknamed him "Little Black Joe."

Riley continued to use federal money to construct or renovate low-income housing, primarily for blacks, and during his administrations more than 500 housing units were rehabilitated, revitalizing the city's depressed east side.

Despite the tremendous gains locally in black-white relations, black Charlestonians resented the segregated school systems, and when the U.S. Justice Department filed suit against the

Charleston County School District in 1981, eight local Afro-American families soon joined the suit. Contending that it was desegregated, the district vigorously defended itself, spending $955,179 on legal fees over a period of seven years.

Litigation also delayed construction of Charleston's hotel-convention complex, and by 1980 the economy of downtown seemed to be moribund. All seven of the theaters that had operated there in the 1930s had moved with the crowds and the shops to the suburban malls.[25]

Ocean-borne tonnage through the Columbus Street Terminal and the North Charleston facility was increasing and the State Ports Authority successfully lobbied the General Assembly for the funds to build a third terminal in order to accommodate the increasing cargoes and to lure commerce to Charleston. Over the protests of environmentalists and after three years of construction costing $81 million, the Wando River Terminal just off the Cooper River and to the north of the city opened for business on October 5, 1981.

Federal spending in the Charleston metropolitan area continued at record levels. In November 1981 a U.S. House-Senate panel authorized $80,300,000 in military construction projects in South Carolina for fiscal year 1982, including projects at the Charleston Naval Station, Naval Weapons Station, Polaris Missile Facility, Charleston Naval Ship Yard, and the Charleston Air Force Base.

Mayor Riley inaugurated a policy of bringing in talented young people from outside the city to help run the various city departments that concerned some of the old aristocracy who believed that there was no longer a family feeling in the mayor's office. And Riley let no one forget his "spiritual kinship" with John P. Grace. A memorial to Mayor Grace created in 1923 was later relegated to the basement of City Hall, where it remained for over forty years until rescued by Mayor Riley, who held a special ceremony to hang the plaque in City Council chambers.

On April 14, 1982, Mayor Riley presided over another gathering in City Council chambers where, before a group of leading black and white citizens, he accepted a gift from the national NAACP of a bronze sculpture in honor of Judge J. Waties Waring and for his "passionate . . . pursuit of justice," despite "continuing personal and public harassment." Placing the sculpture in the southwest corner of the council room overlooking the federal

Members of the National Guard dispatched to Charleston by Governor McNair and the local police force who were ordered to maintain law and order at the intersection of St. Philip's and Radcliffe streets, 1969. *Courtesy of the Black Charleston Photo Collection, College of Charleston Library, Charleston, S.C.*

courthouse, Riley called Waring a man of "uncommon achievement," remarking privately, "It's time to bring him home."[26]

That same year for undetermined reasons and under mysterious circumstances, "Mr. Cool," Charleston's highly esteemed Chief of Police John F. Conroy, committed suicide with his service revolver at his home in Ansonborough. Following a nationwide search, Mayor Riley appointed Reuben Greenberg as Conroy's replacement in April 1982. The eccentric but remarkably effective Greenberg, a black Jew with two Master's degrees from the University of California at Berkeley, attracted the attention of television networks.

After a seven-year fight preservationists failed in their court suit to block construction of the hotel-convention complex, which had been scaled down in size. The hotel, for instance, would contain only 150 rooms. Work began on the project when a giant piledriver pounded into the ground the first of 1,000 eighty-two-foot-long, steel-and-concrete supports on May 27, 1982.

In 1983 Mayor Riley was reelected unopposed. His leadership was both praised and assailed. Although he projected an unassuming nature, Riley has been described by friends and foes alike as "hard-driving and aggressive . . . stubborn, relentless and ambitious." His was not the Charleston style.

The construction of Charleston Place, the hotel-convention center, ignited a building boom in downtown Charleston. The value of new construction in the central business district jumped to over $50 million annually, five times what it averaged in the early 1970s, and many specialty shops, good restaurants, and elegant small inns opened. The three keys to the city's prosperity were federal spending, port activity, and tourism. During 1984 alone the payrolls of the local naval and air bases exceeded $1 billion, imports through the port increased 17 percent, and 2.5 million tourists visited Charleston.

Retail sales doubled in dollar volume between 1980 and 1985, when the populations of Charleston, Dorchester, and Berkeley counties reached almost half a million. The major employers were the U.S. Navy with over 40,000 civilian and military personnel, the U.S. Air Force that employed over 6,000 in both categories, and the Medical University of South Carolina with 5,400 employees. Mayor Riley also continued the vigorous annexation policy of Mayor Gaillard, taking in white middle- and upper-middle-class residential areas west of the Ashley, on James Island, thinly populated black regions of John's Island, and a portion of the Neck. When Riley first took the oath of mayor, the land area of the city embraced 18 square miles and a population of 70,132; by January 1980 the city had grown to 25.48 square miles and 69,855 in population; and by January 1988 the size of the city reached 41.63 square miles and a population of 80,879 of which 40,795 persons lived on the peninsula, 31,627 resided in the West Ashley area, 7,814 on James Island, and 643 on John's Island. At the center of the three-county metropolitan area was downtown Charleston, where Riley's revitalization program had created 2,500 new jobs and $150 million in new private investment by 1985.[27]

From 1980 to late in the decade metropolitan unemployment dropped from 6.2 percent to 4.1 percent. In November 1985 *U.S. News and World Report* picked Charleston out of seventy-four metropolitan areas as the city "where business is best." A Charleston public-housing program also received the *Presidential Award for Design Excellence.* It was one of only thirteen selected from 630 similar projects built with federal money between 1974 and 1984. The national awards jury in its citation noted that the Charleston project included 113 units that were designed along the lines of the traditional Charleston "sidehouse" and they are "exemplary in their social, architectural and urbanistic goals." Both Mayor Riley and the executive director of the city's Housing Authority were at the White House ceremony on January 30 to receive the award from President Reagan.

During 1985 Riley continued his policy of recognizing the contributions of the city's Afro-Americans. On March 15 a portrait of the Reverend Daniel Joseph Jenkins by the black artist Merton D. Simpson, who had been reared in the Jenkins Orphanage and had played in its famous band, and later with Duke Ellington, was hung in the Charleston City Council chambers, the first likeness of a black citizen to be displayed in this historic City Hall. The Jenkins Orphanage was now in its ninety-fourth year and since the 1970s had admitted white children. There were twenty-two boys and girls in residence and the institution was receiving funds from the state and the county, from the Duke Endowment, and $16,250 from the city of Charleston, more annually than it ever had received before, although it was no longer within the city.

In October *Porgy and Bess* again was performed at the Gaillard Auditorium with music by the predominantly white Charleston Symphony Orchestra. The very effective stage sets were exactly the same as those used in the unforgettable 1970 performances, but the 1985 performances were different in two respects: the black singers on stage were professionals—many of whom had been singing in European opera houses—and though there were white tourists in the audience, few blacks attended. For educated, sophisticated Afro-Americans, *Porgy and Bess* had become an offensive reinforcement of stereotyped attitudes toward blacks.

When Charleston Place opened for business in September 1986, more than ten years after Mayor Riley first promoted it, there were thirty historic buildings either restored or scheduled for restoration within three blocks of each other. Few cities can match the diversity, the extent, and the sedate elegance of historic Charleston, where one can walk for miles without ceasing to be pleased with the surroundings.[28]

The city's Establishment is now about 300 years old and a lot quieter than it used to be, but it survives in the Charleston Club, the Carolina Yacht Club, and the St. Cecilia Society, which has enjoyed being described as "the country's oldest and most exclusive society." The society's main activity since the 1820s has been the St. Cecilia Ball, at which the gentlemen wear tails and the ladies still carry cards on which they schedule their dance partners.

Reuben M. Greenberg, Chief of Police, Charleston, 1982–.
Courtesy of the Police Department, Charleston, S.C.

In the 1920s, when the city first began to preserve its beautiful buildings and to attract a steady stream of tourists, it had also
began to collect jokes about itself. When a distinguished editor
from North Carolina declared, "There are two kinds of South
Carolinians: those who've never worn shoes and those who make
you feel that *you've* never worn shoes," Charleston chuckled
while the rest of South Carolina carefully ignored the remark.
Two generations found it agreeable to inform visitors, with a little
smile, that Charlestonians were like Chinese—they ate rice and
worshiped their ancestors—and that in Charleston's harbor the
Ashley and the Cooper came together to form the Atlantic Ocean.
In the 1960s Charlestonians observed with a slight rolling of the
eyes that the city was surrounded by three rivers—the Ashley,
the Cooper, and the Mendel Rivers.

By the 1980s nationally recognized novelists and Charleston-
watchers believed that the city's old elite was threatened. One
wrote that the "requiem for aristocracy is always economic.
There are too many outsiders streaming in . . . with money . . .
[who] are scrappy and brainy and on the move. This influx is making the old Charlestonians rarer." Nevertheless, the local establishment remains as clear as ever on what constitutes the
Charleston style. When Edward Manigault, the millionaire-owner
of the Charleston *News and Courier,* died in the 1980s he was
eulogized as personifying the "real Charlestonian . . . an aristocrat, a descendent of rice planters . . . his grandfather raised a
regiment to fight in the Civil War . . . educated at Porter and the
College he was a member of the St. Cecilia Society. . . . he enjoyed the outdoors . . . and was an accomplished Yachtsman."[29]

Under the gaze of Reuben Greenberg, who often appeared
on the streets on roller skates or on horseback, usually in casual
dress, Charleston's crime rate in the 1980s declined dramatically.
The nabobs of the eighteen century buried in St. Philip's Churchyard would have been pleased with the results, though they
would certainly have been astonished to hear that the city's chief
of police was a black Jew.

But Charleston has learned to expect surprises.

Epilogue

During the first week of September 1989 a cluster of thunderstorms formed in the nursery grounds of hurricanes just off the coast of Senegal, West Africa. Converging trade winds, whirled counterclockwise by the earth's rotation, pushed the growing storms west over the warm Atlantic Ocean. On September 11 the tropical depression was upgraded to a tropical storm named Hugo. A week later the storm had become a powerful category 4 hurricane. With winds of 131 to 155 miles per hour, it left a path of death and destruction across the Leeward Islands and Puerto Rico. Brushing by the Bahamas, the hurricane turned northwest toward the United States mainland on September 20. It was 700 miles southeast of Charleston, South Carolina.

On the morning of September 21, Governor Carroll Campbell ordered the evacuation of all coastal areas. Charleston Mayor Joe Riley asked people living in single story homes to leave the Charleston peninsula. By noon traffic on Interstate 26 between the city and Columbia was bumper-to-bumper. For 54,000 persons with nowhere to go, emergency shelters were opened.

In the late afternoon Hugo was 180 miles off the coast packing 135 mph winds and labeled "extremely dangerous." During the early evening the giant storm headed directly at Charleston.

By 10:30 P.M. fierce gusts of wind were driving sheets of rain horizontally across the city and turning any sort of debris into projectiles that smashed windows and windshields. Ancient oaks and magnolias were split open and uprooted. Power lines swayed crazily, transformers exploded, utility poles snapped and crashed in tangled masses. The city went dark. Roads to the barrier islands were awash and the 44-year-old Sullivan's Island drawbridge sprang upright, rocking in the wind.

Near midnight a 12- to 17-foot wall of water swept over Fort Sumter in the harbor. The storm surge came ashore as the center of the hurricane hit the Isle of Palms just to the east of Charleston. The barrier islands were inundated. Eighty percent of the homes were destroyed on Folly Island south of the city; about an equal percentage collapsed or were badly damaged on Sullivan's

Island and the Isle of Palms. Expensive yachts and sailboats moored at the Wild Dune's Marina were tossed onto a neighboring island.

Along Charleston's King Street glass store fronts exploded. Macabrely twisted mannequins spilled into the sidewalks. Fires erupted from natural gas leaks and water poured through the streets as the tide neared its crest.

Around 1:00 A.M. the screaming winds subsided and an eerie quiet enveloped the city as the eye passed nearby. But the winds soon returned with renewed force and from a different direction.

At the exclusive address 31 East Battery, built about 1835, owner Gene Geer dodged glass shards as eight windows blew out and water rose to two feet on the first floor. Two miles to the north in the barrackslike housing project along the Cooper River, Marcia Glover, a 29-year-old single mother, huddled in her apartment. Much earlier she had sent her children to a shelter. Now the water was rising rapidly. She climbed onto her kitchen counter as her refrigerator began to float. She had only two feet of breathing space left when the waters began to recede.

Others were not so lucky. Charlestonians Robert Lee Page and Harold Hutson drowned trying to pilot their 45-foot shrimp trawler up the Cooper River to safety. The wood-frame houses of Arthur McCloud and Isiah Mack collapsed on them and both died.

The tin, copper, or slate roofs of some of the city's most historic buildings were partially destroyed—the Charleston County Court House, City Hall, Hibernian Hall, the Daughters of the Confederacy Museum, the First Baptist Church, Grace Episcopal Church, and St. Luke and St. Paul's.

Mayor Riley remained at his desk in City Hall managing the crisis by candlelight until part of the roof blew off. As torrents of rain poured in, he and his staff saved the priceless portraits in the Council chambers. When the storm subsided around 4:00 A.M., he lay down on the wood floor and slept for an hour. Before dawn Riley began a tour of his beloved Charleston.

The city resembled a combat zone. The contents of stores, twisted metal roofing, palm fronds, lumber and other storm debris were everywhere. Fallen trees blocked the streets which were covered by a slick of pluff mud, its distinctive smell filling the air. With the exceptions of some damaged roofs, smashed windows, tree-crushed brick-walled gardens, and standing water on

the ground floors, the city's historic homes fared well. There was
far greater devastation in the less affluent neighborhoods on the
peninsula and west of the Ashley River.

That morning Mayor Riley observed: "We have on our hands
a degree of physical destruction that is unprecedented in modern
memory." He invoked a 7:00 P.M. to 7:00 A.M. curfew and ordered the police to patrol the city to prevent looting; the governor sent in 2,500 National Guardsmen to assist them. Within two
days ninety looters were apprehended.

There was no electricity, no water, and for many, no food.
Early Friday morning people began queuing up with jugs and
pails at the artesian well near the corner of Rutledge and Calhoun
streets. Already the sounds of chain saws and hammers could be
heard throughout the city. After reports of price-gouging for ice
and generators, the mayor asked City Council to pass laws prohibiting excessive prices.

By Saturday some people were going hungry. Tired and
dazed after waiting hours outside stores for ice or food, fights
occasionally broke out. When the Red Cross began handing out
hot food, a line of 250 people quickly formed.

On Monday banks began to reopen, a trickle of mail came in,
and trash collection resumed, but downpours of rain hindered the
clean-up efforts. Every chance Mayor Riley had he pleaded on
radio and television for donations of money, clothing, canned
food, and disposable diapers: "We've got a lot of people who are
hurting here and they need our help."

The failure of the Federal Emergency Relief Administration
to respond quickly enough with personnel and equipment, especially generators, brought criticism from Jesse Jackson, Mayor
Riley, and United States Senator Ernest Hollings. This prompted
President George Bush to come to South Carolina and he signed a
$1.1 billion relief package for uninsured victims of the hurricane.

A week after the storm private donations of money, food, and
clothing were coming into the city from all over the nation. People reported that Mayor Riley's appeals had touched their hearts.
That same week the mayor estimated that 50,000 Charlestonians
remained homeless. Since the hurricane, "people's spirits have
been up and down," one resident observed.

The first reports from preservationists were good. Only
twenty to twenty-five historically important buildings were severely damaged, but about three-quarters of the 3,500 significant

structures suffered some damage. This was good news for Charlestonians and Charleston's tourism industry.

People were "mucking out" the pluff mud and hanging water-soaked oriental rugs on the marble steps of the historic homes along the Battery. One local native described the city as looking "surreal. The landscape appears rearranged." She thought that it would "take 100 years to recultivate the city's verdant canopy" of trees, but concluded that "the city's essential character is intact."

Two weeks after Hugo over 1,000 truckloads of debris a day were being removed from the city. "The Oprah Winfrey Show" was televised from Charleston to raise money for the hurricane victims. The city's biggest booster, Mayor Riley, appeared wearing a T-shirt saying:

CHARLESTON, S.C.
WE'RE GOING STRONG

He reported that 90 percent of the city's hotels had reopened, the curfew had been lifted, and the National Guard had departed. "We've bounced back from Hurricane Hugo," he said.

Meanwhile, poor people continued lining up to receive food and clothing outside Gaillard Auditorium, the city's primary relief center. One woman waiting there did not share the mayor's breezy optimism that things were returning to normal. High waters had flooded her apartment in a housing project: "I got no home, my kids are still out of school, and I'm still in this line."

Before the hurricane, Charleston led South Carolina in job growth and ranked twenty-fifth in the nation. After Hugo metropolitan Charleston and the state of South Carolina reeled from damages of $2.8 billion in the city and $4.5 billion across the state. But almost immediately federal money and private insurance funds began flowing in and outside investors started looking for bargains in the ravaged areas.

Some Charlestonians will quickly rebuild their shattered homes and lives while for others it will take much longer. The old sea city has once more survived a major catastrophe.[1]

---

[1]*Atlanta Journal and Constitution*, September 23, 24, 25, 26, 27, 29, 30, October 1, 2, 5, 6, 8, 1989; *Savannah News Press*, September 23, 24, 25, October 1, 5, 1989; *The State* (Columbia, S.C.), September 24, October 1, 1989; *News and Courier/Evening Post*, October 1, 1989; *News and Courier*, October 2, 1989.

Appendix
The Heads of the Government of Charleston

❦ 1. Before Incorporation, 1670–1783

As long as Charles Town was under British rule, the theoretical head of the government was the governor, lieutenant governor, or acting or provisional governor, but the day-to-day governance of the city was managed primarily by various appointed commissioners, none of whom had enough administrative authority to be called the head of government.

❦ 2. The Intendants, 1783–1835

The city was incorporated as Charleston in August 1783, and the head of the city government was elected every two years and until 1836 was called "intendant."

1. Richard Hutson, 1783–85. A member of the Congregational Church, he also served in the state legislature and as lieutenant governor; his opponents called him "Richard I."

2. Arnoldus Vanderhorst, 1785–86; 1790–92. A factor and planter who later served as a governor of the state, 1794–96.

3. John F. Grimké, 1786–88. A judge who owned local real estate and a plantation.

4. Rawlins Lowndes, 1788–89. Former president of the state, Lowndes was a planter and judge who owned five plantations and "scores of slaves."

5. Thomas Jones, 1789–90. A bank president who owned five plantations.

6. John Huger, 1792–94. An owner of a home on Broad Street and four plantations.

7. John Bee Holmes, 1794–95. A member of the Congregational Church, he was an attorney and planter who served in the state House and Senate.

8. John Edwards, 1795–96. A planter who also served in the state legislature.

9. H. W. DeSaussure, 1797–98. An attorney, he also served in the South Carolina House and Senate.

10. Thomas Roper, 1799–1801. A planter who also served in the state legislature, he was a member of the Second Independent Church.

11. John Ward, 1801–2. An attorney and large landowner in the city and on John's Island.

12. David Deas, 1802–3. An attorney who also served in the state legislature.

13. John Drayton, 1803. A Princeton graduate, an attorney and judge, he also served as governor, 1808–10.

14. Thomas Winstanley, 1804–5. An attorney, he owned extensive city real estate.

15. Charles Cochran, 1805–6. A federal marshal and bank president, he also served as state treasurer.

16. John Dawson, Jr., 1806–7. A merchant and rice planter, he resigned as mayor and served in the state House of Representatives.

17. Benjamin Boyd, 1807. He served as interim mayor.

18. William Rouse, 1808–9. A shoemaker and tanner, he was elected to the state House and Senate and was a member of the First Baptist Church.

19. Thomas McCalla, 1810–12. A physician, he owned local real estate and a farm.

20. Thomas Bennett, Jr., 1812–13. An architect and lumber merchant who owned several mills and a mansion in the city and attended the Congregational Church, he also served in the state Senate and as governor, 1820–22.

21. Thomas Rhett Smith, 1813–15. Educated in England, he owned a plantation and served in the South Carolina Senate and House.

22. Elias Horry, 1815–17; 1820–21. He also served in the state legislature and owned eight plantations worked by over 200 slaves.

23. John Geddes, 1817–19; 1823–24. A merchant and attorney who served in the South Carolina House and Senate, he was elected governor in 1818.

24. Daniel Stevens, 1819–20. A planter who also served in the South Carolina House and Senate.

25. James Hamilton, Jr., 1821–23. The owner of seven plantations, a brickyard, and a rice mill, he served in the state House and Senate and was elected governor in 1830.

26. Samuel Prioleau, 1824–25. A graduate of the University of Pennsylvania, a merchant and attorney who owned eighty slaves, he also served in the state legislature.

27. Joseph Johnson, 1825–27. A physician who received his medical degree from the University of Pennsylvania, he owned several houses and lots in the city.

28. John Gadsden, 1827–29. A Yale graduate and attorney, he served in the state legislature.

29. Henry L. Pinckney, 1829–30; 1831–32. A graduate of South Carolina College, an attorney, founder and editor of the Charleston *Mercury,* a member of the Congregational Church, he held extensive real estate in the city and served in the state legislature and the U.S. House of Representatives.

30. James R. Pringle, 1830–31. A collector of the port of Charleston, he owned extensive real estate, sixteen slaves, and served in the state Senate.

31. Edward Y. North, 1833–35. A physician who owned extensive city real estate and twenty-three slaves.

❧ 3. The Mayors, 1836–.

In 1836 the title of the city's chief executive was changed to "mayor," and in 1877 the City Council amended Charleston's Charter, extending the term of office from two to four years.

1. Robert Y. Hayne, 1836–37. A lawyer who served in the South Carolina House and Senate, the U.S. Senate, and as governor, 1832–34.

2. Henry L. Pinckney, 1837–40.

3. Jacob F. Mintzing, 1840–42. A grocer and lumber-mill owner, he served in the state legislature.

4. John Schnierle, 1842–45; 1850–52. A lawyer and planter, he owned valuable local real estate, twenty slaves, and served in the South Carolina House.

5. Thomas Leger Hutchinson, 1846–49; 1852–55. A planter who owned city real estate, he also served in the state legislature.

6. William Porcher Miles, 1855–57. A lawyer and professor at the College of Charleston, he owned modest local real estate, ten slaves, and served in the U.S. House of Representatives and as a member of the Confederate Congress.

7. Charles Macbeth, 1857–65. A planter-lawyer and a Presbyterian who owned local real estate, two plantations, and over 200 slaves; he served in the state legislature and remained the city's chief executive during the Civil War.

8. Peter C. Gaillard, 1865–67. A graduate of West Point, he served as a colonel in the Confederate Army and was removed from office by U.S. General R. S. Canby.

9. General W. W. Burns, 1867–68. Appointed by General Canby.

10. Colonel Milton Cogswell, 1868. Appointed by General Canby.

11. George W. Clark, 1868. Appointed by General Canby.

12. Gilbert Pillsbury, 1868–71. A Massachusetts native, Dartmouth graduate, and one-time abolitionist and Republican who came to Charleston with the Freedmen's Bureau.

13. John A. Wagener, 1871–73. A Democrat, German immigrant, and Lutheran, he was the president of a local insurance company.

14. George I. Cunningham, 1873–75; 1875–77. Twice elected mayor as a Republican, he owned a slaughterhouse business and considerable local property.

15. William W. Sale, 1877–79. A former major in the Confederate Army, he was a native of upcountry Carolina.

16. William Ashmead Courtenay, 1879–83; 1883–87. A captain in the Confederate Army, he was a successful businessman.

17. Christopher S. Gadsden, 1887. A City Council member and great-grandson of the eighteenth-century Charlestonian of the same name, he served briefly as mayor pro-tem.

18. George D. Bryan, 1887–91. A captain in the Confederate Navy, he was an attorney and corporation counsel of the city of Charleston.

19. John F. Ficken, 1891–95. A College of Charleston graduate and a Lutheran, he served in the Confederate Army, became an attorney, and was elected eight times to the state legislature.

20. J. Adger Smyth, 1895–99; 1899–1903. Born and educated in the city, he was a prosperous businessman.

21. R. Goodwyn Rhett, 1903–7; 1907–11. A prominent member of local society, he was president of the city's largest and oldest bank.

22. John P. Grace, 1911–15; 1919–23. The city's first Catholic chief executive and a populist, he practiced law, but his real passion was politics.

23. Tristram T. Hyde, 1915–19. Educated at the High School of Charleston, he was a successful businessman and a Baptist.

24. Thomas Porcher Stoney, 1923–28; 1928–31. A member of the old lowcountry elite of merchants and planters, he was an attorney by profession.

25. Burnet Rhett Maybank, 1931–35; 1935–38. His ancestors were among

the city's earliest settlers and he was educated at the College of Charleston after which he became a successful cotton broker.

26. Henry Whilden Lockwood, 1938–39; 1939–43; 1943–44. A wealthy tugboat-company owner and Lutheran, he was elected by the City Council to serve as interim mayor following Maybank's election as governor and then was elected twice as mayor, dying in office in 1944.

27. E. Edward Wehman, Jr., 1944–47. An alderman and socially prominent Lutheran and businessman, he was elected by the City Council to fill Lockwood's unexpired term of office.

28. William McGillivray Morrison, 1947–51; 1951–55; 1955–59. Born near Charleston, he took a law degree from the University of South Carolina and became corporation counsel for the city of Charleston.

29. J. Palmer Gaillard, Jr., 1959–63; 1963–67; 1967–71; 1971–75. A navy pilot during World War II and afterward a prominent businessman, his grandfather served as mayor nearly 100 years before.

30. Arthur B. Schirmer, Jr., 1975. A local businessman and member of the City Council, he was elected as interim mayor when Gaillard resigned.

31. Joseph P. Riley, Jr., 1975–79; 1979–83; 1983–87; 1987–. Born and educated in Charleston and at the University of South Carolina School of Law, he served in the state legislature and was the city's second Catholic chief executive.

Abbreviations
in Notes and Select Bibliography

AHR   *American Historical Review*

CCA   City of Charleston Archives

DUL   William L. Perkins Library, Duke University, Durham, N.C.

JCHSC   *Journal of the Commons House of Assembly of South Carolina*

JSH   *Journal of Southern History*

LS   Library Society, Charleston, S.C.

NCHR   *North Carolina Historical Review*

PSCHA   *Proceedings of the South Carolina Historical Association*

SCA   South Carolina Department of Archives and History, Columbia, S.C.

SHC   Southern Historical Collection, University of North Carolina, Chapel Hill

SCL   South Caroliniana Library, University of South Carolina, Columbia

SCHGM   *South Carolina Historical and Genealogical Magazine*

SCHM   *South Carolina Historical Magazine*

SCHS   South Carolina Historical Society, Charleston, S.C.

VBSP   Vestry Books, I, II and III, St. Philip's Church, Charleston, S.C.

WMQ   *William and Mary Quarterly*

YCC   *Yearbook of the City of Charleston*

Notes

Chapter I

1. Langdon Cheves (ed.), "The Shaftesbury Papers and Other Records Relating to Carolina . . . prior to the Year 1676," in South Carolina Historical Society *Collections* (Charleston, S.C., 1897), V, 130–31, 224, 248, 261, 348; Robert M. Weir, *Colonial South Carolina: A History* (New York, 1983), 41–42; Patrick Melvin, "Captain Florence O'Sullivan and the Origins of Carolina," *SCHM* 76 (October 1975), 238, 244; Alexander S. Salley, Jr., *The Early English Settlers of South Carolina* (Columbia, S.C., 1945), 5–8; St. Julien R. Childs, "The Naval Career of Joseph West," *SCHM* 71 (April 1970), 110–15.

2. Cheves, "Shaftesbury Papers," V, 134–52, 231; Alexander S. Salley, Jr. (ed.), *Narratives of Early Carolina, 1650–1708* (New York, 1911), 86, 94; David Webster Fagg, Jr., "Carolina, 1663–1683: The Founding of a Proprietary" (Ph.D. dissertation, Emory University, 1970), 201–5; Henry A. M. Smith, "Charleston and Charleston Neck," *SCHGM* 19 (January 1918), 2–5; Joseph I. Waring, *The First Voyage and Settlement at Charles Town, 1670–1680* (Columbia, S.C., 1970), 36.

3. M. Eugene Sirmans, *Colonial South Carolina: A Political History, 1663–1763* (Chapel Hill, N.C., 1966) 3, 6–10; David D. Wallace, *South Carolina: A Short History, 1520–1948* (Chapel Hill, N.C., 1951), 24–25; George C. Rogers, Jr., "The First Earl of Shaftesbury," *SCHM* 68 (April 1968), 76; Fagg, "Carolina," 121–22, 129–30, 184.

4. Waring, *First Voyage*, 22–23; Richard S. Dunn, "The English Sugar Islands and the Founding of South Carolina," *SCHM* 72 (April 1971), 91; Peter Wood, *Black Majority: Negroes in Colonial South Carolina from 1670 through the Stono Rebellion* (New York, 1975), 19; Richard Waterhouse, "South Carolina's Colonial Elite: A Study in the Social Structure and Political Culture of a Southern Colony, 1670–1760" (Ph.D. dissertation, Johns Hopkins University, 1973), 32–35.

5. John D. Duncan, "Servitude and Slavery in Colonial South Carolina, 1670–1766" (2 vols., Ph.D. dissertation, Emory University, 1972), I, 43–47; M. Eugene Sirmans, "Politicians and Planters: The Bull Family of Colonial South Carolina," *PSCHA* (1962), 33; Agnes Leland Baldwin, *First Settlers of South Carolina, 1670–1680* (Columbia, S.C., 1969), see table, "First Settlers of South Carolina"; St. Julien R. Childs, "The First Carolinians," *SCHM* 71 (April 1970), 108; M. Eugene Sirmans, "Masters of Ashley Hall: A Biographical Study of the Bull Family of Colonial South Carolina, 1670–1737" (Ph.D. dissertation, Princeton University, 1959), 26; St. Julien Ravenel, *Charleston: The Place and the People* (New York, 1931), 10–11.

6. Waring, *First Voyage*, 25–31; Joseph I. Waring, *A History of Medicine in South Carolina, 1670–1825* (Columbia, S.C., 1964), 2–3, 10; Wesley Frank Craven, *The Southern Colonies in the Seventeenth Century* (Baton Rouge, La., 1949), 346–47; Sirmans, *Colonial South Carolina*, 20–21; Cheves, "Shaftesbury Papers," V, 196, 283–84; Henry A. M. Smith, "Old Charles Town and Its Vicinity,"

SCHGM 16 (January 1915), 1–3; Theodore H. Jabbs, "The South Carolina Colonial Militia, 1663–1733" (Ph.D. dissertation, University of North Carolina, 1973), 84–85.

7. Waring, *First Voyage*, 36; Wood, *Black Majority*, 21; Clarence L. Ver Steeg, *Origins of a Southern Mosaic* (Athens, Ga., 1975), 103; Sirmans, *Colonial South Carolina*, 22; Weir, *Colonial South Carolina*, 53–59; Frederick Dalcho, *An Historical Account of the Protestant Episcopal Church in South Carolina* (Charleston, S.C., 1820), 28.

8. Richard Waterhouse, "England, the Caribbean, and the Settlement of Carolina," *American Studies* 9 (1975), 271–73, 280–81; John P. Thomas, "The Barbadians in Early South Carolina," *SCHGM* 31 (April 1930), 88–91; Dunn, "The English Sugar Islands," 81–84, 92–93; Sirmans, *Colonial South Carolina*, 27–29; Salley, *Early English Settlers*, 9–13.

9. William R. Snell, "Indian Slavery in Colonial South Carolina, 1671–1795" (Ph.D. dissertation, University of Alabama, 1972), 3, 16–17; David LeRoy Coon, "The Development of Market Agriculture in South Carolina, 1670–1785" (Ph.D. dissertation, University of Illinois at Urbana-Champaign, 1972), 93–95; Converse D. Clowse, *Economic Beginnings in Colonial South Carolina, 1670–1730* (Columbia, S.C., 1971), 62–69; José M. Gallardo, "The Spaniards and the English Settlement in Charles Town," *SCHGM* 37 (April–July 1936), 95–99.

10. Cheves, "Shaftesbury Papers," V, 378–79, 385, 396; A. S. Salley, *Warrants for Lands in South Carolina, 1672–1711* (Columbia, S.C., 1973), 3, 22–23; Wood, *Black Majority*, 22; Craven, *Southern Colonies*, 348–49.

11. "Records in the British Public Record Office Relating to South Carolina" (36 vols., transcripts, SCA), I, 95–96, 118; Gallardo, "The Spaniards," 135–40.

12. "Records," I, 95–96, 104–5, 118–19; Cheves, "Shaftesbury Papers," V, 360–61; Craven, *Southern Colonies*, 353–54; Carl Bridenbaugh, *Cities in the Wilderness: The First Century of Urban Life in America, 1625–1742* (New York, 1964), 12–13. Other colonial American towns—Philadelphia, Williamsburg, and Savannah—were distinguished by broad, straight streets turning at right angles. The oldest of these is Charles Town.

13. Maurice Mathews, "A Contemporary View of Carolina in 1680," *SCHM* 55 (July 1954), 154; Smith, "Charleston Neck," 7; Ravenel, *Charleston*, 15; Dalcho, *Episcopal Church*, 21; Waring, *The First Voyage*, 50–51; Henry A. M. Smith, "Charleston—The Original Plan and the Earliest Settlers," *SCHGM* 9 (January 1908), 16–19, and the accompanying "Plat of Charles Town." Among the first lot-owners were Jacob Waite, Stephen Bull, David Maybank, John Powell, Arthur Middleton, John Coming, James and Thomas Colleton, Thomas Rose, Robert Gibbes, and Henry Hughes.

14. A. O. Halsey, "Historic Charleston in Maps, Book 1, 1682–1770" (ms., SCHS); Salley, *Narratives*, 151, 157–58, 167–71, 182.

15. Mathews, "A Contemporary View," 158; Salley, *Narratives*, 158, 167, 169, 184; Thomas Ashe estimated 1,000–1,200 persons and Samuel Wilson also estimated 100 houses.

16. George Pratt and J. G. Dunlop, "Arrival of the Cardross Settlers," *SCHGM* 30 (April 1929), 71–72; Wood, *Black Majority*, 54, 54n, 67; The immigrant was exposed not only to illness. Judith Giton, who arrived in Charles Town in 1685, wrote: "After our arrival . . . we have been exposed . . . to sickness, pestilence, famine, poverty, and the roughest labor," "Records," I, 293, also II, 4–5, 35–36;

H. Roy Merrens and George D. Terry, "Dying in Paradise: Malaria, Mortality, and the Perceptual Environment in Colonial South Carolina," *JSH* 50 (November 1984), 533–50.

17. Craven, *Southern Colonies*, 354–55; Sirmans, *Colonial South Carolina*, 38–54; "Records," I, 139; Bridenbaugh, *Cities*, 145; Shirley Carter Hughson, *The Carolina Pirates and Colonial Commerce, 1670–1740* (Baltimore, Md., 1894), 18–19; Clowse, *Economic Beginnings*, 88–90.

18. St. Julien R. Childs, *Malaria and Colonization in the Carolina Low Country, 1526–1696* (Baltimore, Md., 1940), 224–25; Waring, *History of Medicine*, 18; John Duffy, "Yellow Fever in Colonial Charleston," *SCHM* 52 (October 1951), 189; Waterhouse, "South Carolina's Colonial Elite," 73.

19. Thomas Cooper (ed.), *The Statutes at Large of South Carolina* (7 vols., Columbia, S.C., 1837–40), II, 1–6; Bridenbaugh, *Cities*, 219; "Records," II, 102–3; A. S. Salley (ed.), *Journal of the Grand Council of South Carolina, April 11, 1692–September 26, 1698* (Columbia, S.C., 1907), 43–44; Daniel H. Usner, Jr., "Rebeckah Lee's Plea on 'Fetching of Drink for an Indian Squaw,' 1684," *SCHM* 85 (October 1984), 317–18.

20. Babette M. Levy, "Early Puritanism in the Southern and Island Colonies," *Proceedings of the American Antiquarian Society* 70 (April 1960), 262–64, 267, 269; Sidney Charles Bolton, "The Anglican Church of Colonial South Carolina, 1704–1754: A Study in Americanization" (Ph.D. dissertation, University of Wisconsin, 1973), 51–54; Hirsch, *Huguenots*, 50–53; George N. Edwards, *A History of the Independent or Congregational Church of Charleston, South Carolina* (Boston, 1947), 8–9; Webber, "Records of the Quakers," 22–23. The municipal parking garage on King Street is on the site of the old "Quaker lot."

21. Jabbs, "Colonial Militia," 147–50, 155–57; J. G. Dunlop, "Spanish Depredations, 1686," *SCHGM* 30 (April 1929), 82–85.

22. Weir, *Colonial South Carolina*, 64–73; Dalcho, *Episcopal Church*, 29–31; Cooper, *Statutes*, II, 131–33.

23. "Records," II, 130, 260; Cooper, *Statutes*, II, 7–9; Hughson, *Carolina Pirates*, 19, 44–45; Hugh F. Rankin, *The Golden Age of Piracy* (Williamsburg, Va., 1969), 58; Sirmans, *Colonial South Carolina*, 56–58; Clowse, *Economic Beginnings*, 125–30; Wood, *Black Majority*, 57–58; Ravenel, *Charleston*, 91.

24. M. Eugene Sirmans, "The Legal Status of the Slave in South Carolina, 1670–1740," *JSH* 28 (November 1962), 462–66, Wood, *Black Majority*, 36–37, 61–62, 88–91.

25. Duncan, "Servitude and Slavery," I, 207–16, II, 510–11; A. S. Salley, "Abstracts from the Records of the Court of Ordinary of the Province of South Carolina, 1692–1700," *SCHGM* 10 (January 1909), 14–15; A. S. Salley (ed.), *JCHSC, 1691* (Columbia, S.C., 1913), 20; A. S. Salley (ed.), *JCHSC, 1698* (Columbia, S.C., 1914), 23; Salley, *Journal of the Grand Council, 1692*, 60. Harsh punishments, floggings, and brandings were sometimes given out for white indentured runaways and convicted white criminals. On September 24, 1692, a court at Charles Town convicted the widow Catherine Bottley of a felony. She was sentenced to be "burnt with the letter T on ye ball of ye Thumb."

26. Sirmans, *Colonial South Carolina*, 60, 66; A. S. Salley (ed.), "Abstracts from Records of the Court of Ordinary for the Province of South Carolina, 1692–1700," *SCHGM* 8 (October 1907), 200–201; Cooper, *Statutes*, VII, 18. In 1703

Carolina had a population of 8,270. Of these 4,220 were white, 3,250 black, and 800 were Indian slaves.

27. Salley, "Abstracts, 1692–1700," 12–18, 137; A. S. Salley (ed.), "Abstracts from the Records of the Court of Ordinary of the Province of South Carolina, 1700–1712," *SCHGM* 12 (April 1911), 72–74, 147–48; Lothrop Withington and H. F. Wates (eds.), "South Carolina Gleanings in England," *SCHGM* 7 (July 1906), 146; "Will Book, Charleston County Wills, 1692–1693" (WPA Records, Charleston County Library, Charleston, S.C.), 15, 52.

28. A. S. Salley (ed.), *JCHSC, January 30, 1696–March 17, 1696* (Columbia, S.C., 1908), 17–19, 34; "Records," III, 142, 169; Cooper, *Statutes,* VII, 6; A. S. Salley (ed.), *Commissions and Instructions from the Lords Proprietors of Carolina to Public Officials of South Carolina, 1685–1715* (Columbia, S.C., 1916), 100, 102; A. S. Salley (ed.), *JCHSC, November 24, 1696–December 5, 1696* (Columbia, S.C., 1912), 13.

29. Salley, *Commissions and Instructions,* 103; John Duffy, *Epidemics in Colonial America* (Port Washington, N.Y., 1972), 16–18, 74; Dalco, *Episcopal Church,* 32n; Edward McCrady, *The History of South Carolina under the Proprietary Government, 1670–1719* (New York, 1897), 307–8; Salley, *Narratives,* 200. A visitor to Charles Town in 1698, William Pratt, reported that "a few days before the fire ther was an earth quak."

30. "Records," IV, 57–58; Salley, *JCHSC, 1698,* 33; Cooper, *Statutes,* VII, 7–11.

31. Duffy, "Yellow Fever," 189–91; Duffy, *Epidemics,* 142–44; Waring, *History of Medicine,* 19–21; Dalcho, *Episcopal Church,* 36, 38n; McCrady, *Proprietary Government,* 309–11; Alexander Hewatt, *An Historical Account of the Rise and Progress of the Colonies of South Carolina and Georgia* (London, 1779), in B. R. Carroll (ed.), *Historical Collections of South Carolina* (2 vols., New York, 1836), I, 128; Ravenel, *Charleston,* 35–36; Salley, *Narratives,* 365. Yellow fever also was raging in Philadelphia at the time. These were the first two major yellow fever epidemics in America.

32. A. S. Salley, Jr. (ed.), *Commissions and Instructions from the Lords Proprietors of Carolina to Public Officials of South Carolina, 1685–1715* (Columbia, S.C., 1916), 147, 152; A. S. Salley, Jr. (ed.), *JCHSC, August 13, 1701–August 28, 1701* (Columbia, S.C., 1916), 3–7, 13; Weir, *Colonial South Carolina,* 75–76; Wallace, *South Carolina,* 66–67; Frederick P. Bowes, *The Culture of Early Charleston* (Chapel Hill, N.C., 1942), 19, 55.

33. A. S. Salley, Jr. (ed.), *JCHSC, 1702* (Columbia, S.C., 1932), 31–32, 37; Sirmans, *Colonial South Carolina,* 83–84; Salley, *Journal, 1701,* 29, 32; Weir, *Colonial South Carolina,* 76–77; "Death Notices in the South Carolina *Gazette,*" *SCHGM* 17 (January 1916), 90–91.

34. Salley, *JCHSC, 1702,* 59–61, 99–101; Sirmans, *Colonial South Carolina,* 84.

35. Mary Julia Curtis, "The Early Charleston Stage: 1703–1798" (Ph.D. dissertation, Indiana University, 1968), 4–6; Wallace, *South Carolina,* 203.

36. Sirmans, *Colonial South Carolina,* 85–86; Verner W. Crane, *The Southern Frontier, 1670–1732* (Ann Arbor, Mich., 1929), 74–77; William J. Rivers, *A Sketch of the History of South Carolina* (Charleston, S.C., 1856), 203; Salley, *Narratives,* 345–47; Dalcho, *Episcopal Church,* 51–52.

37. Crane, *Southern Frontier,* 108; Salley, *Journal, 1703,* 87; Bridenbaugh, *Cit-*

ies, 270; Frank J. Klingberg (ed.), *Carolina Chronicle: The Papers of Commissary Gideon Johnston, 1707–1716* (Berkeley, Calif., 1946), 62.

38. Salley, *Journal, 1703,* 95; Cooper, *Statutes,* II, 224–27; David J. McCord (ed.), *The Statutes at Large of South Carolina* (Columbia, S.C., 1840), VII, 23–24.

39. L. Lynn Hogue, "An Edition of Eight Charges Delivered . . . Held at Charles Town . . . , by Nicholas Trott, Esq.: Chief Justice of the Province of South Carolina" (Ph.D. dissertation, University of Tennessee, 1972), 57–59, 217–24; L. Lynn Hogue, "Nicholas Trott: Man of Law and Letters," *SCHM* 76 (January 1975), 28–29.

40. Sirmans, *Colonial South Carolina,* 87; McCord, *Statutes,* VII, 28–33; Samuel Lapham, Jr., "Notes on Granville Bastion," *SCHGM* 26 (October 1925), 221–27. Today the remains of Granville Bastion lie beneath the Carolina Yacht Club, the Omar Temple of the Masonic Order of the Nobles of the Mystic Shrine, and East Bay Street.

41. McCord, *Statutes,* VII, 19, 38, 41–43; A. S. Salley, Jr. (ed.), *JCHSC, November 20, 1706–February 8, 1706/1707* (Columbia, S.C., 1939), 5; A. S. Salley, Jr. (ed.), *JCHSC, March 6, 1705/6–April 9, 1706* (Columbia, S.C., 1937), 48, 11, 21, 30; Bridenbaugh, *Cities,* 166.

42. Halsey, "Historic Charleston in Maps, Book I"; David Ramsay, *Ramsay's History of South Carolina* (2 vols., Charleston, S.C., 1858), I, 146–47; A. S. Salley, Jr. (ed.), *JCHSC, 1703* (Columbia, S.C., 1934), 90; George C. Rogers, *A South Carolina Chronology: 1497–1970* (Columbia, S.C., 1973), 14; Weir, *Colonial South Carolina,* 76–79.

43. Sirmans, "Masters of Ashley Hall," 101; Salley, *Journals, 1703,* 90; Halsey, "Historic Charleston"; McCord, *Statutes,* VII, 22–26, 32–35.

44. Crane, *Southern Frontier,* 108–12; Philip M. Brown, "Early Indian Trade in the Development of South Carolina," *SCHM* 76 (July 1975), 118–22, 131, 135; Stuart Owen Stumpf, "The Merchants of Colonial Charleston, 1680–1756" (Ph.D. dissertation, Michigan State University, 1971), 69; Richard Waterhouse, "South Carolina's Colonial Elite: A Study in the Social Structure & Political Culture of a Southern Colony, 1670–1760" (Ph.D. dissertation, Johns Hopkins University, 1973), 71–72, 86, 110, 112; Wallace, *South Carolina,* 68, 202; Dalcho, *Episcopal Church,* 64–69.

45. Theodore D. Jervey (ed.), "Items Relating to Charles Town, South Carolina, from the Boston Newsletter," *SCHGM* 40 (July 1939), 73–78; Waring, *A History of Medicine,* 23; Duffy, "Yellow Fever," 192.

46. Frank J. Klingberg (ed.), *The Carolina Chronicle of Dr. Francis Le Jau 1706–1717* (Berkeley, Calif., 1956), 29–30; Hogue, " 'An Edition of Eight Charges Delivered,' " 15–23; Sirmans, *Colonial South Carolina,* 88–89; Wallace, *South Carolina,* 72–73.

47. Klingberg, *Chronicle of Le Jau,* 25–31; Hogue, "Nicholas Trott," 27; N. Johnson (et al.) to Lords Proprietors, September 17, 1708, in Salley, *Records, 1701–1710,* 210; Harry S. Mustard, "On the Building of Fort Johnson," *SCHM* 64 (July 1963), 129–35; McCord, *Statutes,* VII, 43–49; Elmer D. Johnson and Kathleen Lewis Sloan (eds.), *South Carolina: A Documentary Profile of the Palmetto State* (Columbia, S.C., 1971), 63.

48. Bolton, "The Anglican Church," 73–74, 94; Klingberg, *Chronicle: Johnston,* 21–22, 31; Sirmans, *Colonial South Carolina,* 96–98; George C. Rogers, Jr., *Charleston in the Age of the Pinckneys* (Norman, Okla., 1969), 21.

49. Klingberg, *Chronicle: Johnston,* 35–37, 41–42, 55–57, 65, 84–85; Klingberg, *Chronicle of Le Jau,* 72–73; Bolton, "The Anglican Church," 75–76; McCord, *Statutes,* VII, 57.

50. Klingberg, *Chronicle: Johnston,* 48, 58, 60–63; Arthur H. Hirsch, *The Huguenots of Colonial South Carolina* (London, 1962), 306–9; Klingberg, *Chronicle of Le Jau,* 133–34.

51. Klingberg, *Chronicle: Johnston,* 39; Cooper, *Statutes,* II, 342–46, 389–96; Bolton, "The Anglican Church," 216–17.

52. McCord, *Statutes,* VII, 56–57; Dalcho, *Episcopal Church,* 92; Anna Wells Rutledge, "The Second St. Philip's 1710–1835," *Journal of the Society of Architectural Historians* 18 (October 1959), 112. Klingberg, *Chronicle: Johnston,* 99; Klingberg, *Chronicle of Le Jau,* 104; John Duffy, "Eighteenth Century Carolina Health Conditions," *JSH* 18 (August 1952), 298–99.

53. Cooper, *Statutes,* II, 382–85; St. Julien Ravenel Childs, "Notes on the History of Public Health in South Carolina, 1670–1800," *PSCHA* (1932), 17–18.

54. Klingberg, *Chronicle: Johnston,* 109, 142–43, 151; David M. Ludlum, *Early American Hurricanes* (Boston, 1963), 42–43; Klingberg, *Chronicle of Le Jau,* 153, 159, 160–61, 164; Brown, "Early Indian Trade," 121; Crane, *Southern Frontier,* 168–73; Sirmans, *Colonial South Carolina,* 112–13.

55. "Records," VI, 98, 140–41; Richard P. Sherman, *Robert Johnson: Proprietary & Royal Governor of South Carolina,* (Columbia, S.C., 1966), 21–22; Waring, *Medical History,* 27; Wood, *Black Majority,* 126–29; Weir, *Colonial South Carolina,* 84–85.

56. Duffy, "Yellow Fever," 193; Crane, *Southern Frontier,* 184–85; Sherman, *Robert Johnson,* 23, 34; *"Records,"* VII, 19–20; Clowse, *Economic Beginnings,* 186–87; Brown, "Early Indian Trade," 121–22.

57. Rankin, *Age of Piracy,* 96–100, 111–12; Hughson, *Carolina Pirates,* 70–73, 90–98; Sherman, *Robert Johnson,* 31–32.

58. George W. Williams (ed.), "Letters to the Bishop of London from the Commissaries of South Carolina," *SCHM* 78 (January and April 1977), 19; Rankin, *Age of Piracy,* 101, 131; Hughson, *Carolina Pirates,* 99–105, 112–14.

59. Rankin, *Age of Piracy,* 100–102, 131–32; Sherman, *Robert Johnson,* 34–35.

60. "Records," VII, 207–19, 227–28, 255; Sirmans, *Colonial South Carolina,* 120–28; Sherman, *Robert Johnson,* 43–47; Clowse, *Economic Beginnings,* 189–94; Wallace, *South Carolina,* 100–102; Waterhouse, "South Carolina's Colonial Elite," 118–19.

61. McCord, *Statutes,* VII, 72–73; "Records," IX, 70; Sirmans, *Colonial South Carolina,* 128–50; Ravenel, *Charleston,* 95; Richard M. Jellison, "Paper Currency in Colonial South Carolina: A Reappraisal," *SCHM* 62 (July 1961), 138–41; Clowse, *Economic Beginnings,* 194–97.

62. "Records," X, 1, 74–76, 82–86, 93–96, 104–8, 159–60; Sirmans, *Colonial South Carolina,* 143–44; Bolton, "The Anglican Church," 141–45, 148–49, 155, 213–14, 243–44; Williams, "Letters to the Bishop," 19.

63. Edgar Legare Pennington, "The Reverend Thomas Morritt and the Free School in Charles Town," *SCHGM* 32 (January 1931), 36–45; Bolton, "The Anglican Church," 216–20; Sirmans, *Colonial South Carolina,* 142; Wallace, *South Carolina,* 102.

64. Bolton, "The Anglican Church," 244; Williams, "Letters to the Bishop,"

25; Edward McCrady, "Historical Sketch of St. Philip's Church," *YCC, 1895* (Charleston, S.C., 1896), 329–31; Rutledge, "The Second St. Philip's," 112–13; A. S. Salley, Jr. (ed.), *JCHSC, February 23, 1724–June 1, 1725* (Columbia, S.C., 1945), 58–59.

65. Bolton, "The Anglican Church," 231–39, 241, 244–47; Williams, "Letters to the Bishop," 30–31, 128–32, 135–36.

66. Halsey, "Historic Charleston in Maps"; McCord, *Statutes*, VII, 58; Bridenbaugh, *Cities*, 150–51, 212; Alice R. Huger Smith and D. E. Huger Smith, *The Dwelling Houses of Charleston, South Carolina* (Philadelphia, Pa., 1917), 18, 24, 344–46; A. S. Salley (ed.), *JCHSC, November 15, 1726–March 11, 1726* (Columbia, S.C., 1946), 37, 76–78; Salley, *JCHSC, February, 1724–June, 1725*, 50, 55, 100, 116.

67. "James Sutherland to My Lord, [April 14, 1729–January 4, 1731]," in *SCHM* 68 (April 1967), 79–84; Brian J. Enright (ed.), "An Account of Charles Town in 1725," *SCHM* 61 (January 1960), 15–17; Rogers, *Charleston*, 55.

68. Duncan, "Servitude and Slavery," I, 105; Clowse, *Economic Beginnings*, 230–31.

69. Wood, *Black Majority*, 196–97, 220, 272–75, 298–99; McCord, *Statutes*, VII, 375; David Cole, "A Brief Outline of the South Carolina Colonial Militia System," *PSCHA* (1954), 22.

70. Sirmans, *Colonial South Carolina*, 151, 154–58; "Records," XII, 201, XIV, 222; Jellison, "Paper Currency," 141–45; David M. Ludlum, *Early American Winters, 1604–1820* (Boston, Mass., 1966), 139.

71. Carroll, *Historical Collections*, I, 273–74; Waring, *History of Medicine*, 34–35; Duffy, "Yellow Fever," 193; Ludlum, *Early Hurricanes*, 43–44.

72. Sirmans, *Colonial South Carolina*, 158–63; Sherman, *Robert Johnson*, 68–71.

Chapter II

1. Wood, *Black Majority*, 166, 236–37 n62, 298–300; Carroll (ed.), *Historical Collections*, I, 284, 286; Sirmans, *Colonial South Carolina*, 164–67; Sherman, *Robert Johnson*, 71–74, 89; Williams, "Letters to the Bishop of London," 139, 146; Stuart Owen Stumpf, "The Merchants of Colonial Charleston, 1680–1756" (Ph.D. dissertation, Michigan State University, 1971), 157–58; Coon, "The Development of Market Agriculture," 190–93.

2. Governor Robert Johnson to the Lords of Trade, September 28, 1732 and to the Duke of Newcastle, December 15, 1732, in "Records," XV, 229; Duffy, "Yellow Fever," 193–94; William L. King, *The Newspaper Press of Charleston, South Carolina* (New York, 1970), 8–14.

3. Charles Joseph Gayle, "The Nature and Volume of Exports from Charleston, 1724–1774," *PSCHA* (1937), 30–31; Warner Oland Moore, Jr., "The Largest Exporters of Deerskins from Charles Town, 1735–1775," *SCHM* 74 (July 1973), 144–45; Sirmans, *Colonial South Carolina*, 167; Coon, "Development of Market Agriculture," 191; Waterhouse, "South Carolina's Colonial Elite," 134–35, 138; Stumpf, "Merchants of Colonial Charleston," 168, 192; Duncan, "Servitude and Slavery," I, 157–58, 177; Elizabeth Donnan, "The Slave Trade into South Carolina before the Revolution," *AHR* 33 (July 1928), 808–9, 812–13.

4. Carl J. Vipperman, "The Brief and Tragic Career of Charles Lowndes,"

SCHM 70 (October 1969), 211–25; Carl J. Vipperman, *The Rise of Rawlins Lowndes, 1721–1800* (Columbia, S.C., 1978), 3–19; *Gazette,* May 22, 1736.

5. Duncan, "Servitude and Slavery," I, 105; Stumpf, "Merchants of Colonial Charleston," 165–70; Wood, *Black Majority,* 334–41; Donnan, "The Slave Trade into South Carolina," 808–10; Waterhouse, "South Carolina's Colonial Elite," 145, 159–61, 199–202; W. Robert Higgins, "Charles Town Merchants and Factors Dealing in the External Negro Trade, 1735–1775," *SCHM* 65 (October 1964), 206–17; M. Eugene Sirmans, "The South Carolina Royal Council, 1720–1763," *WMQ* 18 (July 1961), 392; Maurice A. Crouse, "The Manigault Family of South Carolina, 1685–1783" (Ph.D. dissertation, Northwestern University, 1964), 25–26; Robert M. Weir, " 'The Harmony We Were Famous For': An Interpretation of Pre-Revolutionary South Carolina Politics," *WMQ* 26 (October 1969), 474–82.

6. *Gazette,* September 13, 1735, May 5, 1736, October 19, 1738, May 1, 15, November 27, December 11, 1740; Bridenbaugh, *Cities,* 344, 347; Walter B. Edgar (ed.), *The Letterbook of Robert Pringle* (2 vols., Columbia, S.C., 1972), I, xviii, 31–32; Walter B. Edgar, "Robert Pringle and His World," *SCHM* 76 (January 1975), 3–7; E. Milby Burton, *South Carolina Silversmiths, 1690–1860* (Charleston, S.C., 1968), 51–73, 96–107, 166–79, 190; E. Milby Burton, *Charleston Furniture, 1700–1825* (Charleston, S.C., 1955), 74–78, 92–95, 107.

7. Beatrice St. Julien Ravenel, *Architects of Charleston* (Charleston, S.C., 1945), 11–15; "Samuel Dyssli to His Mother, Brothers, and Friends in Switzerland," December 3, 1737," in *SCHGM* 23 (July 1922), 89–90; Duncan, "Servitude and Slavery," I, 79, 94, 100, II, 429, 494–96, 501–5, 537–80; William R. Snell, "Indian Slavery," 151–56; "South Carolina Parish of St. Philips, Charles Town, Vestry Book, 1732" (Church Office, St. Philips, Charleston, S.C.); Mabel L. Webber (ed.), "Presentments of the Grand Jury, March, 1733/1734," *SCHGM* 25 (October 1924), 193.

8. Lathan Algerna Windley, "A Profile of Runaway Slaves in Virginia and South Carolina from 1730 through 1787" (Ph.D. dissertation, the University of Iowa, 1974), 41, 65–80, 105, 138, 152–62, 179, 204–6, 218; Daniel E. Meaders, "South Carolina Fugitives as Viewed through Local Colonial Newspapers with Emphasis on Runaway Notices, 1732–1801," *Journal of Negro History* 60 (April 1975), 290–94, 298–99, 306–14; *Gazette,* August 16, November 29, 1735, March 19, May 21, November 5, December 8, 1737, February 9, March 16, 30, June 22, 1738, June 14, 1740.

9. Duncan, "Servitude and Slavery," II, 546–47, 689, 690–91, 693, 772–77; Wood, *Black Majority,* 213–17, 221–23, 283–86; Sirmans, "Legal Status of the Slave," 469.

10. Dyssli to His Mother, December 3, 1737, p. 90; Duncan, "Servitude and Slavery," I, 275, 281–85; Wood, *Black Majority,* 234–38; Winthrop D. Jordan, *White over Black: American Attitudes toward the Negro, 1550–1812* (Baltimore, Md., 1969), 144–50; *Gazette,* September 6, 1735, July 24, 31, 1736.

11. "Letter from Anthony Gordy, Charleston, South Carolina, to His Brother in the Neighborhood of Lausanne, Switzerland, Charleston, May 28, 1733," *SCHGM* 23 (July 1922), 86–88; Gilbert P. Voigt, "Swiss Notes on South Carolina," *SCHGM* 21 (July 1920), 99–103; Bridenbaugh, *Cities,* 303, 359, 397; Jordan, *White over Black,* 129–30; *Gazette,* March 19, 1737; Wood, *Black Majority,*

227–29; J. H. Easterby (ed.), *JCHSC, September 14, 1742–January 27, 1744,* (Columbia, S.C., 1954), 547.

12. Samuel A. Lilly, "The Culture of Revolutionary Charleston" (Ph.D. dissertation, Miami University, 1972), 8–10; James H. Easterby, *The Rules of the South Carolina Society* (Baltimore, Md., 1937), 12–21, 26, 29, 30–32, 94; James H. Easterby, *History of the St. Andrew's Society of Charleston, South Carolina, 1729–1929* (Charleston, S.C., 1929), 21, 30, 34.

13. "St. Philip's Vestry Book, 1732"; Joseph I. Waring, "St. Philip's Hospital in Charleston in Carolina," *Annals of Medical History,* New Series, 4 (1932), 283–85; St. Julien Ravenel Childs, "Notes on the History of Public Health in South Carolina, 1670–1800," *PSCHA* (1932), 20 n29; Benjamin J. Klebaner, "Public Poor Relief in Charleston, 1800–1860," *SCHM* 55 (October 1954), 210; Waring, *History of Medicine,* 48–49; Waterhouse, "South Carolina's Colonial Elite," 247–48.

14. Webber, "Presentment of the Grand Jury," 193–94; J. H. Easterby (ed.), *JCHSC, November 10, 1736–June 7, 1739* (Columbia, S.C., 1951), 47, 51, 164; Bridenbaugh, *Cities,* 385; Voigt, "Swiss Notes," 102; *Gazette,* October 11, 1735, March 26, October 29, 1737, March 23, 1738, March 29, 1740, March 27, 1742; Rogers, *Charleston,* 22; Vipperman, *Rawlins Lowndes,* 36.

15. Henning Cohen, *The South Carolina Gazette, 1732–1775* (Columbia, S.C., 1953), 20, 71–78, Bridenbaugh, *Cities,* 432, 441; Eola Willis, *The Charleston Stage in the XVIII Century with Social Settings of the Time* (New York, 1933), 20; Easterby, *History of the St. Andrew's Society,* 43; Edgar, "Robert Pringle," 5.

16. Julia Curtis, "A Note on Henry Holt," *SCHM* 79 (January 1978), 1–3; Willis, *The Charleston Stage,* 10–15, 21–26; Curtis, "The Early Charleston Stage," 11–16, 22–23; Robert J. Bagdon, "Musical Life in Charleston, South Carolina from 1732 to 1776 as Recorded in Colonial Sources" (Ph.D. dissertation, University of Miami, 1978), 38–39, 59–64, 156–60; Frederick P. Bowes, *The Culture of Early Charleston* (Chapel Hill, N.C., 1942), 102; *Gazette,* August 27, 1737; Bridenbaugh, *Cities,* 381.

17. Cohen, *Gazette,* 3–5, 12, 181–85, 213, 230–41; King, *The Newspaper Press,* 8–14; Bowes, *Culture of Charleston,* 67–69; Bagdon, "Musical Life," 33–34. *Gazette,* May 18, 1734, August 15, 1743.

18. Bowes, *Culture of Charleston,* 56–60, 71–74; Cohen, *Gazette,* 121–32, 159–68; Walter B. Edgar, "The Libraries of Colonial South Carolina" (Ph.D. dissertation, University of South Carolina, 1969), 48–65, 101–12, 144–48, 169, 239; Walter B. Edgar, "Notable Libraries of Colonial South Carolina," *SCHM* 72 (April 1971), 105–10; Walter B. Edgar, "Some Popular Books in Colonial South Carolina," *SCHM* 72 (July 1971), 174–78.

19. Anna Wells Rutledge, "Artists in the Life of Charleston," *Transactions of the American Philosophical Society* (Philadelphia, Pa., 1949), 113–14; Bowes, *Culture of Charleston,* 48; Bagdon, "Musical Life," 23; A. S. Salley (ed.), *JCHSC, November 8, 1734–June 7, 1735* (Columbia, S.C., 1947), 81–82; J. H. Easterby (ed.), *JCHSC, September 12, 1739–March 26, 1741* (Columbia, S.C., 1952), 210; Cohen, *Gazette,* 29–32.

20. Rogers, *Charleston,* 56–57, 66–68; Alice R. Huger Smith and D. E. Huger Smith, *The Dwelling Houses of Charleston, South Carolina* (Philadelphia, Pa., 1917), 43–45; Jack Leland, *60 Famous Houses of Charleston, South Carolina* (Charleston, S.C., 1978), 37; Ravenel, *Architects,* 6–7; Johnson and Sloan, *A Doc-*

umentary Profile, 150; "Ichnography of Charles Town at High Water (1739)," *YCC, 1883* (Charleston, S.C., 1884), frontispiece; Bridenbaugh, *Cities*, 303–14.

21. *Gazette*, August 30, 1735; Easterby, *Journal, 1736–1739*, 258, 288; Easterby, *Journal, 1741*, 252; Webber, "Presentments of the Grand Jury," 194.

22. *Gazette*, May 4, 11, June 1, 15, 29, 1738; Joseph I. Waring, "James Killpatrick and Smallpox Inoculation in Charles Town," *Annals of Medical History*, New Series, 10 (July 1938), 301–4, 306; Waring, "St. Philip's Hospital," 284; Waring, *History of Medicine*, 38–47, 205; Edgar, *Letterbook of Pringle*, I, 33; Duffy, *Epidemics*, 82–83; Williams, "Letters to the Bishop," 296; Duffy, "Yellow Fever," 194; John Duffy, "Eighteenth Century Carolina Health Conditions," *JSH* 18 (August 1952), 301; Wood, *Black Majority*, 313.

23. Duncan, "Servitude and Slavery," II, 501–5, 778–86, 795–800; Wood, *Black Majority*, 271–75, 313–25; Edgar, *Letterbook of Pringle*, I, 135, 163; Easterby, *JCHSC, 1739–1741*, 63–65, 82–83, 86, 184–85; Vipperman, *Rawlins Lowndes*, 37.

24. *Gazette*, March 1742; Sirmans, *Colonial South Carolina*, 209–10; McCord, VII, 397–417; "The Humble Petition and Representation of the Council and Assembly of Your Majestys Province of South Carolina to the Kings Most Excellent Majesty," July 26, 1740, "Records," XX, 300–301.

25. Carroll, *Historical Collections*, I, 341; Kenneth Scott, "Suffers in the Charleston Fire of 1740," *SCHM* 64 (October 1963), 203–11; Edgar, *Letterbook of Pringle*, I, 271–72; Easterby, *JCHSC, 1739–1741*, 479–93; Easterby, *JCHSC, May 18, 1741–July 10, 1742* (Columbia, S.C., 1953), 250–55; *Gazette*, December 4, 18, 1740; Stumpf, "Merchants of Charleston," 190–91, 211; Rogers, *Charleston*, 30; Duncan, "Servitude and Slavery," II, 739–41; Wood, *Black Majority*, 294–95.

26. Bolton, "The Anglican Church," 296–345, 349; David T. Morgan, "The Great Awakening in South Carolina, 1740–1775," *South Atlantic Quarterly* 70 (Autumn 1971), 595–606; Williams, "Letters to the Bishop," 296; Duncan, "Servitude and Slavery," I, 359–70; Sirmans, *Colonial South Carolina*, 231–32; Bowes, *Culture of Charleston*, 222–29; William Howland Kenney III, "Alexander Garden and George Whitefield: The Significance of Revivalism in South Carolina, 1738–1741," *SCHM* 71 (January 1970), 1–16; Elise Pinckney (ed.), *The Letterbook of Eliza Lucas Pinckney* (Chapel Hill, N.C., 1972), 30.

27. Edgar, *Letterbook of Pringle*, I, 280–82, 288–89, 292; Ludlum, *Early American Winters*, 139–141; Scott, "Sufferers in the Fire," 206–8; *Gazette*, November 27, 1740; Bolton, "The Anglican Church," 333; "St. Philip's Vestry Book, 1732."

28. *Gazette*, December 25, 1740; "Postscript" August 15, 1741; Wood, *Black Majority*, 296; Scott, "Sufferers in the Fire," 207; Carl Bridenbaugh, *Cities in Revolt: Urban Life in America, 1743–1776* (New York, 1964), 18–19; Duncan, "Servitude and Slavery," I, 331–37, II, 741–44.

29. Harvey H. Jackson, "Hugh Bryan and the Evangelical Movement in Colonial South Carolina," *WMQ* 43 (October 1986), 594–614; Leigh Eric Schmidt, " 'The Grand Prophet,' Hugh Bryan: Early Evangelicalism's Challenge to the Establishment and Slavery in the Colonial South," *SCHM* 87 (October 1986), 238–50.

30. Edgar, *Letterbook of Pringle*, I, 387–88, 409–10, II, 530; James Glen to My Lords, February 6, 1744, October 10, 1748, "Records," XXI, 30–31, 155–

56, 237, XXIII, 232; Sirmans, *Colonial South Carolina*, 212–13; Easterby, *JCHSC, 1741–1742*, 563–77; Duncan, "Servitude and Slavery," II, 802–3. "St. Philip's Vestry Book, 1732"; Coon, "Development of Market Agriculture," 194; Easterby, *JCHSC, 1742–1744*, 234–38, 547–48.

31. W. E. May, "Capt. Charles Hardy on the Carolina Station, 1742–1744," *SCHM* 70 (January 1969), 2, 4, 9, 12–17; Edgar, *Letterbook of Pringle*, II, 680–85, 790; Stuart O. Stumpf, "Implications of King George's War for the Charleston Mercantile Community," *SCHM* 77 (July 1976), 161–70; Rogers, *Charleston*, 32–33; George C. Rogers, Jr., *Evolution of a Federalist: William Loughton Smith of Charleston, 1758–1812* (Columbia, S.C., 1962), 11; *Gazette*, January 14, 21, March 19, 1745.

32. *Gazette*, May 24, 1740, March 27, 1742; May, "Capt. Charles Hardy," 4, 8–14, 16–17; Philip M. Hamer (ed.), *The Papers of Henry Laurens* (Columbia, S.C., 1968), I, 50, 73; Edgar, *Letterbook of Pringle*, II, 491–92, 569, 734, 762, 815n, 825; Stumpf, "King George's War," 168–78; Vipperman, *Rawlins Lowndes*, 41–46; Rogers, *Evolution of a Federalist*, 12; Waterhouse, "South Carolina's Colonial Elite," 279–99; Weir, " 'The Harmony We Were Famous For,' " 483–85; Coon, "The Development of Market Agriculture," 194–97.

33. George Hunter to Your Lordships, June 30, 1744, "Records," XXI, 281–82; James Glen to My Lords, May 28, 1745, "The Humble Petition of The Governor's Council and Assembly of Your Majesty's Province of South Carolina to the King's Most Excellent Majesty," May 11, 1745, "Records," XXII, 88–93, 104, 274; Easterby, *JCHSC, February 20, 1744–May 25, 1745* (Columbia, S.C., 1955), 230–35, 316–17, 462–79, 489–90, 509–13; Peter Henry Bruce, *The Memoirs of Peter Henry Bruce, Esq.* (London, 1782), 382–84, 433–43, 517–18; Ravenel, *Architects*, 19–21; "Historical Notes," *SCHGM* XII (July 1911), 159–60; Rogers, *Charleston*, 57.

34. "The Presentments of the Grand Jury . . . At Charles Town," March 20, 1744; "Records," XXII, 74–75; James Glen to My Lords, February 6, 1744, "Records," XXI, 237–39; *Gazette*, April 15, 1745, January 15, 19, March 30, 1747; *Sophia Hume's Exhortation and Epistles to the People of South Carolina* (London, 1752), 43; Bridenbaugh, *Cities in Revolt*, 110, 120; David Morton Knepper, "The Political Structure of Colonial South Carolina, 1743–1776" (Ph.D. dissertation, University of Virginia, 1971), 220; Easterby, *JCHSC, September 10, 1745–June 17, 1746*, (Columbia, S.C., 1956), 50–51, 64.

35. Easterby, *JCHSC, September 10, 1746–June 13, 1747* (Columbia, S.C., 1958), 86; Vipperman, *Rawlins Lowndes*, 43, 46–47, 51n, 52, 107; Easterby, *JCHSC, January 19, 1748–June 29, 1748* (Columbia, S.C., 1961), 46–48, 191–92; R. Nicholas Olsberg (ed.), *JCHSC, April 23, 1750–August 31, 1751* (Columbia, S.C., 1974), 232–33; Bridenbaugh, *Cities in Revolt*, 118, 303, 305.

36. Easterby, *JCHSC, 1743–1744*, 532–35; Cooper, *Statutes*, III, 773–74; Easterby, *JCHSC, 1746–1747*, 161.

37. Waring, *History of Medicine*, 51–60, 270–71; Duffy, *Epidemics*, 138–39; 156–57; Hamer, *Laurens Papers*, 171; Duffy, "Yellow Fever," 195–96; Ludlum, *Early American Winters*, 142–43; Waring, "St. Philip's Hospital," 285; Duncan, "Servitude and Slavery," I, 251–52; Easterby, *JCHSC, March 28, 1749–March 19, 1750*, (Columbia, S.C., 1962), 199–200, 276; Cooper, *Statutes*, III, 694. Dr. John Moultrie, Jr., was the first native-born American to graduate from the University

of Edinburgh, His dissertation, written in Ciceronian Latin, described the epidemic of 1745.

38. McCord, *Statutes*, VII, 76; Easterby, *JCHSC, 1749–1750*, 383–88; Terry H. Lipscomb and R. Nichols Olsberg (eds.), *JCHSC, 1751–1752* (Columbia, S.C., 1977), 43, 302–3; Olsberg, *JCHSC, 1750–1751*, 240–41.

39. "Presentments," "Records," XXII, 73–74, 76; Meaders, "South Carolina Fugitives," 306; Duncan, "Servitude and Slavery," II, 693–94, 808–12; James Glen to My Lords, May 28, 1745, April 28, 1747, "Records," XXII, 104, 272–73; Hamer, *Laurens Papers*, 228–29.

40. *Gazette*, June 19, 1749; Vipperman, *Rawlins Lowndes*, 56; Duncan, "Servitude and Slavery," II, 716, 812; Wood, *Black Majority*, 289–91, 297–98.

41. Easterby, *Journal, 1749–1750*, 336, 379, 383–84, 387, 406; Olsberg, *JCHSC, 1750–1751*, 150, 286–87, 292–94; Cooper, *Statutes*, VII, 77, 423.

42. Waring, *History of Medicine*, 62; Stumpf, "King George's War," 173–88; Vipperman, *Rawlins Lowndes*, 52–56; Rogers, *Charleston*, 30–38; James Glen to My Lords, April 28, 1747, "Records," XXII, 274; George W. Williams, *St. Michael's, Charleston, 1751–1951* (Columbia, S.C., 1951), 9–11; Hamer, *Laurens Papers*, 203–4, 241–42.

43. Lionel Chalmers, *An Account of the Weather and Disease of South Carolina* (London, 1776), 16–23; *Gazette*, April 27, September 19, 1752; King, *The Newspaper Press of Charleston*, 15–16; Chapman L. Milling (ed.), *Colonial South Carolina: Two Contemporary Descriptions* (Columbia, S.C., 1940), 107–8; Governor James Glen to My Lords, September 19, 1752, "Records," XXV, 84–86; Lipscomb and Olsberg, *JCHSC, 1751–1752*, 407; "Journal of the Commons House of Assembly, November 12, 1754–March 10, 1755" (ms., SCA), XXX, 197–203; Leland, *60 Famous Houses*, 33–37; Ramsay, *History*, 37–38, 177–82; VBSP, I, 1732 to [1755] (ms., St. Philip's Church, Charleston, S.C.), October 2, 1752.

44. VBSP, II, 1756–1774 (ms., St. Philip's Church, Charleston, S.C.), August 7, October 2, 16, 1758; *Gazette*, October 10, 13, 1752, June 4, 1753, February 6, 1755, February 5, 1756, July 29, 1756, May 5, July 11, 1759; Ludlum, *Hurricanes*, 45–48; Gayle, "The Nature and Volume of Exports," 31; Rogers, *Charleston*, 28–29; Lipscomb and Olsberg, *JCHSC, 1751–1752*, 383–84, 388–89, 411; Vipperman, *Rawlins Lowndes*, 70; VBSP, I, August 6, 1753, August 12, 1754, June 28, 1756, October 2, 16, 1758.

45. James Glen to My Lords, October 10, 1748, "Records," XXIII, 232–36; Jack P. Greene, *The Quest for Power: The Lower Houses of Assembly in the Southern Royal Colonies, 1689–1776* (Chapel Hill, N.C., 1963), 254–58; Sirmans, *Colonial South Carolina*, 293; Lipscomb and Olsberg, *JCHSC, 1751–1752*, 395–96; Louis De Vorsey, Jr. (ed.), *De Brahm's Report of the General Survey in the Southern District of North America* (Columbia, S.C., 1971), 7–14.

46. Williams, *St. Michael's*, 135–39; A. S. Salley, *The State Houses of South Carolina, 1751–1936* (Columbia, S.C., 1936), 4–5; "Ichnography of Charleston . . . for the Use of the Phoenix Fire Company of London" (ms., SCHS); Lipscomb and Olsberg, *JCHSC, 1751–1752*, 410; De Vorsey, *De Brahm's Report*, 16–17, 99–100.

47. "Journal of the Commissioners of the Fortifications, 1755–[1770]" (ms., SCHS), September 1, 1755–June 11, 1756; Marguerite B. Hamer, "The Fate of

the Exiled Acadians in South Carolina," *JSH* 4 (May 1938), 199–204; *Gazette*, March 15, 16, April 12, 17, May 6, July 29, 1756.

48. [George Milligen-Johnston], *A Short Description of South Carolina* (London, 1763), in Milling, *Colonial South Carolina*, xvii–xviii, 145; Pelatiah Webster, "Journal of a Visit to Charles Town, 1765," in H. Roy Merrens (ed.), *The Colonial South Carolina Scene: Contemporary Views, 1697–1774* (Columbia, S.C., 1977), 220; Salley, "The State Houses," 6–7.

49. *Gazette*, May 6, 1756; De Vorsey, *De Braham's Report*, 99–101; Philip M. Hamer and George C. Rogers, Jr. (eds.), *The Papers of Henry Laurens, November 1, 1755–December 31, 1758* (Columbia, S.C., 1970), II, 165, 281; Sirmans, *Colonial South Carolina*, 294, 308–10; "Journal of the Commons House of Assembly," March 5, 1757, XXXI, 56–57, 63, 148–49.

50. William H. Lyttleton to the Lords Commissioners of Trade, May 4, May 24, July 12, 1757, "Records," XXVII, 261–64, 288–89, 305–9; "Journal of the Commissioners of the Fortifications," October 4, 18, 23, December 7, 9, 1756, July 12, August 1, August 11, November 8, December 8, 1757; Rogers, *Charleston*, 59; "Journal of the Commons House," June 27, 1757, XXXI, 142–43; Hamer and Rogers, *Laurens Papers*, II, 449n3; Rogers, *Evolution of a Federalist*, 16–23.

51. Sirmans, *Colonial South Carolina*, 316–23; Alan Calmes, "The Lyttelton Expedition of 1759: Military Failures and Financial Successes," *SCHM* 77 (January 1976), 20–21; Jack P. Greene, "The South Carolina Quartering Dispute, 1757–1758," *SCHM* 60 (October 1959), 193–97; William A. Foote, "The South Carolina Independents," *SCHM* 62 (October 1961), 199; VBSP, II, August 5, 1756, September 27, 1756, December 13, 1757; "Journal of the Commons House," July 2, 1759–June 6, 1759," XXXIV, 325, 340–41; Mabel L. Webber (ed.), "Extracts from the Journal of Mrs. Ann Manigault, 1754–1781," *SCHGM* 20 (April 1919), 128–29; George C. Rogers, Jr., "The Papers of James Grant of Ballindalloch Castle Scotland," *SCHM* 77 (July 1976), 146.

52. "Journal of the Commissioners of the Fortifications," October 14, 1757, February 20, 1758; J. H. Easterby, *A History of the College of Charleston* (New York, 1935), 25–26; "Journal of the Commons House, October 6, 1757–April 7, 1759," October 14, 1757, February 9, 1758, XXXII, 15–16, 101–2; Greene, "Quartering Dispute," 196–204; Sirmans, *Colonial South Carolina*, 321–23.

53. Rogers, *Evolution of a Federalist*, 33; Philip M. Hamer and George C. Rogers, Jr., (eds.),*The Papers of Henry Laurens*, January 1, 1759–August 31, 1763 (Columbia, S.C., 1972), III, 18nn 8–9; Calmes, "Lyttleton Expedition," 13–18, 20–26; Sirmans, *Colonial South Carolina*, 333, 342; Carroll, *Historical Collections*, I, 452; Weir, *Colonial South Carolina*, 269.

54. Waring, *History of Medicine*, 74–76, 221, 235; Ramsay, *History*, 44; Edmund Berkeley and Dorothy Smith Berkeley, *Dr. Alexander Garden of Charles Town* (Chapel Hill, N.C., 1969), 136–39, 140–42; *Gazette*, February 16, March 29, April 14, 1760; Pinckney, *The Letterbook of Pinckney*, 147–48, 153; Diane Meredith Sydenham, "Practitioner and Patient: The Practice of Medicine in Eighteenth Century South Carolina" (Ph.D. dissertation, Johns Hopkins University, 1979), 24, 232; Duffy, *Epidemics*, 94–95; Weir, *Colonial South Carolina*, 270.

55. "Journal of a Visit to Charleston, 1765," in Merrens, *Colonial South Carolina Scene*, 219–20; De Vorsey, *De Brahm's Report*, 90; Robert P. Stockton, "St. Michael's Architect: A Subject for Dispute," *News and Courier*, April 11, 1977;

Robert P. Stockton, "St. Michael's Architect: Unknown," *News and Courier,* October 23, 1978; Ravenel, *Architects,* 27–30; Margaret Simons Middleton, *Jeremiah Theus: Colonial Artist of Charles Town* (Columbia, S.C., 1953), 46; A. S. Salley (ed.), "Diary of William Dillwyn in 1772 during a Visit to Charles Town," *SCHGM* 36 (January 1935), 6; *A History of the Lutheran Church in South Carolina* (Columbia, S.C., 1971), 76.

56. Weir, *Colonial South Carolina,* 271–74; Rogers, *South Carolina Chronology,* 28; Berkeley, *Dr. Alexander Garden,* 169; Duffy, *Epidemics,* 161; Ramsay, *History,* 61.

57. William George Bentley, "Wealth in Colonial South Carolina" (Ph.D. dissertation, Georgia State University, 1977), 6, 77; Waterhouse, "South Carolina's Colonial Elite," 174–77; Rogers, *Evolution of a Federalist,* 18–22; Moore, "The Largest Exporters of Deerskins," 147–50; Rogers and Hamer, *Laurens Papers,* III, 4–6; Rogers, *Charleston,* 37–38; *Gazette,* April 24, November 6, 1762.

58. Gayle, "The Nature and Volume of Exports," 25–33; Leila Sellers, *Charleston Business on the Eve of the American Revolution* (Chapel Hill, N.C., 1934), 9, 11, 154; Donnan, "The Slave Trade into South Carolina," 807, 822, 826; Hamer and Rogers, *Laurens Papers,* II, 427–28; Bentley, "Wealth Distribution," 74, 90, 92.

59. Weir, *Colonial South Carolina,* 292–93; Walter B. Edgar and N. Louise Bailey, *Biographical Directory of the South Carolina House of Representatives; Volume II, The Commons House of Assembly, 1692–1775* (Columbia, S.C., 1977), II, 540–41. The only member of the artisan class to represent Charles Town during the colonial period was Hopkins Price. His career was extraordinary. Immigrating to Charles Town in the 1740s, Price started as a tanner and cobbler, invested in real estate, and was elected as a commissioner of various public works and a churchwarden of St. Philip's. First sent to the Commons House in 1760, he was returned four times.

60. Hamer and Rogers, *Laurens Papers,* III, 416, 467–68; George C. Rogers, Jr., and David R. Chesnutt (eds.), *The Papers of Henry Laurens* (Columbia, S.C., 1974), IV, 85; *Gazette,* April 23, June 14, 18, 1763; Berkeley, *Dr. Alexander Garden,* 137.

Chapter III

1. *Gazette,* November 5, 1763; Webber, "Extracts from the Journal of Ann Manigault," 204–7; Willis, *The Charleston Stage,* 44–47; Carl Bridenbaugh, *Myths and Realities: Societies of the Colonial South* (Baton Rouge, La., 1952), 93.

2. Anna Wells Rutledge, *Artists in the Life of Charleston through Colony and State from Restoration to Reconstruction* (Columbia, S.C., 1980), 114–21; Cohen, *South Carolina Gazette,* 49–57; Thomas J. Tobias (ed.), "Charles Town in 1764," *SCHM* 68 (April 1966), 67–68.

3. Raymond A. Mohl, "Poverty in Early America, a Reappraisal: The Case of Eighteenth Century New York City, *New York History* 50 (1969), 5–27; Allan Kulikoff, "The Progress of Inequality in Revolutionary Boston," *WMQ* 28 (July 1971), 376–411; Gary B. Nash, "Poverty and Poor Relief in Pre-Revolutionary Philadelphia," *WMQ* 33 (January 1976), 3–29; Gary B. Nash, *The Urban Crucible: Social Change, Political Consciousness and the Origins of the American Revolution* (Cambridge, Mass., 1979); John K. Alexander, *Render Them Submissive: Responses*

to *Poverty in Philadelphia, 1760–1800* (Amherst, Mass., 1980). Contemporary townspeople and visitors to these urban centers in the several decades before the American Revolution, like most modern-day historians, have had little to say about the dramatically growing number of poor in the cities. Only recently have historians of the Revolutionary era explored the phenomenon of the increase of poverty in the cities and the impact of the poor on the political and social history of the period.

4. *Gazette,* August 25, 1764, March 9, 1765, July 30, 1772; "Journal of a Visit," in Merrens, *Colonial South Carolina Scene,* 224; A. S. Salley (ed.), *JCHSC, January 9, 1765–August 9, 1765* (Columbia, S.C., 1949), 79–80; Waring, *History of Medicine,* 77–78, 81–90; Ramsay, *History,* 49; Duffy, *Epidemics,* 175–76.

5. Rogers and Chesnutt, *Laurens Papers,* IV, 26, 42, 94, 282, 431, 475, 499n, 598; George C. Rogers, Jr., and David R. Chesnutt (eds.), *The Papers of Henry Laurens, September 1, 1765–July 31, 1768* (Columbia, S.C., 1976), V, 5, 6, 55, 58, 77, 207, 315, 315n, 348, 355, 684; George C. Rogers, Jr., and David R. Chesnutt (eds.), *The Papers of Henry Laurens, August 1, 1768–July 31, 1769* (Columbia, S.C., 1978), VI, 95, 112, 119, 182, 235–36, 256.

6. Rogers and Chesnutt, *Laurens Papers,* VI, 688, 709; Webber, "Extracts from the Journal of Ann Manigault," 128–41, 204–7; Carl Bridenbaugh, "Charlestonians at Newport, 1767–1775," *SCHGM* 41 (April 1940), 43–47; Sydenham, "Practitioner and Patient," 17–18.

7. Sydenham, "Practitioner and Patient," 14; Bridenbaugh, *Cities in Revolt,* 228, 326; Robert V. Wells, "Household Size and Composition in the British Colonies in America, 1767–1775," *Journal of Interdisciplinary History* 4 (Spring 1974), 543–70; Robert V. Wells, *The Population of the British Colonies in America before 1776: A Survey of Census Data* (Princeton, N.J., 1975), 297–333; VBSP, II, May 1, 1764, April 15, 1765, April 17, 1767, April 23, 1770, April 27, 1772; Waring, *History of Medicine,* 67, 79, 90; *Gazette,* June 29, 1767; Hamer and Rogers, *Laurens Papers,* III, 138–40.

8. VBSP I, March 18, 1751; VBSP II, January 7, 1757, January 12, March 13, 1758, June 19, 1766, February 25, 1771, April 27, June 27, August 10, 1772, September 16, 1773; "Journal of the Commons House of South Carolina, October 28, 1765 to May 28, 1767" (ms., SCA), "Schedule of the Charges to the Government, January 1–December 31, 1767, April 6, 1767, XXXVII, 343, 666; Hamer, "Exiled Acadians," 199–204; *Gazette,* July 29, 1756.

9. VBSP I, February 12, April 25, 1751, January 7, 1757, June 5, 1757, April 30, 1759; VBSP II, August 7, 1758, July 14, November 7, 1768. The reform impulse evinced from time to time by the churchmen of St. Philip's conflicts with David J. Rothman's interpretation in *The Discovery of the Asylum: Social Order and Disorder in the New Republic* (Boston, Mass., 1971), 53; Easterby, *History of the St. Andrew's Society,* 36; *Gazette,* June 7, July 18, 1756, October 15, 1758, April 2, 7, 1759, November 12, 1764, July 6, 1767, October 12, 1769, February 1, 1770, November 28, 1771.

10. George D. Sussman, "Parisian Infants and Norman Wet Nurses in the Early Nineteenth Century: A Statistical Study," *Journal of Interdisciplinary History* 7 (Spring 1977), 637–53. "Wet nursing" was a particularly French institution that flourished in the eighteenth and nineteenth centuries. In Paris it appears that most of the wet nurses were unmarried women and that "wet nursing" was "an important source of supplementary income for many women." Interestingly, it appears

that this too was the case in Charles Town; VBSP I, 1751–[1755]; VBSP II, 1756–1773; *Gazette*, December 13, 1760, June 7, 1773.

11. Hamer and Rogers, *Laurens Papers*, III, 416, 416n; Bridenbaugh, *Cities in Revolt*, 374, 379; *Gazette*, November 9, 1769; *South Carolina and American General Gazette*, November 20, 1769; Ramsay, *History*, 199–200; Easterby, *History of the College of Charleston*, 14; David D. Wallace, *The Life of Henry Laurens* (New York, 1915), 182, 463–64; Bowes, *Culture of Charleston*, 44, 50–53; Bridenbaugh, *Myths and Realities*, 103.

12. Rogers, *Charleston*, 100–103; Christopher Gould, "Robert Wells, Colonial Charleston Printer," *SCHM* 79 (January 1978), 23–26.

13. Approximately 25 percent of some 270 persons who served as grand jurors from 1756 to 1774 were members of the "great families" of South Carolina. Included among these were Benjamin Smith, planter-merchant, and the richest man to die in South Carolina before the Revolution; Gabriel Manigault, the wealthiest person in Charles Town by 1776; prominent export-import merchants, large slaveholders and landowners Thomas L. Smith, John Savage, and George Inglis, and members of the Commons House of Assembly Christopher Gadsden, Jacob Motte, Jr., and Richard Beresford. See Grand Jury Lists, *Gazette*, May 1, 1756, April 29, 1763, June 1, October 31, 1765, January 25, 1768, April 13, 22, 1769, May 3, 1770, February 7, 1771, January 24, October 29, 1772, May 24, February 28, June 6, 1774; Waterhouse, "South Carolina's Colonial Elite," 161–62; VBSP II, April 19, 29, 1763, December 7, 22, 1766, April 13, 1769, April 16, 19, 1773; Thomas Anderson to [the St. Andrew's Society] [n/d, early 1760s?], in Easterby, *History of the St. Andrew's Society*, 37.

14. David Merrill Zornow, "A Troublesome Community: Blacks in Revolutionary Charles Town, 1765–1775," (unpublished honors essay, Harvard, 1976, Harvard College Archives), 13–16, 20, 32, 34; Peter H. Wood, " 'Taking Care of Business' in Revolutionary South Carolina: Republicanism and the Slave Society," in Jack R. Censer (ed.), *South Atlantic Urban Studies* (Columbia, S.C., 1978), 54–56; *Gazette*, June 20, 1768; Richard Walsh, "The Charleston Mechanics: A Brief Study, 1760–1776," *SCHM* 60 (July 1959), 137.

15. Donnan, "The State Trade into South Carolina," 808–22; Richard Walsh, *Charleston's Sons of Liberty: A Study of the Artisans, 1763–1789* (Columbia, S.C., 1959), 36, 41–43; *Gazette*, February 2, 1765.

16. Robert McColloch Weir, " 'Liberty and Property, and No Stamps': South Carolina and the Stamp Act Crisis" (Ph.D. dissertation, Case Western Reserve University, 1966), 172–97, 202–3; Jack P. Green, "The Gadsden Election Controversy and the Revolutionary Movement in South Carolina," *Mississippi Valley Historical Review* 46 (December 1959), 469–92. Ramsay, *History*, 253; Richard Walsh, "Christopher Gadsden: Radical or Conservative Revolutionary?" *SCHM* 63 (July 1962), 196–98; Robert H. Woody, "Christopher Gadsden and the Stamp Act," *PSCHA* (1939), 3–5; Rogers and Chesnutt, *Laurens Papers*, IV, 165n1; Laura French, "The Republicanism of Henry Laurens," *SCHM* 76 (April 1975), 73.

17. Woody, "Christopher Gadsden," 3–5; Weir, " 'Liberty and Property, and No Stamps,' " 200–205, 224–40; Robert M. Weir (ed.), "Two Letters by Christopher Gadsden, February, 1766," *SCHM* 75 (July 1974), 169; Edward McCrady, *The History of South Carolina under the Royal Government, 1719–1776* (New York, 1899), 563–67; Walsh, *Charleston's Sons of Liberty, 36–38*.

18. Robert M. Weir, '*A Most Important Epocha' The Coming of the Revolution*

in South Carolina (Columbia, S.C., 1970), 16–18; Rogers and Chesnutt, *Laurens Papers*, V, 24–32, 40; Weir, " 'Liberty and Property, and No Stamps,' " 229–33; on the growing phenomenon of the use of violence as a political weapon by the mobs in Northern cities, see Jesse Lemisch, "The Radicalism of the Inarticulate: Merchant Seamen in the Politics of Revolutionary America," in Alfred F. Young (ed.), *Dissent: Explorations in the History of American Radicalism* (DeKalb, Ill., 1968), 37–82; Wood, " 'Taking Care of Business,' " 58; Rogers, *Evolution of a Federalist, 42–43*.

19. Hennig Cohen (ed.), "Four Letters from Peter Timothy, 1755, 1768, 1771," *SCHM* 55 (July 1954), 162; Weir, " 'Liberty and Property, and No Stamps,' " 237–42; Robert M. Weir, "Who Shall Rule at Home: The American Revolution as a Crisis of Legitimacy for the Colonial Elite," *Journal of Interdisciplinary History* (Spring 1976), 683; Pauline Maier, "The Charleston Mob and the Evolution of Popular Politics in Revolutionary South Carolina, 1765–1784," in *Perspectives in American History* 4 (1970), 176.

20. Donnan, "The Slave Trade into South Carolina," 808–22; W. Robert Higgins, "The Geographical Origins of Negro Slaves in Colonial South Carolina," *South Atlantic Quarterly* 70 (Winter 1971), 34–47; Warner Oland Moore, Jr., "Henry Laurens: A Charleston Merchant in the Eighteenth Century, 1747–1771" (Ph.D. dissertation, University of Alabama, 1974), 159–62, 183–87, 192–96; Rogers and Chesnutt, *Laurens Papers*, IV, 557–59; Duncan, "Servitude and Slavery," I, 134–63, II, 174–75; Weir, " 'Liberty and Property and No Stamps,' " 47n, 47–49; Hamer and Rogers, *Laurens Papers*, III, 195n; Merrens, "Journal of a Visit to Charleston, 1765," 224; Daniel P. Mannix and Malcolm Cowley, *Black Cargoes: A History of the Atlantic Slave Trade* (New York, 1962).

21. Higgins, "Charles Town Merchants and Factors," 205–8; Rogers, *Evolution of a Federalist,* 17–19; Edgar and Bailey, *Biographical Directory,* II, 593–94, 644; Sydenham, "Practitioner and Patient," 6–12, 21–22, 83–84, 94, 105n, 128, 133–46; Chalmers G. Davidson, *Friend of the People: The Life of Dr. Peter Fayssoux* (Columbia, S.C., 1950), 10–11; Bridenbaugh, *Myths and Realities,* 106–7; Bowes, *Culture of Charleston,* 76–78, 91; *Gazette,* February 2, 1765; Walsh, *Charleston's Sons of Liberty,* 103n, 143–45.

22. Rogers, *Evolution of a Federalist,* 25–31; Rogers, *Charleston,* 24–25; Richard Brent Clow, "Edward Rutledge of South Carolina, 1749–1800: Unproclaimed Statesman" (Ph.D. dissertation, University of Georgia, 1976), 31; Knepper, "The Political Structure of Colonial South Carolina," 16–17, 27, 32–33, 205–9; Waterhouse, "South Carolina's Colonial Elite," 162–66; George C. Rogers, Jr., "The Charleston Tea Party: The Significance of December 3, 1773," *SCHM* 75 (July 1974), 153–54; H. Roy Merrens (ed.), "A View of Coastal South Carolina in 1778: The Journal of Ebenezer Hazard," *SCHM* 73 (October 1972), 186; Richard Walsh, "The Charleston Mechanics," 140; Walsh, *Charleston's Sons of Liberty,* 18, 26–27; Bentley, "Wealth Distribution," 77–112; George C. Rogers, Jr., *The History of Georgetown County, South Carolina* (Columbia, S.C., 1970), 55–56.

23. Wood, " 'Taking Care of Business,' " 57–58; Duncan, "Servitude and Slavery," II, 819–26; Zornow, " 'A Troublesome Community,' " 68, 70–80; Rogers and Chesnutt, *Laurens Papers,* V, 53–54; "Extracts from the Journal of Mrs. Ann Manigault," *SCHGM* (July 1919), 209; Ludlum, *Early American Winters,* 143.

24. Maurice A. Crouse (ed.), "The Letterbook of Peter Manigault, 1763–1773," *SCHM* 70 (April 1969), 90–91; D. E. Huger Smith, "Wilton's Statue of

Pitt," *SCHM* 15 (January 1914), 18–32; Woody, "Christopher Gadsden," 10–11; Walsh, *Charleston's Sons of Liberty*, 29–31; Walsh, "The Charleston Mechanics," 143; *Gazette*, June 29, 1767; Yates Snowden, *History of South Carolina* (Chicago and New York, 1920), I, 289–90.

25. Walsh, "The Charleston Mechanics," 128–33, 140; Walsh, *Charleston's Sons of Liberty*, 18, 26, 28; Knepper, "Political Structure of Colonial South Carolina," 207–9; Bentley, "Wealth Distribution," 77–112; Hamer and Rogers, *Laurens Papers*, II, 532–33, 532n; Rogers and Chesnutt, *Laurens Papers*, IV, 261n; Bridenbaugh, *Cities in Revolt*, 351; Burton, *Charleston Furniture*, 76–77, 84–89, 130; Edgar and Bailey, *Biographical Directory*, II, 85–86, 96; 540–41; *Gazette*, November 13, 1755; Burton, *South Carolina Silversmiths, 146–49, 163–69, 208*.

26. Smith and Smith, *The Dwelling Houses of Charleston*, 272–73; Albert Simons, "Architectural Trends in Charleston," *Antiques Magazine* (April 1970), 556, 560; Richard Walsh, "Edmund Egan: Charleston's Rebel Brewer," *SCHM* 56 (October 1955), 201–2; Duncan, "Servitude and Slavery," I, 103, II, 438.

27. Walsh, *Charleston's Sons of Liberty*, 41–45; *Gazette*, June 1, 1765, January 25, 1768; "Journal of the Commons House," April 6, 1767; Easterby, "Public Poor Relief," 81–86; McCord, *Statutes* VII, 90–92; Joseph I. Waring, "The Marine Hospitals of Charleston," *YCC* (Charleston, S.C., 1939), 172–73; VBSP II, December 7, 22, 1766, May 24, 1770, February 23, 1773; "Journal of the Commons House, November 28, 1769–September 18, 1770" (ms., SCA), February 22, 1770.

28. In 1763 Dr. George Milligen-Johnston estimated that there were "about eleven Hundred Dwelling Houses in the Town." Seven years later there were 1,292 "dwelling houses" counted during a census ordered by Royal Lieutenant Governor William Bull. George Milligen-Johnston, "A Short Description of the Province," in Chapman J. Milling (ed.), *South Carolina* (Columbia, S.C., 1940), 31; "Records," XXXII, 380; Bridenbaugh, *Cities in Revolt*, 216, 333; Rogers, "The Charleston Tea Party," 154, 156; Edgar and Bailey, *Biographical Directory*, II, 274–76.

29. John Morrill Bryan, "The Exchange Building, Charleston, 1766–1973: An Architectural History and Restoration Proposal" (ms., SCA), 1–13; Ravenel, *Architects*, 39–146; "Charleston at the End of the Colonial Era, 1774," in Merrens, *Colonial South Carolina Scene*, 282. In 1838 the Guard House was torn down and another built which was in turn demolished for the building of the Post Office that stands on the site today; Ramsay, *History*, 40–41; Rogers, *Charleston*, 58, 62; *Gazette*, August 1, 1768; Mark A. Dewolfe Howe (ed.), "Journal of Josiah Quincy, Junior, 1773," *Proceedings of the Massachusetts Historical Society* 49 (June 1916), 441.

30. McCord, *Statutes*, VII, 85–96; Waring, "The Marine Hospitals of Charleston," 172n3, 173; *Gazette*, November 16, 1767, April 11, 1768, January 17, August 8, 1771; Nora M. Davis, "Public Powder Magazines at Charleston," *YCC, 1942* (Charleston, S.C., 1943), 194; A. S. Salley (ed.), *JCHSC, January 8, 1765–August 9, 1765* (Columbia, S.C., 1949), 101, 128–29; Rogers, *Charleston*, 57–63; Richard Walsh (ed.), *The Writings of Christopher Gadsden, 1746–1805* (Columbia, S.C., 1966), 95; Burton, *South Carolina Silversmiths*, 148; Leland, *60 Famous Houses*, 6; Helen N. Othersen, "History Surrounds 64 Montague Street," *News and Courier*, May 8, 1978.

31. Robert P. Stockton, "Coming Street Home Built on Glebe Lot" and "Com-

ing Street House Has Long History," *News and Courier*, August 18, 1980, September 22, 1980; VBSP, II, March 17, 1771; *Gazette*, October 24, 1771, October 29, 1772; "Journal of the Commons House of Assembly," November 28, 1769, February 20, 1770; Bridenbaugh, *Cities in Revolt*, 237–40; Alfred O. Halsey, "The Passing of a Great Forest and the History of the Mills Which Manufactured It into Lumber," *YCC, 1937* (Charleston, S.C., 1940), 198–203; Smith and Smith, *Dwelling Houses of Charleston*, 93–100, 198–99, 207–8; Simons, "Architectural Trends," 545–49, 561; Edward C. Fennell, "Firm Handles Only Choicest Property," *News and Courier*, November 23, 1980; Robert P. Stockton, "Mansion Resembles 'Single House,' " *News and Courier*, May 29, 1980.

32. *Gazette*, April 29, 1763, November 2, 1767, January 25, May 9, 1768, October 16, April 13, 1769, January 25, November 15, 1770, August 6, October 29, 1772, February 22, April 16, 19, May 24, 1773, June 6, October 31, 1774.

33. *Gazette*, June 1, October 21, 1765, June 2, December 1, 1766, May 11, August 31, 1769, January 25, May 10, 1770, February 7, April 18, 1771, February 22, 1773; Mabel Webber (ed.), "Death Notices from the South Carolina *Gazette* from September 19, 1766 to December 19, 1769," *SCHGM* 34 (January 1933), 57; "Journal of the Commons House of Assembly, March 14, 1769–November 5, 1771" (ms., SCA), XXXVIII, 252.

34. Vipperman, *Rawlins Lowndes*, 128–33, 153–54; "Journal of the Court of General Sessions, 1769–1776" (ms., SCA), 8–328; *Gazette*, October 26, 1769, April 19, May 3, 1770, January 31, February 7, March 26, September 10, October 29, 1772, March 1, 8, 15, May 24, November 1, 1773, February 28, June 6, 1774; the severity of Ramos's punishment and the actions of "an enraged populace" also may have been promoted by feelings of anti-Semitism—Ramos was a Jew. "A Naval Officers View of the Metropolis, 1769," in Merrens, *Colonial South Carolina Scene*, 230–31.

35. Robert M. Calhoon and Robert M. Weir, " 'The Scandalous History of Sir Egerton Leigh,' " *WMQ* 26 (January 1969), 47–74; Weir, *A Most Important Epocha*, 25–28, 39–50; Jack P. Green, "Bridge to Revolution: The Wilkes Fund Controversy in South Carolina, 1769–1775," *JSH* 29 (1963), 19–52; John Drayton, *Memoirs of the American Revolution as Relating to the State of South Carolina* (2 vols., Charleston, S.C., 1821, reprint, New York, 1969), I, 215; Vipperman, *Rawlins Lowndes*, 149–51, 154; John W. Blassingame, "American Nationalism and Other Loyalties in the Southern Colonies, 1763–1775," *JSH* 34 (February 1968), 55–57; Weir, "Who Shall Rule at Home," 693–700; Weir, *Colonial South Carolina*, 275, 309–10.

36. Jack P. Green, " 'Slavery or Independence': Some Reflections on the Relationship among Liberty, Black Bondage, and Equality in Revolutionary South Carolina," *SCHM* 80 (July 1979), 193–216; Kenneth S. Greenberg, "Revolutionary Ideology and the Proslavery Argument: The Abolition of Slavery in Antebellum South Carolina, *SCHM* 42 (August 1976), 365–67; Weir, " 'The Harmony We Were Famous For,' " 474–75; Pauline Maier, "The Road Not Taken: Nullification, John C. Calhoun, and the Revolutionary Tradition in South Carolina," *SCHM* 82 (January 1981), 3–4; Walsh, "The Charleston Mechanics," 142; Woody, "Christopher Gadsden," 10–11; *Gazette*, July 5, 1770; Walsh, *Charleston's Sons of Liberty*, 45–54; Rogers, *Evolution of a Federalist*, 50–51.

37. Sellers, *Charleston Business on the Eve of the Revolution*, 9, 11, 134, 209–16, 220; Maier, "The Charleston Mob," 178; Walsh, *Charleston's Sons of Liberty*,

51–57; Weir, *A Most Important Epocha*, 35–38; Rogers, *Evolution of a Federalist*, 56; Higgins, "The Geographical Origins of Negro Slaves," 40; Donnan, "The Slave Trade into South Carolina," 822–23, 826–27; Gayle, "Nature and Volume of Exports from Charleston," 25–33.

38. Jacob M. Price, "Economic Function and the Growth of American Port Towns in the Eighteenth Century," in *Perspectives in American History* 8 (1974), 123–86; Rogers, "The Charleston Tea Party," 153–57; James P. Petit (ed.), *South Carolina and the Sea* (Charleston, S.C., 1976), I, 83.

39. Bryan, "The Exchange," 1–13; Howe, "Journal of Josiah Quincy," 441; Ravenel, *Architects*, 47–51; Leland, *60 Famous Houses*, 6, 14, 17, 26; Robert P. Stockton, "General Owned Home Briefly," *News and Courier*, September 24, 1979; John Richard Alden, *John Stuart and the Southern Colonial Frontier* (Ann Arbor, Mich., 1944), 167; Helen Othersen, "8 South Battery Dates to Late 18th Century," *News and Courier*, December 26, 1977; Rogers, *Charleston*, 68–69; Frank Winkler Ryan, Jr., "Travelers in South Carolina in the Eighteenth Century," *YCC, 1945* (Charleston, S.C., 1948), 210. The William Gibbes house stands today at 64 South Battery though its view from the river is now blocked by a more recently built row of dwellings.

40. Howe, "Journal of Josiah Quincy," 442–48, 450–51; J. F. D. Smyth and "The English Traveler," in Ryan, "Travelers in South Carolina," 220; Bridenbaugh, *Myths and Realities*, 79–86; *Gazette*, May 3, August 30, 1770, January 17, 1771.

41. Merrens, "A View of Coastal South Carolina," 190; Jordan, *White over Black*, 145; Edgar and Bailey, *Biographical Directory*, II, 540–41; *Gazette*, March 14, 1768, October 5, 1769, March 1, 1773.

42. Wallace, *Henry Laurens*, 31–32; Bridenbaugh, *Myths and Realities*, 73, 84–85, 87; Pinckney, *Letterbook of Eliza Pinckney*, x–xi; Bagdon, "Musical Life in Charleston," 146–54; Cohen, *South Carolina Gazette*, 92–106, 146–69; Ramsay, *History*, 49; Duffy, *Epidemics*, 175–76; Waring, *History of Medicine*, 88–89; Howe, "Journal of Josiah Quincy," 441–42; Merrens, *Colonial South Carolina Scene*, 284.

43. Sydenham, "Practitioner and Patient," 6–12, 21–22, 83–84, 94, 105n, 126–46; Waring, *History of Medicine*, 67–69, 104–8, 268–69, 318–21; Davidson, *Friend of the People*, 10–11; Bridenbaugh, *Cities in Revolt*, 410; Bridenbaugh, *Myths and Realities*, 106–7; Bowes, *Culture of Charleston*, 76–78, 91; Dr. Tucker entered politics and, following the American Revolution, became treasurer of the United States.

44. *South Carolina and American General Gazette*, November 20, 1769; Bridenbaugh, *Myths and Realities*, 113; *Gazette*, March 1, 1773; Howe, "Journal of Josiah Quincy," 441–56; Berkeley, *Dr. Alexander Garden*, 213; Ramsay, *History*, 215–18; Merrens, "A View of Coastal Carolina," 184–92; A. S. Salley (ed.), "Diary of William Dillwyn during a Visit to Charles Town in 1772," *SCHGM* 36 (January 1935), 6; Chalmers, *Weather and Diseases*, I, 38.

45. Walsh, *Charleston's Sons of Liberty*, 56–61; Meaders, "South Carolina Fugitives," 308; "Records," XXXIII, 388; Bridenbaugh, *Cities in Revolt*, 333; VBSP II, [1755] to 1774; Herbert Aptheker, *Early Years of the Republic*, (New York, 1976), 137–38; Lee Soltow, "Socieconomic Classes in South Carolina and Massachusetts in the 1790's and the Observations of John Drayton," *SCHM* 81

(October 1980), 283–305; *Gazette,* February 22, March 8, May 24, June 1, October 25, 1773, February 28, June 6, October 31, 1774.

46. Rogers, "The Charleston Tea Party," 157–58; Maier, "The Charleston Mob," 180; Walter J. Fraser, Jr., *Patriots, Pistols,* and *Petticoats* (Columbia, S.C., 1976), 51–52.

47. Mary Julia Curtis, "Charles-Town's Church Street Theatre," *SCHM* 70 (July 1969), 149–54; Emmett Robinson, "The Dock Street Theatre: A Guide and a Brief Resume of the Theatre in Charleston, S.C. from 1730" (Charleston, S.C., 1975), 16–17. Bridenbaugh, *Myths and Realities,* 94; Willis, *The Charleston Stage,* 63, 66.

48. Walsh, *Charleston's Sons of Liberty,* 60–71; Rogers, "The Charleston Tea Party," 165–67; Maier, "The Charleston Mob," 180; Drayton, *Memoirs,* I, 134–35; Williams, *St. Michael's,* 30–34.

49. Walsh, *Charleston's Sons of Liberty,* 64–67, 73–74; Wallace, *South Carolina,* 254–58; David H. Villers, "The Smythe Horses Affair and the Association," *SCHM* 70 (July 1969), 137–47; Maier, "The Charleston Mob," 180–81; Drayton, *Memoirs,* I, 182–87.

50. B. D. Bargar (ed.), "Charles Town Loyalism in 1775: The Secret Reports of Alexander Innes," *SCHM* 63 (July 1962), 128–34; Wood, " 'Taking Care of Business,' " 61–62; Rogers, "The Papers of James Grant," 159; French, "The Republicanism of Henry Laurens," 73; Raymond G. Starr, "The Conservative Revolution: South Carolina Public Affairs, 1775–1790" (Ph.D. dissertation, University of Texas, 1964), 22–24; Vipperman, *Rawlins Lowndes,* 186–87; *Gazette,* October 17, 1775; Walsh, *Charleston's Sons of Liberty,* 68–71; "Miscellaneous Papers of the General Committee and Provincial Congress 1775," *SCHGM* 8 (July 1907), 141–44; Drayton, *Memoirs,* II, 273–74, 300–302; 132–33; Walsh, "The Charleston Mechanics," 142.

51. Joseph Johnson, *Traditions and Reminiscences Chiefly of the American Revolution in the South* (Charleston, S.C., 1851), 71; Zornow, " 'A Troublesome Community,' " 85–89; Wood, " 'Taking Care of Business,' " 62–66; Maurice A. Crouse (ed.), "Papers of Gabriel Manigault, 1771–1784," *SCHM* 64 (January 1963), 2; R. S. Gibbes (ed.), *Documentary History of the American Revolution* (3 vols., New York, 1853–57) II, 155; Walsh, *Charleston's Sons of Liberty,* 69; Joseph W. Barnwell (ed.), "Correspondence of Hon. Arthur Middleton," *SCHGM* 27 (July 1926), 128–31; Berkeley, *Dr. Alexander Garden,* 265–67; Frances Reece Kepner (ed.), "A British View of the Siege of Charleston, 1776," *JSH* 11 (February 1945), 95; "Miscellaneous Papers of the General Committee, Secret Committee and Provisional Congress, 1775" *SCHGM* 8 (October 1907), 193; *Gazette,* November 7, 1775.

52. Drayton, *Memoirs,* II, 31–40, 70–74; Harriott Horry Ravenel, *Eliza Pinckney* (New York, 1896), 267; "Henry Laurens to His Son John, 1773–1776," *SCHGM* 5 (July 1904), 131; John Laurens to James Laurens, October 24, 1776, *SCHGM* 10 (January 1909), 50.

53. Kepner, "A British View of the Siege," 97; Walsh, *Charleston's Sons of Liberty,* 74–76; "Diary of Captain Bernard Elliott," *YCC, 1888* (Charleston, S.C., 1889); Foster M. Farley, "The South Carolina Negro in the American Revolution, 1775–1783," *SCHM* 79 (April 1978), 75–76; Rogers, *Evolution of a Federalist,* 77n; Starr, "The Conservative Revolution," 36–37.

54. Fraser, *Patriots, Pistols and Petticoats,* 80–94; Weir, *Colonial South Carolina,* 327–30.

55. Wallace, *Henry Laurens,* 225; Starr, "The Conservative Revolution," 43–44, 55, 65, 71–74, 81; Elisha P. Douglas, *Rebels and Democrats: The Struggle for Equal Political Rights and Majority Rule during the American Revolution* (Chapel Hill, N.C., 1955), 33–44; Starr, "The Conservative Revolution," 71–74, 89.

56. Walsh, *The Writings of Christopher Gadsden,* 130; Walsh, *Charleston's Sons of Liberty,* 83–84; Raymond Starr, "Letters from John Gervais to Henry Laurens, 1777–1778," *SCHM* 66 (January 1965), 31–32.

57. Don Higginbotham, "American Historians and the Military History of the American Revolution," *AHR* 70 (October 1964), 33–34; A. S. Salley, Jr., "Records of the Regiments of the South Carolina Line, Continental Establishment," *SCHGM* 5 (January 1904), 15; Edward McCrady, *The History of South Carolina in the Revolution, 1775–1780* (New York, 1969), 10–14, 309; Wilmont G. DeSaussure, *The Names as Far as Can Be Ascertained of the Officers Who Served in the South Carolina Regiments on the Continental Establishment* (Columbia, S.C., 1960), 43–48, 269–99; William E. Hemphill and Wylma Anne Wates (eds.), *Extracts from the Journals of the Provincial Congress of South Carolina, 1776–1780* (Columbia, S.C., 1970), 331–71; A. S. Salley, Jr. (ed.), "Records of the Regiments of the South Carolina Line, Continental Establishment," *SCHGM* 5 (October 1904), 216–17. The names of the officers who rose to be colonels or generals were Christopher Gadsden, Issac Huger, Owen Roberts, William Moultrie, Isaac Motte, William Thompson, James Mayson, William Henderson, Edmund Hyrne, John Laurens, Francis Marion, Thomas Sumter. Joseph W. Barnwell (ed.), "Bernard Elliott's Recruiting Journal, 1775," *SCHGM* 17 (July 1916), 95–98; Jack L. Cross (ed.), "Letters of Thomas Pinckney, 1775–1780," *SCHM* 57 (July 1957), 77; Starr, "Letters from John Gervais," 29; Lee Kenneth (ed.), "Charleston in 1778: A French Intelligence Report," *SCHM* 66 (April 1965), 110.

58. Marvin R. Zahniser, *Charles Cotesworth Pinckney: Founding Father* (Chapel Hill, N.C., 1967), 38; "Order Book of Captain Bernard Elliott" (ms., SCHS); John Bennett, "Charleston in 1774 as Described by an English Traveler," *SCHGM* 47 (July 1946), 179–80; Paul G. Sifton, "Some Sources of South Carolina Revolutionary History, with Two Unpublished Letters of Baron DeKalb," *SCHM* 66 (April 1965), 107; "Moultrie-Lincoln Order Book" (ms., SCHS); Walter J. Fraser, Jr., "Reflections of 'Democracy' in Revolutionary South Carolina? The Composition of Military Organizations and the Attitudes and Relationships of the Officers and Men, 1775–1780," *SCHM* 78 (July 1977), 208–9; Maurer Maurer, "Military Justice under General Washington," *Military Affair* 28 (Spring 1964), 12.

59. A. S. Salley, Jr., *The History of Orangeburg County, South Carolina* (Baltimore, Md., 1969), 342; Gibbes, *Documentary History,* II, 50–51; A. S. Salley (ed.), "Records of the Regiments of the South Carolina Line, Continental Establishment," *SCHGM* 5 (April 1904), 85; "Diary of the Reverend Oliver Hart," *YCC, 1896* (Charleston, S.C., 1897), 395; Don Higginbotham, *The War of American Independence; Military Attitudes, Policies and Practice, 1763–1789* (New York, 1971), 12; Daniel J. Boorstin, *The Americans: The Colonial Experience* (New York, 1958), 365–67.

60. Farley, "The South Carolina Negro," 77–83; Benjamin Quarles, *The Negro in the American Revolution,* (Chapel Hill, N.C., 1961), 142; Zornow, "'A Troublesome Community,'" 91; Gibbes, *Documentary History,* II, 121, 131;

Walsh, *The Writings of Christopher Gadsden,* 166; Peter Maslowski, "National Policy toward the Use of Black Troops in the Revolution," *SCHM* 73 (January 1972), 11–12; Starr, "The Conservative Revolution," 98.

61. Clarence L. Ver Steeg, "Stacy Hepburn and Company: Enterprisers in the American Revolution," *SCHM* 55 (January 1954), 1–5; G. Terry Sharrer, "Indigo in Carolina, 1671–1796," *SCHM* 72 (April 1971), 98–100; W. Robert Higgins, "A Financial History of the American Revolution in South Carolina" (Ph.D. dissertation, Duke University, 1969), 27–38, 40–42; Gibbes, *Documentary History,* II, 121–22; Walsh, *Charleston's Sons of Liberty,* 77–80.

62. VBSP III, April 1775–April 1795 (ms., St. Philip's Church, Charleston, S.C.); William E. Hemphill, Wylma Anne Wates, and R. Nicholas Olsberg (eds.), *Journal of the General Assembly and House of Representatives 1776–1780* (Columbia, S.C., 1970), 96–97, 122–23, 166–67; Gibbes, *Documentary History,* II, 60–66; Harriette K. Leiding, *Charleston: Historic and Romantic* (Philadelphia, Pa., 1931), 195; Starr, "The Conservative Revolution," 82–83.

63. *Gazette,* November 12, 1764, September 21, October 31, 1765, October 1, 1766, December 28, 1769, July 19, 1770, January 31, September 10, 1771, October 22, 29, 1772, March 18, 1779.

64. Petit, *South Carolina and the Sea,* I, 109; King, *The Newspaper Press of Charleston,* 22–24; Walsh, *Charleston's Sons of Liberty,* 80–81; Rogers, *Charleston,* 28; Elkanah Watson, *Men and Times of the Revolution* (New York, 1856), 45–46; McCrady, *History of South Carolina,* 232–33; Webber, "Extracts from the Diary of Ann Manigault," 117.

65. William Wallace, *Appeal to Arms: A Military History of the American Revolution* (New York, 1951), 134–68; John Carroll Cavanagh, "The Military Career of Major General Benjamin Lincoln in the American Revolution, 1775–1781" (Ph.D. dissertation, Duke University, 1969), 153–54; 180–200; Zahniser, *Charles Cotesworth Pinckney,* 58–59; Geraldine M. Meroney, "William Bull's First Exile from South Carolina, 1777–1781," *SCHM* 80 (April 1979), 99; Frances Leigh Williams, *A Founding Family: The Pinckneys of South Carolina* (New York, 1978), 130–31, D. E. Huger Smith, "Nisbett of Dean and Dean Hall," *SCHGM* 24 (January–April 1923), 20–21; Christopher Ward, *The War of the Revolution* (New York, 1952), II, 697, 702; William B. Willcox (ed.), *The American Rebellion: Sir Henry Clinton's Narrative of His Campaigns, 1775–1782, with an Appendix of Original Documents* (New Haven, Conn., 1954), 157–64.

66. Bernhard A. Uhlendorf (ed.), *The Siege of Charleston* (Ann Arbor, Mich., 1938); Joseph P. Tustin (ed.), *Diary of the American War: A Hessian Journal* (New Haven, 1979), 224–27, 237–38; Ravenel, *Charleston,* 267; "The Siege of Charleston: Journal of Captain Peter Russell, December 25, 1779 to May 2, 1780," *AHR* 4 (April 1899), 501; Zahniser, *Charles Cotesworth Pinckney,* 62–64; Richard K. Murdock (ed.), "A French Account of the Siege of Charleston, 1780," *SCHM* 67 (July 1966), 150; Franklin B. Hough (ed.), *The Siege of Charleston by the British Fleet and Army* (Albany, N.Y., 1867), 129.

67. Tustin, *Diary of the American War,* 239–40; Alexander R. Stoesen, "The British Occupation of Charleston, 1780–1782," *SCHM* 63 (April 1962), 72–73; Uhlendorf, *The Siege of Charleston,* 298–99; McCrady, *History of South Carolina,* II, 505n; Willcox, *The American Rebellion,* 174–76; Joseph W. Barnwell (ed.), "Letters of John Rutledge," *SCHGM* 17 (October 1916), 131–34; Ella Pettit Levett, "Loyalism in Charleston, 1761–1784," *PSCHA* (1936), 6–9; Robert W.

Barnwell, Jr., "Addressers of Clinton and Arbuthnot," *PSCHA* (1939), 44; Vipperman, *Rawlins Lowndes*, 229–34.

68. George C. Rogers, Jr., "Aedanus Burke, Nathanael Greene, Anthony Wayne, and the British Merchants of Charleston," *SCHM* 67 (April 1966), 75–76; Walsh, *Charleston's Sons of Liberty*, 90–105; "Petition of Patrick Hind," January 22, 1783; "Petition of Thomas Elfe," January 27, 1783 (SCA); Fraser, *Patriots, Pistols, and Petticoats*, 145–46.

69. "Miscellaneous Proceedings of the Board of Police, 1780–1782," June 13, July 14, 25, August 11, 25, September 8, 10, 22, October 24, 27, 1780, January 5, 10, February 2, October 22, November 24, 1781, April 18, May 14, 18, 1782 (microfilm, SCA); *Royal Gazette*, August 23, March 28, 1782; Moultrie, *Memoirs*, II, 252, 299; Stoesen, "The British Occupation of Charleston," 74–79; Walsh, *Charleston's Sons of Liberty*, 94–100; Ravenel, *Charleston*, 278–79, 304; Rogers, *Charleston*, 30, 103; Ravenel, *Eliza Pinckney*, 282–83.

70. David K. Bowen, *The Execution of Isaac Hayne* (Lexington, S.C., 1977), 15, 20, 29, 30, 32, 34–35, 67–72; Mabel L. Webber (ed.), "Joshiah Smith's Diary, 1780–1781," *SCHGM* 33 (January 1932), 205–6; Ward, *The War of the Revolution*, 826–44; George W. Kyte, "General Greene's Plans for the Capture of Charleston, 1781–1782," *SCHM* 62 (April 1961), 97–99; Jerome J. Nadelhaft, *The Disorders of War: The Revolution in South Carolina* (Orono, Me., 1981), 64–69, 79, 82; Starr, "The Conservative Revolution," 112–16; George Smith McCowen, Jr., *The British Occupation of Charleston, 1780–1782* (Columbia, S.C., 1972), 118n, 151.

71. Aedanus Burke to Arthur Middleton, January 25, 1782, in Joseph W. Barnwell (ed.), "Correspondence of Hon. Arthur Middleton," *SCHGM* 26 (October 1925), 192; Rogers, "The British Merchants," 76–78; Starr, "The Conservative Revolution," 123, 126–27, 132–38, 140, 154–59; Nadelhaft, *Disorders of War*, 55, 72, 76, 79–80, 85–88, 102–19; Wallace, *South Carolina*, 321; Wallace, *Appeal to Arms*, 264; Stoesen, "The British Occupation," 80–82; Rogers, *Evolution of a Federalist*, 101–4; South Carolina *Gazette and General Advertiser*, June 10, 1783; Petit, *South Carolina and the Sea*, I, 155.

Chapter IV

1. *Gazette and General Advertiser*, June 10, 1783; Starr, "The Conservative Revolution," 159–65; McCord, *Statutes*, VII, 97–101; Nadlehaft, *Disorders of War* 129–31, 140–45, 154–58. Information on the seal of the city was supplied by Dr. David Heisser, Head Reference Services, Tufts University, Medford, Massachusetts, who is at work on a history of the seal.

2. N. Louis Bailey and Elizabeth Ivey Cooper (eds.), *Biographical Directory of the South Carolina House of Representatives, 1775–1790* (Columbia, S.C., 1981), III, 364–66; Walsh, *Charleston's Sons of Liberty*, 114–16; Alfred J. Morrison (ed.), *Johann David Schöpf: Travels in the Confederation [1783–1784]* (Philadelphia, Pa., 1911), 204.

3. E. Stanly Godbold, Jr., and Robert H. Woody, *Christopher Gadsden and the American Revolution* (Knoxville, Tenn., 1982), 225–29; Wallace, *South Carolina*, 334–36; Rogers, *Evolution of a Federalist*, 97, 101; Nadelhaft, *Disorders of War*, 143–49; Frank Luther Mott, *American Journalism: A History 1690–1960* (New York, 1962), 135.

4. *Gazette and Public Advertiser,* August 16, September 3, 6, 1785; Starr, "The Conservative Revolution," 179–202; Zahniser, *Charles Cotesworth Pinckney,* 75–76, 76n; Nadelhaft, "Disorders of War, 158–61, 171, 184.

5. Walsh, *Charleston's Sons of Liberty,* 122; Petitions of Inhabitants of the City of Charleston to the Senate of South Carolina, March 1, 1787 (General Assembly Petitions, SCA); Maier, "The Charleston Mob," 193; Godbold and Moody, *Christopher Gadsden,* 130–236.

6. *Gazette and Public Advertiser,* August 27, 1785; Starr, "The Conservative Revolution," 203–32; Wallace, *South Carolina,* 332–33; Rogers, *Evolution of a Federalist,* 133–34; Nadelhaft, *Disorders of War,* 149–72; Ernest M. Lander, "Charleston: Manufacturing Center of the Old South," *JSH* 26 (August 1960), 332–37.

7. Petition of Sundry Widows, Inhabitants of Charleston to the House of Assembly of South Carolina, August 5, 1783 (General Assembly Petitions, 1783, SCA); *Weekly Gazette,* December 12, 1783; Klebaner, "Public Poor Relief," 214–17; J. J. O'Connell, *Catholicity in the Carolinas and Georgia: (Leaves of Its History)* (New York, 1879), 140–41; *Gazette and Public Advertiser,* April 9, June 15, August 25, 1785. For similar conditions in other cities, see Lawrence H. Larsen, "Nineteenth-Century Street Sanitation: A Study of Filth and Frustration," *Wisconsin Magazine of History* 52 (Spring 1969); Morrison, *Travels in the Confederation,* 216; Starr, "The Conservative Revolution," 231.

8. Rogers, *Charleston,* 64–65; Rogers, *South Carolina Chronology,* 48; James H. Dorman, Jr., *Theatre in the Antebellum South, 1815–1861* (Chapel Hill, N.C., 1967); 21; Willis, *The Charleston Stage,* 104–5.

9. George C. Rogers, Jr., "South Carolina Ratifies the Federal Constitution," *PSCHA* (1961), 49–62; Rogers, *Charleston,* 116, 119; Starr, "The Conservative Revolution," 229–30, 238–68; 276–81; Nadlehaft, *Disorders of War,* 167–83; Lacy K. Ford, "Republics and Democracy: The Parameters of Political Citizenship in Antebellum South Carolina" (paper in possession of Walter J. Fraser, Jr.); Ulrich B. Phillips, *American Negro Slavery* (Baton Rouge, La., 1966), 135; Godbold and Moody, *Christopher Gadsden,* 242–42.

10. Rogers, *Charleston,* 83–86.

11. Ibid., 52–65, 114–15, 159; Wallace, *South Carolina,* 347, 362–64; Frederick Cople Jaher, *The Urban Establishment:. Upper Strata in Boston, New York, Charleston and Los Angeles* (Urbana, Ill., 1982), 323–38; Gregory Allen Greb, "Charleston, South Carolina Merchants, 1815–1860: Urban Leadership in the Antebellum South" (Ph.D. dissertation, University of California, Riverside,1978), 5–6, 9–10; Leonard P. Stavisky, "Industrialism in Ante-Bellum Charleston," *Journal of Negro History* 36 (July 1951), 308.

12. Barnett A. Elzas, *The Jews of South Carolina: From the Earliest Times to the Present Day* (Philadelphia, Pa., 1905), 120; Easterby, *History of the College of Charleston,* 20–62.

13. Barbara L. Bellows, "Controlling the Poor in a Slave Society: The Antebellum Charleston Poor House" (paper in possession of Walter J. Fraser, Jr.); Rosser Howard Taylor, "The Gentry of Antebellum South Carolina," *North Carolina Historical Review* 17 (April 1940), 116–17; Raymond A. Mohl, "The Grand Fabric of Republicanism: A Scotsman Describes South Carolina, 1810–1811," *SCHM* 71 (July 1970), 179; Klebaner, "Public Poor Relief," 218–20.

14. John Hammond Moore (ed.), "The Abiel Abbot Journal: A Yankee

Preacher in Charleston, 1818–1827," *SCHM* 68 (July 1967), 68; James P. Petit (ed.), *South Carolina and the Sea* (Mount Pleasant, S.C., 1982), II, 24; Dorman, *Theatre in the Antebellum South,* 23–25; Willis, *The Charleston Stage,* 153–54; 237–38.

15. Alan Frank January, "The First Nullification: The Negro Seaman Acts Controversy in South Carolina, 1822–1860" (Ph.D. dissertation, University of Iowa, 1976), 83–90; Michael Stauffer, "Volunteer or Uniformed Companies in the Antebellum Militia: A Checklist of Identified Companies, 1790–1859,"*SCHM* 88 (April 1987), 108; George D. Terry, "A Study of the Impact of the French Revolution and the Insurrections in Saint Dominque upon South Carolina, 1790–1805" (M.A. thesis, University of South Carolina, 1975), 38–39, 48, 59–61, 64, 80–82.

16. Willis, *The Charleston Stage,* 313–16, 328–29; Charles S. Watson, *Antebellum Charleston Dramatists* (University, Ala., 1976), 11–12. W. Stanley Hoole, *The Antebellum Charleston Theatre* (Tuscaloosa, Ala., 1946), 4–9; Rogers, *Charleston,* 73–75, 110–14, 142; Joseph I. Waring, "Charleston Medicine, 1800–1860," *Journal of the History of Medicine* (July 1976), 337–40; Duke De La Rochefoucault Liancourt,*Travels through the U.S. of North America . . . In the Years 1795, 1796 and 1797,* 2 vols., (London, 1799), I, 566–67; John Hope Franklin, *The Militant South 1800–1861* (Cambridge, Mass., 1956) 77, 174.

17. N. Bowen to Henry Hill, June 17, 1796 (Bowen-Cooke Collection, SCHS); Arnoldus Vanderhorst to Elias Vanderhorst, July 19, 1796 (Vanderhorst Papers, SCHS); Terry, "A Study of the Impact," 104–5, 108, 142–44; January, "The First Nullification," 85–86.

18. "Memorial of Sundry Citizens of Charleston . . . .Respecting the Importation of Negroes, December 11, 1797" (General Assembly Petitions, SCA); *City Gazette,* December 2, 30, 1797; "Salwyn" to Mary M. Singleton, February [?] (Singleton Family Papers, SCL); Patrick S. Brady, "The Slave Trade and Sectionalism in South Carolina, 1787–1808," *JSH* 38 (November 1972), 609–10; Rogers, *South Carolina Chronology,* 52.

19. Jamie W. Moore, *The Lowcountry Engineers: Military Missions and Economic Development in the Charleston District, U.S. Army Corps of Engineers* (Charleston, S.C., 1981), 11–12; Rogers, *Charleston,* 62, 114–15, 132–33; Rogers, *South Carolina Chronology,* 52–53; John Joseph Hindman, "Concert Life in Antebellum Charleston" (Ph.D. dissertation, University of North Carolina, Chapel Hill, 1971), 83–86; Willis, *The Charleston Stage,* 466.

20. Wallace, *South Carolina,* 350, 352, 373–74; Constance McLaughlin Green, *American Cities in the Growth of the Nation* (New York, 1957), 21; Terry, "A Study of the Impact," 144; John Lofton, *Denmark Vesey's Revolt: The Slave Plot That Lit a Fuse to Fort Sumter* (Kent, Ohio, 1983), 5–79.

21. Alfred G. Smith, Jr., *Economic Readjustment of an Old Cotton State: South Carolina 1820–1860* (Columbia, S.C., 1958), 1–6; William W. Freehling, *Prelude to Civil War: The Nullification Controversy in South Carolina, 1816–1836* (New York, 1966), 9–10, 26, 28, 29; Frederick Burtrumn Collins, Jr., "Charleston and the Railroads: A Geographic Study of a South Atlantic Port and its Strategies for Developing a Railroad System, 1820–1860" (M.S. thesis, University of South Carolina, 1977), 17–20; John J. Winberry, "Reputation of Carolina Indigo," *SCHM* 80 (July 1979), 248–50.

22. Richard C. Wade, *Slavery in the Cities: The South, 1820–1860* (New York 1964), 206; Edmund Drago and Ralph Melnick, "The Old Slave Mart Museum,

Charleston, South Carolina: Rediscovering the Past," *Civil War History* 27 (June 1981), 142–43; Harriet Martineau, *Retrospect of Western Travel* (New York, 1838), II, 235.

23. Wallace, *South Carolina*, 350, 365; "The Memorial of John James Negrin . . . to the Senate of the State of South Carolina," [November 23, 1805] (General Assembly Petitions, SCA); Terry, "A Study of the Impact," 162; Rogers, *Charleston*, 138–44; George Rogers believes that only after 1822 Charleston turned "inward." My contention is that the city's elite tried much earlier to isolate the city from "outside" influences that might disturb its institutions.

24. Waring, "Charleston Medicine, 1800–1860," 320–42; Ludlum, *Hurricanes*, 58, 114, 132–34; *Ordinances of the City Council of Charleston, from the Year 1783 to July 1818* (Charleston, S.C., 1818), 26, 48, 226; *Courier*, August 12, 1815, May 26, 1818; "Petition from Charleston City Council for funds to Improve the Health of the City, November 17, 1819" (General Assembly Petitions, SCA); Robert Mills, *Statistics of South Carolina* (Charleston, S.C., 1826), 391–93; Joseph I. Waring, *A History of Medicine in South Carolina, 1825–1900* (Columbia, S.C., 1967), 63.

25. Brady, "The Slave Trade," 615; *Digest of the Ordinances . . . 1783–1818*, 104–19, 178–91; Michael P. Johnson, "Runaway Slaves and the Slave Communities in South Carolina, 1799 to 1830, *WMQ* 38 (July 1981), 418–37, 441; Lofton, *Denmark Vesey's Revolt*, 117–20; Wade, *Slavery in the Cities*, 216–17; Laylon Wayne Jordan, "Police Power and Public Safety in Antebellum Charleston: The Emergence of a New Police, 1800–1860," in *South Atlantic Urban Studies* (Columbia, S.C., 1979), III, 125–28.

26. *Courier*, March 2, 1808, April 4, 1811; Jack Kenny Williams, "The Code of Honor in Ante-Bellum South Carolina," *SCHM* 54 (July 1953), 113–15, 121–27; Bertram Wyatt-Brown, *Southern Honor: Ethics and Behavior in the Old South* (New York, 1982), 167, 350–61; Franklin, *The Militant South*, 33–62; Dickson Bruce, Jr., *Violence and Culture in the Antebellum South* (Austin, Tex., 1979), 20–64; Linda T. Prior, "Ralph Waldo Emerson and South Carolina," *SCHM* 79 (October 1978), 256–58; "Memorial of Citizens of the State to the Senate of South Carolina (1805)" (General Assembly Petitions, SCA); Richard B. Davis, "The Ball Papers: A Pattern of Life in the Low Country, 1800–1825, *SCHM* 65 (January 1964), 14; Anne C. Loveland, *Southern Evangelicals and the Social Order, 1800–1860* (Baton Rouge, La., 1980), 180.

27. Richard W. Griffin, "An Origin of the New South: The South Carolina Homespun Company, 1808–1815," *Business History Review* 35 (Autumn 1961), 411, 413; Lander, "Charleston: Manufacturing Center," 331–32; "Government of the City of Charleston, 1682–1882," in *YCC, 1881* (Charleston, S.C., 1882), 341–51; *Courier*, April 7, 1809, November 14, 1812, February 15, 1815; Hindman "Concert Life in Antebellum Charleston," 79n, 87–89.

28. J. J. Pringle Smith, "Sketch of the History of Charleston," in *YCC, 1880* (Charleston, S.C., 1881), 304–6; Petit; *South Carolina and the Sea*, II, 37–43; Rogers, *Charleston*, 64; Moore, *Lowcountry Engineers*, 14.

29. Bellows, "Controlling the Poor in a Slave Society," 2–3; Klebaner, "Public Poor Relief," 211–12; Rogers, *South Carolina Chronology*, 56; Moore, "The Abiel Abbot Journals," 115, 117; Poor House Journals, October 7, 1808, October 8, November 4, 1821, January 9, 1839 (ms., CCA); *Courier*, August 25, 27, 1814.

30. Rosser H. Taylor, *Ante-Bellum South Carolina: A Social and Cultural His-*

tory (New York, 1970), 39; Wallace, *South Carolina,* 425–26; Dorman, *Theatre in the Antebellum South,* 32–33, 233n; Emmett Robinson (ed.), "Dr. Irving's Reminiscences of the Charleston Stage," *SCHGM* 52 (July 1951), 169; Rogers, *Charleston,* 64–65, 138.

31. *Courier,* February 20, 1817; Chalmers G. Davidson, *The Last Foray: The South Carolina Planters of 1860* (Columbia, S.C., 1971), 170–267; Albert Sidney Thomas, *A Historical Account of the Protestant Episcopal Church in South Carolina, 1820–1957* (Columbia, S.C., 1957), 200–261; Lander, "Charleston: Manufacturing Center," 342–43; Ernest M. Lander, Jr., "Ante-Bellum Milling in South Carolina," *SCHGM* 52 (July 1951), 129–31; "West Point Rice Mills," in *YCC, 1939* (Charleston, S.C., 1940), 211–12; Thomas Weyman to James Weyman, November 25, 1817 (Weyman Family Papers, SCL).

32. John Price Radford, "Culture, Economy and Urban Structure in Charleston" 1860–1880" (Ph.D. dissertation, Clark University, 1974), 211–19; Taylor, "The Gentry of Antebellum South Carolina," 125; Lawrence F. Brewster, "Planters from the Low-Country and Their Summer Travels," *PSCHA* 9(1943), 35; Robert N. Olsberg, "A Government of Class and Race: William Henry Trescot and the South Carolina Chivalry, 1860–1865" (Ph.D. dissertation, University of South Carolina, 1972), 31.

33. Michael P. Johnson, "Planters and Patriarchy: Charleston, 1800–1860," *JSH* 46 (February 1980), 49; Rogers, *Charleston,* 66–67; John R. Welsh, "William Gilmore Simms, Critic of the South," *JSH* 26 (May 1960), 202–14; Morrison, *Travels in the Confederation,* 168; Julien Dwight Martin (ed.), "Letters of Caleb Cotton," *SCHGM* 52 (January 1951), 19; Jane H. Pease and William H. Pease, "Social Structure and the Potential for Urban Change: Boston and Charleston in the 1830's," *Journal of Urban History* 8 (February 1982), 117–78; Thomas Hamilton, *Men and Manners in America* (Philadelphia, Pa., 1833), 350.

34. Thomas D. Clark (ed.), *South Carolina: The Grand Tour, 1780–1865* (Columbia, S.C., 1973), 185, 220; "Letters from Robert Mills," *SCHGM* 39 (July 1938), 117–18; Ravenel, *Architects,* 114–19; Charles Fraser, *Reminiscenses of Charleston* (Charleston, S.C., 1854), 62; Davis, "The Ball Papers," 1–7; Welsh, "William Gilmore Simms," 211–12.

35. Johnson, "Planters and Patriarchy," 56–60; Tyrone Power, *Impressions of America, during the years 1833, 1834 and 1835* (New York, 1971), I, 100; Anna Wells Rutledge (ed.), "Letters from Thomas Pinckney to Harriot Pinckney," *SCHGM* 41 (July 1940), 106; Ramsay, *History,* 226; Arney R. Childs (ed.), *Rice Planter and Sportsman: The Recollections of J. Motte Alston, 1821–1909* (Columbia, S.C., 1953), 60.

36. Paul Stati, "Samuel F. B. Morse in Charleston, 1818–1821," *SCHM* 79 (April 1978), 92–111; Rogers, *Chronology of South Carolina,* 57–58; Smith, *Economic Readjustment;* Freehling, *Prelude to Civil War,* 9–10, 26, 28, 29, 30–32, 36, 39–41; Collins, "Charleston and the Railroads," 17–20; Winberry, "Reputation of Carolina Indigo,"248–250.

37. "Presentations of the Grand Jury of the Charleston District, October, 1820" (Grand Jury Presentments, SCA); Petit, *South Carolina and the Sea,* II, 48; Rutledge, *Artists in the Life of Charleston,* 130–31; Stati, "Morse in Charleston," 110–11; Rogers, *Chronology of South Carolina,* 58–59; Rogers, *Charleston,* 159–60.

38. Gerda Lerner, *The Grimké Sisters from South Carolina: Pioneers for Women's Rights and Abolition* (New York, 1981), 35–37; Elizabeth Muhlenfeld,

Mary Boykin Chesnut: A Biography (Baton Rouge, La., 1981), 110; Joel Williamson, *New People: Miscegenation and Mulattoes in the United States* (New York, 1980), 16–19, 41, 70–71; Marina Wikramanayke, *A World in Shadow: The Free Black in Antebellum South Carolina* (Columbia, S.C., 1973), 76, 82; "Petition of Philippe Stanislaw Noisette to the Senate of South Carolina" [1821] (General Assembly Petitions, SCA).

39. Robert Brent Toplin, "Between Black and White: Attitudes toward Southern Mulattoes, 1830–1861," *JSH* 45 (May 1979), 191; Michael P. Johnson and James L. Roark (eds.), *No Chariot Down: Charleston's Free People of Color on the Eve of the Civil War* (Chapel Hill, N.C., 1984), 3–15; Robert L. Harris, Jr., "Charleston's Free Afro-American Elite: The Brown Fellowship Society and the Humane Brotherhood," *SCHM* 82 (October 1981), 309–10. The civil rights leaders of the 1950s used to say, "We've had nocturnal integration for two-hundred-and-fifty years."

40. "Petition of the Inhabitants of Charleston in Relation to Free Negroes and the Future Emancipation of Slaves, October 16, 1820" (Petitions to House of Representatives, SCA); January, "The First Nullification," 99–100; Wikramanayake, *A World in Shadow*, 122–53; Wade, *Slavery in the Cities*, 17, 229–41; Erskine Clarke, *Westlin' Jacob: A Portrait of Religion on the Old South* (Atlanta, Ga., 1979).

41. Freehling, *Prelude to Civil War*, 53–61; Lofton, *Denmark Vesey*, 144–54; Larry M. Snavley, "Vesey Plot," in David C. Roller and Robert W. Twyman, *The Encyclopedia of Southern History* (Baton Rouge, La., 1979), 1272; Larry Koger, *Black Slaveowners: Free Black Slave Masters in South Carolina, 1790–1860* (Jefferson, N.C. and London, 1985), 160–86; January, "The First Nullification," 19–46, 260; Mark D. Kaplanoff, "Charles Pinckney and the American Republican Tradition," in Michael O'Brien and David Moltke-Hansen, *Intellectual Life in Antebellum Charleston* (Knoxville, Tenn., 1986), 85–87; Richard C. Wade, "The Vesey Plot: A Reconsideration," *JSH* 30 (May 1964), 144, 161; for conflicting interpretations on the evidence and the extent of the "conspiracy," see for one view, Wade, "The Vesey Plot," and Wikramanayake, *A World in Shadow;* for another, see Freehling, *Prelude to Civil War*, Lofton, *Denmark Vesey's Revolt* and Steven A. Channing, *Crisis of Fear: Secession in South Carolina* (New York, 1970), 21, 45, 50, 293.

42. Alan F. January, "The South Carolina Association: An Agency for Race Control in Antebellum Charleston," *SCHM* 78 (July 1977), 191–201.

43. *Charleston City Directory* (Charleston, S.C., 1829), 10; William G. Whilden, "Reminiscenses of Old Charleston," in *YCC* (Charleston, S.C., 1896), 403–4; Ravenel, *Architects*, 145; "Grand Jury Presentments, 1825" (SCA); Lerner, *The Grimké Sisters*, 78; Wade, *Slavery in the Cities*, 99.

44. Rogers, *Chronology of South Carolina*, 60; Moore, "The Abiel Abbot Journals," 70.

45. T. Erskine Clarke, "An Experiment in Paternalism: Presbyterians and Slaves in Charleston, South Carolina," *Journal of Presbyterian History* 53 (Fall 1975), 223; Clarke, *Wrestlin' Jacob*, x–xiii, 20–28, 99, 114–34, 227–28; Jimmy Gene Cobb, "A Study of White Protestants' Attitudes toward Negroes in Charleston, South Carolina, 1790–1845" (Ph.D. dissertation, Baylor University, 1976), 42, 67, 96; Raymond Morris Bost, "The Reverend John Bachman and the Development of Southern Lutheranism" (Ph.D. dissertation, Yale University, 1963),

380; E. Brooks Holifield, *The Gentlemen Theologians: American Theology in Southern Culture, 1795–1860* (Durham, N.C., 1978), 11–12; Wade, *Slavery in the Cities,* 160–61; Charles Joyner, "If You Ain't Got Education": Slave Language and Slave Thought in Antebellum Charleston," in O'Brien and Moltke-Hansen, *Intellectual Life,* 253–78.

46. A Leuasseur, "LaFayette in America in 1824 and 1825," in Clark, *South Carolina: The Grand Tour,* 84–85.

47. Mills, *Statistics of South Carolina,* 420; Robert P. Stockton, "Jail's Octagonal Wing Miscredited to Mills," *Charleston News and Courier,* January 23, 1978; "Presentments of the Grand Jury of the Charleston District, May, 1805 and January 1817," "Presentments of the Grand Jury of the Charleston District, October 7, 1819 and October, 1822" (SCA).

48. Zalon Wildman to Miss Mary Wildman, January 20, 1826 (Wildman Papers, SCL); D. E. Huger Smith, *A Charlestonian's Recollections, 1846–1913* (Charleston, S.C., 1950), 66–67; Jack Kenny Williams, *Vogues in Villainy: Crime and Retribution in Ante-Bellum South Carolina* (Columbia, S.C., 1959), 44–45; Jane H. and William H. Pease, "The Blood-Thirsty Tiger: Charleston and the Psychology of Fire," *SCHM* 79 (October 1978), 295. The latter article stresses the rise of these fears during the 1830s. I believe that they were of far longer duration, having their origin in the early eighteenth century; *Courier,* December 30, 1809, March 9, 1819, January 17, 24, February 3, 7, March 7, 1826, March 22, 1837, April 8, 1853, August 10, 1855; Jordan, "Police Power and Public Safety," 126–27; Edward P. Cantwell, " A History of the Charleston Police Force," in *YCC, 1908* (Charleston, S.C., 1909), 4, 8; George B. Eckhard, *A Digest of the Ordinances of the City Council of Charleston, from the Year 1819 to October, 1844* (Charleston, S.C., 1844), 174–77; Frances Ann Kemble (ed.), *Journal of a Residence on a Georgian Plantation in 1838–1839* (New York, 1961), 39.

49. Rogers, *Charleston,* 67, 87, 149–50, 156–61; Petit, *South Carolina and the Sea,* II, 45, 53; Wallace, *South Carolina,* 376–77, 390–91.

50. Smith, *Economic Readjustment,* 9; Freehling, *Prelude to Civil War,* xii, 41–42, 48; Rogers, *Chronology of South Carolina,* 61; Waring, *History of Medicine,* 71–84; Waring, "Charleston Medicine," 327–30; Moore, *Lowcountry Engineers,* 15–18.

51. Jane H. Pease and William H. Pease, "The Economics and Politics of Charleston's Nullification Crisis," *JSH* 48 (August 1981), 341–62; Wallace, *South Carolina,* 396–403, 419; Rogers, *Chronology of South Carolina,* 62–63; "Memorial of the City Council of Charleston Praying the Establishment of a Poll Tax as a Qualification for Voting at the City Election Instead of the Present Registry Law, October, 1852" (General Assembly Loose Legislative Papers, SCA); Rogers, *Evolution of a Federalist,* 107; Philip F. Wild, "South Carolina Politics" (Ph.D. dissertation, University of Pennsylvania, 1949), 61–64; J. P. Carson (ed.), *Life, Letters, and Speeches of James Louis Petigru: The Union Man of South Carolina* (Washington, D.C., 1920), 85, 102.

52. Samuel G. Stoney (ed.), "The Memoirs of Frederick Adolphus Porcher," *SCHGM* 46 (July 1945), 37; Freehling, *Prelude to Civil War,* 253; Mark D. Kaplanoff, "Making the South Solid: Politics and the Structure of Society in South Carolina, 1790–1815" (Ph.D. dissertation, Cambridge University, 1979), 201, 242; Jaher, *The Urban Establishment,* 371; Pauline Maier, "The Road Not Taken: Nullification, John C. Calhoun and the Revolutionary Tradition in South Carolina,"

SCHM 82 (January 1981), 1–19, and Weir, "The Harmony We Were Famous For," 463–501, label the elitist and deferential politicians of mid-nineteenth-century South Carolina "anachronistic."

53. Wallace, *South Carolina*, 449; Willis, *Charleston Stage*, 153; Dorman, *Theatre in the Antebellum South*, 130–32; Power, *Impressions of America*, I, 93; Hindman "Concert Life in Antebellum Charleston," 86n; Watson *Antebellum Charleston Dramatists*, 1; Hoole, *Antebellum Charleston Theatre*, 34–37.

54. David R. Goldfield, "The Business of Health Planning: Disease Prevention in the Old South," *JSH* 42 (November 1976), 557–70; Barbara L. Bellows, "Dependent upon Her Own Exertions and the Charity of the World: White Working Class Women of Antebellum Charleston" (paper in possession of Walter J. Fraser, Jr.); Taylor, *Antebellum South Carolina*, 97–98; Poor House Journals, December 30, 1830, June 12, 1834, May 20, 1837, February 5, 1840; *Courier*, August 12, 1836, April 29, 1843; Ian R Tyrrell, "Drink and Temperance in the Antebellum South: An Overview and Interpretation," *JSH* 48 (November 1982), 502–10; "Jacob Schirmer Diary" (SCHS), April 13, December 10, 1843; Loveland, *Southern Evangelicals*,131.

55. Smith, "Sketch of the History of Charleston," 304–306; Pease, "The Blood-Thirsty Tiger," 282–284; Rogers, *Chronology of South Carolina*, 64.

56. [E. Vanderhorst] to "My Dear Sister," to "My Dear Wife," August 13, September 19, 1835; A. V. Huff, Jr., "The Eagle and the Vulture: Changing Attitudes toward Nationalism in Fourth of July Orations Delivered in Charleston, 1778–1860," *South Atlantic Quarterly* 73 (Winter 1974), 18; Schirmer, "Diary," July 29, 31, 1835; Frank O. Gatell (ed.), "Postmaster Huger and the Incendiary Publications," *SCHM* 64 (October 1963), 193–201; Rogers, *Charleston*, 163; *Proceedings of the Citizens of Charleston on the Incendiary Machinations Now in Progress against the Peace and Welfare of the Southern States* (Charleston, S.C., 1835), 6–12.

57. Dorman, *Antebellum Charleston Theatre*, 133; Kenneth Severens, *Southern Architecture: 350 Years of Distinctive American Buildings* (New York, 1981), 140. The New Charleston Theatre was destroyed during the great fire of 1861.

58. Stavisky, "Industrialism in Antebellum Charleston," 307; Laylon Wayne Jordan, "Education for Community: C. G. Memminger and the Origination of Common Schools in Antebellum Charleston," *SCHM* 83 (April 1982), 99–106; Petit, *South Carolina and the Sea*, II, 62; Wallace, *South Carolina*, 459–60.

59. Muhlenfeld, *Mary Boykin Chesnut*, 24–27, 33; Stoney, "Memoirs of Frederick Adolphus Porcher," 84; *Courier*, October 17, 1839; Easterby, *History of the College*, 89–97, 141; Pease, "The Blood-Thirsty Tiger," 281–95.

60. Pease, "The Blood-Thirsty Tiger," 281–95; *Courier*, May 31, June 2, 4, 8, 1838, August 29, 1859; Channing, *Crisis of Fear*, 43; Hamilton, *Men and Manners*, 347–48; Taylor, *Ante-Bellum South Carolina*, 39; "Petition of the Aetna Fire Engine Company of Charleston . . . November 17, 1829" (SCA); Greb, "Charleston, South Carolina Merchants," 20–23; Jaher, *The Urban Establishment*, 339–40.

61. Radford, "Culture, Economy and Urban Structure," 134–37, 153; H. L. Pinckney, *A Report, Relative to the Proceedings for the Relief of the Sick Poor, during the Late Epidemic; and on the Subject, Generally, of the Public Health: To Which Is Annexed the Report of the Commissioners of the Temporary Hospital* (Charleston, S.C., 1838), 4, 10–13, 18, 25–26, 53–54, 58–59; William H. Pease and Jane H. Pease, *The Web of Progress: Private Values and Public Styles in Boston*

and Charleston, 1827–1843 (New York, 1985), 196; *Courier,* May 11, July 20, September 11, 1838, September 1, 1839.

62. Poor House Journals, March 23, 1836, November 14, 1838, January 9, 1839, December 10, 1842; Bellows, "Controlling the Poor in a Slave Society," 10–11; Rutledge, *Artists in the Life of Charleston,* 153; Severens, *Southern Architecture,* 138–39; Robert P. Stockton, "Building's Demolition Was a Loss," *News and Courier,* February 16, 1981; [William Gilmore Simms], "Charleston: The Palmetto City," *Hapers New Monthly Magazine* 15 (June 1857), 18.

63. "West Point Rice Mills," 211–12; *Courier,* April 6, 1841, Hindman, "Concert Life in Antebellum Charleston, 21, 76–94, 119, 123, 142n, 169–170, 175–75,180–85; R. C. Carson to [?], April 14, 1840 (Joseph Harvey Wilson Papers, SCL); Clark, "A Theatrical Visit, 1842," 109–99; Hoole, *The Antebellum Charleston Theatre,* 39–40, 41n; Severens, *Southern Architecture,* 140; Dorman, *Antebellum Charleston Theatre,* 136–37; Fraser, *Reminiscences of Charleston,* 59–61; Charlotte Curtis, in "St. Cecilia Party Recalls the Past for Chosen Few," *New York Times,* January 17, 1964, quotes from a former president of the organization in the 1930s who offered one explanation for the society's passion for anonymity: "Publicity concerning the society is injurious to the community as a whole because it tends to stir up jealousies and animosities which seriously impair the goodwill normally existing between members and non-members."

64. "The Memorial of the Board Appointed to Establish a Municipal Guard for the Protection of Charleston and Its Vicinity, to the Senate of South Carolina" (Memorials 1825, SCA); Taylor, *Antebellum South Carolina,* 49, 122; Franklin, *The Militant South,* 151–53; Robert P. Stockton, "Citadel Architectural Style: A Combination," *News and Courier,* May 11, 1981; "The South Carolina Military Academy," in *YCC, 1892* (Charleston, S.C., 1893), 207–8; Ravenel, *Architects,* 142; Rogers, *Charleston,* 147; Rollin G. Osterweis, *Romanticism and Nationalism in the Old South* (Baton Rouge, La., 1949), 125–26.

65. Radford, "Culture, Economy and Urban Structure," 32–31, 119–25; Jane H. Pease and William H. Pease, "If All the South Were Charleston and Boston, All the North" (paper in possession of Walter J. Fraser, Jr.); Taylor, *Ante Bellum South Carolina,* 149; Olsberg, "A Government of Class and Race," 31, 180–82; Wallace, *South Carolina,* 452–54.

66. Greb, "Charleston, South Carolina, Merchants," 28–38, 45, 82–84, 110–25, 146–83, 231–37; Jaher, *The Urban Establishment,* 338–39, 344–49, 350–53. The Bank of Charleston in the twentieth century became the South Carolina National Bank, a statewide banking system.

67. Collins, "Charleston and the Railroads," 26–27, 31–36, 41, 58–59, 67–68, 84–85, 92–95; Donald A. Grinder, Jr., "Building the South Carolina Railroad," *SCHM* 77 (April 1976), 84–97; Johnson, "Planters and Patriarchy," 47–65; Stavisky, "Industrialism in Antebellum Charleston," 314–15; Captain Basil Hall, *Travels in North America in the Years 1827 and 1828* (Philadelphia, Pa., 1829), 191; *Courier,* January 28, 1841, August 30, 1845, September 21, October 18, 1849; Goldfield, "The Business of Health Planning," 565–69; Waring, "Charleston Medicine," 340.

68. January, "The First Nullification," 300–302; Clement Eaton, *The Growth of Southern Civilization, 1790–1860* (New York, 1961), 323; Wallace, *South Carolina,* 430, 436.

69. Anna Hays Johnson to Elizabeth Haywood as quoted in Wyatt-Brown,

Southern Honor, 201; Olsberg, "A Government of Class and Race," 176–77; Welsh, "William Gilmore Simms," 209–10; Jane H. Pease and William H. Pease, "Intellectual Life in the 1830's: The Institutional Framework and the Charleston Style," in O'Brien and Moltke-Hansen, *Intellectual Life,* 233–54.

70. Eaton, *Growth of Southern Civilization,* 16–17; Harriet Martineau, *Retrospect of Western Travel* (London, 1838), I, 236–40; Drew Faust, *A Sacred Circle: The Dilemma of the Intellectual in the Old South* (Baltimore, Md., 1977), xi, 6, 47–48, 90, 171n; John Dewey Lane, "The Charleston Club" (M.S. thesis, University of Virginia, 1924), 3, 9–13; Paul Hamilton Hayne, "Ante-Bellum Charleston," *The Southern Bivouac* 1 (November 1885), 3, 327–29; William Henry Longton, "Some Aspects of Intellectual Activity in Ante-Bellum South Carolina, 1830–1860: An Introductory Study" (Ph.D. dissertation, Chapel Hill, N.C., 1969), 28–29; John McCardell, "Poetry and the Practical: William Gilmore Simms," in O'Brien and Moltke-Hansen, *Intellectual Life,* 186–210; Jay B. Hubbell, *The South in American Literature* (Durham, N.C., 1954), 577–84, 745–47.

71. Holifield, *The Gentlemen Theologians,* 10–12, 128; Samuel G. Stoney (ed.), "The Memoirs of Frederick Adolphus Porcher," *SCHGM* 44 (April 1943), 49; Pease, "Intellectual Life in the 1830's," Bost, "The Reverend John Bachman," 233–54; 380–81; Clyde Norman Wilson, "Carolina Cavalier: The Life of James Johnson Pettigrew (Ph.D. dissertation, University of North Carolina at Chapel Hill, 1971).

72. Edmund Gifford, Jr., "The Charleston Physician-Naturalists," *Bulletin of the History of Medicine* (Winter 1975), 564–71; Thomas Cary Johnson, Jr., *Scientific Interests in the Old South* (New York, 1936), 136–37, 145–51; Lester D. Stephens, "Scientific Societies in the Old South" (paper in possession of Walter J. Fraser, Jr.); Lester Stephens, "Lewis R. Gibbes and Scientific Activity in Charleston" (paper in possession of Walter J. Fraser, Jr.); Lester D. Stephens, "The Mermaid Hoax: Indications of Scientific Thought in Charleston, South Carolina in the 1840's" (paper in possession of Walter J. Fraser, Jr.); David Moltke-Hansen, "The Expansion of Intellectual Life: A Prospective," and Pease, "Intellectual Life in the 1830's," in O'Brien and Moltke-Hansen, *Intellectual Life,* 3–44, 233–54.

73. Rutledge, *Artists in the Life of Charleston,* 160–66.

74. Stavisky, "Industrialism in Antebellum Charleston," 307; "Memorial of the Mechanics of Charleston Petition . . . for an Amendment of the Law as to Colored Negro Tradesman" (n.d., General Assembly Petitions, SCA); "Petition of the Mechanics and Working Men of the City of Charleston to Provide More Efficiently for the Prevention of Slaves Hiring Their Own Time" (Loose Legislative Petitions, SCA). Christopher Silver, "A New Look at Old South Urbanization: The Irish Worker in Charleston, South Carolina, 1840–1860," in Hines and Hopkins (eds.), *South Atlantic Urban Studies,* 157; "Presentments of the Grand Jury District of Charleston, May, 1846" (General Assembly Grand Jury Presentments, SCA).

75. Wallace, *South Carolina,* 501–03; Wade, *Slavery in the Cities,* 157–59; Robert F. Durden, "The Establishment of Calvary Protestant Episcopal Church for Negroes in Charleston," *SCHM* 65 (April 1964), 73; Pease, "The Blood-Thirsty Tiger," 295.

76. Rogers, *Charleston,* 167–68; Wallace, *South Carolina,* 448, 509.

77. John P. Radford, "Social Structure and Urban Form: Charleston, 1860–

1880," in Fraser and Moore, *From the Old South to the New,* 84; John P. Radford, "Race, Residence, and Ideology: Charleston, South Carolina in the Mid-Nineteenth Century," *Journal of Historical Geography* 2 (1976), 334–39; Kemble, *Journal of a Residence on a Georgia Plantation,* 38–40; S. A. Hulburt (ed.), *Charleston One Hundred Years Ago: Being Extracts from the Letters of Fredricka Bremer during Her Visit to Charleston in 1850* (Charleston, S.C., 1951), 2, 10–11; Ravenel, *Charleston,* 480, describes the Battery in antebellum Charleston as "a cool and cheerful walk" of "large gardens" and "arbours where tea-tables were set" and "gentlemen smoked tobacco then forbidden in dining rooms"; George A. Gordon to "Krilla," June 25, 1857 (George A. Gordon Papers, DUL).

78. *Courier,* December 17, 1850, October 7, 8, 1853; Leonard P. Curry, *The Free Black in Urban America 1800–1850; The Shadow of the Dream* (Chicago, Ill., 1982), 59–60; Davidson, *The Last Foray,* 185; Leland, *60 Famous Houses,* 28–29; Severens, *Southern Architecture,* 73–76; G.M., "South Carolina," in Eugene L. Schwaab (ed.), *Travels in the Old South* (Lexington, Ky., 1973), I, 231; Alston Deas (ed.), "A Ball in Charleston," *SCHM,* 75 (January 1974), 49;. [Simms], "Charleston: The Palmetto City," 18–19.

79. Wallace, *South Carolina,* 456, 511–13.

80. Jaher, *The Urban Establishment,* 350–55; Lander, "Charleston: Manufacturing Center," 331–32, 339–43; Lander, "Ante-Bellum Milling," 129–31; "West Point Rice Mills," 211–12; Radford, "Culture, Economy and Urban Structure," 128; Halsey, "The Passing of a Great Forest," 203–7; Greb, "Charleston, South Carolina, Merchants," 110–25, 146–86.

81. Collins, "Charleston and the Railroads," 68–71, 92, 95; Greb, "Charleston, South Carolina, Merchants," 134; Taylor, *Ante-Bellum South Carolina,* 149.

82. Smith, "The Government of the City," 342–51; Wallace, *South Carolina,* 436, 522; Hubbell, *The South in American Literature,* 438–45; Ford, "Republics and Democracy"; M. Foster Farley, "The Mighty Monarch of the South: Yellow Fever in Charleston and Savannah," *The Georgia Review* 27 (1973), 58; Goldfield, "The Business of Health Planning," 564.

83. Jaher, *The Urban Establishment,* 356; Allan Pred, *Urban Growth and City-Systems in the United States, 1840–60* (Cambridge, Mass., 1980), 115–18; Ivan D. Steen, "Charleston in the 1850's: As Described by British Travelers," *SCHM* 71 (January 1970), 43, 45.

84. "Minutes," Poor House Journals, 1800–1860; "Comparative Costs of Paupers to the City of Charleston," December 23, 1856 (Loose Legislative Papers, SCA); Johnson, "Wealth and Class in Charleston," 70–74; Frederick Law Olmstead, *A Journey in the Seaboard Slave States* (New York, 1856), 404; "Petition of City Council of Charleston, September 4, 1855" (Loose Legislative Papers, SCA); "Presentments of the Grand Jury for the District of Charleston, May 10, 1847" (SCA); Robert P. Stockton, "Relic of Racy Past Has Uncertain Fate," *News and Courier,* January 3, 1977, May 12, 1980; "Diary of John Berkeley Grimball, 1858–65" (SCHS), 42.

85. Pease, "If All of the South were Charleston," 20–21; Stanley K. Schultz, *The Culture Factory: Boston Public Schools, 1789–1860* (New York, 1973), 9, 309; Wallace, *South Carolina,* 464, 475, 575; Jordan, "Education for Community," 99, 106–111; Ford, "Republics and Democracy"; Laylon Wayne Jordan, "Between Two Worlds: Christopher G. Memminger of Charleston and the Old South in Mid-Passage, 1830–1861," *PSCHA* (1981), 64–66.

86. Klebaner, "Public Poor Relief," 214, 218–20; *Mayor's Report on City Affairs* (Charleston, S.C., 1857), 53; *The Proceedings of the Sixty-Sixth Anniversary of the Orphan House of Charleston, South Carolina, October 18, 1855* (Charleston, S.C., 1855), 25, 47, 50, 61–62; Newton B. Jones, "The Charleston Orphan Home, 1860–1876," *SCHM* 62 (October 1961), 203–4; Charleston "Commissioners Minutes—Orphan House" (CCA), June 14, 1855.

87. Jordan, "Police Power and Public Safety," 124–30, 131–33n12, 135–36; Cantwell, "History of Charleston Police," 12–13; *Mayor's Report* (1857), 39–41.

88. "Petition of the City Council of Charleston for the Building of a New Jail," [1853] (Loose Legislative Papers, SCA); Stockton, "Jail's Octagonal Wing"; Pease and Pease, *The Web of Progress*, 196–97; Steen, "Charleston in the 1850s," 38; "Presentments of the Grand Jury of the Charleston District, April, 1857 and May, 1858 and October 1859" (SCA); Williams, *Vogues in Villany*, 106–15, 551; *Mercury*, December 13, 1953; *Courier*, March 26, 1859.

89. Lacy Ford, "James Louis Petigru: The Last South Carolina Federalist," in O'Brien and Moltke-Hansen, *Intellectual Life*, 176–77; Rogers, *Charleston*, 160; Wallace, *South Carolina*, 523; *Mayor's Report* (1857), 27–28, 30, 43–45; George A. Gordon to "Dear Krilla," August 28, 1858, Gordon Papers; Farley, "the Mighty Monarch of the South," 61; Goldfield, "Health Planning in the Old South," 565; Frederick L. Olmstead, *The Cotton Kingdom: A Traveler's Observations on Cotton and Slavery in the American Slave States* (New York, 1861), 499.

90. Michael P. Johnson, "Wealth and Class in Charleston in 1860," in Walter J. Fraser, Jr., and Winifred B. Moore, Jr. (eds.), *From the Old South to the New: Essays on the Transitional South* (Westport, Conn., 1981), 66–67, 73; *List of the Taxpayers of the City of Charleston for 1859* (Charleston, S.C., 1860), 169, 273, 280, 308; Steen, "Charleston in the 1850's," 43; Radford, "Culture Economy and Urban Structure in Charleston," 173–74; Richard B. Morris, "White Bondage in Antebellum South Carolina," *SCHGM* 49 (October 1948), 206; "An Englishman in South Carolina," Schwaab, *Travels in the Old South*, II, 569; James David Altman, "The Charleston Marine School, *SCHM* 88 (April 1987), 76–79.

91. Olmstead, *The Cotton Kingdom*, 574; Olmstead, *A Journey in the Seaboard Slave States*, 404; Huff, "The Eagle and the Vulture," 19–21; Greenberg, "Revolutionary Ideology and the Proslavery Argument" 369, 382; Channing, *Crisis of Fear*, 18–58, 207–8, 231, 241, 251–73, 282n61, 291; Barnwell, "Love of Order," 294–96, 440; Wallace, *South Carolina*, 433, 525, 529; John C. Roberson, "The 1860 Association: Catalyst of Secession" (paper in possession of Walter J. Fraser, Jr.).

92. Wikramanayake, *A World in Shadows*, 155, 168–71; Ira Berlin, *Slaves without Masters: The Free Negro in the Antebellum South* (New York, 1976), 14–15, 163–78; Johnson and Roark, *No Chariot Let Down*, 5–15; Michael P. Johnson and James L. Roark, *Black Masters: A Free Family of Color in the Old South* (New York, 1984), 194–286.

93. Ralph Wooster, "Membership of the South Carolina Secession Convention," *SCHGM* 55 (October 1954), 185, 189, 192; Wallace, *South Carolina*, 526; Grimball, "Diary," December 20, 21, 1860; *Mercury*, December 22, 28, 1860; "An Englishman in South Carolina, December, 1860," as reprinted in *Travels in the Old South*, II, 564, 572; Olsberg, "A Government of Class and Race," 11–16, 35; Robert M. Weir, "The South Carolinian as Extremist," *South Atlantic Quarterly* 74 (Winter 1975), 93, 96–97, 99–103; George C. Rogers, Jr., "South Caro-

lina and the Origins of the Nullification Movement," *SCHM* 71 (January 1970), 27–32; Rogers, *Charleston,* 164–66; Ford, "James Louis Petigru," 182.

94. *The War of the Rebellion: A compilation of the Official Records of the Union and Confederate Armies* (series 1, vol. I, Washington, D.C., 1880), pp. 2, 3, 71, 74–77, 90, 91, 100, 129, 252; Rogers W. Young, "Castle Pinckney, Silent Sentinel of Charleston Harbor, *SCHM* 39 (January 1938), 1–2, 7–8, 12, 14; E. Milby Burton, *The Siege of Charleston, 1861–1865,* (Columbia, S.C. 1976), 5, 9–16; Moore, *Lowcountry Engineers,* 40; Bruce Catton, *The Coming Fury* (New York, 1961), 143, 153–60; W. A. Swanberg, *First Blood: The Story of Fort Sumter* (New York, 1957), 89–101, 108; Charles E. Cauthen, *South Carolina Goes to War, 1860–1865* (Chapel Hill, N.C., 1950), 99.

Chapter V

1. Burton, *Siege,* 17–18; John F. Marszalek (ed.), *The Diary of Miss Emma Holmes, 1861–1866* (Baton Rouge, La., 1979), 10–11; Martin Abbott and Elmer L. Puryear (ed.), "Beleaguered Charleston: Letters from the City, 1860–1864," *SCHM* 61 (April 1960), 30, 32, 61–63; *Official Records,* ser. 1, vol. I, 136; Hartwell Perry Spain Diary, February 19, 1861 (SHC); Schirmer, "Diary," January 29, 1861; Howard T. Oedel, "Lincoln Takes the Pulse of the Confederacy at Charleston in March, 1861," *Lincoln Herald* 73 (1971), 156–62.

2. T. Harry Williams, *P. G. T. Beauregard: Napoleon in Gray* (Baton Rouge, La., 1954), 1–8, 49–54, 56–61; Burton, *Siege,* 31–39, 41–45; Charles W. Ramsdell, "Lincoln and Fort Sumter," *JSH* 3 (August 1937), 280; John B. Edwards, Jr., "Francis W. Pickens and the War Begins," *PSCHA* (1970), 28; Robert Rosen, *A Short History of Charleston* (San Francisco, 1982), 101–2; Marszalek, *Diary,* 11, 24–26; "Your Brother" to "Dear Charlie" and "Doc," April 5, 1861 (Willis Grady Briggs Papers, SHC); C. Vann Woodward (ed.), *Mary Chesnut's Civil War* (New Haven, Conn., 1981), 41–46; *Official Records,* ser. 1, vol. I, 14; Muhlenfeld, *Mary Boykin Chesnut,* 107; Schirmer, "Diary," April 12, 1861; Ron Chepesiuk (ed.), "Eye Witness to Fort Sumter: The Letters of Private John Thompson," *SCHM* 85 (October 1984), 278; Marszalek, *Diary,* 29; F. L. Parker, "The Battle of Fort Sumter as Seen from Morris Island," *SCHM* 62 (April 1961), 70.

3. William Howard Russell, *My Diary North and South* (New York, 1969), 56–57, 60; Frank B. Williams, Jr., "From Sumter to the Wilderness: Letters of Sergeant James Butler Suddath, Co. E. 7th Regiment, S.C.V.," *SCHM* 63 (January 1962), 2; William M. Still, Jr., *Confederate Shipbuilding* (Athens, Ga., 1969), 9; William F. Barney, *Flawed Victory: A New Perspective on the Civil War* (Washington, D.C., 1980), 32–35; Willie Lee Rose, *Rehearsal for Reconstruction: The Port Royal Experiment* (New York, 1964), 4–6, 11–12.

4. Grimball, "Diary," 158, 160; Cauthen, *South Carolina Goes to War,* 81n, 137; Olsberg, "A Government of Class and Race," 312–16; Mary Elizabeth Massey, *Refugee Life in the Confederacy* (Baton Rouge, La., 1964), 13; 252–53; *Official Records,* ser. 1, vol. I, XIV, 42, 479–480.

5. Marszalek, *Diary,* 105–12; *Courier,* December 12, 13, 1861; Carson, *Petigru,* 416–18; Burton, *Siege,* 82–84; Smith, "Sketch of the History of Charleston," 306–7; Van Woodward, *Mary Chesnut's Civil War,* 266–67; Arney R. Childs (ed.), *Rice Planter and Sportsman: The Recollections of J. Motte Alston, 1821–1909* (Columbia, S.C., 1953), 133–35. Friend Street is Legare Street today.

6. Bernard E. Powers, Jr., "Black Charleston: A Social History, 1822–1855" (Ph.D. dissertation, Northwestern University, 1982), 77–80; *Courier,* May 14, 1962; Still, *Confederate Shipbuilding,* 16, 40, 69; J. Thomas Scharf, *History of the Confederate States Navy from Its Organization to the Surrender of Its Last Vessel* (New York, 1887), 670; Jack A. Sutor, "Charleston, South Carolina, during the Civil War Era, 1858–1865" (M.A. thesis, Duke University, 1942), 144–46, 201–5, 213–16; *Official Records,* ser. 1, vol. I, XIV, 491–92, 832; Arney Robinson Childs (ed.), *The Private Journal of Henry William Ravenel, 1859–1887 (Columbia, S.C., 1947), 101–2, 121.*

7. B. S. Caleb, "Prison-Life," *Harper's New Monthly Magazine* 30 (July 1865), 144; *Courier,* October 25, 1862; *Official Records,* ser. 1, vol. VI, 42.

8. Marszalek, *Diary,* 56, 74, 91, 97, 123, 138–39, 141; E. Huger Smith (ed.), *Mason Smith Family Letters, 1860–1868* (Columbia, S.C., 1950); 28; Isabella M. Leland (ed.), "Middleton Correspondence, 1861–1865," *SCHM* 65 (January 1964), 34, 41, 44; Isabella M. Leland (ed.), "Middleton Correspondence, 1861–1865," *SCHM* 64 (July 1963), 158; Sutor, "Charleston," 194–95, 219, 225–26; Burton, *Siege,* 261–62; Van Woodward, *Mary Chesnut's Civil War,* 323; James Morris Morgan, *Recollections of a Rebel Reefer* (Boston, Mass., 1917), 91; Mrs. E. C. Ball to "My Dear Son," January 21, 1863 (Ball Family Papers, SCL); Bettie R. Brown to "My Dear Bersha," March 5, 1863 (Bettie R. Brown Papers, DUL).

9. Okon Edet Uya, *From Slavery to Public Service: Robert Smalls, 1839–1915* (New York, 1971), 12–16; Benjamin Quarles, *The Negro in the Civil War* (New York, 1953), 70–74; Burton, *Siege,* 94–97, 100–112; 142; Carson, *Petigru,* 452–53.

10. *Courier,* September 21, November 17, 1862, September 28, December 8, 1864; Smith, *Mason Smith Letters,* 22n; Olsberg, "A Government of Class and Race," 325–26, 345, 365–66; William Middleton to "My Dear Wife," September 17, 1863 (William Middleton Papers, SCL); Leland "Susan to Harriott, July 17, 20, 1863," in "Middleton Correspondence," 164–65; Schirmer, "Diary," June 16, 1862.

11. Williams, *Beauregard,* 64–67, 166–68; Burton, *Siege,* 132; William Middleton to "My Dear Sue," November 2, 1862, Middleton Papers; W. F. G. Peck, "Five Years under Fire at Charleston," *Harper's New Monthly Magazine* 31 (August 1865),359; Smith, *Mason Smith Letters,* 68–69; James Conner to General Pender, November 5, 1862 (William Dorsey Pender Papers, SHC); M. L. Bonham to General G. T. Beauregard, October 27, and Colonel D. B. Davis to General Beauregard, October 31, 1863 (P.G.T. Beauregard Papers, SCL); Elmer L. Puryear (ed.), "The Confederate Diary of William John Grayson," *SCHM* 63 (July 1962), 142–43; Sutor, "Charleston," 113–20, 226–33; E. Merton Coulter, *George Walton Williams: The Life of a Southern Merchant and Banker, 1820–1903* (Athens, Ga., 1976), 79–82.

12. Herman Hattaway and Archer Jones, *How the North Won: A Military History of the Civil War* (Urbana, Ill., 1983), 126, 360–61, 426–27; Frank F. Vandiver, *Plough Shares into Swords: Josiah Gorgas and Confederate Ordnance* (Austin, Tex., 1952), 61, 82, 148n, 152; Still, *Confederate Shipbuilding,* 13–16, 28, 72; William N. Still, Jr., *Iron Afloat: The Story of the Confederate Armorclads* (Nashville, Tenn., 1971), 98, 212, 219; Lynda Worley Skelton, "the Importing and Exporting Company of South Carolina," *SCHM* 75 (January 1974), 24–32;

Marcus W. Price, "Blockade Running as a Business in South Carolina during the War between the States, 1861–1865," *American Neptune* 8 (1948), 196–241; Clement Eaton, *Jefferson Davis* (New York, 1977), 237.

13. Shelby Foote, "DuPont Storms Charleston," *American Heritage* 14 (June 1963), 28–34, 89–92; Burton, *Siege*, 64, 77–78, 117, 135–45, 252–60; Williams, *Beauregard*, 170, 262–63, 270–72; Howard G. Westwood, "Captive Black Soldiers in Charleston—What to Do?" *Civil War History* 28 (March 1982), 28–29, 33–34, 37, 39, 44–45; Joseph T. Durkin, *Stephen R. Mallory: Confederate Navy Chief* (Chapel Hill, N.C., 1954), 258, 177–78, 185–91; William Garland to "My Dear Father," February 7, 1863 (William Harris Garland Papers, SHC).

14. Mary Ravenel to Mrs. Snowden, July 30, 1863 (Snowden Papers, SCL); Charlotte R. Holmes, *The Burckmyer Letters, 1863–1865* (Columbia, S.C., 1926), 50; Mrs. "G.D." to Mrs. Joseph Glover, August 1863 (Henry W. DeSaussure Papers, DUL); Dr. Robert Lebby to Surgeon N. S. Crowell, December 8, 1863 (Letter Book, Wayside Hospital, SCL); Sutor, "Charleston," 146, 165–67; Leland, "Susan to Harriot, April 13, 1862," in "Middleton Correspondence," 62; Marszalek, *Diary*, 386.

15. Abbott and Puryear, "Beleaguered Charleston," 169, 210, 212; Burton, *Siege*, 251–53; Rosen, *Charleston*, 108–9; W. Stanley Hoole, *Vizetelly Covers the Confederacy* (Tuscaloosa, Ala., 1957), 94–99; Schirmer "Diary," August 31, 1863.

16. Holmes, *Burckmyer Letters*, 161–66, 191, 213–15, 275, 309, 428, 430; Cochran, *Blockade Runners*, 165; Childs, *Journal of Ravenel*, 205; *Courier*, December 16, 29, 1863; Arthur Grimball to "My Dear Father," December 31, 1864 (Grimball Family Papers, SHC); Olsberg, "A Government of Class and Race," 359–61; Durkin, *Stephen Mallory*, 274–79; Burton, *Siege, 202*.

17. Petit, *South Carolina and the Sea*, II, 126–27; *Courier*, May 19, 1863, July 9, August 27, September 12, 19, 30, October 10, 15, 1864; Nathaniel Hughes, Jr., *General William J. Hardee: Old Reliable* (Baton Rouge, La., 1965), 250–54; 268, 272–78; Burton, *Siege*, 236–41, 303–15; Wallace, *South Carolina*, 359–60, 551; Still, *Confederate Shipbuilding*, 56, 72; John G. Barrett, *Sherman's March through the Carolinas* (Chapel Hill, N.C., 1956), 39, 40, 52–53; Alfred Ayer to "Dear Father," January 6, 1865 (Lewis Malone Ayer Papers, SCL); Yates Snowden, "Charleston in War-Time, 1861–1865," *YCC, 1908* (Charleston, S.C., 1909), 57–58.

18. Edmund Rhett to William P. Miles, February 3, 1865 (William Porcher Miles Papers, SHC); *Courier*, May 19, 1863, February 11, 13, 20, 1865; Still, *Iron Afloat*, 219–21; John E. Duncan (ed.), "The Correspondence of a Yankee Prisoner in Charleston, 1865," *SCHM* 66 (January 1965); Viola Caston Floyd (ed.), " 'The Fall of Charleston,' " *SCHM* 66 (January 1965), 1–7; *Official Records*, ser. 1, vol. LIII, 60–61; ser. 1, vol. XLVII, pt. 2, pp. 659–60.

19. *Official Records*, ser. 1, vol. XL, 60–61; ser. 1, vol. XLVII, pt. 1, 1007–8, 1019–20; ser. 1, vol. XLVII, pt. 11, p. 711; Petit, *South Carolina and the Sea*, II, 137, 141–42; Francis Butler Simkins and Robert H. Woody, *South Carolina during Reconstruction* (Chapel Hill, N.C., 1932), 18–19; Burton, *Siege*, 322–23.

20. Coulter, *George Williams*, 91–95; Rev. Philip G. Clarke, *Anglicanism in South Carolina* (Easley, S.C., 1976), 56, 58; John Hall, "A Pilot of People," *State Magazine*, May 17, 1987, 10; Powers, "Black Charleston," 80–82; Joel Williamson, *After Slavery: The Negro in South Carolina during Reconstruction, 1861–1877* (Chapel Hill, N.C., 1965), 45–51, 258–59.

21. W. Stanley Hoole, "Charleston Theatricals during the Tragic Decade, 1860–1869," *JSH* 11 (November 1945), 541–42; *Courier*, December 21, 1865, May 2, 9, October 10, November 9, 10, 27, 1866, April 9, October 30, 1867; Harriet P. and Albert Simons, "The William Burrows House of Charleston," *SCHM* 70 (July 1969), 175; Herbert Ravenel Sass, *Outspoken: 150 Years of the News and Courier* (Columbia, S.C., 1953), 34–36. The Mills House stood until 1969 when it was demolished to make way for building another hotel on the site. The Mansion House operated as a roominghouse in the early twentieth century. In the 1920s the structure that had first been built there in the early 1770s and known as the William Burrows House was dismantled and moved.

22. Olsberg, "A Government of Class and Race," 381; E. Vanderhorst to J. B. Grimball, June 5, 1865 (Grimball Papers, SHC); Powers, "Black Charleston," 85–88, 91–92, 98–118, 146–58, 245, 283–87, 317–22; *Courier*, June 29, July 7, September 5, 1865; George S. Pelzer, *Annual Report of the Health Department for . . . 1866* (Charleston, S.C., 1867), 17, 39, 43, 47; Simkins and Woody, *South Carolina*, 119; Waring, *A History of Medicine*, 161–64, 173, 176; Elias Horry Deas to "My Dear Daughter," August 12, 1865 (Elias Horry Deas Papers, SCL); Howard N. Rabinowitz, "Southern Urban Development, 1860–1900," in Brownell and Goldfield, *City in Southern History*, 117.

23. Marszalek, *Diary*, 441–42, 455; Schirmer, "Diary," June 19, 1866; Eliza Fludd to "My Dear Friend," September 25, October 24, 1865, and to "My Beloved Sister, November 14, 1865, July 4, 1867 (Eliza Fludd Papers, DUL); Martin Abbott, *The Freedmen's Bureau in South Carolina, 1865–1872* (Chapel Hill, N.C., 1967), 120–27; C. Vann Woodward, *Origins of the New South,* (Baton Route, La., 1951), 429–31.

24. Carl Schurz, *The Reminiscences of Carl Schurz* (New York, 1908), III, 164–65; Simkins and Woody, *South Carolina,* 30, 57, 60; W. A. Swanberg, *Sickles the Incredible* (New York, 1956), 217.

25. Powers, "Black Charleston," 273–74, 276–79; Williamson, *After Slavery,* 46–51, 211, 216, 258–59; *Daily Courier,* July 26, 28, 1865, December 28, 1868, May 20, 1869; William C. Hine, "Frustration, Factionalism and Failure: Black Political Leadership and the Republican Party in Reconstruction Charleston, 1865–1877" (Ph.D. dissertation, Kent State University, 1979), 31–49, 33n, 51n, 52n, 56–57, 74; Coulter, *George Williams,* 94; Swanberg, *Sickles,* 276–79; James E. Sefton, *The United States Army and Reconstruction, 1865–1877* (Baton Rouge, La., 1967), 54; Rosen, *Charleston,* 111–18; *An Historical and Descriptive Review of the City of Charleston, South Carolina* (New York, 1884), 166–67.

26. W. L. Trenholm, *The South: An Address on the Third Anniversary of the Charleston Board of Trade* (Charleston, S.C., 1869), 1–18; Swanberg, *Sickles,* 287n7; Don H. Doyle, "Leadership and Decline in Postwar Charleston, 1865–1910," in Walter J. Fraser, Jr., and Winfred B. Moore, Jr. (eds.), *From the Old South to the New: Essays on the Transitional South* (Westport, Conn., 1981), 93, 98–99; John McCardell, "William Gilmore Simms and His World after the Civil War: A New Look at Joscelyn" (paper in possession of Walter J. Fraser, Jr.); Coulter, *George Williams,* 134, 138.

27. Robert P. Stockton, "King St. Victorian Dates to 1870s," *News and Courier,* August 10, 1981; Robert P. Stockton, "Elliot House Hotel Preserved through Adaptive Development," *News and Courier,* April 13, 1981, "House Was Built with City Loan," *News and Courier,* August 25, 1980.

28. Tom W. Schick and Don H. Doyle, "The South Carolina Phosphate Boom and the Stillbirth of the New South, 1867–1920," *SCHM* 86 (January 1985), 1–31; W. L. Trenholm, *The Centennial Address before the Charleston Chamber of Commerce* (Charleston, S.C., 1884), 35.

29. Jones, "The Charleston Orphan House," 210; Eileen M. Miller, "The Charleston Orphan House: An Historical Study of Personnel and Policies" (M.A. thesis, University of South Carolina, 1982), 26, 29; *YCC, 1880* (Charleston, S.C., 1881), 58; George B. Tindall, *South Carolina Negroes, 1877–1900* (Baton Rouge, La., 1966), 278–79; [?] *Historical Sketch of the Confederate Home and College* (Charleston, S.C., 1921), 1–22.

30. Russell Middleton to "My Dear Alicia," December 26, 1868, Middleton Family Papers; Schirmer, "Diary," July 4, 1868; Simkins and Woody, *South Carolina*, 346–47; *Courier*, March 22, June 4, 5, September 4, 5, 1865, May 21, June 5, 1867, June 4, 15, 1868; *News and Courier*, September 4, 10, 1872, July 4, 1881; The Rutledge Avenue Pond later became Colonial Lake. Today Hampton Park is located on the site of the Washington Race Course, and Marion Square is the name of the former Citadel green.

31. Powers, "Black Charleston," 156, 289–91; 305; Simkins and Woody, *South Carolina*, 64–68, 82–83, 93; Swanberg, *Sickles*, 290, 292; Sefton, *Army and Reconstruction*, 159, 186–87, 251, 262; Hine, "Black Leadership," 130–32, 135–36, 144–48, 163–76, 184–86, 493–96; Coulter, *George Williams*, 104; Thomas Holt, *Black over White: Negro Political Leadership in South Carolina during Reconstruction* (Chicago, 1977), 117; Schirmer, "Diary," May 30, 1868; William C. Hine, "The 1867 Charleston Streetcar Sit-Ins: A Case of Successful Black Protest," *SCHM* 77 (April 1977), 110–14.

32. Peggy Lamson, *The Glorious Failure: Black Congressman Robert Brown Elliott and the Reconstruction in South Carolina* (New York, 1974), 47–63, 66–69; J. J. Pringle Smith to W. P. Miles, January 25, 1868, William P. Miles Papers; Simkims and Woody, *South Carolina*, 82–83; "Pillsbury Genealogy" (in possession of Walter J. Fraser, Jr.); *Courier*, November 9, 14, 17, 1868; Hine, "Black Leadership," 168–76, 184–86, 254; Coulter, *George Williams*, 105.

33. Schirmer, "Diary," December 30, 1869, December 29, 1870; "Reminiscences of Thomas Pinckney Lowndes" (SHC); Williamson, *After Slavery*, 292; Robert Somers, *The Southern States since the War,* (London and New York, 1872), 41–43, 280–81; Doyle, "Leadership and Decline," 93, 98–99.

34. Hoole, "Charleston Theatricals," 541–47; Charleston *Daily Republican,* July 5, 1868; *Courier*, April 17, 1866, June 9, December 4, 29, 1868, April 12, 24, 1869, February 22, 1870, December 1, 14, 1871, January 1, 25, February 23, April 8, July 19, 22, 1872.

35. *News and Courier*, September 4, 8, 10, 1872, December 9, 1875, September 11, 1876; Robert P. Stockton, "281 Meeting Street," *News and Courier*, September 28, 1980; Rosen, *Charleston*, 114–15; Simkins and Woody, *South Carolina*, 118, 189–99, 208–10, 222, 271–72, 280, 313–16, 354; Edward King, "The Great South," *Scribner's Monthly* 8 (June 1874), 142–43; Jamie W. Moore, "The Low Country in Economic Transition: Charleston since 1865," *SCHM* 80 (April 1979), 157–58; Powers, "Black Charleston," 143, 273–79, 311; Robert Preston Stockton, "The Evolution of Rainbow Row" (M.A. thesis, University of South Carolina, 1979), 1, 9–10, 146–47; Holt, *Black over White*, 116–19, 158–60. The structure built for the German Friendly Alliance currently serves as the

headquarters of the Washington Light Infantry, a local military organization dating from the Chesapeake–Leopard Affair of 1807.

36. Lamson, *Glorious Failure,* 101; Hine, "Black Leadership," 270, 273, 277–78, 293n218, 296–99, 302, 321–26, 363, 486; Schirmer, "Diary," August 31, 1871; Waring, *A History of Medicine,* 174–75; Holt, *Black over White,* 119–20; *Cyclopedia of Eminent and Representative Men of the Carolinas* (Spartanburg, S.C., 1972), I, 541–42.

37. Moore, "Low Country in Economic Transition," 157; King, "The Great South," 143; E. Culpepper Clark, *Francis W. Dawson and the Politics of Restoration: South Carolina, 1874–1889* (University, Ala., 1980), 148; Simkins and Woody, *South Carolina,* 271–72, 337; Somers, *Southern States,* 280–81; Asa H. Gordon, *Sketches of Negro Life and History in South Carolina* (Columbia, S.C., 1971), 260–65; Petit, *South Carolina and the Sea,* II, 149.

38. Hine, "Black Leadership," 365–68, 441; Almshouse Records, City of Charleston (CCA), August 31, October 10, 12, 1874, June 21, 1875, March 15, April 10, May 22, 1876, May 25, 1877, May 5, 1879, January 8, 1883, April 4, 1887; Powers, "Black Charleston," 305–11, 323–24; Williamson, *After Slavery,* 161–63, 176–77, 294–97; Jones, "The Charleston Orphan House," 213; Laylon W. Jordan, " 'The Method of Modern Charity': The Associated Charities Society of Charleston, 1888–1920" (paper in possession of Walter J. Fraser, Jr.); *Report of the Special Committee of the City Council, 1875* (Charleston, S.C., 1875), 20; Wallace, *South Carolina,* 583, 609; *Sholes' Directory of the City of Charleston for 1877–1878* (Charleston, S.C., 1878), 41.

39. Snowden, *South Carolina,* 923; *YCC, 1870, 1880, 1890, 1900; Report of the Special Committee of the City Council, 1875,* 20; *Courier,* March 9, 1870; Simkins and Woody, *South Carolina,* 315–16, 370–76.

40. Robert P. Stockton, "Church Designed in Classic Mode," *News and Courier,* March 31, 1981; Clark, *Dawson,* 41, 54–56; Hine, "Black Leadership," 367–78; Holt, *Black over White,* 107, 116–19; Wallace, *South Carolina,* 578–79, 596n; Williamson, *After Slavery,* 384n, 402; Coulter, *George Williams,* 153–56, 192–93; Moore, *The Lowcountry Engineers,* 36; Gustavus G. Williamson, "Francis W. Dawson and South Carolina Politics" (paper in the possession of Walter J. Fraser, Jr.); *YCC, 1880,* 309–11; *News and Courier,* January 10, 1876.

41. Williamson, *After Slavery,* 268–72; *News and Courier,* November 16, 1876; Lamson, *Glorious Failure,* 154–59, 239–46, 249–50; Hine, "Black Leadership," 231–37, 428–33, 440, 460; Roller and Twyman, *Encyclopedia of Southern History,* 180, 340, 570–71; Rosen, *Charleston,* 119–21; Holt, *Black over White,* 210; Laylon W. Jordan, "Police and Politics: Charleston in the Gilded Age, 1880–1900," *SCHM* 81 (January 1980), 42n20; Wallace, *South Carolina,* 602; Schirmer, "Diary," November 21, 1876, June 28, 1877; King, "The Great South," 149; Sefton, *Army and Reconstruction,* 262.

42. Theodore Hemmingway, "Beneath the Yoke of Bondage: A History of Black Folks in South Carolina, 1900–1940" (Ph.D. dissertation, University of South Carolina, 1976), 34; Moore, *Low Country Engineers,* 31–39; Robert Goodwyn Rhett, *Charleston: An Epic of Carolina* (Richmond, Va., 1940), 333; *YCC, 1880,* 309–11; Radford, "Culture, Economy and Urban Structure," 234–236; Powers, "Black Charleston," 305–11, 317–24; Williamson, *After Slavery,* 177, 294–97; Hine, "Black Leadership," 437–41, 451–61, 493–97; Theodore Hemmingway, "Paternalism, Protest, and Progress: Race Relations in Charleston,

South Carolina, 1900–1930" (paper in possession of Walter J. Fraser, Jr.); William Watts Ball, *The State That Forgot* (Indianapolis, Ind., 1932), 149.

43. Clark, *Dawson*, 138–39, 147–52; *News and Courier*, November 21, 30, December 5, 7, 11, 12, 18, 1877, October 17, 30, November 3, 27, December 10, 1879, August 26, 1954; *Cyclopedia of Eminent and Representative Men of the Carolinas*, 367–72; Rhett, *Charleston*, 312, 333; Moore, "Low Country in Economic Transition," 158, 160–63; Moore, *Low Country Engineers*, 31–39, 58–59; Collins, "Charleston and the Railroads," 10, 55, 144; Coulter, *George Williams*, 229.

44. *YCC, 1880*, 26, 30–38, 41–56; George E. Waring, Jr., *Report on the Social Statistics of Charleston, South Carolina* (Washington, D.C., 1888), 99–102; *YCC, 1892*, 5–6; *YCC, 1893*, 10; Arthur Mazyck and Gene Waddell, *Charleston in 1883*, (Easley, S.C., 1973) xviii; "Journal of City Council, 1883–1887," 183, 193; *The City of Charleston and the State of South Carolina* (New York, 1889), 16–17; *YCC, 1885* (Charleston, S.C., 1886), 144; Radford, "Culture, Economy and Urban Structure," 208; Powers, "Black Charleston," 237–38; *News and Courier*, February 11, 1883.

45. Jordan, " 'The Method of Modern Charity' "; *YCC, 1895*, 14; Waring, *History of Medicine*, 23–24, 180–83, 189; *YCC, 1900* (Charleston, S.C., 1901), 278; *The Charleston City Directory, 1887* (Charleston, S.C., 1887), 683; Jones, "The Charleston Orphan House," 213n32.

46. Cantwell, "History of Charleston Police," 14–15; Jordan, "Police and Politics," 35–50; Lawrence H. Larsen, *The Rise of the Urban South* (Lexington, Ky., 1985), 136; *YCC, 1880*, 91–92, 131–32; *YCC, 1883*, 202–13; *YCC, 1900*, xviii; Waddell, *Charleston*, xxi, xxiii; Karen Greene, *Porter-Gaud School: The Next Step* (Easley, S.C., 1985), 12–13; *Twelfth Census of the United States Population, Taken in the Year 1900, Part II* (Washington, D.C., 1902), 388, 390, 392, 394, 442, 444, 446, 448; Easterby, *History of the College of Charleston*, 154–58, 163, 168, 170.

47. William J. Cooper, Jr., *The Conservative Regime: South Carolina, 1877–1890* (Baltimore, Md., 1968), 20, 39; Waring, *History of Medicine*, 163–164; Powers, "Black Charleston," 305–11, 323–24; Williamson, *After Slavery*, 294–97; Lamson, *Glorious Failure*, 283–85. Black Charlestonians crowded into an area just west of King Street between Beaufain and Queen streets and into residences behind the wharves along Stoll's Alley, St. Michael's Alley, and Cordes Court; also into a low, marshy area bounded by Calhoun, Anson, and Laurens streets, known derisively as "Rottenborough." The black population in the early 1880s also expanded rapidly into the northwestern portion of the city as low-lying lots were filled in and streets like Radcliffe, Spring, Bogard, and Race were laid out between Vanderhorst and Congress streets.

48. Shick and Doyle, "The South Carolina Phosphate Boom," 1–31; Coulter, *George Williams*, 153–56; Waddell, *Charleston*, xii–xv, xxiii; Waring, *Social Statistics*, 104; Robert P. Stockton, "King St. Victorian Dates to 1870s," *News and Courier*, August 10, 1981, "Research Undercuts Preservation Theory," *News and Courier*, July 26, 1981, "East Battery Home Dates to Mid-'80's, *News and Courier*, August 3, 1981; Moore, "Low Country in Economic Transition," 160–63; Petit, *South Carolina and the Sea*, II, 156–57; Hine, "Black Leadership," 440.

49. *Charleston's Annual Travel Review, 1886–1887* (Charleston, S.C., 1887), 1–6; Clark, *Dawson*, 146; Rhett, *Charleston*, 322; David L. Carlton, *Mill and Town in South Carolina, 1880–1920* (Baton Rouge, La., 1982), 44–46; Doyle "Leader-

ship and Decline," 96–102; Jonathan E. Land, *Charleston: Her Trade, Commerce and Industries, 1883–84* (Charleston, S.C., 1884), 12; Trenholm, *Centennial Address*, 24; Waddell, *Charleston*, ix.

50. Thomas della Torre, *A Sketch of the Charleston Club with Its Constitutions and By-Laws, and a List of Its Members, 1852–1938* (Charleston, S.C., 1938), 11–15, 30–41; *News and Courier*, July 4, 1884, June 25, 1885, May 11, 1890, February 17, 1891, July 3, 5, 1895, May 9, July 5, 1896; Powers, "Black Charleston," 143–44, 170–71; Marshall, "Gentlemen without a Country," 40–49, 278–79; 281–82; *City Directory, 1887*, 700–701; Schirmer, "Diary," July 4, 1882, July 4, 1885.

51. Vernon W. Crane, "Edward McCrady," *Dictionary of American Biography* (New York, 1933), 1–2. Charleston's annual yearbook, published almost continuously from 1880 until it was discontinued in 1951 during the administration of Mayor William McGillivray Morrison, and a vast reservoir of information for historians of Charleston, reflects the divided mind of the city. Sometimes page after page of documents in the yearbooks nostalgically recall the city's celebrated past, while the boosterism of a mayor pervades other pages.

52. Carl McKinley, "The August Cyclone: A Descriptive Narrative of the Memorable Storm of 1885," *YCC, 1885*, (Charleston, S.C., 1885), 6–12; Clark, *Dawson*, 138–39; Ellen W. Hard, "An Account of the Earthquake in Charleston in 1886," in Charles F. and Ellen Whilden Hard, "Recollections" (ms., SCL); Coulter, *George Williams*, 231–32; [?] to "My Dear Julie," September 8, 1886 (Hatch Papers, SHC); C. P. Porcher to "My Dear Daughter," September 7, 1886 (Frederick Adolphus Porcher Papers, SCL); George Marshall Allen, "Charleston: A Typical City of the South," *Magazine of Travel* 1 (February 1895), 124–25; Kenneth E. Peters, "Disaster Relief Efforts Connected with the 1886 Charleston Earthquake" (paper in possession of Walter J. Fraser, Jr.).

53. *Charleston's Annual Travel Review, 1886–1887* (Charleston, S.C., 1887), 1–27; Williams, *St. Michael's*, 109; *Cyclopedia of Eminent and Representative Men of the Carolinas*, 367–72; Clark, *Dawson*, 178–79, 206–31; "Our New Fire Department," *News and Courier*, January 20, 1883; Robert P. Stockton, "Fire Stations," *News and Courier*, September 7, 1981; Thomas R. Waring, Jr., (ed.), *The Way It Was in Charleston*, (Old Greenwich, Conn., 1980), 70–71.

54. Clark, *Dawson*, 178–79, 206–8; *News and Courier*, October 28, 29, 1887; *Cyclopedia of Eminent and Representative Men of the Carolinas*, 367–72.

55. Clark, *Dawson*, 215–32. The Dawson-McDow-Burdayron affair was the stuff of novels, one of which appeared in 1958, Robert Molloy's *An Afternoon in March*.

Chapter VI

1. Ben Robertson, *Red Hills and Cotton: An Upcountry Memory* (New York, 1942), 103–4; Ball, *The State That Forgot*, 243, 249.

2. *News and Courier*, October 21, December 9, 11, 15, 1891; Geddings H. Crawford (ed.), *Who's Who in South Carolina* (Columbia, S.C., 1921), 58–59; Francis Butler Simkins, *Pitchfork Ben Tillman: South Carolinian* (Baton Rouge, La., 1944), 365; Doyle W. Boggs, "John Patrick Grace and the Politics of Reform in South Carolina, 1900–1931" (Ph.D. dissertation, University of South Carolina, 1977), 13–15; Rosen, *Charleston*, 127–28.

3. "Oliver James Bond Diary, 1889–94" (ms. SCL), March 23, 1890; Easterby, *History of the College of Charleston,* 163–74; Torre, *A Sketch of the Charleston Club,* 11–15, 30, 41; Wallace, *South Carolina,* 660–65; Allen, "Charleston," 108; Waring, *The Way It Was,* 70–71; *News and Courier,* March 31, July 15, 1891, September 8, 1892, October 23, 1894.

4. Robert P. Stockton, "German Built Building," *News and Courier,* July 8, 1979, " 'One of the Handsomest' Marked a New Era," *News and Courier,* August 24, 1981, "King St. Hardware Store Cited as 'Model of Beauty in 1892,' " *News and Courier,* December 28, 1981; Shick and Doyle, "The South Carolina Phosphate Boom," 1–31; Coulter, *George Williams,* 153–56, 229; *YCC, 1890,* 76–77; *YCC, 1892,* 12; Waddell, *Charleston,* xiv–xv; Tindall, *South Carolina Negroes,* 278–79.

5. Allen, "Charleston," 124; Fennell, "Hurricanes;" *YCC, 1892,* 5–6; *YCC, 1893* (Charleston, S.C., 1894), 23–24; Doyle, "Leadership and Decline," 93.

6. Moore, *Low Country Engineers,* 58–59; Clark, *Dawson,* 147–52; Rhett, *Charleston,* 312; Collins, "Charleston and the Railroads," 10, 55, 114; Radford, "Culture, Economy, and Urban Structure in Charleston," 227–29; Moore, "Low Country in Economic Transition," 159–63.

7. Jones, "Charleston Orphan House," 211–13; *YCC, 1885,* 100–105; *YCC, 1890* (Charleston, S.C., 1891), 66–77; *YCC, 1892,* 12; *News and Courier,* September 30, 1890, December 31, 1891, December 27, 1898, September 6, 1899; Tindall, *South Carolina Negroes,* 277–79; Jordan, " 'The Method of Modern Charity,' " 3–17, *YCC, 1896* (Charleston, S.C., 1897), 13; *YCC, 1897,* 284–86; Margaret Simons Middleton, "The Ladies' Benevolent Society of Charleston, South Carolina," *YCC, 1941* (Charleston, S.C., 1942), 216–39.

8. *News and Courier,* November 2, 12, December 6, 11, 17, 1895; *YCC, 1920* (Charleston, S.C., 1921), 635–37; Boggs, "Politics of Reform," 16–17; *YCC, 1893* (Charleston, S.C., 1894), 10–14, *YCC, 1894* (Charleston, S.C., 1895), 9, 10–11, *YCC, 1895* (Charleston, S.C., 1896), 10–11, *YCC, 1897* (Charleston, S.C., 1898), xxi; Waddell, *Charleston,* xviii; Rhett, *Charleston,* 343; "Journal of City Council, 1883–1887," 183, 193; *The City of Charleston and the State,* 16–17; *YCC, 1898* (Charleston, S.C., 1899), xxi.

9. *Annual Report Department of Health and the City of Charleston, 1892* (Charleston, 1893), 1–15; Leon Banov, *As I Recall: The Story of the Charleston County Health Department* (Columbia, S.C., 1970), 7; *YCC, 1900,* 61–65, 262–67; *YCC, 1880,* 100; *YCC, 1883,* 52–53; *YCC, 1892,* 10, *YCC, 1897,* 57, 66–67; Waring, *History of Medicine,* 166, 173–79, 182–83; *YCC, 1883,* 54–56; *YCC, 1885,* 60; *YCC, 1886,* 45–46; *YCC, 1890,* 42–43, 88; *YCC, 1897,* 60–61.

10. *YCC, 1899* (Charleston, S.C., 1900), 125; *News and Courier,* July 23, 1897, January 24, 25, 1899; Coulter, *George Williams,* 137.

11. James Russell, "Homicide and the Violent Ideal in Atlanta, 1865–1890" (paper in possession of Walter J. Fraser, Jr.); "Police Reports" in *YCC, 1880–1900;* Waring, *The Way It Was,* 75; *YCC, 1880,* 58; *YCC, 1883,* 98; *YCC, 1890,* 76–77; *YCC, 1892,* 12; Jordan, " 'The Method of Modern Charity,' " 15; *YCC, 1896,* 13; *YCC, 1897,* 284–86; Jordan, "Police and Politics," 49–50.

12. *News and Courier,* March 20, 29, April 10, May 1, December 27, 1898, March 18, 1899; John Moore, *History of the South Carolina Highway Department* (Columbia, S.C., 1988).

13. *Twelfth Census, Part II,* 388, 392, 394, 442, 444, 446; Coulter, *George*

Williams, 137; John J. Duffy, "Charleston Politics in the Progressive Era" (Ph.D. dissertation, University of South Carolina, 1963), 10–14, 32–36, 155–57.

14. Moore, "The Lowcountry in Economic Transition," 166–67; Moore, *Lowcountry Engineers,* 58–60; Peter J. Scialabba, "The Charleston Naval Shipyard" (paper in possession of Walter J. Fraser, Jr.).

15. Doyle, "Leadership and Decline," 103–4; Jamie W. Moore, "The Great South Carolina Inter-State and West Indian Exposition of 1901," *Sandlapper* 11 (July 1978), 11–15; *News and Courier,* December 2, 1901, June 1, 17, July 2, 1902; *Official Guide, South Carolina Interstate and West Indian Exposition* (Charleston, S.C., 1901), 1, 20, 23; Rosen, *Charleston,* 126–28.

16. Marvin L. Cann, "Burnet Rhett Maybank and the New Deal in South Carolina, 1931–1941" (Ph.D. dissertation, University of North Carolina, 1967), 13–15; Boggs, "John P. Grace," 13–17, 25–30, 32–37; Duffy, "Charleston Politics," 14–15, 29–30, 43–50, 119–22, 142–54, 214, 252–56; *News and Courier,* January 5, 6, October 19, 1900, August 7, 1901, June 22, 1902, May 13, 1903; Thomas Petigru Lesesne, *History of Charleston County, South Carolina* (Charleston, S.C., 1931), 131–33; Willard B. Gatewood, "Theodore Roosevelt and Southern Republicans: The Case of South Carolina, 1901–1904," *SCHM* 70 (October 1969), 262.

17. Lesesne, *Charleston County,* 174–75; Margaret C. Adkins, "Charleston's Political Anomaly: John Patrick Grace" (paper in possession of Walter J. Fraser, Jr.); Boggs, "John P. Grace," 6–8, 12, 17–22, 28–31, 37–47; Petit, *South Carolina and the Sea,* II, 170; *Walsh's City Directory, 1905* (Charleston, S.C., 1904), 72; Jaher, *Urban Establishment,* 401; *YCC, 1905* (Charleston, S.C., 1906), 132; Samuel Hopkins Adams, "Guardians of the Public Health," *McClure's Magazine* 31 (July 1908), 250.

18. Rhett, *Charleston,* 344; Duffy, "Charleston Politics," 4, 24–28, 30, 61–66. 102–19, 164, 170–78, 184–85, 211–12, 218, 273–78; Wallace, *South Carolina,* 653–54; Miss O'Neill to Mayor R. G. Rhett, October 8, 1911 (R. Goodwyn Rhett Papers, CCA); *News and Courier,* June 1, 1906; C. C. Blocker to Tristram T. Hyde, July 8, 1916, Thomas R. Heyward to Tristram T. Hyde, September 30, 1916 (Tristram T. Hyde Papers, CCA); Theodore Hemmingway, "Prelude to Change: Black Carolinians in the War Years, 1914–1920," *Journal of Negro History* 65 (Summer 1980), 212–13.

19. Duffy, "Charleston Politics," 17, 28–29, 48–49, 53–66, 71–76, 102–19, 170–78, 229–37, 272–78, 345, 356; Boggs, "John P. Grace," 37–47, 184–86.

20. *YCC, 1909* (Charleston, S.C., 1910), 261; *YCC, 1910* (Charleston, S.C., 1911), 194, 332–45, 363–64; *YCC, 1912* (Charleston, S.C., 1913), 256, 308–12, 321–24, 330–39; *YCC, 1908* (Charleston, S.C., 1909), xiii–xiv; Ernest M. Lander, Jr., *A History of South Carolina, 1865–1960* (Chapel Hill, N.C., 1960), 126–28; Louis R. Harlen, *Separate and Unequal: Public School Campaigns and Racism in the Southern Seaboard States, 1901–1915* (Chapel Hill, N.C., 1958), 208–9; Easterby, *History of the College of Charleston,* 185–86.

21. Hemmingway, "Prelude to Change," 211–12; Brownell and Goldfield, *City in Southern History,* 146, 186; August Kohn, *Charleston, South Carolina: Business, Trade, Growth, Opportunity* (Charleston, S.C., 1910), 3–5; "Petition to the Hon. R. Goodwyn Rhett," July 26, 1911, Rhett Papers.

22. Charleston *Evening Post,* August 28, 1911; *A New Guide to Modern Charleston, 1912* (Charleston, S.C., 1911), 5; *YCC, 1912,* xxvii–xxviii; Duffy,

"Charleston Politics," 48–57, 119–22, 229–30, 283–321; *YCC, 1914* (Charleston, S.C., 1915), xxxiii; Boggs, "John P. Grace," 13, 35, 47–48, 68–69, 71–84, 236–37; Rosen, *Charleston,* 129.

23. *YCC, 1906* (Charleston, S.C., 1907), 262; *YCC, 1912,* 299, 321–30; Duffy, "Charleston Politics," 59–61, 78, 236–37, 353, 377–78; Chief of Police W. A. Boyle to Mayor R. G. Rhett, March 24, 1910, Rhett Papers; Records of the Almshouse, CCA; Jordan, " 'The Method of Modern Charity.' "

24. Headley M. Cox, Jr., "The Charleston Poetic Renascence, 1920–1930" (Ph.D. dissertation, University of Pennsylvania, 1958), 1–8; Rhett, *Charleston,* 348–50.

25. Alan Coleman, "The Charleston Bootlegging Controversy, 1915–1918," *SCHM* 75 (April 1974), 77–94; Vincent Chicco to Mayor John P. Grace, August 28, 1913, John P. Grace to Hon. Richard I. Manning, April 21, 1915 (John P. Grace Papers, CCA); W. A. Boyle to Hon. R. G. Rhett, June 4, 1909, Rhett Papers; Duffy, "Charleston Politics," 250–51, 354–58; Boggs, "John P. Grace," 208.

26. Elwood Street, "When the Soldiers Come to Town," *The Survey,* August 18, 1917, 433–35; *Special Report of the Law and Order League of Charleston, S.C.* (Charleston, S.C., 1913), 19; John Hammond Moore, "Charleston in World War I: Seeds of Change," *SCHM* 86 (January 1985), 45–49; "Another Red Light District Gone," *Survey,* October 13, 1917, 84; Moore, *Lowcountry Engineers,* 110.

27. Louis D. Rubin, Jr. (ed.), *The American South: Portrait of a Culture* (Baton Rouge, La., 1980), 8; Mildred Cram, *Old Seaport Towns of the South* (New York, 1917), 125–26.

28. Duffy, "Charleston Politics," 321–32, 342–59; Boggs, "John P. Grace," 88–101, 128–32; Robert Milton Burts, *Richard Irvine Manning and the Progressive Movement in South Carolina* (Columbia, S.C., 1974), 102–7; Crawford, *Who's Who,* 87–88.

29. Thomas R. Heyward to Mayor Tristram T. Hyde, August 7, 1916, Hyde Papers; John Hammond Moore, "South Carolina's Reaction to the Photoplay, *The Birth of a Nation,*" *PSCHA* (1963), 38; Committee of the Colored Civic League to Mayor T. T. Hyde, January 12, 1916, Mayor T. T. Hyde to Mr. W. D. McGuire, July 17, 1916, Hyde Papers.

30. Boggs, "John P. Grace," 47, 111–12, 184–86; Mooe, "Lowcountry in Economic Transition," 166–67; Moore, *Lowcountry Engineers,* 58–60, 76; Scialabba, "The Charleston Naval Shipyard"; Petit, *South Carolina and the Sea,* II, 182–83; Robert Yarborough Davis, *The Pilgrimage* (Albuquerque, N.M., 1980), 34–39; Mamie Garvin Fields with Karen Fields, *Lemon Swamp and Other Places: A Carolina Memoir* (New York, 1983), 31, 192.

31. Theodore Hemmingway, "Prelude to Change," 220; Moore, "Charleston in World War I," 41–49; "Another Red Light District Gone," 97; Petit, *South Carolina and the Sea,* II, 187; Duffy, "Charleston Politics," 229–30, 345–56.

32. *YCC, 1918,* (Charleston, S.C., 1919), 166–67; *News and Courier,* October 6, 14, 18, 22, November 11, 18, 19, 1918; Banov, *As I Recall,* 22–24; R. Mack Mulholland, "The Jenkins' Orphanage Band" (paper in possession of Walter J. Fraser, Jr.); *News and Courier,* August 18, 20, 24, December 10, 1919.

33. Hemmingway, "Paternalism, Protest, and Progress"; John C. Roberson, "Sailors against Blacks: The Charleston Race Riot of 1919" (paper in possession of Walter J. Fraser, Jr.); Septima Clark, *Echo in My Soul* (New York, 1962), 3, 14–19,

23–30, 61; *The State,* December 17, 1987; *YCC, 1918,* 357; Fields, *Lemon Swamp,* 192, 203.

34. Duffy, "Charleston Politics," 355, 366–72, 378; *News and Courier,* February 15, 1919, June 9, 1965; Boggs, "John P. Grace," 102–43, 149.

35. Boggs, "John P. Grace," 12, 163–67, 179–81, 208–9; John P. Grace to "My Dear Lieutenant," June 21, 1922, Grace Papers; *YCC, 1920* (Charleston, S.C., 1921); 412, *YCC, 1924* (Charleston, S.C., 1925), lii, liv; Thomas R. Waring, "Red Light Reflections," *News and Courier,* January 11, 1981; Admiral A. H. Robertson to John P. Grace, March 20, 1922, Grace Papers.

36. Charles B. Hosmer, Jr., *Preservation Comes of Age: From Williamsburg to the National Trust, 1926-1949* (Charlottesville, Va., 1981), 231–50; William Henry Hanckel, "The Preservation Movement in Charleston, 1920–1962" (M.A. thesis, University of South Carolina, 1961), 1–49; Rosen, *Charleston,* 130–32, 140; Robert P. Stockton, "Charleston: The Preservation of a City," in C. Edward Kaylor, Jr., *A Consideration of Growth in the Trident Area: From the Academy to the Marketplace* (Charleston, S.C., 1982), 20–21.

37. Cox, "The Charleston Poetic Renascence," 8–66, 198–201; Duffy, "Charleston Politics," 344, 377; Frank Durham, "The Poetry Society of South Carolina's Turbulent Year: Self-Interest, Atheism, and Jean Toomer," *Southern Humanities Review* 5 (Winter 1971), 76–80; William Henry Slavick, "DuBose Heyward: The Rhythms of Charleston" (Ph.D. dissertation, University of Notre Dame, 1971), 452–53.

38. Duffy, "Charleston Politics," 344, 369–87; Adkins, "Charleston's Political Anomaly"; Boggs, "John P. Grace," 163–208; Lesesne, *Charleston County,* 238–42; Crawford, *Who's Who,* 188–89; *News and Courier,* June 28, 1923; *YCC, 1923* (Charleston, S.C., 1924), xv–xvi; Margaret R. Canady, "An Era in Charleston Politics: 1923–1931" (Senior thesis, University of South Carolina, 1961), 6.

39. Cann, "Burnet Maybank," 18–19; Carl E. McCombs, "Charleston Breaks with the Past in Public Welfare Work," *National Municipal Review* (June 1924), 341–46; Ellen Barr, "A History of the Junior League of Charleston" (paper in possession of Walter J. Fraser, Jr.); Duffy, "Charleston Politics," 24–28, 63, 345, 356; Boggs, "John P. Grace," 184–86, 251.

40. Banov, *As I Recall,* 64–69, 107; "Journal of City Council," April 12, 1927; *YCC, 1925* (Charleston, S.C.., 1926), xlvi; *YCC, 1924* (Charleston, S.C., 1925), x, lxix, 140–45.

41. *YCC, 1927* (Charleston, S.C., 1928), xx, 171–72; Hemmingway, "Paternalism, Protest, and Progress"; Grace to "My Dear Lieutenant," June 21, 1922, Grace Papers; Waring, "Red Light Reflections"; *Special Report of the Law and Order League,* 19; Admiral A. H. Robertson to Grace, March 20, 1922, Grace Papers; Boggs, "John P. Grace," 166; Robert Lee Frank, "The Economic Impact of Tourism in Charleston, South Carolina, 1970" (M.A. thesis, University of South Carolina, 1972), 34.

42. Blaine A. Brownell, *The Urban Ethos in the South, 1920-1930* (Baton Rouge, La., 1975), 198–99; Smith, *The Dwelling Houses of Charleston,* 374; Hosmer, *Preservation Comes of Age,* 231–50; Hanckel, "The Preservation Movement," 1–49; Stockton, "Charleston: The Preservation of a City," 20–21.

43. Durham, "The Poetry Society of South Carolina's Turbulent Year," 76–80; Tindall, *New South,* 291–93, 308–12; Cox, "Poetic Renascence," 8–66, 198–201; Slavick, "DuBose Heyward," 14, 26–28, 41, 452–53; Rhett, *Charleston,*

349–53; Jaher, *The Urban Establishment*, 415–16; Harold A. Mouzon, "The Carolina Art Association: Its First Hundred Years," *SCHM* 59 (January 1959), 125–38; *News and Courier*, November 28, 1927, November 25, 1929, January 25, 1930; *YCC, 1925*, 161.

44. Duffy, "Charleston Politics," 43–50, 345, 356, 377, 386–90; Boggs, "John P. Grace," 208–16, 221–40, 243–44; Adkins, "Charleston's Political Anomaly"; Rosen, *Charleston,* 141; Canady, "Era in Charleston Politics," 37–42; *News and Courier,* November 9, 10, 16, December 14, 1927; *YCC, 1927*, xxxiii; *YCC, 1930* (Charleston, S.C., 1931), xxxvii; *YCC, 1932–1935 (Charleston, S.C., 1936),* 67, 158–59.

45. Moore, *Lowcountry Engineers,* 108–10; Brownell, *Urban Ethos,* 12–13; Hosmer, *Preservation Comes of Age,* 231–50; *News and Courier,* March 9, 1976; Hanckel, "Preservation Movement," 1–49.

46. Cann, "Burnet Maybank," 13–50, 110–23, 200; Tinsley Yarborough, *A Passion for Justice: J. Waties Waring and Civil Rights* (New York, 1987), 10; Boggs, "John P. Grace," 179–86, 245–53; *YCC, 1900–1930; News and Courier,* June 15, 1953; *YCC, 1932–1935,* 12, 144, 152; Banov, *As I Recall,* 107; *YCC, 1936* (Charleston, S.C., 1937), 67; *YCC, 1938* (Charleston, S.C., 1940), 13–14.

47. Boggs, "John P. Grace," 181–83, 253–57; Cann, "Burnet Maybank," 51–55, 68, 72–87, 90–94, 101–8; *News and Courier,* July 10, 1935; *YCC, 1930,* xxi, xxxvii; *YCC, 1932–1935,* 19, 67, 226–31.

48. Fields, *Lemon Swamp,* 194–95; *YCC, 1936,* 13, 16–18; *YCC, 1937,* 14, 132–33, 159; *YCC, 1940* (Charleston, S.C., 1941), 11; *YCC, 1942* (Charleston, S.C., 1943), 18; *YCC, 1944* (Charleston, S.C., 1946), 139; Cann, "Burnet Maybank," 121–36; Frank, "Economic Impact of Tourism," 35; Duffy, "Charleston Politics," 377; Banov, *As I Recall,* 57.

49. Robert P. Stockton, "The Riviera: Art Deco Architecture," *News and Courier,* May 26, 1980; *YCC, 1932–1935,* 19; *YCC, 1936,* 18, 181–82; *YCC, 1937,* 14; *YCC, 1938,* 15, 182–90; *YCC, 1940,* 17; Cann, "Burnet Maybank," 121, 126; Stockton, "Charleston: The Preservation of a City," 20–23; Rosen, *Charleston,* 133–34; Edward Twig, "Charleston: The Great Myth," *Forum and Century* 102 (January 1940), 1, 4.

50. Twig, "Charleston," 1–7; Lesesne, *Charleston County,* 162–63; Petit, *South Carolina and the Sea,* II, 199–200; W. W. Ball to McMaster, May 31, 1940 (Fitz Hugh McMaster Papers, SCL); *Evening Post,* July 31, 1941; *News and Courier,* June 15, 1953.

51. Moore, *Lowcountry Engineers,* 83–86, 110–13; Cann, "Burnet Maybank," 114–16, 154; Jack Irby Hayes, Jr., "South Carolina and the New Deal, 1932–1938" (Ph.D. dissertation, University of South Carolina, 1971), 277.

52. Drucilla Berkham, "The Charleston Home Front: December 7, 1941–June 6, 1944" (paper in possession of Walter J. Fraser, Jr.); Peter Collier and David Horowitz, *The Kennedys: An American Drama* (New York, 1984), 122–24; Petit, *South Carolina and the Sea,* II, 191–93; *YCC, 1940,* 14.

53. John Hammond Moore, "No Room, No Rice, No Grits: Charleston's 'Time of Trouble,' 1942–1944," *South Atlantic Quarterly* 85 (Winter 1986), 23–28; Scialabba, "Charleston Naval Shipyard"; Enid Ewing, "Charleston Contra Mundum," *The Nation* (November 20, 1943), 579; Berkham, "The Charleston Home Front"; Omar Hill, "Charleston's New Industry Board," *Manufacturers Re-*

cord 115 (August 1946); Petit, *South Carolina and the Sea*, II, 202–8; *YCC, 1942*, 16; *YCC, 1945*, 13, 15.

54. *YCC, 1943*, 17; Banov, *As I Recall*, 72–77; *News and Courier*, February 19, June 4, July 18, September 27, 1942, November 5, December 2, 1943, February 6, 1944; Ewing, "Charleston," 579; Moore, "No Room, No Rice, No Grits," 27; Admiral W. G. Allen to H. J. Mann, September 19, 1941, Lt. Peyton Anderson to Mayor Henry W. Lockwood, September 25, 1941, Henry W. Lockwood to James M. Coleman, February 11, 1942 (Henry W. Lockwood Papers, CCA); *YCC, 1942*, 14–15; Banov, *As I Recall*, 70–72; *YCC, 1942*, 14–15; "Minutes of the Social Protection Committee, September 3, 1943," Lockwood Papers; *YCC, 1944*, 11–14.

55. Berkham, "The Charleston Home Front"; *News and Courier*, May 7, 8, August 15, 1945; Rosen, *Charleston*, 141; Petit, *South Carolina and the Sea*, II, 214–20.

Chapter VII

1. Robert Lewis Terry, "J. Waties Waring, Spokesman for Racial Justice in the New South" (Ph.D. dissertation, University of Utah, 1970), iv, 1–20, 29, 34, 48–49, 50–53, 61, 71, 74, 83, 85–87, 90–91, 95–96, 98–99, 103, 106–9, 113; Yarborough, *A Passion for Justice*, 30–31, 42–47, 53–54, 67.

2. John Lewis, "Strong Medicine from a Native Son" (paper in possession of Walter J. Fraser, Jr.); Robert Winter, "Celebration," *Charleston Magazine* (April 1976), 8–11; Lander, *South Carolina*, 176–77; *News and Courier*, May 29, 1945, June 9, 19, 1945, December 9, 19, 1947.

3. Shirley M. Gibson, "Personal Recollections on Charleston City Government from John P. Grace to J. Palmer Gaillard" (paper in possession of Walter J. Fraser, Jr.); John D. Stark, *Damned Upcountryman: William Watts Ball, a Study in American Conservatism* (Durham, N.C., 1968), 211–12, 220n75, 226; William B. Scott, "Judge J. Waties Waring: Advocate of 'Another' South," *South Atlantic Quarterly* 27 (Summer 1978), 320–34; I. A. Newby, *Black Carolinians: A History of Blacks in South Carolina from 1895 to 1968* (Columbia, S.C., 1973), 280–85.

4. *News and Courier*, February 23, April 19, 1950; Rosen, *Charleston*, 141; *YCC, 1945* (Charleston, S.C., 1947), 15; *YCC, 1948* (Charleston, S.C., 1949), 13, 158; *YCC, 1949–1951* (Charleston, S.C., 1952), 12–13, 16, 113; Frank, "Economic Impact of Tourism," 36–50.

5. Barr, "A History of the Junior League"; Miller, "The Charleston Orphan Home," 40–54.

6. Lewis, "Strong Medicine"; Clark, *Echo in My Soul*, 95–101; Gibson, "Personal Recollections."

7. Terry, "J. Waties Waring," iv, 134–42, 146–54, 180–83, 199–201, 220–21, 231, 246–58; Yarborough, *A Passion for Justice*, 110–14, 141, 162, 168; Winter, "Celebration," 8–11; "Brickbats at the Judge," *Newsweek*, October 23, 1950, p. 29; Andrew M. Secrest, "In Black and White: Press Opinion and Race Relations in South Carolina, 1954–1964" (Ph.D. dissertation, Duke University, 1971), 182, 413–14.

8. Gibson, "Personal Recollections"; *YCC, 1949–1951*, 16, 301, 329; *News and Courier* July 1, 2, 5, 8, 17, 19, 20, 25, 1951; Petit, *South Carolina and the Sea*, II, 219–26.

9. "Conference of Mayor and City Officials with Naval Shore Patrol Officers,

October 26, 1951" (William McG. Morrison Papers, CCA); "Minutes: Charleston Social Protection Committee, March 29, 1946," E. Edward Wehman to George Gould, February 8, 1947 (E. Edward Wehman Papers, CCA); *News and Courier,* June 19, 1953; Raymond Arsenault, "The End of the Long Hot Summer: The Air Conditioner and Southern Culture," *JSH* 50 (November 1984), 597–628; Mouzon, "The Carolina Art Association," 125–38; Nancy Press, "Cultural Myth and Class Structuration: The Downtown Group of Charleston, South Carolina" (Ph.D. dissertation, Duke University, 1985), 300–301.

10. Secrest, "In Black and White," 26, 104; Terry, "J. Waties Waring," 268, 272–73; Yarborough, *A Passion for Justice,* 227.

11. Moore, *Lowcountry Engineers,* 110; Petit, *South Carolina and the Sea,* II, 228–30, 232, 235; *News and Courier,* January 12, June 11, December 14, 1955; *Charleston Evening Post,* January 1, 1960.

12. Lander, *South Carolina,* 230; William Peters, *The Southern Temper* (Garden City, N.Y., 1959), 123; Slavick, "DuBose Heyward," 14n24; Secrest, "In Black and White," 27–28, 196–97, 210, 217, 421; Clark, *Echo in My Soul,* 31, 107–18, 177; Harry Ashmore, *An Epitaph for Dixie* (New York, 1957), 87.

13. *News and Courier,* July 25, 1957, June 5, 7, 9, 10, 11, December 7, 1959, December 10, 1969, February 22, 1971; Rosen, *Charleston,* 145, 147; Gibson, "Personal Recollections"; Petit, *South Carolina and the Sea,* II, 235; John C. Purvis and H. Landers, *South Carolina Hurricanes or a Descriptive Listing of Tropical Cyclones That Have Affected South Carolina* (Columbia, S.C., 1973), 39.

14. Gibson, "Personal Recollections"; Secrest, "In Black and White," 259–85, 290, 309; Benjamin Muse, *Ten Years of Prelude: The Story of Integration since the Supreme Court's 1954 Decision* (New York, 1964), 257–58.

15. Rosen, *Charleston,* 147–48; Purvis and Landers, *South Carolina Hurricanes,* 41; Frank, "The Economic Impact of Tourism," 36–50; Petit, *South Carolina and the Sea,* II, 236–45.

16. Secrest, "In Black and White," 313–14, 369–73, 377, 380, 400–414; *News and Courier,* June 10, July 6, 16, 17, 18, 20, 21, 24, December 11, 1963; Gibson, "Personal Recollections."

17. Clarke, *Anglicanism,* 133; Clark, *Echo in My Soul,* 31, 107–18, 177; Don Oberdorfer, " 'Rivers Delivers,' " *New York Times Magazine,* August 19, 1965; "The Muckraker," *Newsweek,* June 27, 1966, 97; Marshall Frady, "The Sweetest Finger This Side of Midas," *Life* magazine, February 27, 1970, pp. 52–60.

18. *News and Courier,* June 12, 14, 16, December 11, 12, 13, 1967; "Interview with Septima Poinsette Clark, July 25, 1976, by Jacquelyn Dowd Hall for the Southern Oral History Program" (copy in possession of Walter J. Fraser, Jr.); Gibson, "Personal Recollections"; Rosen, *Charleston,* 147–51; Yarborough, *A Passion for Justice,* 241–42; Frady, "Sweetest Finger," 52–60.

19. "Southern Gothic," *The Nation,* December 29, 1969; W. Ellison Chalmers, "Racial Negotiations: Potentials & Limitations" (Ann Arbor, Mich., 1974), 50–71; Jack Bass, "Strike at Charleston," *New South* (Summer 1969), 1–10; *Evening Post,* July 21, 1969; Clarke, *Anglicanism,* 141–42.

20. Gibson, "Personal Recollections"; Hall, "Interview with Septima Clark"; *News and Courier,* June 1–15, December 1–15, 1971.

21. Press, "Cultural Myth and Class," 292–94; *Hills Charleston City Directory, 1973* (Richmond, Va., 1973), 1; Moore, "Lowcountry in Economic Transition," 170; Petit, *South Carolina and the Sea,* II, 239–46, 256–59; *News and*

Courier, January 25, 1975, December 5, 1976, May 23, 1982; Mouzon, "The Carolina Art Association," 125–38.

22. *News and Courier,* February 11, December 5, 7, 10, 1975; Rosen, *Charleston,* 132, 151; Margaret Corvini, "Joseph P. Riley, Jr's. Charleston: He's in the Business of Cities," *The State* [Columbia, S.C.], May 11, 1986.

23. Lofton, *Denmark Vesey's Revolt,* vii–ix; Stockton, "Charleston: The Preservation of a City," 23–26; Corvini, "Riley's Charleston."

24. Petit, *South Carolina and the Sea,* II, 265–66, 270–72, 274, 282; Barbara Gervais Street, "Charleston's Southern Comforts," *Travel and Leisure* 16 (February 1986), 170; Gary D. Ford, "Charleston Preserved," *Southern Living* 23 (March 1988), 112–15.

25. *News and Courier,* March 16, 1979, January 15, 1980, May 29, 1988; Yarborough, *A Passion for Justice,* 242–43; Rosen, *Charleston,* 152–53; Robert N. Rosen, "The Charleston Center," *News and Courier,* January 7, 1980.

26. Moore, "Lowcountry in Economic Transition," 170; Petit, *South Carolina and the Sea,* II, 284–87; Corvini, "Riley's Charleston"; Moore, *Lowcountry Engineers,* 113–16; Yarborough, *A Passion for Justice,* 243; Rosen, *Charleston,* 132.

27. Frank, "The Economic Impact of Tourism," 2–3, 28–32, 36–50; Petit, *South Carolina and the Sea,* II, 284–85, 287, 313–18; "Still Empty Lot Seeded a City's Revival," *New York Times,* October 17, 1982; Marshella Wallace, City Planner, to Mayor Joseph P. Riley, Jr., January 27, 1988 (copy in possession of Walter J. Fraser, Jr.).

28. Joseph P. Riley, Jr., to the author, July 18, 1986; Petit, *South Carolina and the Sea,* II, 315–18; "Cities Where Business Is Best," *U.S. News and World Report,* November 11, 1985; William E. Schmidt, "City Ports Prosperity Sign of Boom in Dixie," *Savannah Morning News,* October 20, 1986; *Atlanta Journal and Constitution,* December 27, 1987.

29. Anne Rittenhouse, "America's Social House of Peers," *Ainslee's Magazine* (October 1905), 76–79; Albert Goldman, "Charleston! Charleston!" *Esquire* 87 (June 1977), 154; Pat Conroy, "Shadows of the Old South," *Geoliving* 3 (May 1981), 71–72; "Edward Manigault," *News and Courier,* June 4, 1983.

Select Bibliography

Manuscripts

City of Charleston Archives

Almshouse Records.
City Council Journal, 1883–87.
John P. Grace Papers.
Tristram T. Hyde Papers.
Henry W. Lockwood Papers.
William McGillivray Morrison Papers.
Orphan House, Commissioners Minutes.
Poor House Journals, Minutes, 1800–1860.
R. Goodwyn Rhett Papers.
E. Edward Wehman Papers.

Duke University

Bettie R. Brown Papers.
Henry W. DeSaussure Papers.
Eliza Fludd Papers.
George A. Gordon Papers.
Augustin Louis Taveau Papers.

St. Philip's Church, Charleston

South Carolina Parish of St. Philip's, Charles Town, Vestry Book, 1732.
Vestry Books, St. Philip's, vols. I–III.

South Carolina Department of Archives and History

Board of Police, Miscellaneous Proceedings, 1780–82.
Charleston District, Presentments of the Grand Jury.
Commons House of Assembly of South Carolina, Journal.
Court of General Sessions, Journal, 1769–76.
General Assembly Petitions.
Loose Legislative Papers.
Transcripts of Records Relating to South Carolina in the British Public Record Office.

South Carolina Historical Society

Bowen-Cooke Collection.
Commissioners of the Fortifications, Journal, 1755–70.
Elliott, Captain Barnard, Order Book.
Grimball, John Berkeley, Diary, 1858–65.
Moultrie-Lincoln Order Book.
Schirmer, Jacob, Diary.

Select Bibliography

Vanderhorst Family Papers.

University of North Carolina, Southern Historical Collection
Willis Grady Briggs Papers.
William Harris Garland Papers.
Grimball Family Papers.
Charles F. and Ellen Whilden Hard Recollections.
Hatch Family Papers.
William Porcher Miles Papers.
William Dorsey Pender Papers.
Hartwell Perry Spain Diary.

University of South Carolina, South Caroliniana Library
Adger–Smythe–Flynn Papers.
Lewis Malone Ayer Papers.
Ball Family Papers.
P. G. T. Beauregard Papers.
Oliver James Bond Diary, 1889–94.
Elias Horry Deas Papers.
Fitz Hugh McMaster Papers.
Middleton Family Papers.
Frederick Adolphus Porcher Papers.
Singleton Family Papers.
Snowden Papers.
Wayside Hospital, Letter Book.
Weyman Family Papers.
Wildman Papers.
Joseph Harvey Wilson Papers.

Government Documents

An Historical and Descriptive Review of the City of Charleston, South Carolina. New York: Empire Publishing Company, 1884.

Annual Report of the Health Department for . . . 1866. Charleston: Courier Job Press, 1867.

Annual Reports: Department of Health of the City of Charleston, 1892. Charleston: Walker, Evans & Cogswell, 1893.

Charleston, South Carolina: The Advantages of the City as a Port. Charleston: News & Courier Book Presses, 1880.

Charleston City Directory, 1887. Charleston: Walker, Evans & Cogswell, 1887.

Charleston's Annual Travel Review, 1886–87. Charleston: Walker, Evans & Cogswell, 1887.

Cooper, Thomas, and David J. McCord, eds. The Statutes at Large of South Carolina. 10 vols. Columbia: A. S. Johnston, 1838–41.

Digest of the Ordinances of the City Council of the City of Charleston from the Year 1783 to October 1818. Charleston: Archibald E. Miller, Printer, 1818.

Digest of the Ordinances of the City Council of the City of Charleston from the Year 1783 to October 1844. Charleston: Walker & Burke, 1844.

Easterby, J. H., ed. *JCHSC. May 18, 1741–July 10, 1742.* Columbia: State Company, 1953.

———. *JCHSC. February 20, 1744–May 25, 1745.* Columbia: State Company, 1955.

———. *JCHSC. January 19, 1748–June 29, 1748.* Columbia: State Company, 1961.

———. *JCHSC. September 10, 1745–June 17, 1746.* Columbia: State Company, 1956.

———. *JCHSC. September 14, 1742–January 27, 1744.* Columbia: State Company, 1954.

———. *JCHSC. November 10, 1736–June 7, 1739.* Columbia: State Company, 1951.

———. *JCHSC. September 12, 1739–March 26, 1741.* Columbia: State Company, 1952.

———. *JCHSC. March 28, 1749–March 19, 1750.* Columbia: State Company, 1962.

Lipscomb, Terry H., and R. Nicholas Olsberg, eds. *JCHSC, 1751–1752.* Columbia: University of South Carolina Press, 1977.

List of the Taxpayers of the City of Charleston for 1859. Charleston: Evans & Cogswell, 1860.

Mayor's Report Respecting the General Condition of City Affairs. Charleston: W. Riley, 1839.

Mayor's Report on City Affairs. Charleston: A. E. Miller, 1857.

Ordinances of the City of Charleston from the 19th of August 1844, to the 14th of September 1854. Charleston: A. E. Miller, 1854.

Ordinances of the City of Charleston from October 20, 1865, to September 6, 1870. Charleston: Charleston Courier Book & Job Presses, 1871.

Pinckney, H. L. *A Report Containing a Review of the Proceedings of the City Authorities from First September, 1838, to First August, 1839.* Charleston: W. Riley, 1839.

———. *A Report, Relative to the Proceedings for the Relief of the Sick Poor, during the Late Epidemic; and on the Subject, Generally, of the Public Health: To Which Is Annexed the Report of the Commissioners of the Temporary Hospital.* Charleston: W. Riley, 1838.

———. *Remarks Addressed to the Citizens of Charleston on the Subject of Interments, and the Policy of Establishing a Public Cemetery, beyond the Precincts of the City.* Charleston: Walker, Evans & Company, 1858.

Proceedings of the Citizens of Charleston on the Incendiary Machinations Now in Progress against the Peace and Welfare of the Southern States. Charleston: A. E. Miller, 1835.

Proceedings of the Sixty-Sixth Anniversary of the Orphan House of Charleston, South Carolina. Charleston: A. E. Miller, 1855.

Report of the Chief of the Fire Department of the City of Charleston, S.C. . . . 1871. Charleston: Courier Book & Job Presses, 1871.

Report of the Special Committee of the City Council. . . . 1875. Charleston: News & Courier Job Presses, 1875.

Salley, A. S., ed. *Commissions and Instructions from the Lords Proprietors of Carolina to Public Officials of South Carolina, 1685–1715.* Columbia: State Company, 1916.

_____. *JCHSC. November 24, 1696–December 5, 1696.* Columbia: State Company, 1912.

_____. *JCHSC. November 8, 1734–June 7, 1735.* Columbia: State Company, 1947.

_____. *JCHSC. February 23, 1724–June 1, 1725.* Columbia: The State Company, 1945.

_____. *JCHSC. January 8, 1765–August 9, 1765.* Columbia: State Company, 1949.

_____. *JCHSC. January 30, 1696–March 17, 1696.* Columbia: State Company, 1908.

_____. *JCHSC. 1703.* Columbia: State Company, 1934.

_____. *JCHSC. 1702.* Columbia: State Company, 1932.

_____. *JCHSC. August 13, 1701–August 28, 1701.* Columbia: State Company, 1916.

_____. *JCHSC. 1691.* Columbia: State Company, 1913.

_____. *JCHSC. January 9, 1765–August 9, 1765.* Columbia: State Company, 1949.

_____. *JCHSC. March 6, 1705/6–April 9, 1706.* Columbia: State Company, 1937.

_____. *JCHSC. November 20, 1706–February 8, 1707.* Columbia: State Company, 1939.

_____. *JCHSC. November 15, 1726–March 11, 1726.* Columbia: State Company, 1946.

_____. *JCHSC. 1698.* Columbia: State Company, 1914.

_____. *Journal of the Grand Council of South Carolina, April 11, 1692–September 26, 1698.* Columbia: State Company, 1907.

Special Report of the Law and Order League of Charleston, S.C. Charleston: Executive Committee Law and Order League, 1913.

The War of the Rebellion: A Compilation of the Official Records of the Union and Confederate Armies. 128 vols. Washington, D.C.: U.S. Government Printing Office, 1880–1901.

Twelfth Census of the United States Population, Taken in the Year 1900, Part II. Washington, D.C.: U.S. Government Printing Office, 1902.

Waring, George E., Jr. *Report on the Social Statistics of Charleston, South Carolina Compiled as Part of the Tenth Census.* Washington, D.C.: U.S. Government Printing Office, 1888.

Yearbook, City of Charleston. Charleston: various publishers, 1880–1951.

Newspapers

Charleston *Courier*
Charleston *Daily Republican*
Charleston Evening Post
Charleston *Mercury*
Charleston *News and Courier*
City Gazette
South Carolina and American General Gazette
South Carolina *Gazette and General Advertiser*
South Carolina *Gazette*
South Carolina Royal Gazette
South Carolina *Weekly Gazette*

Diaries, Memoirs, Travel Accounts, and Other Printed Sources

A Little History of St. Andrew's Parish. Charleston: Charleston Bridge Company, 1889.

A New Guide to Modern Charleston, 1912. Charleston: Walker, Evans & Cogswell, 1912.

Abbott, Martin, and Elmer, L. Puryear, eds. "Beleaguered Charleston: Letters from the City, 1860–1864." *South Carolina Historical Magazine* 61 (July 1960): 164–175.

Bargar, B. D., ed. "Charlestown Loyalism in 1775: The Secret Reports of Alexander Innes." *South Carolina Historical Magazine,* 63 (July 1962): 125–36.

Barnwell, Joseph W., ed. "Correspondence of Hon. Arthur Middleton." *South Carolina Historical and Genealogical Magazine* 26 (October 1925): 183–213.

———. "Diary of Timothy Ford," 1785–1786." *South Carolina Historical and Genealogical Magazine* 13 (October 1912): 174–204.

———. "Correspondence of Hon. Arthur Middleton." *South Carolina Historical and Genealogical Magazine* 27 (July 1926): 107–37.

———. "Bernard Elliott's Recruiting Journal, 1775." *South Carolina Historical and Genealogical Magazine* 17 (July 1916): 95–100.

———. "Letters of John Rutledge." *South Carolina Historical and Genealogical Magazine* 17 (October 1916): 131–39.

———. "Addressers of Clinton and Arbuthnot." *Proceedings of the South Carolina Historical Association* (1939): 44.

Bennett, John. "Charleston in 1774 as Described by an English Traveler." *South Carolina Historical and Genealogical Magazine* 47 (July 1946): 179–80.

Bernard, Duke of Saxe Weimar Eisenach. *Travels through North America during the Years 1825 and 1826.* 2 vols. Philadelphia: Carey, Lea & Carey, 1828.

Bruce, Peter Henry. *The Memoirs of Peter Henry Bruce, Esq.* London: Printed by the author's widow and sold by T. Payne and Son, 1782.

Bulger, William T., ed. "Sir Henry Clinton's 'Journal of the Siege of Charleston, 1780.' " *South Carolina Historical Magazine* 66 (July 1965): 147–82.

Caleb, B. S. "Prison-Life." *Harper's New Monthly Magazine* 30 (July 1865): 137–49.

Carroll, B. R., ed. *Historical Collections of South Carolina.* 2 vols. New York: Harper & Bros., 1836.

Carson, J. P., ed. *Life, Letters, and Speeches of James Louis Petigru: The Union Man of South Carolina.* Washington, D.C.: W. H. Loudermilk & Company, 1920.

Charleston City Directory, 1938. Charleston: Baldwin Directory Company, 1938.

Charleston, S.C., City Directory for 1901. Charleston: Lucas & Richardson, 1901.

Chepesiuk, Ron, ed. "Eye Witness to Fort Sumter: The Letters of Private John Thompson." *South Carolina Historical Magazine* 85 (October 1984): 271–79.

Cheves, Langdon, ed. "The Shaftesbury Papers and Other Records Relating to Carolina . . . prior to the Year 1676." South Carolina Historical Society *Collections,* Vol. 5. Charleston: 1897.

Childs, Arney R., ed. *Rice Planter and Sportsman: The Recollections of J. Motte Alston, 1821–1909.* Columbia: University of South Carolina Press, 1953.

———. *The Private Journal of Henry William Ravenel, 1859–1887.* Columbia: University of South Carolina Press, 1947.

Select Bibliography

Clark, Thomas D., ed. *South Carolina: The Grand Tour, 1780–1865* Columbia: University of South Carolina Press, 1973.

Cohen, Henning. *The South Carolina Gazette, 1732–1775.* Columbia: University of South Carolina Press, 1953.

Crouse, Maurice A., ed. "Papers of Gabriel Manigault, 1771–1784." *South Carolina Historical Magazine* 64 (January 1963): 1–12.

Dawson, J. L., and H. W. DeSaussure. *Census of the City of Charleston for the Year 1848.* Charleston: J. B. Nixon, 1849.

Deas, Alston, ed. "A Ball in Charleston." *South Carolina Historical Magazine* 75 (January 1974): 49.

De Vorsey, Louis Jr., ed. *De Brahm's Report of the General Survey in the Southern District of North America.* Columbia: University of South Carolina Press, 1971.

Drayton, John. *Memoirs of the American Revolution as Relating to the State of South Carolina.* 2 vols. Charleston: A. E. Miller, 1821.

Duncan, John E., ed. "The Correspondence of a Yankee Prisoner in Charleston, 1865." *South Carolina Historical Magazine* 66 (January 1965): 215–24.

Edgar, Walter B., ed. *The Letterbook of Robert Pringle.* Columbia: University of South Carolina Press, 1972.

Enright, Brian J., ed. "An Account of Charles Town in 1725." *South Carolina Historical Magazine* 61 (January 1960): 13–18.

"Extracts from the Diary of the Reverend Oliver Hart." *Yearbook of the City of Charleston, 1896* (Charleston, 1897): 375–401.

Fraser, Charles. *Reminiscenses of Charleston.* Charleston: Garnier & Company, 1854.

Gibbes, R. W., ed. *Documentary History of the American Revolution.* 3 vols. 1853–1857. New York: D. Appleton & Co.

Glen, James, and George Milligen-Johnston. *Colonial South Carolina: Two Contemporary Descriptions.* Columbia: University of South Carolina Press, 1951.

Hall, Basil. *Travels in North America in the Years 1827 and 1828.* London: Simpkin & Marshall, 1829.

Hamer, Philip M., and George C. Rogers, Jr., eds. *The Papers of Henry Laurens, Vol. 2: November 1, 1755–December 31, 1758.* Columbia: University of South Carolina Press, 1970.

Hamer, Philip M., and George C. Rogers, Jr., et al., eds. *The Papers of Henry Laurens, Vol. 3: January 1, 1759–August 31, 1763.* Columbia: University of South Carolina, 1972.

Hamilton, Thomas. *Men and Manners in America.* Philadelphia: Carey, Lee & Blanchard, 1833.

Hayne, Paul Hamilton. "Ante-Bellum Charleston." *Southern Bivouac* 1 (November 1885): 194–201.

"Henry Laurens to His Son John, 1773–1776." *South Carolina Historical and Genealogical Magazine* 5 (July 1904): 125–42.

Hewatt, Alexander. *An Historical Account of the Rise and Progress of the Colonies of South Carolina and Georgia.* London: A. Donaldson, 1779.

Hill's Charleston City Directory, 1973. Richmond: Hill's Directory Company, 1973.

Historical Sketch of the Confederate Home and College. Charleston: Walker, Evans & Cogswell, 1921.

Holmes, Charlotte R. *The Burckmyer Letters, 1863–1865.* Columbia: State Company, 1926.

Hough, Franklin B., ed. *Siege of Charleston by the British Fleet and Army.* Albany: J. Munsell, 1867.

Howe, Mark A. DeWolfe, ed. "Journal of Josiah Quincy, Junior, 1773." *Proceedings of the Massachusetts Historical Society* 49 (June 1916): 424–81.

Hulburt, S. A., ed. *Charleston One Hundred Years Ago: Being Extracts from the Letters of Fredricka Bremer during Her Visit to Charleston in 1850.* Charleston: St. Albans Press, 1951.

Jervey, Theodore D., and Mrs. Waveland FitzSimons, eds. "Items Relating to Charles Town, South Carolina, from the Boston Newsletter." *South Carolina Historical and Genealogical Magazine* 40 (July 1939): 73–78.

"John Laurens to James Laurens, October 24, 1776." *South Carolina Historical and Genealogical Magazine* 10 (January 1909): 49–53.

Johnson, Elmer D., and Kathleen Lewis Sloan, eds. *South Carolina: A Documentary Profile of the Palmetto State.* Columbia: University of South Carolina Press, 1971.

Johnson, Joseph. *Traditions and Reminiscences Chiefly of the American Revolution in the South.* Charleston: Walker & James, 1851.

Kemble, Frances Ann, ed. *Journal of a Residence on a Georgian Plantation in 1838–1839.* New York: Alfred A. Knopf, 1961.

Kepner, Frances Reece, ed. "A British View of the Siege of Charleston, 1776." *Journal of Southern History* 11 (February 1945): 93–105.

King, Edward. "The Great South." *Scribner's Monthly* 8 (June 1874): 130–60.

Klingberg, Frank J., ed. *Carolina Chronicle: The Papers of Commissary Gideon Johnson, 1707–1716.* Berkeley: University of California Press, 1946.

——. *The Carolina Chronicle of Dr. Francis Le Jau 1706-1717.* Berkeley: University of California Press, 1956.

Land, Jonathan E. *Charleston: Her Trade, Commerce and Industries, 1883–84.* Charleston: Published by the author, 1884.

Leland, Isabella M., ed. "Middleton Correspondence, 1861–1865." *South Carolina Historical Magazine* 64 (July 1963): 158–68.

——. "Middleton Correspondence, 1861–1865." *South Carolina Historical Magazine* 65 (January 1964): 33–44.

"Letters from Robert Mills." *South Carolina Historical and Genealogical Magazine* 39 (July 1938): 110–24.

La Rochefoucault-Liancourt, François Alexandre Frederic, Duc de. *Travels through the U.S. of North America . . . In the Years 1795, 1796 and 1797.* 2 vols. London: R. Phillips, 1799.

Marszalek, John F., ed. *The Diary of Miss Emma Holmes, 1861–1866.* Baton Rouge: Louisiana State University Press, 1979.

Martin, Julien Dwight, ed. "Letters of Caleb Cotton." *South Carolina Historical and Genealogical Magazine* 52 (January 1951): 17–25.

Martin, Sidney W. "Ebenezer Kellogg's Visit to Charleston, 1817." *South Carolina Historical and Genealogical Magazine* 49 (January 1948): 1–14.

Martineau, Harriet. *Retrospect of Western Travel.* 2 vols. London: Saunders & Otley, 1838.

Mathews, Maurice. "A Contemporary View of Carolina in 1680." *South Carolina Historical Magazine* 55 (July 1954): 153–59.

McKinley, Carl. *The August Cyclone: A Descriptive Narrative of the Memorable Storm of 1885*. Charleston: News & Courier Book Presses, 1886.

Merrens, H. Roy, ed. "A View of Coastal South Carolina in 1778: The Journal of Ebenezer Hazard." *South Carolina Historical Magazine* 73 (October 1972): 177–93.

Mills, Robert. *Statistics of South Carolina*. Charleston: Hurlburt & Lloyd, 1826.

Moffatt, Lucius Gaston, and Joseph M. Carriere. "A Frenchman Visits Charleston." *South Carolina Historical and Genealogical Magazine* 49 (July 1948): 131–54.

Mohl, Raymond A. "The Grand Fabric of Republicanism: A Scotsman Describes South Carolina, 1810–1811." *South Carolina Historical Magazine* 71 (July 1970): 170–88.

Moore, John Hammond, ed. "The Abiel Abbot Journal: A Yankee Preacher in Charleston, 1818–1827." *South Carolina Historical Magazine* 68 (October 1967): 232–54.

Morgan, James Morris. *Recollections of a Rebel Reefer*. Boston: Houghton-Mifflin, 1917.

Morrison, Alfred J., ed. *Johann David Schöepf: Travels in the Confederation [1783–1784]*. Philadelphia: W. J. Campbell, 1911.

Murdock, Richard K., ed. "A French Account of the Siege of Charleston, 1780." *South Carolina Historical Magazine* 67 (July 1966): 138–54.

Oliphant, Mary C. Simms, Alfred Taylor Odell, and T. C. Duncan Eaves, eds. *The Letters of William Gilmore Simms*. 5 vols. Columbia: University of South Carolina Press, 1952–56.

Olmstead, Frederick Law. *A Journey in the Seaboard Slave States*. New York: Dix & Edwards, 1856.

―――. *The Cotton Kingdom: A Traveler's Observations on Cotton and Slavery in the American Slave States*. New York: Alfred A. Knopf, 1953.

Peck, W. F. G. "Five Years under Fire at Charleston." *Harper's New Monthly Magazine* 31 (August 1865): 358–66.

Pinckney, Elise, ed. *The Letterbook of Eliza Lucas Pinckney*. Chapel Hill: University of North Carolina Press, 1972.

Power, Tyrone. *Impressions of America, during the Years 1833, 1834 and 1835*. New York: Benjamin Blom, 1971.

Pringle, Elizabeth W. Allston. *Chronicles of Chicora Wood*. Boston: Christopher Publishing House, 1940.

Puryear, Elmer L., ed. "The Confederate Diary of William John Grayson." *South Carolina Historical Magazine* 63 (July 1962): 137–49.

Ramsay, David. *Ramsay's History of South Carolina from Its First Settlement in 1670 to the Year 1880*. 2 vols. Newberry, S.C.: W. J. Duffie, 1858.

Rogers, George C., Jr., and David R. Chesnutt, eds. *The Papers of Henry Laurens*. Vol. 5: *September 1, 1765–July 31, 1768*. Columbia: University of South Carolina Press, 1976. Vol. 6: *August 1, 1768–July 31, 1769*. Columbia: University of South Carolina Press, 1978.

Russell, William Howard. *My Diary North and South*. Gloucester, Mass: Peter Smith, 1969.

Rutledge, Anna Wells, ed. "Letters from Thomas Pinckney to Harriot Pinckney." *South Carolina Historical and Genealogical Magazine* 41 (July 1940): 99–116.

Salley, A. S., ed. "Diary of William Dillwyn in 1772 during a Visit to Charles

Town." *South Carolina Historical and Genealogical Magazine* 36 (January 1935): 1–6.

———. *Narratives of Early Carolina, 1650–1708.* New York: Barnes & Noble, 1911.

———. "Records of the Regiments of the South Carolina Line, Continental Establishment." *South Carolina Historical and Genealogical Magazine* 5 (January 1904): 20–26.

———. "Records of the Regiments of the South Carolina Line, Continental Establishment." *South Carolina Historical and Genealogical Magazine* 5 (April 1904): 69–74.

———. *The State Houses of South Carolina, 1751–1936.* Columbia: Carey Printing Company, 1937.

"Samuel Dyssli to His Mother, Brothers, and Friends in Switzerland, December 3, 1737." *South Carolina Historical and Genealogical Magazine* 23 (July 1922): 89–91.

Schurz, Carl. *The Reminiscences of Carl Schurz.* 3 vols. Garden City, N.Y.: Doubleday, 1908.

Schwaab, Eugene L., ed. *Travels in the Old South.* 2 vols. Lexington: University Press of Kentucky, 1973.

Shecut, J. L. E. W. *Medical and Philosophical Essays: Containing Topographical, Historical, and Other Sketches of the City of Charleston from Its First Settlement to the Present Period.* Charleston: A. E. Miller, 1819.

Sholes' Directory of the City of Charleston for 1877–1878. Charleston: Evans & Cogswell, 1879.

Sifton, Paul G. "La Caroline Meridionale: Some Sources of South Carolina Revolutionary History, with Two Unpublished Letters of Baron DeKalb." *South Carolina Historical Magazine* 66 (April 1965): 102–8.

[Simms, William Gilmore]. "Charleston: The Palmetto City." *Harpers New Monthly Magazine* 15 (June 1857): 1–22.

Smith, D. E. Huger. *A Charlestonian's Recollections, 1846–1913.* Charleston: Walker, Evans, & Cogswell, 1950.

———, ed. *Mason Smith Family Letters, 1860–1868.* Columbia: University of South Carolina Press, 1950.

Somers, Robert. *The Southern States since the War.* London and New York, Macmillan, 1871.

Steen, Iva D. "Charleston in the 1850's: As Described by British Travelers." *South Carolina Historical Magazine* 71 (January 1970): 36–45.

Stoney, Samuel G., ed. "The Memoirs of Frederick Adolphus Porcher." *South Carolina Historical and Genealogical Magazine* 44 (April 1943): 83–119.

The City of Charleston and State of South Carolina. New York: Engelhardt Series, 1889.

"The Siege of Charleston: Journal of Captain Peter Russell, December 25, 1779 to May 2, 1780." *American Historical Review* 4 (April 1899): 478–501.

Tobias, Thomas J., ed. "Charles Town in 1764." *South Carolina Historical Magazine* 68 (April 1966): 63–74.

Trenholm, W. L. *The South: An Address on the Third Anniversary of the Charleston Board of Trade.* Charleston: Walker, Evans & Cogswell, 1869.

———. *The Centennial Address before the Charleston Chamber of Commerce.* Charleston: News & Courier Book Presses, 1884.

Tustin, Joseph P., ed. *Diary of the American War: A Hessian Journal.* New Haven: Yale University Press, 1979.

Voigt, Gilbert P. "Swiss Notes on South Carolina." *South Carolina Historical and Genealogical Magazine* 21 (July 1920): 93–104.

Walsh, Richard, ed. *The Writings of Christopher Gadsden, 1746–1805.* Columbia: University of South Carolina Press, 1966.

Walsh's Charleston, South Carolina 1905 City Directory. Charleston: Walker, Evans & Cogswell, 1904.

Waring, Thomas R., Jr., ed. *The Way It Was in Charleston.* Old Greenwich, Conn.: Devin-Adair Company, 1980.

Watson, Winslow C., ed. *Men and Times of the Revolution; or Memoirs of Elkanah Watson.* New York: Dana & Company, 1856.

Webber, Mabel L., ed. "Extracts from the Journal of Mrs. Ann Manigault, 1754–1781." *South Carolina Historical and Genealogical Magazine* 20 (April 1919): 128–41.

———. "Josiah Smith's Diary, 1780–1781." *South Carolina Historical and Genealogical Magazine* 33 (January 1932): 1–207.

Weir, Robert M., ed. "Two Letters by Christopher Gadsden, February, 1766." *South Carolina Historical Magazine* 75 (July 1974): 169–76.

Whilden, William G. "Reminiscences of Old Charleston." *Year Book City of Charleston, 1896* (Charleston, 1897): 402–23.

Willcox, William B., ed. *The American Rebellion: Sir Henry Clinton's Narrative of His Campaigns, 1775–1782, with an Appendix of Original Documents.* New Haven: Yale University Press, 1954.

Williams, George W., ed. "Letters to the Bishop of London from the Commissaries in South Carolina." *South Carolina Historical Magazine* 78 (April 1977): 120–47.

———. "Letters to the Bishop of London from the Commissaries of South Carolina." *South Carolina Historical Magazine* 78 (January 1977): 1–31.

Williams, Frank B., Jr. "From Sumter to the Wilderness: Letters of Sergeant James Butler Suddath, Co. E. 7th Regiment, S.C.V." *South Carolina Historical Magazine* 63 (January 1962): 1–12.

Books

Abbott, Martin. *The Freedmen's Bureau in South Carolina, 1865–1872.* Chapel Hill: University of North Carolina Press, 1967.

Alden, John Richard. *John Stuart and the Southern Colonial Frontier.* Ann Arbor: University of Michigan Press, 1944.

Alexander, John K. *Render Them Submissive: Responses to Poverty in Philadelphia, 1760–1800.* Amherst: University of Massachusetts Press, 1980.

Ashmore, Harry. *An Epitaph for Dixie.* New York: Norton, 1958.

Baldwin, Agnes Leland. *First Settlers of South Carolina, 1670–1680.* Columbia: University of South Carolina Press, 1969.

Ball, William Watts. *The State That Forgot.* Indianapolis: Bobbs-Merrill, 1932.

Banov, Leon. *As I Recall: The Story of the Charleston County Health Department.* Columbia: R. L. Bryan Company, 1970.

Barrett, John G. *Sherman's March through the Carolinas.* Chapel Hill: University of North Carolina Press, 1956.

Berkeley, Edmund, and Dorothy Smith Berkeley. *Dr. Alexander Garden of Charles Town*. Chapel Hill: University of North Carolina Press, 1969.

Berlin, Ira. *Slaves without Masters: The Free Negro in the Antebellum South*. New York: Pantheon Books, 1974.

Boorstin, Daniel J. *The Americans: The Colonial Experience*. New York: Random House, 1958.

Bowden, David K. *The Execution of Isaac Hayne*. Lexington, S.C.: Sandlapper Press, 1977.

Bowes, Frederick P. *The Culture of Early Charleston*. Chapel Hill: University of North Carolina Press, 1942.

Bridenbaugh, Carl. *Myths and Realities: Societies of the Colonial South*. Baton Rouge: Louisiana State University Press, 1952.

_____. *Cities in Revolt: Urban Life in America, 1743–1776*. New York: Capricorn, 1964.

_____. *Cities in the Wilderness: The First Century of Urban Life in America, 1625–1742*. New York: Alfred A. Knopf, 1964.

Brownell, Blaine A. *The Urban Ethos in the South, 1920–1930*. Baton Rouge: Louisiana State University Press, 1975.

Brownell, Blaine A., and David R. Goldfield, eds. *The City in Urban History: The Growth of Urban Civilization in the South*. Port Washington, N.Y.: Kennikat Press, 1977.

Bruce, Dickson D., Jr. *Violence and Culture in the Antebellum South*. Austin: University of Texas Press, 1979.

Burton, E. Milby. *South Carolina Silversmiths, 1690–1860*. Rutland, Vt.: Charles Tuttle, 1968.

_____. *The Siege of Charleston, 1861–1865*. Columbia: University of South Carolina Press, 1970.

Burts, Robert Milton. *Richard Irvine Manning and the Progressive Movement in South Carolina*. Columbia: University of South Carolina Press, 1974.

Carlton, David L. *Mill and Town in South Carolina, 1880–1920*. Baton Rouge: Louisiana State University Press, 1982.

Catton, Bruce. *The Coming Fury*. Garden City, N.Y.: Doubleday, 1961.

Cauthen, Charles E. *South Carolina Goes to War, 1860–1865*. Chapel Hill: University of North Carolina Press, 1950.

Channing, Steven A. *Crisis of Fear: Secession in South Carolina*. New York: Simon & Schuster, 1970.

Chalmers, Lionel. *An Account of the Weather and Disease of South Carolina*. London: E. & C. Dilly, 1776.

Chalmers, W. Ellison. *Racial Negotiations: Potentials and Limitations*. Ann Arbor, Mich.: Institute of Labor and Industrial Relations, 1974.

Childs, St. Julien R. *Malaria and Colonization in the Carolina Low Country, 1526–1696*. Baltimore: Johns Hopkins University Press, 1940.

Clark, Septima. *Echo in my Soul*. New York: Dutton, 1962.

Clark, E. Culpepper. *Francis W. Dawson and the Politics of Restoration: South Carolina, 1874–1889*. University, Ala.: University of Alabama Press, 1980.

Clarke, Erskine. *Wrestlin' Jacob: A Portrait of Religion in the Old South*. Atlanta: John Knox Press, 1979.

Clarke, Rev. Philip G. *Anglicanism in South Carolina*. Easley, S.C.: Southern Historical Press, 1976.

Clowse, Converse D. *Economic Beginnings in Colonial South Carolina, 1670–1730.* Columbia: University of South Carolina Press, 1971.

Cochran, Hamilton. *Blockade Runners of the Confederacy.* Indianapolis & New York: Bobbs-Merrill, 1958.

Cooper, William J., Jr. *The Conservative Regime: South Carolina, 1877–1890.* Baltimore: Johns Hopkins University Press, 1968.

Coulter, E. Merton. *George Walton Williams: The Life of a Southern Merchant and Banker, 1820–1903.* Athens, Ga.: Hibriten Press, 1976.

Cram, Mildred. *Old Seaport Towns of the South.* New York: Dodd, Mead, 1917.

Crane, Verner W. *The Southern Frontier, 1670–1732.* Ann Arbor: University of Michigan Press, 1929.

Craven, Wesley Frank. *The Southern Colonies in the Seventeenth Century.* Baton Rouge: Louisiana State University Press, 1949.

Crawford, Geddings H., ed. *Who's Who in South Carolina.* Columbia: McCaw, 1921.

Curry, Leonard P. *The Free Black in Urban America 1800–1850: The Shadow of the Dream.* Chicago: University of Chicago Press, 1982.

Dalcho, Frederick. *An Historical Account of the Protestant Episcopal Church in South Carolina.* Charleston: E. Thayer, 1820.

Davidson, Chalmers G. *The Last Foray: The South Carolina Planters of 1860: A Sociological Study.* Columbia: University of South Carolina Press, 1971.

――――. *Friend of the People: The Life of Dr. Peter Fayssoux.* Columbia: Medical Association of South Carolina, 1950.

Davis, Robert Yarborough. *The Pilgrimage.* Albuquerque, N.M.: CEC Publishers, 1980.

Dorman, James H., Jr. *Theatre in the Antebellum South, 1815–1861.* Chapel Hill: University of North Carolina Press, 1967.

Douglas, Elisha P. *Rebels and Democrats: The Struggle for Equal Political Rights and Majority Rule during the American Revolution.* Chapel Hill: University of North Carolina Press, 1955.

Drago, Edmund L. *Initiative, Paternalism, and Race Relations: Charleston's Avery Normal Institute.* Athens: University of Georgia Press, 1990.

Drayton, John. *Memoirs of the American Revolution as Relating to the State of South Carolina.* 2 vols. Charleston 1821; reprinted New York: New York Times Books, 1969.

Duffy, John. *Epidemics in Colonial America.* Port Washington, N.Y.: Kennikat Press, 1972.

Durkin, Joseph T. *Stephen R. Mallory: Confederate Navy Chief.* Chapel Hill: University of North Carolina Press, 1954.

Easterby, James H. *History of the College of Charleston.* New York: Scribners, 1935.

――――. *History of the St. Andrew's Society of Charleston, South Carolina, 1729–1929.* Charleston: Walker, Evans & Cogswell, 1929.

Eaton, Clement. *The Growth of Southern Civilization, 1790–1860.* New York: Harper & Row, 1961.

――――. *Jefferson Davis.* New York: Free Press, 1977.

Edgar, Walter B., ed. *Biographical Directory of the South Carolina House of Representatives.* Vol 1: *Sessions Lists, 1692–1973.* Columbia: University of South Carolina Press, 1974.

———. and N. Louise Bailey, eds. *Biographical Directory of the South Carolina House of Representatives. Vol. 2: The Commons House of Assembly, 1692–1775.* Columbia: University of South Carolina Press, 1977. N. Louise Bailey and Elizabeth Ivey Cooper, eds. *Biographical Directory of the South Carolina House of Representatives. Vol. 3: 1775–1790.* Columbia: University of South Carolina Press, 1981.

Edwards, George N. *A History of the Independent or Congregational Church of Charleston, South Carolina.* Boston: Pilgrim Press, 1947.

Elzas, Barnett A. *The Jews of South Carolina: From the Earliest Times to the Present Day.* Philadelphia: J. B. Lippincott, 1905.

Faust, Drew. *A Sacred Circle: The Dilemma of the Intellectual in the Old South.* Baltimore: Johns Hopkins University Press, 1977.

Fields, Mamie Garvin, with Karen Fields. *Lemon Swamp and Other Places: A Carolina Memoir.* New York: Free Press, 1983.

Franklin, John Hope. *The Militant South 1800–1861.* Cambridge, Mass.: Harvard University Press, 1956.

Fraser, Walter J., Jr. *Patriots, Pistols,* and *Petticoats.* Columbia, S.C.: R. L. Bryan Company, 1976.

Fraser, Walter J., Jr., and Winfred B. Moore, Jr., eds. *From the Old South to the New: Essays on the Transitional South.* Westport, Conn.: Greenwood Press, 1981.

Freehling, William W. *Prelude to Civil War: The Nullification Controversy in South Carolina, 1816–1836.* New York: Harper & Row, 1966.

Godbold, E. Stanly, Jr., and Robert H. Woody. *Christopher Gadsden and the American Revolution.* Knoxville: University of Tennessee Press, 1982.

Gordon, Asa H. *Sketches of Negro Life and History in South Carolina.* 2nd ed. Columbia: University of South Carolina Press, 1981.

Greene, Jack P. *The Quest for Power: The Lower Houses of Assembly in the Southern Royal Colonies, 1689–1776.* Chapel Hill: University of North Carolina Press, 1963.

Green, Karen. *Porter-Gaud School: The Next Step.* Easley, S.C.: Southern Historical Press, 1985.

Harlen, Louis R. *Separate and Unequal: Public School Campaigns and Racism in the Southern Seaboard States, 1901–1915.* Chapel Hill: University of North Carolina Press, 1958.

Hattaway, Herman, and Archer Jones. *How the North Won: A Military History of the Civil War.* Urbana: University of Illinois Press, 1983.

Hemphill, James C., ed. *Men of Mark in South Carolina.* 4 vols. Washington, D.C.: Men of Mark Publishing Company, 1907.

Higginbotham, Don. *The War of American Independence: Military Attitudes, Policies and Practice, 1763–1789.* New York: Macmillan, 1971.

Hirsch, Arthur H. *The Huguenots of Colonial South Carolina.* Hamden, Conn.: Archon Books, 1962.

Holifield, Brooks. *The Gentlemen Theologians: American Theology in Southern Culture, 1795–1860.* Durham, N.C.: Duke University Press, 1978.

Holt, Thomas. *Black over White: Negro Political Leadership in South Carolina during Reconstruction.* Urbana: University of Illinois Press, 1977.

Hoole, W. Stanley. *Vizetelly Covers the Confederacy.* Tuscaloosa, Ala.: Confederate Publishing Company, 1957.

――――. *The Antebellum Charleston Theatre.* Tuscaloosa, Ala.: University of Alabama Press, 1946.

Hosmer, Charles B., Jr. *Preservation Comes of Age: From Williamsburg to the National Trust, 1926–1949.* 2 vols. Charlottesville: University of Virginia Press, 1981.

Hubbell, Jay B. *The South in American Literature.* Durham, N.C.: Duke University Press, 1954.

Hughes, Nathaniel, Jr. *General William J. Hardee: Old Reliable.* Baton Rouge: Louisiana State University Press, 1965.

Hughson, Shirley Carter. *The Carolina Pirates and Colonial Commerce, 1670–1740.* Baltimore: Johns Hopkins University Press, 1894.

Jaher, Frederic Cople. *The Urban Establishment: Upper Strata in Boston, New York, Charleston and Los Angeles.* Urbana: University of Illinois Press, 1982.

Johnson, Michael P., and James L. Roark, eds. *No Chariot Down: Charleston's Free People of Color on the Eve of the Civil War.* Chapel Hill: University of North Carolina Press, 1984.

Johnson, Michael P., and James L. Roark. *Black Masters: A Free Family of Color in the Old South.* New York: W. W. Norton, 1984.

Johnson, Thomas Cary, Jr. *Scientific Interests in the Old South.* New York: D. Appleton Century, 1936.

Jordan, Winthrop D. *White over Black: American Attitudes Toward the Negro, 1550–1812.* Chapel Hill: University of North Carolina Press, 1968.

King, William L. *The Newspaper Press of Charleston, South Carolina.* Charleston: Edward Perry Book Press, 1970.

Koger, Larry. *Black Slaveowners: Free Black Slave Masters in South Carolina, 1790–1860.* Jefferson, N.C., and London: McFarland & Company, 1985.

Kohn, August. *Charleston, South Carolina: Business, Trade, Growth, Opportunity.* Charleston: Walker, Evans & Cogswell, 1910.

Lamson, Peggy. *The Glorious Failure: Black Congressman Robert Brown Elliott and the Reconstruction in South Carolina.* New York: W. W. Norton, 1974.

Lander, Ernest M., Jr. *A History of South Carolina, 1865–1960.* Chapel Hill: University of North Carolina Press, 1960.

Larsen, Lawrence H. *The Rise of the Urban South.* Lexington: University of Kentucky Press, 1985.

Leiding, Harriette K. *Charleston: Historic and Romantic.* Philadelphia: J. B. Lippincott, 1931.

Leland, Jack. *60 Famous Houses of Charleston, South Carolina.* Charleston: News & Courier and the Evening Post, 1978.

Lerner, Gerda. *The Grimké Sisters from South Carolina: Pioneers for Women's Rights and Abolition.* New York: Schocken Books, 1971.

Lesesne, Thomas Petigru. *History of Charleston County, South Carolina.* Charleston: A. J. Cranston, 1931.

Lofton, John. *Denmark Vesey's Revolt: The Slave Plot That Lit a Fuse to Fort Sumter.* Kent, Ohio: Kent State University Press, 1983.

Loveland, Anne C. *Southern Evangelicals and the Social Order, 1800–1860.* Baton Rouge: Louisiana State University Press, 1980.

Ludlum, David M. *Early American Winters, 1604–1820.* Boston: American Meteorological Society, 1966.

――――. *Early American Hurricanes, 1492–1870*. Boston: American Meteorological Society, 1963.

Mannix, Daniel P., and Malcolm Cowley. *Black Cargoes: A History of the Atlantic Slave Trade*. New York: Viking Press, 1962.

Massey, Mary Elizabeth. *Refugee Life in the Confederacy*. Baton Rouge: Louisiana State University Press, 1964.

Mazyck, Arthur, and Gene Waddell. *Charleston in 1883*. Easley, S.C.: Southern Historical Press, 1983.

McCrady, Edward. *The History of South Carolina in the Revolution, 1775–1780*. New York: Macmillan, 1896.

――――. *The History of South Carolina under the Proprietary Government, 1670–1719*. New York: Macmillan, 1897.

――――. *The History of South Carolina under the Royal Government, 1719–1776*. New York: Macmillan, 1899.

McCrady, Edwards, and Samuel A. Ashe. *Cyclopedia of Eminent and Representative Men of the Carolinas of the Nineteenth Century*. Vol. 1. Madison, Wis.: Brant & Fuller, 1892.

McGowen, George Smith, Jr. *The British Occupation of Charleston, 1780–1782*. Columbia: University of South Carolina Press, 1972.

Merrens, H. Roy, ed. *Colonial South Carolina Scene*. Columbia: University of South Carolina Press, 1977.

Middleton, Margaret Simons. *Jeremiah Theus: Colonial Artist of Charles Town*. Columbia: University of South Carolina Press, 1953.

Moore, Jamie W. *The Lowcountry Engineers: Military Missions and Economic Development in the Charleston District, U. S. Corps of Engineers*. Charleston: U.S. Corps of Engineers, Charleston District, 1981.

Muhlenfeld, Elizabeth. *Mary Boykin Chesnut: A Biography*. Baton Rouge: Louisiana State University Press, 1981.

Muse, Benjamin. *Ten Years of Prelude: The Story of Integration since the Supreme Court's 1954 Decision*. New York: Viking Press, 1964.

Nadelhaft, Jerome J. *The Disorders of War: The Revolution in South Carolina*. Orono: University of Maine at Orono Press, 1981.

Nash, Gary B. *The Urban Crucible: Social Change, Political Consciousness and the Origins of the American Revolution*. Cambridge, Mass.: Harvard University Press, 1979.

Newby, I. A. *Black Carolinians: A History of Blacks in South Carolina from 1895 to 1968*. Columbia: University of South Carolina Press, 1973.

O'Brien, Michael, and David Moltke-Hansen, eds., *Intellectual Life in Antebellum Charleston*. Knoxville: University of Tennessee Press, 1986.

O'Connell, Jeremiah J. *Catholicity in the Carolinas and Georgia: Leaves of Its History*. New York: D. & J. Sadlier & Company, 1879.

Osterweis, Rollin G. *Romanticism and Nationalism in the Old South*. New Haven: Yale University Press, 1949.

Pease, William H., and Jane H. Pease. *The Web of Progress: Private Values and Public Styles in Boston and Charleston, 1827–1843*. New York: Oxford University Press, 1985.

Peters, William. *The Southern Temper*. Garden City, N.Y.: Doubleday, 1959.

Petit, James P., ed. *South Carolina and the Sea*. 2 vols. Charleston, S.C.: Ashley Printing & Publishing Company, 1976, 1982.

Phillips, Ulrich B. *American Negro Slavery*. Baton Rouge: Louisiana State University Press, 1966.

Pred, Allan. *Urban Growth and City-Systems in the United States, 1840–1860*. Cambridge, Mass.: Harvard University Press, 1980.

Purvis, John C., and H. Landers. *South Carolina Hurricanes, or a Descriptive Listing of Tropical Cyclones That Have Affected South Carolina*. Columbia: University of South Carolina Press, 1973.

Quarles, Benjamin. *The Negro in the American Revolution*. Chapel Hill: University of North Carolina Press, 1961.

———. *The Negro in the Civil War*. New York: Russell & Russell, 1953.

Rankin, Hugh F. *The Golden Age of Piracy*. New York: Holt, Rinehart, & Winston, 1969.

Ravenel, St. Julien. *Architects of Charleston*. Charleston: Carolina Art Association, 1945.

Ravenel, Beatrice St. Julien. *Charleston: The Place and the People*. New York: Macmillan, 1906.

Ravenel, Harriott Horry. *Eliza Pinckney*. New York: Scribners, 1896.

Rhett, Robert Goodwyn. *Charleston: An Epic of Carolina*. Richmond, Va.: Garrett & Massie, 1940.

Robertson, Ben. *Red Hills and Cotton: An Upcountry Memory*. New York: Alfred A. Knopf, 1942.

Rogers, George C., Jr. *Evolution of a Federalist: William Loughton Smith of Charleston 1758–1812*. Columbia: University of South Carolina Press, 1962.

———. *The History of Georgetown County, South Carolina*. Columbia: University of South Carolina Press, 1970.

———. *Charleston in the Age of the Pinckneys*. Norman: University of Oklahoma Press, 1969.

———. *A South Carolina Chronology: 1497–1970*. Columbia: University of South Carolina Press, 1973.

Rose, Willie Lee. *Rehearsal for Reconstruction: The Port Royal Experiment*. Indianapolis: Bobbs-Merrill Company, 1964.

Rosen, Robert. *A Short History of Charleston*. San Francisco: Lexikos, 1982.

Rubin, Louis D., Jr., ed. *The American South: Portrait of a Culture*. Baton Rouge: Louisiana State University Press, 1980.

Rutledge, Anna Wells. *Artists in the Life of Charleston through Colony and State from Restoration to Reconstruction*. Philadelphia: American Philosophical Society, 1980.

Salley, A. S. *The Early English Settlers of South Carolina*. Charleston: National Society of Colonial Dames of America in the State of South Carolina, 1946.

Sass, Herbert Ravenel. *Outspoken: 150 Years of the News and Courier*. Columbia: University of South Carolina Press, 1953.

Scharf, J. Thomas. *History of the Confederate States Navy from Its Organization to the Surrender of Its Last Vessel*. New York: Rogers & Sherwood, 1887.

Sefton, James E. *The United States Army and Reconstruction, 1865–1877*. Baton Rouge: Louisiana State University Press, 1967.

Sellers, Leila. *Charleston Business on the Eve of the American Revolution*. Chapel Hill: University of North Carolina Press, 1934.

Severens, Kenneth. *Southern Architecture: 350 Years of Distinctive American Buildings*. New York: Dutton, 1981.

Sherman, Richard P. *Robert Johnson: Proprietary & Royal Governor of South Carolina*. Columbia: University of South Carolina Press, 1966.

Simkins, Francis Butler. *Pitchfork Ben Tillman: South Carolinian*. Baton Rouge: Louisiana State University Press, 1944.

Simkins, Francis Butler, and Robert H. Woody. *South Carolina during Reconstruction*. Chapel Hill: University of North Carolina Press, 1932.

Sirmans, M. Eugene. *Colonial South Carolina: A Political History, 1663-1763*. Chapel Hill: University of North Carolina Press, 1966.

Smith, Alice R. Huger, and D. E. Huger Smith. *The Dwelling Houses of Charleston, South Carolina*. Philadelphia: J. B. Lippincott, 1917.

Smith, Alfred G., Jr. *Economic Readjustment of an Old Cotton State, South Carolina, 1820-1860*. Columbia: University of South Carolina Press, 1958.

Snowden, Yates. *History of South Carolina*. 5 vols. Chicago: Lewis Publishing Co., 1920.

Stark, John D. *Damned Upcountryman: William Watts Ball, a Study in American Conservatism*. Durham, N.C.: Duke University Press, 1968.

Still, William N., Jr. *Iron Afloat: The Story of the Confederate Armorclads*. Nashville, Tenn.: Vanderbilt University Press, 1971.

———. *Confederate Shipbuilding*. Athens: University of Georgia Press, 1969.

Swanberg, W. A. *First Blood: The Story of Fort Sumter*. New York: Scribners, 1957.

———. *Sickles the Incredible*. New York: Scribners, 1956.

Taylor, Rosser H. *Ante-Bellum South Carolina: A Social and Cultural History*. Chapel Hill: University of North Carolina Press, 1970.

Thomas, Albert Sidney. *A Historical Account of the Protestant Episcopal Church in South Carolina, 1820-1957*. Columbia: R. L. Bryan, 1957.

Tindall, George B. *South Carolina Negroes, 1877-1900*. Baton Rouge: Louisiana State University Press, 1966.

———. *The Emergence of the New South*. Baton Rouge: Louisiana State University Press, 1967.

Torre, Thomas della. *A Sketch of the Charleston Club with Its Constitutions and By-Laws, and a List of Its Members, 1852-1938*. Charleston: Charleston Club, 1938.

Uhlendorf, Bernard A., ed. *The Siege of Charleston*. Ann Arbor: University of Michigan Press, 1938.

Uya, Okon Edet. *From Slavery to Public Service: Robert Smalls, 1839-1915*. New York: Oxford University Press, 1971.

Vandiver, Frank F. *Plough Shares into Swords: Josiah Gorgas and Confederate Ordnance*. Austin: University of Texas Press, 1952.

Ver Steeg, Clarence L. *Origins of a Southern Mosaic*. Athens: University of Georgia Press, 1969.

Vipperman, Carl J. *The Rise of Rawlins Lowndes, 1721-1800*. Columbia: University of South Carolina Press, 1978.

Wade, Richard C. *Slavery in the Cities: The South, 1820-1860*. New York: Oxford University Press, 1964.

Wallace, David D. *South Carolina: A Short History, 1520-1948*. Chapel Hill: University of North Carolina Press, 1951.

Walsh, Richard. *Charleston's Sons of Liberty: A Study of the Artisans, 1763-1789*. Columbia: University of South Carolina Press, 1959.

Ward, Christopher. *The War of the Revolution.* 2 vols. New York: Macmillan, 1952.

Waring, Joseph I. *A History of Medicine in South Carolina, 1670–1900.* 2 vols. Columbia: R. L. Bryan & Company, 1964, 1967.

_____. *The First Voyage and Settlement at Charles Town, 1670–1680.* Columbia: University of South Carolina Press, 1970.

Watson, Charles S. *Antebellum Charleston Dramatists.* University, Ala.: University of Alabama Press, 1976.

Weir, Robert M. *"A Most Important Epocha": The Coming of the Revolution in South Carolina.* Columbia: University of South Carolina Press, 1970.

_____. *Colonial South Carolina: A History.* New York: KTO Press, 1983.

Wells, Robert V. *The Population of the British Colonies in America before 1776: A Survey of Census Data.* Princeton, N.J.: Princeton University Press, 1975.

Wikramanayake, Marina. *A World in Shadow: The Free Black in Antebellum South Carolina.* Columbia: University of South Carolina Press, 1973.

Williams, George W. *St. Michael's, Charleston, 1751–1951.* Columbia: University of South Carolina Press, 1951.

Williams, Jack Kenny. *Vogues in Villainy: Crime and Retribution in Ante-Bellum South Carolina.* Columbia: University of South Carolina Press, 1959.

Williams, T. Harry. *P. G. T. Beauregard: Napoleon in Gray.* Baton Rouge: Louisiana State University Press, 1954.

Williamson, Joel. *After Slavery: The Negro in South Carolina during Reconstruction, 1861–1877.* Chapel Hill: University of North Carolina Press, 1965.

_____. *New People: Miscegenation and Mulattoes in the United States.* New York: Free Press, 1980.

Willis, Eola. *The Charleston Stage in the XVIII Century with Social Settings of the Time.* Columbia: State Company, 1924.

Wood, Peter H. *Black Majority: Negroes in Colonial South Carolina from 1670 through the Stono Rebellion.* New York: Alfred A. Knopf, 1975.

Woodward, C. Vann. *Origins of the New South.* Baton Rouge: Louisiana State University Press, 1951.

Woodward, C. Vann, ed. *Mary Chesnut's Civil War.* New Haven: Yale University Press, 1981.

Wyatt-Brown, Bertram. *Southern Honor: Ethics and Behavior in the Old South.* New York: Oxford University Press, 1982.

Yarborough, Tinsley. *A Passion for Justice: J. Waties Waring and Civil Rights.* New York: Oxford University Press, 1987.

Zahniser, Marvin R. *Charles Cotesworth Pinckney: Founding Father.* Chapel Hill: University of North Carolina Press, 1967.

Articles

Adams, Samuel Hopkins. "Guardians of the Public Health." *McClure's Magazine* 31 (July 1908): 251–52.

Aldredge, Robert Croom. "Weather Observers and Observations at Charleston, South Carolina, 1670–1871." *Year Book City of Charleston 1940.* (1940): 190–257.

Allen, George Marshall. "Charleston: A Typical City of the South." *Magazine of Travel* 1 (February 1895): 99–129.

Altman, James David. "The Charleston Marine School." *South Carolina Historical Magazine* 88 (April 1987): 76–82.

Arsenault, Raymond. "The End of the Long Hot Summer: The Air Conditioner and Southern Culture." *Journal of Southern History* 50 (November 1984): 597–628.

Bass, Jack. "Strike at Charleston." *New South* (Summer 1969): 1–10.

Becker, Robert A. "Sales Populi Suprema Lex: Public Peace and South Carolina Debtor Relief Laws, 1783–1788." *South Carolina Historical Magazine* 80 (January 1979): 65–75.

Blassingame, John W. "American Nationalism and Other Loyalties in the Southern Colonies, 1763–1775." *Journal of Southern History* 24 (February 1968): 50–75.

Brady, Patrick S. "The Slave Trade and Sectionalism in South Carolina, 1787–1808." *Journal of Southern History* 38 (November 1972): 601–20.

Brewster, Lawrence F. "Planters from the Low-Country and Their Summer Travels." *Proceedings of the South Carolina Historical Association* (1943): 35–41.

Bridenbaugh, Carl. "Charlestonians at Newport, 1767–1775." *South Carolina Historical and Genealogical Magazine* 41 (April 1940): 43–47.

Brown, Philip M. "Early Indian Trade in the Development of South Carolina." *South Carolina Historical Magazine* 76 (July 1975): 118–28.

Calhoon, Robert M., and Robert M. Weir. " 'The Scandalous History of Sir Egerton Leigh.' " *William and Mary Quarterly* 26 (January 1969): 47–74.

Calmes, Alan. "The Lyttelton Expedition of 1759: Military Failures and Financial Successes." *South Carolina Historical Magazine* 77 (January 1976): 10–33.

Cantwell, Edwin P. "History of the Charleston Police Force." *Year Book City of Charleston, 1908* (Charleston, 1909): 3–19.

"Charles Macbeth—1805–1881." *Year Book City of Charleston, 1881* (Charleston, 1882): 251–53.

"Charleston a Century Ago." *Year Book City of Charleston, 1881* (Charleston, 1882): 378–80.

Childs, St. Julien Ravenel. "Notes on the History of Public Health in South Carolina, 1670–1800." *Proceedings of the South Carolina Historical Association* (1932): 13–22.

———. "The Naval Career of Joseph West." *South Carolina Historical Magazine* 71 (April 1970): 109–16.

———. "The First Carolinians." *South Carolina Historical Magazine* 71 (April 1970): 101–8.

Clarke, T. Erskine. "An Experiment in Paternalism: Presbyterians and Slaves in Charleston, South Carolina." *Journal of Presbyterian History* 53 (Fall 1975): 223–38.

Cole, David. "A Brief Outline of the South Carolina Colonial Militia System." *Proceedings of the South Carolina Historical Association* (1954): 14–23.

Coleman, Alan. "The Charleston Bootlegging Controversy, 1915–1918." *South Carolina Historical Magazine* 75 (April 1974): 77–94.

Conroy, Pat. "Shadows of the Old South." *Geoliving* 3 (May 1981): 64–82.

Crane, Vernon W. "Edward McCrady." In Dumas Malone, ed., *Dictionary of American Biography*, pp. 1–2. New York: Charles Scribner's Sons, 1933.

Curtis, Julia. "A Note on Henry Holt." *South Carolina Historical Magazine* 79 (January 1978): 1–5.

————. "Charles-Town's Church Street Theatre." *South Carolina Historical Magazine* 70 (July 1969): 149–54.

Davis, Nora M. "Public Powder Magazines at Charleston." *Year Book City of Charleston, 1942* (Charleston, 1942): 184–210.

Davis, Richard B. "The Ball Papers: A Pattern of Life in the Low Country, 1800–1825." *South Carolina Historical Magazine* 65 (January 1964): 1–15.

Donnan, Elizabeth. "The Slave Trade into South Carolina before the Revolution." *American Historical Review* 33 (July 1928): 804–28.

Doyle, Don H. "Leadership and Decline in Postwar Charleston, 1865–1910." In Walter J. Fraser, Jr., and Winfred B. Moore, Jr., eds., *From the Old South to the New: Essays on the Transitional South,* pp. 93–106. Westport, Conn.: Greenwood Press, 1981.

————. "Urbanization and Southern Culture: Economic Elites in Four New South Cities (Atlanta, Nashville, Charleston, Mobile) c. 1865–1910." In Orville Vernon Burton and Robert C. McMath, Jr., eds. *Toward a New South?: Studies in Post Civil War Southern Communities,* pp. 11–36. Westport, Conn.: Greenwood Press, 1982.

Drago, Edmund, and Ralph Melnick. "The Old Slave Mart Museum, Charleston, South Carolina: Rediscovering the Past." *Civil War History* 27 (June 1981): 138–54.

Duffy, John. "Yellow Fever in Colonial Charleston." *South Carolina Historical Magazine* 52 (October 1951): 189–97.

————. "Eighteenth Century Carolina Health Conditions." *Journal of Southern History* 18 (August 1952): 289–302.

Dunn, Richard. "The English Sugar Islands and the Founding of South Carolina." *South Carolina Historical Magazine* 72 (April 1971): 81–93.

Durden, Robert F. "The Establishment of Calvary Protestant Episcopal Church for Negroes in Charleston." *South Carolina Historical Magazine* 65 (April 1964): 63–84.

Durham, Frank. "The Poetry Society of South Carolina's Turbulent Year: Self-Interest, Atheism, and Jean Toomer." *Southern Humanities Review* 5 (Winter 1971): 76–80.

Easterby, J. H. "Public Poor Relief in Colonial Charleston: A Report to the Commons House of Assembly about the Year 1767." *South Carolina Historical and Genealogical Magazine* 42 (April 1941): 83–86.

Edgar, Walter B. "Notable Libraries of Colonial South Carolina." *South Carolina Historical Magazine* 72 (April 1971): 105–10.

————. "Robert Pringle and His World." *South Carolina Historical Magazine* 76 (January 1975): 1–11.

————. "Some Popular Books in Colonial South Carolina." *South Carolina Historical Magazine* 72 (July 1971): 174–78.

Edwards, John B., Jr. "Francis W. Pickens and the War Begins." *Proceedings of the South Carolina Historical Association* (1970): 21–29.

Eisterhold, John A. "Charleston: Lumber and Trade in a Declining Southern Port." *South Carolina Historical Magazine* 74 (April 1973): 61–72.

Ewing, Enid. "Charleston Contra Mundum." *The Nation* (November 20, 1943): 579–81.

Farley, Foster M. "The South Carolina Negro in the American Revolution, 1775–1783." *South Carolina Historical Magazine* 79 (April 1978): 75–86.

———. "Stranger's Fever." *South Carolina History Illustrated* 1 (February 1970): 54–61.

———. "The Mighty Monarch of the South: Yellow Fever in Charleston and Savannah." *Georgia Review* 27 (1973): 56–70.

Floyd, Viola Caston, ed. " 'The Fall of Charleston.' " *South Carolina Historical Magazine* 66 (January 1965): 1–14.

Foote, Shelby. "Du Pont Storms Charleston." *American Heritage* 14 (June 1963): 28–92.

Foote, William A. "The South Carolina Independents." *South Carolina Historical Magazine* 62 (October 1961): 185–191.

Ford, Gary D. "Charleston Preserved." *Southern Living* 23 (March 1988): 112–15.

Ford, Lacy. "James Louis Petigru: The Last South Carolina Federalist." In Michael O'Brien and David Moltke-Hansen, eds., *Intellectual Life in Antebellum Charleston*, pp. 152–85. Knoxville: University of Tennessee Press, 1986.

Fraser, Walter J., Jr. "Reflections of 'Democracy' in Revolutionary South Carolina? The Composition of Military Organizations and the Attitudes and Relationships of the Officers and Men, 1775–1780." *South Carolina Historical Magazine* 78 (July 1977): 202–12.

French, Laura. "The Republicanism of Henry Laurens." *South Carolina Historical Magazine* 76 (April 1975): 68–79.

Frady, Marshall. "The Sweetest Finger This Side of Midas." *Life* magazine (February 27, 1970): 52–60.

Gallardo, José M. "The Spaniards and the English Settlement in Charles Town." *South Carolina Historical and Genealogical Magazine* 37 (April–July 1936): 49–64.

Gatell, Frank O., ed. "Postmaster Huger and the Incendiary Publications." *South Carolina Historical Magazine* 64 (October 1963): 193–201.

Gatewood, Willard B. "Theodore Roosevelt and Southern Republicans: The Case of South Carolina, 1901–1904." *South Carolina Historical Magazine* 70 (October 1969): 251–66.

Gayle, Charles Joseph. "The Nature and Volume of Exports from Charleston, 1724–1774." *South Carolina Historical Society Proceedings* (1937): 25–33.

Gifford, Edmund, Jr. "The Charleston Physician-Naturalists." *Bulletin of the History of Medicine* 45 (Winter 1975): 556–74.

Goldfield, David R. "The Business of Health Planning: Disease Prevention in the Old South." *Journal of Southern History* 42 (November 1976): 555–65.

Goldman, Albert. "Charleston! Charleston!" *Esquire* 87 (June 1977): 110–13, 154–56.

Gould, Christopher. "Robert Wells, Colonial Charleston Printer." *South Carolina Historical Magazine* (January 1978): 23–49.

Greene, Jack P. "Bridge to Revolution: The Wilkes Fund Controversy in South Carolina, 1769–1775." *Journal of Southern History* 29 (February 1963): 19–52.

———. " 'Slavery or Independence': Some Reflections on the Relationship among Liberty, Black Bondage, and Equality in Revolutionary South Carolina." *South Carolina Historical Magazine* 80 (July 1979): 193–214.

———. "The Gadsden Election Controversy and the Revolutionary Movement in

South Carolina." *Mississippi Valley Historical Review* 46 (December 1959): 469–92.

―――. "The South Carolina Quartering Dispute, 1757–1758." *South Carolina Historical Magazine* 60 (October 1959): 193–204.

Greenberg, Kenneth S. "Revolutionary Ideology and the Proslavery Argument: The Abolition of Slavery in Antebellum South Carolina." *Journal of Southern History* 42 (August 1976): 365–84.

Gregorie, Anne King. "The First Decade of the Charleston Library Society." *Proceedings of the South Carolina Historical Association* (1935): 3–10.

Griffin, Richard W. "An Origin of the New South: The South Carolina Homespun Company, 1808–1815." *Business History Review* 35 (Autumn 1961): 402–14.

Grinde, Donald A., Jr. "Building the South Carolina Railroad." *South Carolina Historical Magazine* 77 (April 1976): 84–96.

Halsey, Alfred O. "The Passing of a Great Forest and the History of the Mills Which Manufactured It into Lumber." *Yearbook City of Charleston, 1937* (Charleston, 1938), pp. 198–218.

Hamer, Marguerite B. "The Fate of the Exiled Acadians in South Carolina." *Journal of Southern History* 4 (May 1938): 199–208.

Hemmingway, Theodore. "Prelude to Change: Black Carolinians in the War Years, 1914–1920." *Journal of Negro History* 65 (Summer 1980): 212–27.

Higginbotham, Don. "American Historians and the Military History of the American Revolution." *American Historical Review* 70 (October 1964): 18–34.

Higgins, W. Robert. "The Geographical Origins of Negro Slaves in Colonial South Carolina." *South Atlantic Quarterly* 70 (Winter 1971): 34–47.

―――. "Charles Town Merchants and Factors Dealing in the External Negro Trade, 1735–1775" *South Carolina Historical Magazine* 65 (October 1964): 205–17.

Hill, Omar. "Charleston's New Industry Board." *Manufacturers Record* 115 (August 1946): 37–38.

Hine, William C. "The 1867 Charleston Streetcar Sit-Ins: A Case of Successful Black Protest" *South Carolina Historical Magazine* 77 (April 1977): 110–14.

―――. "Black Politicians in Reconstruction Charleston, South Carolina: A Collective Study." *Journal of Southern History* 49 (November 1983): 555–84.

Hogue, L. Lynn. "Nicholas Trott: Man of Law and Letters." *South Carolina Historical Magazine* 76 (January 1975): 25–34.

Hoole, W. Stanley. "Charleston Theatricals during the Tragic Decade, 1860–1869." *Journal of Southern History* 11 (November 1945): 538–46.

Huff, A. V., Jr. "The Eagle and the Vulture: Changing Attitudes toward Nationalism in Fourth of July Orations Delivered in Charleston, 1778–1860." *South Atlantic Quarterly* 73 (Winter 1974): 10–22.

Insh, George Pratt. "Arrival of the Cardross Settlers." *South Carolina Historical and Genealogical Magazine* 30 (April 1929): 69–80.

Jackson, Harvey H. "Hugh Bryan and the Evangelical Movement in Colonial South Carolina." *William and Mary Quarterly* 43 (October 1986): 594–614.

Jaher, Frederick C. "Antebellum Charleston: An Anatomy of an Economic Failure." In Orville Vernon Burton and Robert C. McMath, Jr., eds., *Class, Conflict and Consensus: Antebellum Southern Community Studies*, pp. 207–31. Westport, Conn.: Greenwood Press, 1982.

January, Alan F. "The South Carolina Association: An Agency for Race Control in Antebellum Charleston." *South Carolina Historical Magazine* 78 (July 1977): 191–201.

Jellison, Richard M. "Paper Currency in Colonial South Carolina: A Reappraisal." *South Carolina Historical Magazine* 62 (July 1961): 134–47.

Johnson, Michael P. "Runaway Slaves and the Slave Communities in South Carolina, 1799 to 1830." *William and Mary Quarterly* 38 (July 1981): 418–41.

————. "Planters and Patriarchy: Charleston, 1800–1860." *Journal of Southern History* 46 (February 1980): 45–72.

Jones, Newton B. "The Charleston Orphan Home, 1860–1876." *South Carolina Historical Magazine* 62 (October 1961): 203–14.

Jordan, Laylon Wayne. "Between Two Worlds: Christopher G. Memminger of Charleston and the Old South in Mid-Passage, 1830–1861." *Proceedings of the South Carolina Historical Association* (1981): 56–76.

————. "Education for Community: C. G. Memminger and the Origination of Common Schools in Antebellum Charleston." *South Carolina Historical Magazine* 83 (April 1982): 99–115.

————. "Police and Politics: Charleston in the Gilded Age, 1880–1900." *South Carolina Historical Magazine* 81 (January 1980): 35–50.

————. "Police Power and Public Safety in Antebellum Charleston: The Emergence of a New Police, 1800–1860." In Samual M. Hines and George W. Hopkins, eds., *South Atlantic Urban Studies*, vol. 3, pp. 122–40. Columbia: University of South Carolina Press, 1979.

Joyner, Charles. "If You Ain't Got Education": Slave Language and Slave Thought in Antebellum Charleston." In Michael O'Brien and David Moltke-Hansen, eds., *Intellectual Life in Antebellum Charleston.*, pp. 255–78. Knoxville, University of Tennessee Press, 1986.

Kenneth, Lee, ed. "Charleston in 1778: A French Intelligence Report." *South Carolina Historical Magazine* 66 (April 1965): 109–11.

Kenney, William Howland III. "Alexander Garden and George Whitefield: The Significance of Revivalism in South Carolina, 1738–1741." *South Carolina Historical Magazine* 71 (January 1970): 1–16.

Klebaner, Benjamin J. "Public Poor Relief in Charleston, 1800–1860." *South Carolina Historical Magazine* 55 (October 1954): 210–20.

Kulikoff, Allan. "The Progress of Inequality in Revolutionary Boston." *William and Mary Quarterly* 28 (July 1971): 375–412.

Kyte, George W. "General Greene's Plans for the Capture of Charleston, 1781–1782." *South Carolina Historical Magazine* 62 (April 1961): 96–128.

Lander, Ernest M., Jr. "Charleston: Manufacturing Center of the Old South." *Journal of Southern History* 26 (August 1960): 331–42.

————. "Ante-Bellum Milling in South Carolina." *South Carolina Historical and Genealogical Magazine* 52 (July 1951): 125–31.

Lapham, Samuel, Jr. "Notes on Granville Bastion." *South Carolina Historical and Genealogical Magazine* 26 (October 1925): 221–27.

Levett, Ella Pettit. "Loyalism in Charleston, 1761–1784." *Proceedings of the South Carolina Historical Association* (1936): 3–17.

Levy, Babette M. "Early Puritanism in the Southern and Island Colonies." *Proceedings of the American Antiquarian Society* 70 (April 1960): 69–348,

Lewisohn, Ludwig. "South Carolina: A Lingering Fragrance." *The Nation* 115 (July 12, 1922): 36–38.

Maier, Pauline. "The Road Not Taken: Nullification, John C. Calhoun, and the Revolutionary Tradition in South Carolina." *South Carolina Historical Magazine* 82 (January 1981): 1–19.

———. "The Charleston Mob and the Evolution of Popular Politics in Revolutionary South Carolina, 1765–1784." *Perspectives in American History* 4 (1970): 173–96.

Maslowski, Peter. "National Policy toward the Use of Black Troops in the Revolution." *South Carolina Historical Magazine* 73 (January 1972): 1–17.

May, W. E. "Capt. Charles Hardy on the Carolina Station, 1742–1744." *South Carolina Historical Magazine* 70 (January 1969): 1–19.

McCardell, John. "Poetry and the Practical: William Gilmore Simms." In Michael O'Brien and David Moltke-Hansen, eds., *Intellectual Life in Antebellum Charleston*, pp. 186–210. Knoxville: University of Tennessee Press, 1986.

McCombs, Carl E. "Charleston Breaks with the Past in Public Welfare Work." *National Municipal Review* (June 1924): 341–45.

McCrady, Edward. "Historical Sketch of St. Philip's Church." *Yearbook City of Charleston, 1897* (Charleston, 1897), pp. 319–74.

Meaders, David E. "South Carolina Fugitives as Viewed through Local Colonial Newspapers with Emphasis on Runaway Notices." *Journal of Negro History* 60 (April 1975): 288–319.

Melvin, Patrick. "Captain Florence O'Sullivan and the Origins of Carolina." *South Carolina Historical Magazine* 76 (October 1975): 235–49.

Meroney, Geraldine M. "William Bull's First Exile from South Carolina, 1777–1781." *South Carolina Historical Magazine* 80 (April 1979): 91–104.

Merrens, H. Roy, and George D. Terry. "Dying in Paradise: Malaria, Mortality, and the Perceptual Environment in Colonial South Carolina." *Journal of Southern History* 50 (November 1984): 533–50.

Middleton, Margaret Simons. "The Ladies' Benevolent Society of Charleston, South Carolina." *Yearbook City of Charleston, 1941* (Charleston, 1942), pp. 216–39.

Mohl, Raymond A. "Poverty in Early America, a Reappraisal: The Case of Eighteenth Century New York City." *New York History* 50 (1969): 5–27.

Moltke-Hansen, David. "The Expansion of Intellectual Life: A Prospectus." In Michael O'Brien and David Moltke-Hansen, eds., *Intellectual Life in Antebellum Charleston*, pp. 3–44. Knoxville: University of Tennessee Press, 1986.

Moore, Jamie W. "The Great South Carolina Inter-State and West Indian Exposition of 1901." *Sandlapper* 11 (July 1978): 11–15.

———. "The Low Country in Economic Transition: Charleston since 1865." *South Carolina Historical Magazine* 88 (April 1979): 156–71.

Moore, John Hammond. "South Carolina's Reaction to the Photoplay, *The Birth of a Nation*." *South Carolina Historical Association Proceedings* (1963): 30–40.

———. "No Room, No Rice, No Grits: Charleston's 'Time of Trouble,' 1942–1944." *South Atlantic Quarterly* 85 (Winter 1986): 23–31.

———. "Charleston in World War I: Seeds of Change." *South Carolina Historical Magazine* 86 (January 1985): 39–49.

Moore, Warner Oland, Jr. "The Largest Exporters of Deerskins from Charles

Town, 1735–1775." *South Carolina Historical Magazine* 74 (July 1973): 144–50.

Morgan, David T. "The Great Awakening in South Carolina, 1740–1775." *South Atlantic Quarterly* 70 (Autumn 1971): 595–606.

Morris, Richard B. "White Bondage in Antebellum South Carolina." *South Carolina Historical and Genealogical Magazine* 49 (October 1948): 191–207.

Mouzon, Harold A. "The Carolina Art Association: Its First Hundred Years." *South Carolina Historical Magazine* 59 (January 1959): 125–38.

Mustard, Harry S. "On the Building of Fort Johnson." *South Carolina Historical Magazine* 64 (July 1963): 129–35.

Nash, Gary B. "Poverty and Poor Relief in Pre-Revolutionary Philadelphia." *William and Mary Quarterly* 33 (January 1976): 3–30.

Oberdorfer, Don. " 'Rivers Delivers.' " *New York Times Magazine* (August 19, 1965): 30–40.

Oedel, Howard T. "Lincoln Takes the Pulse of the Confederacy at Charleston in March, 1861." *Lincoln Herald* 73 (1971): 156–62.

Olsberg, Nicholas. "Ship Registers in the South Carolina Archives." *South Carolina Historical Magazine* 74 (October 1973): 189–97.

Parker, F. L. "The Battle of Fort Sumter as Seen from Morris Island." *South Carolina Historical Magazine* 62 (April 1961): 65–71.

Pease, Jane H., and William H. Pease. "The Economics and Politics of Charleston's Nullification Crisis." *Journal of Southern History* 48 (August 1981): 335–62.

——. "The Blood-Thirsty Tiger: Charleston and the Psychology of Fire." *South Carolina Historical Magazine* 79 (October 1978): 281–95.

——. "Social Structure and the Potential for Urban Change: Boston and Charleston in the 1830's." *Journal of Urban History* 8 (February 1982): 171–96.

——. "Intellectual Life in the 1830's: The Institutional Framework and the Charleston Style." In Michael O'Brien and David Moltke-Hansen, eds., *Intellectual Life in Antebellum Charleston*, pp. 233–54. Knoxville: University of Tennessee Press, 1986.

Pennington, Edgar Legare. "The Reverend Thomas Morritt and the Free School in Charles Town." *South Carolina Historical and Genealogical Magazine* 32 (January 1931): 34–45.

Phillips, Ulrich B. "The Slave Labor Problem in the Charleston District." *Political Science Quarterly* 22 (1907): 416–39.

Price, Jacob M. "Economic Function and the Growth of American Port Towns in the Eighteenth Century." *Perspectives in American History* 8 (1974): 123–88.

Price, Marcus W. "Blockade Running as a Business in South Carolina during the War between the States, 1861–1865." *American Neptune* 8 (1948): 196–241.

Prior, Linda T. "Ralph Waldo Emerson and South Carolina." *South Carolina Historical Magazine* 79 (October 1978): 253–63.

Rabinowitz, Howard N. "From Exclusion to Segregation: Southern Race Relations, 1865–1890." *Journal of American History* 63 (September 1976): 325–50.

Radford, John. "The Charleston Planters in 1860." *South Carolina Historical Magazine* 77 (October 1976): 227–35.

———. "Race, Residence and Ideology: Charleston, South Carolina in the Mid-Nineteenth Century." *Journal of Historical Geography* 2 (1976): 329–46.

———. "Social Structure and Urban Form: Charleston, 1860–1880." In Walter J. Fraser, Jr., and Winfred B. Moore, Jr., eds., *From the Old South to the New: Essays on the Transitional South*, pp. 81–91. Westport, Conn.: Greenwood Press, 1981.

Rittenhouse, Anne. "America's Social House of Peers." *Ainslee's Magazine* (October 1905): 75–84.

Robinson, Emmett, ed. "Dr. Irving's Reminiscences of the Charleston Stage. *South Carolina Historical and Genealogical Magazine* 52 (July 1951): 166–79.

Rogers, George C., Jr. "The Charleston Tea Party: The Significance of December 3, 1773." *South Carolina Historical Magazine* 75 (July 1974): 153–68.

———. "Aedanus Burke, Nathanael Greene, Anthony Wayne, and the British Merchants of Charleston." *South Carolina Historical Magazine* 67 (April 1966): 75–83.

———. "The First Earl of Shaftesbury." *South Carolina Historical Magazine* 68 (April 1968): 74–78.

———. "South Carolina and the Origins of the Nullification Movement." *South Carolina Historical Magazine* 71 (January 1970): 17–32.

———. "South Carolina Ratifies the Federal Constitution." *South Carolina Historical Association Proceedings* (1961): 41–61.

Rutledge, Anna Wells. "The Second St. Philip's, Charleston, 1710–1835." *Journal of the Society of Architectural Historians* 18 (October 1959): 112–14.

Ryan, Frank Winkler, Jr. "Travelers in South Carolina in the Eighteenth Century." *Year Book City of Charleston, 1945* (Charleston, 1945), pp. 184–256.

Schmidt, Leigh Eric. " 'The Grand Prophet,' Hugh Bryan: Early Evangelicalism's Challenge to the Establishment and Slavery in the Colonial South." *South Carolina Historical Magazine* 87 (October 1986): 238–50.

Scott, Kenneth. "Sufferers in the Charleston Fire of 1740." *South Carolina Historical Magazine* 64 (October 1963): 203–11.

Scott, William B. "Judge J. Waties Waring: Advocate of 'Another' South." *South Atlantic Quarterly* 27 (Summer 1978): 320–34.

Sherrer, G. Terry. "Indigo in Carolina, 1671–1796." *South Carolina Historical Magazine* 72 (April 1971): 94–103.

Shick, Tom W., and Don H. Doyle. "The South Carolina Phosphate Boom and the Stillbirth of the New South, 1867–1920." *South Carolina Historical Magazine* 86 (January 1985): 1–31.

Silver, Christopher. "A New Look at Old South Urbanization: The Irish Worker in Charleston, South Carolina, 1840–1860." In Samuel M. Hines and George W. Hopkins, eds., *South Atlantic Urban Studies*, vol. 3, pp. 141–72. Columbia: University of South Carolina Press, 1979.

Simons, Albert. "Architectural Trends in Charleston." *Antiques Magazine* 97 (April 1970): 545–55.

Simons, Harriet P., and Albert Simons. "The William Burrows House of Charleston." *South Carolina Historical Magazine* 70 (July 1969): 155–76.

Sirmans, M. Eugene. "The Legal Status of the Slave in South Carolina, 1670–1740." *Journal of Southern History* 28 (November 1962): 462–73.

———. "Politicians and Planters: The Bull Family of Colonial South Carolina." *South Carolina Historical Association Proceedings* (1962): 32–41.

————. "The South Carolina Royal Council, 1720–1763." *William and Mary Quarterly* 18 (July 1961): 375–92.

Skelton, Lynda Worley. "The Importing and Exporting Company of South Carolina." *South Carolina Historical Magazine* 75 (January 1974): 24–32.

Smith, D. E. Huger. "Wilton's Statue of Pitt." *South Carolina Historical and Genealogical Magazine* 15 (January 1914): 18–38.

Smith, Henry A. M. "Old Charles Town and Its Vicinity." *South Carolina Historical and Genealogical Magazine* 16 (January 1915): 1–15, 49–67.

————. "Charleston—The Original Plan and the Earliest Settlers." *South Carolina Historical and Genealogical Magazine* 9 (January 1908): 12–27.

————. "Charleston and Charleston Neck." *South Carolina Historical and Genealogical Magazine* 19 (January 1918): 3–76.

Smith, J. J. Pringle, and William A. Courtenay. "Sketch of the History of Charleston." *Year Book City of Charleston, 1880* (Charleston, 1880), pp. 239–79.

————. "Some Account of the Government of the City of Charleston Before and After the Revolution of 1776." *Year Book City of Charleston, 1881* (Charleston, 1881), pp. 325–67.

Smith, Clarence M. "William Porcher Miles, Progressive Mayor of Charleston, 1855–1857." *Proceedings of the South Carolina Historical Association* (1942): 30–39.

Snavley, Larry M. "Vesey Plot." In David C. Roller and Robert W. Twyman, eds., *The Encyclopedia of Southern History*. Baton Rouge: Louisiana State University Press, 1979.

Snowden, Yates. "Charleston in War-Time, 1861–1865." *Year Book City of Charleston, 1908* (Charleston, 1909): 41–58.

Soltow, Lee. "Socioeconomic Classes in South Carolina and Massachusetts in the 1790's and the Observations of John Drayton." *South Carolina Historical Magazine* (October 1980): 283–305.

Stati, Paul. "Samuel F. B. Morse in Charleston, 1818–1821." *South Carolina Historical Magazine* 79 (April 1978): 87–112.

Stavisky, Leonard P. "Industrialism in Ante-Bellum Charleston." *Journal of Negro History* 36 (July 1951): 302–22.

Stockton, Robert P. "St. Michael's Architect: A Subject for Dispute." *News and Courier*, April 11, 1977.

————. "Coming Street Home Built on Glebe Lot" and "Coming Street House Has Long History." *News and Courier*, August 18, 1980.

————. "St. Michael's Architect: Unknown." *News and Courier*, October 23, 1978.

————. "Jail's Octagonal Wing Miscredited to Mills." *News and Courier*, January 23, 1978.

————. "House Was Built with City Loan." *News and Courier*, August 25, 1980.

————. "King St. Victorian Dates to 1870s." *News and Courier*, August 10, 1981.

————. "Relic of Racy Past Has Uncertain Fate." *News and Courier*, January 3, 1977.

————, "Charleston: The Preservation of a City." In C. Edward Kaylor, Jr., *A Consideration of Growth in the Trident Area: From the Academy to the Marketplace*. Charleston: Medical University Press, Medical University of South Carolina, 1982.

————. "Fire Stations." *News and Courier*, September 7, 1981.

———. "The Riviera: Art Deco Architecture." *News and Courier,* May 26, 1980.

Stoesen, Alexander R. "The British Occupation of Charleston, 1780–1782." *South Carolina Historical Magazine* 63 (April 1962): 71–82.

Street, Elwood. "When the Soldiers Come to Town." *The Survey.* August 18, 1917.

Stumpf, Stuart O. "Implications of King George's War for the Charleston Mercantile Community." *South Carolina Historical Magazine* 77 (July 1976): 161–81.

———. "South Carolina Importers of General Merchandise, 1735–1765." *South Carolina Historical Magazine* 84 (January 1983): 1–10.

Taylor, Rosser Howard. "The Gentry of Antebellum South Carolina." *North Carolina Historical Review* 17 (April 1940): 114–31.

Thomas, John P. "The Barbadians in Early South Carolina." *South Carolina Historical and Genealogical Magazine* 31 (April 1930): 75–92.

Toplin, Robert Brent. "Between Black and White: Attitudes toward Southern Mulattoes, 1830–1861." *Journal of Southern History* 55 (May 1979): 185–200.

Twig, Edward. "Charleston: The Great Myth." *Forum and Century* 102 (January 1940): 2–7.

Tyrrell, Ian R. "Drink and Temperance in the Antebellum South: An Overview and Interpretation." *Journal of Southern History* 48 (November 1982): 485–510.

Usner, Daniel H., Jr. "Rebeckah Lee's Plea on 'Fetching of Drink for an Indian Squaw,' 1684." *South Carolina Historical Magazine* 85 (October 1984): 317–18.

Ver Steeg, Clarence L. "Stacy Hepburn and Company: Enterprisers in the American Revolution." *South Carolina Historical Magazine* 55 (January 1954): 1–5.

Villers, David H. "The Smythe Horses Affair and the Association." *South Carolina Historical Magazine* 70 (July 1969): 137–48.

Vipperman, Carl J. "The Brief and Tragic Career of Charles Lowndes." *South Carolina Historical Magazine* 70 (October 1969): 211–25.

Wade, Richard C. "The Vesey Plot: A Reconsideration." *Journal of Southern History* 30 (May 1964): 143–61.

Walsh, Richard. "Edmund Egan: Charleston's Rebel Brewer." *South Carolina Historical Magazine* 56 (October 1955): 200–204.

———. "The Charleston Mechanics: A Brief Study, 1760–1776." *South Carolina Historical Magazine* 60 (July 1959): 123–44.

———. "Christopher Gadsden: Radical or Conservative Revolutionary?" *South Carolina Historical Magazine* 63 (July 1962): 195–203.

Waring, Joseph I. "St. Philip's Hospital in Charleston in Carolina." *Annals of Medical History,* New Series 4 (1932): 283–88.

———. "Charleston Medicine, 1800–1860." *Journal of the History of Medicine* 31 (July 1976): 320–42.

———. "James Killpatrick and Smallpox Innoculation in Charles Town." *Annals of Medical History,* New Series 10 (July 1938): 301–8.

———. "The Marine Hospitals of Charleston." *Yearbook City of Charleston, 1939* (Charleston, 1940), pp. 172–82.

Waring, Thomas R. "Red Light Reflections." *News and Courier,* January 11, 1981.

Waterhouse, Richard. "England, the Caribbean, and the Settlement of Carolina." *American Studies* 9 (1975): 259–81.

Webber, Mabel L., ed. "Spanish Depredations, 1686." *South Carolina Historical and Genealogical Magazine* 30 (April 1929): 81–89.

Weir, Robert M. " 'The Harmony We Were Famous For' ": An Interpretation of Pre-Revolutionary South Carolina Politics." *William and Mary Quarterly* 26 (October 1969): 473–501.

―――. "The South Carolinian as Extremist." *South Atlantic Quarterly* 74 (Winter 1975): 86–103.

―――. "Who Shall Rule at Home: The American Revolution as a Crisis of Legitimacy for the Colonial Elite." *Journal of Interdisciplinary History* 6 (Spring 1976): 679–700.

Welsh, John R. "William Gilmore Simms, Critic of the South." *Journal of Southern History* 36 (May 1960): 201–14.

Westwood, Howard G. "Captive Black Soldiers in Charleston—What to Do?" *Civil War History* 28 (March 1982): 28–44.

Williams, Jack Kenny. "The Code of Honor in Ante-Bellum South Carolina." *South Carolina Historical Magazine* 54 (July 1953): 113–28.

Winberry, John J. "Reputation of Carolina Indigo." *South Carolina Historical Magazine* 80 (July 1979): 242–50.

Winter, Robert. "Celebration." *Charleston Magazine* 2 (April 1976): 8–11.

Wood, Peter H. " 'Taking Care of Business' in Revolutionary South Carolina: Republicanism and the Slave Society." In Jeffery J. Crow and Larry Tise, eds., *The Southern Experience in the American Revolution*, pp. 268–93. Chapel Hill: University of North Carolina Press, 1978.

Woody, Robert H. "Christopher Gadsden and the Stamp Act." *Proceedings of the South Carolina Historical Association* (1939): 2–12.

Young, Rogers W. "Castle Pinckney, Silent Sentinel of Charleston Harbor." *South Carolina Historical and Genealogical Magazine* 39 (January 1938): 1–14.

Theses, Dissertations, and Unpublished Papers

Adkins, Margaret C. "Charleston's Political Anomaly: John Patrick Grace." Paper in possession of Walter J. Fraser, Jr.

Bagdon, Robert J. "Musical Life in Charleston, South Carolina, from 1732 to 1776 as Recorded in Colonial Sources." Ph.D. dissertation, University of Miami, 1978.

Barnwell, John G., Jr. "Love of Order: The Origins and Resolution of South Carolina's First Secession Crisis." Ph.D. dissertation, University of North Carolina, 1979.

Barr, Ellen. "A History of the Junior League of Charleston." Paper in possession of Walter J. Fraser, Jr.

Bellows, Barbara L. "Controlling the Poor in a Slave Society: The Antebellum Charleston Poor House." Paper in possession of Walter J. Fraser, Jr.

―――. "Dependent upon Her Own Exertions and the Charity of the World: White Working Class Women of Antebellum Charleston." Paper in possession of Walter J. Fraser, Jr.

Bentley, William G. "Wealth in Colonial South Carolina." Ph.D. dissertation, Georgia State University, 1977.

Berkham, Drucilla. "The Charleston Home Front: December 7, 1941–June 6, 1944." Paper in possession of Walter J. Fraser, Jr.

Select Bibliography

Boggs, Doyle W. "John Patrick Grace and the Politics of Reform in South Carolina, 1900–1931." Ph.D. dissertation, University of South Carolina, 1977.

Bolton, Sidney Charles. "The Anglican Church of Colonial South Carolina, 1704–1754: A Study in Americanization." Ph.D. dissertation, University of Wisconsin, 1973.

Bost, Raymond M. "The Reverend John Bachman and the Development of Southern Lutheranism." Ph.D. dissertation, Yale University, 1963.

Bryan, John Morrill. "The Exchange Building, 1766–1973: An Architectural History and Restoration Proposal." Paper in the South Carolina Department of Archives and History.

Canady, Margaret R. "An Era in Charleston Politics: 1923–1931." Senior thesis, University of South Carolina, 1961.

Cann, Marvin L. "Burnet Rhett Maybank and the New Deal in South Carolina, 1931–1941." Ph.D. dissertation, University of North Carolina, 1967.

Cavanagh, John Carroll. "The Military Career of Major General Benjamin Lincoln in the American Revolution, 1775–1781." Ph.D. dissertation, Duke University, 1969.

Clow, Richard Brent. "Edward Rutledge of South Carolina, 1749–1800: Unproclaimed Statesman." Ph.D. dissertation, University of Georgia, 1976.

Cobb, Jimmy Gene. "A Study of White Protestants' Attitudes toward Negroes in Charleston, South Carolina, 1790–1845." Ph.D. dissertation, Baylor University, 1976.

Collins, Frederick Burtrumn, Jr. "Charleston and the Railroads: A Geographic Study of a South Atlantic Port and Its Strategies for Developing a Railroad System, 1820–1860." M.S. thesis, University of South Carolina, 1977.

Coon, David LeRoy. "The Development of Market Agriculture in South Carolina, 1670–1785." Ph.D. dissertation, University of Illinois, Urbana-Champaign, 1972.

Cox, Headley M., Jr. "The Charleston Poetic Renascence, 1920–1930." Ph.D. dissertation, University of Pennsylvania, 1958.

Crouse, Maurice A. "The Manigault Family of South Carolina." Ph.D. dissertation, Northwestern University, 1964.

Curtis, Mary Julia. "The Early Charleston Stage: 1703–1798." Ph.D. dissertation, Indiana University, 1968.

Duffy, John J. "Charleston Politics in the Progressive Era." Ph.D. dissertation, University of South Carolina, 1963.

Duncan, John D. "Servitude and Slavery in Colonial South Carolina, 1670–1776." Ph.D. dissertation, Emory University, 1972.

Edgar, Walter B. "The Libraries of Colonial South Carolina." Ph.D. dissertation, University of South Carolina, 1969.

Fagg, David Webster, Jr. "Carolina, 1663–1683: The Founding of a Proprietary." Ph.D. dissertation, Emory University, 1970.

Ford, Lacey K. "Republics and Democracy: The Parameters of Political Citizenship in Antebellum South Carolina." Paper in possession of Walter J. Fraser, Jr.

Frank, Robert Lee. "The Economic Impact of Tourism in Charleston, South Carolina, 1970." M.A. thesis, University of South Carolina, 1972.

Gibson, Shirley M. "Personal Recollections on Charleston City Government from

John P. Grace to J. Palmer Gaillard." Paper in possession of Walter J. Fraser, Jr.

Greb, Gregory Allen. "Charleston, South Carolina Merchants, 1815–1860: Urban Leadership in the Antebellum South." Ph.D. dissertation, University of California, Riverside, 1978.

Hanckel, William Henry. "The Preservation Movement in Charleston, 1920–1962." M.A. thesis, University of South Carolina, 1961.

Hayes, Jack Irby, Jr. "South Carolina and the New Deal, 1932–1938." Ph.D. dissertation, University of South Carolina, 1971.

Hemmingway, Theodore. "Beneath the Yoke of Bondage: A History of Black Folks in South Carolina, 1900–1940." Ph.D. dissertation, University of South Carolina, 1976.

_____. "Paternalism, Protest, and Progress: Race Relations in Charleston, South Carolina, 1900–1930. Paper in possession of Walter J. Fraser, Jr.

Higgins, W. Robert. "A Financial History of the American Revolution in South Carolina." Ph.D. dissertation, Duke University, 1969.

Hindman, John Joseph. "Concert Life in Antebellum Charleston." Ph.D. dissertation, University of North Carolina, Chapel Hill, 1971.

Hine, William C. "Frustration, Factionalism and Failure: Black Political Leadership and the Republican Party in Reconstruction Charleston, 1865–1877." Ph.D. dissertation, Kent State University, 1979.

Hogue, L. Lynn. "An Edition of Eight Charges Delivered . . . Held at Charles Town . . . , by Nicholas Trott, Esq.: Chief Justice of the Province of South Carolina." Ph.D. dissertation, University of Tennessee, 1972.

Jabbs, Theodore H. "The South Carolina Colonial Militia, 1663–1733." Ph.D. dissertation, University of North Carolina, 1973.

January, Alan Frank. "The First Nullification: The Negro Seaman Acts Controversy in South Carolina, 1822–1860." Ph.D. dissertation, University of Iowa, 1976.

Jordan, Laylon W. " 'The Method of Modern Charity': The Associated Charities Society of Charleston, 1888–1920." Paper in possession of Walter J. Fraser, Jr.

Kaplanoff, Mark D. "Making the South Solid: Politics and the Structure of Society in South Carolina, 1790–1815." Ph.D. dissertation, Cambridge University, 1979.

Knepper, David Morton. "The Political Structure of Colonial South Carolina, 1743–1776." Ph.D. dissertation, University of Virginia, 1971.

Lane, John Dewey. "The Charleston Club." M.S. thesis, University of Virginia, 1924.

Lewis, John. "Strong Medicine from a Native Son." Paper in possession of Walter J. Fraser, Jr.

Lilly, Samuel A. "The Culture of Revolutionary Charleston." Ph.D. dissertation, Miami University, 1972.

Longton, William Henry. "Some Aspects of Intellectual Activity in Ante-Bellum South Carolina, 1830–1860: An Introductory Study." Ph.D. dissertation, University of North Carolina, Chapel Hill, 1969.

Marshall, Howard Joseph. "Gentlemen without a Country." Ph.D. dissertation, University of North Carolina, Chapel Hill, 1979.

McCardell, John. "William Gilmore Simms and His World after the Civil War: A New Look at Joscelyn." Paper in possession of Walter J. Fraser, Jr.

Miller, Eileen M. "The Charleston Orphan House: An Historical Study of Personnel and Policies." M.A. thesis, University of South Carolina, 1982.

Moore, Warner Oland, Jr. "Henry Laurens: A Charleston Merchant in the Eighteenth Century, 1747–1771." Ph.D. dissertation, University of Alabama, 1974.

Mulholland, R. Mack. "The Jenkins' Orphanage Band." Paper in possession of Walter J. Fraser, Jr.

Olsberg, Robert N. "A Government of Class and Race: William Henry Trescot and the South Carolina Chivalry, 1860–1865." Ph.D. dissertation, University of South Carolina, 1972.

Pease, Jane H., and William H. Pease. "If All the South Were Charleston and Boston, All the North." Paper in possession of Walter J. Fraser, Jr.

Peters, Kenneth E. "Disaster Relief Efforts Connected with the 1886 Charleston Earthquake." Paper in possession of Walter J. Fraser, Jr.

Powers, Bernard E., Jr. "Black Charleston: A Social History, 1822–1885." Ph.D. dissertation, Northwestern University, 1982.

Press, Nancy. "Cultural Myth and Class Structuration: The Downtown Group of Charleston, South Carolina." Ph.D. dissertation, Duke University, 1985.

Radford, John Price. "Culture, Economy and Urban Structure in Charleston, 1860–1880." Ph.D. dissertation, Clark University, 1974.

Roberson, John C. "Sailors against Blacks: The Charleston Race Riot of 1919." Paper in possession of Walter J. Fraser, Jr.

————. "The 1860 Association: Catalyst of Secession." Paper in possession of Walter J. Fraser, Jr.

Russell, James "Homicide and the Violent Ideal in Atlanta, 1865–1890." Paper in possession of Walter J. Fraser.

Scialabba, Peter J. "The Charleston Naval Shipyard." Paper in possession of Walter J. Fraser, Jr.

Secrest, Andrew M. "In Black and White: Press Opinion and Race Relations in South Carolina, 1954–1964." Ph.D. dissertation, Duke University, 1971.

Sirmans, M. Eugene. "Masters of Ashley Hall: A Biographical Study of the Bull Family of Colonial South Carolina, 1670–1737." Ph.D. dissertation, Princeton University, 1959.

Slavick, William Henry. "Dubose Heyward: The Rhythms of Charleston." Ph.D. dissertation, University of Notre Dame, 1971.

Snell, William R. "Indian Slavery in Colonial South Carolina, 1671–1795." Ph.D. dissertation, University of Alabama, 1972.

Starr, Raymond G. "The Conservative Revolution: South Carolina Public Affairs, 1775–1790." Ph.D. dissertation, University of Texas, 1964.

Stockton, Robert P. "The Evolution of Rainbow Row." M.A. thesis, University of South Carolina, 1979.

Stumpf, Stuart O. "The Merchants of Colonial Charleston, 1680–1756." Ph.D. dissertation, Michigan State University, 1971.

Sutor, Jack A. "Charleston, South Carolina during the Civil War Era, 1858–1865." M.A. thesis, Duke University, 1942.

Sydenham, Diane Meredith. "Practitioner and Patient: The Practice of Medicine in Eighteenth Century South Carolina." Ph.D. dissertation, Johns Hopkins University, 1979.

Terry, George D. "A Study of the Impact of the French Revolution and the Insurrections in Saint Dominque upon South Carolina, 1790–1805." M.A. thesis, University of South Carolina, 1975.

Terry, Robert Lewis. "J. Waties Waring, Spokesman for Racial Justice in the New South." Ph.D. dissertation, University of Utah, 1970.

Waterhouse, Richard. "South Carolina's Colonial Elite: A Study in the Social Structure and Political Culture of a Southern Colony, 1670–1760." Ph.D. dissertation, Johns Hopkins University, 1973.

Weir, Robert M. " 'Liberty and Property, and No Stamps': South Carolina and the Stamp Act Crisis." Ph.D. dissertation, Case Western Reserve University, 1966.

Wild, Philip F. "South Carolina Politics." Ph.D. dissertation, University of Pennsylvania, 1949.

Williamson, Gustavus G. "Francis W. Dawson and South Carolina Politics." Paper in possession of Walter J. Fraser, Jr.

Wilson, Clyde Norman. "Carolina Cavalier: The Life of James Johnson Pettigrew." Ph.D. dissertation, University of North Carolina, Chapel Hill, 1971.

Windley, Lathan Algerna. "A Profile of Runaway Slaves in Virginia and South Carolina from 1730 through 1787." Ph.D. dissertation, University of Iowa, 1974.

Index